ACCIDENTAL GAMBLERS

Vidarbha, a major cotton growing region in central India, has been the epicentre of a protracted agrarian crisis. Chronic indebtedness and farmers' suicides continue unabated despite decades of state intervention. Going beyond the contemporary discourse that finds fault in neoliberal policies and integration with global markets, this fascinating book tells the story of how nineteenth-century 'accidents', particularly in the form of events and processes, ushered in institutional transformations that shaped the region's cotton economy.

By drawing insights from the authors' longitudinal study in villages of the region spanning twelve years, *Accidental Gamblers* presents the 'gambles' that farmers are part of in addition to the detailed historical account of the political economy and development of the cotton economy of the region. The novelty of combining a long view of history and evidence based on primary field research results in a book that underscores the importance of investigating roots of agrarian crisis and paying attention to adjustments of farm households, at a crucial juncture in India's economic transformation.

Sarthak Gaurav is an associate professor in economics in the Shailesh J. Mehta School of Management at IIT Bombay. He has worked on risk and vulnerability of agricultural households in Vidarbha and Gujarat since 2008 and cofounded the Behavioural Lab and Geospatial Information Science and Engineering (GISE) Hub at IIT Bombay.

Thiagu Ranganathan is an associate professor at the Centre for Development Studies, Thiruvananthapuram. He has worked on various issues in agricultural economics and development economics, including agricultural price risk management and implications of water scarcity on rural livelihood diversification.

ACCIDENTAL GAMBLERS

RISK AND VULNERABILITY IN VIDARBHA COTTON

SARTHAK GAURAV
THIAGU RANGANATHAN

CAMBRIDGE
UNIVERSITY PRESS

CAMBRIDGE
UNIVERSITY PRESS

Shaftesbury Road, Cambridge CB2 8EA, United Kingdom

One Liberty Plaza, 20th Floor, New York, NY 10006, USA

477 Williamstown Road, Port Melbourne, vic 3207, Australia

314 to 321, 3rd Floor, Plot No.3, Splendor Forum, Jasola District Centre, New Delhi 110025, India

103 Penang Road, #05–06/07, Visioncrest Commercial, Singapore 238467

Cambridge University Press is part of the University of Cambridge.

It furthers the University's mission by disseminating knowledge in the pursuit of education, learning and research at the highest international levels of excellence.

www.cambridge.org
Information on this title: www.cambridge.org/9781108832298

First published 2023
Reprint 2025

Printed in India by Avantika Printers Pvt. Ltd.

A catalogue record for this publication is available from the British Library

ISBN 978-1-108-83229-8 Hardback

CONTENTS

List of Illustrations vii
List of Tables xi
Acknowledgements xiii
List of Abbreviations xix

Introduction 1

Part I

1 A Brief History of Vidarbha 13
2 Accidents and Gambles in Colonial Vidarbha 60

Part II

3 Field and Fieldwork 161
4 Gambles of Farmers 218
5 Inputs in the Cotton Gamble 269
6 Risk and Vulnerability 315
7 Conclusion 373

Glossary 411
Bibliography 417
Index 466

ILLUSTRATIONS

GRAPHS

2.1	Cotton imports into Britain from India and the United States	63
2.2	Rainfall variability in Vidarbha (annual)	75
2.3	Rainfall variability in Vidarbha (monsoon months)	75
2.4	Price of Indian cotton (Surats) at Liverpool market	79
2.5	Price of US cotton at Liverpool market	84
2.6	Real price of cotton and acreage index in the Bombay Province	86
2.7	Index of relative prices of cotton, wheat, and *jawari* in the Bombay Presidency	87
2.8	Area under major crops in the Central Provinces	89
2.9	Real wages in Berar (kilograms of *jawari* per daily wage in rupees)	92
2.10	Mortality per 1,000 in Berar	92
2.11	Population and average land owned in Berar	99
2.12	Cotton area and production in Vidarbha	120
2.13	Area under cotton cultivation in Wardha and Yavatmal	121
2.14	Cotton production in Wardha and Yavatmal	122
3.1	Interest rate on loans by household type	203
4.1	Cultivated area	222

4.2 Area under major crops in Wardha 227
4.3 Area under major crops in Yavatmal 227
4.4 Area share of crops in cultivated area 231
4.5 Major intercropping patterns 232
4.6 Economics of cotton cultivation 238
4.7 Economics of soybean cultivation 238
4.8 Economics of *tur* cultivation 239
4.9 Yield of major kharif crops 241
4.10 Price of major kharif crops 241
4.11 Share of major cost components: Cotton 242
4.12 Share of major cost components: Soybean 243
4.13 Share of major cost components: *Tur* 243
4.14 Area under major rabi crops in Wardha 245
4.15 Area under major rabi crops in Yavatmal 245
4A.1 Economics of kharif cultivation 261
5.1 Year of Bt cotton adoption in Wardha sample: 2009 273
5.2 Plot-level number of cotton seed brands: 2016 278
5.3 Plot-level number of cotton seed brands: 2017 278
5.4 Seed brands used by cultivators 280
6.1 Yield variations 341
6.2 Trajectories of income from cotton cultivation 343
6.3 Trajectories of income from cultivation 343
6.4 Monthly per capita food consumption expenditure and losses 345
6.5 Monthly per capita non-food consumption expenditure and losses 345
6.6 Share of PDS cereals in household cereal consumption: 2019 346

MAPS

2.1 Annual mean rainfall 74
2.2 Population and area of the Central Provinces and Berar 93

2.3 The Great Indian Peninsular Railway, 1870 102
3.1 India, Maharashtra, Vidarbha region, study districts 172
3.2 Study villages where AWS were installed in 2016 176

IMAGES

2.1 Cotton stacks and *churka* in operation 83
3.1 Gaurav during a field visit to Wardha 172
3.2 Resident investigator demonstrating non-pesticidal management 183
3.3 A father and son operating a bullock pair during *dawran* 193
3.4 A cattle fair in Deoli, Wardha 199
4.1 Brick kiln along the road to Wardha villages 224
4.2 *Hamal* labour wage rates in Yavatmal APMC yard 250
5.1 Labourer spraying insecticides on *tur* in a cotton–*tur* intercropping 291
5.2 *Yeli*, a lining tool used in *patta paddath* 293
5.3 Land preparation before rabi sowing 299
5.4 Women agricultural workers engaged in cotton-picking 300
6.1 Cotton bales to be transported from a ginning and pressing unit 335
6.2 Ranganathan at a cotton gin 336

TABLES

2.1	Mean and CV of monsoon and annual rainfall	74
3.1	Survey rounds, villages, and survey instruments	166
3.2	Summary of sample households	185
3.3	Farm and non-farm assets	192
3.4	Financial assets	195
3.5	Livestock ownership	195
3.6	Livestock ownership by size-class of land owned	197
3.7	Loan outstanding	201
3.8	Source of credit	204
3.9	Purpose of loan	205
4.1	Economics of kharif cultivation	235
4.2	Household income from livestock and non-farm enterprises	248
4.3	Earnings from livestock and non-farm enterprises by social group	249
4.4	Earnings from livestock and non-farm enterprises by size-class of land owned	249
4.5	Labour supply by non-cultivator and cultivator households	251
4.6	Labour supply by non-cultivator and cultivator households in own farm and off-farm	253
4.7	Average wage rates of agricultural labour by gender	254
4.8	Labour income	256

4A.1 Kharif cultivation economics across land-size classes 262
4A.2 Employment of household members 264
5.1 Expenditure on pesticides 287
5.2 Variations in pesticide expenditure per acre 288
5.3 Economics of cotton cultivation by *paddath* 295
5.4 Cost per acre for cotton and *tur* intercropping 297
6.1 Distribution of monsoon rainfall in Wardha 321
6.2 Probability of a dry day in Wardha 322
6.3 Average rainfall and dry days in AWS villages 322
6.4 Fertilizer use among farmers of different land-size classes 327
6.5 Content of N, P, and K in fertilizers 328
6.6 Cotton yield response to fertilizer 329
6.7 Fertilizer use among farmers of different land-size class 330
6.8 Yield losses 341
6.9 Risk perceptions 348
6.10 Risk coping mechanisms 350
6A.1 Monthly household expenditure on food and non-durables 361
6A.2 Annual household expenditure on durables 362

ACKNOWLEDGEMENTS

This book is the culmination of our dabbling with several troubling questions about economic development and society for over twelve years. As we began drafting the book proposal in the winter of 2019, we could not help but wonder about the series of extraordinary coincidences that piqued our interest in agricultural risk. We believe it is important to briefly mention two coincidences that played their part in our commitment to the historical inquiry and longitudinal study that forms the foundation of this book.

First, we joined and quit the Centre for Insurance and Risk Management (CIRM), Institute for Financial Management and Research (IFMR), Chennai, around the same time. The experience at CIRM sensitized us to the limits of market-based risk management solutions and the centrality of the state in enabling farmers to manage risks. Gaurav went on to pursue his doctoral research on the risk and vulnerability of agricultural households at the Indira Gandhi Institute of Development Research (IGIDR), Mumbai, that resulted in the study of five villages in Vidarbha region of Maharashtra from 2009 to 2013. Then he worked on the longitudinal study of Palanpur village over the next two years spent at the London School of Economics and Political Science (LSE) and Centre de Sciences Humaines (CSH), New Delhi. Second, Ranganathan completed his PhD on Soybean futures markets at the Indian Institute of Technology Bombay (IIT Bombay). He joined the Agricultural Economics Research Unit (AERU) at the Institute of Economic Growth (IEG), New Delhi and subsequently joined the Indian Institute of Management Nagpur (IIM Nagpur)—at the heart of Vidarbha and the winter capital of Maharashtra—as a faculty in 2017. As luck would have it, Gaurav had joined IIT Bombay by then as a faculty. These serendipitous developments not only reinforced our resolve to continue our research in Vidarbha but also continued our collaboration that was in its eighth year by then. The next few years saw intensive data collection and fieldwork interspersed over the calendar years. We ensured that either of us conducted fieldwork at the beginning and end of a cropping season; and intermittent and short visits to study villages continued. We have nevertheless had our share of accidents and gambles in bringing the book project to fruition.

* * *

I am indebted to my doctoral advisor Srijit Mishra of IGIDR, Mumbai, for his encouragement and constant support in studying questions of risk and vulnerability in Vidarbha, and for introducing me to the joys of fieldwork in economic research. I have benefitted from constant support and discussions with Sripad Motiram, Nicholas Stern, Shawn Cole, Jeremy Tobacman, Reinhard Mechler, Stefan Hochrainer-Stigler, Spencer Xiao, N. C. Narayanan, Pankaj Sekhsaria, and Himanshu. I have benefitted from discussions with Laxman D. Satya, Michael Lipton, S. Mahendra Dev, Manoj Panda, Jaideep Hardikar, Satish Agnihotri, Milind Sohoni, Anush Kapadia, Vaishnavi Surendra, Ruchira Bhattacharya, Japneet Kaur, Bhavna Joshi, Priyanka Pande, Rishav K. Thakur, Jayaseelan Raj, Sven Beckert, and Vinish Kathuria. K. D. Khandare at the Vidarbha Archives in Nagpur has been extremely helpful in navigating archival materials. I would like to thank Ruth Kattumuri for her support during my research on the Palanpur village study at the Asia Research Centre (ARC) at LSE. I am grateful to the staff at the two wonderful libraries where I have spent considerable amount of time—LSE and IGIDR.

During the pandemic that more or less overlapped with our writing period, digitized archives of the National Archives of India and Internet Archive were valuable sources of information. DSpace repository of Gokhale Institute of Politics and Economics (GIPE) was equally informative. Vijay Jawandhia has been a source of valuable information on the dynamics of Vidarbha agriculture, and I owe him my deep-felt gratitude.

I am thankful to Rupalee Ruchismita at CIRM, IFMR, for introducing me to the issues of rural insurance. The current director of the Central Institute for Cotton Research (CICR), Nagpur, Y. G. Prasad, and the scientists there gave rich insights into the institutional effort at seed development and improving agricultural extension in the region. I also owe a lot of my understanding of the cotton crop to ex-director of CICR, Keshav R. Kranthi. G. V. Ramanjaneyulu of the Centre for Sustainable Agriculture (CSA), Hyderabad, and their team members in 2008, Vijay Barapatre and Chandrasekhar Dorlikar, were instrumental in starting the first round of survey in Wardha, and I owe my gratitude to them.

I have benefitted from interactions with researchers at several other research institutions such as the Centre de Sciences Humaines (CSH), New Delhi, during my research journey. I am fortunate to have had excellent research assistance from Rahul Kumar Singh, Rayees Ahmad Sheikh, Khushboo Balani, Neha Durga, Rohit Shah, Vrishal Yelegaonkar, Ramraj Bharti, Priya Noronha, and Shweta Kalla. Mihir Narayan and Gopal Golhar provided valuable assistance in data entry. I would like to thank Pravin Mankar for his generous hospitality and guidance about the Vidarbha economy over these years, and for a family away from home during field visits. I thank Atul Sharma and Varada Ranjane for their insights on Vidarbha agriculture. This book would not have been possible without the consternation as well as the support of my family members—Bapa, Maa, Apa, Anne, and all the pets of my family for accommodating and tolerating my absence and inattention during family events. Hope they understand that the troubles they had to go through were worth it.

Friends at IGIDR—Nirupam Datta, Priya Rampal, Sarbojit Pal, Kiran Limaye, Nayantara Sarma, Shaz Hoda, Upasak Das, Avitosh Panda, and Ashish Singh—were a constant sounding board. Over the years, my friends Asis Senapati, Anubhab Pattanayak, and Manas Mohanty have been extremely supportive. At IIT Bombay, I am thankful for the company of Ashish Singh, Arti Kalro, Trupti Mishra, Dinesh Sharma, Shishir Kumar Jha, who also provided much-needed comic relief and humour during the research and writing journey. Owen Berkeley-Hill, a stalwart of the Ford Production System reinforced my belief in the principle of the Toyota Production System—'Genchi Genbutsu', Japanese for 'real location, real thing'—and introduced me to the terms 'Babuji' and 'Behenji' for the shop floor workers in his elucidation of Lean Operations at the Shailesh J. Mehta School of Management (SJMSOM), IIT Bombay. He also rekindled my interest in the Indian Railways, and I owe him my gratitude for the memorable interactions over the years.

Sarthak Gaurav

I am deeply indebted to T. V. Venkateswaran who encouraged me and accompanied me to work on the question of pesticide use in Vidarbha. His support and encouragement has meant a lot to me. My stint at CIRM based out of IFMR introduced me to issues related to Weather Insurance and Agricultural

Risk Management. I am grateful to Rupalee Ruchismita for providing me with that opportunity. Researchers from various places I have worked with during these twelve years have been a source of constant support and encouragement—Usha Ananthakumar, Gajendra Kumar Adil, Shishir Kumar Jha, Prabhusekaran Muthappan at IIT Bombay; Manoj Panda, and Sabyasachi Kar at the Institute of Economic Growth (IEG); L. S. Murty, Rahul Kumar Sett, Preeti Ghasad, Vijay Kumar Medi, and Neerpal Rathi at IIM Nagpur. I thank S. Krithi and Avina Mendonca for the insightful academic discussions over the years. Atul Sharma provided valuable inputs in the field. Pravin Mankar at Wardha has become a part of my family over the course of these twelve years.

I am unlikely to come across a place better than the Centre for Development Studies (CDS) to work on this book. Along with a tranquil campus, I am fortunate to have had some wonderful colleagues—Jayaseelan Raj, Tirtha Chatterjee, Praveena Kodoth, T. Abhilash, Rajit Biswas, Ritika Jain, M. Parameswaran, P. L. Beena, and Vinoj Abraham. I would like to thank Ramesh Dangol and Malabika Biswas for providing their feedback on the draft chapters. I would also like to thank T. Maheshkumar and John Kujur, the doctoral students at CDS, for their valuable research assistance. Special thanks are due to Gajanand Ahirwal, Bhaskar Nehare, and Anil *bhau* who have been working with us for what seems like forever. I express my profound gratitude to participants in our survey without whose patience this study would not have been possible. I would, most importantly, like to thank my family—Amma, Appa, Esther, Thilak, and Addhu for their constant support and patience.

Thiagu Ranganathan

We would also like to express our gratitude and special thanks to Anwesha Rana at Cambridge University Press for being extremely patient with us overshooting certain deadlines. We are grateful for her support at all stages of this book's journey. We wish to thank Priya Das and Nilanjana Dey for the excellent editing of this book. We would also like to thank the two anonymous readers for reviewing the book proposal. Aniruddha De provided valuable guidance about the production process.

Most importantly, this book would not have been possible without the hard work and commitment of our resident investigators Bhaskar Nehare, Gajanand Ahirwal, and Anil Golhar. Special thanks are in place to all our field enumerators and data entry operators over the long span of time. Last but not least, we will ever be grateful for the patience and kindness of all the participants in our surveys and fieldwork. We have benefitted from the financial support of the Indian Council of Social Science Research (ICSSR) and IIT Bombay for their generous grants. Part funding for the research was provided through two major research proposal grants from ICSSR to Ranganathan in 2015 (Code: SC-02/15-16/ICSSR/RPS) and ICSSR-IMPRESS and Ministry of Education grant to Gaurav in 2019 (Project No.P2276, Code: RS/0119-ICSSR00-001), which we sincerely acknowledge. Gaurav would like to especially thank IIT Bombay for the financial support as well as the administration of seed grant support in 2016 (RD/0516-IRCCSHO-022). We would like to thank Anita Narwade, Archana Joshi, and all the staff at SJMSOM and IRCC, IIT Bombay, for their administrative help during the course of our research.

Sarthak Gaurav and **Thiagu Ranganathan**
3 March 2023

ABBREVIATIONS

ADWDRS	Agricultural Debt Waiver and Debt Relief Scheme
AERC	Agro-Economic Research Centre
AICIL	Agriculture Insurance Company of India Ltd
APL	above poverty line
APMC	Agricultural Produce Market Committee
ASHA	accredited social health activist
ATMA	Agricultural Technology Management Agency
AWS	automated weather station
BJP	Bharatiya Janata Party
BPL	below poverty line
Bt	Bacillus thuringiensis
CACP	Commission for Agricultural Costs and Prices
CAGR	compound annual growth rate
CAIM	Convergence of Agriculture and Industry in Maharashtra
CCEA	Cabinet Committee for Economic Affairs
CCI	Cotton Corporation of India
CIBRC	Central Insecticides Board and Registration Committee
CICR	Central Institute for Cotton Research
CIRCOT	Central Institute for Research on Cotton Technology
CSA	Centre for Sustainable Agriculture
CV	coefficient of variation

DAP	di-ammonium phosphate
DBT	Direct Benefit Transfer
DCCB	District Central Cooperative Bank
EIC	East India Company
ETL	economic threshold limit
FAS	Foundation for Agrarian Studies
FAQ	fair average quality
FCI	Food Corporation of India
FGD	focus group discussion
FPC	Farmer Producer Company
FYM	farmyard manure
GCA	gross cropped area
GEAC	Genetic Engineering Appraisal Committee
GIPR	Great Indian Peninsular Railway
GKU	Girni Kamgar Union
HAD	Hyderabad Assigned Districts
HDPS	high density planting system
HTBt	herbicide tolerant Bt cotton
HYV	high yielding variety
ICAR	Indian Council of Agricultural Research
ICDS	Integrated Child Development Scheme
ICRISAT	International Crops Research Institute for the Semi-Arid Tropics
IFAD	International Fund for Agricultural Development
IMD	India Meteorological Department
INC	Indian National Congress
INTUC	Indian National Trade Union Congress
IPM	integrated pest management
IPR	intellectual property right
IRM	insecticide resistance management
ITI	industrial training institute

JJAS	four monsoon months of June, July, August, and September
JSA	Jalyukt Shivar Abhiyaan
JSY	Janani Suraksha Yojana
KCC	*kisan* credit card
KVK	Krishi Vigyan Kendra
LFPR	labour force participation rate
MAP	mono ammonium phosphate
MCPS	Monopoly Cotton Procurement Scheme
MDG	Millennium Development Goal
MDMS	Mid-day Meal Scheme
MFI	microfinance institution
MGNREGS	Mahatma Gandhi National Rural Employment Guarantee Scheme
MLA	member of the Legislative Assembly
MMBL	Mahyco–Monsanto Biotech Ltd
MNAIS	Modified National Agricultural Insurance Scheme
MOP	muriate of potash
MP	member of parliament
MPCE	monthly per capita consumption expenditure
MRP	mixed recall period
MSCCGMF	Maharashtra State Cooperative Cotton Growers Marketing Federation Ltd
MSP	minimum support price
MSRLM	Maharashtra State Rural Livelihoods Mission
MVA	Maha Vikas Aghadi
NABARD	National Bank for Agriculture and Development
NAFED	National Agricultural Cooperative Marketing Federation of India Ltd
NAIS	National Agricultural Insurance Scheme
NBFC	non-banking financial company
NCAER	National Council of Applied Economic Research
NCDEX	National Commodity & Derivatives Exchange Limited

NCP	Nationalist Congress Party
NDA	National Democratic Alliance
NEP	National Education Policy
NGO	non-governmental organization
NHC	new history of capitalism
NPK	nitrogen phosphorous potassium
NPM	non-pesticidal management
NREGS	National Rural Employment Guarantee Scheme
NSSO	National Sample Survey Office
NT	nomadic tribe
OBC	other backward classes
OGL	Open General Licence
PARI	Project on Agrarian Relations in India
PBW	pink bollworm
PDKV	Dr Panjabrao Deshmukh Krishi Vidyapeeth
PDS	Public Distribution System
PMFBY	Pradhan Mantri Fasal Bima Yojana
PMJDY	Pradhan Mantri Jan-Dhan Yojana
PM-KISAN	Pradhan Mantri Kisan Samman Nidhi (Prime Minister's Farmer's Tribute Fund)
POCRA	Project on Climate Resilient Agriculture
RCT	randomized control trial
RMMS	Rasthriya Mill Mazdoor Sangh
RSBY	Rashtriya Swasthya Bima Yojana
RWBCIS	Restructured Weather-Based Crop Insurance Scheme
RWS	reference weather station
SAS	situation assessment survey
SBC	special backward classes
SC	scheduled caste
SEBC	socially and economically backward class
SHC	soil health card
SHG	self-help group

SIT	special investigation team
SOPA	Soybean Processors Association of India
SPNF	Subhash Palekar Natural Farming
SRC	States Reorganization Commission
SRTT	Sir Ratan Tata Trust
SSP	single super phosphate
ST	scheduled tribe
UPA	United Progressive Alliance
VDSA	Village Dynamics Studies in South Asia
VER	vulnerability as uninsured exposure to risk
VIDC	Vidarbha Irrigation Development Corporation
VIIDP	Vidarbha Intensive Irrigation Development Programme
VLS	village-level study
VNSS	Vasantrao Naik Sheti Swavlamban Mission
WBCIS	Weather-Based Crop Insurance Scheme
WTO	World Trade Organization
WTP	willingness to pay
WUA	Water User Association
ZBNF	zero budget natural farming

INTRODUCTION

As this book goes to print, life is slowly returning to normalcy in India following multiple waves of a debilitating pandemic that took the lives of more than half a million. Debates on the true extent of deaths notwithstanding, the pandemic infected above 40 million in the country and impacted lives and livelihoods across the globe. There is considerable uncertainty in Europe with the Russian invasion of Ukraine; political instability in neighbouring Pakistan with the ousting of the incumbent prime minister in a no-trust vote; mass protests following the economic crisis in Sri Lanka; strict lockdown in China as it grapples with another wave of COVID-19 outbreak; and inflationary pressures remain a concern worldwide amidst supply disruptions as recovery from the pandemic-induced recession had commenced. By contrast there is exuberance in the Indian financial sector, 'unicorns' are disrupting the market with their technological innovation and the initial public offering market spanning diversified industries is buoyant with unprecedented proceeds and a robust pipeline for the near future.[1] While most struggle to make sense of how the platform economy creates value or how the digital transformation has created nouveau dollar billionaires, a 'crypto mania' is sweeping through the country. Not surprisingly the Government of India has announced that it will issue a digital rupee as central bank digital currency and that incomes from crypto assets will be taxed. In stark contrast to the exuberance in the financial markets and the ongoing digital transformation, the farm sector has witnessed prolonged large scale agitation.

In an unanticipated move in November 2021, the Government of India repealed three controversial farm laws enacted in September 2020 that were at the centre of protracted protests by farmers: mostly from the north Indian states.

As agitating farmers and farmer unions demanded repeal of the farm laws and that the minimum support price (MSP) be made the legal guarantee as the floor price for all market purchases, the deep-rooted agrarian distress in regions such as Vidarbha in Maharashtra faded into oblivion as if those in crisis were unable to protest vehemently or end their lives tragically enough to draw media and policy attention. Of course, the issue of agrarian crisis has to be seen in the larger context of the changing structure of the economy and society. The underlying structural transformation of the economy has undoubtedly resulted in millions moving out of agriculture, and rising non-farm employment.[2] However, those who were unable to or unwilling to move out of agriculture face the idiosyncrasies of agriculture and its attendant worries—uncertainty, drudgery, loss, and indebtedness—season after season. For cotton farmers of the Vidarbha region in central India that has gained infamy for the spate of farmers' suicides, the 'record-high' prices in cotton this marketing season was accompanied by looming yield losses from excess rains in 2021 despite the season starting off with prospects of a 'good monsoon'.[3] So often do the erratic interplay between crop yields and prices of the output worry the farmers that losses attributed to them no longer surprise them as they either carry on with resilience and fortitude or give in to despair and fatalism. Policy uncertainties such as those around the implementation of the repealed farm laws or trade policies become a source of adverse fluctuations of farm incomes as well as a constant source of duress. That these routine struggles of the farmers and their households persist in the context of the narrative of a chronic agrarian distress raises several questions.

Is the crisis in Vidarbha agriculture a consequence of the stunted structural transformation of the economy? Is it an outcome of the deceleration in agricultural growth since the economic liberalization that began three decades ago? Why is it that despite years of state interventions the agrarian crisis continues unabated? Does the region's geography and climate predispose it to agrarian crisis? Have strong inclusive institutions failed to emerge in the region? If there is a protracted crisis, why do ginners and traders continue to throng the local cotton marts in hordes year after year to procure cotton? Is there indeed a crisis in Vidarbha or is it make-believe orchestrated by the media, politicians, farm activists, academics, and policymakers? What are the experiences of Vidarbha's cotton farmers amidst the din and roar? Why, despite all the stress and anxiety associated with growing cash crops such as cotton, do the farmers continue to grow cotton?

In this book, we attempt to answer these questions and investigate the affinity of farmers in the region to cotton despite the overarching evidence on its complicity in the agrarian crisis. This book is a penetrating examination of the twists and turns in the fate of the region rooted in the 'accidents' affecting generations of farmers in the region who have engaged with the 'gamble' in cotton cultivation as the economy and society has transformed. It aims at unravelling a deeper understanding of the region's cotton economy that is enmeshed in the history of the region and that of regions far from it. It also examines why it has not been easy to let go of the commodity that has pushed many to ruination and, as contemporary evidence indicates, forced thousands to committing suicide because of the complex interactions associated with growing the crop. We posit that the several historical 'accidents' that we throw light on institutionalized the 'gamble' with cotton in a region whose heterogeneities have been understudied despite its importance in the domestic and global cotton economy. These accidents primarily took the form of radical institutional changes and integration of global economy and local markets in the building blocks of present-day Vidarbha in the colonial period—Berar and the Central Provinces. Present-day Vidarbha became an important source of raw cotton to feed the mills of Lancashire before and after the American Civil War during 1861–1865. While indigenous raw cotton varieties—*desi kapas*—had been grown in the region for millennia, the transition to highly commercialized farming using *hirsutum* varieties occurred in the colonial period, hybrid cotton since the 1970s, and genetically modified cotton over the past two decades—Bt cotton—all became gambles that generations of crisis-ridden farmers became party to. The agrarian transition left no section of the rural population untouched as social institutions also transformed with the inveterate economic changes. In pre-colonial India, the accidentality in this agrarian transition is attributed to institutional changes that accompanied changing political fortunes, and during the colonial era, to the colonial state transforming local institutions, fostering railway expansion, persistently introducing new varieties, and several other measures. Even before the colonial agenda for cotton expansion, institutional changes and political instability over centuries influenced the socio-economic development of the region. The period of interest traverses the influence of the Delhi sultanates, the Bahamani sultanates, the Mughals, the Marathas, and colonial rule in the pre-independence era. In the post-independence era, the accidentality is ascribed to the introduction of high input intensive systems of production espoused in the Green Revolution, and the introduction of Bt cotton, among several others. Viewed through this lens, cotton in Vidarbha is a legacy that has passed on over generations; transferring the traits of its deep link with capitalism and imperialism that goes beyond national boundaries and involvement of diverse set of stakeholders.

This book is an account of how hope frequently gives way to despair if farmers are unable to earn enough to pay off their debt and meet major consumption requirements. It is a chronicle of the struggles to make ends meet with whatever remains after repaying the debt partially or totally so that they save enough, spend enough, invest enough, and survive enough to repeat the same another season. In this book we document the struggles of farmers as they navigate the country's economic development and of which they are an integral part. In doing so, we bring to light the routine adaptation of farmers to changes in the economy, markets, environment, and politics. Surprisingly, how the story of risk and vulnerability of the farmers of Vidarbha have panned out over centuries has not been narrated to the extent that the enormity of the crisis warrants. An important facet of this story is the resilience and enterprise of the Vidarbha farmers so that the gambles with cotton can also be interpreted as the performance of 'cotton specialists'. That the cotton specialists routinely navigate high-stake risks in a production system that is the consequence of historical accidents and that institutional reforms do not necessarily mitigate risks for the farmers as they gamble with cotton is the core subject of this book.

Through the body of evidence and arguments presented in this book, we posit that there is a need to reimagine the story of cotton farming in the region in a manner that recognizes the bets that the farmers wager in the context of the interplay of capital, institutions, and nature. Historically, upheavals and disturbances far away have been the hallmark of being a cotton grower in the region. For centuries, cotton growers have been exposed to booms and busts of cotton, the vagaries of monsoon, and the uncertainties of the prices. Successive governments at the centre and the state have intervened to support in the form of agricultural input subsidies, procurement of produce at MSP, debt waivers, and several other programmes and schemes. However, the past three and a half decades have been unforgiving for the region's cotton farmers. What went wrong? Why have policies, programmes, and schemes been unable to alleviate the woes of the farm sector? Why have civil society organizations' efforts to sustain farm livelihoods not worked? Why do farmers continue to end their lives despite the concerted efforts to address agrarian distress?

In this book that was conceived as an attempt to articulate the complexity of risk and vulnerability in Vidarbha cotton, we present two core arguments.

First, we argue that it is necessary to locate the antecedents of institutions and agrarian conditions in historical circumstances in the distant past. That these events were beyond the anticipation or control of the generations of cotton farmers, renders them accidental. Second, we characterize the gambles of Vidarbha cotton farmers owing to them routinely undertaking risky production and marketing decisions in a high-stakes environment. That farmers' ex ante and ex post management of risks is situated in the context of multiple market failures is testimony to them being fundamentally similar to entrepreneurs in the formal sector. However, unlike the formal sector entrepreneurs, the odds are egregiously stacked against the cotton farmers. In the absence of fall-back options or cushions to absorb adverse income shocks, farmers have specialized in cropping patterns, developed agronomic practices, and relied on informal mechanisms that help them wager their bets repeatedly.

In part due to the insights from our engagement with farmers over a decade, and partly due to our frustration with limitations of top-down policies that ignore the insights from the field, this book proposes a 'people-centric' approach to developing agricultural policies and debating pathways of agricultural development. An important theme of the book is that merely focusing on the farmer and farm household as a producer and discounting the needs of the farmer and farm household as a consumer neglects their vulnerability. In doing so, it rests the case for accommodating the hopes, aspirations, and concerns of farmers in agricultural policy rather than simple production-centric target fixation like 'doubling agricultural credit', 'doubling farmers' income', or 'doubling the number of farmer-producer organizations', and so on.

Although the emphasis of the book is on cotton farmers of Vidarbha, we also present insights on the lives and livelihoods of agricultural labour households and comment on the scope of non-farm activities in augmenting household incomes. Furthermore, in the light of the political economy considerations shaping the role of the state in agricultural development, it argues for the need to deepen our understanding of unmitigated risks in agriculture as well as the vulnerability of agricultural households. We believe this is necessary for a critical assessment of the limitations of informal risk-management strategies and failures of existing formal risk-management structures in place to protect incomes of agricultural households. Taken together, the arguments presented in the book call for a reimagination of the market-based approach to risk management with an eye on the changing structures of society and economy.

One might wonder how we arrived at the title of the book. There is an anecdote that will help explain our choice of the book's title. During fieldwork in Wardha in 2015, we asked a farmer in his fifties about what he believed needed to change for the farmers to be satisfied with farming policies. He answered: 'Sheti sodun dhya' (Give up farming). The bemusing response was followed by the farmer proudly showing us the packets of a new brand of Bt cotton seeds that he said he had never used earlier. Upon asking why someone utterly frustrated with policies and farming would be exuberant while displaying the seeds which were likely to add to his woes, his response baffled us even more than the earlier response: 'Kahinna romanch avadoto' (Some like the thrill). His emotive responses about cotton or the cotton seeds notwithstanding, it made us ponder over the possibility of the 'thrill' associated with cotton growing.

In a region where generations of cotton growers have risked their assets and lives in growing cotton; a cash crop that has irrefutably shaped the world in more ways than one, it was not surprising for us that while conducting an opinion poll to name a board game Gaurav had designed to simulate riskiness in production in Vidarbha, the most popular response was 'Baazigar' (Gambler). It was on that day that we decided if we ever wrote a book based on our work in Vidarbha, it would refer to this 'Gambler' as a mark of our work's dedication to those who are routinely gambling by undertaking cash crop production in a high-risk environment year after year. There are however fundamental conceptual distinctions between a gamble, bet, and lottery that we will delve into while describing how cotton farmers qualify to be gamblers.

Regarding the 'Accidental' part of the title, we have long held the view that the importance of historical accidents in the story of cotton in Vidarbha is understudied. Furthermore, the history of the Vidarbha region itself is not completely understood; even among administrators, academics, journalists, policymakers and the protagonists of the book—the farmers. The contemporary discourse on agrarian crisis and rural distress explains the crisis through developments in the recent past. There is limited engagement with agrarian history of the region which has been the epicentre of agrarian crisis and long before that, the stage of major geopolitical upheavals. Therefore, we dug deeper into the region's history from archival and secondary sources with the hope that there may be clues in the region's history that might explain how it became a major centre for global cotton supply. Our primary obsession with the region's history arose out of our interest in figuring out how institutions and markets evolved in the pre-colonial and colonial periods. This is not to suggest that there was a lack of design or deliberation on part of the rulers, state or forces beyond the region in these transformative changes. Rather the emphasis on the unfolding of history foregrounds the lives of farmers for whom these changes were mostly unanticipated and external. Although there were elements of design in policies and stakeholders anticipated upheavals to a certain extent, for the protagonists of our story, that is cotton farmers of Vidarbha, the events of interest retained attributes of accidents. Indeed, how farmers responded to the changes exemplifies their agency albeit with considerable temporal and spatial variation. The analytical approach in this book also does not undermine the commendable research that scholars have conducted over the decades from their respective perspectives in the realm of agriculture, agrarian crisis, cotton, economic history, and other related themes that we delve into. In fact, much of our insights on the question of agrarian crisis as well as the region are informed by contemporary as well as historical scholarship.

STRUCTURE OF THE BOOK

This book is structured into two parts. In Part I (Chapters 1 and 2), we delve into the geography, political changes and reconfiguration of the territorial boundaries of Vidarbha from a long historical point of view. We stress on the need to distinguish between the history of Berar and Central Provinces that are building blocks of present-day Vidarbha, and examine the pre-colonial developments since the thirteenth century in particular and identify the major forces and institutional factors that influenced the circumstances in which the commercialization of cotton took place. We dwell on the veritable institutional changes that shaped not only the trade expansion but also agricultural development outcomes over time. By investigating the details of the colonial takeover of the region since the mid-nineteenth century, we give a sneak peek into the changes in institutions—particularly land revenue administration, property rights, traditional agrarian relations, credit markets and expansion of railways. The most significant historical event that we dwell on is the American Civil War that lasted between 1861 and 1865. Relying on colonial administrative records, limited archival materials, and secondary sources, we reconstruct the circumstances under which present-day Vidarbha's agrarian transformation occured.

In Part II, we examine developments in relatively more recent history: over the past twelve years based on our primary research in the districts of Wardha and Yavatmal in Vidarbha. The task of Chapter 3 is to present the study design and characteristics of sample households in our longitudinal study between 2009 and 2021. The analysis over the next three chapters is based on the data from a pooled sample of households over the eight years (2009–2011, 2015–2017, and 2019–2020) and a panel data over the five years (2015–2017 and 2019–2020). For the sake of brevity, we have broken up the set of findings into three chapters allowing a comprehensive coverage of the underlying issues: cropping patterns, costs, and incomes (Chapter 4); dynamics of agricultural inputs in cotton cultivation (Chapter 5); and vulnerability of farm households by emphasizing the farm household as a unit of production as well as consumption (Chapter 6). In the last chapter of the book (Chapter 7), we conclude with a synthesis of the findings from both parts and articulate policy implications as well as our vision for the agricultural development of Vidarbha. Taken together, these chapters present a nuanced understanding of aspects of change and continuity in our narrative of the 'accidental gamblers' as individuals with elements of agency who routinely adapt to changing environment, markets, and policies. Through the body of evidence from the multiple rounds of surveys and fieldwork over the years, we raise questions on the nature of choice and agency as well as the lack thereof in the story of the persistence of cotton in Vidarbha.

Despite a rich heritage of the commodity and its inherent relationship with the narrative of agrarian crisis and farmers' suicides, there is a dearth of detailed investigation on questions that have motivated our research. Given the primacy of a risky production environment and a chronic developmental backwardness of the region, the habitual act of growing cotton is essentially a gamble, but there are gaps in the literature in systematically characterizing the gambles. The fact that the gamble with cotton is an artefact of the historical accidents that we emphasize characterizes cotton farmers of Vidarbha as 'accidental gamblers'—hence the seemingly dramatic title of the book. Furthermore, discerning readers who may have engaged with the discourse on agrarian crisis and farmers' suicides would have observed that official statistics on farmers' suicides is reported under 'Accidental Deaths and Suicides in India'. Our reference to 'accident' is also an implicit reference to this artefact.

Our methodology allows for a critical examination of the narrative of agrarian crisis. Undoubtedly, the nature of cotton production has undergone drastic changes compared to what it was over half a century ago. The real cost of cultivation has increased but real returns to cultivation have fallen, resulting in lower profitability. That farmers continue to increase the area allocated to cotton or at best make marginal reductions in response to changing prices or other sources of adverse variability in the region compels us to wonder if the characterization of agrarian crisis in Vidarbha is valid. That despite facing losses, sometimes multiple losses in a short period, farmers do not merely cultivate cotton but 'perform' all the new 'tricks of the trade' made available to them, raises questions about the oversimplified characterization of farmers in the region. By relying on research of primary and secondary historical materials, ethnography, and longitudinal survey data, we present a novel description of the journey of cotton in the region and how farmers adapted to it.

The set of findings from Part I and Part II underscores our hypothesis that there is an agrarian crisis in Vidarbha irrespective of how one characterizes it. We find that the crisis in Vidarbha is nested in the broader institutional, macroeconomic, and political economy forces that have not only been shaped by historical developments beyond the control of the farmers but also continue to shape history continually. By drawing attention to the major dimensions of risk and vulnerability, particularly agricultural production and price risks, we find that over the centuries, they have essentially remained unchanged while there are dimensions of change. For instance, the near-universal diffusion of transgenic seeds—Bt cotton—two decades since their commercialization is a clear break from the narrative of technological backwardness. However, emerging issues with Bt cotton's ability to protect farmers against pink bollworm infestation and the growing issue of secondary pests suggests the inherent risks and uncertainties embedded in new technologies. The commoditization of agricultural inputs including seeds and fertilizers has intensified over time. Credit market imperfections and shift from dirigiste continue to have distributional impacts in the village economy. The abuse of soil health and groundwater resources persists unabated. In addition, income shocks are not fully insured, and level of awareness about formal insurance remains low. The COVID-19 pandemic also showed the multiple dimensions of vulnerability to covariate as well as idiosyncratic risks. The inability to garner labour resources to undertake sowing or weeding within a critical window continues to bother farmers while gendered division of labour persists despite structural changes in the village economy.

Our book situates the story of cotton in a region that has become the hotspot for the sordid manifestation of agrarian distress—farmers' suicides. What went wrong in the story of cotton needs an examination from both its historical developments as well as the interplay of markets and policies that have shaped the fates of millions of cotton growers. We argue that the story of cotton in Vidarbha cannot be narrated in isolation from the history of Vidarbha as well as how Vidarbha cotton has been embedded in the global trends over centuries.

Our expectations from this set of arguments are modest. We hope that our conceptualization and empirical evidence contributes to the body of knowledge and the discourse of agrarian crisis. If there are solutions, it would be a source of joy. This book, although comprehensive in its assessment of the risk and vulnerability of Vidarbha cotton, is by no means all-inclusive. It is likely that there are historical materials and studies pertaining to several aspects of the complex systems under inquiry that we may not have referred to. All errors of omission and commission are ours. Usual disclaimers apply.

NOTES

1. Unicorn refers to start-ups valued at 1 billion US dollars or higher. The number of unicorns has been on the rise in recent times. The technology start-up trends suggest an increasing reliance on the platform economy. Platform economy refers to a diverse set of businesses based on radical digital systems connecting buyers and sellers. Affordable internet services and smart phones have enabled the growth of the platform economy.
2. H. P. Binswanger-Mkhize, 'The Stunted Structural Transformation of the Indian Economy: Agriculture, Manufacturing and the Rural Non-Farm Sector', *Economic and Political Weekly* 48, nos. 26/27 (2013): 5–13.
3. S. Arya, 'Cotton Rates at an All-Time High but No Bonus for Vid's Farmers', *Times of India*, 3 November 2021, https://timesofindia.indiatimes.com/city/nagpur/cotton-rates-at-an-all-time-high-but-no-bonus-for-vids-farmers/articleshow/87495612.cms (accessed on 20 November 2021).

PART I

1

A BRIEF HISTORY OF VIDARBHA

Vidarbha is a major cotton-growing region in central India.[1] On the political map of India, it is located in the eastern part of the state of Maharashtra, the richest state in India in terms of gross state domestic product and home to the country's financial and commercial capital—Mumbai.[2] It has been a frontier, not only geographically and culturally but also in terms of recasting the global system of cotton growing and manufacturing since the second half of the nineteenth century. It is however a land of several contradictions.

First, despite being home to the winter capital of the state, Nagpur, there has been long-standing demand for separate statehood on grounds of political negligence resulting in significant developmental backlogs.[3] Ethos of being separate from rest of the state are also reflected in the arena of cricket as Vidarbha has one of the three first-class cricket teams in the state, the other two being Mumbai and Maharashtra. Second, it is one of the most mineral-rich regions in the country and contributes to over two-thirds of mineral deposits of the state and most of its forest resources.[4] Yet, as if there were a 'resource curse', it is one of the most backward regions.[5] Third, far from the popular imagination of Vidarbha as a homogenous region, it is an amalgamation of two administrative divisions having distinct linguistic and sociocultural histories. Whilst the Amravati division (western part) has a shared history with the erstwhile Berar Province, the Nagpur division (eastern part) has a shared history with what comprised districts of the Central Provinces during colonial era. The cotton tracts of the former have primarily been the epicentre of agrarian distress and witnessed a spate of farmers' suicides over the past two and a half decades whereas the densely forested areas of the latter are afflicted with Naxalite–Maoist insurgency. In fact, the parts of eastern Vidarbha that have been witnessing Naxal extremism for over half a century continue to have meaning in the political assertion of Gonds as erstwhile rulers of the kingdom of Nagpur, but they are conspicuous by their absence in the agricultural development discourse on Vidarbha that is primarily concentrated on western Vidarbha. Fourth, it became a prominent centre of Buddhism, but it has witnessed centuries of bloody power struggles that shaped the history of India.[6] For constructing the history of cotton in the region, one has to give proper concern to the geographical setting and the political scrambles that shaped the region.

The identification of the region while based on present-day boundaries of administrative units comprising Vidarbha, nevertheless, is not assumed to be fixed in different phases of history of interest. Beyond the political identity, the geographical region corresponding to Vidarbha and its socio-cultural identity are crucial strands in our narrative. While we are not inclined towards periodizing the regional history into ancient, medieval, and modern, the broader time bracket of interest is based on our judgment about major events within and beyond the region that influenced the region over a long historical scale rather than mere chronological occurrence. Using the evolution of political boundaries in the region between the thirteenth century and mid-nineteenth century as well as the pre-colonial history of agrarian condition as the backdrop, this chapter explores three broad questions.

First, what can a deeper understanding of the long-range historical account inform us about the forces that shaped the political contours of the region? Second, what were the antecedents of the institutions relevant to contemporary agricultural development? Third, how do the reconfigurations of geopolitics help us characterize 'geographic luck' in the context of the development of the cotton economy?[7] This chapter explores these questions and offers insights into the region and its transformation during the pre-colonial period that helps establish the antecedents of the cotton economy of the region during the colonial era. It presents a brief history of the pre-colonial era in the form of dramatic power struggles and contestation for political supremacy in the region of Berar and the Central Provinces to piece together the larger picture. In doing so, it situates the narrative of agrarian distress in a historical setting. From the perspective of the scale of our historical narrative and emphasis on deep-seated structures shaping historical change, it resembles the *longue durée* tradition of the Annales School as we seek a wide perspective on historical change in the region by acknowledging the role of a complex range of factors. However, we also recognise the importance of episodic events as well as individuals and cultural groups. While it is preposterous to even claim that an exhaustive presentation of the historical developments over this long period can be presented in a chapter, we nevertheless weave together major political developments that are likely to have shaped institutions and agricultural development in territories corresponding to present-day Vidarbha.[8]

THE REGION

Vidarbha features prominently in India's history, literature, and mythology. There are literary references to Vidarbha in ancient Hindu scriptures including the Rig Veda and Puranas apart from several references in the epics Mahabharata and Ramayana. In antiquity, it was an important centre of learning and culture.[9] Human archaeological excavations in the region indicate considerable prehistoric and protohistoric human activity.[10] Iron technology in ancient megalithic communities of the region was well developed.[11] Even the effect of climatic changes in the late Holocene is well documented.[12] However, millions of years before human settlement, the land was home to dinosaurs.[13] The region shares large swathes with the Gondwana region—home to the Gond (also Gondi) ethnic group.[14] It is thus part of the Neoproterozoic Era geological landmass—Gondwanaland or Gondwana—meaning forests of the Gonds.[15] Gondwana even became a landscape for colonial imagination about primitivism.[16]

Present-day Vidarbha comprises eleven districts that were once part of two provinces—Berar or Varhad in the west and the Central Provinces in the east. Berar largely coincides with the Amravati administrative division of Vidarbha that includes five districts: Amravati, Buldhana, Akola, Yavatmal, and Washim.[17] The Nagpur division comprises six districts: Nagpur, Wardha, Chandrapur, Gadchiroli, Bhandara, and Gondia, which were carved out of the Central Provinces.[18] These districts were part of Nag Vidarbha under the Maratha Bhonsales until the colonial takeover of the region.[19] There is considerable heterogeneity between the two divisions of Vidarbha. However, this aspect has not received the attention it deserves in the discourse on agrarian crisis afflicting the region. Nevertheless, the following distinctions between the two divisions are noteworthy.

First, districts in the erstwhile Berar Province along with present-day Nagpur and Wardha have had a long history of cotton cultivation whilst the remaining districts of eastern Vidarbha have been paddy-growing regions. This distinction based on the importance of cotton in agriculture correlates with the patterns of farmers' suicides discussed earlier. Second, while the Amravati division and the two districts of Nagpur division, Wardha and Nagpur, continue to be hotspots of farmers' suicides, three districts of Nagpur division, Gondia, Gadchiroli, and Chandrapur, grapple with Naxalite–Maoist insurgency. Not attributing causality, the latter districts, with a greater share of scheduled tribes (STs) in the population, dense forest cover, and rich mineral deposits are considerably underdeveloped compared to the former.[20] Third, as elaborated in Chapter 2, infrastructural development, particularly the expansion of railways and integration with major markets such as Bombay during the colonial period, not only began earlier but also has been concentrated in western Vidarbha. Fourth, local institutions of eastern and western Vidarbha have been historically very different.

During the colonial era, farmers in the former became owners of the land under the *ryotwari* system whilst alternative land administration systems such as *malguzari* persisted in the latter. The nature of the institutions not only had a bearing on the political developments of the region but also the patterns of economic development across the region as discussed later. That the Central Provinces came to be known as the 'Cinderella of the Indian Provinces' speaks of the state of general deprivation during the colonial period. Yet despite the state of deprivation in the colonial period, the province offered stark contrasts as captured by John O. Miller's reading on the Central Provinces to the Royal Society of Arts. Miller says:[21]

> And yet it is extremely interesting, and no Province perhaps brings into such vivid juxtaposition the contrasts and diversities that characterise India as a whole. It is a microcosm of India, of India's history, and of India's problems.

Although we refer to eastern and western Vidarbha as if there were clear-cut demarcations between the two and their composition, it should not be inferred that the east and the west of the region have had distinct and stable boundaries; rather, territorial boundaries in the region have been dynamic.

Berar had a much longer existence as an administrative province whilst the Central Provinces came into existence in 1861.[22] From the perspective of our narrative, it is fascinating that expansion of cotton cultivation in the region was a primary reason for the administrative restructuring that resulted in the formation of the Central Provinces.[23] Such was the lure of Berar that despite Hyderabad State being a British protectorate, in 1902, territories of Berar—Akola, Amravati, Buldana (Buldhana), and Yeotmal (Yavatmal)—were leased out to the British by the nizam of Hyderabad for an annual payment of 25 lakh rupees.[24] In fact, Berar, with its fertile cotton tracts, was the richest part of the nizam's dominion—the largest and wealthiest princely state in India in the early twentieth century. Consequently, these territories were attached to the Central Provinces, forming the Central Provinces and Berar. The administration of the cotton economy in the two parts of present-day Vidarbha also underwent historical changes as the chief commissioner of the Central Provinces took charge of the administration of Berar as the chief commissioner of the Central Provinces and Berar.[25]

Despite being assigned a singular administrative identity by the British, Berar and the Central Provinces had distinct political histories and sociocultural identities that have manifested in demands for separation of the two provinces.[26] The Central Provinces itself is a heterogeneous territory with diversity in culture as well as geography, with parts of present-day Maharashtra, Madhya Pradesh, Chhattisgarh, and Orissa (now Odisha) being carved out of the province. Commenting on the merging of Berar and the Central Provinces, the first director of the Department of Agriculture of the Central Provinces, and later the Central Provinces commissioner of settlements and agriculture, J. B. Fuller wrote:

> … a veritable territorial puzzle was pieced together, and tracts were united which differed widely from each other in circumstances, people, and language.[27]

In light of the 'veritable territorial puzzle', it is not surprising that there have been popular movements for separate statehood for over a century, stoking tensions based on these diversities. As recent as 2017, an incumbent chief minister belonging to the Bharatiya Janata Party (BJP) publicly expressed his and his party's support for separate statehood of Vidarbha whilst the majority party in the Maha Vikas Aghadi coalition, Shiv Sena, opposed the idea of separate statehood on grounds of its emphasis on a unified Maharashtra.[28]

Two years prior, the advocate general of the state had courted political controversy by calling for a referendum on Vidarbha's statehood. The demand for a separate state of 'Maha Vidarbha' dates to 1905. In the backdrop of claims about discrimination and negligence in resource allocation, there was a demand to separate the Marathi-speaking areas from the Hindi-speaking areas of the Central Provinces. The proposal for a separate state of Vidarbha was approved by the All India Congress Committee in 1918 and by the Madhya Pradesh Legislative Assembly in 1938. A week before India's independence, the Akola Pact of 8 August 1947, an agreement between the Congress leaders from the two parts, envisaged the formation of two provinces—Vidarbha and Western Maharashtra—under one government. In 1950, Berar and the Central Provinces became part of the state of Madhya Pradesh, with Nagpur as its capital, but the movement to separate the Marathi-speaking areas persisted. The Nagpur Pact of 28 September 1953 envisaged the creation of a Maharashtra state that would include the bilingual Bombay State and the Marathi-speaking areas of Madhya Pradesh and Hyderabad State. However, the States Reorganization Commission (SRC), in its report in 1955, recommended a separate state of Vidarbha after considering arguments put forward by parties demanding integration with Maharashtra and those demanding separation.[29] It recognized the changing political fortunes along the following lines:

> The history of Berar falls into certain distinct periods; and it may be useful to indicate briefly the political fortunes of Berar in each one of these periods, since it will facilitate an understanding of the demand for autonomy.[30]

The SRC also envisioned the new state of Vidarbha to be an important cotton-growing state of the country. In 1956, when states were reorganized along linguistic lines, Berar as well as the Marathi-speaking parts of Central Provinces (present-day Nagpur division) were separated from Madhya Pradesh and integrated with the Bombay State.[31] This integration necessitated a constitutional amendment to ensure the constitutionality of the Nagpur Pact. Section 371(2) was added to the Constitution of India, assuring equitable allocation of funds for development, adequate arrangements for education and vocational training, and provision of adequate employment opportunities in services under the state government.[32] Vidarbha was retained as part of Maharashtra when the bilingual Bombay State was bifurcated into Gujarat and Maharashtra on 1 May 1960 following the struggles of the Samyukta Maharashtra movement.[33] Nagpur—the city of oranges—became the winter capital of the state, and a bench of the Bombay High Court was located there.[34] However, despite assurances of equitable distribution of resources across the regions, humongous 'developmental backlogs' persist—an issue that we will explain in detail in the context of the region's agricultural development. The region elects 10 members of parliament (MPs) (out of 48) and 60 members of the Legislative Assembly (MLAs) (out of 288) but the political mobilization from the region is also limited, and there is yet to be a consensus among major political parties on the separate statehood question.[35]

Having described how present-day Vidarbha, with deep-rooted heterogeneities across the districts, weathered recurrent demands for separate statehood over a century, it remains to be seen what factors drove the political instability in the pre-independence times in particular. In what follows, we summarize the key developments from mainly medieval history until the colonial takeover of the region in the nineteenth century that shaped the conditions of agriculture in Vidarbha. This historical account, although brief, provides an understanding of the preconditions of agrarian transformation that the colonial rule ushered in. Furthermore, it also highlights the changes and continuities in what we characterize as 'outsider influence' in the region.

AGE OF UNSTABLE KINGDOMS

The ancient history of Vidarbha spanning the Vedic period as well as Mauryan and Shunga dynasty until the second century BC is well recorded.[36] The fertile basin of the Wardha and Wainganga rivers experienced prosperity in the first half of the first millennium. Under the Satavahana Empire, urban settlements flourished, only to decay following its fall. By the early third century, under the Satavahana rule, feudal chiefs raised revenue from taxes on land, property, and trade.[37] Analysis of artefacts of the Vakataka period suggests de-urbanization and growth of rural settlements in Vidarbha in the fifth century.[38] The existence of feudal levy in feudatory territories added to the suffering of peasants. Transformation of the free and revenue-paying peasantry into sharecropping and rent-paying peasantry in rural areas resulted due to extant land grant arrangements.[39] These arrangements suggest that agrarian distress in the region is not a twentieth-century phenomenon. In fact, in subsequent sections, we will present insights on how agrarian distress is deeply linked to the local institutions of the times.

There was decadence for about four centuries from about AD 500 in the post-Gupta period.[40] Until the thirteenth century, the region came under the rule of several Deccan kingdoms, such as the Satavahanas, Vakatakas, Chalukyas, Rashtrakutas, and Yadavas.[41] Over the next several centuries, prolonged contestations for imperial dominance shaped the political boundaries of the region. Although cotton is believed to have been grown at several places and trade in white calico flourished during these long stretches of the region's history,[42] the political instability in the region has been aptly summarized by the *Amravati Gazetteers*:

> Long wasting wars, bloody feuds, revolts, massacres, assassinations, cruel and barbarous punishments, sad stories of death….[43]

In comparison with Berar, the Central Provinces was a much larger territory (see Map 2.2). The Narmada flowing along the northern stretches of the province separates the Vindhya and Satpura mountain ranges.[44] It is a natural boundary for the geographical separation of India's north from the south.[45] Endowed with densely forested highlands along with river valleys and plains, the province has been the frontier of dynasties of yore discussed thus far. Princely states also ruled tracts of the province independently or as subordinates of other powerful empires that ruled over the region. With the decline of the Yadavas in medieval India, the Muslim sultanates attained considerable control over the region. However, the later centuries witnessed the power struggles involving the Mughals, Marathas, and the British East India Company (or EIC; 'Company' henceforth, unless otherwise stated). Between the thirteenth and nineteenth centuries, the region came under the control of several empires ranging from the Muslim sultanates to the British Crown. A brief history of the political instability in the pre-colonial period follows.

THE MUSLIM SULTANATES

While the Kalachuris and Rashtrakutas ruled over parts of present-day Vidarbha in the second half of the first millennium, the Chalukyas had their influence on the region from the sixth to the thirteenth century. This was followed by dominance of the Yadavas (Seuna dynasty) with their capital at

Devagiri in the Deccan (*dakhin*; literally, Sanskrit *daksina* meaning south) that included the territory associated with Berar.[46] What may be considered as a watershed moment in the region's history, in 1296 the Yadavas of Devagiri surrendered in the raid by Ala-ud-din Khalji (also Khilji), who went on to usurp the throne of the Delhi sultanate in a coup financed by the plunder from *dakhin*. This was the first raid by the Delhi sultanate in the south, or *dakhin*, and the Yadava raja Ramadeva (also Ramachandra) continued to pay tribute until Ala-ud-din Khalji's unsuccessful raids against the Kakatiyas of Warangal (present-day Telangana) in 1303.[47] In 1307, Khalji's slave lieutenant—Malik Kafur—raided Devagiri.[48] Devagiri became the base for Khalji's military advances in the peninsula, and Malik Kafur defeated the Kakatiyas in a raid in 1310 in alliance with Ramadeva. Apart from the guarantee for annual tribute and elephants to be sent to Delhi by the Kakatiyas, it is speculated that Malik Kafur returned to Delhi in 1310 with the famed Peacock Throne and the Koh-i-Noor diamond.[49] In 1313, Devagiri was annexed to the Delhi sultanate when Ramadeva's successor Raja Simhana III was killed during the recapture campaign of Malik Kafur.[50] Following a series of successful raids in southern India that amounted to unprecedented loot, Malik Kafur became the governor of Devagiri until 1315.[51] The following year, Ala-ud-din Khalji died and Malik Kafur, who had become *naib* (viceroy), became the regent.[52] However, Malik Kafur was assassinated by the very soldiers he had sent to blind Ala-ud-din Khalji's imprisoned son Mubarak Shah.[53] Mubarak Shah usurped power and became the sultan of Delhi for four years.[54]

With the death of Ala-ud-din Khalji and Malik Kafur, the Yadavas got some respite from the frequent raids from the north. However, the last Yadava ruler Harapaladeva was defeated by Mubarak Shah in a raid on the Devagiri in 1318.[55] At its peak, the Yadava Kingdom included parts of present-day southern Gujarat, the Marathi-speaking regions of Madhya Pradesh and Berar, western Maharashtra, the western half of Hyderabad State, Karnataka (parts in Old Bombay Province), and the northern districts of Mysore.[56] The annihilation of the Yadavas however set the course for bloody and brutal territorial contests in the Deccan that lasted over five centuries. The Deccan conquests also transformed the demographic structure as they created a migration corridor between the north and the south. There was large-scale coerced migration of the Muslim population including the nobles and clergies of Delhi migrating to Tughlaq's (also Tughlak) second administrative capital Daulatabad.[57] While there was large-scale reverse migration to Delhi, the presence of elites in Daulatabad played an important role in the subsequent rise of the Bahamani sultanate in the Deccan.[58]

After the fall of the Khalji dynasty, the Tughluqs took over the Delhi sultanate in 1320. The founder of the Tughluk sultanate, Ghazi Malik (also Ghiyas-ud-Din Tughluq), sent his son Ulugh Khan (also Jauna) to invade the Kakatiyas in the south. In 1325, Ulugh Khan became the sultan following Ghiyas-ud-Din Tughluq's demise in a bizarre accident during a grand reception to commemorate his successful Bengal raid.[59] He ruled under the name of Muhammad bin Tughluq. During his reign, several independent states emerged from the rebellion by Tughlaq *amir*s (nobles). One such kingdom founded by an *amir* Ala-ud-din Husain Bahamani Gangu (also Hasan Shah and Bahaman Shah) was the Bahamani sultanate in the Deccan.[60] The sultanate had its capital in the fort-city of Gulbarga (in present-day Karnataka) and ruled over Berar from 1347. Though it may seem like the most turbulent fifty years in Vidarbha's history spanning the end of the Yadava dynasty to the influence of three Muslim sultanates, the developments in the following centuries would be punctuated by periods of several turbulent five decades.

Berar was also known as Waradatat (literally, the banks of river Varada, that is, Wardha). It was one of the four *taraf*s, or administrative divisions, of the Bahamani sultanate that were governed by the *tarafdar*s, or governors, having extensive administrative, civil, revenue, and military powers.[61] Achalpur (also Elichpur, now in Amravati district) was the seat of Berar *taraf*, and the first *tarafdar* of Berar was Safdar Khan Sistani.[62] In the second half of the fourteenth century, the second Bahamani sultan Muhammad Shah I's reign witnessed high administrative efficiency. The governor of Berar (Majlis-i-Aaali) had unfettered power over the provincial administration, and later Bahamani rulers curtailed his powers through administrative subdivisions and frequent visits to the province.

In the northern and eastern frontiers of Berar, the Gond principalities have been recorded to be in control from the fourteenth century with five branches of Gond kingdoms ruling over parts of central India. In the late fourteenth century, when Firuz (also Firoz) Shah Bahamani campaigned against the Vijayanagara Kingdom, the Gonds helped Narasingdeva, the ruler of Khedala (Kherla, now in Betul district of Madhya Pradesh), in his raids against the Bahamanis. However, the Gonds were defeated and Narasingdeva accepted Bahamani supremacy. Remarkably, Firuz inducted Deccani Brahmins into his administration, especially in revenue administration. This inclusion of Hindus provided a 'balance against the influx of foreigners *afaqis* or *gharibs*'.[63] In 1419, Firuz lost to Deva Raya I of the Vijayanagara Kingdom.[64] Under Sultan Ahmad Shah who reigned from 1422–1436, the Bahamanis eventually dominated the Krishna–Godavari basin after eliminating the ruler of Warangal and annexing large parts of its territory. Although there were several decades of Bahamani consolidation, the Bahamani stronghold over the Deccan weakened in the last two decades of the fifteenth century.

The Bahamani sultanate reached its peak in the time of Mahmud Gawan (also Gavan) in the late fifteenth century as territories and trade expanded. Berar was divided into north Berar with the headquarters at Gavligad (also Gawlighur) and south Berar with the headquarters at Mahur for administrative convenience.[65] In what stands out as a beacon of hope during crisis in a conflict-ridden land, albeit lasting briefly, Gawan also introduced several land reforms following the devastating Deccan famine in 1474. However, with Gawan's assassination in 1481, the Bahamani sultanate that ruled over the region for nearly 150 years went into disarray.[66] In 1490, eight years before Vasco da Gama landed in the Malabar Coast of India, five independent kingdoms emerged following the disintegration of the Bahamani sultanate, and Berar was one among them.[67] The governor of Gawlighur (also Gawligarh or Gawligad)—Fathullah Imad-ul-Mulk—founded the Imad Shahi dynasty that ruled over Berar from 1490 to 1574.[68] In the sixteenth century, Berar was constantly under attack from the Nizam Shahi sultanate of Ahmednagar, but Imad-ul-Mulk's descendants resisted the attacks. In 1568, the teenage ruler Burhan Imad Shah was deposed by a noble of the dynasty—Tufail Khan. However, Tufail Khan's rule was short-lived as he failed to defend the invasion by Murtaza Nizam Shah I.[69] The Nizam Shahi rule that ensued saw two decades of contestation in the region in which the Mughals and *amir*s of the Nizam Shahi sultanate reshaped the power structure in Berar.[70] Following decades of attempts by the Mughals to control Berar, it was ceded to Mughal Emperor Akbar by Sultana Chand Bibi of the Nizam Shahi of Ahmednagar and Bijapur sultanate in 1596.[71] Thus began the most turbulent epoch in Vidarbha's history that spanned over 250 years.

THE MUGHAL AND MARATHA CONTEST

Despite the annexation of Berar by the Mughals in 1596, conquests of strategically important forts continued until 1600.[72] In 1601, Malik Ambar—the Siddi mercenary having allegiance to the Nizam Shahi sultanate—revolted against the Mughals. This resulted in Akbar's successor Jahangir—who gave the Company permission to trade and set up factory in Surat—sending the Rajput king Man Singh I and other generals to regain the three Deccan provinces namely Berar, Khandesh, and Ahmednagar under one viceroyalty.[73] The struggle for supremacy in the Deccan continued, and in 1628 Berar returned to Mughal subordination following Jahangir's third son, Shah Jahan's campaigns.[74] Over the next four years, Deccan was ravaged by a deadly famine. Shah Jahan carved out the province of Telangana from Berar, but it was merged with Bidar to form Bidar *subah* in 1657.[75] Within four decades of the Mughal conquest of Berar, Shah Jahan's successor—Aurangzeb—took charge of Berar in 1636 as the viceroy. Berar became a Mughal *subah*, with Ellichpur (or Achalpur) in present-day Amravati district as its capital.[76]

Upon becoming the emperor of the Mughal Empire in 1658, Aurangzeb introduced several administrative changes in the Deccan as discussed later. However, his protracted conflict with his nemesis—the Marathas—eventually contributed to the downfall of the Mughal Empire.[77] The Maratha Empire was founded by Shivaji Bhonsale I (also Bhosle and Bhonsala), son of a nobleman of the Nizam Shahi (Ahmednagar) and Adil Shahi (Bijapur) sultanate, Shahaji Bhonsale.[78] The nearly three-decade-long 'Deccan wars' between the Mughals and the Marathas were financed by revenues from Berar.[79] Extraction of tribute from neighbouring kingdoms also filled the coffers of the imperial (Mughal) exchequer. For instance, in 1661, the *subahdar* of Berar and the *faujdar* of the province attacked the Gond kingdom of Chanda (present-day Chandrapur in Vidarbha) under the command of Aurangzeb's general Diler Khan. The Gond raja paid 1 crore rupees,[80] promised to pay an annual tribute of 2 lakh rupees, and saw his fortifications razed.[81] The fate of the region was also determined by several treaties among the axis of powers.

In 1665, amidst the Mughal–Maratha skirmishes, the Treaty of Purandhar (also Purandar) was signed between the Mughal governor of Deccan and raja of Amber—'Mirza Raja' Jai Singh I and Shivaji. As per the pact, Shivaji retained twelve forts and area equivalent to revenue of 1 lakh *hon*s, along with an obligation to come to the aid of the Mughals whenever sought.[82] Shivaji's son Sambhaji was made a *mansabdar* of rank 5,000 and was given a *jagir* in Berar comprising the *pargana*s of Balapur in present-day Akola district of Vidarbha.[83] Shivaji also visited Agra in 1666 upon Aurangzeb's invitation (also a clause in the Treaty of Purandhar) and made an ingenious escape from house arrest. He was coronated in 1674 as Chhatrapati *maharaj*, thereby formally founding the Maratha Empire. Following Shivaji's death, Sambhaji conquered the Berar *subah* in 1680.[84] However, Sambhaji was executed following his capture by the Mughals in 1689. His son (Shahu) and widow Yesubai were besieged in Raigarh. In that decade, several notable developments took place in kingdoms to the north and east of Berar.

In 1686, the Gond raja of Deogarh (also Devagad in present-day Chhindwara, Madhya Pradesh)—Bakht Buland Shah—fled to Delhi to seek Aurangzeb's support in regaining his territory from local contenders.[85] With Aurangzeb's backing, he established Nagpur as the capital of the eponymous kingdom.[86] He brought parts of what would later comprise the Central Provinces under his rule. Quite similar to the twist and turn of fate of the region, he had a love-and-hate relationship with Aurangzeb as he served the Mughals in their campaigns against the Marathas in the Deccan but became belligerent against the Mughal forces in due course.[87] Consequently, Bakht Buland Shah was dethroned, resulting in skirmishes between the kingdom of Chanda which was in alliance with the Mughals. Under these circumstances, the deposed Bakht Buland Shah joined hands with the Marathas in attacking the governor of Berar, Ali Mardan Khan, but the joint forces were defeated.[88] For five decades since Aurangzeb's viceroyalty of Berar, Vidarbha witnessed the dominance of Mughals over Marathas along with the weakening of the Gond rulers. However, with Aurangzeb's death in 1707, political structures of the region underwent a transformation that had a strong impact on the development of the region's cotton economy in the eighteenth century.

Aurangzeb's death was a significant event in the history of the subcontinent. Upon his death, Sambhaji's son—Shahu—was released by Mughal courtiers. He went on to thwart the plans of his aunt Tarabai (Sambhaji's half-brother, Rajaram's widow) to instate her son as the next Chhatrapati. He appointed his aide Balaji Vishwanath Bhat as the peshwa in 1713.[89] The peshwa's son—Baji Rao I—who is considered next to Shivaji among the great Maratha heroes became the peshwa in 1720 by heredity.[90] The Maratha invasions of Bengal Subah over a decade since 1741 significantly weakened the Mughal dominance and established the Marathas as a force to reckon with in the subcontinent. The Maratha Empire reached its zenith when Baji Rao I was the peshwa as it expanded across the north and western coast of India. The Marathas became de facto rulers of Delhi by installing Shah Alam II as the Mughal emperor in 1760. However, the loss to the Afghan invader Ahmad Shah Abdali (founder of the Durrani Empire) and his allies from the subcontinent in the Third Battle of Panipat in 1761 stalled the Maratha expansion. By this time, the Company had gained strength in

Bengal following its victory against Siraj-ud-Daulah and his French allies at the Battle of Plassey on 23 June 1757. The next four decades were tumultuous from the perspective of political stability in the Deccan as well as rest of India. The dynamics of relationships among the Marathas, the nizam, and the kingdom of Mysore created ample opportunities for the Company to successfully employ the 'divide and rule' strategy in attaining supremacy.

RISE OF THE COMPANY

In the decade following the Maratha loss in the Third Battle of Panipat, a period known as the 'Maratha Resurrection', the Marathas regained authority in the Deccan and north India. Madhavrao Bhat I became the peshwa under the regency of his uncle Raghunathrao Bhat (also Raghoba). However, following Madhavrao's death in 1772, court intrigue and internecine wars plunged the Maratha Confederacy into disarray.[91] Raghoba become the peshwa for a short period as the Machiavellian minister and general Nana Phadnavis led a council of twelve Maratha sardars (generals) called Barabhai to instate the infant son of the deceased Narayanrao Bhat—Sawai Madhavrao II—as the peshwa.[92] In his bid to be reinstated as the peshwa, Raghoba sought the aid of the Bombay government. This is where British interference in the Deccan became imminent. By this time, the Company's dominance over Bengal had been established, following victory over the Nawab of Bengal and his French allies in the Battle of Plassey in 1757.

In 1775, the Treaty of Surat was signed in which Raghoba, still a claimant to the throne of the peshwa, ceded Salsette and Bassein (Vasai) Island (Greater Bombay) as well as a share of the revenue from Surat and Broach (Bharuch) to the Bombay government in return for 2,500 soldiers promised by the Company.[93] However, the Supreme Council of Bengal did not recognize the treaty, and Governor-General Warren Hastings sent Colonel Upton to Pune to annul the Treaty of Surat. Consequently, the Treaty of Purandar was executed in 1776. This was a crucial treaty as Raghoba was pensioned; Sawai Madhavrao II was recognized as the peshwa; and the Marathas were barred from recognizing the French in India.[94] However, the Marathas violated the Treaty of Purandar as Nana Phadnavis allowed French ships to dock on the western coast. In response, the Bombay government attempted to reinstate Raghoba in Poona, starting the First Anglo-Maratha War. However, relentless attacks by the Marathas resulted in their victory in 1779.[95]

As the Deccan and Berar were undergoing sweeping political changes in the eighteenth century, what were the developments in the Gond dominated territories? In territories that became part of the Central Provinces during the colonial rule, the tribal Gond principality flourished from the fifteenth century to 1739—the year Bakht Buland Shah's son Chand Sultan died.[96] Following Chand Sultan's death, there was a struggle for power among his sons that saw the involvement of the Maratha Bhonsales (also Bhonsle) in the Nagpur Kingdom. The Bhonsales were one of the five chieftains of the Maratha Confederacy at that time and governed Berar on behalf of the Maratha Chhatrapati. Unlike Berar, which had come under direct Maratha influence for several decades, the princely states of the Central Provinces were not under Maratha rule until 1743. That year, Raghoji (also Raghuji) I Bhonsale made the last Gond raja—Burhan Shah—a state pensioner, thereby becoming the first Maratha ruler of Nagpur. By the time of his death in 1755, Raghoji I Bhonsale had annexed Deogarh, Chanda, and territories of Chhattisgarh along with territories in Bengal.[97] For a perspective on the timeline, this was six years before the Maratha loss in the Third Battle of Panipat. In the late eighteenth century a bloody battle of succession among the Marathas destabilized the Nagpur Kingdom. Raghoji's successor Janoji supported the Nizam of Hyderabad in his assault against the peshwa but subsequently betrayed both. The consequence of this betrayal was devastating for Nagpur, as described in the *Imperial Gazetteer of India*:

> Janoji sold his support to each side by turns. At last, disgusted by his treachery, the Peshwa and the Nizam in 1765 united their forces against Janoji, burned down Nagpur, and forced the Raja to disgorge the greater part of the money he had received.[98]

Following Janoji's death in 1772, his brothers got embroiled in a fight for succession in which Mudhoji Bhonsale emerged as the victor.[99] He became the regent for Janoji's adopted son Raghoji II Bhonsale. Mudhoji annexed Mandla and the upper Narmada valley to the Nagpur Dominion in 1785. Following his death in 1788, Raghoji II Bhonsale became the raja of Nagpur, under whom the kingdom of Nagpur expanded to a great extent. In 1799, in a bid to negotiate an alliance with the Bhonsales, H. T. Colebrooke was appointed by the Company as the first British resident to Nagpur.[100] During the Fourth Anglo-Mysore War, Raghoji II obliged the Company's requests for passage of troops from Oudh (Awadh) and Cuttack through Berar. Governor-General Richard Wellesley urged Colebrooke to impress upon Raghoji II to form a quadruple alliance to defeat the eponymous 'Tiger of Mysore', Tipu Sultan.[101] Raghoji II briefly practised the policy of favouring the Company as he hoped it would be instrumental for his autonomy from the peshwa in Poona. However, following Tipu's death on 4 May 1799, pressures on Nagpur to accede to a subsidiary alliance grew.[102] Raghoji II fought alongside Dowlat Rao Scindia (also Daulatrao Shinde) of Gwalior in the Second Anglo-Maratha War (1803–1805). With the defeat of the Maratha chiefs, Raghoji II ceded territory including Cuttack, Balasore, Sambalpur (in present-day Odisha), and southern Berar to the Company.[103]

Raghoji II's defeat brought extreme hardship upon the people of the region. In the two-thirds of villages that Raghoji II retained according to the Treaty of Deogaon, a pact concluded by Sir Arthur Wellesley and Raghoji II, there was exploitative taxation and rack-renting to compensate for the loss of revenue. To make matters worse, cultivators were sacked by Maratha troops whose arrears remained unpaid given the inability of the fiscally strained ruler to pay their salaries.[104] In 1816, following Raghoji II's death, his brother Mudhoji II became the ruler by dispatching Raghoji II's heir Parsoji. Mudhoji II formed an alliance with the last peshwa Baji Rao II and Malharrao Holkar III of Indore in the Third Anglo-Maratha War in 1817. In three decisive battles of the war that ended the Maratha dominance, the Bhonsale lost in the Battle of Sitabuldi in Nagpur; Holkar lost in the battle of Mahidpur; and the peshwa lost in the battle of Koregaon and Khadki in Pune.[105] The Nagpur Kingdom was annexed by the British, and northern parts of the kingdom became part of the Saugor and Narmada territories. Around the same time, the Pindaris—autonomous militia outfits—were raiding areas in and around Nagpur.

Before gaining autonomy, the Pindaris accompanied the armies of the Mughals and Marathas, and they plundered villages on cavalry as well as foot.[106] The loot was their pay, and they are documented to have committed atrocities against their allies including the Marathas time and again.[107] The Pindaris challenged authority across the kingdoms as well as the British territories. However, during the Third Anglo-Maratha War, they were protected by the Scindias of Gwalior until the latter were compelled to sign a treaty with the British revising the Treaty of Surji–Anjangaon, which granted power to Scindias in return for their support to the Company in its fight against the Pindaris. Ultimately, it took the Pindari Wars (1816–1818) during the Third Anglo-Maratha War under the command of Governor-General Francis Rawdon-Hastings for the scourge of the Pindaris to be terminated.[108] The Anglo-Maratha War irrevocably reconfigured the territorial contours of present-day Vidarbha. With the Maratha defeat in 1818, Nagpur came under the suzerainty of the Company. Having lost much of their dominion, the Bhonsales were confined to Narsinghpur which became a princely state of the British Empire. Far away, in Pune, the peshwa was captured, and a large part of his territory was annexed as part of the Bombay Presidency. In 1853, the last Bhonsale ruler Raghoji III died heirless, and Nagpur was annexed by the Company under the 'doctrine of lapse'.[109]

With the colonial takeover of Berar and the territories that would later form Central Provinces, districts having considerable differences but hitherto one commonality—the Maratha rule—underwent a process of standardization and extensive administrative reforms. Nevertheless, colonial commentators such as Baden-Powell were overtly critical of the commonality of Maratha rule as is evident from his statement:

> One of the few features which the bulk of the districts possess in common, is the fact they passed under 'the Maratha plough'—the iron share of that relentless and greedily rule having left its mark almost everywhere; old rights were ignored, old differences levelled down under the uniform pressure of the revenue-demand, and new men were put over the villages, with such powers as, in the end, were thought to represent, or amount to, a landlord right.[110]

THE NIZAM RULE

Mir Qamaruddin Ali Khan (also Asaf Jah I, Chin Qilich Kamaruddin Khan, and Nizam-ul-Mulk), who became the first nizam of Hyderabad, was a Mughal noble with Persian ancestry, born in Agra, having ancestral ties with Mughal emperors and considerable loyalty toward Aurangzeb. He was an important presence in eighteenth-century Deccan, and his successor would go on to amass unprecedented levels of wealth over the next two centuries.[111] He gained administrative control of Berar after the Mughal emperor Farrukhsiyar made him the viceroy of Deccan and *faujdar* of Carnatic in 1714.[112] The Mughal emperor Muhammad Shah made him the *wazir* (grand vizier or prime minister) as a reward for his role in assassinating the troublesome Sayyid brothers in the early 1720s.[113] However, apprehending the rise in Mir Qamaruddin's power, Muhammad Shah ordered him to be transferred from the court in Delhi to Awadh in 1723.[114] In 1724, Mir Qamaruddin revolted against the imperial order and marched towards Hyderabad; a decision that resulted in the Battle of Shakar Kheda in Berar in which the Mughal governor of Hyderabad in south-central India was defeated by Mir Qamaruddin who had allied with Baji Rao I.[115] Mir Qamaruddin became the first nizam of Hyderabad, and Berar became Hyderabad Assigned Districts (HAD)—under the nizam's dominion—the largest princely state in India with an area larger than Bengal and Bombay. Endowed with rich mineral resources and diamond mines of Golconda, Hyderabad was the wealthiest princely state.

With the nizam controlling large parts of south-central India, arrangements of splitting the revenues of Berar between the Marathas and the nizam emerged. Accordingly, Peshwa Baji Rao I obtained the grant to collect taxes from the nizam.[116] The Marathas collected *chauth*—annual tax or tribute levied at a quarter of the produce or revenue from lands that were nominally under Mughal rule. They also collected *sardeshmukhi*—a cess of one-tenth levied over and above the *chauth*.[117] In due course, despite garnering Maratha support in his victory against the Mughals, the nizam took military action to oust Maratha tax collectors from the Carnatic. The Marathas responded with military campaigns against the nizam but they failed.[118] Also, taking advantage of the struggle for power between Baji Rao I and Sambhaji II of Kolhapur in the Maratha Confederacy, the nizam invaded Pune—the seat of the peshwa. In retaliatory attacks and widespread plunder by the Marathas under the command of Baji Rao I, Berar became collateral damage as the Marathas pillaged the nizam's territory. The nizam was defeated by the Marathas in the Battle of Palkhed in 1728, and the former regained their right to be tax collectors of the Deccan.[119] In subsequent years, there was considerable intervention by the Company, and a British resident was posted in Hyderabad in 1798. The growing British control over the nizam and the weakening of the Marathas since the early nineteenth century were significant factors in India's colonial history.

Having discussed the arc of the remarkable political developments in Vidarbha over a long period covering India's late medieval and early modern history, we characterize the agrarian conditions in the region until the colonial takeover of Berar in 1853 in what follows. To reconstruct the agrarian conditions, we focus on revenue administration and local institutions as these institutions shaped the agrarian conditions of the region.

AGRARIAN SYSTEM IN PRE-COLONIAL VIDARBHA

LAND REVENUE ADMINISTRATION

Over the centuries, the agrarian conditions have undoubtedly been influenced by the ravages of war, political upheavals, and natural calamities. However, the land revenue administration in practice had a direct impact on the surplus for cultivators and incentives for agricultural development. As in the rest of the regions, revenue administration systems and extractive revenue arrangements instituted during different regimes discussed so far shaped the agrarian system that was by no means primitive. Instead of delving into the details of the agrarian conditions under a certain rule, we present a summary of contemporary practices since the Muslim conquest of Vidarbha.

By the early fourteenth century, Ala-ud-din Khalji imposed the annual *jizya* tax on non-Muslim subjects (*dhimmi*) and made an annual charitable donation (*zakat*) mandatory for the Muslim population under his rule. He levied taxes on housing (*ghari*) and grazing (*charai*). He usurped four-fifth of the loot of the war (*khums*) from his soldiers instead of the norm of one-fifth.[120] However, he brought an end to the feudal land grants as well as the practice of 'revenue farming' (*iqta*) in which the holder of such a right (*iqtedar*/*muqti*) had temporary revenue rights over a unit of land.[121] However, he taxed half of the agricultural produce in the form of *kharaj* tax and levied poll tax.[122] Famines during Khalji's reign resulted in the introduction of food rationing.[123] Since the contemporary rulers of the region—the Yadavas—did not cede territory to the Khaljis but paid annual tribute as discussed earlier, cultivators were squeezed by the raja whenever the revenue demands from Delhi emerged. To make matters worse, extraction of accumulated arrears in the tribute payments also depleted the farmers' surplus. Frequent raids from Delhi also hampered agricultural development.

Agrarian conditions under the Tughlaqs were quite harsh as well. Muhammad bin Tughlaq imposed regressive land taxes, and non-Muslims (*dhimmis*) paid unfair crop taxes, with more than half of their produce taken away by the state. This distressed cultivators and mass abandonment of farming was commonplace. Nonetheless, state response to famine in the form of relief measures seems to have been extant. During a famine in the early fourteenth century, accounts of the Moroccan traveller Ibn Battuta suggest that Muhammad bin Tughlaq's famine relief policy included the digging of wells and supply of seeds to peasants.[124] Firuz Shah Tughluq renewed the *iqtadari* system and made the assignment of *iqta* hereditary.[125] The assignment of heredity in *iqtadari* and the development of a sense of ownership rights, unlike in earlier periods, is considered by some scholars as an important factor in urban development in medieval India.[126]

As far as the conditions of Berar under the Bahamani, Imad Shahi, and Nizam Shahi rule in the pre-Mughal period spanning the fourteenth and fifteenth century are concerned, there are limited accounts. One of the most notable developments of the Bahamani period from an agrarian system perspective however was innovation in land surveys. Mahmud Gawan, the *wazir* of the Bahamani sultanate, of Persian origin, introduced systematic land surveys that resulted in land being classified into culturable and fallow land. Concerns for risks in cultivation and covariate shocks such as famines is also evident in the revenue policy of Bahamani Malik-ut-Tujar (Mahmud Gawan) around the mid-fifteenth century. He attempted to resettle villages depopulated by the famines and promoted tax-free cultivation in the first year, and revenue was gradually raised to the normal rate.[127] A century and half later, when Berar became a Mughal *subah*, contemporary historians have documented that food crop production was widespread and so was the practice of crop rotation with an understanding of fertilizing qualities of legume. Cotton and sugarcane were major cash crops, belonging to the *jins-i-kaamil* or *jins-i-aalaa* category in Mughal records (high-grade crops grown for the market). Contemporary European travellers document several varieties of cotton produced in the region.[128] The villages had division of labour and several kinds of wage arrangements were in place.[129] While wages in kind and cash were common, there existed caste-based master–servant relations in Berar called *balutedari* as discussed later. As we will elaborate in Chapter 2, dismantling of *balutedari* during the colonial period can be characterized as a significant historical accident for the cultivators of Vidarbha.

Scholars such as Irfan Habib argue that the main objective of the agrarian system of Mughal India was to 'obtain land revenue on an ever-ascending scale' that left little in terms of subsistence for the peasants.[130] To achieve this, the administration and revenue division (*sarkar*) included a panoply of administrative agents such as *amil*s, *dewan*s, *deshmukh*s, *deshpandiya*s, *qanungo*s, *desai*s, *sardeshmukh*s, *sardeshkat*s, *sardesai*s, *muqqadam*s, *patel*s, *patwari*s, *tahsildar*s, *munsif*s, and *chaudhuri*s.[131] Each *subah* was under the administrative control of a governor (*subahdar* or *nazim*), and its subdivisions (*paragana*s) were headed by a *deshmukh* and it had an accountant, *deshpandiya*.[132] Key state appointees such as *mansbadar*s, *faujdar*s, and *jagirdar*s were central to the exercise of administration of land revenue, imperial military powers, and maintenance of law and order. Under the *mansabdari* system, the emperor-appointed *mansabdar*s had the responsibility of maintaining troops for the emperor. Their rank was based on the number of soldiers under their command (*zat*) and their status was based on the number of horsemen under their command (*sawar*).[133] *Mansabdar*s who received salary in cash were called *naqdi* and those receiving rights to land revenue from estates were called *jagirdar*s. Tenants were not in direct contact with the state and paid their rents to the *jagirdar*. Upon the *jagirdar*'s death, the land passed on to the state.[134] Chronicling the distress and suffering peasants had to face due to ill-treatment by seventeenth-century Mughal governors, the French traveller Bernier notes:

> These poor people, when incapable of discharging the demands of their rapacious lords, are not only often deprived of the means of subsistence, but are bereft of their children, who are carried away as slaves. Thus it happens that many of the peasantry, driven to despair by so execrable a tyranny, abandon the country and seek a more tolerable mode of existence, either in the towns, or camps; as bearers of burdens, carriers of water, or servants to horsemen. Sometimes they fly to the territories of a Raja, because they find less oppression, and are allowed a greater degree of comfort.[135]

In the sixteenth century, notable revenue reforms were introduced by Raja Todar Mal—Akbar's finance minister and counsellor of the empire. Todar Mal introduced the *dahshala* (ten years) system that helped standardize measurements for revenue assessment.[136] As per this system, crop produce was estimated, and revenue was assessed for 1570–1580 to arrive at decadal averages. This became the basis for revenue rates per unit of area (*bigha*) and the total revenue demand for the village(s) (*tankhwa*) was calculated accordingly. Quite futuristic for its times, there was variation in tax rate by crop, and irrigation status also existed. Todar Mal is believed to have set the revenue demand (*jama*) at half the produce for rain-fed crops; one third for food grains irrigated by well and artificial sources; and lower shares for cash crops. Soil fertility also influenced the *tankhwa* rate.

In Berar, a general rate was fixed based on each of the three types of soils: *ainkali* (deep black soil), *miankalas* (black soil mixed with lighter soil), and *kalaspati* (highland soil).[137] Under this system, one-third of the crop output in cash equivalent was the share of the state whilst the remaining was the peasant's share (*kharaj*)—a rate presumably inherited from Sher Shah Suri—the founder of the Suri Empire in present-day Bihar, and the one who introduced rupee as the currency.[138] Records of later periods of Shah Jahan's reign show that for cotton (as rabi harvest) under the *kankut* system in which the share of produce was demanded by the state based on its estimate following inspections, the rate was one-half whilst for wheat the rate was one-third of the produce. By contrast, the share of the state for kharif crops in crop-sharing (*ghalla-bakshi* or *batai*) was one-third.[139] Since cash revenue replaced grain revenue, grain had to be commuted to cash for payment of land revenue. This system contributed to the development of grain markets in Berar and fostered the commercialization of agriculture.[140] During Aurangzeb's governorship of the Deccan in the mid-seventeenth century, the diwan of Berar-Balaghat, Murshid Quli Khan, followed the *zabt* system of assessment. *Amin*s (assessors) and surveyors were involved in land measurement, and records of individual holdings (*raqba*) were collected.[141]

Yield slumps and droughts were recurrent due to the dependence on monsoon and pestilence in the pre-colonial period. Famines such as those during the Khalji and Tughlaq period discussed earlier, and the Durgadevi Famine of 1396–1407 during the Bahamani rule and the Deccan Famine of 1630–1632 during the Mughal rule were the outcome of prolonged monsoon and harvest failure.[142] To make matters worse for the farmers, taxes levied by the state left little margin, and there was a wide gap between the farm harvest prices and what the merchants received. Over this period, there was also a remarkable fluctuation in the price of cotton. During Aurangzeb's reign, a period which has rich official records of revenue administration in the form of Dastur-ul-Amals, these positions were mostly assigned to erstwhile *zamindar*s. *Zamindari* entailed permanent revenue rights that were conferred upon payment of *peshkash*—paid in instalments or in full. Arrears of *peshkash* running into thousands of rupees in the late seventeenth century was common.[143]

Among other notable experiments with land settlement in the Deccan, land reforms by the Siddi military leader Malik Ambar in the early seventeenth century stands out. Based on survey and settlement, this mechanism stood in contrast with the earlier attempts at reforming the revenue administration by Todar Mal. In this system, there were multiple stages of assessing the land revenue based on detailed classification of the type of cultivable land.[144] An advantage of such a system of settlement was that assessing officers (*amil*s) as well as the peasants were better informed about the cultivable land available for taxation. Moreover, the powers of intermediaries in the revenue collection were curtailed significantly. By contrast, in the Mughal system, property rights were vested with the state and land was measured but not surveyed.[145] Land revenue administration under the Nizam Shahi rule prior to the land revenue assessment reforms by Malik Ambar in the early seventeenth century comprised an exploitative system of measurement by ropes (*zabt*) and settlement of revenues at the village level at customary rates based on a number of ploughs under the *nasaq* system.[146] Under the *nasaq* system followed in the *zabt* system of assessment, there was no relationship of the revenue demand with area or harvest.

In the last four decades of the seventeenth century, whilst the Mughal skirmishes with the Marathas in the Deccan persisted, the Company caught up with its primary competitor, the Dutch VOC (Vereenigde Oostindische Compagnie), in terms of its share in the trade with India. It went on to out-compete its European partners over the next eight decades.[147] For instance, by the end of the 1660s, cotton textiles from the Coromandel coast, Gujarat, and Bengal—in that order of their share in the trade—comprised over half of its imports; the quantity of and share in imports for cotton cloth growing meteorically over the next three decades.[148] Among several factors, a crucial one behind the growth of the Company's dominance in the subcontinent was the *farman* (also *firman*) or imperial decree by Mughal emperors. Be it the first purported *farman* in 1612 by Jahangir permitting the Company to trade from its factory in Surat, or the one by Jahangir and Prince Khurram that Thomas Roe secured in 1618, the growing competition among the European traders in India in the seventeenth century considerably owe their origins to these imperial orders.[149] Following Aurangzeb's prolonged Deccan campaign and his death, the Mughal Empire weakened considerably.[150] Nevertheless, the later Mughals continued issuing imperial decrees that strengthened the Company's economic and political strength. As a case in point, a *farman* by the tenth Mughal emperor Farrukhsiyar in 1716 granted the Company duty-free trading rights in Bengal. With this *farman*, the Company's fortunes soared. So did its contestation with rulers of the provinces in these regions that set the stage for political dominance over the next five decades.

In parts of the Central Provinces, during Bakht Buland Shah's reign in the early eighteenth century, agriculture developed in areas to the south of Deogarh—between the river Wainganga and its tributary Kanhan. Cultivators were encouraged to settle on equal terms with the Gonds. Several towns and villages were founded, and economic activity intensified. For instance, the town of Pauni in Bhandara was famous for its handloom-based cotton fabrics.[151] Following Aurangzeb's death, Bakht Buland Shah regained territories and established dominance of the house of Deogarh in the region that overlapped with the Central Provinces.[152] With the nizam becoming an important axis of power in the Deccan, the Marathas had elaborate arrangements of taxes levied on the Mughal and nizam territories, the prominent being *chauth* and *sardeshmukhi*. As discussed earlier, the extractive arrangement of *do amli*, or double government, unquestionably squeezed the producers of Berar.[153] An additional levy for horse fodder (*ghas dana*) was also part of the *do amli* arrangement. In case the nizam failed to pay the dues, Maratha raids were certain. The fear of the Maratha raids ensured that the nizam avoided failure of paying the dues. Such extractive arrangements for revenue and taxation are likely to have had adverse effects on agricultural development in the region.

It is believed that pre-medieval kingdoms including the Satavahanas did not invest in irrigation in the Deccan because of the notion that 'the cotton growing black soil did not stand in need of heavy irrigation'.[154] However, the Ishvakus and Pallavas built masonry waterworks and long canals in eastern and southern Deccan respectively.[155] In terms of state investment in irrigation, the fourteenth-century sultan of Delhi Firuz Shah Tughlaq stands out for building and renovating aqueducts, reservoirs, and *nahar*s (canals) for irrigation in the Doab region of north India. His renovation of the Western Yamuna Canal is legendary. In Deccan, however, there is no evidence of the Tughlaqs building water management structures.

Traditional diversion systems of irrigation known as *phad* were common in northwestern parts of present-day Maharashtra as well as in Yavatmal, Vidarbha. The system includes a built *bandhara* (check dam or diversion weir) across a river, from which *kalva*s (contour canals) branch out. *Chari*s (distributaries) from the canals feed water into *sarang*s (field channels) that carry the water to the fields in the command area divided into *phad*s (blocks).[156] In these community-based irrigation systems, the village community decided which *phad*s to cultivate and which to leave fallow in a season. In the seventeenth century, the Gond kings of eastern Vidarbha built *tank* irrigation systems that were later built and maintained by the *malguzar*s (land-owning class) and came to be known as 'Malguzari tanks'.[157] The Bhonsale kings gave free water rights to the community that allowed the cultivation of sugarcane and jaggery production. It also allowed pisciculture.[158] Ramtek in Nagpur district is well known for the 'Ramtek Model' of irrigation.[159] In this system, water tanks connected by underground and surface canals form a network extending from the foothills to the plains. These tanks became important water conservation structures in the high rainfall zone of the Wainganga River basin.

Concessions from the state during contingencies was not uncommon as the Mughal administration demonstrated adjustments in revenue collection in the eventuality of natural calamities. A *farman* acknowledging risks in agriculture was issued by Aurangzeb in 1665. This *farman* to Rasikdas—a revenue official—offers valuable insights into how riskiness of agricultural production due to natural calamity as well as the distinction between wilful and non-wilful abandonment of operations by the cultivator was well acknowledged in the late seventeenth century.[160] Another Mughal institution that provided *riaya/raiyat* (cultivators) relief during distress due to natural calamities was the *taccavi* loan. In the aftermath of natural calamities, revenue collections were minimized or suspended, and *taccavi* (literally, strength-giving) loans were short-term loans advanced for the recovery of the cultivators. The administration of these loans was undertaken by village headmen (*chaudhuri*s) or other officials such as *zamindar*s and *talukdar*s, who collected the outstanding loans when the distress was over.[161] In terms of credit arrangements in the Mughal period, there is evidence at hand to suggest that indebtedness of peasants to usurious lending at even 150 per cent per annum by *mahajan*s (moneylenders) was common, and revenue demand was an important reason for indebtedness.[162] Another *farman* by Aurangzeb in the early 1680s also shows exemption granted to poor peasants who were indebted for seeds and cattle, and Aurangzeb equating indebtedness of peasants to pauperization.[163]

The sensitivities of the Mughal administration to natural calamities notwithstanding, historians have debated the effect of the Mughal administration on the peasantry in India. According to scholars such as Irfan Habib and Shireen Moosvi, the centralized and extractive institutions of the Mughals impoverished peasants. On the contrary, scholars including David Washbrook and Sanjay Subrahmanyam challenge this view of the Mughal 'state as an insatiable Leviathan'.[164] The latter group believes that much of the revenue was redistributed back to local interests and that there were thriving regional and, for some goods, national markets. They also argue that central control was weak in many areas, especially southern India, and that the proportion of agricultural produce collected was much less than that claimed by Irfan Habib. Others argue that whilst the product and money market were sophisticated, land and labour markets remained underdeveloped.[165]

BALUTEDARI

Although extractive systems discussed above affected the village economy, there was no change in the exploitative system of organization of production in villages namely *balutedari*. In this system, the organization of agricultural production was based on caste affiliation along master–servant lines.[166] The dominant clan namely *balutedar*, usually belonging to the upper caste, and wielded considerable power. The *balutedar*s gave baluta (gift in kind, usually grain) to the *asami*—agricultural labourer, artisans, and other service providers.[167] The *balutedar* generally used services of around thirty castes following hereditary occupation. A dozen of these were considered most important and were called *bara balutedar*.[168] The rights of distribution of the annual produce were with the *balutedar*, who he divided the produce according to ranking in the caste hierarchy.[169] The share of the twelve *asami*s would be around 4 per cent of the produce with wide variation by services. The remaining share was appropriated by the *balutedar*.[170]In Berar, this arrangement was known as *aykari*.[171] This mode of organization of production resembles the *jajamani* system of north India where customary services were based on heredity.[172]

The *balutedari* system was a system of control over the labour of the lower castes based on norms and strict enforcement of punishments for deviation from these norms. Although the agricultural production system in the nineteenth-century Vidarbha was devoid of slavery unlike the cotton plantations of the American South, the *balutedari* system resembled slavery but for the social obligation of *asami*s to serve the *balutedar*s rather than being his property. An important aspect of *balutedari* is that it allowed the subjugation of the *asami*s by the dominant clan because of which the *asami*s, usually belonging to the lower caste, comprised the lower class. There were certain norms through which the power asymmetries embodied in *balutedari* could be sustained.

First, the *balutedar*s' ability to exercise control in the village society emerged from *dimmat*, *watan*, *khel*, and *ghurry*.[173] The dominant clan (*dimmat*) and its kinship network had control over the estates (*khel*). The *balutedar*s had rights control over the produce in their *watan* or territory as a hereditary right. They built fortifications called *ghurr*ies to coerce labour from migrating as well as defend against aggressors given the political instability of the times as discussed earlier. Second, *balutedar*s captured the village council or *panchayat* that gave them considerable power in an estate (*khel*). Third, the *balutedar* had the exclusive rights to grow horticultural crops whereas the *asami*s were not allowed to do so. Forms of free labour (*atari*) were also extracted from the *asami*s in village economic activity, such as the construction of temples. Fourth, the *balutedar*s destroyed permanent irrigation structures and neglected maintenance of anicuts and dams that sustained rain-fed agriculture in the region for centuries. They employed *asami*s to build small dams and drainage systems that were not durable, requiring frequent rebuilding. This ensured that the *balutedar*s could continue to use *asami* labour and hold on to their power to distribute the produce.

It is evident that the caste–class juxtaposition due to the *balutedari* system left little surplus for the labourers in a Berar village. The mobility of *asami*s was constrained and they were coerced into services of the *balutedar*. Thus, the exercise of power by controlling rights over distribution of water suggests that the *balutedari* system had characteristics of the 'agromanagerial bureaucracy' of a hydraulic society 'oriental despotism'.[174] As we will see in Chapter 2, systematic dismantling of *balutedari* and its vestiges of power namely *dimmat, watan, khel,* and *ghurry* was a central feature of the colonial transformation of the region. Accidents such as these institutional transformations not only allowed deep integration of Vidarbha with the global trade but also fostered fundamental changes in institutions that prevailed since the colonial take over—factors crucial for the gambles with cotton in Vidarbha.

CONCLUSION

This chapter presented a brief history of the Vidarbha region of central India. Vidarbha is an ancient civilization with diverse geological as well as sociocultural characteristics. We focused on the period of history ranging from the thirteenth century when the Muslim sultanates dominated the geopolitics to the mid-nineteenth-century colonial takeover of Berar and the Central Provinces—the building blocks of Vidarbha. It is evident that the region that is concomitant with present-day Vidarbha has been a frontier territory that was at the crossroads of long-standing contests and relentless influence of 'outside forces' to establish supremacy in the Deccan as well as southern India.

Berar came under the control of the Delhi sultanates and witnessed the rise and fall of the Muslim sultanates in the Deccan that shaped the power distribution in the region as well as peninsular India. It became a Mughal *subah* during Akbar's reign. Following Mughal Emperor Aurangzeb's demise in the early eighteenth century, the Marathas wielded considerable influence over Berar and the kingdom of Nagpur that had experienced prolonged rule by Gond kings. Maratha influence under the Bhonsales since the mid-eighteenth century significantly shaped the agrarian conditions and the village economy. However, with Maratha defeat in the last Anglo-Maratha war, the region came under colonial domination. Maratha rule in the region ended abruptly in 1853 with the Bhonsale of Nagpur dying without an heir, thereby bringing the region under direct British rule. Since 1724, the nizams of Hyderabad influenced the regional geopolitics for over two centuries. Hyderabad came under British influence since the turn of the nineteenth century, and ceded Berar (HAD) to the British in 1853, never to regain the territory. The region was under British rule until India's independence in 1947. However, it took decades of reorganization and political parlays before the region was incorporated into the state of Maharashtra in 1960 when the Bombay State was split into Gujarat and Maharashtra along linguistic lines.

The vicissitudes of the Central Provinces and Deccan's political instability meant that Vidarbha was an important theatre for centuries of scramble for power in pre-colonial India. The institutions that emerged in the region were largely the outcome of the shifting power structures. Frequent internecine wars, struggle for dominance over the Deccan, and unstable alliances among the Mughals, Marathas, the kingdom of Mysore, and the nizam of Hyderabad gave an opportunity to the Company to emerge as victors over their nemesis—the kingdom of Mysore and the Maratha Confederacy by the early nineteenth century. Both Nagpur and Berar came under British administrative control in 1853, thereby halting the centuries of territorial reconfiguration.

The chapter summarizes the dramatic power struggles and transformation of local institutions in pre-colonial Vidarbha. The political turbulence in the region over the seven centuries suggest that unstable kingdoms between the thirteenth and nineteenth centuries did not augur well for the economic development of the region. To put the economic development in the region over the period in a perspective, India's per capita gross domestic product (GDP) steadily declined between 1600 and 1871, with the timing of the 'Great Divergence' debated among economic historians.[175] For six centuries since 1200, the standard of living in Maharashtra and Deccan was low, and the majority were poor.[176] Real wages declined since the seventeenth century to such an extent that late twentieth-century real wages were considered to be lower than those of the late sixteenth century.[177]

Our characterization of the agrarian conditions of pre-colonial Vidarbha suggests that although there were intermittent attempts at land reforms by Malik Ambar of the Bahamani sultanate, Todar Mal of the Mughal Empire, and the system of surveying land and settlement by the Mughals, peasants were heavily taxed and imposition of myriad taxes by the rulers stymied agricultural surplus. Levy of *chauth* and *sardeshmukhi* by the Marathas or 'revenue farming' by the nizam exploited the peasantry, and it is not surprising that there were no breakthroughs in agriculture or manufacturing that could be fostered in a population that struggled to make ends meet. The extractive tax regimes no doubt squeezed the cultivators and created significant uncertainties. History however suggests few rulers allowed for adjustments in taxations in the eventuality of natural calamities. There is also evidence of the state providing loans (for example, *taccavi* loans) to cultivators to wade over a crisis, only for the revenue to be exacted at a later stage. In terms of the organization of agricultural production in the eighteenth century, the prevalence of the caste–class-based *balutedari* system further constrained the region's agricultural development. More importantly, the *balutedar*s sustained their control over labour, production, and water rights—aspects that are critical for the development of any agrarian society.

Such a long-range historical account of the developments in the region helps identify elements of change and continuity. The significant historical events set the stage for the evolution of institutions and agricultural development of the region. These developments are likely to have influenced the incentives to farmers and their adoption of new agricultural practices. From a political ecology perspective, it also raises questions on how to interpret the unprecedented ecological transformation given the power tussle in the region. In Chapter 2, we will examine in detail how the changing geopolitics of the region impacted the region in terms of the introduction of new institutions aimed at boosting cotton production. In our attempt to identify antecedents of agricultural development in general and the cotton economy, we will also contextualize the 'accidental' and 'gambling' with reference to the title of the book. We will find answers to the following questions: How were traditional institutions impacted? Did the institutional changes transform the agrarian system? How did the industrial revolution of the late eighteenth century impact the material conditions of the region? How did the region become embedded in the world system for cotton production?

NOTES

1. The region is home to over 22 million which is equal to the population of New Zealand and about four times the population of Norway. It also encompasses an area more than twice of Netherlands, Denmark, and Switzerland; and higher than that of over half of the countries in the world.
2. Maharashtra's gross state value added in 2020–2021 is nearly a quarter of India's gross value added at 2011–2012 (constant) prices. See data released by the Ministry of Statistics and Programme Implementation (MOSPI), available at http://mospi.nic.in/GSVA-NSVA (accessed on 18 March 2021).
3. See P. F. McEldowney, 'Colonial Administration and Social Developments in Middle India, the Central Provinces, 1861–1921' (PhD thesis, Corcoran Department of History, University of Virginia, USA, 1980).
4. Government of India, *Indian Minerals Yearbook 2013 (Part-I) 52nd edition: State Reviews (Maharashtra) (Final Release)* (Ministry of Mines, Indian Bureau of Mines, 2015).
5. P. Amrutkar, 'The Backwardness and Demand for a Statehood of Vidarbha', *Indian Journal of Political Science* 70, no. 2 (2009): 521–528.
6. S. B. Deo, 'New Evidence of Hinayana Buddhism in Vidarbha', *Purātattva* 1972–1973, no. 6 (1972): 84–86; and B. C. Deotare, G. Shete, R. Sawant, V. Kathale, and S. Naik, 'Discovery of Structural Stupa at Bhon, District Buldana, Maharashtra', *Purātattva* 2006–2007, no. 37 (2007): 177–185.
7. Our reference to geographic luck alludes to geography, climate, and ecology as in Diamond (1997) that influence economic outcomes separate from the effect of institutions à la Acemoglu and Robinson (2012). For an excellent study on disentangling the web of causality between geography, institutions, and integration on the one hand and income of nations on the other, see D. Rodrik, A. Subramanian, and F. Trebi, 'Institutions Rule: The Primacy of Institutions over Geography and Integration in Economic Development', *Journal of Economic Growth*, no. 9 (2004): 131–165.

8. The Annales School approach to historiography was developed in the twentieth century by French historians including Lucien Febvre and Marc Bloch. It focuses on long-term and slowly evolving structures instead of short-term and episodic histories that is of interest to chroniclers and journalists. See, for example, F. Braudel and I. Wallerstein, 'History and the Social Sciences: The Longue Durée', *Review (Fernand Braudel Center)* 32, no. 2 (2009): 171–203.
9. The literary style of Vidarbha-*riti* that scholars of the region used was considered the best style in Sanskrit and Prakrit literature. See Berar All-Parties Committee, *Berar's Position in Indian Federation: A Case*, prepared by the Berar All-Parties' Committee for consideration by the members of the Round Table Conference (Bombay: Vaibhav Press, 1931), 1.
10. See R. Sawant, 'Review of Archaeological Investigations in the Protohistoric and Historical Archaeology of Vidarbha', *Man and Environment* 35, no. 2 (2010): 45–65. For a description of domestication of animals in the Iron Age and early historical settlements in the region, see A. Deshpande-Mukherjee, P. K. Thomas, and R. K. Mohanty, 'Faunal Remains from the Iron age and Early Historical Settlement at Mahurjhari, District Nagpur, Maharashtra', *Man and Environment* 35, no. 1 (2010): 87–102.
11. J.-S. Park and V. Shinde, 'Iron Technology of the Ancient Megalithic Communities in the Vidarbha Region of India', *Journal of Archaeological Science* 40, no. 11 (2013): 3822–3833.
12. B. C. Deotare, 'Late Holocene Climatic Change: Archaeological Evidence from Purna Basin, Maharashtra', *Man and Environment* 35, no. 1 (2006): 87–102.
13. For the fossils of dinosaurs (*Titanosaurus indicus*) found in the region, see G. V. R. Prasad and A. Sahni, 'First Cretaceous Mamma from India', *Nature* 332, no. 6165 (April 1988); and Matthew Carrano, Jeffrey Wilson, and Paul Barrett, 'The History of Dinosaur Collecting in Central India, 1828–1947', *Geological Society London Special Publications* 343, no. 1 (2010): 161–173. For an interesting note on Stephen Hislop, a Scottish missionary who contributed much to discovering dinosaur fossil in Central India, see A. Bhagat, 'Stephen Hislop: Discovering the Wonders of Central India', *Live History India*, 19 May 2022, https://www.livehistoryindia.com/story/people/stephen-hislop (accessed on 25 October 2022).
14. Other ethnic groups including the Korku, Korwa, Maida, Baiga, Binjhari are also natives of the region. For colonial explorations that shaped early colonial perspectives on the region, see J. T. Blunt, 'Narrative of a Route

from Chunarghur, to Yertnagoodum, in the Ellore Circar', *Asiatic Researches* 7 (1803): 11, 96. Also see E. Thornton, *A Gazetteer of the Territories under the Government of the East-India Company, and of the Native States on the Continent of India: Compiled by the Authority of the Hon. Court of Directors, and Chiefly from Documents in their Possession*, 4 vols. (London: William H. Allen & Co., 1854), 355.

15. Mughal texts refer to it as 'Gondwanah'. For example, see Abul Fazl-i-Allami, *The Ain-i-Akbari*, trans. from the original Persian by Colonel H. S. Jarrett, annotated by Rev. J. N. Sarkar, vol. 2 (Calcutta: The Asiatic Society, 1949), 222–223, 309.
16. For a critical discussion on how the term 'Gondwana' has geological, anthropological, and historical connotations but not philosophical, political, and cultural ones, see Pratik Chakrabarti, 'Gondwana and the Politics of Deep Past', *Past and Present* 242, no. 1 (2019): 119–153. Akash K. Prasad, 'Gondwana Movement in Post-colonial India: Exploring Paradigms of Assertion, Self-determination and Statehood', *Journal of Tribal Intellectual Collective India* 3, no. 1 (2015): 37–45. For a rich social historical account, see B. H. Mehta, *Gonds of the Central Indian Highlands*, vol. 1 (New Delhi: Concept, 1984).
17. Washim was not named as part of Berar by the State Reorganization Commission of 1955 (Government of India, *Report of the States Reorganisation Commission* [New Delhi, 1955], 123) as it was bifurcated into Akola and Yavatmal districts by the British in early twentieth century. In *Ain-i-Akbari*, it was a revenue district named Bashim. The present-day Washim district was carved out of Akola in 1998.
18. Gadchiroli was part of Chandrapur district until 1982 whereas Gondia was carved out of Bhandara district in 1999.
19. The Nag Vidarbha Andolan Samiti (NVAS) is a political outfit that has been demanding separate statehood for Vidarbha.
20. At a conceptual level, one may be inclined to consider this as some form of a resource curse.
21. J. O. Miller, *Journal of the Royal Society of Arts* 60, no. 3103 (1912): 611–630, 612.
22. The Central Provinces came into being as an administrative province of British India in 1861 with the amalgamation of the Nagpur division and the Saugor and Nerbudda (also Narmada) territories—the Mahakoshal region—including districts in present-day Madhya Pradesh. The Nagpur division became part of the Nagpur Province following the annexation of the Nagpur Kingdom by the British in 1853.

23. McEldowney, 'Colonial Administration and Social Developments'.
24. 'Lakh' is a unit followed in the South Asian numbering system, where 1 lakh = 100,000.
25. The Raj Bhavan or Governor House in Nagpur was the residence of the chief commissioner of the Central Provinces. It was also known as 'Gondwana Gubernatoris'. In 1920, a Governor Council took over the administration of the Central Provinces. Available at 'Raj Bhavan Nagpur', Raj Bhavan Maharashtra, https://rajbhavan-maharashtra.gov.in/en/raj-bhavan-nagpur/ (accessed on 20 February 2021).
26. D. E. U. Baker, *Changing Political Leadership in an Indian Province: The Central Provinces and Berar, 1919–1939* (Delhi: Oxford University Press, 1979). For a detailed historical sketch of the Central Provinces and Berar, see V. N. Aiyar, *A Historical Sketch of the Central Provinces and Berar from the Earliest Times* (Allahabad: The Pioneer Press, 1914). Aiyar derives the dynastic sketch based on epigraphical and numismatic records near the province along with literacy sources such as the Mahabharata, Vishnupurana, and Kali Dasa's *Malavikagnmitra*, among others.
27. Cited in B. H. Baden-Powell, *The Land-Systems of British India: Being a Manual of the Land-Tenures and the Systems of Land-Revenue Administration Prevalent in the Several Provinces*, vol. 2, book 3, *The System of Village or Mahal Settlement*s (Oxford: Clarendon Press, 1892), 369.
28. M. Phadke, 'I Am for a Separate Vidarbha State: Maharashtra CM Fadnavis', *The Print*, 16 November 2017, https://theprint.in/theprint-otc/separate-vidarbha-maharashtra-fadnavis/16582/ (accessed on 16 July 2021).
29. Government of India, *Report of the States Reorganisation Commission*, 123–125.
30. Ibid., 123.
31. The Hindi-speaking parts of the Central Provinces remained as part of the new Madhya Pradesh. Parts of the Central India Agency—Madhya Bharat, Vindhya Pradesh, and Bhopal—merged with Madhya Pradesh State to form the largest state of India, Madhya Pradesh.
32. H. G. Ahir, The Commission for the Formation of the State of Vidarbha Bill (2008), http://164.100.47.4/billstexts/lsbilltexts/asintroduced/153ls-8.pdf (accessed on 6 January 2021).
33. The movement was spearheaded by the Samyukta Maharashtra Samiti based in Pune. The samiti supported the 'one language–one state' principle as against the 'one state–one language' principle. It witnessed several political contestations with the Indian National Congress over the issue

of state formation. Despite the bifurcation of Bombay State into Gujarat and Maharashtra on 1 May 1960, factions within the samiti continued to demand for merging Marathi-speaking areas of northern Karnataka as well as the Portuguese colonies of Goa and Daman with Maharashtra. However, in 1967, a referendum in Goa decided against the merger, and the Marathi-speaking parts of northern Karnataka did not become part of Maharashtra.

34. It is also where the 'Zero Mile Stone' monument was built during the Great Trigonometrical Survey of India in 1907 for which it became a standard benchmark. In 1956, B. R. Ambedkar—the father of India's constitution—converted to Buddhism at Nagpur along with nearly 0.4 million followers.
35. Coalitions, such as the Vidarbha Nirman Mahamanch (VNM), and fledgling parties, such as the Vidarbha Maza, champion the cause of separate statehood but they have not yet attained political success necessary to act as effective pressure groups nor garner popular support.
36. See S. Aney, *Vidarbhanama: Early Period to British Rule* (Nagpur: Vidarbha Mirror Prakashan, 2021), 1–7. Aney has references to important Marathi literature on the history of the region including Y. M. Kale, S. G. Deogaonkar, Satish Pawde, and G. M. Purandare, among others.
37. For a brief description of economy and society under Satavahana rule, see Aney, *Vidarbhanama*, 8–11.
38. For an account of the structure of Vidarbha villages in the fifth century during the Vakataka era including the caste composition of rural society where *brahmana*s (Brahmins) dominated, see R. Vajpeyi, 'Areas of Set-Back and Tension in Agrarian Relations in Vidarbha in the Fifth Century: A Causality Analysis', *Proceedings of the Indian History Congress* 50 (1989): 96–104.
39. Ibid., 99.
40. Sawant, 'Review of Archaeological Investigations', 45–65, 52.
41. S. V. Fitzgerald and A.E. Nelson, eds., *Central Provinces District Gazetteers: Amraoti District* (Pune: The Government Photozinco Press, 1983 [1911]), 290.
42. Aney, *Vidarbhanama*, 21.
43. *Amraoti Gazetteers* (1911), 290.
44. For a classification of the Central Provinces into six geographical regions, see O. H. K. Spate and A. T. A. Learmonth, *India and Pakistan: A General and Regional Geography* (London: Methuen, 1954), 352–353.
45. Winfred M. Day, 'Relative Permanence of Former Boundaries in India'. *Scottish Geographical Magazine* 65, no. 3 (1949): 114–116.

46. Devagiri (also Deogir) was renamed Daulatabad in 1327 when it became the second capital of the Tughluqs; the successors of the Khaljis in the Delhi sultanate. A visit to the remnants of Daulatabad fort near present-day Aurangabad by the first author in 2016 had coincidentally raised questions about how dynamic the Deccan frontier would have become following the encounters with the Delhi sultanate. For details of Alauddin Khalji's first campaign against Devagiri, see P. M. Joshi, 'Alauddin Khalji's First Campaign against Devagiri', in *Dr Ghulam Yazdani Commemoration Volume*, ed. H. K. Sherwani (Hyderabad: Maulana Abul Kalam Azad Oriental Research Institute, 1966). For details of the 1307 campaign, see J. Keay, *India: A History* (New York: Atlantic Monthly Press, 2010), 252–257.
47. This disastrous expedition was commanded by Fakhr-ud-din Jauna, who would go on to become Muhammad bin Tughluq. See P. Jackson. *The Delhi Sultanate: A Political and Military History* (Cambridge: Cambridge University Press, 2003), 201. See Satish Chandra, *Medieval India: From Sultanat to the Mughals-Delhi Sultanat (1206–1526)*, part 1 (New Delhi: Har-Anand Publications, 2004), 89.
48. The king Ramadeva was detained in Delhi along with his family, but he became Khalji's subordinate and returned to Devagiri as Rai-i-Rayan ('King of Kings')—a title bestowed upon him by Ala-ud-din Khalji. A. Eraly, *The Age of Wrath: A History of the Delhi Sultanate* (New Delhi: Penguin, 2015), 114.
49. Ibid., 116. For a description of the siege of Warangal by Malik Kafur in 1310, and the 1318 assault by Khusrau Khan against Pratapa Rudra for going delinquent on his annual tribute payments, see R. M. Eaton, *A Social History of the Deccan, 1300–1761: Eight Indian Lives*, part 1, vol. 8 (New York: Cambridge University Press, 2005), 18–19.
50. Simhana was a prince who was away with a large part of the Yadava army when Ramadeva agreed to sign the peace treaty with Ala-ud-din Khalji in his first raid in 1296. He put up a resistance before the treaty was signed but was defeated by Khalji. See A. S. Altekar, *The Early History of the Deccan. VIII: Yādavas of Seuṇadeśa*, ed. Ghulam Yazdani (London: Oxford University Press, 1960), 516–551.
51. Malik Kafur was the governor for two years but he had to return to Delhi in 1315 given Ala-ud-din Khalji's ill health. See S. S. Ali, *The African Dispersal in the Deccan: From Medieval to Modern Times* (New Delhi: Orient Blackswan, 1996), 84.
52. Malik Shihab-ud-din, Ala-ud-din Khalji's minor son by the Yadava princess, was made the 'sultan'. B. P. Saksena, 'The Khaljis: Alauddin Khalji', in

A Comprehensive History of India: The Delhi Sultanat (1206–1526), ed. Mohammad Habib and Khaliq Ahmad Nizami, 2nd ed. (New Delhi: The Indian History Congress/People's Publishing House, 1992 [1970]), 408–410.

53. Eraly, *The Age of Wrath*, 133.
54. Ibid., 133–139, for the developments leading to the decline of the Khalji dynasty.
55. Saksena, 'The Khaljis', 555–556.
56. Ibid., 557.
57. C. W. Ernst, *Eternal Garden: Mysticism, History, and Politics at a South Asian Sufi Center* (Albany, New York: SUNY Press, 1992).
58. P. M. Holt, A. K. S. Lambton, and B. Lewis, *The Cambridge History of Islam: Islamic Society and Civilization*, vol. 2B (Cambridge, UK: Cambridge University Press, 1977), 15.
59. Some notable chroniclers of the time such as the Moorish traveller Ibn Battutah claim that Muhammad bin Tughluq conspired to kill his father by designing an ingenuous collapsible stage in Afghanpur village near the capital of Tughluqabad that Ghiyas-ud-Din had built to the south of Delhi. See Ibn Battutah and T. Mackintosh-Smith, *The Travels of Ibn Battutah* (London: Picador, 2002), 65–166. Others such as Ferishta (also Firishta) and the chief chronicler of Muhammad bin Tughluq's reign Zia-ud-Din Barani, however, disagree.
60. Gangu named the sultanate in honour of his Brahmin (Bahaman) master whom he had served earlier. Allami, *Ain-i-Akbari*, 236.
61. The other three *taraf*s were Gulbarga, Daulatabad, and Bidar.
62. T. W. Haig, *Imperial Gazetteers of India: Berar* (Calcutta: Calcutta Superintendent of Govt Printing, 1909), 374–375.
63. S. Chandra, *History of Medieval India: 800–1700* (New Delhi: Orient BlackSwan, 2007), 184; emphasis added.
64. Muhammad Qasim Hindu Shah Astarabadi (Firishtah), *History of the Rise of the Mahomedan Power in India*, trans. John Briggs, vol. 2 (New Delhi: Oriental Books Reprint Corp., 1981), 232–233.
65. Ibid., 383. The forts of Gavligad and Narnala in Satpura Range protected the northern frontier while Mahur was on the southern frontier. In essence, these fortifications provided the Bahamani sultanate protection from kingdoms including the Gonds. It was the successor of Bahamani Gangu, Muhammad Shah Bahamani, who gave the title of Majlis-i-Aali to the four *tarafdar*s. See *Gazetteer of Buldhana*, available at https://cultural.maharashtra.gov.in/english/gazetteer/BULDHANA/his_mediaeval%20period.html (accessed on 10 April 2021).

66. Chandra, *History of Medieval India*.
67. The five independent kingdoms were Berar, Bidar, Bijapur, Golconda, and Ahmednagar. See S. Sen, *A Textbook of Medieval Indian History* (Delhi: Primus Books, 2013), 117–119.
68. There is scant official record of the Imad Shahi rule. Most contemporary writings about the Imad Shahi rule can be found in *Burhan-i-Maasir* and *Tarikh-i-Firishta*. See M. Y. Quddusi, *Berar under the Mughals* (Nagpur: Vishwabharti, 2007), 47–48, for a brief account of the administration of Berar under the Imad Shahi rule.
69. Tufail Khan was punished for not allying with Murtaza Nizam Shah I and Ali Adil Shah of Bijapur in their assault against the Vijayanagara Kingdom. S. V. Fitzgerald and A. E. Nelson, eds., *Central Provinces District Gazetteers: Amraoti District* (Pune: The Government Photozinco Press), 99.
70. Quddusi, *Berar under the Mughals*, 3–12.
71. Several decades later, son of a nobleman of the Nizam Shahi (Ahmednagar) and Adil Shahi (Bijapur) sultanates Shivaji Bhonsale I would go on to be the nemesis of the Mughals. Eaton, *A Social History of the Deccan*, 128–221.
72. One of the forts to be surrendered was Paunar—also known as Pavnar—10 kilometres from Wardha. Pavnar would go on to be the site for an ashram by the Gandhian reformer, Acharya Vinobha Bhave who championed the *bhoodan* (land gift) movement in the early 1950s.
73. Man Singh I, one of the *navaratnas* (nine gems) in Akbar's court and the raja of Amer (also Amber) that later became Jaipur, died in Achalpur in present-day Amravati district of Vidarbha.
74. McEldowney, 'Colonial Administration and Social Developments'.
75. R. A. Alvi, 'Mughal Geographical Accounts of Khandesh', *Medieval India: A Miscellany* 3 (1975): 127–151.
76. The same year, Aurangzeb annexed Ahmednagar which was the seat of the Nizam Shahi dynasty.
77. For details of succession among Mughal princes, see M. D. Faruqui, *The Princes of the Mughal Empire, 1504–1719* (New York: Cambridge, 2012), 24–45.
78. For a brief account of Shivaji's life, see Eaton, *A Social History of the Deccan*, 128–221.
79. Aurangzeb died in his Deccan headquarters, Aurangabad. He was interred at Rauza near the famous Ajanta and Ellora caves in present-day Aurangabad. At Aurangabad, one would also find the 'Bibi ka Maqbara'—a grandiose mausoleum that Aurangzeb built in memory of his beloved first

wife Dilras Banu Begum. The mausoleum has an uncanny resemblance to the Taj Mahal that his father Shah Jahan built in memory of Aurganzeb's mother Mumtaz Mahal. It is also known as *dakhin* Taj, or 'Taj of the Deccan'. In fact, the chief architect Ata-ullah was the son of the chief architect of the Taj Mahal—Ustad Ahmad Lahauri. The construction was undertaken around 1669 and was well within the budgeted 7 lakh rupees. Maharashtra (India) Gazetteers Dept, *Maharashtra State Gazetteers* (Director of Govt Printing, Stationery and Publications, Maharashtra State, 1977), 951.

80. 'Crore' is a unit followed in the South Asian numbering system, where 1 crore = 10,000,000.
81. *Gazetteer of Akola*, https://cultural.maharashtra.gov.in/english/gazetteer/AKOLA/his_mediaeval%20period.html (accessed on 20 April 2021).
82. *Hon* is the gold coin issued by Chhatrapati Shivaji, probably on his coronation in 1647. See C. Brown and A. E. Nelson, *Central Provinces and Berar District Gazetteers: Akola District* (Calcutta: Baptist Mission Press, 1910), https://indianculture.gov.in/gazettes/central-provinces-and-berar-district-gazetteers-akola-district-vol-descriptive (accessed on 16 April 2021).
83. This Treaty of Purandhar should not be confused with the later Treaty of Purandhar that was signed between the Maratha peshwa and the Company in Calcutta on 1 March 1771. Under the former, Sambhaji also received the *jagirdari* of the *pargana* of Avandhe. The treaty was confiscated later due to the recovery of the amount of 1 lakh *hon*s sanctioned to Shivaji as expenses when he visited Agra in 1666. For more on the first Treaty of Purandhar, see G. Stewart, 'The Marathas 1600–1818', in *The New Cambridge History of India*, ed. Gordan Stewart, vol. 2 (Cambridge, UK: Cambridge University Press, 1993), 73–74.
84. J. L. Mehta, *Advanced Study in the History of Modern India: Volume One: 1707–1813* (Noida: Sterling, 2005), 4, 47.
85. Gond mythology suggests there are three kinds of Gonds—Raj Gonds, Sur Gonds, and Nand Gonds. The Raj Gonds practised settled agriculture and were better educated. See Smita Yadav, *Precarious Labour and Informal Economy: Work, Anarchy, and Society in an Indian Village* (New York: Springer, 2018), 10–11.
86. Aurangzeb converted him to Islam and baptized him as Bakht Buland Shah ('the lucky one'). When the relationship turned sour, Aurangzeb changed his name to Nagun Bakht ('the unlucky one'). See *Gazetteer of Bhandara*,

https://cultural.maharashtra.gov.in/english/gazetteer/BHANDARA/his_mediaeval%20period.html (accessed on 24 October 2021).

87. J. Sarkar, *History of Aurganzib: Based on Original Sources*, vol. 5, *The Closing Years, 1689–1707* (Calcutta: M. C. Sarkar & Sons Ltd, 1924), 107–108.
88. Bakht Buland found allies in several Muslim vassals who resisted the imperial forces. See *Gazetteer of Bhandara*.
89. The peshwas in the Maratha empire were considered prime ministers, but their powers relative to the Maratha rulers changed fundamentally since the appointment of the Bhat peshwas who were 'Chitpavan Brahmins'. The first peshwa, Moropant Pingle was appointed by Shivaji in 1674. He, along with the later peshwas under Sambhaji and Rajaram, were 'Deshashta Brahmins'.
90. S. Gordon, *Marathas, Marauders, and State Formation in Eighteenth-Century India* (New Delhi: Oxford University Press, 1994).
91. Madhavrao Bhat I's teenaged brother Narayanrao was assassinated within a year of becoming the peshwa. Madhavrao Bhat's youngest son Sawai Madhavrao II, who was born after his death, was instated as the peshwa with the support of the Barabhai council that Nana Phadnavsi forged. See S. R. Sharma, *The Making of Modern India: From AD 1526 to the Present Day* (New Delhi: Orient Longman, 1951), 302.
92. S. Kulkarni, *The Satara Raj, 1818–1848: A Study in History, Administration, and Culture* (New Delhi: Mittal Publications, 1995), 74.
93. It may be surprising that the interaction between the Marathas and Europeans was not always about extortion, conflict, and trade. Several Maratha leaders including Shivaji had collaborated with Europeans for knowledge about naval technology. Many peshwas had a penchant for English clocks, watches, and items of luxury. See P. L. Saswadkar, 'The Dawn of Modernization in the Maratha State on the Eve of Its Extinction, 1790–1840', *Proceedings of the Indian History Congress* 29, no. 2 (1967): 127–131.
94. This should not be confused with another Treaty of Purandar that was signed 110 years before this treaty. The parties included the founder of the Maratha Empire, Shivaji and the Rajput king Jai Singh I who was commander of the Mughals. See M. N. Pearson, 'Shivaji and the Decline of the Mughal Empire', *Journal of Asian Studies* 35, no. 2 (1976): 221–235.
95. The Treaty of Wadgaon was signed by the Company in 1779, giving the upper hand to the Marathas in establishing supremacy in the Deccan. For

a historical account of the three Anglo-Maratha Wars, and counterview points compared to arguments for motivations and outcomes in these wars, see M. S. Naravane, *Battles of the Honourable East India Company: Making of the Raj* (New Delhi: APH Publishing, 2006), 49–148.

96. This was also the year the Persian invader Nadir Shah looted Mughal Delhi. The invasion that included the loot of the Peacock Throne with the Koh-i-Noor diamond left the Mughal coffers empty.
97. It is well known how fearing the Bhonsale advances into Bengal in the 1740s the Company had built the 'Maratha Ditch'—a nearly 5-kilometre-long moat outside Calcutta. For description of the Maratha Ditch, see N. P. Thankappan, 'The Growth and Development of Old Calcutta', in *The Living City*, ed. S. Chaudhuri, vol. 1 (New Delhi: Oxford University Press, 1990), 12.
98. S. W. W. Hunter, *Imperial Gazetteer of India*, vol. 10, *Multan to Palhalli* (London: Trubner & Co, 1886), 167.
99. Mudhoji II killed his brother Sabaji in the battle of Panchgaon (near Nagpur) in 1775.
100. K. N. Sinha, 'British Relations with the Nagpur Court (1799–1806)', *Proceedings of the Indian History Congress* 28 (1966): 346–353.
101. The second nizam, Nizam Ali Khan or Asaf Jah II; Peshwa Madhavrao I of Poona; and Haidar Ali of the kingdom of Mysore had formed an alliance against the Company in the Second Anglo Mysore War of 1780–1784. However, under Lord Cornwallis, the British formed a triple alliance involving the Company, Nizam Ali, and the peshwa to defeat Tipu Sultan after Tipu attacked Travancore. Ironically, a quadruple alliance was formed by Tipu's father Haidar Ali during the First Anglo-Mysore War, 1766–1769. It included Mysore, the nizam, peshwa, and Bhonsale.
102. The subsidiary alliance was designed on the same lines as the British resident at Hyderabad J. A. Kirkpatrick negotiated with the second nizam, Nizam Ali Khan. Hyderabad was the first princely state to accede to the Company's protection under the subsidiary alliance that Governor-General of India Lord Wellesley instituted in 1798.
103. Available at https://web.archive.org/web/20140531051603/http://nagpur.nic.in/zpnagpur/English/history.htm (accessed on 20 April 2022).
104. See M. Desai, D. Kumar, T. Raychaudhuri, and I. Habib, eds., *The Cambridge Economic History of India: Volume 1, c.1200–c.1750* (Cambridge, UK: Cambridge University Press, 1982), 192–193.

105. J. Black, *A Military History of Britain: From 1775 to the Present* (Westport, Connecticut: Greenwood Publishing Group, 2006).
106. Historians speculate that Pindaris are from Bidar, and the Pindaris are also referred to as 'Bidaris'. They were known to accompany the Mughal campaigns and received Maratha patronage before gaining autonomy. See P. F. McEldowney, 'Pindari Society and the Establishment of British Paramountcy in India' (master's thesis, Department of History, University of Wisconsin–Madison, 1966), https://asianstudies.github.io/area-studies/SouthAsia/Ideas/pindaris.html (accessed on 14 March 2021). For the relationship between Marathas and Pindaris, see T. Banerjee, 'The Marathas and the Pindaris: A Study in Their Relationship', *Quarterly Review of Historical Studies* 11, no. 2 (1972): 71–82.
107. Banerjee, 'The Marathas and the Pindaris', 71–82, 77. For information on some prominent Pindari leaders, see R. S. Chaurasia, *History of the Marathas* (New Delhi: Atlantic Publishers, 2004), 158–159.
108. J. Ross, *The Marquis of Hastings, K. G. and the Final Overthrow of the Maratha Power* (Oxford: Clarendon Press, 1900).
109. Lord Dalhousie, who was the governor-general of the Company between 1848 and 1856, annexed several princely states under this doctrine that posited that the princely state status of any princely state under suzerainty of the Company would be abolished if the ruler died without a male heir or was manifestly incompetent.
110. Baden-Powell, 'The Land-Systems of British India', 369.
111. For details about the relationship between the origins and end of the life of the first nizam of Hyderabad, see M. D. Faruqui, 'At Empire's End: The Nizam, Hyderabad and Eighteenth-Century India', *Modern Asian Studies* 43, no. 1 (2009): 5–43.
112. This is how Mir Qamaruddin acquired the titles of Asaf Jah I, Nizam-ul-Mulk, and Fateh Jung. His grandfather Qilich Khan was a close aide of Aurangzeb and lost his life in the siege of Golconda in 1687.
113. Following the death of Aurangzeb in 1707, the Sayyid brothers were instrumental as king-makers in Delhi.
114. J. F. Richards, *The Mughal Empire*, vol. 5 (Cambridge, UK: Cambridge University Press, 1993), 279–281.
115. Historians have differing views on the nizam's separation from the Mughals as indicative of an act of strength or weakness. For example, see Faruqui, 'At Empire's End', 17, and references therein.
116. J. L. Mehta, *Advanced Study in the History of Modern India*, 492–494.

117. J. G. Duff, *History of the Mahrattas* (New Delhi: Times of India Office, 1878), 1:333.
118. S. Gordon, *The Marathas 1600–1818* (Cambridge, UK: Cambridge University Press, 2007), 120–131.
119. G. S. Sardesai, *New History of the Marathas: The Expansion of the Maratha Power, 1707–1772* (Bombay: Phoenix Publications, 1948), 98. Also see J. Sarkar, *Military History of India* (Calcutta: M. C. Sarkar and Sons), 143.
120. K. S. Lal, *History of the Khaljis (1290–1320)* (Allahabad: The Indian Press, 1950), 250.
121. Ibid., 102. For a discussion on how this system ensured the flow of revenue and bullion in rural garrison towns, see A. Wink, *Al-Hind, Vol. 2: Slave Kings and the Islamic Conquest, 11th–13th Centuries* (Leiden, Netherlands: E. J. Brill, 1997), 216.
122. Irfan Habib, 'Northern India under the Sultanate: Agrarian Economy', in *The Cambridge Economic History of India: Volume 1, c.1200–c.1750*, ed. T. Raychaudhuri and I. Habib (Cambridge, UK: Cambridge University Press, 1982), 62.
123. *Tarikh-i-Firoz Shahi*, 212, cited in A. Rashid, 'Famine in the Turco-Afghan Period', *Proceedings of the Indian History Congress* 26, no. 2 (1964): 84–89, 86.
124. Ibid., 85.
125. S. J. Raza, 'Tughlaq Administration in the Light of Epigraphic Evidence', *Proceedings of the Indian History Congress* 69 (2008): 230–239.
126. D. Kaur, 'Iqtadari System and the Growth of Towns in Medieval India', *India Quarterly* 46, nos. 2/3 (1990): 188–196, 194–195.
127. See *Gazetteer of Poona*, https://cultural.maharashtra.gov.in/english/gazetteer/Poona/PART%20II/Chap%20(2)/Muslim%20Period.htm (accessed on 23 March 2021).
128. See, for example, William Foster, ed., *Early Travels in India, 1583–1619* (London: Munshiram Manoharial Publishers Pvt. Ltd, 1927), 17.
129. S. Moosvi, 'The World of Labour in Mughal India (c.1500–1750)', *International Review of Social History* 56, no. S19 (2010–2011): 245–261.
130. I. Habib, *The Agrarian System of Mughal India 1556–1707* (Oxford: Oxford University Press, 1963), 231, 290.
131. In Berar subah, *chaudhuri*, *qanungo*, *muqaddam*, and *patwari* were termed as *deshmukh*, *deshpande*, *patil*, and *kulkarni*, respectively.
132. The *subahdar* was supported by several administrators including the *diwan*, *bakshi*, *sadr*, *qazi*, *kotwal*, *mir bahr*, and *waqa-i-navis*, *patwari*, and *qanungo*.

See V. D. Mahajan, *History of Medieval India, Part 2* (New Delhi: S. Chand, 2007), 236.

133. M. Athar Ali, *The Mughal Nobility under Aurangzeb* (Bombay: Oxford University Press, 1966), 84–86. The *jagidari* system was founded by the Delhi Sultanate.
134. Catherine B. Asher and Cynthia Talbot, *India before Europe* (New York: Cambridge University Press, 2006), 125–127. Unlike *jagirdari, zamindari* rights were hereditary. Nevertheless, hereditary transfers of *jagir* to the male lineal heirs were also practised in some places. See Richards, *The Mughal Empire*, 292–293.
135. F. Bernier, *Travels in the Mogul Empire AD 1656–1668*, trans. Archibald Constable (Westminster, UK: Archibald Constable & Co., 1891), http://www.columbia.edu/cu/lweb/digital/collections/cul/texts/ldpd_6093710_000/pages/ldpd_6093710_000_00000265.html (accessed on 14 February 2021).
136. Records of *dahshala* can be found in the *muwazana-i dah-shala* that records revenue and area of the last ten years as well as the records of the previous year or the average of the assessed revenue. Habib, *The Agrarian System of Mughal India*, 259.
137. L. D. Satya, *Cotton and Famine in Berar 1850–1900* (New Delhi: Manohar, 1997), 29.
138. W. H. Moreland, 'Sher Shah's Revenue System', *Journal of the Royal Asiatic Society* 58, no. 3 (1926): 447–459, 452–454.
139. Habib, *The Agrarian System of Mughal India*, 237–239.
140. Central Provinces and Berar (India), *Central Provinces and Berar: A Review of the Administration of the Provinces*, vol. 2 (Nagpur: Govt Printing, 1922), 207. For evidence of cash orientation of early medieval India, see W. H. Moreland, *The Agrarian System of Moslem India* (Cambridge, UK: Cambridge University Press, 2011; reprint of 1929), 114, 136–137.
141. The rates varied from half of the produce for rain-fed crops; one-third for food grains; and between one-ninth and one-fourteenth for cash crops irrigated by wells and canals. Available at https://egyankosh.ac.in/bitstream/123456789/44525/1/Unit-19.pdf (accessed on 14 March 2020).
142. For details of the Durgadevi famine, see James M. Campbell, I. C. S, *Gazetteer of the Bombay Presidency: Nasik*, vol. 16 (Bombay: Printed at the Govt Central Press, 1883), 105; and G. Hugo and B. Currey, *Famine as a Geographical Phenomenon* (Boston, MA: GeoJournal library/D. Reidel, 1984), 72. For details of the Deccan famine in the first half of the

seventeenth century, see C. Ó. Gráda, 'Making Famine History', *Journal of Economic Literature* 45, no. 1 (2007): 5–38, 7. For a perspective on how Deccan irrigation canals ended famines in the 1920s but carry concerns about efficiency of resource use, see D. W. Attwood, 'Big Is Ugly? How Large-Scale Institutions Prevent Famines in Western India', *World Development* 33, no. 12 (2005): 2067–2083.

143. Z. Husain, 'The "Zamindars" in the Deccan under Aurangzeb', *Proceedings of the Indian History Congress* 60 (1999): 315–331. Apart from Habib, *The Agrarian System of Mughal India*, for seminal scholarly works on revenue administration during Akbar's reign, see Raychaudhuri and Habib, *Cambridge Economic History of India*, 235–249; S. Moosvi, *The Economy of the Mughal Empire, c. 1595* (Oxford: Oxford University Press, 1987), 95–126. Compared to Aurangzeb's reign, there is scant official record of the revenue administration for the period of the later Mughals. For instance, see N. A. Siddiqi, 'The Dastur-Ul-Amal-I-Baikas: An Administrative Manual of Muhammad Shah's Reign', *Proceedings of the Indian History Congress* 23 (1960): 243–247.

144. It was remarkable that distinction between kharif and rabi crops as well as that between *zirayati* (rain-fed) and *baghati* (irrigated) lands was central to the revenue assessment; the latter being further classified based on the source of irrigation. The tax rate was one-third of the produce in the case of *zirayati* lands and two-fifth of the produce in the case of *baghati* lands. The rates differed in the case of commercial crops such as sugarcane and grapes, and expenses incurred in irrigation until the plants bore fruits determined the rates. The share of the state on the estimate of produce per *bigha* (yield) commuted to cash value was a significant development in the history of land administration.

145. For pros and cons of the reforms by Malik Ambar, see T. B. Jervis, *Report: Historical and Geographical Account of the Western Coast of India, Revenue and Land Tenure*, cited in G. T. Kulkarni, 'Land Revenue Settlement under the Nizam Shahis (1489–1636), With Special Reference to Malik Ambar – A Preliminary Study', *Proceedings of the Indian History Congress* 52 (1991): 369–377, 376–377.

146. Ibid.

147. For details of how the Company went on to dominate trade with India by surpassing its European trading rivals such as the VOC over a century since 1668, see O. Prakash, *European Commercial Enterprise in Pre-Colonial India* (New Delhi: Cambridge University Press, 2000), 115, 121.

148. N. Robins, *The Corporation That Changed the World: How the East India Company Shaped the Modern Multinational*, 2nd ed. (London: Pluto Press, 2012), 44.
149. See P. N. Chakrabarti, 'Myth of the Date of Establishment of the First English Factory (1613) and Its Baneful Effect on Mughal Economy', *Proceedings of the Indian History Congress* 40 (1979): 487–490.
150. Aurangzeb's death in 1707 and the 'anarchy' it resulted in was a pivotal moment in the rise of supremacy of the Company in Deccan. See W. Dalrymple, *The Anarchy: The East India Company, Corporate Violence, and the Pillage of an Empire* (London: Bloomsbury Publishing, 2019).
151. *Gazetteer of Bhandara.*
152. For a detailed review of the developments resulting in Bakht Buland Shah falling in and out of favour with Aurangzeb, see the *Gazetteer of Bhandara.*
153. *Central Provinces and Berar*, 208.
154. N. K. Kumar, 'Hydraulic Agriculture in Peninsular India (c.300 BC–1300 AD)', *Proceedings of the Indian History Congress* 40 (1979): 211–214, 212.
155. Ibid., 212.
156. Available at http://www.rainwaterharvesting.org/Rural/Traditional2.htm#Phad (accessed on 21 April 2022).
157. M. Rajankar, 'Traditional Water Management Systems of Eastern Vidarbha: Community Conservation–1', *South Asia Network on Dams, Rivers and People* 9 (December 2011): 5–8, 5. Also see 'Rejuvenation of Malguzari Tanks', http://cgwb.gov.in/Bhujal-manthan/bm3-file10.pdf (accessed on 17 March 2020).
158. M. Purohit, 'Rejuvenating Traditional Water System in Maharashtra', *Down to Earth*, 2016, https://www.indiawaterportal.org/articles/rejuvenating-traditional-water-system-maharashtra (accessed on 17 March 2020).
159. A. Kumar, 'Ramtek's Water Woes', *Economic and Political Weekly* 38, no. 3 (2003): 186–187.
160. The text of the *farman* was edited and first published by noted historian Jadunath Sarkar in 1906 in the *Journal of the Asiatic Society of Bengal.* See J. Sarkar, 'Aurangzeb's *Farman* to Rasikdas', *Journal of the Asiatic Society of Bengal* (1906).
161. Usually paid in two instalments after harvest or at first two harvests. Practice of local officials earning a commission from the peasants cannot be ruled out.
162. I. Habib, 'Usury in Medieval India', *Comparative Studies in Society and History* 6, no. 4 (1964): 393–419, 394.

163. Ibid., 394–395.
164. D. A. Washbrook, 'Progress and Problems: South Asian Economic and Social History c. 1720–1860', *Modern Asian Studies* 22, no. 1 (1988); T. Raychaudhuri, 'State and the Economy: The Mughal Empire', in *Cambridge Economic History of India*, ed. Raychaudhuri and Habib, 173.
165. C. A. Bayly, 'State and Economy in India over Seven Hundred Years', *Economic History Review* 38, no. 4 (1985): 587. For a review of the literature on the role of Mughal rule on India's economic development, see F. W. Ellis, 'In What Way, and to What Degree, Did the Mughal State Inhibit Smithian Growth in India in the Seventeenth Century?' (working paper no. 14/05, London School of Economics and Political Science, London, UK).
166. For an analysis of agrarian relations in rural Maharashtra, see M. B. McAlpin, *Subject to Famine: Food Crises and Economic Change in Western India, 1860–1920* (Princeton: Princeton University Press, 1983).
167. Habib, *The Agrarian System of Mughal India*, 155–157.
168. The twelve (*bara* in Marathi) services were categorized into three hierarchical groups: *paheeli ol*, *dusari ol*, *tisari ol* (*ol* means row) that determined the payment structure. Although payments were usually in kind and food, monetary payments were also provided. The remaining eighteen types of services providers were called *alutedar* who received their payment *alut* in kind after annual harvest. Not all the caste groups would be present in a village.
169. A. R. Kulkarni, 'Village Life in the Deccan in the Seventeenth Century', *Indian Economic and Social History Review* 4, no. 1 (1967): 38–52.
170. Satya, *Cotton and Famine in Berar*, 35.
171. For a general description of social organization in rural Maharashtra, see I. K. Karve, 1968, *Maharashtra—Land and Its People* (Directorate of Government Printing, Stationery and Publications, Maharashtra State). In *varhadi* (Berari) dialect of Marathi, *ay* is income and *kari* is service. Therefore, *aykari* can be interpreted as remuneration for service. Different regions of Maharashtra have different names for the same system. Synonyms of *baluta* include *ghugari* (grains), *pendikadi* (bundle of unthreshed crops), *ser* (certain share of grains), and *hakk* (right). The *ay* system in northern Karnataka resembles the *aykari* system. See K. Ishwaran, *Tradition and Economy in Village India* (New York: Routledge and Kegan Paul Ltd, 1966).
172. For differences between the *balutedari* and *jajamani* systems, see H. Fukazawa, 'Rural Servants in Eighteenth-Century Maharashtrian

Village: Demiurgic or Jajmani System?', *Hitotshubashi Journal of Economics* 12, no. 2 (1972): 14–40.

173. Much of our discussion on how *balutedar*s sustained their control over labour is based on Satya, *Cotton and Famine in Berar*, 41–43.
174. K. Wittfogel, *Oriental Despotism: A Comparative Study of Total Power* (New Haven, CT: Oxford University Press, 1957).
175. For real wage trends over the period between the sixteenth and mid-nineteenth centuries, see S. N. Broadberry and B. Gupta, 'The Early Modern Great Divergence: Wages, Prices and Economic Development in Europe and Asia, 1500–1800', *Economic History Review* 59, no. 1 (2006): 2–31; and S. N. Broadberry and B. Gupta, 'Lancashire, India and Shifting Competitive Advantage in Cotton Textiles, 1700–1850: The Neglected Role of Factor Prices', *Economic History Review* 62, no. 2 (2009): 279–305.
176. H. Fukazawa, 'Standard of Living 2: Maharashtra and the Deccan', in *The Cambridge Economic History of India*, ed. Raychaudhuri and Habib, 471–477.
177. For arguments that started the debate, see A. V. Desai, 'Population and Standards of Living in Akbar's Time', *Indian Economic and Social History Review* 9, no. 1 (1972), 43–62; and A. V. Desai, 'Population and Standards of Living in Akbar's Time: A Second Look', *Indian Economic and Social History Review* 15, no. 1 (1978): 53–79. For a retort of such stark conclusions about real wage differentials over the centuries, see A. W. Heston, 'The Standard of Living in Akbar's Time: A Comment', *Indian Economic and Social History Review* 14, no. 3 (1977): 391–396.

2

ACCIDENTS AND GAMBLES IN COLONIAL VIDARBHA

By now, we have a fair understanding of the history of Vidarbha until the colonial takeover. Regardless of the political instability that marred the region over centuries, it remains to be seen why and how cotton became the mainstay of the region's economy ever since.[1] Is it possible that the developments in cotton economy in one region structurally transformed cotton economy in faraway regions? Were there transnational impacts that the commodity has had over centuries that have not been analysed? In this context, major upheavals in the world cotton trade need to be accounted for. Prominent among these upheavals was the American Civil War that broke out in 1861. Furthermore, British trade policy—during and following the Company's prolonged domination over India—also influenced the directions and quantum of cotton trade of the region.

In this chapter, we present a sketch of how cotton became the staple of the American South and how the United States became the leading exporter of raw cotton in the world by the middle of the nineteenth century—a watershed in Vidarbha's economic history. In doing so, we examine how 'King Cotton' and its retainers were central to the American Civil War that disrupted the supply of raw cotton to the growing demand of the Lancashire mills. We locate the emergence of India in general and Berar and the Central Provinces in particular, on the world map of cotton through these tectonic developments. We also delve into changes in contemporary institutions and agrarian systems of the region following the colonial takeover. In essence, we give an account of the major events that shaped the extent and nature of expansion of cotton cultivation in the region. This account will demonstrate how Vidarbha farmers entered the metaphorical casino of gambling with cotton.

We posit that to characterize the cotton economy in colonial-era Vidarbha, it is necessary to identify underlying developments that fostered cotton expansion. We draw attention to major historical developments in faraway lands—the United States, Britain, and China—in conjunction with domestic factors that shaped the cotton economy even before the colonial takeover. Since the colonial takeover in 1853, there was a transformation of local institutions in the region. Traditional land revenue assessment and agrarian relations were dismantled, and property rights on cultivated land developed. Credit markets also underwent significant changes. There was considerable expansion of the railways and communication systems. There were several efforts to introduce new seed varieties. Beyond the changes taking place domestically, there were major upheavals in the world cotton trade in the second half of the nineteenth century. The American Civil War that broke out within eight years of the region's colonial takeover is a historical accident that warrants attention. There was an extraordinary upsurge in the export of raw cotton from India and the price of cotton increased until the war lasted. The prospects of profits also led to the widespread practice of adulteration of raw cotton meant for exports that resulted in laws to counter the issue. The 'cotton mania' and the subsequent crash of prices in the late nineteenth century demonstrated the significance of speculative bubbles in the story of cotton. The late nineteenth century also saw the rise of cotton mills in Bombay, Ahmedabad, and Vidarbha. By the turn of the twentieth century, the stage was set for the capitalist development of India's cotton economy and cotton growers of Vidarbha became increasingly integrated with the domestic and world markets. This integration however came at the cost of their exposure to the vicissitudes of cotton demand and supply. The growth of the cotton economy also had environmental and ecological consequences that irrevocably transformed the region. The economic and social transformation also influenced the ability of rural households to cope with debilitating famines of the Victorian era.

Indeed, it is beyond the scope of a few pages to comprehensively chronicle all changes in technology, institutions, trade, commerce, and political upheavals that directly or indirectly had a bearing on our topic of interest. Nevertheless, an exposition of the complex systems that enabled the commercialization of cotton cultivation in Vidarbha is necessary. For the sake of brevity, we will not delve into finer details of historical developments of the post-bellum reconstruction of the North American and global cotton economy that have been extensively documented in the literature.[2] Rather, we present an account of the antecedents of the growth of Vidarbha's cotton economy by establishing a link with the developments in the region with that in Europe and North America in the nineteenth century.

THE BOOM AND BUST IN COTTON ECONOMY

It is not a coincidence that following the colonial takeover of the region that we know of as Vidarbha, nearly 170 years ago, there was a phenomenal rise in the area under cotton as farmers began growing cotton for world markets extensively. However, around the time this transformation occurred, farmers were not strangers to growing different varieties of cotton, having grown the indigenous (*desi*) cotton *Gossypium arboreum* and *Gossypium herbaceum* on tracts with fertile black cotton soil.[3] By the second half of the nineteenth century, colonial experimentation with exotic varieties such as New Orleans, Egyptian, and Brazilian cotton had been systematically implemented for decades.[4] However, early years of experimentation with the exotic cotton varieties was a failure.[5] These experimentations were part of the cotton improvement programme that attempted to relieve Britain's dependence on the American South for raw cotton.[6] Nevertheless, during the American Civil War of 1861–1865, there was a remarkable surge in exports of raw cotton from India. The euphoria around cotton arose out of the shift in England's dependence on raw cotton from America to India during the war years.

In 1860, India exported 497,649 bales of raw cotton to Europe whilst the export to China—the most important destination in the previous century—was a little over 200,000 bales. At the start of the war in 1861, exports surged to 955,030 bales to the former and fell to around 67,000 bales to the latter.[7] It is in this context of rising raw cotton exports to Europe in general and Britain in particular that Bombay became the leading port for the cotton trade in the late nineteenth century, and cotton-growing regions including Berar and the territories that would later become part of the Central Provinces became important suppliers of raw cotton. Since 1866 there was a precipitous fall in the cotton exports to Britain as the United States recovered from the Civil War (Graph 2.1).[8] Even though the United States gradually regained its leading position as supplier of raw cotton in global cotton exports after the Civil War, India remained at the second position until the end of the nineteenth century.

These developments resulted in a profound transformation of the agrarian system of the region. Tales of prosperity of cultivators in the region during the Civil War period and the first decade of the twentieth century are well

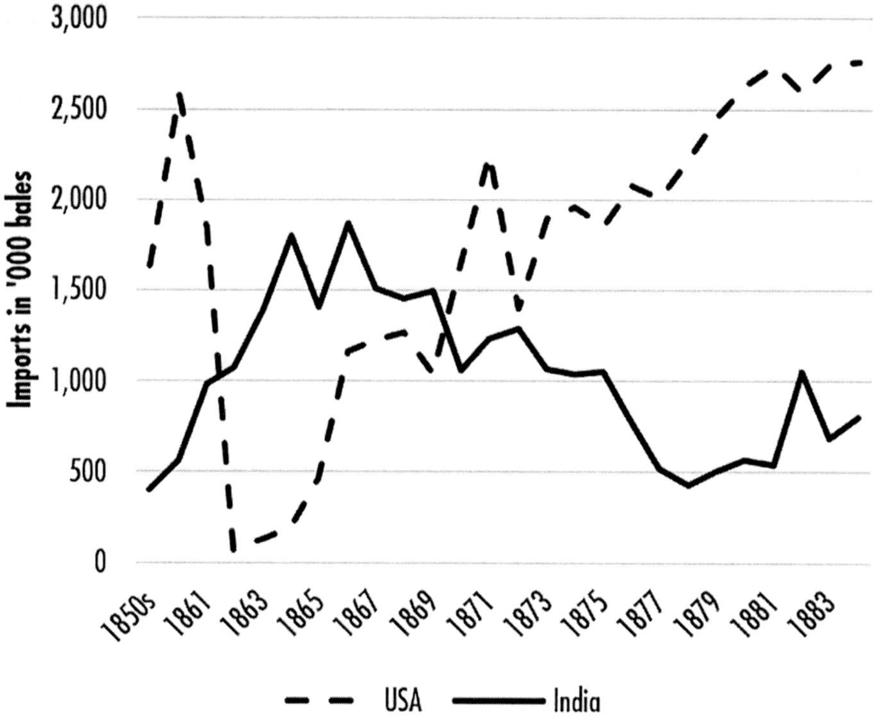

Graph 2.1 Cotton imports into Britain from India and the United States: 1850–1883

Source: G. Wright, 'Cotton Competition and the Post-bellum Recovery of the American South', *Journal of Economic History* 34, no. 3 (1974): 610–635, 611, table 1.

Note: For data on cotton imports of Britain from India for the period 1840–1858 in pounds, see J. F. Watson, 'On the Growth of Cotton in India: Its Present State and Future Prospects, With Special Reference to Supplies to Britain', *Journal of the Society of Arts* 7, no. 331 (1859): 277–293, 286, table 2. '1850s' refers to the average of the 1850s.

recorded. In what might seem a stark contrast to the narrative of agrarian distress in recent times, there are accounts of cultivators of the cotton tracts silver-plating their cartwheels. Also, in what might seem like a bizarre manifestation of the prosperity from cotton production in the early twentieth century, farmers committed suicide 'in a delirium of joy at the extraordinary profits of agriculture'.[9] One might wonder how these tales of prosperity can be reconciled with the tragedies that accompanied the agrarian change? What is striking that despite limited historical record of how the Civil War and colonial era policies transformed the history of cotton and global capitalism, not much is known about how these forces became a 'tipping point' in the history of cotton farmers of Vidarbha.[10]

The transformation of Vidarbha's cotton economy is a remarkable story of how the Civil War linked it with the developments in distant territories. Indeed, it may seem preposterous that developments in the American South in the late nineteenth century catalysed the process of global integration of the cotton growers of central India. However, that is precisely what the acute scarcity of raw cotton because of the American Civil War resulted in. The *Amravati Gazetteer* aptly comments on this transformation of the cotton economy due to the American Civil War, and developments three decades thereafter:

> Since 1857 the history of the district has been the record of a steady increase of prosperity, which received a sudden stimulus from the American Civil War, which increased the demand for Indian cotton, and was only temporarily checked by the season of scarcity in 1896–97 and the famine of 1899–1900.[11]

How did such prosperity come about? How long did the prosperity last? What distinguished the region from other cotton-growing tracts of the country? What distinguished the export-oriented cotton economy from the American South? Were there episodes of agrarian crisis? To find answers to these questions, we examine how geopolitical developments related to 'King Cotton' and the American Civil War put Berar and the Central Provinces on the world cotton map. We also delve into major institutional changes that accompanied the colonial takeover of the region. Central to our characterization of the changes sweeping through the region since the late nineteenth century is the story of how 'King Cotton' policy and the 'Cotton Famine' of the late nineteenth century weaved the destinies of actors in the global supply chain of cotton across multiple continents. Although much has been written about these topics, we briefly present a summary to contextualize how Vidarbha arrived in the world stage of cotton production.

'KING COTTON' AND ITS GLOBAL RETAINERS

British protectionist policies of the late seventeenth and early eighteenth centuries as well as the technological innovations played a vital role in the proliferation of cotton manufacturing in the northwest counties of England, especially Lancashire.[12] Concerns of competition from cheap imported calicoes and chintzes that the Company introduced to the British market following the Restoration in 1660 threatened the survival of domestic linen and woollen manufacturers.[13] Alarmed by the growing share of imports of cotton, linen, and silks from Asia, the woollen and silk industry in England lobbied against the competition.[14] Consequently, several protectionist policies to safeguard the woollen and worsted cloth manufacturers of eastern and southern England were enacted between 1665 and 1721.[15] Protectionist legislations such as the Calico Acts of 1701 and 1721 banned the import of white cotton cloth for finishing in England.[16] Import tariffs incentivized mass production of white cloth for the calico printing industry.[17] However, as imports of prohibited textiles grew following a temporary dip, the Parliament succumbed to growing public unrest, and further prohibitions were legislated.[18] Subsequent legislations such as the Manchester Act of 1736 allowed printing of fustians made using coloured weft and linen warp, causing a rise in demand for woven cloth, and thereby cotton.[19] In due course, Lancashire became more competitive compared to Indian cotton manufacturing—the world leader at the time.[20]

It was not just British protectionist policies but also the Industrial Revolution that catalysed the cotton economy of a young United States of America. The Industrial Revolution transformed how cotton was ginned, spun, and woven.[21] By the late eighteenth century, the slew of innovations including Eli Whitney's gin spawned mass production of cotton manufactures, creating an immense demand for raw cotton.[22] With the growing demand for raw cotton exports from the American South to Britain and continental Europe, there was a concerted attempt by European capitalists to have a stake in the growing cotton business.[23] Agents of European import merchants frequented the major cotton centres in the South, deepening the networks of trade and commerce. Also, British industrialists travelled to North America in the late eighteenth century to promote cotton growing.[24] Until 1785, American cotton was barely recognized in European markets as a source of raw cotton, and incidents of impounding of consignments imported by British merchants were not uncommon.[25] Such incidents would soon be a thing of the past as the United States became the largest supplier of raw cotton to Britain.

With the rise in raw cotton prices because of growing British demand, American planters grabbed the opportunity of a lucrative business.[26] Long-staple varieties such as 'Sea Island' cotton—whose seeds were brought from the Bahamas—became popular in plantations of coastal Georgia and South Carolina in 1786.[27] By contrast, farther inland, upland cotton, one that required labour-intensive ginning, became popular.[28] In facilitating the production and trade of cotton in the American South, mercantile capital played a significant role.[29] States such as Georgia, Alabama, Mississippi, and Louisiana became the major cotton-producing states, and cotton was grown in large areas of Arkansas, Texas, and Tennessee. Port cities and river mouths—particularly of the Mississippi—grew with the growing cotton trade.[30] Intermediaries such as 'factors' who supplied the raw cotton to manufacturers and agents abroad emerged as powerful actors in the global supply chain of cotton.[31] However, at the heart of the cotton expansion in the American South was an institution of immense significance in the global history of cotton—slavery.[32]

Slavery in North America had been in vogue since the tobacco boom. As profits from tobacco rose, there was an increase in migrants and settlements in the tidewater coastal plains and Piedmont on the eastern coast. Between 1630 and 1700, there was a manifold rise in the share of blacks in the population of several tobacco-growing areas.[33] The formal banning of slavery of the Native Americans in 1705 intensified the Atlantic slave trade.[34] As the slave labour-based tobacco economy grew, it worsened inequality in wealth distribution; with the planter aristocracy including the likes of Thomas Jefferson and George Washington receiving an increasingly higher share of the profits.[35] Subsequent legislation institutionalized the racialization of slave labour. When the 'Deep South'—South Carolina, Georgia, Alabama, Mississippi, and Louisiana—began the expansion of tobacco owing to cheaper land and conducive climate and soil, the availability of abundant slave labour was a catalyst.[36] The underlying forces for the propagation of slavery in cotton were similar.

America's cotton planters enthusiastically responded to the growing demand of Lancashire which in turn was rising due to the rapid expansion of British cotton cloth and yarn exports.[37] By 1800, cotton production in the United States increased thirtyfold over the past decade and continued to rise exponentially over the next several decades.[38] Raw cotton exports from the American South to England grew to such an extent that the United States became the leading supplier of raw cotton as early as 1802.[39] Why did the United States dominate the world cotton markets in the nineteenth century instead of the traditional leaders in supply of raw cotton—the New World or China or India? Both demand and supply of cotton played a role. As far as the demand is concerned, American upland cotton was not only suitable for Whitney's gin but also in high demand among British manufacturers for the production of cheap cloth out of the coarse yarns and fabrics that this cotton was appropriate for. Regarding supply, the ability of planters to bring under the plough lands with climate and soil suitable for cotton production was crucial. Command over slave labour and access to mercantile capital created a combination of factors that were conducive to the unprecedented cotton expansion. Indeed, historians debate the role of slavery in the growth of cotton in the American South and that of capitalism. For instance, the new history of capitalism (NHC) school attributes the comparative advantage of the American South's cotton exports to slavery. It also argues that 'war capitalism' shaped the 'periphery' to meet the dynamics of industrial demand in the nineteenth century.[40] Critics however disagree with the argument of slavery as a necessary condition of expansion of American cotton as well as ambiguity around definitions of capitalism eschewed by the NHC camp.[41]

American raw cotton exports received a fillip as the Napoleonic Wars over the period 1803–1815 interrupted the supply of raw cotton from Asian colonies such as China and Egypt. However, the booming cross-Atlantic cotton trade was interrupted due to Thomas Jefferson's Embargo Act in 1807 and the War of 1812.[42] Within a few years, the discovery of cotton varieties such as *G. barbadense* in North America, popularly known as 'Petit Gulf' in Mississippi in 1820, boosted cotton production in the South as it was better suited for the cotton gin and could be more densely grown.[43] These developments played an important role in the South American replacing the New World as the most important source of raw cotton for cotton manufacturing in North America as well as Europe. However, the 'Cotton Panic' of 1837 in the United States hit the profitability of cotton and worsened the indebtedness of planters, particularly in the South. Following the depressed prices since the recovery from the Cotton Panic of 1837, cotton growers were relieved by technological innovations. In addition, export demand resurged as English markets opened. In the story of the South's dominance in world cotton, expansion of railroads and improvement in steamboat transportation was crucial.[44]

As the British economy recovered from a slump on account of a low interest rate regime, there was a 'railway mania' in Britain in the early 1840s. There was an extraordinary rise in the number and price of railway securities in the London Stock Exchange that subsided by the latter part of 1845 as the speculative bubble began to burst.[45] Poor harvest of grains in England and

Ireland in 1846 resulted in growing food imports that depleted gold bullion reserves, prompting the Bank of England to eventually tighten its monetary policy, that is, raising interest rates.[46] Speculation grew on account of rising food prices (mostly corn) but the derivatives markets crashed on account of prospects of good harvest in 1847. By mid-1847, with further monetary tightening by the Bank of England, a financial panic gripped Britain as the speculators and bankers bit the dust. The crisis was also aggravated by the short cotton crop in the American South in 1845 and 1846. As cotton prices rose from 4.5 pence per pound in 1845 to 6.5 pence per pound in 1847[47] and domestic demand contracted, Lancashire experienced high unemployment.[48]

Following recovery from the 'Cotton Panic' of 1847, by the mid-nineteenth century, market expansion gained prominence in the American South as cotton emerged as America's most valuable crop, and its export share in the British trade increased markedly.[49] Cotton mills developed in New England, and subsequently in the South, in the first half of the nineteenth century given the growing profitability in cotton manufacturing.[50] The railroad expansion accentuated the transport of raw materials to ports and reduced transportation costs drastically. This also spurred the growth of cities such as Memphis, Atlanta, Dallas, Columbus, and Jackson. As cotton could be produced at considerably low costs owing to slavery, planters, merchants, exporters, and bankers benefited from the growing transoceanic trade. However, by the mid-nineteenth century, there was increased recognition of the evils of slavery that was the backbone of the Southern economy.[51] For several decades, abolitionists had attempted to persuade the federal government to bring an end to slavery without success. Ultimately, the reorganization of British abolitionism across the Atlantic and renewed pressures on the South to abolish slavery following the election of Abraham Lincoln as the US president in 1860 created tensions between the North and the South.[52] The following year, with the bombardment of Fort Sumter in South Carolina on 12 April 1861, the American Civil War broke out.[53]

With the outbreak of the Civil War, the supply of raw cotton to the mills of England was disrupted by a Southern-imposed embargo and a Union blockade that ensued. It is not surprising that the strategic embargo on cotton by the Confederate states rested on the assumption that given the importance of Southern cotton for New England as well as England's textile industry, an embargo would result in European recognition of the Confederacy. Such recognition was presumed to result in an inevitable alliance.[54] That the South was grossly mistaken in its assumption of such alliance based on the primacy of 'King Cotton' cannot be questioned.[55] There was a strategic blunder on the South's part in their 'King Cotton diplomacy' as they miscalculated the bumper crops in recent years as well as surplus cotton stocks in England in anticipation of possibilities of a civil war in the United States.[56] Nonetheless, the moniker of 'King Cotton' is testimony to the power of cotton. The following boast by the senator of South Carolina in 1858 is indicative of the power wielded by cotton in the whole scheme of things:

> What would happen if no cotton were furnished for three years? I will not stop to depict what everyone can image, but this is certain: old England would topple headlong and carry the whole civilized world with her.... No, you dare not make war on cotton. No power on earth dares to make war on cotton. Cotton is king![57]

Cotton not only financed warships of the Confederates; it also became a mode of payment for armament procured by the South despite the naval blockade by the North. The use of blockade runners—lightweight steamships built in England and Scotland—to pass through the blockade, carrying arms and supplies to the South in exchange for cotton for England, is yet another example of the supremacy of cotton among all commodities.[58] Long before the Civil War, catalysed by increased traffic of steamships and the telegraph, information from England reached America earlier than cotton shipments, thereby fostering cotton futures trading.[59] Despite adversities brought upon by the Civil War, cotton financing continued in innovative ways. During the Civil War period, cotton was the basis for the only foreign loans effected. Cotton-backed, that is, redeemable in cotton bales bonds—'Erlanger bonds'—launched in Europe in March 1863, is a case in point.[60] Furthermore, investors were given the additional option of taking payment in cotton at a fixed price on this high-risk bond.[61]

Surprisingly, cotton was also central to rampant corruption in the Mississippi valley as federal permits were issued to cotton in the Confederate states.[62] The North made federal permits mandatory for buying cotton in the South with the objective of thwarting the cotton-backed financing power of the South. The confederate cotton that was to be confiscated could be bought extremely cheap and sold dear. This created prospects of hitherto unseen windfalls. Not surprisingly, a 'cotton mania' ensued given the possibility of overnight fortune reversals.[63] The quirks of King Cotton notwithstanding and its susceptibility to panics and manias, the effects of the Confederacy's defeat in the American Civil War were profound.[64] Before examining the impact of the Civil War on the Indian cotton economy, a glimpse into how it changed the Southern economy is illustrative of how cotton is intricately linked with the economy and society of regions with an overarching dependence on it.

With emancipation, the slavery-based model of mass cotton production came to an end. There was a recasting of the structure of the global supply chain of cotton.[65] Most freed slave labourers rented land and became sharecroppers. The newly freed black plantation worker families—'freedman families'—increasingly became sharecroppers instead of becoming owners of land.[66] Wartime orders such as 'forty acres and a mule' that could have potentially transformed land ownership structures were also short-lived.[67]

There were changes in cropping patterns as well. While the area under corn and soybean increased, cotton continued to be the main crop of the South. Mills for oil extraction from soybean and cottonseed flourished. However, post-bellum cotton exports occurred in a highly competitive trade environment with competition from larger suppliers such as India, Brazil, and Egypt. Appreciation of the dollar owing to capital inflows and economic expansion of the American North have also been propounded as alternative explanations for the weakening of postbellum cotton exports related to the antebellum period.[68] The slump in world cotton demand was also an impediment to the Southern recovery.[69] Nevertheless, the cotton belt became increasingly industrialized in the post-bellum period.[70] Another significant consequence of the Civil War was the end of the factorage system that had begun in the antebellum period following improvement in transportation, particularly with the expansion of railroads that forced the factors to become buyers of cotton. This was in stark contrast to their traditional role of sales force, suppliers, and creditors for planters. The railroads changed the trading patterns as well as the nature of the Southern cotton trade. Eventually the factorage system was replaced by a new actor—a furnishing merchant. The furnishing merchant procured directly from the farmers and linked manufacturers to the cotton growers.[71]

In the post-bellum markets, buyers could bypass the factors and merchants as they could directly procure cotton from the interiors. In this change, several innovations became instrumental. First, the provision of bills of lading by railroad companies in connection with the steamship lines on the East Coast fostered direct shipment to manufacturers. Aiding the transformation ushered in by railroads, innovations such as cotton compressors installed in the interiors gained prominence as it obviated the need for recompressing at the ports. Even freight rates reduced as the capacity of railroad cars increased.[72] Second, innovations in communication technology such as the telegraph, the trans-Atlantic cable, and the telephone made the price discovery role of the factor redundant as merchants across markets could have better information about prices and production.[73] Because of its deep links with global capitalism, cotton helped finance the repayment of federal debts and financed development, particularly railroads after the Civil War ended in 1865.[74] As we will see later, most of these structural changes that transformed the post-bellum cotton economy of the American South were remarkably at work in the development of the cotton economy of Berar and the Central Provinces.

THE LANCASHIRE COTTON FAMINE

As if the American Civil War was not disruptive enough for global cotton supply chains, the 'Cotton Famine' or 'Cotton Panic' that was associated with the depressed textile industry of Lancashire was critical in the history of cotton. How the 'Cotton Famine' affected capitalist production systems and the livelihood of workers of the cotton manufacturing industry is an artefact of the susceptibility of the cotton economy to economic forces of demand, supply, and speculation. How the path dependencies in the cotton economy crossed the paths of Vidarbha, Britain, and the American South is a fascinating story.

Since 1850 there had been a surge in cotton manufacturing in England as thousands of mills sprung up in Lancashire and its vicinity.[75] However, there were concerns about the viability of the Lancashire mills because the price of finished cloth was depressed due to the glut from overproduction. In 1860, over 1 billion pounds of raw cotton were imported and nearly 3 billion yards of cotton cloth along with about 200 million pounds of twist and yarn were exported.[76]

As the Civil War erupted, there was a fall in American demand for printed imports produced by these mills. At the same time, there was severe negative supply shock as raw cotton exports from the South were disrupted. To make matters worse for Lancashire, apprehending supply shortages from political upheavals in the American South, there was large-scale speculative storage of baled cotton in the entrepôts. Speculation was rife as merchants in entrepôts hoarded cotton and prices of finished goods slumped. These developments resulted in very high prices of raw cotton, which in the face of the glut implied a reduction in production. As production fell, the employment of mill workers in Lancashire was grievously affected. By the later part of 1862, a 'cotton panic' or 'cotton famine' ensued.[77] In response, public relief and welfare schemes were implemented to support the impoverished, and since 1864 the imports of raw cotton reverted to earlier high levels. It was in this chaotic setting that India emerged as a major supplier of cotton to Lancashire.[78]

Beyond doubt, the Civil War had far-reaching consequences on the American South as well as other parts of the world including India that substituted for the American supply of raw cotton. The shift induced technology developments that augmented Indian cotton.[79] It also created an environment in which the state increasingly played an important role along with traders, merchants and textile manufacturers. In what follows, we use this backdrop to describe the evolution of Vidarbha's cotton economy.

Within a decade of the end of the Civil War, the United States regained its position as the leading exporter of cotton. Consequently, the fortunes of those who experienced a windfall during the Civil War period reversed.[80] Indeed, the Civil War stimulated the cotton economy, but by that time farmers of the region had already been introduced to high-value cash crop production—one that offered prospects of high returns albeit with the risk of considerable adverse possibilities.[81] The region was however by no means alien to cotton-growing or international trade in raw cotton. In what follows, we describe the factors that made Vidarbha conducive to cotton cultivation and the familiarity of the region with cotton before its colonial takeover.

ASCENT OF COTTON IN VIDARBHA

There is archaeological evidence of cotton growing and weaving in the subcontinent for the past three millennia. The earliest literary reference to threads and looms in the subcontinent is found in a hymn in the Rig Veda. A later Vedic text (*Vedanga*) believed to be around 1000 BC, has perhaps the first literary reference to cotton. The *Manusmriti*, dating to around 800 BC prescribes *karpashi* (Sanskrit for cotton) as the material for the sacred thread of Brahmins.[82] While a variety related to *G. arboreum* cotton, native to the Indian subcontinent, was cultivated during the Indus valley civilization, to our knowledge, there is no antiquarian reference to cotton cultivation in the Vidarbha region.[83] Nonetheless, there is considerable archaeological evidence of changing cropping patterns in the region—from paddy to *jawari* (sorghum) and *bajra* (pearl millet)—which is most likely due to climatic changes of the late Holocene. In multiple excavation sites in semi-arid regions of eastern Vidarbha, there is ample evidence of cereals: paddy, *jawari*, wheat, *bajra*; legumes and pulses: *tur* (pigeon pea), *jawari*, black gram, green gram, grass pea, and common pea over the period 200 BC–AD 200, commensurate with the pre- and post-Satavahana periods.[84]

The agro-climatic variations in the region along with the variability in soils have undoubtedly influenced the cropping patterns over millennia. Soils in the region are classified as vertisols derived from the 'trap' and vary across the region. The 'Deccan Traps' derived from volcanic lava comprise soils developed over the sub-soil stratum of weathered or fractured basalts and provide a natural system of drainage. However, the soil offers considerable challenges in its management if not tilled when the moisture content is appropriate. The broad soil types are deep black soil (*bharkali*), the richest soil with good moisture retention property—a characteristic suitable for cotton; medium black soil containing lime (*murmad*) found in the southern plateau that is less fertile than *bharkali*; and coarse shallow soils and very shallow soils in higher lands that are black, brown, and reddish in colour (*barad*) and less suitable for cotton compared to *bharkali* and *murmad*. Most soils in the region are alkaline, low in organic matter and nitrogen, but well supplied with potash and phosphate.[85]

The fertile plateau between Melghat in the Satpura Range in the north and Ajantha Range in the south (Payanghat) is drained by four rivers: Wardha, Wainganga, Penganga, and Purna. The eastern part covering Gondia, Bhandara, Gadchiroli, Chandrapur, Nagpur, and Wardha districts comprise the narrow alluvial plains of Wainganga, Penganga, and Wardha rivers. It is not surprising that the region has been an important cotton-growing tract given its endowment of black soil—*regur* or black cotton soil—having good water retention properties.[86]

While the soils of the region are suitable for cotton production, has the climate been favourable? Map 2.1 shows the spatial variation in annual mean rainfall for the region using daily data for a long rainfall series spanning 118 years: 1901–2018. Using the same data, Table 2.1 shows the annual and monsoon rainfall means and coefficient of variation (CV) of rainfall for the region across sub-periods of three decades from 1901 to 2018. Four key patterns

Table 2.1 Mean and CV of monsoon and annual rainfall in Vidarbha by thirty-year sub-periods: 1901–2018

	JJAS (Monsoon months)		Annual		JJAS rainfall as percentage of annual rainfall (mean)
	Mean	*CV (%)*	*Mean*	*CV (%)*	
1901–1930	943.5	17.0	1,080.7	17.2	87.3
1931–1960	1,074.5	16.0	1,227.6	16.7	87.5
1961–1990	958.6	19.6	1,084.8	17.9	88.4
1991–2018	959.6	17.6	1,073.8	17.3	89.4

Source: Authors' calculation based on daily 0.25° gridded data from the IMD (India Meteorological Department) between longitudes 76° E to 81° E and latitudes 18°75' N to 21°75' N extracted for the period 1901–2018.

Note: JJAS denotes the four monsoon months of June, July, August, and September. CV denotes the coefficient of variation.

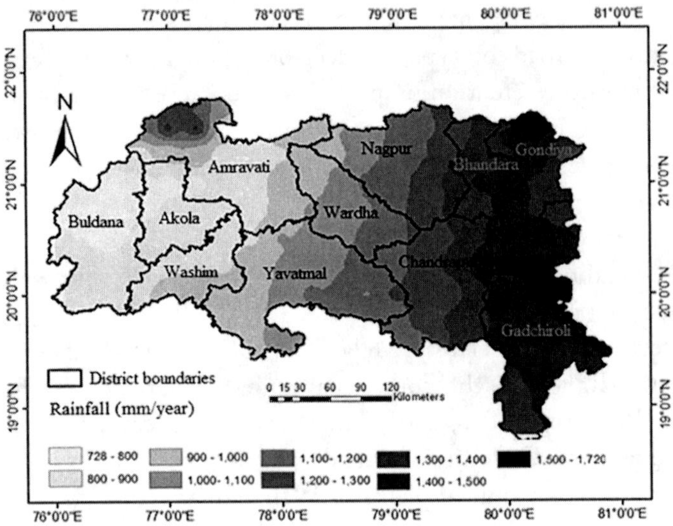

Map 2.1 Annual mean rainfall 1901–2018

Source: Prepared by authors; base map from Survey of India (OVSF/1M/9 shapefile up to state and district level).

emerge. First, the region has considerable variability in the distribution of precipitation; with the eastern part receiving relatively higher rainfall than the western part over the southwest monsoon period that lasts from June to September (JJAS). The former is primarily the paddy belt whereas the latter is the cotton belt. Nevertheless, variation within the western and eastern parts is evident. Second, since the 1931–1960 period, there has been a decline in mean precipitation over the long term, but the CV—a measure of dispersion around the mean—is relatively low. Third, the CV however is below 100 per cent in all the subperiods. The CV of the region varies by season, and the low CVs here are not surprising as studies using a shorter rainfall series (1901–2006) have found the monsoon period CV for these districts to be below 100 per cent.[87] Fourth, although the share of monsoon period rainfall (JJAS) to annual total has been increasing, there are significant seasonal variations in distribution of precipitation. In Chapter 6 we will demonstrate weather variability and its effect on crop yields and household vulnerability to weather shocks in detail.

Graphs 2.2 and 2.3 show the variability in rainfall in Vidarbha over a century, along with a linear trend for annual rainfall and monsoon rainfall, respectively. Both annual rainfall and monsoon rainfall series have a decreasing trend. The variability around the trend also suggests the frequent

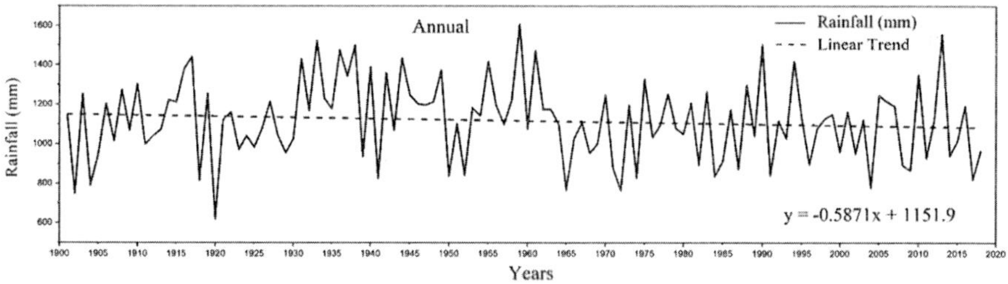

Graph 2.2 Rainfall variability in Vidarbha (annual): 1901–2018

Source: Authors' calculation based on daily 0.25° gridded data from the IMD between longitudes 76° E to 81° E and latitudes 18°75' N to 21°75' N extracted for the period 1901–2018.

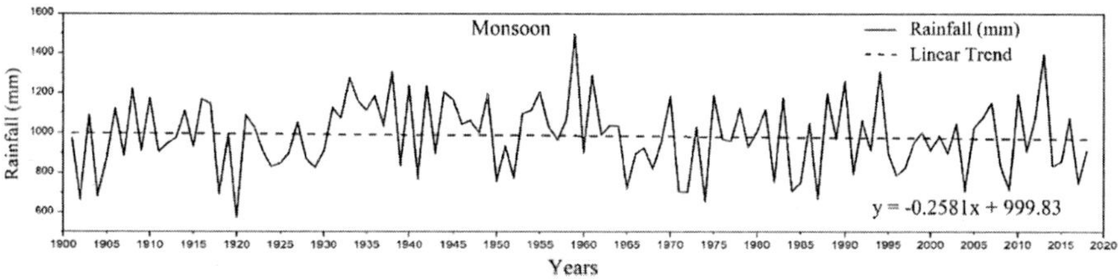

Graph 2.3 Rainfall variability in Vidarbha (monsoon months): 1901–2018

Source: Authors' calculation based on daily 0.25° gridded data from the IMD between longitudes 76° E to 81° E and latitudes 18°75' N to 21°75' N extracted for the period 1901–2018.

fluctuations that generations of farmers in the region have experienced. In Chapter 6 we will examine the vulnerability of households to weather risks that will offer a rich description of the seasonal variability and its effect on household welfare. Studies have also shown the adverse effects of temperature change on crop yield in different districts of the region.[88] Vulnerability to climate change is in fact considerable.[89] An analysis of trends of average temperature and rainfall has found seven districts of Vidarbha among the top ten climate hotspots: Chandrapur, Bhandara, Gondia, Wardha, Nagpur, Yavatmal, and Gadchiroli.[90] These findings suggest that while soils of the region are conducive to cotton cultivation, climate change and climatic variability pose uncertainties for the region's agriculture and those dependent on it for livelihood.

Before examining the developments in Vidarbha's cotton economy since the middle of the nineteenth century, it is important to understand its role in the flourishing raw cotton trade between India and China in the eighteenth and early nineteenth centuries. This is an often-neglected aspect of the region's integration with global supply chains and warrants attention for improved characterization of the preconditions for colonial cotton expansion agenda.

RAW COTTON EXPORTS TO CHINA

Western India was an important centre of seaborne trade with Southeast Asia in the sixteenth and seventeenth centuries. However, it was not until four decades since the first consignment of raw cotton from the port city of Surat in Gujarat to the Chinese port of Amoy in 1704 that Company vessels frequently plied to China via India.[91] By the second half of the eighteenth century, raw cotton from Gujarat was imported into China by merchants from Surat.[92] Cotton grown in Gujarat was increasingly shipped to Canton (present-day Guangzhou) from Bombay as well as via Calcutta and Madras.[93] This was largely driven by the decline in supply of Gujarat raw cotton to Bengal following political turbulence in both the regions between 1740 and 1785 in general, and since the Battle of Plassey in 1757 in particular.[94] In 1757, the same year as the Battle of Plassey, Qing China banned all foreign trade except at Canton, following which all trade was carried out under the 'Canton System'.[95] During the 1760s the Company primarily relied on private traders as it took decades to establish itself in the 'country trade'—the inter-Asian trade—owing to financial turmoil caused by its growing military and civil expansion in India.[96] With opening of the China market in 1770, there was a gradual shift in the shipping and trade from Surat to the port of Bombay that was suitable for large vessels carrying the bulky cargo to China.

While British protectionist trade policies boosted the growth of Lancashire mills, its trade laws such as the Commutation Act of 1784 bolstered the export of raw cotton from India to China to counter the trade deficit on account of growing British tea imports from China.[97] It is not well known that until the end of the eighteenth century, China was more or less the only market for Indian raw cotton exports. Given the relatively inelastic supply of cotton and growing domestic demand in China as well as demand in overseas markets for manufactured cotton goods, there was over a threefold rise in the price of raw cotton in western India and Bengal for three decades ending in between 1785 and 1818.[98] As discussed earlier, Bombay dominated the shipping of raw cotton to meet the growing Chinese demand.[99] In the late eighteenth century, the raw cotton exported from Bombay was mostly 'Surat' cotton—a medium-staple variety from north Gujarat that traders from Surat supplied to Bombay merchants for transhipment to Canton. This was also a period of food shortage in China that resulted in a greater area under food grain at the cost of cotton, leading to a sharp rise in cotton prices in China. Consequently, cotton exports from Bombay became sought after due to their relative cheapness compared to native cotton.[100] This expansion of the country trade saw Bombay becoming the major entrepôt for the country trade.[101] Beyond the domain of trade, there were several experiments in popularizing American cotton varieties by the British to meet the demands of the Lancashire. As a case in point, by 1790 an exotic American variety of cotton—Bourbon—was introduced as a potential replacement for indigenous varieties of cotton that were concerted 'inferior' for Lancashire mills.[102] In the early 1790s, there was a conscious attempt by the British government to increase cotton cultivation in India as evident from the efforts of the Board of Directors of the Company such as sending the saw gin to improve cotton ginning in the Bombay Presidency.[103] Around this time, legislations such as the 1793 act allowed reservation of cargo space for private traders in the Company's ships facilitating the country trade.[104] This phase of expansion of the raw cotton trade however was plagued by several problems. Cotton merchants of Bombay were heavily dependent on the intermediaries who procured raw cotton from the hinterland. In addition, collusion among the dealers inflated the price of cotton, thereby affecting the export demand in Canton.[105]

Taking advantage of this window of opportunity, Calcutta merchants met the shortfall in shipment to Canton from Bombay.[106] Although speculative buying of raw cotton for the Chinese trade from Calcutta had commenced in the late eighteenth century in marts such as Mirzapur (present-day Uttar Pradesh) that encouraged raw cotton trade between Berar and Nagpur, the Calcutta raw cotton exports are likely to have gained momentum after Wellesley's annexation of parts of Awadh in 1801. The territorial expansion brought cotton-producing regions under imperial control. Consequently, cotton expansion in Awadh, Bundelkhand, and parts of the Central Provinces including those in the Maratha territories resulted in an increased supply of raw cotton in Calcutta via Mirzapur through the river route.[107] Furthermore, lessons from the issues with quality of cotton from Bombay enabled Calcutta traders to invest in cleaning, processing, and packing to improve the quality of the cotton shipped to Canton.[108]

At this juncture, when the future of Bombay as the most important centre of raw cotton trade came under threat owing to the myriad issues in the trade, large parts of western India including the Deccan came under the Company's control, as discussed in the preceding chapter. This shift in political fate of the Deccan was indeed an accident that played an important role in the revival of Bombay's fortune in the cotton trade.[109] However, as a harbinger of the twists and turns in the fortunes associated with the cotton trade and cultivation, for a decade since 1805, raw cotton exports from India fell precipitously due to the Napoleonic Wars and the growth of raw cotton exports to Britain from the American South. These adversities notwithstanding, by 1811 Bombay was a major centre of trade in the Indian Ocean as well as the domestic market. Moreover, since the Charter Act of 1813, with the monopoly of the Company for trade in India extended by two decades, there was a reorientation of Bombay's trade towards China. Consequently, raw cotton exports to Liverpool and China increased over the next few years, with the former having a smaller share in the total raw cotton exports from Bombay than the latter. However, the boom in foreign trade was short-lived, and by the early 1820s considerable quantities of imported cotton goods namely foreign yarn and cloth began appearing in the home markets; thereby setting into motion forces that would decimate the indigenous spinning and weaving industry.

The first half of the nineteenth century witnessed remarkable price volatility that would go on to become a defining feature of raw cotton. The price of Indian cotton soared and then slumped over the period 1801–1851 (Graph 2.4). The rise in prices until 1815 was on account of inelastic supply in the face of growing demand from England. The precipitous fall in cotton prices for the next four decades was the consequence of the weakening rupee, which increased exports (Graph 2.1). Between 1819 and 1850, there was a prolonged period of decline in raw cotton prices, but substantial reduction in transportation costs in India as well as a weak rupee contributed to the growth of raw cotton exports.[110] It was in this context of the declining price of cotton that opium cultivation in India was encouraged by the British, and opium became a major item of export to China.[111]

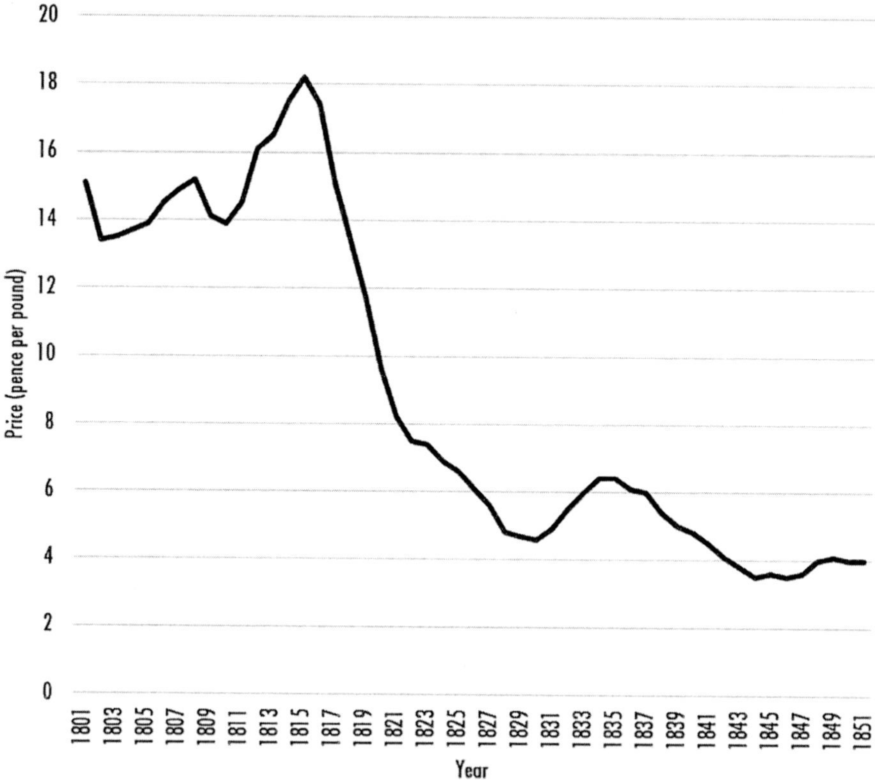

Graph 2.4 Price of Indian cotton (Surats) at Liverpool market: 1801–1851

Source: A. Guha, 'Raw Cotton of Western India: 1750–1850', *Indian Economic and Social History Review* 9, no. 1 (1972): 1–41, 35. Prices are a five-year moving average for average prices of Surats variety of cotton.

Note: One rupee was equal to 30 pence until 1815, 27 pence from 1816 to 1822, and 24 pence since 1823. In the late nineteenth century, the currency exchange rate between pound sterling and rupees was as follows: 1 pound sterling was equivalent to 10 rupees until 1873. In 1873 the rupee was devalued, and 1 pound sterling became equivalent to 15 rupees.

One of the most remarkable transformations in India's trade composition in the first half of the nineteenth century was the domination of opium in the Asian trade. By 1840, opium comprised around 30 per cent of India's exports, and its value exceeded that of other commodities including raw cotton.[112] However, China banned the import of opium in the first half of the nineteenth century, resulting in the Opium Wars.[113] This was also a period when the share of imports of piece goods from Britain to Bombay as well as Calcutta witnessed a marked increase, affecting the survival of the domestic cotton textiles manufacturing that was far from being mechanized, unlike its Lancashire counterparts.

Did Berar and Nagpur have a stake in the booming China trade? Indeed, in the late eighteenth century Berar was an important supplier in the raw cotton trade of China that was exported from Calcutta via the great mart of Mirzapur.[114] There are contemporary accounts of prevailing prices of cotton in cities of present-day Vidarbha, such as Nagpur and Amravati. For instance, at the close of the eighteenth century, the average price in Nagpur was 2.5 pence per pound whilst that in Mirzapur was around 4.8 pence per pound.[115] Over the years, as Bengal increasingly failed to absorb surplus Berar cotton owing to the decline of its cotton manufacturing industry, Bombay became the main destination of Berar cotton via Khamgaon (that is depicted in the cover of the book) for foreign export. By 1825, Berar's integration with the overseas trade with Britain began as cotton from the region made its way to Bombay for the growing cotton trade.[116]

Several indigenous traders pioneered the Bombay trade from Khamgaon. For instance, in 1825–1826, Parsi merchants exported what is believed to be the first raw cotton exports from Berar to Bombay. Messrs Vikaji and Pestanji—a firm with offices across India, Singapore, and Canton, exported raw cotton consisting of '500 bullock-loads, being 120,000 lbs. weight, valued at Rs. 25,000'.[117] Exports to Bombay from Berar, then under the nizam's rule, grew substantially over the decade—to nearly 50 million pounds, valued at 0.6 million pound sterlings.[118] The decade since 1826 was marred by an economic crisis, which put a dent on the trend of growing exports from India. Bombay developed as an important centre of trade and commerce to such an extent that as early as 1836 the Bombay Chambers of Commerce and Industry was set up to safeguard the interests of the mercantile community of the Bombay Presidency. However, by 1837, there was a decline in Berar's Bombay trade due to the opening of a new cartable road between Narsinghpur in the

Central Provinces and Mirzapur, diverting supply to the China trade from Calcutta via Mirzapur.[119]

Oddly enough, long before developments in the United States impacted the cotton economy of the region, the decline in the Bombay trade from Berar was also an outcome of the 'Cotton Panic' of 1837 in the United States.[120] R. H. Fenwick, a Hyderabad-based cotton trader, reported of a decline in the exports of raw cotton from Berar to Bombay to around 29 million pounds in 1841, which was significantly lower than the quantity exported five years ago. As we will scrutinise the impact of the American Civil War on the region's cotton economy two decades since these developments, it is essential to acknowledge the shifting patterns of trade as well as varying degrees of integration of the region with Bombay and Calcutta since the late eighteenth century. Evidence from the antebellum period raw cotton trade from the region suggests that it had developed strong trade ties with Bombay. In the post-bellum period the cotton textile industry in India grew phenomenally, which is not surprising as by the middle of the nineteenth century cotton capitalism had taken root. We will examine in detail how the growth of cotton manufacturing in Bombay that followed its success with cotton trade and commerce shaped capitalist development in Berar and Nagpur as well the deepening of railway infrastructure. Modern factories sprung up in Bombay since the middle of the nineteenth century, thereby reviving the indigenous textile export industry.[121]

As the British cotton industry boomed, there were considerable attempts by its manufacturing interests to expand cotton cultivation in India. Since the 1840s the colonial cotton development programme had begun in India by order of the Court of Directors of the Company. It was an outcome of the efforts of the British textile manufacturing interests that had begun exploring the source of raw materials to feed its growth.[122] The 'Cotton Famine' of 1847 described earlier started the conscious search for cheaper raw materials in Indian cotton country by Manchester traders. By the middle of the nineteenth century, cotton manufacturers in England grew wary of the potentially catastrophic consequences of the outbreak of a civil war in the United States—the major supplier of raw cotton. Since the 1850s, the search for a reliable alternative source of raw cotton had generated interest in India as a substitute for the United States.[123] With the aim of encouraging cotton cultivation in all parts of India, the Cotton Supply Association was formed by the Lancashire manufacturers in 1857—the year of the Sepoy Mutiny.[124] Another organization having the same objective, namely the Manchester

Cotton Company, was set up by the Manchester Chamber of Commerce in 1860.[125] Following surveys of cotton-growing areas in British colonies across the world, India was identified as the 'cotton hope'—the most suitable source of cotton supply in case the American supply were to be disrupted.[126] The growing interest in Indian raw cotton as a potential substitute for American cotton in the eventuality of the war garnered the support of the colonial state. For instance, the Government of India resolved to

> do all within its 'legitimate' power towards facilitating 'an immediate increase' in the production of cotton….[127]

The annexation of Berar was clearly motivated by prospects of cotton expansion and mineral resources of the region. While changes in institutions and the rapid expansion of the area under cotton increased cotton production, investment in the railways and communication boosted movement of cotton from the hinterlands of Berar to Bombay and Calcutta. Cotton became a source of considerable revenue for the state. Capital flowed in from all parts of the world for establishment of cotton gins, spinning and weaving mills, presses, and financing of a bustling trade and commerce. There is no doubt that the colonial takeover of Berar and the Central Provinces allowed cotton expansion to satiate the needs of Lancashire's cotton mills. However, this process resulted in cultivators of the region growing a cash crop under a predominantly rain-fed environment. As we show in what follows, cotton was germane to frenzied speculation and fortune reversals but the transformation of the cotton economy rendered the population vulnerable to ecological and environmental degradation.[128] Recurrent famines resulted in a terrible human tragedy in the region; one which perhaps the region has yet to come out of.

COTTON MANIA AND FORTUNE REVERSALS

By 1853, when Berar came under colonial control as discussed at length in Chapter 1, it was not only a well-known centre of raw cotton exports but also a thriving centre of spinning and weaving. Farmers picked and ginned cotton using *charkha* (also *churka*)—traditional Indian spinning wheel—that Mahatma Gandhi popularized decades later.[129] It was common for cleaning and carding to be done by itinerant labour communities as well as members of the households (Image 2.1). At that time, markets such as Khamgaon in present-day Buldhana district and Amravati in present-day Amravati

Image 2.1 Cotton stacks and *churka* (or cotton gin) in operation, Berar, circa 1866

Source: © The British Library Board (Photo 1000/52(4892)). For a description of the source of the image, see http://www.bl.uk/onlinegallery/onlineex/apac/photocoll/c/019pho001000s52u04892000.html (accessed on 17 April 2021).

Note: In late nineteenth-century Berar, division of labour based on gender was common. Spinning was usually done by women as shown in the middle ground, whereas weaving was mostly undertaken by men as shown in the foreground. The spun yarn was stored at farmers' houses or often kept in the open—to be sold in the market or supplied to the local weaver.

district were established raw cotton marts. It is important to reiterate that while cotton cultivation had begun considerably with the growing trade, the American Civil War stimulated the expansion of cotton cultivation in Berar and the Central Provinces in a manner and extent that was unprecedented.[130]

Berar had long been identified as a fertile cotton tract that could relieve Britain's overdependence on raw cotton from the American South. Writing about Britain's enthusiasm about Berar as a cotton tract par excellence, a contemporary scholar notes:

> But of the eventual power of Berar and the adjacent country to supply more than one-third of the thousand million pounds of raw material now yearly required for our factories, I believe there can be no doubt. Looking into the capabilities of the huge tract of country, which may be considered, *par excellence*, the great cotton field of India, having regard to the great skill of the cultivators, and the cheap rate at which it can be

> grown, we are warranted in looking to it with much hope, and in the full expectation that it will yet materially assist in cotton. The whole history of this portion of the country bears out the view entertained of it.[131]

Raw cotton exports to Britain from India (that is, Britain's imports from India) fell as the Civil War ended, and the United States resumed its exports to Lancashire (see Graph 2.1). During the Civil War, the price of US cotton in Liverpool—the most important port in the world cotton market and the place where the price of cotton was determined—increased by over five times and fell sharply as the supplies resumed (see Graph 2.5). During the war period, although Britain's total imports of raw cotton fell, India's share in the exports rose sharply, resulting in higher prices of Indian cotton. This surge in raw cotton prices of Indian cotton resulted in a 'cotton mania'.

Graph 2.5 Price of US cotton at Liverpool market: 1850s–1884

Source: G. Wright, 'Cotton Competition and the Post-bellum Recovery of the American South', *Journal of Economic History* 34, no. 3 (1974): 610–635, 611, table 1.

Between 1861 and 1865, the price of Indian cotton suddenly grew by leaps and bounds. Prices reached nearly five times the pre-war level. In western India, at certain markets, prices saw an eightfold increase.[132] Such spectacularly high prices resulted in a frenzy among cotton farmers in Berar and other cotton tracts to supply cotton to Bombay. Undoubtedly, the 'Cotton Famine' of 1861–1865 resulted in a frantic rush to grow cotton and profit from the cotton trade. In his memoir, Sir Richard Temple, the first chief commissioner of the Central Provinces and later the British resident at Hyderabad and the governor of the Bombay Presidency, comments:

> The produce of all the great cotton fields in India, Nagpur, Berar, Guzerat, the South Maratha Country, found its way to Bombay in order to be exported to England with all possible despatch, while the high prices ruled and the blockade of the South American ports lasted. So sudden was the demand, so high the range of price, so vast the profits, that an economic disturbance set in. Money seemed to lose its purchasing power, the prices of almost all articles rose simultaneously and the wages of labour were enhanced in proportion.[133]

Graph 2.6 shows the rise in acreage and prices of cotton in the 1860s in the Bombay Province (1860–1861 = 100) to give a perspective on the extent of the variation within a short period of time. The area under cotton rose with rising prices during the Civil War period but declined following the crash in prices as the Civil War ended; rising again toward the end of the decade.

Apart from farmers, traders and merchants were also lured into the cotton economy given the prospects of profit. Brokers, primarily from the Parsi and Gujarati communities, had been trading in shares for nearly a decade in Bombay and the market was bullish about cotton.[134] As early as 1855, the Indian cotton merchants and *muccadums* had formed a collective called the Bombay Cotton Dealers Association.[135] They laid down various *laga* (cess) and set of rules for conducting the transactions of cotton business.[136] With the emergence of the Trans-Atlantic cable, speculation and futures contracts in cotton developed around 1866.[137] The period saw the emergence of a speculator—Premchand Roychand, known as the 'Cotton King'—who went on to establish the Native Share and Stock Brokers Association, now known as the Bombay Stock Exchange (BSE), in 1875.[138] The period also saw the share values of companies such as Backbay Reclamation and Bank of Bombay soaring astronomically.[139] Such was the impact of the 'cotton mania' that even

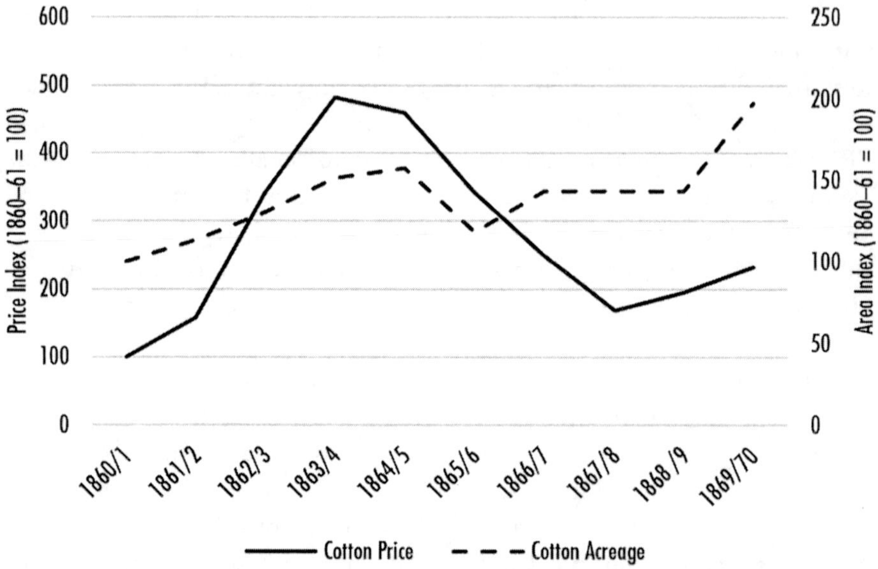

Graph 2.6 Real price of cotton and acreage index in the Bombay Province: 1860–1861 to 1869–1870 (1860–1861 = 100)

Source: A. Heston, 'The Impact of Cotton and Wheat Exports on Deccan Agriculture' (paper presented at the Conference on Patterns of Change in Nineteenth-Century Maharashtra, University of Chicago, 6–8 June 1969), cited in P. Harnetty, 'Cotton Exports and Indian Agriculture, 1861–1870', *Economic History Review* 24, no. 3 (1971): 414–429, 418, table 5.

Note: Primary axis is price index whereas secondary axis is area (acreage) index with 1860–1861 as the base year.

the price of land in Bombay surged in line with the rising cotton prices. On the prospects of profit that the Civil War presented before cotton interests in Bombay, a contemporary commentator observed:

> Shrewd merchants of Bombay prognosticated that the war cloud may soon burst [in America] which will have the effect of Lancashire making a large and unlimited demand on India for the supply of cotton.[140]

An economic consequence of the cotton boom was the rise in wages in response to the growing demand for labour in the cotton trade. Rents also shot up, and so did the price of land. In Bombay, there was also a real estate boom during the cotton mania.[141] Unbeknownst to the cotton interests, the windfall would be short-lived. As the Civil War ended in 1865, cotton prices crashed. The period of high cotton prices was associated with the inflationary

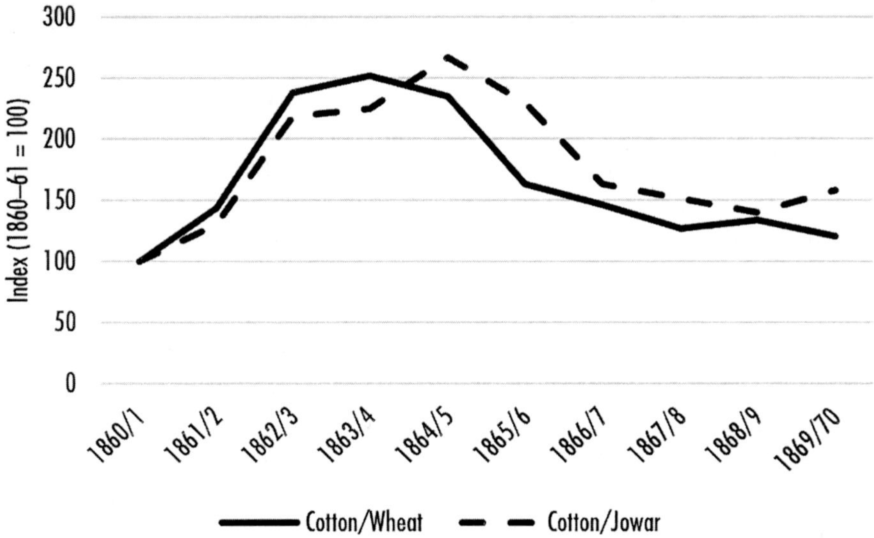

Graph 2.7 Index of relative prices of cotton, wheat, and *jawari* (or *jowar*) in the Bombay Province: 1860–1861 to 1869–1870 (1860–1861 = 100)

Source: Heston, 'The Impact of Cotton and Wheat Exports on Deccan Agriculture', cited in Harnetty, 'Cotton Exports and Indian Agriculture', 418, table 5.

tendency for food grains as well. During the decade of the 1860s, comparing the changes in the relative price of cotton and food grains such as wheat and *jawari* in the Bombay Province is illustrative (see Graph 2.7). Cotton prices were relatively higher than both the food grains but the sharp rise in cotton prices in early phases of the Civil War period was followed by a sharp fall. Over this period, cotton's price relative to food grains remained high, reflected in the growing acreage of cotton as seen in Graph 2.6.

Adulteration became a scourge as the prospects soared. Adulteration and generally poor quality of cotton marketed from Gujarat thwarted the reputation of Indian cotton. One Bombay newspaper noted in April 1862:

> The quality of Bombay cotton has notoriously become worse instead of better. The rise in prices has no other effect than of stimulating the practice of adulteration. Every trick … is used to swell the bulk and lower the intrinsic value of cotton. Sometimes the bales are wetted in the sea, sometimes their weight is increased by keeping seed in the cotton and loading it besides with stones and dirt, sometimes there is

> a systematic substitution of an inferior for a better kind of cotton, or a mixture of two kinds.[142]

Both Company and private merchants in Bombay bore the brunt of the poor quality raw cotton that required considerable labour to clean and process. In response, the Company resorted to imported machinery for 'better cleaning, screwing, and packing of cotton'.[143] Despite the introduction of the Cotton Frauds Bill in 1863, and later the Act in 1869 with stringent measures to address the issues, adulteration continued unabated.[144] In addition to these problems, there were sharp inter-annual fluctuations in the volume of exports due to a host of factors including vagaries of weather, piracy, and logistical uncertainties associated with a complex network of intermediaries.[145]

During the crash in March 1865, price of Indian cotton fell suddenly. It resulted in widespread losses and financial disaster as the 'cotton mania' was the basis for a 'share mania'. Several speculators and commercial interests became bankrupt. By May of 1865, Byramji (also Behramji) Hormusji Cama, the largest shipper of raw cotton, found himself unable to pay banks for his consignments. He lost over 30 million rupees. Many other cotton merchants such as Rustomjee Jamsetjee Jejeebhoy lost heavily.[146] It took five more years for Bombay to recover from the collapse. In fact, the 'share mania' in Bombay was an unintended consequence of the 'cotton mania'.[147] The large-scale bankruptcies associated with the cotton mania notwithstanding, the American Civil War catalysed the process of global integration of the cotton growers of Berar and the Central Provinces in an unprecedented manner.

While cotton made and marred fortunes in Bombay, which had become the second largest city in the British Empire by 1870, and other cities of western India, it had deeply transformed the hinterland including Berar. The *Amravati Gazetteer* summarizes the transition of the cotton economy in Berar on the following lines:

> Since 1857 the history of the district has been the record of a steady increase of prosperity, which received a sudden stimulus from the American Civil War, which increased the demand for Indian cotton, and was only temporarily checked by the season of scarcity in 1896–97 and the famine of 1899–1900.[148]

As in the case of Berar, cotton cultivation in the Central Provinces gained momentum during the Civil War period. In the Central Provinces,

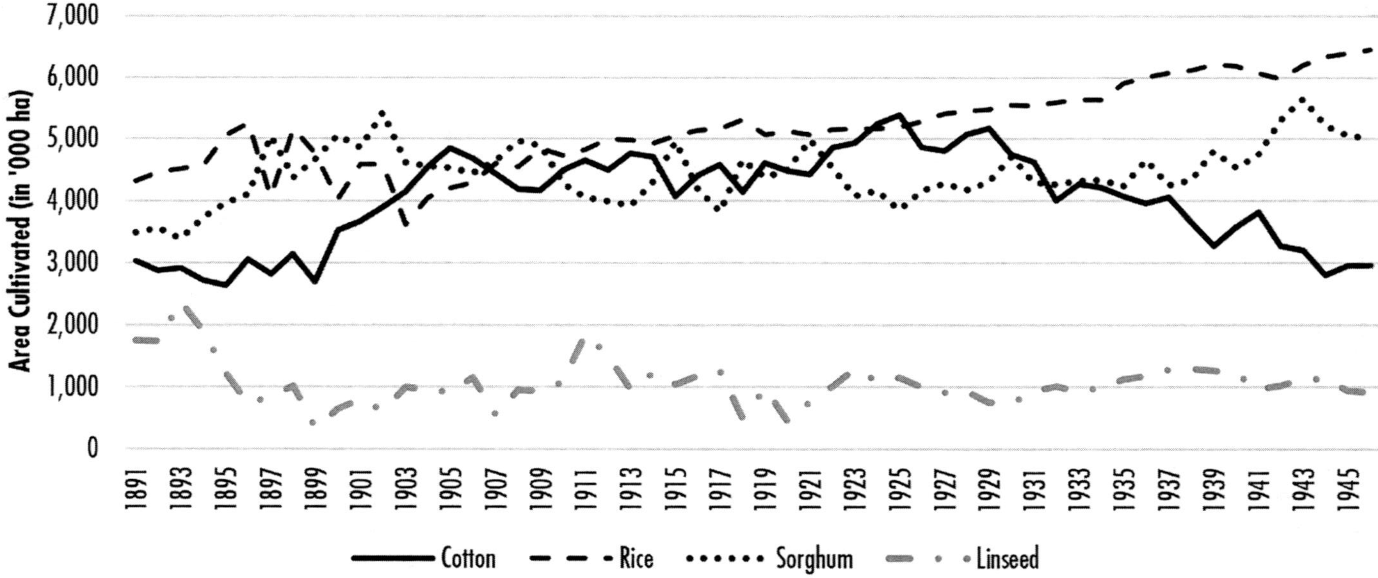

Graph 2.8 Area under major crops in the Central Provinces: 1891–1946

Source: G. Blyn, *Agricultural Statistics of British India, 1891–1947* (Philadelphia: University of Pennsylvania, 1966), 256, 264, 289, 308–309.

cotton experienced an increase in cultivation in the mid-1870s but by 1884, acreage as well as exports declined markedly.[149] The value of exports had also been a fraction of what it used to be during the mid-1860s. Cotton regained its importance in the early twentieth century, with the resurgence of demand from Lancashire. The profitability of cotton elevated it to the status of principal crop in intercropping and crop rotation. Farmers grew cotton continuously and more as a monocrop, increasing the risk of pest infestation.

In terms of agronomic practices, intercropping was common. Farmers followed the practice of sowing two lines of *tur* to twelve or more of cotton. These practices have stood the test of time as discussed in Chapter 5. Furthermore, agronomic practices from other cotton-growing regions such as Dharwad in Bombay Presidency also informed colonial administrators about the adjustments necessary to grow in different agro-climatic conditions including Berar and the Central Provinces.[150] In the following discussion, we elaborate the colonial effort to secure cheap cotton from the region to feed the mills of Lancashire.

Jowar/*jawari* (sorghum), a sturdy crop suitable for rain-fed areas and source of food as well as fodder, was largely grown on poor lands. The proportion of *tur* to *jawari* was generally about one-seventh. Since this method of cultivation did not reduce the outturn of *jawari*, it evolved as an insurance mechanism for cultivators. However, it was susceptible to locust attacks as cotton was to weevil attacks. In the Central Provinces there was a large switch from *jawari* to cotton between 1861 and 1921. Graph 2.8 exhibits the changes in area of crops between 1891 and 1945 in the province.

The changing cropping patterns and the concomitant institutional changes had three serious ramifications for farmers. First, farmers increasingly became reliant on purchased inputs, and hence cultivation expenses grew drastically. The Indian Famine Commission, 1880, captures the transformation on the following lines:

> The cultivator is now put to expenses which in former times he did not know. His pecuniary wants are so pressing that often the whole produce of a crop is disposed of by him without provision being made from it for his own subsistence, and very often without his even reserving from it a sufficiency of seed grain for future sowing. He now pays more for his cattle than he did yore, and he can no longer fell a tree from any place he likes to provide him with a shaft for his plough, or a yoke for his oxen. He has now practically to expend coin where before he needed only to

> labour, and the grass with which he annually thatches his hut has to be bought, and not merely cut and carried as it used to be.[151]

Second, the rise in use of purchased inputs in agriculture along with the revenue demands on the cultivator became a major reason for the indebtedness of the Vidarbha farmers in the early twentieth century. While colonial accounts suggest that cotton brought prosperity for the cultivators in the region, poverty and destitution were not uncommon.[152] Furthermore, it cannot be denied that it introduced cultivators to a new category of production and credit risks that were borne by generations of cotton farmers and continues to afflict them to this day. The uncertainties that farmers faced has been captured in the writings of contemporary colonial administrators such as the first cotton commissioner of the Central Provinces and Berar, John Harry Rivett-Carnac. Rivett-Carnac says:

> The great rise and the sudden fall in the price of cotton, and the constant fluctuations in the market, by which the cultivator, in even the most remote of the cotton-growing villages is affected, has led some of the less intelligent to regard cotton not only with distrust, but with a certain degree of awe.[153]

Third, the rising area under cotton came at the cost of production of food crops such as *jawari*.[154] There were several environmental and ecological impacts along with falling real wages in the villages that affected the entitlements of rural households as discussed later. With considerable variation in the wages of women and children involved in specific tasks in cotton production, these entitlement failures were nonetheless heterogeneous. From a vulnerability perspective, entitlement failures made the population susceptible to damages and adverse fluctuations during years of scarcities and famines such as those in 1868–1869, 1871–1872, 1897–1898, and 1899–1900.

While there were no food shortages in Berar before the famine, the disproportionately higher food grain prices compared to the nominal wages in the last quarter of the nineteenth century are likely to have resulted in the decline of exchange entitlements that led to the famines.[155] Since 1873, real wages experienced a steady decline until 1900 (Graph 2.9). When the severe famine of 1899–1900 occurred, the real wages were at historic lows. Over the period, the expansion of the railways and improvement in roads however meant that food grain exports continued unabated, and the famines were an

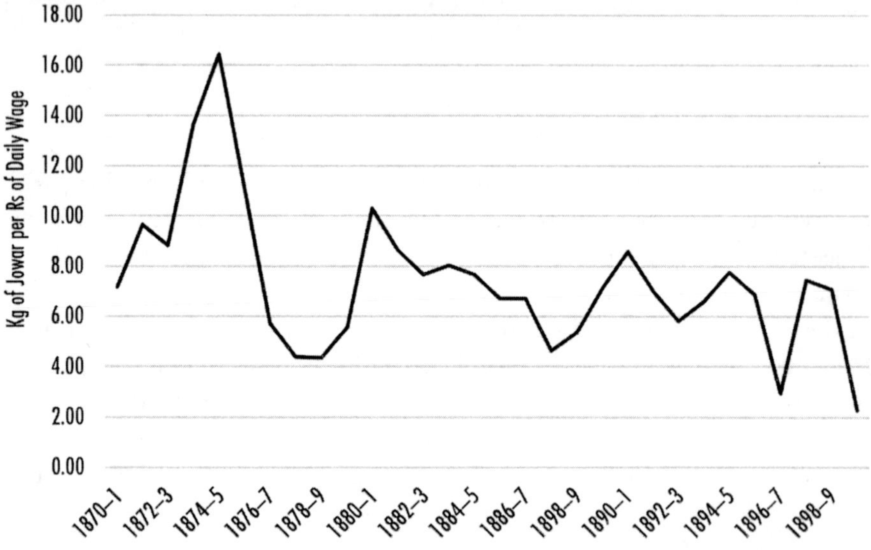

Graph 2.9 Real wages in Berar (kilograms of *jawari* per daily wage in rupees): 1870–71 to 1899–1900

Source: L. D. Satya, *Cotton and Famine in Berar 1850–1900* (New Delhi: Manohar, 1997), 284, table 34.

Note: Satya reports wages in annas per day and *jawari* (sorghum) quantities in seer; 1 rupee = 16 annas and 1 seer = 2.057 pounds or 0.435 kilograms has been used as the conversion factor in our calculation of real wages in kilograms of *jawari* per rupee wages in a day.

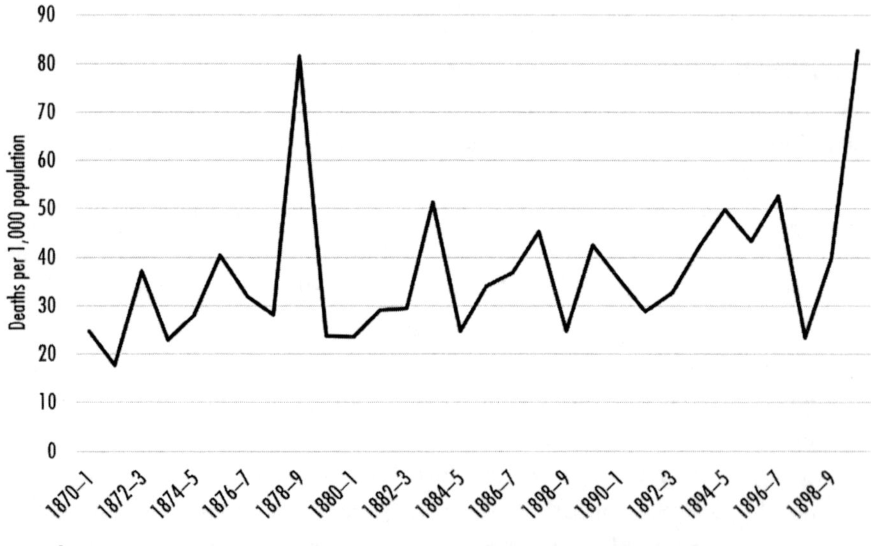

Graph 2.10 Mortality per 1,000 in Berar: 1870–71 to 1899–1900

Source: Satya, *Cotton and Famine in Berar*, 284, table 34.

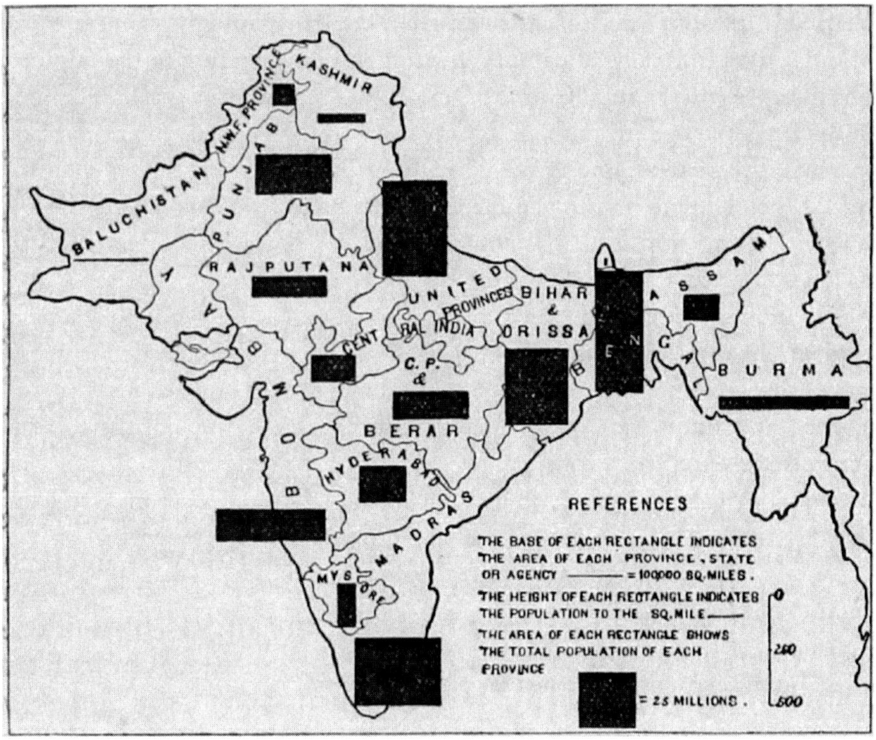

Map 2.2 Population and area of the Central Provinces and Berar, Census 1911

Source: This image is a public domain image, which means either that the copyright has expired in the image or the copyright holder has waived their copyright.

Note: The population of the Central Provinces and Berar approaches that of Brazil; Hyderabad had as many inhabitants as Egypt (Government of India, *Census of India 1911* [New Delhi: Office of the Registrar General and Census Commissioner, 1911], 175). Berar was a much smaller province in comparison with the Central Provinces. Old Berar, the province before amalgamation with the Central Provinces and Berar in 1903, was as a region in the southwestern part of the Central Provinces and Berar that shared its borderr with Hyderabad States.

outcome of flawed food distribution rather than environmental shocks alone. The consequences of the famines and diseases that ravaged the region over the same period were staggeringly high death rates in general, and in years of famines and pandemics in particular (Graph 2.10).

Administrative records of the late nineteenth-century famines that ravaged the region suggest the occurrence of major and minor famines causing scarcity and mortality in varying degrees. These records however present an account of proactive state intervention through relief works and charitable activities in the affected districts to seemingly exonerate the colonial state from any culpability or inaction in responding to the famines. For instance, the Famine Commission of 1898 reports that the 1896 famine in Berar was not severe and that it was caused by high prices rather than food scarcity. The distress among the agricultural labourers was higher than the rest of the population. The Famine Commission of 1898 documents the low wages that were given to women and children ('D wage') as Berar did not have a famine code and applying the Bombay codes seemed to result in higher wages and ran the risk of attracting unaffected persons to work on the relief works.[156] In some districts, railway work failed to attract workers due to low wages that were not indexed to food inflation.[157] Loans and advances as well as charitable funds were operationalized during the famine but the colonial administrative records exonerate any failures of the state in the distress that prevailed. Mortality was attributed not to the failure of relief measures but due to issues with the population accepting relief. Commenting on the economic condition of the agricultural population in Berar, a late nineteenth-century commentator noted:

> Cotton agriculture became the curse of Berar.[158]

To understand if indeed the cotton expansion became the curse of Berar, we need to understand the institutional transformation of the region imposed by the force of British colonialism.

CHANGES IN LAND ADMINISTRATION

Following the annexation of Berar in 1853—a region endowed with fertile black soil suitable for cotton expansion and rich mineral resources—a new bureaucratic machinery was established. The Berar Commission was set up with the objective of settling Europeans for the cultivation of cotton—as in the case of indigo in Bengal and Bihar, and tea in Assam. District and sub-districts (*taluka*s) were formed for administration, and cantonments were established.[159] The expansion of the railways connected the hinterland to major ports such as Bombay to not only transport raw cotton, coal, and other valuable minerals from the interior but also open Indian markets for British cotton textiles.[160]

Land revenue comprised a major source of revenue for the state along with several taxes (including poll tax on fairs and festivals) and duties (including those on alcohol and opium). Elaborate land surveys and settlement operations were undertaken to assign plots of cotton-rich land to individuals who bore the burden of revenue on the land. This allowed the colonial system to introduce inheritable property rights. *Khatedar*s, or holders of land title, became the unit of revenue assessment, with survey numbers, or *sanad*s (deeds), granted to them.[161] Revenue from private property became the primary source of revenue for the colonial state. Was the colonial state autonomously transforming the institutions of the region in a bid to increase revenue, or were there other forces at work that pushed it to do so? Unsurprisingly, as in the role played by the state in territorial expansion by planters in the American South, interests related to cotton influenced the state's policy in Berar. As a case in point, the Manchester Chamber of Commerce put immense pressure on the state to introduce and enforce property rights in the rich cotton tracts of Berar. The colonial state however did not simply succumb to these pressures. There were tensions between the laissez-faire doctrine of the secretary of state of India during the Civil War period, Sir Charles Wood and the proposals of the Manchester Chamber of Commerce.[162] The state was nevertheless invested in public works whenever its finances allowed rather than unequivocally complying with the demands of the Manchester interests.

There was considerable churning of the land administration in the early years of Berar's annexation: from the *mouzawur* system where *muqqadam*s, or village heads, were given the task of revenue collection, to the dismantling of powerful village actors, the *deshpandia*s and *deshmukh*s. New revenue administrators in the form of *patil*s/*patel*s (village headmen) and *patwari*s (village accountants) were appointed. In 1855, a five-year settlement was initiated with the *jama* (rent roll) increasing annually; the *patil*s *and patwari*s playing an important role in the preparation of the annual *jamabandi*—rent roll directory. However, because of rent seeking by the *patil*s and *patwari*s, revenues stagnated. Consequently, the two positions were discontinued.[163] Patronage grants such as those under granted to *inamdar*s under the *inamdari* system offered exemptions and privileges that were a drain on colonial revenue, and they were gradually brought under revenue assessment.

After much debate and deliberation about the merit of alternate revenue systems, the *ryotwari* system was adopted in Berar following the colonial takeover in 1853.[164] We have already discussed the *malguzari* system in the context of 'Malguzari Tanks' in the Central Provinces. The first cotton commissioner of the Central Provinces and Berar John Harry Rivett-Carnac in his memoir has rich descriptions about his administrative experience in assigning proprietary land rights to hardworking tenants rather than the absentee landlords (*malguzar*s) who

> ... had never helped them—tenants [*sic*] in any way, and who would not even contribute when necessary towards repairing the embankment of the lake on which the village lands depended for irrigation.[165]

Even before the colonial takeover, the region witnessed the implementation of the *mahalwari* system by William Bentinck in 1833. As was in the case of Thomas Munro's concern in the Madras Presidency, whether *ryotwari*, *zamindari*, or *malguzari* would generate more revenues was debated by colonial officials.[166] This mode of revenue payment was consolidated through survey and settlement operations between 1862 and 1877.[167] The survey and settlement operations had a considerable impact on the Berar economy. The move for standardization and regularization of land revenue assessment resulted in the replacement of *beegha* (also *bigha*) by acre as the unit of land, and weights and measures were standardized.[168] There was also an elaborate categorization of villages based on their revenue potential. In the scheme of things, proximity to the railways and major markets was an important consideration in the assessment rate.[169]

An important change in land administration was the pruning of the power of *deshmukh*s and *deshpandia*s, and the creation of a new class, namely the *khatedar*—registered tenant in a village. The *khatedar* had the right to occupancy as long as the annual revenue was paid. The *khatedar* did not have the right to divert the holding for non-agricultural purposes. However, subletting the holding was permitted, and these subtenants were known as *bhagindar*. There was widespread rack-renting, which was the rent paid by the *bhagindar* to the *khatedar*. The rent was generally more than three–four times the land revenue rate paid by the *khatedar* to the state. On the changed revenue arrangements, the *Berar Gazetteer* of 1870 notes:

> 'A man who had carefully formed and prepared his fields saw them sold to the highest bidder; Whole taluks and parganas were let and sublet to the speculators for sums far above the ancient standard assessment.' The revenue was then farmed out to either deshmukhs (hereditary paragana officials) or sahukars (money lenders) who did not recognize the rights of occupancy.

In the new institutional setting, the power of the state depended upon the loyalty of the *khatedar*s, but their loyalty was assured more by threat than by persuasion.[170] The *khatedari* system and the survey and settlement exercise nevertheless had three major effects. First, there was a tendency towards fragmentation of holdings primarily due to the subdivision by the survey teams. Moreover, the state dealt with the *khatedar* but the *khatedar* had an incentive to engage in rack-renting. Some estimates suggest that over half of the *khatedari* land was operated by the *bhagindar*s.[171] Second, it changed the agrarian relations in the region as it reorganized caste–class relations. The preponderant peasant population were Kunbis—a lower caste as per the prevailing caste hierarchy. Some of them became *khatedar*s. As many subtenants (*bhagindar*s) of the *khatedar*s were Kunbis, the new system created a class hierarchy within the same caste. At the same time, agricultural labourers belonging to lower-caste groups such as Mahar or Bhangi could also undertake cultivation as subtenants and attain the same class status as Kunbi subtenants. Third, defaults in revenue payment resulted in loss of rights of the *khatedar*, and forfeiture of land and associated property was common.[172] This was an important factor in the growing indebtedness in the region.

Institutional change also occurred in the form of changes in the role of caste in the village and property rights were redefined. A major change occurred in the form of the dismantling of the *balutedari* system, which created confusion about property rights for the colonial administrators. The process of demilitarization of the *balutedar*s, who locally held considerable power, ensued. *Watan* rights of the *watandar* were nullified.[173] The annihilation of the traditional local power structures meant that the power that the *balutedar*s commanded over water resources and their management came to an end.

The prodigious expansion of area under cotton in Berar due to high cotton prices as well as the growth of private property over land with continuous revenue demand exacted on the produce had drastic ecological consequences. First, there were several reports of exhaustion of fertile land due to successive crop production.[174] Second, a scarcity of grass and firewood due to privatization of culturable lands and wastelands based on surveys and measurement resulted in farmers using cattle dung as fuel. Consequently, there was lack of availability of manure for crops that affected soil fertility. In fact, manure, which used to be free, had to be purchased by the cultivators. The scramble for land acquisition for cotton expansion resulted in the destruction of wastelands that acted as a buffer in times of famines or scarcity.[175] Third, without access to commons—pastures for cattle to graze—the cattle economy of Berar was severely impacted. A colonial report of the 1912–1913 comments on the fodder crisis brought upon by the expansion of cotton along these lines:

> But the extension of cotton cultivation has been at the expense of food crops such as juari and has begun to react upon the supply of fodder.[176]

New laws were enacted to lease out wastelands for up to thirty years under the *izara* tenure system. Cultivators were incentivized to settle wastelands in the lure of being made *patil*, and multiple land tenure arrangements prevailed.[177] As the extraction of cotton from the fields of Berar intensified, the vulnerability of its rural population to droughts and famines increasingly worsened. Although farmers could manage to reap higher profits and the state's revenue expanded unlike ever before, the ability of the village economy to withstand droughts and famines weakened. In 1869, when the original revenue settlement was introduced into almost the whole *taluka*, the area of culturable and assessed land lying unoccupied was about 67,100 acres. In 1896–1897, the unoccupied area was only 11 acres.[178] The gross cropped area in Berar which was about 3.4 million acres (average of 1862–63 to 1864–65) more than doubled to 7.4 million acres (average of 1905–06 to 1909–10) in a matter of four decades.[179]

During the same period, the area cultivated under cotton more than trebled from 1 million acres to 3.1 million acres. This led to so severe environmental degradation that by the 1890s not a single perennial river or stream was left in Berar; a harbinger of the terrible famines that were to ravage the lands over the next decade.[180] This dimension of ecological degradation is perhaps one of the most significant costs of the gamble with extensive production of cotton in the region. There was also growing population pressure on land with an increase in population in the period between 1860 and 1880 with Berar registering a 1.8 per cent average annual growth rate between 1867 and 1881, largely due to in-migration.[181]

The changes in land revenue administration altered the scale of agricultural production. As the population pressure on land increased, there was a sharp decline in the size of landholdings or fall in the land–man ratio. By 1903, a *khatedar* had around 18 acres of land, compared to 24 acres in 1870—the total number of *khatedar*s increasing from 2,26,307 to 3,94,644 in Berar over the period.[182] While the population of Berar grew steeply since

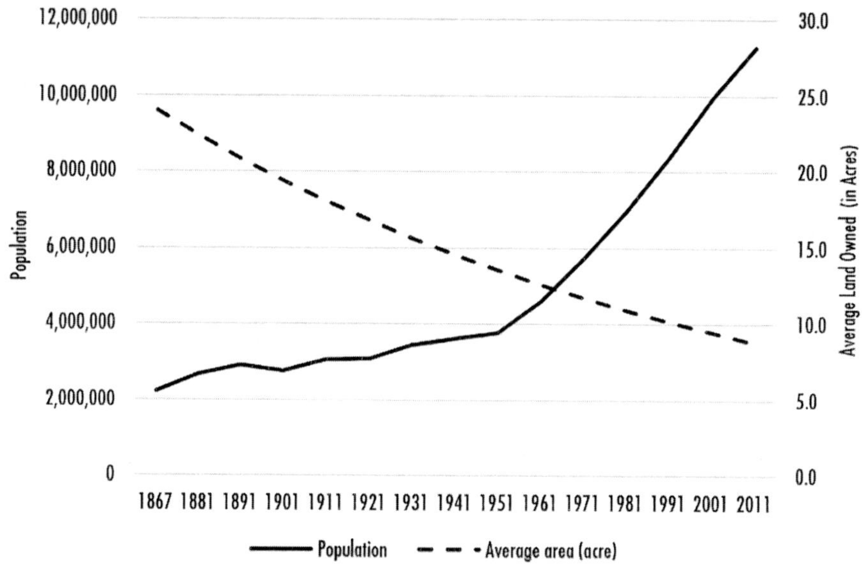

Graph 2.11 Population and average land owned in Berar: 1867–2011

Source: Population data from 1867 to 1981 are from various census years as cited in T. Dyson, 'The Population History of Berar since 1881 and its Potential Wider Significance', *Indian Economic and Social History Review* 26, no. 2 (1989): 167–201, 169, table 1. Population data from 1991 to 2011 are based on the Census of India. Average land size is calculated by authors based on computed compound annual growth rate (CAGR) of 6.94 per cent using data for 1867 and 1901 as endpoints as provided in Satya, *Cotton and Famine in Berar*, 72, table 3.

Note: Population of Berar since 1961 is assumed to be that of Amravati division. Washim district was carved out of the Akola and Buldhana districts in 1998. The population of Washim was included in the 2001 Census.

independence, there was a steady decline in the average land size since 1867. Berar's population grew from about 2 million in 1867 to almost 7 million in 1981. Among phases of decline, the population declined due to famines by 5 per cent in the period between 1891 and 1901. The influenza pandemic also slowed down the population growth rate from 1911 to 1921, after which the population growth has been steady. The growth of population and estimate of decline in average land size since 1901 is shown in Graph 2.11.

The falling size of landholdings and growing demand of land revenue in cash contributed to a high incidence of indebtedness during the period. Often, land revenue was paid by moneylenders on behalf of the *khatedars*, which not only led to the proliferation of moneylending classes but also debt bondage and usurping of crops pledged by the peasants.[183]

The changing land administration was also a reason for growing indebtedness and incidence of land grabs.

Evidence from the Bombay Deccan during the period establishes that the new colonial land system that allowed commercial agriculture also resulted in land mortgages and indebtedness for the cultivators. Forfeiture of land by moneylenders and the state became commonplace. Despite legislation such as the Deccan Agricultural Relief Act of 1879 and the Loan Limitation Act of 1859, indebtedness and dispossession from land continued.[184] The processes of in-migration and dispossession also led to an early breakdown of the caste-occupation nexus in the region. As early as 1881, almost half of the agricultural labour population belonged to the intermediate peasant caste in the region.[185] Apart from dismantling *balutedari*, another traditional institution that was ended was *hoondakuri*. *Hoondakur*s comprised collectors of tolls along the cotton routes by merchants and bankers.[186] Freeing up the cotton routes fostered the cotton trade. However, the growth of cotton trade and increase in land revenue due to the expansion of cotton cultivation exacerbated the vulnerability in years of scarcity and famines as the burgeoning tax rate skimmed cultivator surplus.

Although the close historical connection between Berar's hinterland and flourishing cotton trade and cotton textiles industry in Bombay played a role in its commercial development, and a few decades earlier, the embattled land of Berar also suffered considerably due to the practice of 'revenue farming' during the prime ministership of Raja Chandu Lal between 1809 and 1843, which is also notorious for bringing 'ruin and disaster to Berar'. The adverse effects of this form of extortion on cultivated acreage and villagers abandoning their fields have been chronicled by the *Amraoti Gazetteer*.[187] The mercantile house formed in Hyderabad by Brigadier General of the nizam's bodyguard William Palmer and Gujarati banker Benkati Das, Palmer and Co. that had spread their roots deep into the hinterland, made a fortune advancing loans to revenue farmers to pay off Chandu Lal.[188]

In what follows, we summarize the developments related to the expansion of the railways in the region and explore how its existence and growth was motivated by the colonial objective of extracting raw cotton and minerals, particularly coal from the region.

THE RAILWAY EXPANSION

We have already discussed how by the middle of the nineteenth century, a 'railway mania' had gripped Britain. In this context, development of the railways in India may seem like a logical extension to its colony. However, promotion of the railways in India was driven by the need to supply raw cotton to the ports for export to Britain as well as its potential as a market for ready-made manufactures from Britain. Since the early 1840s, proposals for constructing a viable railway network in India had been mulled. Dissatisfaction with inland transport affecting the Indo-British trade aside, administrative and military justifications were also extended as important concerns in the case put forth to the government.[189] However, it was not the Company, with its slipping control over India, but the thrust on private railway enterprises by merchants and manufacturers of cotton textiles in Britain and merchant firms in Indian entrepôts that shaped the development of railways in India. On the factors leading to the introduction of modern railways in India, Daniel Thorner writes:

> The key groups whose pressure led to the launching of modern railways in India were the great English and Scottish mercantile houses trading with the East and the smaller British merchant firms in the Indian port towns with which they were in correspondence.[190]

There were several committees for promotion of the railways that not only deliberated on the justification of introducing the railways but also the virtues of private enterprise related to the raising of capital, ownership, and operation of the railways. At the same time there were demands for state (Government of India) guarantees in the risky undertaking. When the expansion of roads was financed through levies and cess, British capital financed the construction and operation of the railways, with the Indian government guaranteeing 5 per cent dividends. Much has been written about the details of the prolonged deliberations since the early 1840s.

In the fascinating story of the railways in India, the role of luminaries such as John Chapman, George T. Clark, G. T. Henry Coneybeare, R. M. Stephenson, John Stuart Wortley, Sir Bartle Frere, Lord Dalhousie, Lord Canning, and Lord Elgin stands out. Even a few Indian merchants were present in the important committees in the mid-nineteenth century that decided in favour of the introduction of the railways.[191] John Chapman, who was a pioneer of the railways in western India, visited India in 1845 to research the feasibility of his proposal for the railway line from Bombay to the important centres of cotton in Berar and other commercial centres.[192] In 1849, the British Cabinet, the Company, and promoters of the railways

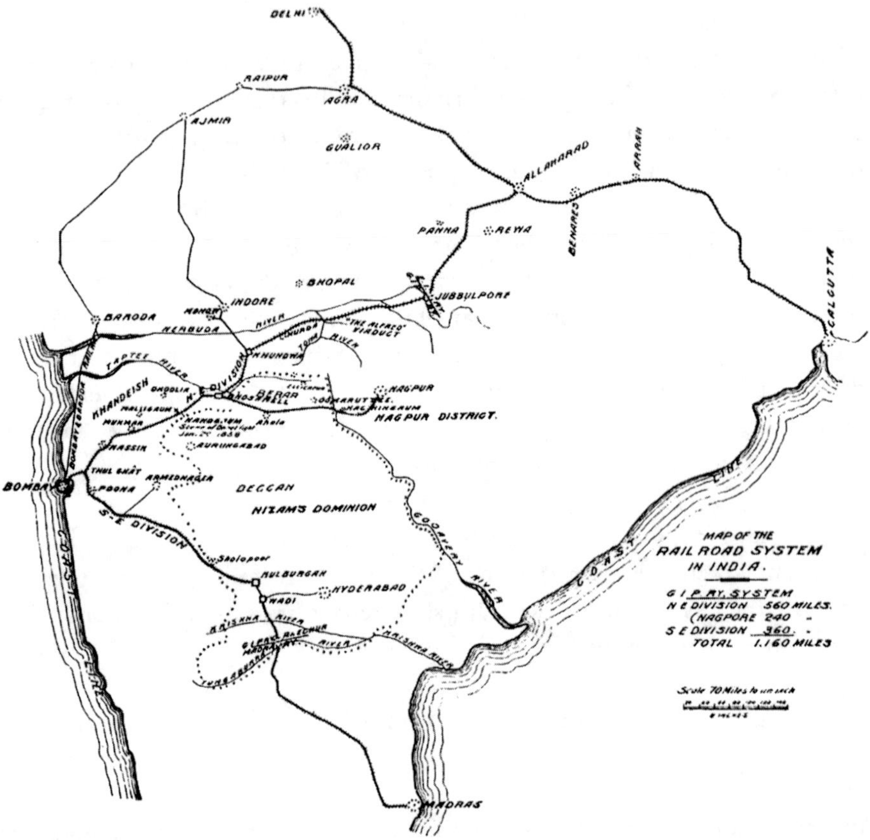

Map 2.3 The Great Indian Peninsular Railway, 1870, by R. M. Brereton, 1907

Source: Wikimedia Commons (https://commons.wikimedia.org/wiki/File:Great_Indian_Peninsula_Railway_1870.png [accessed on 20 December 2021]). This work is in the public domain as the copyright holder R. M. Brereton passed away in 1911 and it has been over 70 years since his passing.

agreed upon two experimental projects; one of the two to run between Bombay and the cotton fields in the hinterland.

In 1853, the year Berar was annexed to the British Crown, the Great Indian Peninsular Railway (GIPR henceforth) (Map 2.3) launched the first passenger train from Bombay to Thane—a precursor to the eastward expansion into the cotton country including the extension of the Bombay–Bhusawal line up to Nagpur. In the last two decades of the nineteenth century, the Government of India acquired a majority stake in the private railways including the major trunk lines. Although some private companies remained functional, the guarantees were lowered.[193] By 1900, India had the fourth largest railway network in the world, but the pace of route mileage expansion slowed down by the 1920s. Despite the slowdown, all the major ports were connected, and rail freight increased from about 20 million tons to 120 million from 1890 to 1930.[194] However, railway mileage per capita and connectivity among the interior locations were low.

In the light of the railway expansion in colonial India, its economic impact was immense. Studies suggest railway expansion had a significant impact on trade and prices of commodities.[195] Although it was a major source of employment at different levels of skills, wage convergence was not to the extent of convergence of prices of commodities such as cotton and food grains. Apart from raw cotton, it also became the main mode of export of food grains from the region even during the famine years.[196]

How did the introduction of the railways transform the cotton economy of Vidarbha? Before the road infrastructure improved or the railways became the main mode of transporting raw cotton from the hinterland to entrepôts such as Bombay, pack bullocks transported the valuable cargo. As expected, the price differences of commodities within a region were stark. For instance, within the Central Provinces, wheat sold for 80 seers per rupee in Chhattisgarh, but it was 44 seers per rupee in Jabalpur, and 21 seers per rupee in Nagpur.[197] The first consignment of cotton from Berar to Bombay was made in 1824–1825. The leading Bombay merchant and Parsi Baronet—Jamsetjee Jejeebhoy—oversaw 'establishing a traffic in cotton between Berar and Bombay'.[198]

Before the introduction of the railways, much of Indian cotton used to be exported to China via the Mirzapur–Calcutta route as discussed in Chapter 1. With the decline of the Bengal trade, a veritable trade link was established between Berar and Bombay. In 1846, around 180,000 bullocks were employed in the transportation business for that route.[199] Construction of the railways fundamentally altered the movement of people and produce from the region. It not only connected the hinterland to Bombay but also to Calcutta. It also became a corridor to connect the north and south of India, providing access to markets for hitherto underdeveloped parts of the plains.

The railways played a crucial role in the transformation of Berar's cotton economy, before and during the American Civil War. It brought about a structural shift in the way cotton was grown and exported in the late nineteenth century. During the Civil War, railroad expansion along the GIPR gained prominence. The Malkapur and Shegaon lines were open by 1864. The GIPR connected Bombay with the important cotton marts of

Berar which produced a quarter of exports from Bombay by 1870.[200] By 1870 the markets such as Khamgaon were connected to Bombay, but ox carts still had to haul cotton over long distances on the roads that were built for the transport of cotton to the railway towns. The phenomenal railway expansion is evident from the fact that 400 miles of railway track were interspersed with two 10-mile feeder lines until the twentieth century.[201]

The railways catalysed the changes in cropping patterns considerably. Up to 1870 the Central Provinces was a net importer of oilseeds. But the extension of rail line to Nagpur (1867) and Jubbulpore (1870) had an immediate effect on both the cultivation and exports of oilseeds. By 1873 oilseed exports from the Central Provinces outstripped cotton exports in bulk and in 1875 far surpassed cotton in value as well.[202]

Telegraph connectivity also followed, resulting in improved communication about prices and demand for cotton. However, despite improvements in communication, several infrastructures for the cotton market were left wanting. At the end of the American Civil War, there were no presses in Berar. Consignments of raw cotton loosely packed in *dokra*s were an obstacle to delivering quality cotton in Bombay. Nonetheless, there was growing investment in pressing and baling infrastructure in the railway stations.[203] The expansion of branch lines on the GIPR such as that the one between Khamgaon and Jalamb stimulated this investment. European firms such as Ralli Brothers and Volkart Brothers set up gins and presses in Berar. These firms established a strong network of agencies across the region, and there was growing investment in railways as well as cotton textile mills in the first half of the twentieth century, particularly in periods of cotton boom..

However, these infrastructural developments conceal two major changes in the local economy that had structural consequences. First, the infrastructural development meant that now cheap English piece goods inundated the local markets. As a result, the local cotton textiles industry failed to compete with the imported goods, and weavers and cotton trading communities became agricultural labourers in hordes as their livelihoods took a hit. Second, by the early twentieth century, Berar produced more cotton than Egypt, and had become what some considered 'the perfect garden of cotton'.[204] This transformation of the cash crop economy rode the expansion of credit in the local economy. Indeed, administration changes, particularly in land revenue administration and property rights, underwent glaring transformation but the expansion of cotton could not have been achieved without the credit cultivators took from merchants and moneylenders.

CREDIT AND INDEBTEDNESS

Despite several land reform measures introduced by the colonial administration, land revenue payments and cultivation costs became a source of indebtedness for *khatedars* as well as tenants. It was anticipated that the cotton price boom and clarity on property rights would free the cultivators from the clutches of moneylenders. On the contrary, indebtedness was exacerbated in the cotton country. The problem of indebtedness was compounded by high levels of illiteracy in the hinterland and a lack of institutional reforms in human capital.[205] Of course, periods of rise in cotton prices created opportunity for debt-ridden farmers to repay partially or completely the outstanding loans, as noted by the cotton commissioner of the Central Provinces and Berar, John Harry Rivett-Carnac in his report in 1867–1868:

> In the Wurdha district, the price of the cotton rose from Rs. 23 a 'bhoja'[206] to Rs. 140; and although there have been many disappointing fluctuations, it still stands at what, even making allowance for the increased expense of cultivation, is a remunerative rate. And although unfortunately, many cultivators may be met with, who, believing the golden age would never end, spent fabulous sums of money on marriages, pairs of fancy bullocks, and other extravagancies, and ran even more deeply into debt than before, still the mass of the agricultural population seized the opportunity of ridding themselves of the burden of debt which had so long weighed them down, and affected so injuriously their produce.[207]

It was also anticipated that the establishment of railways would encourage direct trade of cotton from the farmer with the Bombay merchant thereby reducing any interlinked transactions in the village. These promises though did not materialize for the farmers. The decline of prices during the end of the slump following the cotton boom only increased the strangle of the proverbial Shylock, the moneylender on the farmers. Instead of the Bombay merchant and farmers meeting face to face, it was observed in the Khamgaon market that cultivators rarely brought the produce directly to the market—a high estimate puts this at one-fifth of their crop owing to significant intermediation by the middlemen.[208] An Indian official, in the midst of the cotton boom, noted:

> ... the Berar raiat is generally very poor, and they are not at present in a position to cultivate the farms without the assistance of the

> capitalist.... The bania, or village sahukar, is a person to whom they look for assistance, ... and most of the proceeds of the year's produce is taken off by the lender, leaving scarcely sufficient for the next year's maintenance.[209]

An important aspect of the credit markets associated with cotton in the late nineteenth century was the interlocking of credit, goods, and trade. The cotton price boom attracted money lenders (*sahukar*s) from different parts of the country into the region.[210] Since a high proportion of moneylenders were outsiders and not involved in cultivation, the crop was typically the security for the credit advanced by the moneylender. It is in this context that development of land markets provided an opportunity for moneylenders to keep land as a collateral.[211] When the prices were high, moneylenders found it attractive to gain control over the produce rather than have land as collateral. As discussed earlier, the pressure of land revenue also necessitated farmers to borrow from moneylenders. The *sahukar* acted as an intermediary between the farmers and agents from market towns. The agents, mostly Marwari and Gujarati tradesmen, were typically representatives of the merchants from Bombay and the European firms that had considerable presence in the towns. Indebtedness was inevitable in such a scenario as payment was made by moneylenders on behalf of the registered occupants of the land. Moneylenders and large landlords provided operating capital and cash for the payment of land revenue. It is common to characterize the *sahukar* as unscrupulous and greedy, but the mechanism of the cotton trade permitted the *sahukar* to behave in that manner. Prices were determined in Liverpool or Bombay and the *sahukar* procured the raw cotton from the farmer at a pre-determined rate, bearing the possibility of downside risks. Capital for the moneylender was provided by the European merchant firms under the *sutta* contract, that is, cotton had to be supplied to the firm on a stipulated date at a pre-agreed price. It is not difficult to see why a low pre-agreed price squeezed the *sahukar*, who in turn put pressure on the cultivator. In the gamble of cotton with the demands of the colonial state and the activities of the trading firms, the moneylender was just a 'fly hovering around the twin wheel'.[212]

There were different types of loans provided in the Berar region—*sawai*, *nimi sawai*, and *lawani*. The typical money loan was given to the cultivator for an interest calculated every month. The lending between moneylenders was at the interest of 6 per cent while the lending rate to the cultivator was typically 12 per cent per annum. The rates though could vary from 9 to 24 per cent per annum. *Sawai* and *nimi sawai* were loans given in kind where the borrower had to repay one-fourth or one-eighth more, respectively, of whatever was produced. In such loans, seed grains or food was typically lent. *Lawani* was a loan of seed that was repaid in cash at the prevailing market rates and was sometimes referred to as a loan repaid in kind (grain or cotton) at a fixed rate. Apart from seeds, the loans in agriculture were typically taken for weeding operations.[213]

As the markets developed, apart from the moneylenders, loans were also provided by the colonial government (British Raj or Raj) under the Land Improvement Act, 1871, and Agricultural Loans Act, 1891. The first type of loans was intended to be for making permanent improvements to the land while the second type of loans was more temporary in nature. The temporary loans were typically advanced towards the purchase of cattle and seeds. Typically, a very small amount was totally given as loans in these acts (an average of 1,300 rupees from 1901 to 1906), but a loan amount of about eighteen times this amount was disbursed in the two famine years, 1899 and 1900.[214] Though the interest rates were lower for the government loans, there were often excessive delays, and bureaucratic red tape in obtaining the loans made farmers borrow money from the moneylenders.

The system of providing *taccavi* loans was also dismantled in many *taluka*s which increased the dependence on moneylenders for consumption loans in bad years. Cooperative credit emerged as a formal source of credit for the farmers in about the second decade of the twentieth century. Much has been written about the idiosyncrasies and limitations of cooperative credit institutions that need not be reiterated here. To deal with the growing discontent and usurious practices of moneylenders, the Raj implemented anti-usury laws such as the Berar Protector of Debtors Act of 1934 and the Central Provinces and Berar Moneylenders Act of 1934, which regulated the money-lending business and put a ceiling on the interest rates that registered moneylenders could charge to farmers. After the reorganization of states, the Bombay Money-Lenders Act of 1946 came to be applicable to Vidarbha districts since 1960, there were amendments to the law regulating moneylenders in the state.

Regulation of moneylenders comprising individuals, companies, unincorporated bodies, and undivided Hindu families was a significant step in reducing *mala fide* activities and awareness about the laws among the debtors. Several laws and subsequent amendments also regulated lending by co-operative societies in pre-independence Vidarbha. Decades since, as we will discuss later, these cooperative institutions were in bad shape in Vidarbha while in western Maharashtra they were captured by the sugar barons.[215]

Interestingly, the cooperative officers were required to keep a watch on factories and mills in several parts of the state. Hundreds of cases of illicit moneylending and court cases were common. Moneylenders had to maintain accounts that were frequently scrutinized. They were not allowed to charge interest exceeding 9 per cent per annum on secured loans and 12 per cent per annum on unsecured loans. According to the law, moneylenders could charge an interest payment of 1 rupee per year if total interest chargeable within the prescribed limits in respect to loans advanced during a year amounted to less than a rupee. Moneylenders in both Vidarbha and Bombay demanded increasing the rates for several years. In 1965, the interest rates were revised to 18 per cent per annum for secured loans and 21 per cent per annum for unsecured loans—for persons other than agriculturists. Another development that shaped Vidarbha's cotton economy was the trajectory of cotton mills as part of the spurt in capitalist development in India since the late nineteenth century.

RISE AND FALL OF COTTON MILLS

The first cotton mill in India, Bowreah Mills, was set up near Calcutta, supposedly in 1817.[216] However, it took over four decades for the cotton manufacturing industry to take off. The first cotton mill in Bombay—Bombay Weaving and Spinning Company—was set up in 1854 by Cowaszee Nanabhoy Davar, a Parsi connoisseur, and his business partners in the Tardeo district of Bombay. As the American Civil War broke out, there was a large-scale diversion of capital from cotton mills to investment in raw cotton; the boom being associated with unprecedented accumulation of capital. However, in the post-Civil War period, there was a considerable increase in investment in mills. By 1880, around 40,000 workers were employed in 58 functioning cotton mills across the country with over 13,000 looms and nearly 1.5 million spindles.[217] By 1890, nearly 60,000 workers toiled at the cotton mills of Bombay alone. However, since then and the end of World War I, only 17 additional mills were set up in the city albeit with a phenomenal rise in mill workers.[218] Much has been written about the organization of labour in the textile mills of Bombay.[219] Changes in the structure of the industrial labour force including a decline in the role of the 'jobber' have also been documented.[220]

Ahmedabad saw its first mill in 1861 founded by Ranchhodlal Chhotalal.[221] Entrepreneurs, local financiers belonging to the Bania and

Saraf (Shroff) community, played a crucial role in the city's growth in the cotton economy. Deep networks of social capital and trust-based lending were critical not only for the marketing of cotton to meet export demand but also in setting up cotton mills. The 'managing agency' system, reliance on British technical expertise and machinery imported by firms such as Greaves Cotton played a crucial role in the expansion of cotton mills.[222] At the end of the Civil War, while the fortunes of many crashed, that of others remained unaffected. The latter became a source of finance for cotton mills.

Several institutional developments also catalysed the growth of cotton manufacturing in Ahmedabad, but it lagged Bombay as an important centre of the international cotton trade. The Ahmedabad Mill Owners Association was set up in 1891, twenty-six years later than the mill owners' association in Bombay.[223] Between 1891 and 1905, there was a growth spurt in cotton manufacturing in the city. Protective tariffs of 1894 resulted in the growth of cotton mills. Parsi entrepreneurs also set up shop in the city during this period. In fact, the first mill by the Tatas in Ahmedabad was set up in 1903.

While there was a boom in the spinning and weaving mills in Bombay and Ahmedabad, what was the situation in the Central Provinces and Berar? Even in Wardha and Nagpur, spindles were set up. Jamsetji Nusserwanji Tata set up Alexandria Mill in 1869 by acquiring a dilapidated oil mill in Chinchpokli, Bombay. He followed it by setting up the Central India Spinning, Weaving and Manufacturing Company in Nagpur in 1874, which began functioning as the Empress Mill in 1877.[224] Incentivized by the rising prices of cotton and buoyant global demand, there was a surge in ginning and pressing factories in the region. In 1902, 20 new ginning and pressing factories came up in Wardha and 13 in Nagpur. Around 20,800 workers were employed in the 107 cotton gins and presses in the Central Provinces.[225] By 1903, the number of factories increased to 379 across the region: 51 new factories in the former and 25 in the latter. This was concomitant with the growth of employment to around 42,000 workers including considerable child labour employment.[226]

As in Bombay and Ahmedabad, local capitalists, primarily Marwari and Gujarati traders and cotton agents for British mills who were encouraged to settle in the region following the railway expansion, also invested in industrial growth of Vidarbha. Prominent among them was Bachhraj Bajaj—a rich Marwari moneylender and Bania from Wardha who established a cotton ginning factory in Wardha in 1905, and whose adopted grandson Jamnalal Bajaj went on to found the Bajaj group of companies and invited Mahatma

Gandhi to Wardha.[227] This phase of industrialization was not only a departure from the colonial policy of deindustrialization under the diktats of the interest of capitalists in Lancashire three decades before but also the emergence of local capitalist interests in cotton manufacturing. While the origins of this phase of capitalist development is known, several questions about labour embedded in the industrialization centred around cotton manufacturing arise. Where did the mill workers of Bombay come from? Did migrants from Berar and the Central Provinces participate in the cotton manufacturing in Bombay?

Despite the lack of reliable estimates of the proportion of the rural population in India in the late nineteenth century that was landless or worked on submarginal lands, it can be surmised that these subgroups were the preponderant labour force in Bombay's cotton mills. From the seminal work of Rajnarayan Chandavarkar on the development of industrial capitalism and social relations in Bombay's cotton textile industry, we glean that Marathi speaking workers from Ratnagiri in the Konkan region (western coastal region of Maharashtra) comprised the majority of immigrants working in the cotton mills of Bombay, but by the early 1920s their proportion declined whilst that of immigrants from the United Provinces (present-day Uttar Pradesh) increased.[228] The departments in the mills employed mostly adult men. Although around a fifth to a quarter of the workers were women, there was a sharp decline in participation of women since the introduction of night shifts in 1931 and mechanization of the reeling department which predominantly employed women. Employment of children varied around 5 per cent for the period between 1884 and 1947.[229] The squalor and living conditions in the tenements, where mill workers resided, are well documented.[230] Hard times fell upon the cotton textile industry due to the outbreak of World War I.[231]

The twentieth century saw booms and busts of the cotton economy with the Great Depression sandwiched between two World Wars. There was considerable growth in indigenous capitalism through investment in cotton ginning and pressing as well as the textile industry. Substitution of American cotton by Indian cotton was an important agenda in Indo-Japanese trade relations around World War I. Archival information gleaned from then 'confidential' telegraphic exchanges (now declassified) between the India Office, London and the British Embassy in Tokyo reveals the importance of cotton in Indo-Japanese trade. Apprehensions about the imposition of export duty on raw cotton and the imposition of restrictions on Council Bills—means for Japan to finance purchase of Indian cotton—were major concerns for Japan. Because of the restrictions on Council Bills, Japan had to pay for cotton with gold but the embargo on species by the US government had put Japan in a 'very difficult position'.[232] It is also evident from the exchanges that newspapers took considerable interest in the speculation about Japan supplanting Indian cotton by the American variety.

The Japan Cotton Trading Company played an important role in this trade. The nexus between state and capital is evident from the following declassified exchange between Japan and pre-independence India:

> ... that American cotton is about 16% more expensive than Indian cotton and that Japanese Bankers [*sic*] would thereby voluntarily handicap the cotton industry to this extent in order to protect their accumulation of gold which at present are very large.

Even as the war raged, the Textiles Committee of the Board of Trade on the supply of raw cotton to the British Empire worried about supply of quality of cotton seeds and improvement in the local cotton markets in the Central Provinces and Berar.[233] Throughout the 1917–1918 season during the World War I, raw cotton prices reached 'unprecedented heights' due to anticipated buying and partly on account of believed unfavourable season and high world prices. Since the middle of November 1917, a 'very heavy fall occurred'. However, Japanese demand was soaring.[234]

Following the fall of the mills after the war, there was a widespread working-class struggle. In January 1918, mill owners in Ahmedabad stopped the 'Plague bonus' that was given to workers since the outbreak of the bubonic plague in 1917.[235] Consequently, workers demanded a dearness allowance of half their wages in their July salary to cope with the war-related inflation. Mill owners sacked striking workers and hired weavers from Bombay, which resulted in the agitated workers seeking the help of Anusuya Sarabhai—sister of the president of the Ahmedabad Mill Owners' Association, Ambalal Sarabhai. Anusuya Sarabhai sought Gandhi's intervention.[236] Gandhi's mediation resulted in his 'fast unto death' and the ultimate acceptance of the demands for arbitration and wage increase that Gandhi proposed.[237] The effects of the first general textile strike of 1919 and 1920 are well documented.[238] The 1918 influenza pandemic also exacted a heavy human toll as millions perished.[239] At the same time, this was also a period in which the nationalistic movement gained momentum. The nationalistic movement that had commenced since the late nineteenth century in the backdrop of destruction of the domestic cotton economy and the Swadeshi movement of the early nineteenth century intricately linked cotton and India's struggle for independence. In particular, in the 1920s, Gandhi's resistance against the British rule and message of self-reliance through spinning of the *charkha* (hand spinning of cotton) closely linked the cotton and cotton industry to India's freedom struggle.[240] The decade of 1920s saw the formation and politicization of powerful trade unions in the cotton mills such as the Girni Kamgar Union (GKU), a Communist workers' union that were central to trade union activism decades before India's independence.

With the depression in the late 1920s and early 1930s, there was a slowdown in the mill expansion and the industrial dispute problem continued to be a concern for the cotton capitalists.[241] Later, we will summarize the developments in cotton economy in the post-independence period that will augment the context of structural shifts in cotton manufacturing industry. However, before doing so, we will shed light on the persistent seed experiments and trade integration orchestrated by the colonial state.

SEED EXPERIMENTS

An important aspect of early nineteenth-century cotton expansion was the colonial attempts to popularize American varieties and agronomic practices. Unlike the long staple American cotton, the Indian short staple varieties had lower quality. The short staple Indian cotton, generally called 'Surat' cotton or 'Surats', was considered low quality owing to rampant adulteration, requiring cleaning and preparation for use in the mills. It was also unsuitable for spinning in Lancashire mills. The issues of adulteration of 'Surat' cotton—the label of short staple Indian cotton that was transported from the port of Bombay—was a serious matter as discussed earlier. In terms of developments relatively more proximate to the outbreak of the American Civil War, the export demand for Indian cotton was on the decline.[242] One of the important reasons for the decline in demand for Indian cotton in world markets in the 1840s was the growth of cotton supplies from the American South. Second, the quality of Indian cotton was a concern for the mills of Manchester and towns in east and south Lancashire. In fact, there was a substantial investment for re-equipping the mills to spin Indian cotton.[243] In a bid to diversify trade, there were several unsuccessful attempts at cotton expansion by establishing agricultural research institutions and experimental farms in the 1820s and 1830s.[244] There were several attempts to plant American varieties in the Dharwar region of the Bombay Presidency.[245] In the decade before the outbreak of the Civil War, as discussed earlier, experiments with New Orleans cotton in Berar by Dr Riddel was a source of hope for contemporary commentators.[246]

Gazetteers of districts of the region record several varieties of indigenous varieties. *Bani*, formerly known as Hinganghat, and *ghat kapas* (*G. indicum*) was a long staple variety that was exported to England before the cotton boom. Another variety, *jari* (*G. neglectum*), was favoured in the native textile mills and cultivators whereas the 'soft and silky' *bani* fetched a high price in the export market. Cultivators preferred *jari* as it was hardy and profitable compared to the long staple *bani* that was preferred by the Lancashire mills. The coarse cotton had a good market in India, Japan, and Europe whilst the finer cotton *bani* had a greater risk of failure, gave smaller yield, and had a lower percentage of lint–seed ratio.[247] The *Indian Cotton Report* (1913) notes the following:

> Bani is a silky, fine cotton, of 1 inch staple, perhaps the finest cotton grown in India. It was largely exported at one time under the name of 'Hinganghats', but the yield per acre is about one-quarter less than that of the local Jari, and the ginning out-turn is only 26 per cent, for Bani against 35 per cent, for Jari. Taking the yield per acre and the ginning out-turn into consideration, the advantages for the grower are considerably in favour of Jari cotton, and consequently Bani has practically been given up.[248]

Average cotton yield in the late 1850s was two-thirds of a quintal per acre for cotton of the best quality, half quintal for second-best quality, and quarter of a quintal for third-best quality.[249] It is only after the mid-nineteenth century that exotic varieties such as *buri* (*G. hirsutum*) or upland Georgian acclimatized in Bengal and *ghogli* (*G. hirsutum*) gained prominence.[250] *Buri* was found to be more robust against the wilt disease in cotton as noted in the *Indian Cotton Report* of 1913:

> Buri is now only grown on the rich village lands, and in those districts where cotton is generally affected by wilt. Buri is entirely immune from this disease. About 600,000 acres of this cotton are grown, which produce 1,500 bales. These have been bought every year by a Nagpur spinning mill.[251]

It should not be assumed that India's importance in global cotton manufacturing was a recent phenomenon at the time when these experiments took place because the late fifteenth century Indian cotton had long established its centrality in world trade. Indian cotton textiles were the most important manufacturing industry in the world, and there is little reason to doubt that the Indian subcontinent was the original centre of cotton growing, spinning, and weaving. Merchants and intermediaries took Indian cotton cloth—calicoes, muslin, chintzes—on caravans and over the sea to the Middle East where they were sent to markets even in the Ottoman Empire. There was a vibrant export of cotton cloth from ports in Gujarat, the Coromandel Coast, and Calcutta—to long-distance markets in Africa and Southeast Asia. By the early sixteenth century, when the Portuguese traders arrived in the Malacca straits, Gujarati merchants dominated the trade. However, in the late eighteenth century, England emerged as the new centre of cotton textiles manufacturing for reasons described earlier.

In the first decade of the twentieth century, there was a boom in spinning and weaving mills and exports trade was brisk. Cotton fetched remunerative prices, and all these factors contributed to the growing popularity of the cash crop.[252] The variety of seeds and their quality were emphasized. Peter Harnetty writes:

> Lancashire was once again becoming interested in India as a source of raw cotton, and in 1904 the Government of India raised the old question of improving cotton cultivation in this part of India. It declared that it should be government policy to introduce better varieties of cotton, to improve methods of cultivation, and to provide and distribute good seed.[253]

Experiments with 'seed gardens' and trials with exotic varieties were common in even Wardha. Describing the administrative attempt to expand the spread of specific seed varieties, the Indian Cotton Committee, 1919, notes:

> Isolated experiments with exotic, more especially with Egyptian and Brazillian varieties, date from about 1839. In 1866, a 'Superintendent of Cotton Affairs' was appointed for the Wardha district but, later on in the same year, his duties were absorbed in those of the new post of Cotton Commissioner for the Central Provinces and Berar, of which Mr. J. H. Rivett Carnac was the first and only holder.[254]

Seed varieties did not diffuse on their own. An important factor in the growth of cotton in these parts in the early twentieth century was the colonial effort for cotton expansion. The value of extension and demonstration in agrarian practices to farmers was not only well recognized but also practised. Beyond cotton, the emphasis on livestock research resulted in a cattle-breeding farm at Telinkheri in the outskirts of Nagpur.[255] The varietal improvement agenda in cotton began as early as 1904 (a year following the formation of the Central Provinces and Berar) with the establishment of agriculture departments. In 1906, five cotton seed farms were established in Wardha and Nagpur to promote American varieties. In 1923, the Indian Central Cotton Committee (ICC) was constituted.

As seen earlier, institutional attempts to extend cotton cultivation in the region had been long established by this time. An office of the cotton commissioner for the Central Provinces and Berar in 1866 had a robust system of information gathering for the cotton-growing areas. At the national level, in 1873, the Fibres and Silk Branch was created to gather detailed statistical information on cotton production. The emphasis on agricultural administration in the British Raj is evident from the setting up of the Department of Revenue and Agriculture and Commerce as early as 1871; and following the recommendation of the Famine Commission in 1881, a dedicated Department of Revenue and Agriculture was established. According to the Voelcker Report,[256] the production of cotton for export in India increased over fivefold since the end of the 1850s to 1914, which was achieved to a large extent by the institutional impetus that area expansion of cotton received in cotton tracts including Vidarbha. Interestingly, by this time, the emphasis on productivity improvement through scientific approaches had taken form in the United States since the setting up of the Department of Agriculture in 1862 and the Land Grant college system that along with other American institutions would go on to shape the efficiency mandate of agriculture in India in the twentieth century.[257]

RISKS IN COLONIAL COTTON ECONOMY

India's dominance in export markets, particularly in the coarse goods market, continued until 1876 but supply to domestic cotton mills also grew considerably. Much of the investment in cotton mills was by Indian merchants. With the cotton boom, the construction of the railways, and the deeper integration of colonial cotton trade, the region became the heartland of cotton production in India. This attracted European capitalists such as the Swiss firm Volkart Brothers to Berar. The Volkart Brothers set up sixteen cotton presses in Berar by 1883. These presses supplied ginned and pressed cotton by rail to Bombay. Several other European merchants such as Rallis, Knoops, and Siegfrieds also dominated cotton manufacturing and trade in the late nineteenth century.[258] In the early twentieth century, Japanese trading firms such as Toyo Menka Kaisha deepened their network with hundreds of Indian subagencies and intensified trading activities in the region. These changes in the economic organization of the cotton economy also intensified the culture of moneylenders and dealers providing usurious loans to the Vidarbha farmer—to buy agricultural inputs, pay taxes, and manage liquidity.

From the late nineteenth century, Wardha, Nagpur, Nimar, and Chhindwara began to specialize heavily in cotton cultivation. This development was stimulated by the large demand for cotton owing to the establishment of numerous gins and spinning mills in these districts to meet the growing domestic demand for manufactured cotton. We have already seen how responding to the rise in prices of cotton, between 1891 and 1902, there was an increase in area under cotton production relative to paddy and sorghum in the Central Provinces (see Graph 2.6). In the early twentieth century, as the region was recovering from the 1899–1900 famine, there was an unprecedented expansion of area under cultivation (see Graph 2.7). This trend was noted in a colonial administrative report:

> The remarkable and unabated expansion of cotton cultivation of late years is perhaps the most important feature of the recent agricultural history of the Central Provinces and Berar.[259]

Interannual fluctuations in prices influenced farmers' acreage as in the Civil War period described earlier. For instance, cotton prices jumped from 13 rupees 3 annas to 15 rupees 6 annas per maund in 1902, which was a substantial incentive for farmers to increase area under cotton.[260] In 1902, despite a deficit monsoon due to late arrival (early July) and a prolonged break in early August, good rain towards the end of the month resulted in good yields in the cotton-sorghum tracts. By contrast, paddy tracts could not escape the famine due to poor rains that affected transplantation. The deficit in late monsoon showers (ending in early September) in the southern part of the province left land dry for rabi sowing. However, October storms brought showers that helped rabi crops in the north and west. The state's intervention in the form of remission of rents and revenue as well as generally low prices is likely to have helped cultivator households who had a precarious existence in bad years. Commenting on the state of agriculture and cultivators in the Central Provinces at the start of the twentieth century, a colonial report notes:

> Over the greater part of the Province the agricultural classes have been more fortunate than for years past, and even in the distressed south they have shown far more recuperative vigour than might have been expected. The area occupied for cultivation is the largest ever recorded, cotton and juar cropping has increased enormously....[261]

1n 1903 heavy rains resulted in the failure of cotton and sorghum in Nagpur and Berar. This resulted in a large decline in the area which was compensated for by wheat.[262] However, as the prices of food grains and linseed declined due to bumper production, cotton prices increased owing to American speculation. Exports and value of exports of raw cotton increased. Unfavourable as the rains were for the cotton growers, the higher prices mitigated any yield losses. It was the high price commanded by raw cotton that helped cultivators avoid huge losses despite the poor produce of cotton. As a case in point, these two years show that the vagaries of monsoon have always been a defining factor for cotton yield in the region, and the level of prices along with the cost of cultivation eventually determine the profits accruing to farmers.

Commensurate with the growing prices of cotton, the number of mills in the region grew to 391 and the provision of the Factories Act was in force.[263] However, unlike in the Central Provinces, Berar's reliance on the import of food grains assumed relevance in the aftermath of the famine as most of the good quality land in the region had been taken up for cotton cultivation. Also, rising wealth from cotton exports allowed the import of cotton manufactures, metals, oils, provisions, and sugar in larger-than-before quantities.[264] There was also a marked increase in the cattle population among tenant cultivators whenever there was prosperity due to high prices. Colonial administrative reports repeatedly refer to 'prosperity', 'content', and 'affluence' of the cotton farmers of Berar whenever the circumstances were favourable.[265]

COTTON ECONOMY IN THE POST-INDEPENDENCE PERIOD

In post-colonial India, the Green Revolution of the 1960s resulted in greater emphasis on input-intensive agriculture. Farmers started intensifying their use of hybrid seeds, fertilizers, pesticides, and irrigation.[266] Land reforms including imposition of land ceilings and consolidation of landholdings have had heterogeneous effects across the country and over time. Vidarbha inherited various land administration systems as legacy of the institutions in both the Central Provinces and Berar. Taken together, this meant increased complexity of implementing land reforms. Compared to other states, parts of Maharashtra (that was formed in 1960) experienced proactive implementation of land reforms following the Bombay Tenancy and Agricultural Lands Act, 1948, and a flurry of laws related to tenancy, land ceiling, landholding consolidation, and distribution.[267] In particular, the state used the financial assistance for assigning the surplus ceiling land that was provided by the central government in 1975–1976 very effectively. Vidarbha performed better than other regions in land distribution from 1981–1982 to 1991–1992. The overall land distribution and the proportion of land owned by the scheduled caste (SC) and ST population improved significantly in this period.[268]

Distortions in the trade and pricing policy of Indian seed-cotton (*kapas*) also played a role in making it challenging for the state to protect the incomes of cotton cultivators.[269] The late twentieth century also saw declining public investment in agriculture, and a narrative of agrarian crisis and chronic agrarian distress emerged. Perhaps the most significant development of the previous century that had ramifications on farmers' welfare was trade liberalization under the World Trade Organization (WTO) framework. Following the Uruguay Round in 1993, the Agreement on Agriculture—aimed at minimizing market distortions and fostering international trade—was ratified in the Morocco round in 1994. It was implemented in 1995 with the agreement that developed country members were to reduce the base-period volume of subsidized exports by 21 per cent and the budgetary outlays for export subsidies by 36 per cent in equal annual reductions over six years as compared to 14 per cent and 24 per cent, respectively, for developing country members over a decade. However, a discriminatory WTO subsidy regime meant that smallholders from developing country members were particularly affected by developed economies resorting to producer protection limits beyond the cap of 10 per cent. As developed economies dumped cheap exports in world markets, the competitiveness of Indian commodity exports was affected. Commodity prices including cotton took a hit. Import duties on the other hand left the domestic textiles industry worse off.

Since 1986, when the first mass suicide among farmers was reported, the region became the epicentre of farmers' suicides. Several studies confirm the complex interplay of social, political, and environmental constraints. Institutional changes such as the dismantling of the Monopoly Cotton Procurement Scheme (MCPS) and intensification of globalization aggravated the downside price risks that the farmers were exposed to. It is in this backdrop that the commercialization of genetically modified seeds, namely Bt cotton seeds in 2001, set the stage for the most significant technological transformation in our story of cotton.[270] With all these developments, farmers in contemporary Vidarbha (carved out of the erstwhile Central Provinces and Berar) have been constantly engaging with cotton cultivation. Cotton is cultivated in lakhs of hectares across the districts in the region and a very large amount of cotton is produced every year (Graph 2.12). The variability in production being much higher than variability in area indicates the rain-fed nature of cultivation that makes weather a key intermediary in the fortunes of the farmers.

In Part II, we will analyse cotton cultivation in a district each from the erstwhile Central Provinces (Wardha) and Berar (Yavatmal) using primary data collected over twelve years. The share of area cultivated and cotton produced by both these districts in cotton cultivation and production is quite significant. As of 2018–2019, the area of cotton cultivated in Wardha and Yavatmal was 50 per cent of the total area of cotton cultivation in the region and cotton production was 42 per cent of the cotton production in the region (Graphs 2.13 and 2.14).

As the structure of agriculture changed and Bt cotton become a potential game-changer in the cotton industry, indebtedness among cotton farmers reached epidemic proportions. It is evident that skewed distribution of rural and agricultural credit markets aggravated the structural dependence on credit for meeting the growing operating costs in cultivation.[271] Since 2000 there has been a revival of the growth of agricultural credit following a slowdown in the previous decade. However, distributional inequalities remain unabated. After 2000, indirect agricultural credit dominated agricultural credit, and urban and metropolitan branches had a higher share in outstanding loans that are concentrated on large business.

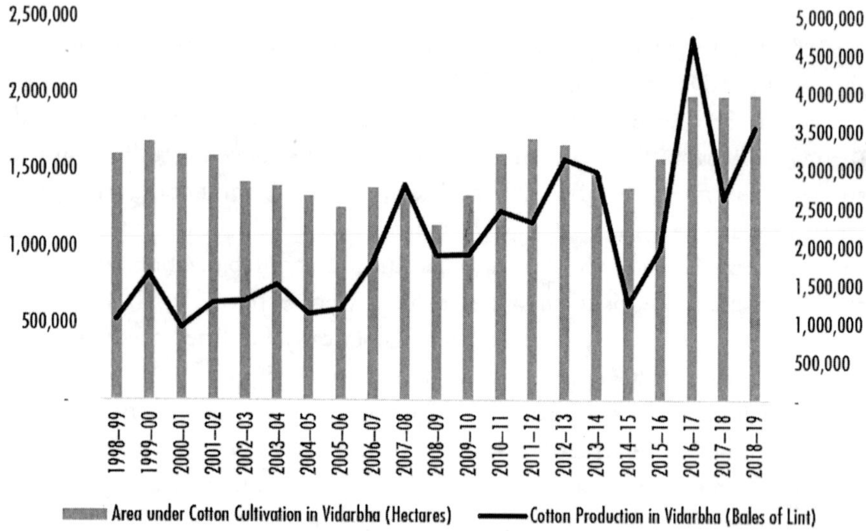

Graph 2.12 Cotton area and production in Vidarbha

Source: Directorate of Economics and Statistics, Department of Agriculture and Farmers Welfare, Ministry of Agriculture and Farmers Welfare, Government of India, https://aps.dac.gov.in/APY/Public_Report1.aspx (accessed on 22 September 2021).

Note: Cotton is cultivated in all districts of Vidarbha except Gondia. Primary vertical axis refers to area in hectares and secondary vertical axis refers to cotton production in bales of lint. One bale equals 170 kilograms.

From the prospects of agricultural credit to finance farm productivity, the seasonality of credit demand should be accounted for, which unfortunately is an exception rather than the rule. Lastly, there has been a fall in the share of long-term credit in the past three decades.[272] A slew of debt waivers and debt reliefs were announced along with 'packages' for relief. However, cotton farmers continue to be vulnerable to debt traps, and debt waiver and debt relief measures remain politically salient. Despite growing agricultural subsidies, the profitability of agriculture remains circumspect. Meanwhile, in the period from 2001 to 2018, the Amravati division in Vidarbha witnessed 13,640 farmer suicides while the Nagpur division accounted for 3,907 farmer suicides in the same period.[273] Indebtedness has been closely related to farmer and farm labour suicides happening in the region. Apart from distress in agriculture, various sociological explanations of suicides in the region have also emerged.[274] In the next part of the book, we will examine the agrarian crisis and related issues in the context of findings from our primary research in Vidarbha.

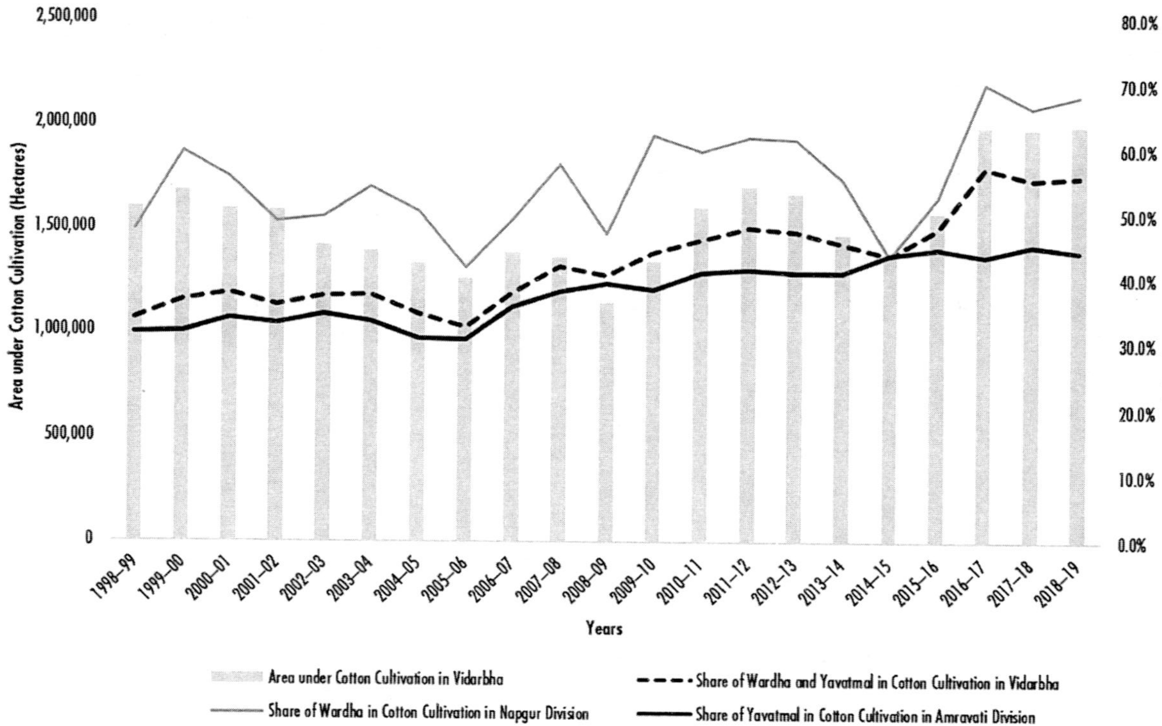

Graph 2.13 Area under cotton cultivation in Wardha and Yavatmal: from 1998–1999 to 2018–2019

Source: Directorate of Economics and Statistics, Department of Agriculture and Farmers Welfare, Ministry of Agriculture and Farmers Welfare, Government of India, https://aps.dac.gov.in/APY/Public_Report1.aspx (accessed on 22 September 2021).

Note: Cotton is cultivated in all districts of Vidarbha except Gondia.

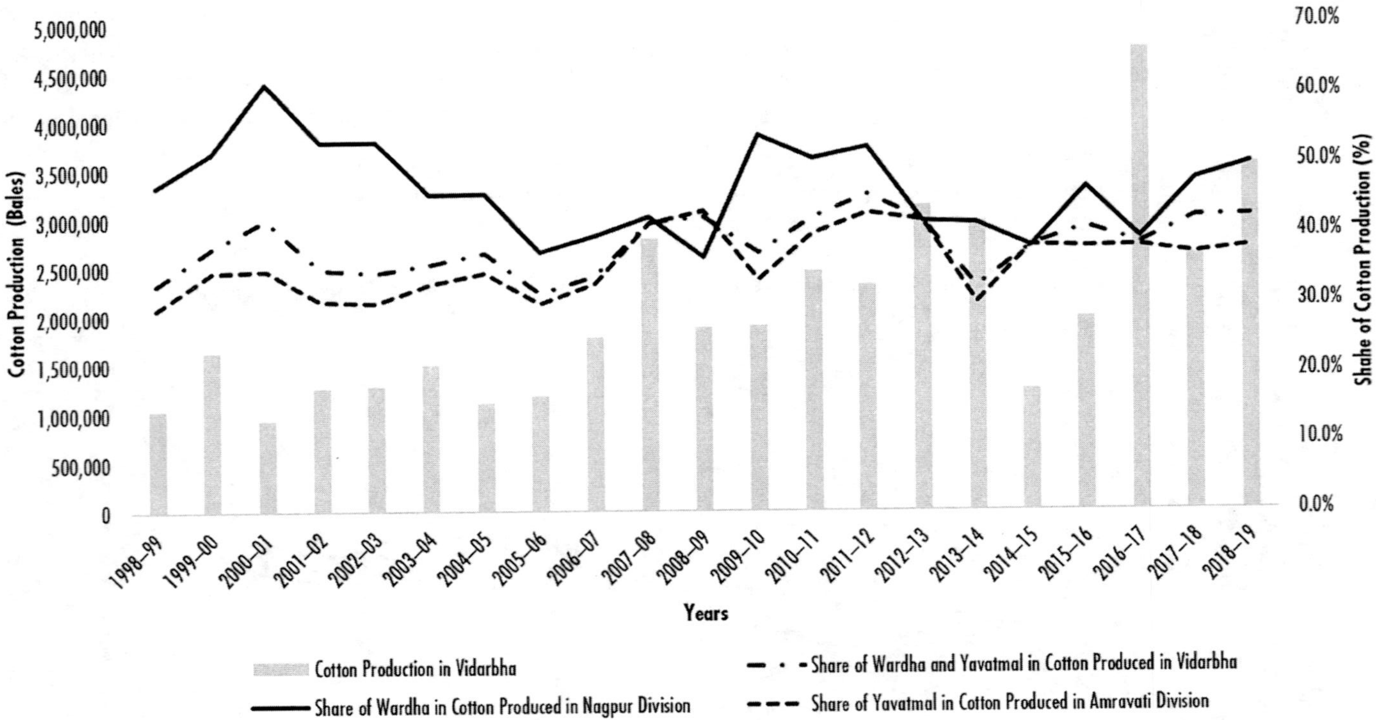

Graph 2.14 Cotton production in Wardha and Yavatmal: from 1998–1999 to 2018–2019

Source: Directorate of Economics and Statistics, Department of Agriculture and Farmers Welfare, Ministry of Agriculture and Farmers Welfare, Government of India, https://aps.dac.gov.in/APY/Public_Report1.aspx (accessed on 23 September 2021).

Note: Cotton is cultivated in all districts of Vidarbha except Gondia.

CONCLUSION

In this chapter, we analysed evidence from different sources to bear on the question of how commercialization of cotton became a central feature of the Vidarbha economy since the middle of the late nineteenth century. We demonstrated how imperialism and capitalism played their part in the reorganization of the cotton economy. We emphasized the emergence of the American South as the leading exporter of raw cotton to Britain by the middle of the nineteenth century and discussed how the American Civil War disrupted the global supply chain for raw cotton. Our description of the antecedents of the cotton economy in Berar and the Central Provinces—the regions out of which present-day Vidarbha is carved—showed that the region became an important supplier of raw cotton in the China trade of the late eighteenth century, and that Bombay and Calcutta had distinct as well as varying importance in overland raw cotton trade from Berar and Nagpur region ever since. It is clear that British trade policies along with the industrial revolution of late eighteenth-century Europe and the United States had an unprecedented impact on the material condition of the region. In fact, the late eighteenth century transformation of cotton industry of western Europe, particularly Lancashire in England, marked a global shift in the cotton economy that had far-reaching ramifications. The most significant repercussion of the rise of European cotton industry was the phenomenal decline in Indian cotton industry in the nineteenth century.[275]

In the course of our scrutiny of the antecedents of the rise of Vidarbha's cotton economy, we presented the historical 'accidents' that can be considered as turning points in the region's agrarian history. It may be recalled that in Chapter 1, we qualified our reference to historical accidents. However, it is worth reiterating what we aim to attain through our emphasis on accidents in history. To answer the question as to why cotton gained prominence in Vidarbha, we have identified several antecedents—proximate as well as distant events in the past—that we believe are crucial for our explanation. However, we do not imply determinism or inevitability in the sense of 'absolute determinism', whereby events could have occurred. This leaves open the possibility of the cotton economy to have developed through alternative path dependencies.

Our arguments about the phenomenal increase in cotton cultivation since the colonial takeover and episodes such as the American Civil War also requires us to clarify our position regarding the choices of farmers. Indeed, the changes observed in the region were a culmination of external forces as discussed as well as agency of the farmers. In this context, Karl Marx's comment, published a year before Berar's colonial takeover, conveys the essence of the interaction between circumstances and agency succinctly: 'Men make their own history, but they do not make it as they please; they do not make it under self-selected circumstances, but under circumstances existing already, given and transmitted from the past.'[276] It is in this spirit that we described in detail how the colonial takeover in 1853 transformed the cotton economy of Berar and the Central Provinces.

The colonial period saw several changes in local institutions. The *balutedari* system of agrarian relations based on caste–class lines was dismantled. In the colonial states' attempt to establish property rights to cultivators and increase land revenue, the *khatedari* system was introduced. With this, new agrarian classes such as *khatedar*s in Berar and renewed *malguzar*s in the Central Provinces emerged.[277] Before the American Civil War of 1861 transformed the cotton economy, colonial experiments with seeds had commenced with the search for alternative sources of raw cotton for Lancashire's mills. The expansion of railways and communication enabled the deeper integration of the region with global markets which the American Civil War accelerated. Additionally, the introduction of courts and regulation of moneylenders since the late nineteenth century was central to the commercialization of cotton on the one hand, and strengthening of the relationship between agricultural credit and debt on the other hand.

As described earlier, a central theme underpinning our description in this part is the importance of chance or accidental events that were exogenous from the vantage point of the cotton farmers of the region. Indeed, seemingly inconsequential events as well as watershed events occurring suddenly have altered outcomes of interest in the region's cotton economy. However, historians such as E. H. Carr dismiss the study or inclusion of accidents as irrelevant in causation on the grounds that they are not of significance in drawing generalizations in as much as generalizability is concerned.[278]

On the contrary, we agree with Brien's view that

> 'accidents' have often played a very important role in determining the course of past events. If present, they must be considered when attempting to provide an adequate and complete explanation as they help to explicate just why events unfolded as they did. Instead of offering

them as an explanation in themselves, accidents may lead the way to further causal investigations.[279]

We argue that the colonial experimentation with seed varieties, railways, telegraph, institutional reforms, and the American Civil War became the basis for the emergence of late nineteenth-century Vidarbha as a major supplier of raw cotton on the global stage. Although investment in railways, roadways, irrigation, and the telegraph preceded the American Civil War, the nature and scale of expansion of cotton following the latter were transformational for farmers as well as capitalists wagering their stake in the cotton economy.

As cotton prices surged, there was an unprecedented increase in area under cotton in the hinterland and a 'cotton mania' gripped Bombay. The speculative boom that saw land prices skyrocket and share prices of new banks and companies reach euphoric heights ended with the crash of cotton prices in 1865 as the Civil War ended. The enormous profits accrued over the short span were replaced by widespread bankruptcy and loss. The financial crisis or the Bombay Crash became one of the many speculative booms and busts that occurred in the early twentieth century, making and marring fortunes in cotton. Not surprisingly, the fortunes made in cotton mills and cotton speculation in the first half of the twentieth century also resulted in cotton capitalists financing Bollywood—Bombay's eponymous film industry.[280]

While the integration with the global supply chain created prospects of higher prices, the nature of the transformation made cotton farmers vulnerable to the growing cost of production due to the marketization of inputs. Also, the expansion of area under cotton came at the cost of large-scale deforestation and ecological damages.[281] Changing cropping patterns and dramatic reduction in pastures devastated the local cattle economy.[282] Furthermore, the systematic replacement of indigenous seed varieties by exotic varieties since the late eighteenth century sheds light on the historical roots of the crisis of agricultural science.

We present connections between the historical transformation of present-day Vidarbha following the colonial takeover and the roots of agrarian crisis. We argue that the process of integration of the region with the global cotton economy corresponded with diminished entitlements through the replacement of food grains such as *jawari* (sorghum) due to cotton-area expansion and loss of control over wastelands due to institutional changes introduced by the colonial state. The late nineteenth-century famines and pandemics ravaged the population, but vulnerability was accentuated by such entitlement failures.

In the course of our explanation of the multiple changes sweeping through the region and western India since the late eighteenth century, we also discussed the development of the cotton mills in Vidarbha as well as the Bombay Presidency, backed by the indigenous capitalists. Whilst specific communities such as Jains in Ahmedabad and an eclectic group comprising Marwaris, Banias and Parsis were pioneers in the cotton textile industry at the turn of the twentieth century, the domestic cotton textiles industry went through major ups and downs, particularly in the context of the relationship between labour unions and the mill owners. By contrast, with the dependence on exports to Britain in the nineteenth century, the early twentieth century experienced a resurgence of cotton, mostly due to the growing Japanese demand. The fortunes of Vidarbha's cotton farmers swayed as the cotton trade experienced cyclical fluctuations and speculative bubbles.

Be as it may, farmers in the region had not experienced the level of profits they experienced during the cotton boom between 1861 and 1865, and their response was remarkable. A 'cotton mania' ensued, and the crash of 1865 demonstrated the fragility of the exuberance around the windfalls to be reaped from cotton. Undertaking the production of cash crops with deep interconnections with global markets also meant farmers had to experience frequent volatility in prices. In the context of the expansion of cotton in the late nineteenth century, it is evident that events in the distant past have had a profound impact on the lives of generations of farmers.

It can be asserted that it was not a single event that put the Vidarbha farmer on the late nineteenth-century map of world cotton. Several events including British policies creating a conducive environment for raw cotton trade with China, the annexation of Berar and the Central Provinces, and the American Civil War transformed the region's cotton economy. Therefore, it was of particular importance to sketch the historical developments in the eventful nineteenth and early twentieth centuries as it shows the complex economic and social environment in which cotton gained significance in Vidarbha.

Our examination suggests that compared to the increasing role of European merchant capital the local merchant capital played a very important role in domestic cotton trade as well as international export business. Parsis and Banias played a crucial role in developing cotton manufacturing in the region as well as major entrepôts.[283] However, the nature of the cotton trade and revenue demands of the colonial state resulted in cotton farmers surviving from harvest to harvest—as they continue to do so even seventy-five years since the end of the British Raj.

By 1947, when India attained independence, Vidarbha had become a major supplier of raw cotton to the domestic textile industry. As discussed, there were several developments relevant to the cotton economy of Vidarbha in the post-independence period which were set in the context of India's agricultural development trajectory. However, Vidarbha did not experience the agricultural development that the paddy and wheat belts of Punjab, Haryana, and western Uttar Pradesh experienced in the post-Green Revolution era. Even within the state of Maharashtra, there was considerable regional variation in agricultural development and several manifestations of regional imbalances continue despite concerted attempts by the state to alleviate the woes of the farmers. For instance, the irrigated sugarcane tracts of western Maharashtra experienced high agricultural growth unlike the cotton tracts of Vidarbha and Marathwada.

These developments, taken in their entirety, contributed to Vidarbha emerging as a major source of raw cotton in the twentieth century, and subsequently, closer to the present, as an arena for agrarian crisis manifesting in the form of a spate of farmers' suicides. These developments also set the stage for Part II of the book that delves into our primary research that began in the first decade of the twenty-first century. We believe, the understanding developed thus far will provide sound background to the context of the broader questions of institutional development and changing agrarian conditions in the region that are necessary to understand the 'gambles' farmers in the region routinely participate in.

NOTES

1. Unless otherwise stated, cotton means raw cotton or seed cotton (*kapas*). Ginned cotton or lint cotton is the processed cotton following separation of seeds from the fibre, which is an input for the cotton industry downstream.
2. For an excellent analysis of the relationship between emancipation and emergence of the global cotton empire, see S. Beckert, 'Emancipation and Empire: Reconstructing the Worldwide Web of Cotton Production in the Age of the American Civil War', *American Historical Review* 109, no. 5 (2004): 1405–1438.

3. *G. arboreum* and *G. herbaceum* are diploid (2n = 26), and native to the Old World. The other two species of cultivated cotton—*G. hirsutum* and *G. barbadense*—are tetraploid (2n = 52) and known as 'New World Cotton'. American cotton or upland cotton are *G. hirsutum* and comprise the most common cotton species in the world. Long-staple and extra-long staple Egyptian cotton, 'Pima cotton' and 'Sea Island cotton'—which is the rarest of all cottons—belong to the *G. barbadense* species. For a description of cotton varieties and hybrids in India, see P. Singh and M. S. Kairon, 'Cotton Varieties and Hybrids', CICR Technical Bulletin no. 13, Central Institute for Cotton Research (CICR), Nagpur, https://www.cicr.org.in/pdf/cotton_varieties_hybrids.pdf (accessed on 24 November 2020).
4. W. R. Cassell, *Cotton: An Account of Its Culture in the Bombay Presidency, Prepared from Government Records and Other Authentic Sources, in Accordance with a Resolution of the Government of India*, vol. 103 (Bombay: Bombay Education Society's Press, 1862).
5. F. A. Logan, 'The American Civil War: An Incentive to Western India's Experiments with Foreign Cotton Seeds?', *Agricultural History* 30 (1956): 35–40.
6. P. Harnetty, 'The Imperialism of Free Trade: Lancashire, India, and the Cotton Supply Question, 1861–1865', *Journal of British Studies* 6, no. 1 (2014): 70–96.
7. *Times of India*, 3 October 1862, 2, cited in S. Beckert, *Empire of Cotton: A Global History* (New York: Vintage; Penguin, 2014), 526. Based on figures in G. Wright, 'Cotton Competition and the Post-bellum Recovery of the American South', *Journal of Economic History* 34, no. 3 (1974): 610–635, 6. Alternative sources of raw cotton exports from India in the antebellum and post-bellum period are F. A. Logan, 'India's Loss of the British Cotton Market after 1865', *Journal of Southern History* 31, no. 1 (1965): 40–50, 40; T. Ellison, *The Cotton Trade of Great Britain* (New York: Augustus M. Kelley, 1968); and P. Harnetty, 'Cotton Exports and Indian Agriculture, 1861–1870', *Economic History Review* 24, no. 3 (1971): 414–429. There are discrepancies among multiple sources for the period under consideration. Note that the quantity of pounds in a bale increased steadily from 300 pounds in the 1830s to 420 pounds in the 1850s in Britain whilst it rose from 340 pounds to 450 pounds in the United States over the same period. Oxford University Press, 'Statistics of Iron and Cotton 1830–1860', *Quarterly Journal of Economics* 2, no. 3 (1888): 379–384, 383.

8. Following a deficient rainfall year in 1868, inflation was high in 1869. The peak of exports is likely due to a combination of high domestic inflation and high import demand. See F. J. Atkinson, 'Rupee Prices in India, 1870 to 1908; With an Examination of the Causes Leading to the Present High Level of Prices', *Journal of the Royal Statistical Society* 72, no. 3 (1909): 496–573, 499. Supplies of raw cotton from the United States were low in 1869 due to bad weather as well, which increased demand for Indian raw cotton in the world markets. For trends of terms-of-trade and changing composition of cotton piece goods between India and Britain between 1858 and 1947, see D. J. Appleyard, 'The Terms of Trade between the United Kingdom and British India, 1858–1947', *Economic Development and Cultural Change* 54, no. 3 (2006): 635–654. The worsening barter terms-of-trade between British India and Britain since 1858 was also an important argument the 'drain theory' attributed to nationalists such as Dadabhai Naoroji and Romesh C. Dutt. See D. Naoroji, *Poverty and Un-British Rule in India* (London: Swan Sonnenschein, 1901); and R. C. Dutt, *The Economic History of India*, vol. 2 (New York: Augustus M. Kelley, 1969).
9. J. O. Miller, 'The Central Provinces', *Journal of the Royal Society of Arts* 60, no. 3103 (1912): 611–630, 624.
10. We refer to 'tipping point' in the sense of M. Gladwell, *Tipping Point: How Little Things Can Make a Big Difference* (New York: Little Brown, 2000).
11. *Amravati Gazetteer*, 130.
12. The growth of the cotton industry does not necessarily imply the decline of the British woollen industry, which lobbied for protectionist policies. Some historians argue that in the late eighteenth and early nineteenth centuries both industries boomed because of complementarities of style, production, and trade. For a description of the woollen industry of the period, see David Jenkins, 'The Western Wool Textile Industry in the Nineteenth Century', in *The Cambridge History of Western Textiles*, ed. David Jenkins, vol. 2 (Cambridge: Cambridge University Press, 2003), 761–789.
13. This was also a period when the Company expanded its factories in the Indian subcontinent. This is documented to have boosted the demand for cotton in India but the re-exports of finished cotton goods to the Indian market became the death knell for India's cotton industry. See A. Reid, 'Southeast Asian Consumption of Indian and British Cotton Cloth, 1600–1850', in *How India Clothed the World: The World of South*

Asian Textile, 1500–1850, ed. Giorgio Riello and Tirthankar Roy (Leiden; Boston: Brill, 2013).

14. Mercantilist lobbying with the British Parliament to thwart competition resulted in sumptuary laws, and legislations such as the Burial Act of 1666 (renewed in 1678) that made the use of shrouds other than wool illegal for burials. See P. O'Brien, T. Griffiths, and P. Hunt, 'Political Components of the Industrial Revolution: Parliament and the English Cotton Textile Industry, 1660–1774', *Economic History Review New Series* 44, no. 3 (1991): 395–423, 397. For studies on lobbying and interest groups in the emergence of free-trade regime in Britain, see G. M. Anderson and R. D. Tollison, 'Ideology, Interest Groups, and the Repeal of the Corn Laws', *Zeitschrift für die gesamte Staatswissenschaft/Journal of Institutional and Theoretical Economics* 141, no. 2 (1985): 197–212; and C. Schonhardt-Bailey, 'Lessons in Lobbying for Free Trade in 19th-Century Britain: To Concentrate or Not', *American Political Science Review* 85, no. 1 (1991): 37–58. For an analysis of welfare impacts of specific laws such as the repeal of the Corn Laws in 1846, see D. A. Irwin and M. G. Chepeliev, 'The Economic Consequences of Sir Robert Peel: A Quantitative Assessment of the Repeal of the Corn Laws' (NBER Working Paper, NBER, 2020). See C. Schonhardt-Bailey, *From the Corn Laws to Free Trade: Interests, Ideas, and Institutions in Historical Perspective* (Cambridge, MA: MIT Press, 2006) for the political economy dimensions of the transition towards free trade following the Corn Laws.
15. Prohibitions of printed cotton fabrics and cotton goods of various kind were also in force in France for over seven decades from 1686. See E. F. Heckscher, *Mercantilism*, vol. 1 (London; New York: Routledge, 1994), 172.
16. The Calico Act of 1721 prohibited import and use of dyed and printed calicoes from Asian countries, especially India. Calico-dyed blue muslins, neck cloths, and fustians were exempted. It however allowed imports of white cotton cloth for re-export purposes. See O'Brien, Griffiths, and Hunt, 'Political Components of the Industrial Revolution', 409.
17. A. P. Wadsworth and J. de L. Mann, *The Cotton Trade and Industrial Lancashire, 1600–1780* (Manchester: Manchester University Press, 1931), 144.
18. For an account of such unrests, see P. Mantoux, *The Industrial Revolution in the Eighteenth Century: An Outline of the Beginnings of the Modern Factory System in England* (Oxfordshire: Routledge, 1963), 200.
19. O'Brien, Griffiths, and Hunt, 'Political Components of the Industrial Revolution', 395–423.

20. For dynamics of the competitiveness of cotton textiles between the eighteenth and the mid-nineteenth centuries, see S. Broadberry and B. Gupta, 'Lancashire, India, and Shifting Competitive Advantage in Cotton Textiles, 1700–1850: The Neglected Role of Factor Prices', *Economic History Review* 62, no. 2 (2009): 279–305.
21. Early innovations of the eighteenth century such as John Kay's flying shuttle in 1733 resulted in rise in yarn demand and prices. See M. Beggs-Humphreys, H. Gregor, and D. Humphreys, 'The Revolution in Spinning and Weaving', in *The Industrial Revolution*, Economic History (Oxfordshire: Taylor and Francis, 2005), 19. The Paul-Wyatt's roller-spinning machinery patented in 1738 prompted the setting up of cotton mills in England in the early 1740s. See J. de L. Mann and Al. P. Wadsworth, *The First Cotton Spinning Factories: The Cotton Trade and Industrial Lancashire, 1600–1780* (Manchester: Manchester University Press, 1931), 433–448; and T. T. Harman and W. Showell, 'Calico, Cotton, and Cloth', in *Showell's Dictionary of Birmingham: A History and Guide Arranged Alphabetically* (Project Gutenberg, 2004 [1885]), ebook. Decades later, inventions such as James Watts' modifications of the Newcomen steam engine in 1781, which the firm Boulton & Watt commercialized, ushered in the late Industrial Revolution in England where innovations such as Crompton's spinning mule, Hargreave's spinning jenny, and Arkwright's water frames in the late eighteenth century transformed the cotton textile industry. See J. L. Hammond and B. Hammond, *The Skilled Labourer 1760–1832* (London: Longmans, Green and Co., 1919), 50. For insights on the role of institutions and culture in driving the technological progress associated with the industrial revolution, see J. Mokyr, 'Technological Inertia in Economic History', *Journal of Economic History* 52, no. 2 (1992); and J. Mokyr, *A Culture of Growth: The Origins of the Modern Economy* (Princeton, NJ: Princeton University Press, 2016). For scholarship on the role of ideas and culture as crucial drivers of the 'Great Enrichment' in Europe, see D. N. McCloskey, *D. N. Bourgeois Dignity: Why Economics Can't Explain the Modern World* (Chicago: University of Chicago Press, 2010).
22. A. Lakwete, *Inventing the Cotton Gin: Machine and Myth in Antebellum America* (Baltimore: Johns Hopkins University, 2003). For an analysis of the productivity increases in the UK cotton industry following the eighteenth-century innovations in cotton-spinning technologies, see P. Maw, P. Solar, A. Kane, and J. S. Lyons, 'After the Great Inventions: Technological

Change in UK Cotton Spinning, 1780–1835', *Economic History Review* 75, no. 1 (2022): 22–55, https://doi.org/10.1111/ehr.13082.

23. By the early seventeenth century, European settlers had introduced cash crops such as rice, indigo, tobacco, and cotton in American colonies to cater to the growing European demand. Although cotton had been planted in present-day Virginia, Florida, and South Carolina in the early seventeenth century, it had to wait for two centuries to emerge as the leading cash crop of America. See J. E. Chaplin, 'Creating a Cotton South in Georgia and South Carolina, 1760–1815', *Journal of Southern History* 57, no. 2 (1991): 171–200; N. Foley, *The White Scourge: Mexicans, Blacks, and Poor Whites in the Cotton Culture of Central Texas* (Oakland, CA: University of California Press, 1997), 32.
24. M. M. Edwards, *The Growth of the British Cotton Trade, 1789–1815* (Manchester: Manchester University Press, 1967), 87.
25. See, for example, Morris R. Chew, *History of the Kingdom of Cotton and Cotton Statistics of the World* (New Orleans: W. B. Stansbury & Co., 1884), 37.
26. Long before cotton assumed significance in the export trade of the United States, tobacco was first grown as an export crop in Virginia in 1611. An English settler in Jamestown named John Rolfe planted tobacco seeds he had received from the Caribbean where the Spanish had already introduced it. Rolfe, who had married the Powhatan chief's daughter Pocahontas, died in 1622, the year in which the Algonquian tribes massacred hundreds of English settlers in the infamous Indian Massacre at Jamestown. See G. S. Woodward, *Pocahontas* (Oklahoma: University of Oklahoma Press, 1976), 190. For details on the development of Jamestown as a colony, see Joseph Kelly, *Marooned: Jamestown, Shipwreck, and a New History of America's Origin* (New York: Bloomsbury Publishing, 2018).
27. S. G. Stephen, 'The Origins of Sea Island Cotton', *Agricultural History* 50, no. 2 (1976): 391–399.
28. N. Turnbull, 'The Beginning of Cotton Cultivation in Georgia', *Georgia Quarterly History* 2, no. 1 (1917): 39–45.
29. J. Hoppit, *Risk and Failure in English Business, 1700–1800* (Cambridge, UK: Cambridge University Press, 1987), 76–78.
30. For details of how sediment-rich soils and facilities for cheap transportation of freight to key ports such as New Orleans contributed to its dominance in American cotton production, see S. Bruchey, ed., *Cotton and the Growth of the American Economy, 1790–1860* (New York: Harcourt, Brace & World, 1967),

80–81. For a discussion on speculation and land policy, see R. P. Swierenga, *Pioneers and Profits: Land Speculation on the Iowa Frontier* (Ames: Iowa State University Press, 1968). For a discussion on how religion intertwined with the cotton capitalism in the American South, see J. Lindbeck, 'Slavery's Holy Profits: Religion and Capitalism in the Antebellum Lower Mississippi Valley' (electronic theses and dissertations, no. 1424, PhD dissertation, Department of History, University of Mississippi, 2018).

31. Factors were commissioning agents who got a commission on the sale of the cotton they procured from the planters. They also arranged for supplies, such as agricultural equipment, food, luxury items for the planters, receiving commission on them as well. The factors also acted as an important source of market information in the global supply chain of cotton. Other intermediaries, such as buying agents and selling agents, were also crucial intermediaries of the cotton supply chain. See S. Beckert, *The Monied Metropolis: New York City and the Consolidation of the American Bourgeoisie, 1850–1896* (Cambridge, UK: Cambridge University Press, 2001), ch. 5, 6, and 10.
32. Willie Lee Nichols Rose, *A Documentary History of Slavery in North America* (Athens, Georgia: University of Georgia Press, 1999), 25–27.
33. Slavery had been in existence in North America since the early sixteenth century. See Jane Landers, *Black Society in Spanish Florida* (Illinois: University of Illinois Press, 1999), 11–12. However, slavery was legalized in Virginia by way of late seventeenth-century legislations. For instance, in 1705, the Virginia Slave Codes promulgated by the House of Burgesses regulated interactions between slaves and citizens of the colony. See Jonathan A. Bush, 'The British Constitution and the Creation of American Slavery', in *Slavery and the Law*, ed. Paul Finkelman (Lanham, MD: Rowman & Littlefield, 2002), 391–392. Around the same time, slavery in rice cultivation was also widespread in present-day South Carolina.
34. All the thirteen original colonies enslaved native Indians. For details of Indians in the colonial South, see Edmund S. Morgan, *American Slavery, American Freedom: The Ordeal of Colonial Virginia* (New York: W. W. Norton and Company, 1975); and K. M. Shefveland, 'The Many Faces of Native Bonded Labor in Colonial Virginia', *Native South* 7 (2014): 68–91; for a description of Indian slavery in South Carolina, see K. J. Berteselen, 'Indian Slavery in Colonial Virginia and South Carolina' (masters' thesis, College of William & Mary-Arts & Sciences, Williamsburg, Virginia, 1984).
35. Both Jefferson and Washington inherited plantations and slaves. See C. Dierksheide, 'The Great Improvement and Civilization of that Race:

Jefferson and the "Amelioration" of Slavery, ca. 1770–1826', *Early American Studies* 6, no. 1 (2008): 165–197; P. K. Longmore, *The Invention of George Washington* (Berkeley, California: University of California Press, 1988); and J. E. Ferling, *Setting the World Ablaze: Washington, Adams, Jefferson, and the American Revolution* (Oxford, United Kingdom: Oxford University Press, 2002).

36. The Deep South or 'cotton states' includes present-day South Carolina, Georgia, Alabama, Louisiana, and Mississippi. For a discussion on the racialization of the trans-Atlantic slavery, see L. Edmondson, 'Trans-Atlantic Slavery and the Internationalization of Race', *Caribbean Quarterly* 22, nos. 2/3, 'Essays on Slavery' (1976): 5–25.
37. Between 1780 and 1810, there was a 50-fold expansion in the value of exports from Britain, and a 200-fold increase in quantity exported that was possible on account of the labour productivity brought about by the Industrial Revolution. See Reid, 'Southeast Asian Consumption of Indian and British Cotton Cloth', 44.
38. Beckert, *Empire of Cotton*, 104.
39. Ibid., 105.
40. Central arguments of the NHC revolve around a narrative of cotton textile industrialization to the agricultural periphery as well as the innovations linking source of raw materials to manufacturers. For a few recent studies, see W. Johnson, *River of Dark Dreams: Slavery and Empire in the Cotton Kingdom* (Cambridge, MA: Harvard University Press, 2013); and Beckert, *Empire of Cotton*.
41. For a critique of the NHC that argues slavery-based raw cotton production as the basis of industrial capitalism, see A. L. Olmstead and P. W. Rhode, 'Cotton, Slavery, and the New History of Capitalism', *Explorations in Economic History* 67 (2018): 1–17. Also see K. Rönnbäck and D. Theodoridis, 'Cotton Cultivation under Colonial Rule in India in the Nineteenth Century from a Comparative Perspective', *Economic History Review* 75, no. 2 (2021): 374–395, DOI: 10.1111/ehr.13094.
42. D. R. Hickey, 'American Trade Restrictions during the War of 1812', *Journal of American History* 68, no. 3 (1981): 517–538.
43. J. S. Otto, *The Southern Frontiers, 1607–1860: The Agricultural Evolution of the Colonial and Antebellum South* (Westport, CT: Greenwood, 1989), 94–96.
44. V. M. Conway, 'The Panic of 1837' (master's thesis, Loyola University, Chicago, 1939), 58.

45. See G. Campbell, 'Deriving the Railway Mania', *Financial History Review* 20, no. 1 (2013): 1–27.
46. A crucial legislation in monetary dominance of the Bank of England was the Bank Charter Act of 1844. Also known as the Peel Bank Act of 1844, it was legislated during the prime ministership of the newly elected Robert Peel. It separated banking and currency issue roles of banks, giving monopoly of currency issue to the Bank of England and institutionalized bullionism. See P. B. Whale, 'A Retrospective View of the Bank Charter Act of 1844', *Economica New Series* 11, no. 43 (1944): 109–111.
47. 12 pennies made a shilling, and 20 shillings made a pound of the currency.
48. C. Ward-Perkins, 'The Commercial Crisis of 1847', *Oxford Economy Papers* 2, no. 1 (1950): 75–94, 78.
49. Board of Governors of the Federal Reserve System (US), 1935–, and Federal Reserve Board, 1914–1935, 'American Cotton Production, Exports and Percentages of Cotton Exported', *Federal Reserve Bulletin: 'May 1923'*, 566–567.
50. For details of the two principal types of textile firms in New England during the early nineteenth century—the Massachusetts type and the Rhode Island type—see Caroline F. Ware, *The Early New England Cotton Manufacture* (Boston, MA: Houghton Mifflin Company, 1931). During the mid-1840s, the structure of the industry underwent a change resulting in the Rhode Island type small and specialized mills producing medium-grade cloth while the Massachusetts type large-scale integrated units producing low-grade cloth. See L. E. Davis and H. L. Stetller III, 'The New England Textile Industry, 1825–60: Trends and Fluctuations', in *Output, Employment, and Productivity in the United States after 1800*, ed. Dorothy S. Brady, Studies in Income and Wealth Series (Cambridge, MA: NBER, 1966), 215.
51. Literary works such as *Uncle Tom's Cabin* by Harriet Beecher Stowe (1852) revived the abolitionist mood in England as slavery was banned several decades earlier—abolition of international slave trade in 1808 and emancipation in 1833 that outlawed slavery. H. B. Stowe, *Uncle Tom's Cabin; or, Life Among the Lowly*, vol. 1 (Boston: John P. Jewitt, 1852).
52. For an analysis of the rhetoric of the anti-slavery and pro-slavery movements in the antebellum period, particularly since the 1830s, see D. F. Ericson, *The Debate over Slavery: Antislavery and Proslavery Liberalism in Antebellum America* (New York: NYU Press, 2000).

53. For developments leading to the onset of the Civil War, see W. J. Cooper, *We Have the War upon Us: The Onset of the Civil War, November 1860 – April 1861* (New York City, NY: Vintage, 2012).
54. Even Jefferson Davis, the president of the Confederacy, was a Mississippi cotton planter—a member of the 'plantation elite'. He was also a staunch supporter of the 'King Cotton diplomacy'.
55. D. Tripathi, 'A Shot from Afar: India and the Failure of Confederate Diplomacy', *Indian Journal of American Studies* 10, no. 2 (1980): 75.
56. Anticipating an impending conflict, an inventory of a million bales of cotton was already stockpiled in England, and acreage of cotton in 1861 was high despite the crisis, resulting in a glut that led to internal oversupply. See D. G. Surdam, 'King Cotton: Monarch or Pretender? The State of the Market for Raw Cotton on the Eve of the American Civil War', *Economic History Review* 51, no. 1 (1998): 113–132.
57. Congressional Globe (Washington, DC), 1858, 35th Congress, 1st Session, 961. Cited in Surdam, 'King Cotton'.
58. S. Lebergott, 'Through the Blockade: The Profitability and Extent of Cotton Smuggling, 1861–1865', *Journal of Economic History* 41, no. 4 (1981): 867–888.
59. S. Dumbel, 'The Origin of Cotton Futures', *Economic Journal* 37, suppl. 1 (1927): 259–267.
60. Named after the powerful French banking house Emile Erlanger & Co., it was a dual currency (pound sterling and French francs), one commodity bond through which the Confederates could borrow the much-needed capital to sustain their War effort. The bonds were valid for two decades and promised an interest of 7 per cent. Investors could receive coupon and principal payments in either pound sterling or French francs. J. F. Gentry, 'A Confederate Success in Europe: The Erlanger Loan', *Journal of Southern History* 36, no. 2 (1970): 157–188.
61. For a discussion on Erlanger bonds and the loan arrangements during the Civil War, see R. Lester, 'An Aspect of Confederate Finance during the American Civil War: The Erlanger Loan and the Plan of 1864', *Business History* 16, no. 2 (1974): 130–144. Also see J. Sexton, *Debtor Diplomacy: Finance and American Foreign Relations in the Civil War* (Oxford: Oxford University Press, 2005).
62. L. H. Johnson, 'Northern Profit and Profiteers: The Cotton Rings of 1864–1865', *Civil War History* 12, no. 2 (June 1966): 101–115.

63. Joshua D. Rothman, *Flush Times and Fever Dreams: A Story of Capitalism and Slavery in the Age of Jackson* (Athens: University of Georgia Press, 2012), 5. For a description of the rush to the cotton belt in the antebellum expansion of cotton in the South, see W. H. Sparks, *Memories of Fifty Years* (Philadelphia: Claxton, Remsen and Haffelfinger, 1870), 364.
64. For a general discussion of the global impact of the American Civil War, see B. J. Fields, 'The Advent of Capitalist Agriculture: The New South in a Bourgeois World', in *Essays on the Postbellum Southern Economy*, ed. Thavolia Glymph and John J. Kushma (Tex.: College Station, 1985), 73–94; Eric Foner, *Reconstruction: America's Unfinished Revolution, 1863–1877* (New York: HarperCollins, 1988); Steven Hahn, *The Roots of Southern Populism: Yeoman Farmers and the Transformation of the Georgia Upcountry, 1850–1890* (New York: Oxford University Press, 1983).
65. For a rich description of the political economy aspects of the cotton economy in the South, see G. Wright, *The Political Economy of the Cotton South: Households, Markets and Wealth in the Nineteenth Century* (New York: Norton, 1978).
66. Forty acres of land and a mule were part of wartime proclamations by General W. T. Sherman, known as Special Field Orders no. 15. President Andrew Johnson annulled the orders. Typically, land allocated under the programme was returned to the white owners. For the conditions of sharecroppers, peasants, and plantation workers in post-bellum period, see L. N. Powell, *New Masters: Northern Planters during the Civil War and Reconstruction* (New Haven: Yale University Press, 1980).
67. J. D. Smith, 'The Enduring Myth of "Forty Acres and a Mule"', *Chronicle of Higher Education* 49, no. 24 (2003), https://www.chronicle.com/article/the-enduring-myth-of-forty-acres-and-a-mule/ (accessed on 27 February 2021).
68. M. Aldrich, 'Flexible Exchange Rates, Northern Expansion, and the Market for Southern Cotton: 1866–1879', *Journal of Economic History* 33 (June 1973): 399–416.
69. Wright, 'Cotton Competition and the Post-bellum Recovery of the American South'.
70. In the industrial transformation of the cotton belt, institutional factors played a major role. In the agriculture that survived this transformation, degradation of soil fertility resulted in increasing application of fertilizers. Insect pests such as bollworm weevil from Mexico ravaged crops, which increased damage control expenses over years. Price uncertainty, growing

expenses, and falling incomes forced farmers to leave agriculture and migrate to towns for non-farm work. In parts of Alabama and Mississippi—the 'black belt'—those who left cotton resorted to dairy and beef production. At this juncture, farm mechanization in the form of tractors for land preparation, weeding, and harvesters began an expansion. Mules were replaced by machines. This period also saw the growth of agricultural experiment farms that helped farmers grow cotton with more profitability. Cotton started becoming profitable for the fewer farmers who stayed back. Tenancy arrangements, particularly sharecropping, were associated with land utilization patterns where a small number of American farmers held on to large swathes of land

71. H. D. Woodman, 'The Decline of Cotton Factorage after the Civil War', *American Historical Review* 71, no. 4 (1966): 1219–1236.
72. Joseph Nimmo, Jr., 'First Annual Report on the Internal Commerce of the United States (1877)' (House Executive Document, 44 Cong., 2 sess., No. 46, Pt. 2, 143), cited in Woodman, 'The Decline of Cotton Factorage', 1224.
73. R. Somers, *The Southern States since the War, 1870–1* (London; New York: Macmillan & Co., 1871), 260.
74. H. D. Woodman, *King Cotton and His Retainers: Financing and Marketing the Cotton Crop of the South, 1800–1925* (Lexington: University Press of Kentucky, 1968).
75. The mills of Lancashire were a major source of employment for men, women, and children involved in several tasks, at varying wage rates. For a discussion on wage differentials by age and gender, as well as debates among economic historians on the skill formation among the workforce in the Lancashire cotton mills in the first half of the nineteenth century, see H. M. Boot, 'How Skilled Were Lancashire Cotton Factory Workers in 1833', *Economic History Review* 48, no. 2 (1995): 283–303.
76. Sir Arthur Arnold, *The History of the Cotton Famine, from the Fall of Sumter to the Passing of the Public Works Act (1864)* (London: Saunders, Otley and Co., 1864), 37–38.
77. D. A. Farnie, *The English Cotton Industry and the World Market, 1815–1896* (Oxford: Clarendon Press, 1979), 135–170. Some scholars however argue that demand was not depressed as previously thought. For example, see Surdam, 'King Cotton'.
78. For raw cotton exports from India to Britain between 1861 and 1870, see Harnetty, 'Cotton Exports and Indian Agriculture'. Apart from India, Egypt and Brazil also regained their importance as sources of raw cotton.

See E. M. Earle, 'Egyptian Cotton and the American Civil War', *Political Science Quarterly Review* 41, no. 4 (1926): 520–545.

79. For econometric analysis of how the large 'exogenous' shift relative prices of Indian and American cotton reverted to pre-war levels despite an increase in supply of Indian raw cotton, see W. W. Hanlon, 'Necessity Is the Mother of Invention: Input Supplies and Directed Technical Change', *Econometrica* 83, no. 1 (2015): 67–100. For insights on directed technical change, that is, how shifts in relative supply of inputs influence the direction of technological progress, see D. Acemoglu, P. Aghion, L. Bursztyn, and D. Hemous, 'The Environment and Directed Technical Change', *American Economic Review* 102, no. 1 (2012): 131–166.
80. References to Vidarbha imply Berar and the districts of Central Provinces in present-day Vidarbha as per the period discussed in Chapter 2.
81. The distinction among a gamble, betting, and lottery is in place. Betting implies wagering money or something of value by the better on the odds of an uncertain event, against a second party (operator or the house such as sportsbook in sports betting). It involves skill of prediction but active participation does not influence the outcomes of the event of interest. Gambling, on the other hand, involves both chance and skill where one party (the gambler) risks losing something of value to win (gain) a prize of higher value. In gambling, there may be cases where an operator or the house wants to win against the player (poker, slot machine, blackjack without card counting, or roulette at a casino or online fantasy cricket), that is, it is a negative expected value gamble. There could be gambles such as farming cotton where the players gamble autonomously without a second party wanting to win against them, that is, it is not a negative expected value gamble. On the contrary, lottery is purely a game of chance where probability of winning is determined by chance or accident and the operator or the house does not play against the one participating in it.
82. V. Santhanam and V. Sundaram, *Agri-history of Cotton in India: An Overview* (Central Institute for Cotton Research, Nagpur, 2015), 2–3. Also see V. Sundaram, 'Antiquity of Cotton', in *Fifty Years of Research at the Cotton Technological Research Laboratory, Bombay, 1924–1974* (New Delhi: Indian Council of Agricultural Research, 1974), 212. For other ancient literary references to cotton and the age-old cotton manufacturing process in pre-industrial India, see D. Schlingoff, 'Cotton-Manufacture in Ancient India', *Journal of the Economic and Social History of the Orient/Journal de l'histoire Economique et Sociale de l'Orient* 17, no. 1 (1974): 81–90.

83. G. Watt, *Commercial Products of India, London* (London: J. Murray, 1908), 577, cited in I. Habib, 'The Peasant in Indian History', *Social Scientist* 11, no. 3 (1983): 21–64.
84. B. C. Deotare, P. S. Joshi, and C. N. Parchure, *Glimpses of Ancient Maharashtra through Archaeological Excavations* (Pune: Bharatiya Itihas Sankalan Samitee and Deccan College PBRI, 2013); Himani Patel, Anil K. Pokharia, N. Nihildas, Niraj Rai, and Rajeshwar P. Sinha, 'Rithi Ranjana: Reconstructing Crop Economy Based on Archaeobotanical Evidence and Radiocarbon Dates from An Early Iron Age Site in Semi-arid Vidarbha, Maharashtra, India', *Current Science* 120, no. 11 (2021): 1728–1739.
85. A. S. Tingre, 'Cropping Pattern Behaviour in Vidarbha' (PhD thesis, Dr Panjabrao Deshmukh Krishi Vidyapeeth, Akola, India, 2005), 63–64.
86. S. W. W. Hunter, *The Imperial Gazetteer of India (Volume XVII) Mahbubabad to Moradabad*, new ed. (New Delhi, 1839), 100.
87. P. Guhathakurta and E. Saji, 'Detecting Changes in Rainfall Pattern and Seasonality Index Vis-à-Vis Increasing Water Scarcity in Maharashtra', *Journal of Earth System Science* 122, no. 3 (2013): 639–649.
88. D. Swami, P. Dave, and D. Parthasarathy, 'Analysis of Temperature Variability and Extremes with Respect to Crop Threshold Temperature for Maharashtra, India', *Theoretical and Applied Climatology* 144, nos. 3/4 (2021): 861–872.
89. For a study on the vulnerability of the districts of Maharashtra taking into account multiple dimensions of exposure, sensitivity, and adaptive capacity, see D. Swami and D. Parthasarathy, 'Dynamics of Exposure, Sensitivity, Adaptive Capacity and Agricultural Vulnerability at District Scale for Maharashtra, India, 2021', *Ecological Indicators* 121, no. 107206 (2021): 1–17, DOI: 10.1016/j.ecolind.2020.107206.
90. M. Mani, S. Bandyopadhyay, S. Chonabayashi, A. Markandya, and T. Mosier, *South Asia's Hotspots: The Impact of Temperature and Precipitation Changes on Living Standards* (Washington, DC: World Bank, 2018).
91. H. B. Morse, *The Chronicles of the East India Company Trading to China, 1635–1834*, vol. 1 (Cambridge, UK: Harvard University Press, 1926), 130, 132.
92. For the presence of Gujarati merchants in China in the early sixteenth century, see K. N. Chaudhuri, *The Trading World of Asia and the English East India Company, 1660–1760* (Cambridge, UK: Cambridge University Press, 1978), 197. For the presence of Muslim private merchants from Surat in China in the early eighteenth century, see M. N. Pearson and Ashin

Das Gupta, eds., *India and the Indian Ocean, 1500–1800* (Oxford: Oxford University Press, 1987), 192; and C. T. Smith and P. A. Van Dyke, 'Muslims in the Pearl River Delta, 1700 to 1930', *Review of Culture* 3, no. 10 (2004): 6–15. There was also raw cotton trade between India and Nanyang operated by Indian and Portuguese merchants in the late seventeenth century; see, for example, H. V. Bowen, 'British Exports of Raw Cotton from India to China during the Late Eighteenth and Early Nineteenth Century', in *How India Clothed the World*, ed. Riello and Roy, 120–121.

93. For Chinese dependence on Indian raw cotton given its domestic production during the period, see Morse, *The Chronicles of the East India Company Trading to China*, 3:2. Also see Kenneth Pomeranz, *The Great Divergence: China, Europe, and the Making of the Modern World Economy* (Princeton: Princeton University Press, 2000), 227; and P. Parthasarathi, 'The Great Divergence', *Past and Present* 176 (August 2002): 282–283.
94. Gujarat and Bengal had a flourishing sea trade. However, political turmoil in both the regions over the period 1740–1785 deeply affected the trade.
95. For details of the Canton System of trade, see J. M. Carroll, 'The Canton System: Conflict and Accommodation in the Contact Zone', *Journal of the Royal Asiatic Society Hong Kong Branch* 50, fiftieth anniversary issue (2010): 51–66. Also see A. Schottenhammer, *The East Asian Maritime World 1400–1800: Its Fabrics of Power and Dynamics of Exchanges*, East Asian Economic and Socio-cultural Studies (Wiesbaden, Germany: Harrassowitz, 2007), 33.
96. Bowen, 'British Exports of Raw Cotton', 122.
97. The trade balance of Britain with China deteriorated with the outflow of silver to pay for the growing imports of tea. As the trade deficit worsened and concerns of smuggling of tea into Britain heightened, the British Parliament enacted the Commutation Act of 1784 that lowered import duties on tea from China by one-tenths. Although tea smuggling plummeted due to the growth of legal tea exports from China, it gave a fillip to raw cotton exports from India to China. In fact, the raw cotton exports to China from India helped balance the trade deficit that Britain had with China primarily due to imports of tea and silk.
98. Bowen, 'British Exports of Raw Cotton', 118–119.
99. A. Bulley, *The Bombay Country Ships, 1790–1833* (Richmond, VA: Curzon, 2000), 101–123.
100. The cheapness persisted despite adding packing, transport, and freight. See G. Macartney, *An Embassy to China: Being the Journal Kept by Lord*

Macartney during His Embassy to the Emperor Ch'ien-lung, 1793–1794 (London; Toronto: Longmans, 1962), 263.

101. Surat and Calcutta, and to a lesser extent, Madras, were the other ports from which raw cotton shipments left for China in the early nineteenth century.
102. C. S. Prasad, 'Suicide Deaths and Quality of Indian Cotton: Perspectives from History of Technology and Khadi Movement', *Economic and Political Weekly* 34, no. 5 (1999): PE12–PE21, PE12.
103. C. Deshmukh, 'Bombay Cottons On (A Case Study of the Economic Revolution in Bombay with Special Reference to Cotton and the Textile Industry, 1850–1914)', *Proceedings of the Indian History Congress* 37 (1976): 321–326.
104. Subsequent legislation such as the 1812 and 1833 acts enabled the growth of the intra-Asian trade, and the gradual end of the trading privileges of the EIC. See K. Sugihara, 'The Resurgence of Intra-Asian Trade, 1800–1850', in *How India Clothed the World*, ed. Riello and Roy, 147–148.
105. P. Nightingale, *Trade and Empire in Western India, 1784–1806* (Cambridge, UK: Cambridge University Press, 2008), 188.
106. Markets for yarn and cloth trade in seventeenth-century Calcutta had been well established, but merchants, traders, and bankers immigrated to the city in the early eighteenth century to seek fortune in the city's expansion. See B. Ghose, 'The Colonial Beginnings of Calcutta: Urbanisation without Industrialisation', *Economic and Political Weekly* 12, no. 33 (August 1960): 1255–1260.
107. For the importance of Mirzapur (Mirzapore) in the first half of the nineteenth century, see J. F. Royle, *On the Culture and Commerce of Cotton in India and Elsewhere: With an Account of the Experiments Made by the Hon. East India Company Up To the Present Time* (London: Smith, Elder, & Co., 1851), 42.
108. It should not be assumed that Bengal was experiencing growth of cotton trade for the first time. In fact, handloom cotton manufactures of Bengal were world renowned, and the region had experienced prosperity since the Battle of Plassey in 1757 because of rising foreign demand as well-established deep trading networks of the Company. The industry however experienced prolonged depression since 1803–1804 on account of the Napoleonic War affecting exports from Britain into France on the one hand, and mushrooming cotton mills in Lancashire, on the other hand. There was a recovery in trade, and by 1811 it was a major exporter of cotton

cloth whilst imports of cotton cloth from Britain were low. However, by 1840, years of influx of piece goods from Lancashire had weakened the cotton textile mill of Bengal, which had considerably declined by the mid-nineteenth century. On debates on the periodicity and explanations for the decline of the Bengal cotton textiles industry, see I. Ray, 'Identifying the Woes of the Cotton Textile Industry in Bengal: Tales of the Nineteenth Century', *Economic History Review* 62, no. 4 (2009): 857–889. For arguments on the catastrophic deindustrialization of Bengal during the period, see A. K. Bagchi, 'Deindustrialization in India in the Nineteenth Century: Some Theoretical Implications', *Journal of Development Studies* 12, no. 2 (1976): 135–164. For an alternative view, see M. J. Twomey, 'Employment in Nineteenth Century Indian Textiles', *Explorations in Economic History* 20, no. 1 (1983): 37–57.

109. For a rich account of the depression and recovery of trade from Bombay in the early nineteenth century, see Bowen, 'British Exports of Raw Cotton', 128–137.
110. 'Reports and Documents Connected with the East India Company in Regard to the Culture and Manufacture of Cotton Wool, Raw Silk and Indigo in India (1836), 132', cited in R. D. Choksey, *Economic Life in the Bombay and Gujarat 1800–1939* (Bombay: Asia Publishing House, 1968), 128.
111. The Company's monopoly in trade with China ended in 1831. Other western merchants including American and European merchants had to trade through thirteen Chinese *hong* merchants—authorized by Beijing and organized into the guild of merchants called Cohong in 1720. Following the Opium War, this system was dismantled.
112. Sugihara, 'The Resurgence of Intra-Asian Trade', 128–137, 160–161.
113. P. W. Fay, *The Opium War, 1840–1842: Barbarians in the Celestial Empire in the Early Part of the Nineteenth Century and the Way by Which They Forced the Gates Ajar* (Chapel Hill, North Carolina: University of North Carolina Press, 2000), 73–74. For an account of opium trade in an earlier period, see M. Greenberg, *British Trade and the Opening of China, 1800–1842* (New York: Cambridge University Press Archive, 1969).
114. Royle, *On the Culture and Commerce of Cotton in India*, 41. Also see Major General Briggs, 'The Cotton Trade of India, Its Past and Present' (paper read before the Royal Asiatic Society on 16 November 1839), 7, cited in N. Lal, 'Mirzapur: Did the Railways Change Its Commercial Narrative', *Proceedings of the Indian History Congress* 76 (2015): 408–425; and *London General Gazetteer*, vol. 2 (London, 1825), 743. Historians have debated

whether the decline of the central mart of Mirzapur as an important town in the cotton trade during the colonial period can be attributed to the Railways. See C. A. Bayly, *Rulers, Townsmen and Bazaars: North Indian Society in the Age of British Expansion –1770–1870* (Cambridge, UK: Cambridge University Press, 1988 [1983]). Also see Lal, 'Mirzapur'.

115. H. T. Colebrooke, *Remarks on the Husbandry and Internal Commerce of Bengal* (Calcutta: Hard Press, written in 1794; revised 1st ed. 1804; reprint 1884), 206, cited in A. Guha, 'Raw Cotton of Western India: 1750–1850', *Indian Economic and Social History Review* 9, no. 1 (1972): 1–41, 6.
116. Cited in Beckert, *Empire of Cotton*, 295.
117. *Buldhana District Gazetteer*, https://cultural.maharashtra.gov.in/english/gazetteer/BULDHANA/bank_trade_history.html (accessed on 17 January 2021). The *Buldhana District Gazetteer* refers to the presence of indigenous bankers with *kothi*s in distribution networks such as Gopaldas Manohardas in the cotton trade of Berar. For efforts of traders such as Vikaji Meherji, Pestonji Meherji, Jamsetji Jijibhai, Gopalji, Runmul Shankar, and Karuna Shankar in establishing Khamgaon as a major cotton town is well documented, see Chapman, cited in M. L. Dantwala, *A Hundred Years of Indian Raw Cotton* (Bombay: East India Cotton Association, 1947), 31.
118. Guha, 'Raw Cotton of Western India', 9.
119. Guha, 'Raw Cotton of Western India'.
120. R. H. Timberlake, 'Panic of 1837', in *Business Cycles and Depressions: An Encyclopedia*, ed. David Glasner and Thomas F. Cooley (New York: Garland Publishing, 1997), 514–516.
121. For a description of the development of cotton textiles industry in India since the seventeenth century, see D. A. Farnie, 'The Role of Cotton Textiles in the Economic Development of India, 1600–1990', in *The Fibre That Changed the World: The Cotton Industry in International Perspective, 1600–1990s*, ed. D. A. Farnie and D. J. Jeremy (Oxford: Oxford University Press, 2004), 395–430.
122. S. Leacock and D. G. Mandelbaum, 'A Nineteenth Century Development Project in India: The Cotton Improvement Program', *Economic Development and Cultural Change* 3, no. 4 (1955): 334–351.
123. F. A. Logan, 'India—Britain's Substitute for American Cotton, 1861–1865', *Journal of Southern History* 24, no. 4 (1958): 472–480.
124. The Association wound up in 1871 after the formation of the Department of Agriculture in India.

125. 'Fifth Annual Report of the Cotton Supply Association (Manchester, 1862), 5', cited in Earle, 'Egyptian Cotton and the American Civil War'.
126. Hansard, third series, 163:350–373, cited in Logan, 'India—Britain's Substitute for American Cotton', 473.
127. Ibid., 474.
128. M. Davis, *Late Victorian Holocausts: El Niño Famines and the Making of the Third World* (London: Verso Books, 2001), 288–289.
129. In 1936, Mahatma Gandhi set up his ashram in Sevagram, near Wardha. He popularized the *charkha* as the symbol of nationalism in the freedom struggle. However, in the post-independence period, the khadi movement that emphasized self-reliance and hand-spinning the course yarn to make clothes locally failed to gather momentum despite the emphasis on Khadi and village industries in Wardha. Jamnalal Bajaj donated the land where Sevagram was set up, and it became Gandhi's residence for the last twelve years of his life. Gandhi's trusted aide and economist, J. C. Kumarappa also proposed an alternative model of sustainable development while based in Wardha. See https://www.mkgandhi.org/articles/UN-sustainable-development-goals.html (accessed on 28 December 2021). On our visits to Wardha, time spent at the Magan Sangrahalaya (Magan Museum) as well as Sevagram was an important source of history of how Gandhi changed Wardha and how Wardha changed Gandhi.
130. Harnetty, *Imperialism and Free Trade.*
131. J. F. Watson, 'On the Growth of Cotton in India: Its Present State and Future Prospects, with Special Reference to Supplies to Britain', *Journal of the Society of Arts* 7, no. 331 (1859): 277–293, 283.
132. P. Shashtri, 'American War Set Gujarat Cotton Afire 150 Years Ago', *Times of India*, 23 June 2015, https://timesofindia.indiatimes.com/city/ahmedabad/american-war-set-gujarat-cotton-afire-150-years-ago/articleshow/47790075.cms (accessed on 12 July 2021).
133. Sir Richard Temple, *Men and Events of My Time in India* (London: J. Murray, 1882), 268–269, https://archive.org/details/menandeventsofmy034939mbp/page/n7/mode/2up (accessed on 18 September 2020).
134. BSE was set up in 1875.
135. *Muccadum* in cotton trading means a carting agent and a warehouseman.
136. In a meeting held on 1 September 1855, it was decided to impose a cess of 1¼ annas per candy on all cotton brought into Bombay. The proceeds of the same were to be used for charity to be given to mendicants who otherwise

were given a handful of cotton. See M. Pavaskar, *Saga of The Cotton Exchange* (Bombay: Popular Publications, 1985), 19–20.

137. Pavaskar, *Saga of The Cotton Exchange,* 20.
138. A. K. Mishra, 'Premchand Roychand: Mumbai's Original Share King', *Mint*, 29 May 2015, https://www.livemint.com/Sundayapp/R5BUHntOmItyIJ2yE4G09M/Premchand-Roychand-Mumbais-original-share-king.html (accessed on 10 October 2021).
139. F. Watson, *Report on Cotton Gins and on the Cleaning and Quality of Indian Cotton,* part 1 (London: William H. Allen & Co., 1879), 31.
140. Logan, 'India—Britain's Substitute for American Cotton'.
141. For details of the 'cotton mania', see D. Tripathi, *The Oxford History of Indian Business* (New Delhi: Oxford University Press, 2004), 55–56. Also see D. E. Wacha, *A Financial Chapter in the History of Bombay City* (Bombay: Commercial, 1910).
142. *Bombay Saturday Review* 3 (April 1862): 22, cited in Logan, 'India's Loss of the British Cotton Market', 40–50, 42.
143. BL, IOR, H/374, passim, cited in Bowen, 'British Exports of Raw Cotton', 129.
144. See Logan, 'India's Loss of the British Cotton Market', 40–50.
145. Bowen, 'British Exports of Raw Cotton', 127, 130.
146. Not to be confused with India's first knight and baronet and Parsi philanthropist Jamsetjee Jejeebhoy of Bombay, who anyway had considerable stake in the cotton economy of his times.
147. S. P. Mampatta and R. Bhayani, 'How Abraham Lincoln Triggered India's First Stock Market Crash', *Business Standard*, 22 July 2015, https://www.business-standard.com/article/beyond-business/150-years-later-115071001354_1.html (accessed on 17 July 2021).
148. *Amraoti Gazetteer*, 130.
149. At the peak of the American Civil War, cotton comprised less than one-tenths of the cultivated area in the districts of the Central Provinces for which figures were available. The Central Provinces, Administration Report, 1866–1867, 82.
150. On potential of the New Orleans variety in Berar, see ibid.,14–15.
151. Indian Famine Commission (1880), 299.
152. L. D. Satya, *Cotton and Famine in Berar 1850–1900* (New Delhi: Manohar, 1997), 81.
153. J. H. Rivett-Carnac, *Report on the Cotton Department for the year 1868-69* (Bombay: Education Society's Press, 1869), 52.

154. The share of cotton in the total area cultivated varied considerably in a year during the period of interest. It was typically around 40 per cent of the cultivated area. However, there were annual and regional variations.
155. Using analysis of twentieth-century famines such as the Great Bengal Famine of 1943, Sen argued that it was not food shortages that caused the famine but rather the decline of what he considered 'exchange entitlements'. See A. K. Sen, *Poverty and Famines: An Essay on Entitlement and Deprivation* (Oxford: Oxford University Press, 1982).
156. *Report of the Indian Famine Commission, 1898, Part 4, Central Provinces and Berar* (London: Her Majesty's Stationery Office, 1899), para. 153, 96, 191–193.
157. Ibid., 97.
158. J. B. Piele, 'Note on the Economic Condition of the Agricultural Population of India', in Indian Famine Commission (1881), 162.
159. J. Gray, *General Administration Report of Hyderabad Assigned Districts, 1856–57* (Calcutta: John Gray, 1858), para. 10; and J. Gray, *General Administration Report of Hyderabad Assigned Districts, 1861–62* (Calcutta: John Gray, 1863), para. 96.
160. See D. Thorner, 'The Pattern of Railway Development in India', *Far Eastern Quarterly* 14, no. 2 (1955): 201–206.
161. L. D. Satya, 'Colonial Encroachment and Popular Resistance: Land Survey and Settlement Operations in Berar (Central India), 1861–1877', *Agricultural History* 72, no. 1 (1998): 55–76. For details of formidable challenges and resistance to the survey and settlement operations in the region, see Satya, 'Colonial Encroachment and Popular Resistance', 84–86.
162. A. W. Silver, *Manchester Men and Indian Cotton, 1847–1872* (Manchester: Manchester University Press, 1966).
163. *General Administration Report on the Hyderabad Assigned Districts for the Year 1856–1857*, para. 10.
164. The *ryotwari* system was introduced in Madras, Bombay, and parts of Assam by Thomas Munro in 1820. Under this system, the peasants had proprietary rights on land. The revenue rate varied from 50 per cent to 60 per cent depending on whether the land was unirrigated or irrigated, respectively. The *zamindari* system, introduced by Lord Cornwallis in Bengal, Bihar, Odisha, and Varanasi through the Permanent Settlement Act of 1793, differed from the *zamindari* system of the Mughal period in the sense that the landlords became owners of the land in perpetuity rather than being just intermediaries for revenue collection. They were permitted

to rent out lands to tenant farmers and retain one out of eleven parts of the produce, with the rest shared with the state. See J. B. Fuller, *Introduction to the Land Revenue and Settlement Systems of the Central Provinces* (Nagpur: Government Press, 1922, reprint).

165. J. H. Rivett-Carnac, *Many Memories of Life in India at Home and Abroad* (Scarborough; London: Blackwood and Sons, 1910), 148. For a recent work on techno-politics of irrigation in colonial times in Bombay Deccan, refer to A. Tozzi, S. Bouzarovski, and C. Henry, 'Colonizing the Rains: Disentangling More-Than-Human Technopolitics of Drought Protection in the Archive', *Geoforum* 135: 12–24.
166. There is an interesting debate in development economics on the classification of land revenue system of the former Central Provinces. Although there is evidence of differences in historical colonial land revenue systems explaining the current state of agricultural development in the context of the Central Provinces, new research has shown that the differences arise out of misinterpretation of the land revenue of the Central Provinces.
167. Elphinstone was the survey chief from 1862 to 1870.
168. Satya, *Cotton and Famine in Berar*, 62. At that point of time in Berar, one *bigha* was little more than two-thirds of an acre.
169. 'Central Provinces and Berar: A Review of the Administration of the Province, 1921–1923', part 2, para. 219.
170. Satya, *Cotton and Famine in Berar*, 65.
171. The Census of 1891 indicates that the population of *bhagindar*s were more than twice that of the *khatedar*s.
172. *Report on the Administration of Hyderabad Assigned Districts for the Year 1882–1883* (Hyderabad: Residency Government Press), para. 25; 'Central Provinces and Berar, 1921–1923', part 2, para. 221.
173. *Watandar* grants of land or share of village revenue were hereditary and rent free whereas *inamdar* was land granted as gift to recognize past services to the state. The latter was a perpetual grant whereas the former was not. A. R. Kulkarni, 'The Mahar Watan: A Historical Perspective', in *Intersections: Socio-Cultural Trends in Maharashtra*, ed. Meera Kosambi (London: Sangam, 2000), 121–140.
174. *Report of the Famine Commission 1880, London: 1881*, cited in L. D. Satya, *Cotton and Famine in Berar 1850–1900* (New Delhi: Manohar, 1997), 79.
175. Ibid., 78–83.

176. J. H. Morris, *Report on the Administration of the Central Provinces, for the Year 1912–1913*, 9.
177. See *Gazetteer of Yavatmal*, https://cultural.maharashtra.gov.in/english/gazetteer/YAVATMAL/agri_tenures.html (accessed on 3 February 2020).
178. *Central Provinces District Gazetteers: Buldana Gazetteer* (Calcutta: Baptist Mission Press, 1910), 368–369.
179. See C. R. Reddy, 'The Incidence of Agricultural Labourers in India: Variations over Time and Space (with a Study of Varhad in Maharashtra)' (doctoral dissertation, Jawaharlal Nehru University, New Delhi, 1990), 183, table 6.2.
180. Satya, *Cotton and Famine in Berar*, 81.
181. This increase could be partly due to the improvements in the coverage of census as noted in T. Dyson, ed., *Studies in Famine, Disease and Society*, 1st ed. (London: Routledge, 1989), 168–169, table 1.
182. Satya, *Cotton and Famine in Berar*, 72, table 3.
183. Ibid., 80.
184. I. Klein, 'British Reforms, Commercial Agriculture, and Agrarian Distress in India', *The Historian* 70, no. 4 (2008): 732–752, 743.
185. Reddy, 'The Incidence of Agricultural Labourers in India', 213, table 6.13.
186. A. C. Lyall, *Gazetteer of Haidarbad Assigned Districts* (New Delhi: Archaeological Survey of India, 1870), 136.
187. *Amraoti Gazetteer*, 295.
188. Chandu Lal was deputy prime minister of Hyderabad State from 1809–1832, and *diwan* (prime minister) from 1832–1843. He turned over the Hyderabad Contingent, originally part of the nizam's military forces in Berar to the Company. The nizam had to pay the contingent without using them, compelling him to build his own forces to counter it. Revenue from Berar financed these forces. K. Leonard, 'Palmer and Company: An Indian Banking Firm in Hyderabad State', *Modern Asian Studies* 47, no. 4 (2013): 1157–1184, 1160–1163.
189. Thorner, 'The Pattern of Railway Development in India'.
190. D. Thorner, 'Capital Movement and Transportation: Great Britain and the Development of India's Railways', *Journal of Economic History* 11, no. 4 (1951): 389–402, 389.
191. R. P. Bhambi, *The Great Indian Peninsula Railway: A Journey Through Time (1853–1871)* (New Delhi: Bharti Publications, 2016), 23–31.
192. He was also the author of the book *Cotton and Commerce in India*.

193. For evolution of the ownership and financing aspects of the Indian Railways in its first wave of expansion, see D. Bogart and L. Chaudhary, 'Railways in Colonial India: An Economic Achievement?', in *A New Economic History of India*, ed. L. Chaudhary, B. Gupta, T. Roy, and A.V. Swamy (New Delhi: Routledge, 2015), 140–160. For insights on financial infrastructure in developing countries through the evidence from the Railway era, see B. Eichengreen, 'Financing Infrastructure in Developing Countries: Lessons from the Railway Age', *World Bank Research Observer* 10, no. 1 (1995): 75–91.
194. See D. H. Buchanan, *The Development of Capitalistic Enterprise in India* (New York: The Macmillan Company, 1934), 196.
195. For studies on price convergence, see J. Hurd II, 'Railways and the Expansion of Markets in India, 1861–1921', *Explorations in Economic History* 12, no. 3 (1975): 263–288; M. B. McAlpin, 'Railroads, Prices and Peasant Rationality: India, 1860–1900', *Journal of Economic History* 34, no. 3 (1974): 662–684; and D. Donaldson, 'Railroads and the Raj: Estimating the Economic Impact of Transportation Infrastructure', *American Economic Review* 108, nos. 4/5 (2018): 899–934. For evidence against price convergence, see T. Andrabi and M. Kuehlwein, 'Railways and Price Convergence in British India', *Journal of Economic History* 70, no. 2 (2010): 351–377.
196. Satya, *Cotton and Famine in Berar*, 284.
197. Miller, 'The Central Provinces', 611–630, 623.
198. Watson, 'On the Growth of Cotton in India', 282.
199. Ibid., 282.
200. Rivett-Carnac, *Report on the Cotton Department*, 28.
201. Satya, *Cotton and Famine in Berar*, 173.
202. P. Harnetty, 'Crop Trends in the Central Provinces of India, 1861–1921', *Modern Asian Studies* 11, no. 2 (1977): 341-377, 355.
203. Rivett-Carnac, *Report of the Cotton Department*, 11, 13, 131.
204. Alfred Comyn Lyall, ed., *Gazetteer for the Haidarabad Assigned Districts*, Commonly Called Berar, 1870 (Bombay, 1870), 137, cited in S. Beckert, 'Emancipation and Empire: Reconstructing the Worldwide Web of Cotton Production in the Age of the American Civil War', *American Historical Review* 109, no. 5 (2004): 1405–1438.
205. How low investment in human capital by the British sustained existing hierarchies in the country and how it provided very few avenues for vertical mobility across classes and only made horizontal mobility within the classes

are dealt with in Klein, 'British Reforms, Commercial Agriculture, and Agrarian Distress in India'.

206. 1 bhoja = 280 pounds.

207. Rivett-Carnac, *Report on the Cotton Department*, 132–133.

208. Cotton report for the Hyderabad Assigned Districts, 8, cited in Sumit Guha, 'Commodity and Credit in Upland Maharashtra, 1800–1950', *Economic and Political Weekly* 22, no. 52 (1987a): A126–A140.

209. Letter no. 979, from Nago Rao Jeyakrishna, Assistant Cotton Commissioner, East Berar, to Deputy Commissioner, Oomraottee District, Oomraottee, dated 24 June 1872, in the Proceedings of the Hyderabad Administration for the month of October 1874, submitted to the Home Department, no. 99, 26 October 1874. Cited in Satya, *Cotton and Famine in Berar*, 235.

210. Satya, *Cotton and Famine in Berar*, 204. Though the dominant moneylenders in the region were Marwaris and Banias, there were also moneylenders belonging to other social groups—Brahmins, Kunbis, Khatris, Telis, Sonars, and Muhamadans, Agarwals, Bhatias, Chhatrapuris, Bhoras, Pathans, Afghans, and Rohillas. Refer to C. Brown and R. V. Russell, eds., *Central Provinces District Gazetteers (Facsimile Reproduction): Yeotmal District*, vol. A (Government Photozinco Press: Pune), https://indianculture.gov.in/gazettes/central-provinces-district-gazetteers-facsimile-reproduction-yeotmal-district-1908-vol (accessed on 24 May 2021), 382. Apart from this, some of the wealthy farmers also lent to other tenants and farmers. See Satya, *Cotton and Famine in Berar*, 218.

211. For a detailed description of this point, refer to Guha, 'Commodity and Credit in Upland Maharashtra'; S. Guha, 'The Land Market in Upland Maharashtra c. 1820-1960-I', *Indian Economic and Social History Review* 24, no. 2 (1987b): 117–144. This finding largely pertains to the Bombay Deccan region and its applicability to the Central Provinces and Berar is questioned in Satya, *Cotton and Famine in Berar*.

212. Ibid., 224–225, 246.

213. *Maharashtra Gazetteers*, 382–383.

214. Ibid., 403. For details of moneylending in the region before India's independence and early decades of post-independence, see https://gazetteers.maharashtra.gov.in/cultural.maharashtra.gov.in/english/gazetteer/WARDHA/bank_money_lenders.html (accessed on 23 December 2021).

215. S. Sukhtankar, 'Sweetening the Deal? Political Connections and Sugar Mills in India', *American Economic Journal: Applied Economics* 4, no. 3 (2012): 43–63.

216. For doubts about the veracity of the commonly believed establishment year to be 1818, and archival evidence on Bowreah Cotton Mills as well as Fort Gloster Jute Mills, see S. Rungta, 'Bowreah Cotton and Fort Gloster Jute Mills, 1872–1900', *Indian Economic and Social History Review* 22, no. 2 (1985): 109–137.
217. Ibid., 111.
218. S. B. Upadhyay, 'Cotton Mill Workers in Bombay, 1875 to 1918: Conditions of Work and Life', *Economic and Political Weekly* 25, no. 30 (1990): PE87–PE99.
219. M. D. Morris, *The Emergence of an Industrial Labour Force in India: A Study of the Bombay Cotton Mills, 1854–1947* (Berkeley; Los Angeles: University of California Press, 1965); and Upadhyay, 'Cotton Mill Workers in Bombay'.
220. See R. Chandavarkar, 'The Decline and Fall of the Jobber System in the Bombay Cotton Textile Industry, 1870–1955', *Modern Asian Studies* 42, no. 1 (2008): 117–210.
221. Initial investment in the mill was half a million rupees at 1853 prices. The mill began production on 7 February 1856 under the supervision of British engineers and skilled cotton operatives. P. Mantoux, 'The Beginnings of Machinery in the Textile Industry', in *The Industrial Revolution in the Eighteenth Century: An Outline of the Beginnings of the Modern Factory System in England* (Oxfordshire: Routledge, 1963), 212.
222. H. Spodek, 'The "Manchesterisation" of Ahmedabad', *Economic and Political Weekly* 17, no. 11 (1965): 485–486.
223. Even the Ahmedabad Stock Exchange was set up in 1894, much later than the BSE.
224. The mill was rechristened as the Empress Mills on 1 January 1877; the day Queen Victoria was proclaimed the empress of India. While easy access to coal, water, railways, and cheap land drove the decision to locate the industry, the mill is legendary for Jamsetji's adoption of innovation and foresight. See https://www.tata.com/newsroom/through-the-mill (accessed on 22 December 2021).
225. J. H. Morris, *Report on the Administration of the Central Provinces for the Year 1902–03*, n.d., 12.
226. J. H. Morris, *Report on the Administration of the Central Provinces for the Year 1903–04*, n.d., 26.
227. Bachhraj Bajaj and his wife adopted Jamnalal Bajaj, the founder of the Bajaj industrial conglomerate, as their grandson. Jamnalal Bajaj learned the ropes about cotton trading after inheriting Bachhraj Bajaj's business and was a

close associate of Mahatma Gandhi while he was at Sevagram. Gandhi adopted Jamnalal as his son. Today, the Bajaj Foundation is involved in several developmental initiatives in the district.

228. Morris, *The Emergence of an Industrial Labor Force in India*, 62–63.
229. Ibid., 65–68.
230. For an excellent socio-cultural description of life in 'Girangaon'—mill village—where most mills of Bombay were located, see R. Chandavarkar, *The Origins of Industrial Capitalism: Business Strategies and the Working Classes in Bombay, 1900–1940* (Cambridge: Cambridge University Press, 1994). Also see, D. D'Monte, *Mills for Sale* (Mumbai: Marg Publications, 2006). For a novel interactive archive of the mill district of Bombay through the eyes of workers and residents, see 'Mythologies of Mumbai' (interactive documentary, HELM), https://www.helmstudio.org/portfolio_page/mythologies-of-mumbai/ (accessed on 8 March 2021).
231. For a contemporary account of the cotton mill industry, see D. E. Wacha, 'Indian Cotton and the Cotton-Mill Industry', *Journal of the Royal Society of Arts* 66, no. 3426 (1918): 544–564.
232. See despatch dated 29 October 1917 from the commercial attaché to the British Embassy, E. F. Crow addressed to C. Greene at the British Embassy. On 1 November 1917, Greene, in a letter to the Foreign Office at London, conveys the importance of substituting American cotton by Indian cotton given the state of crisis Japanese cotton industry.
233. See 'Further Papers from the R and A Department Regarding the Appointment of a Committee in India to investigate the Possibility of Increasing the Production of Long Stapled Cotton in India', Department of Commerce and Industries, National Archives of India (1918a), PR_000004008643, file no. 25, 1–2.
234. 'Papers Regarding the Import of Cotton into Japan from India', PR_000004008644, file no. 7, National Archives of India (1918b), accessed through *Abhilekh Patal*.
235. During World War I, there were substantial crop losses due to heavy monsoon in 1917 and outbreak of the plague epidemic between August 1917 and January 1918, resulting in workers being offered a 'Plague Bonus' equivalent to 80 per cent of their wages to keep them from quitting work. See H. Spodek, *Ahmedabad: Shock City of Twentieth-Century India* (Bloomington, IN: Indiana University Press, 2011).
236. Mahatma Gandhi made the Sabarmati Ashram at Ahmedabad his base from 1915 to 1931. His championing of the Swadeshi movement gave a

significant boost to the industrial development and optimism in the city. Following the end of World War I, Ahmedabad saw a phenomenal growth of cotton manufacturing.

237. Based on the description of the 1918 labour strike in Ahmedabad as described in https://nvdatabase.swarthmore.edu/content/ahmedabad-textile-laborers-win-strike-economic-justice-1918 (accessed on 15 January 2021).
238. See S. B. Upadhyay, 'Communalism and Working Class: Riot of 1893 in Bombay City', *Economic and Political Weekly* 24, no. 30 (1989): PE69–PE75.
239. In 1918, excess mortality due to fever and respiratory diseases was over 1 million in the Bombay Presidency and 941,076 in the Central Provinces, compared to 1913–1917. See I. D. Mills, 'The 1918–1919 Influenza Pandemic. The Indian Experience', *Indian Economic and Social History Review* 23, no. 1 (1986): 1–40, 39.
240. See P. Parthasarathi and I. Wendt (2012: 401–405), for succinct account of the links between decline of Indian cotton industry and nationalism.
241. In the post-independence period, the Indian National Trade Union Congress (INTUC) created the Rasthriya Mill Mazdoor Sangh (RMMS) that sided with mill owners during industrial disputes of the 1950s to the 1970s. Decades later, the Great Bombay Textile Strike of 1982 under the aegis of GKU resulted in shutting down of nearly fifty mills. This marked the decimation of Bombay's cotton mills.
242. Guha, 'Raw Cotton of Western India'.
243. Farnie, *The English Cotton Industry*, 135–170.
244. Leacock and Mandelbaum, 'A Nineteenth Century Development Project in India', 334–351, 338–339.
245. S. Hazareesingh, '"Your Foreign Plants Are Very Delicate": Peasant Crop Ecologies and the Subversion of Colonial Cotton Designs in Dharwar, Western India, 1830–1880', in *Local Subversions of Colonial Cultures: Commodities and Anti-commodities in Global History*, ed. S. Hazareesingh and H. Maat, Cambridge Imperial and Post-colonial Studies Series (London: Palgrave Macmillan, 2016), 97–124.
246. Watson, 'On the Growth of Cotton in India', 283.
247. *Jari* was a taller variety and had larger number of bolls compared to *bani* but the latter's bolls were larger, and owing to its export demand, fetched a higher price per *khandi* (candy). Captain Meadows Taylor spells *bani* and *jari* as *bhunnee* and *jhurree*, respectively. He mentions that the former grows on the gravelly soil, and the latter on rich black soil. See M. Taylor, 'Sketch of the Topography of East and West Berar, in Reference to the Production

of Cotton', *Journal of the Royal Asiatic Society of Great Britain and Ireland* 20 (1863): 5.

248. *Indian Cotton Report* (1913), 129, https://archive.org/details/indiancotton00inte/page/128/mode/1up?view=theater (accessed on 8 August 2020).
249. Average values are averages of cleaned cotton (lint) on 'newly ploughed virgin soil' based on an average of the lower and upper bounds of yield (in pounds) by variety from *panchayat*s of all *taluka*s. The averages were much lower for lands already growing cotton. 1 pound = 0.453 kilogram. Ibid., 6.
250. *Buri*'s lint was comparable to that of *bani*. The former had a lint–seed ratio of 33 compared to 26 for the latter. It also fetched 50 per cent higher value than *jari*. See *Gazetteer of Buldhana*, https://gazetteers.maharashtra.gov.in/cultural.maharashtra.gov.in/english/gazetteer/Buldhana%20District/agriculture_crops.html# (accessed on 25 November 2020).
251. Ibid.
252. For example, see *Report on the Administration of the Central Provinces, for the Year 1902–03*, 10.
253. Harnetty, 'Crop Trends in the Central Provinces of India', 341–377, 359.
254. *Report of the Indian Cotton Committee*, 1919, 62, https://archive.org/details/reportoftheindia031916mbp/page/n5/mode/2up (accessed on 28 March 2021).
255. *Report on the Administration of the Central Provinces for the Year 1903–04*, 24.
256. J. A. Voelcker, *Report on the Improvement of Indian Agriculture* (London: Eyre and Spottiswoode, 1893).
257. See R. Kumar, *Rethinking Revolutions: Soyabean, Choupals, and the Changing Countryside in Central India* (New Delhi: Oxford University Press, 2016), 113–120, for an excellent discussion on the evolution of the colonial and American emphasis on productivity and efficiency logic in agricultural policy that influence post-independence agricultural policies in India considerably.
258. Beckert, *Empire of Cotton*, 314–315.
259. *Report on the Administration of the Central Provinces for the Year 1903–04*, 26.
260. *Report on the Administration of the Central Provinces for the Year 1902–03*, 12.
261. Ibid., 6.
262. *Report on the Administration of the Central Provinces for the Year 1903–04*, 11.
263. Ibid., 11.
264. Ibid., 32.
265. Ibid., 12.

266. P. L. Pingali, 'Green Revolution: Impacts, Limits, and the Path Ahead', *PNAS* 109, no. 31 (2012): 12302–12308.
267. K. R. Nanekar, *Land Reforms in the Vidarbha Region: An Enquiry into the Implementation of Land Reforms in the Vidarbha Region* (Calcutta: Oxford and IBH Publishing Company, 1968); V. M. Rao, 'Land Transfers in Rural Communities: Some Findings in a Rayatwari Region', *Economic and Political Weekly* 7, no. 40 (1972).
268. N. Rajasekaran, 'Land Reforms in Maharashtra: A Regional Analysis', *Review of Development and Change* 3, no. 2 (1998): 238–263.
269. A. Gulati, 'Effective Incentives and Subsidies for Cotton Cultivators in India', *Economic and Political Weekly* 22, no. 52 (1987): A177–A179, A181–A187.
270. For early narratives in the Bt cotton debate a decade ago, see D. Glover, 'Exploring the Resilience of Bt Cotton's "Pro-poor Success Story"', *Development and Change* 41, no. 6 (2010a): 955–981; D. Glover, 'The Corporate Shaping of GM Crops as a Technology for the Poor', *Journal of Peasant Studies* 37, no. 1 (2010b): 67–90; D. Glover, 'Is Bt Cotton a Pro-poor Technology? A Review and Critique of the Empirical Record', *Journal of Agrarian Change* 10, no. 4 (2010c): 482–509. There were heated debates around introducing Bt brinjal (eggplant) in India but given the uncertainty around its effects, there was an embargo on its commercial release. See V. V. Krishna and M. Qaim, 'Estimating the Adoption of Bt Eggplant in India: Who Benefits from Public–Private Partnership?', *Food Policy* 32, nos. 5/6 (2007): 523–543; V. V. Krishna and M. Qaim, 'Potential Impacts of Bt Eggplant on Economic Surplus and Farmers' Health in India', *Agricultural Economics* 38, no. 2 (2008): 167–180.
271. For critical perspective on microfinance in terms of technological improvements, see P. Chavan and R. Ramkumar, 'Micro-credit and Rural Poverty: An Analysis of Empirical Evidence', *Economic and Political Weekly* 37, no. 10 (2002): 955–965.
272. R. Ramkumar and M. Chavan, 'Bank Credit to Agriculture in India in the 2000s: Dissecting the Revival', *Review of Agrarian Studies* 4, no. 1 (2014), http://www.ras.org.in/bank_credit_to_agriculture_in_india_in_the_2000s (accessed on 19 September 2020).
273. For details of farm suicides in the Vidarbha and Marathwada regions of Maharashtra, refer to D. Talule, 'Farmer Suicides in Maharashtra, 2001–2018: Trends across Marathwada and Vidarbha', *Economic and Political*

Weekly 55, no. 10 (2020): 116–125; also see S. Mishra, 'Farmers' Suicides in Maharashtra', *Economic and Political Weekly* 41, no. 16 (2006): 1538–1545; D. N. Reddy and S. Mishra, eds., *Agrarian Crisis in India* (Nagpur: Oxford University Press, 2010).

274. See B. B. Mohanty and S. Shroff, 'Farmers' Suicides in Maharashtra', *Economic and Political Weekly* 39, no. 52 (2004): 5599–5606; B. B. Mohanty, 'Farmer Suicides in India: Durkheim's Types', *Economic and Political Weekly* 48, no. 21 (2013): 45–54; N. Kumar, 'Egoism, Anomie and Masculinity: Suicide in Rural South India (Andhra Pradesh)' (PhD thesis, London School of Economics and Political Science, 2011).
275. See P. Parthasarathi and I. Wendt, 'Decline in Three Keys: Indian Cotton Manufacturing from the Late Eighteenth Century', in *The Spinning World: A Global History of Cotton Textiles, 1200-1850*, ed. G. Riello and P. Parthasarathi (Delhi: Primus Books, 2012), 398–407.
276. K. Marx, 'The Eighteenth Brumaire of Louis Bonaparte', 1852, https://www.marxists.org/archive/marx/works/1852/18th-brumaire/ch01.htm (accessed on 10 April 2021). Also see J. Brien, 'The Role of Causation in History', *History in the Making* 2, no. 1 (2013): 78–79.
277. For the *malguzari* system in the Narmada valley of the Central Provinces, and market developments in the wheat and paddy system, see C. Bates, 'Class and Economic Change in Central India: The Narmada Valley 1820–1930', in *Arrested Development in India: The Historical Dimension*, ed. Clive Dewey (New Delhi: Manohar, 1988); R. Bates, 'Regional Dependence and Rural Development in Central India: The Pivotal Role of Migrant Labour', *Modern Asian Studies* 19, no. 3 (1985): 573–592.
278. E. H. Carr, *What Is History?* (London: Penguin, 1961), 85.
279. Brien, 'The Role of Causation in History', 80.
280. D. Mukherjee, *Bombay Hustle: Making Movies in a Colonial City* (New York: Columbia University Press, 2020).
281. Satya, *Cotton and Famine in Berar*.
282. Satya, 'Colonial Encroachment and Popular Resistance', 55–76.
283. Parsis dominated the cotton trade in all aspects: spinning, weaving, and dyeing. Surat was the hub for the textile market due to its proximity to towns teeming with weaving, such as Navsari and Bardoli. It was also served by far-off places along the important inland trade routes of the times. The Banias paid advance to Indian intermediaries who procured finished cloth from the weaver. The European factors did not command

such control over the supplies of raw cotton and cloth as they did not have commercial ties with farmers and weavers further inland. Among the merchant communities, the Marwaris were averse to anti-usury regulations. They were dominant moneylenders and stood to lose from stringent measures. Marwari families with loyalty to the British during the Revolt of 1857 and later periods made considerable commercial gains from their loyalty.

PART II

3

FIELD AND FIELDWORK

The two preceding chapters provided an expansive historical background of Vidarbha and elucidated the transformation of its cotton economy. The colonial takeover resulted in the dismantling of traditional institutions such as *balutedari* and introduction of the *khatedari* system that bestowed property rights on the farmers who became central to the revenue of the state. With expansion of railways, there was growth of 'cotton towns' along the railroads such as Khamgaon and Murtizapur (in present-day Akola) as well as market towns such as Amravati and Akola. The local economy was stimulated by the American Civil War but with later changes such as crackdown on usury; and introduction of courts, Vidarbha became increasingly integrated with global markets in a manner that increased dependence of the farmers and agricultural labourers on cash and credit. Consequently, the colonial state's attempts to settle cultivators for cotton expansion irrevocably altered the rhythms of Vidarbha society.

Communities such as the Banjaras, who were pivotal in the movement of raw cotton and food grains on carts and pack bullocks, lost out with the expansion of railways and decline of the cattle economy in the second half of the nineteenth century. They were also coerced into settling down for cotton cultivation by the colonial state that was suspicious of their mobility. Mobility restrictions for Banjara communities based on 'pass system' became increasingly punitive, thereby adversely impacting the culture of fairs and bazaars in the region that had been facilitated by logistics services offered by the Banjaras.[1] We also briefly described the developments since India's independence in the context of the plight and predicament of cotton farmers of the region that has been the epicentre of farmers' suicides in the past twenty-five years.

As seen in Chapter 2, in the late nineteenth century, the region was ravaged by famines, crushing revenue demands, widespread undernourishment, disease, and mortality, but farmers' suicides were unheard of. Indeed, the American Civil War–induced boom in the cotton economy made fortunes for many in Vidarbha as well as Bombay, but it also marred fortunes owing to crashes and panics. Moreover, far from having similar impacts on different communities in Vidarbha society, the cotton boom generated unprecedented wealth for merchants, traders, moneylenders, and large *khatedar*s in particular. Kunbi peasants and agricultural labourers, on the other hand, were even more vulnerable to food inflation and adverse income shocks as traditional forms of social insurance weakened.

The colonial state's indifference to investment in irrigation as well as the political economy of the late nineteenth and early twentieth centuries contributed to decadence of the cotton economy. Despite the troubles, the region's tryst with cotton continued well into the early twentieth century with rising Japanese demand for raw cotton. Cotton was crucial in the economy when Gandhi set up his residential ashram near Wardha in 1936, and it continues to be so several decades later.[2] Of course, a long historical perspective aids in identifying multiple causes and accidental turning points that may explain phenomena such as the allure of cotton in the region. However, contemporary first-hand account of the developments in the recent past offers an opportunity to delve into the facets of continuity and change, and dwell upon relatively proximate events. While the knowledge of society, economy, and politics is essential for studying contemporary circumstances and choices of actors, valuable insights emerge from first-hand observations and data gathered over an extended period. In this chapter, following a rather unusual approach, we bridge our narrative of the past and present by introducing our study that began with the objective of understanding the gambles with cotton, and in doing so, the story of risk and vulnerability of agricultural households in Vidarbha that has entered its thirteenth year at the time of writing.

When we began our doctoral research, having worked on issues in the microinsurance sector, farmers' suicides in Vidarbha troubled us as we presumed it was the outcome of a collective failure to insure unmitigated risks. In an attempt to find answers to our questions about risk and vulnerability of agricultural households in Vidarbha, what began as an exploratory fieldwork in 2008 took the form of an ongoing study that we have been administering across villages. In our research spanning over twelve years from 2009 to 2021, we have administered several rounds of surveys and conducted fieldwork in the districts that witnessed the astounding changes described at length in the preceding chapters. In all these rounds, the overarching objective pertained to the theme of risk and vulnerability of agricultural households in the region. Nonetheless, our enquiries espoused a holistic perspective on the region, its people, culture, climate, politics, and of course, history that informed the two preceding chapters. Much of our discussion in this part of the book draws upon our findings over the period. These surveys have not only enriched our understanding of lives and livelihoods associated with Vidarbha cotton but have also been a source of considerable learning about the challenges involved in administering longitudinal study in a village setting.

In this chapter we present the rationale for our research methodology and describe the characteristics of the villages and households that are part of our study. We also articulate our motivation for conducting the study and our vision to conduct longitudinal village-level studies (VLS) that aims to complement the decades of evidence on agrarian transformation and economic development from large-scale longitudinal studies by institutions such as the International Crops Research Institute for the Semi-Arid Tropics (ICRISAT) or the National Council of Applied Economic Research (NCAER) among others. Without doubt, the kind of research undertaking we embarked upon entails several intellectual choices, and we believe it is crucial to present a thumbnail sketch of the same. In this regard, we concur with Maurice Punch when he says: 'But we are often left in the dark as to the personal and intellectual path that led researchers to drop one line of inquiry and pursue another. We require more intellectual autobiographies to clarify why academics end up studying what they do.'[3] This chapter is written with the intent of explaining why we ended up studying what we did and how we went about it.

The remainder of this chapter is structured as follows. We begin by elaborating the methodological considerations that have guided our research along with the challenges that we faced in operationalizing it. We delve into the rationale for our choice of unit of analysis and method of data collection. As we progress, we explain the thematic focus of investigation in different rounds of our surveys. In addition, we present details of the village setting: profile of the villages from which the households were sampled as well as household-level summary statistics that help characterize the setting of our longitudinal study. Last but not least, we discuss various challenges we faced in the collection and analysis of data over the years, and our attempts at circumventing them.

METHODOLOGICAL CONSIDERATIONS

As discussed in the genesis of the book in the Introduction, our studies on cotton farmers in Vidarbha began as part of our doctoral research from a quantitative methodological perspective informed by mainstream literature on farmers' decision-making under risk and uncertainty. Our initial explorations were planned as empirical investigations from a hypothetico-deductive paradigm. We began with an urge to 'model' the decision-making and 'test' hypotheses that our training suggested. However, experiences during fieldwork and pilot studies in 2008–2009 in the region convinced us about the limitations of viewing the phenomena of interest: decisions of farmers, risk, vulnerability, and agricultural development, exclusively through the lens of mainstream economics; replete with its deductive paradigms.[4]

Back then, our exposure to qualitative research was also limited as our training took place in an academic milieu that valued quantitative over qualitative pursuits. Moreover, as the effects of the global financial crisis began fading away from public consciousness, big data analytics and advanced econometric methods were gaining popularity.[5] Gradually it became apparent that unpacking the underlying processes and choices by decision-makers in an agrarian setting called for a deeper engagement rather than taking recourse to a cross-sectional survey or evaluation of a programme. That deeper engagement took shape in the form of a longitudinal study in the villages of Wardha and Yavatmal—districts of Vidarbha. In our bid to benefit from the complementarities of quantitative and qualitative research as social scientists, our research design evolved to accommodate structured questionnaires, unstructured questionnaires, and ethnography. We relied on semi-structured interviews and focus group discussions (FGDs) as well as structured questionnaires to gather data. Our broad research programme necessitated 'understanding' as well as 'explaining' phenomena rather than a singular focus on meaning-making or hypothesis-testing.

Since our first field visit to Wardha in 2008, before the first round of surveys began, we decided to follow quantitative and qualitative research, albeit without committing to a specific mode of mixing the two. This decision was motivated by the following reasons. First, given the centrality of understanding the risk and vulnerability of agricultural households over a period, quantification of inputs to the production process and outcomes in agriculture and livelihood would allow tracking intertemporal variations. Information on household characteristics could be correlated with the constructs of interest. Data such as agricultural inputs, cost of cultivation, crop yields, loss distribution, household expenditure and consumption patterns are amenable to quantitative analysis. Second, qualitative research in the form of ethnography and FGDs had the promise of complementing the explanatory ability based on quantitative exercises. Every visit to the villages reaffirmed our belief that the insights from the field would also deepen understanding. Indeed, there is no novelty in this approach, as such complementarities from multi-strategy as well as multidisciplinary studies have long been argued to be of considerable value in similar inquires.

'Underscoring the emphasis on fieldwork, we were influenced by the perspective that fieldwork comprises more than data collection.'[6] Fieldwork at different stages of our research allowed a 'thick-description' of the social setting—one of the most valuable components of our research.[7] However, given the nature of inquiries in agricultural economics—the primary focus of our research—we prioritized surveys for analysing agricultural outcomes in conjunction with circumstances of households involving their demography, caste, assets and liabilities, cropping patterns, cost of cultivation, production, value of products and by-products, incomes, and labour supply among other things. Following iterations based on feedback from pilot testing, survey questionnaires were finalized. All questionnaires were in the vernacular, Marathi. Although our working knowledge of Marathi helped us in striking conversations and comprehending detailed responses, resident investigators came to our rescue whenever dialects varied across areas of two districts. Typically, villagers in Wardha were more comfortable conversing in Hindi relatively to their counterparts in Yavatmal. During the longitudinal study, we also attempted to measure risk attitudes and perceptions. We even conducted a randomized control trial (RCT). Table 3.1 presents details of the information captured through the survey instruments and qualitative inquiries over the period of primary research.

Although much of what we report in the following chapters are based on our quantitative analysis, the latter was immensely shaped by our insights from the qualitative research. Moreover, our interpretations of findings from quantitative analysis as well as ecological validation relied on insights gathered during fieldwork over the years. Before discussing further aspects

Table 3.1 Survey rounds, villages, and survey instruments

Rounds of Survey	Year	Villages Covered	Survey Modules
Round 1	2009–2012	5 villages in Wardha district	Household demographics, risk attitudes, cultivation inputs and outputs (plot level), assets and liabilities, livestock, consumption expenditure, risk perceptions, risk coping mechanisms
Round 2	2015–2018	16 villages in Wardha and Yavatmal districts	Household demographics, cultivation inputs and outputs (plot level), land, liabilities, pesticide use, perceptions of pesticide use
Round 3	2019–2021	10 villages in Wardha and Yavatmal districts	Household demographics, cultivation inputs and outputs (plot level), land, assets and liabilities, livestock, consumption expenditure for cultivator and non-cultivator households, risk perceptions, risk coping mechanisms
Special Surveys			
Input Dealer Survey	2017–2018	Wardha city	Market insights, perception survey, pesticide inventory
Basis Risk (RCT)	2018	6 villages in Wardha and Yavatmal districts	Weather insurance adoption
Women Participation in Socio-economic Activities (Qualitative Study)	2019–2020	10 villages in Wardha and Yavatmal districts	Agency of women, participation in public life, employment constraints, health and nutrition including reproductive and child health (RCH) issues
COVID-19 Survey (Qualitative Study)	2020	6 villages in Wardha and Yavatmal districts	Coping with COVID-19 pandemic, migration

Source: Authors' compilation.

of our longitudinal study, we recall an important epistemological lesson that stayed with us throughout. While undertaking our investigations, we not only experienced but also were constantly reminded of the following comment of Martin Shubik:

> The study of risk in different societies, given what we know at this time from the social sciences, is much like the theme of the film Rashomon, where a murder was reported and re-enacted through the eyes of several different witnesses and the murdered man himself.[8]

While studying a village society or the village economy, we present our interpretations based on our observations. However, wherever quantitative insights are not available, the interpretations may not be undermined along the lines of the situation in the movie *Rashomon*. Furthermore, our knowledge of the history of the region and that of cotton that was covered in the last two chapters developed in response to questions that often erupted in the course of quotidian observations during fieldwork or ruminations while we were away from the field. In what follows, we describe the unit of analysis and administration of the surveys in the villages.

UNIT OF ANALYSIS

A preliminary concern in our research design related to the choice of the unit of analysis as to whether it should be the household or the village. The Indian 'village' has been an important site as well as object of study by anthropologists, sociologists, historians, and economists.[9] The village has been imagined as a microcosm of the changes taking place in the country.[10] Although village studies serve as a valuable historical record, that the village can be a representative unit for understanding Indian society has been critiqued.[11] A combination of quantitative approach and village case studies reveal the dynamics of rural transformations that are complex.[12] There have also been critical views on imagining villages as what Charles Metcalfe considered as 'little republics'.[13] These perspectives aside, village studies offer a deeper understanding of the process of rural transformation in general, and agrarian change in particular.[14]

Another fascinating feature of village studies is the vast literature on the revisits to the villages that scholars themselves surveyed in the past or those that were studied by other scholars.[15] In what may be considered as a intriguing approach to village studies, examining a single village over an extended period of time has also been an approach to understanding development and change. For instance, Palanpur—a well-known site for village studies in western Uttar Pradesh—was initially studied by the Agro-Economic Research Centre (AERC) of the University of Delhi in 1957–1958 and 1963–1964. This was followed by surveys in 1983–1984, 1993, 2008–2010.[16] In the context of Vidarbha, surprisingly, village studies administered by economists are scant.[17] There are few ethnographic studies by anthropologists and sociologists.[18] There are also several contributions by resolute journalists who have studied the agrarian issues in the region for a long period of time.[19] A few governmental inquiries into the agrarian crisis in the region present insights into the conditions in the villages of the region.[20]

Despite the intellectual tradition of village studies that could have allowed an intimate study of the village economy and the social phenomena, we chose households as the unit of analysis. To a large extent, we were heavily influenced by prior scholarship. Two studies had a lasting impression on us, and we envisioned our longitudinal research project in line with these detailed and long-running studies: ICRISAT's village-level studies—VDSA (Village Dynamics Studies in South Asia)—in India's semi-arid tropics in particular and the Townsend Thai Project.[21] Both these studies offer rich insights into household-level decision-making and the socio-economic and institutional context in which these decisions are made. The village profiles, though detailed, become secondary to the analysis of household data. Moreover, understanding heterogeneity in exposure to risk as well as risk management by households across different villages was of considerable interest. Therefore, we considered households as the unit of analysis. This form of longitudinal study nevertheless meant compromises in terms of merits of a deeper examination of a single village or extended field immersion. We will elaborate on these later.

METHOD OF DATA COLLECTION

Following exploratory visits to Vidarbha in the winter of 2008, we had a dilemma, namely whether to conduct a village census or sample surveys to address our research questions. A village census would undoubtedly generate data on all the households in the village(s) and also provide an opportunity to understand transactions among all the households in the study village(s).

It would further allow an understanding of relational aspects in the village society. However, typically this understanding comes with a census of few villages, even a single village such as Vilyatpur in Punjab or a pair of villages as in Harold H. Mann's studies in the Deccan, Maharashtra.[22]

Despite offering rich details of the village life and understanding its transformation, we believed that conducting a village census over an extended period would entail a trade-off with broader representativeness and require considerable resources, as we operated out of shoestring budgets in the absence of financial support in the early stages of our study.[23] Budgetary considerations aside, we believed that resorting to survey of households would be in line with the general strategy of the ICRISAT-VDSA and the Townsend-Thai Project mentioned earlier.[24] In this endeavour, fieldwork with dependence on our resident investigators was central to making sense of the village setting as well as developing ecologically valid interpretation of survey findings. On the question of representativeness, we assumed that a sample survey in the villages complemented with ecological validation from prolonged and extensive fieldwork would suffice given our research objectives. Having decided the unit of analysis and method of data collection, the strategy of research design narrowed down to the mechanics of collecting longitudinal data, which was essential to understanding changes over time. The uncertain environment and seasonality inherent in agriculture and village life meant collecting data at a single point of time will only provide a limited picture of intertemporal dynamics. It was evident to us that the chronicles of farmers having to indulge in the gambles year after year cannot be well captured by collecting data at only one time period. Common sense, insights from the literature and interactions with experts indicated that the vagaries of nature, market, actions of the state and the households are typically well understood through data collected over time. A longitudinal study also opens up the possibility to obtain panel data having observations on the same households over time, which allows for econometric analysis controlling for the year-specific and household-specific effects.

Compared to cross-sectional studies, longitudinal studies offer several advantages. First, they aid data quality through a process of continuous validation owing to the repeated visits. They allow verification of responses in a manner that is not feasible with a one-shot cross-sectional survey. The scope for multiple visits and extended stays in the field also obviates the need for long questionnaires as multiple visits with short questionnaires far outweigh the former in terms of quality of data. Apart from additional resources utilized (including time), painfully long questionnaires induce respondent fatigue. Second, they contribute to the completeness of the survey data. Repeated visits in the same as well as subsequent seasons allowed completing questions earlier left unanswered. Third, they are amenable to course correction based on feedback from the field. Lastly, from an econometric analysis perspective, longitudinal studies also allow the possibility of estimation using panel data, that is, having observations on the same households over time—data that allow analysis of both intra-household and inter-household variations unlike in cross-sectional or time-series data.

In hindsight, fieldwork within the setting of a longitudinal study taught us the importance of reflexivity. Reflexivity has allowed us to think critically about our research. The process of reflexivity nevertheless has been a source of discomfort many a time as we questioned our assumptions, data collection pathways, and overall judgment about the contours of the longitudinal study. Reflexivity has also helped us recognize the importance of carefully listening to what the stakeholders in our research have to say, rather than selectively seeking conformation of our priors. In doing so, we have often incorporated changes in our research design—aspects that we will describe in this chapter. In hindsight, we can confess that as students of economics with a quantitative indoctrination, temptations to quantify were difficult to resist. Our belief in the merit of fieldwork in the social sciences was a driving force in extending the duration of our longitudinal study nearly a decade beyond the end of our doctoral research.

Looking back on our approach to the research, we have understood that although we were involved in an active process of reflexivity, we did not resort to thematic analysis of the copious transcripts of text from our interviews as is standard in qualitative research despite having contemplated the same at different rounds. The reason for the same may be attributed to our approach of complementing the findings of the surveys with insights from fieldwork rather than dedicated qualitative research aimed at meaning making from the text data. Indeed, we consider this a missed opportunity in our research strategy but one that will be taken up in future research as described in Chapter 7. We would also like to clarify that we do not consider our research as mixed methods in the strictest sense as we did not follow the conventions of the mixed-methods strategy. From an analytical perspective, the methodology was critical for resisting our temptations to model farmers' decision-making from the neoclassical framework where rational choices entail utility maximization or profit maximization. To quip Kalyan Sanyal in this context, we avoided the following logic: 'Peasant behaviour is assumed to be guided by a utility function (with say, leisure and agricultural output as the arguments) where the first derivative is positive and the second derivative is negative and so on.'[25]

SURVEY ROUNDS

In the monsoon season of 2008, fieldwork in Wardha villages was motivated by broader questions about the agrarian crisis in Vidarbha, and a stupefying news story about a village named Dorli that was up for sale in 2005. In essence, our momentous train journey from Mumbai to Wardha was all about figuring out what pushed the farmers to put their village on sale. The topic of investigation aside, there was also a sense of romanticism following our reading of classic ethnographies including those described later. Weeks of 'hanging around' in the villages, aimless or otherwise, during fieldwork gave rich insights that aided understanding, and fuelled our scepticism about received knowledge in the textbooks.[26] What began with an exploratory recce of sorts became an academic preoccupation that has entered its fourteenth year at the time of writing. Indeed, over the years, qualitative insights from fieldwork not only improved contextual understanding but also allowed active validation and triangulation of quantitative results. Often, reminiscing about our enthusiasm for fieldwork in Vidarbha, images such as what is presented in Image 3.1 comes to mind.

In the first part of the book, we delved into the history of the region, and identified several turning points in history. A detailed history of the study region Vidarbha was presented in Chapters 1 and 2. The present-day Vidarbha region comprises eleven districts that are part of two administrative divisions—Nagpur and Amravati (Map 3.1). The former belongs to the erstwhile Central Provinces whereas the latter belongs to Berar. Two of the districts from these two divisions—Wardha and Yavatmal—have been the epicentre of farmers' suicides in this region. Wardha district is predominantly rain-fed with only 7 per cent of its net sown area irrigated, although the region falls under an assured rainfall zone with an average annual rainfall of 1,041 millimetres; with around fifty-three rainy days a year, the dependence on the monsoon rains makes agricultural activities in the region particularly vulnerable to the distributional vagaries of the southwest monsoon over the period June–September (JJAS henceforth).[27] Yavatmal district is also part of

Image 3.1 Gaurav during a field visit to Wardha, circa 2009

Source: Sarthak Gaurav.

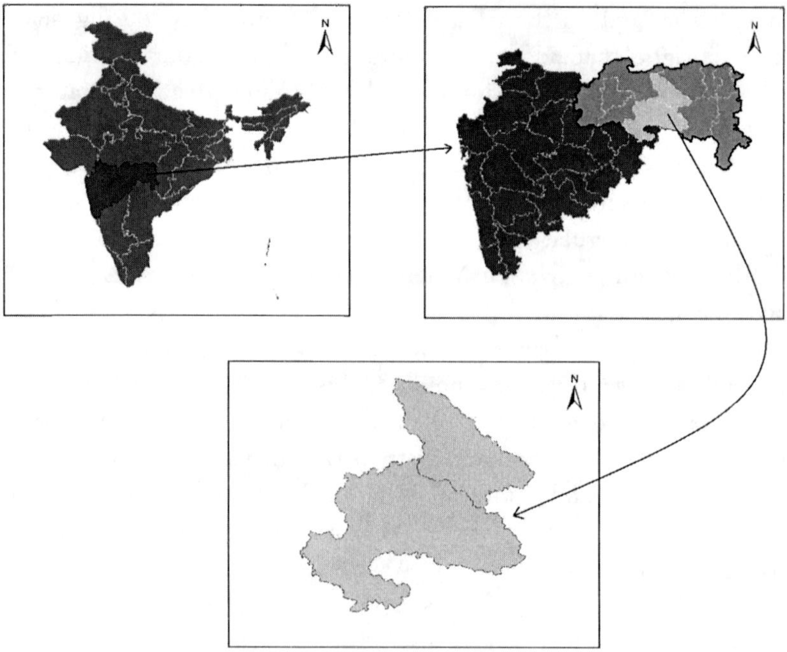

Map 3.1 India, Maharashtra, Vidarbha region, study districts

Source: Prepared by authors; base map from https://www.diva-gis.org/gdata (accessed on 28 March 2021).

Notes: In the third panel, the upper district is Wardha, and the lower district is Yavatmal. Maps not to scale and the map of India does not represent authentic international boundaries.

the same agroclimatic zone as discussed in Chapter 2. In both the districts, the southwest monsoon is received in the period June–September. The distributional vagaries within this monsoon season also have a huge impact on crop cultivation in the region.

When it comes to how we selected the study villages, as discussed earlier, exploratory fieldwork in Wardha in 2008 introduced us to civil society organizations and farmers in the villages nearby. The circumstances that influenced our earlier decision to locate our study in Wardha were partly accidental and partly sentimental given that the broader topic of our doctoral dissertations dealt with risk and vulnerability of agricultural households. The villages that we chose for our surveys fit the requirements we sought: considerable acreage of cash crops such as cotton and soybean under rain-fed conditions, contiguity, proximity to town, and possibility of having resident investigators stationed in the villages.

In the first round of our survey spanning 2009–2012, we chose five contiguous villages in Wardha district: Dhamangaon-Wathoda, Amla, Lonsavli, Dorli, and Shekapur. These villages were situated near the district headquarter Wardha. Amla was the village nearest to this town while Shekapur was the farthest. The advantage of contiguity was mostly in commonality of exposure to covariate shocks, that is adverse events simultaneously affecting a large area or population such as drought, pest outbreak, or pandemic. Contiguity of villages was expected to ensure that not only were terrain, soil, and agroclimatic conditions common but socio-cultural attributes and institutions of the villages also did not differ significantly. Indeed, this is not always true as heterogeneities within a village can arise in the form of microclimates and variations in soil typology even within a village. The year 2009 turned out to be a drought year, and farmers in particularly the rain-fed regions like those in the study villages were badly affected.

One hundred and twenty cultivators who were head of households in the panel survey were randomly selected from a sample frame comprising all land-owning cultivators in the five villages. The sampling frame for the cultivators was based on official land-ownership documents called *saatbaara utara*, or colloquially *saatbaara* (7/12),[28] which is an extract from the land register maintained by the revenue department of the state government. Confining our sample to land-owning cultivators meant that landless cultivators who leased in land for agricultural operations would be excluded in our sample. Nevertheless, we studied tenancy arrangements in the village independent of our sample. In a later round, we could overcome this lacuna with inclusion of landless non-cultivator households in our sample. Apart from the criterion of land ownership, it was also necessary for at least one member of the household to be involved in cultivation as the primary occupational activity in the past 365 days for the selected household to be considered as cultivator household. Importantly, the notion of a household that was relevant for our study was a group of individuals normally residing together and having food from a common kitchen. The head of the household was the customary head who may or may not be primary earning member, and he or she was the primary respondent in our surveys.

The second round of the surveys that spanned 2015–2018 was motivated by our interest in studying the use of pesticides and the role of knowledge and perceptions of farmers in this regard. We selected villages across the districts of Wardha and Yavatmal. The sample as well as villages in the second round differed from the earlier round. While we retained some of the villages in Wardha that were included in the first round, new villages from both districts were added for the first time. This was a crucial period in the decade because of impactful changes in the economy and polity including regime change at the federal level, introduction of the goods and services tax (GST), demonetization, and loan waiver by the state government.

However, resampling resulted in the loss of several Wardha households in the first round. In each of the two districts, three *taluka*s were randomly selected, out of which eighteen villages (nine each from Wardha and Yavatmal) were selected based on variations in distance from the respective headquarters. Following the merging of two contiguous villages that were considered as one, sixteen villages remained in our sample. Out of these sixteen villages, 600 farmer households were randomly selected from the sampling frame. During the second round of surveys, among the villages surveyed from Wardha and Yavatmal, we surveyed about 30 per cent of the households in the villages. There was notable heterogeneity in the demographic and social profile of villages. While the smallest village in Wardha sample, Dorli had a population of 70 households, the largest village in the district sample, Lonsavli had a population of 327 households. Few villages like Shankarpur in Yavatmal had an SC population of 35 per cent while Borkhedi in Wardha had an ST population of 49 per cent. But, when it came to attributes of agriculture and irrigation patterns, the villages were quite similar. Only 14 per cent of cultivated area was irrigated across all villages except Waldhur in Yavatmal that had high levels of irrigation. Although there is nothing peculiar in the study villages compared to agriculture and village economy in other parts of the region, wherever there are distinctions relevant to our discussion, we will highlight the same.

In September 2016 we installed six automated weather stations (AWSs) in six villages; three in each district. The locations in Yavatmal district are Inzapur, Sankarpur, and Ichora whereas those in Wardha district are Wathoda, Shekapur, and Sawad. The AWS records daily rainfall, temperature, soil moisture, relative humidity, and wind speed. An RCT was conducted in 2019 to to analyse the impact of an informational intervention on farmers' adoption of weather insurance. As we elaborate in Chapter 6, variability of weather, unseasonal weather events, and weather insurance are important facets of risk and vulnerability that our study investigates.

For the third round of survey conducted between 2019 and 2021, a sample of 190 cultivator households and 180 non-cultivator households were sampled from 10 of the study villages in the second round. The sampling frame for cultivators included all the landowners in the villages, and at least one member in the selected household had to undertake cultivation as primary activity in the past 365 days. To have a deeper understanding of the social organization of work in the villages as well as the production relations, we included non-cultivator households belonging to diverse caste groups and occupational categories. Non-cultivators are farm labourers whose primary activity is labourers in agricultural and allied activities, but they may supply labour to non-farm activities as well. By non-cultivator household, we imply that the head of the household is a non-cultivator. In the absence of a sampling frame for selection of non-cultivator households, the sample of non-cultivator samples was non-random. Non-cultivator households were recruited through a purposive sample having representation of key occupations of non-cultivator households based on information provided by key informants in each of the study villages. When the first survey of the third round was completed, a nationwide lockdown due to the COVID-19 pandemic was enforced. Over the period of this study, administration of the surveys and field visits was frequently affected by intermittent localized lockdowns as well as an extended lockdown from mid-April 2021.[29] At the time of writing, survey for the agricultural year 2021–2022 was in progress. This will help understand how lives and livelihoods were affected during the multiple waves of the pandemic, thereby adding a dimension of risk and vulnerability that we could not have anticipated back in 2008 when we decided to conduct the longitudinal study.

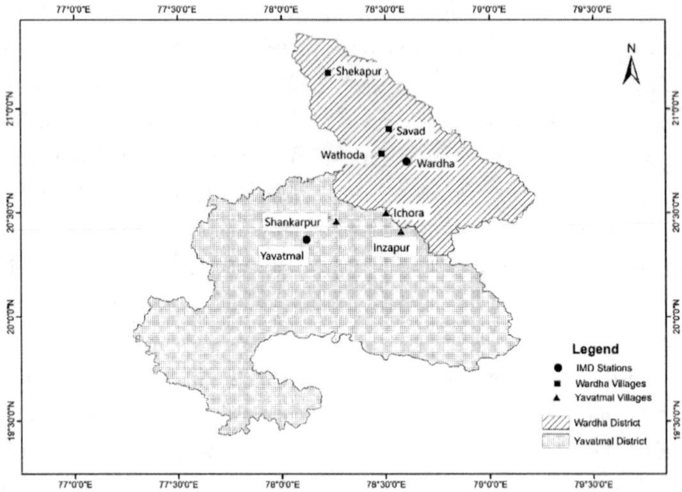

Map 3.2 Location of study villages where AWS were installed in 2016

Source: Prepared by authors; base map from polygon shapefiles of districts of India, available at https://geodata.lib.utexas.edu/catalog/stanford-sh819zz8121 (accessed on 28 March 2021).

Notes: Map not to scale and does not represent authentic national boundaries. AWS data collected daily weather data on six parameters for three years. Following the rabi season of 2019, no data has been collected due to difficulties in reactivation of the data subscription and maintenance challenges because of the COVID-19 pandemic.

In summary, over twelve years the longitudinal study comprised eight years of data from the sampled households. The first round, second round, and third round provided continuous data for three years, three years, and two years, respectively. The twelve years during which our surveys were spread, of which two are prominent, we did not conduct a survey in 2012, 2013, 2014, and 2018. We have described the characteristics of the sample households as well contemporary developments in the Vidarbha region later. This indeed provides a sense of change over the study regions, and wherever evident—a link between the past and the present. Next, we discuss issues related to administration of the surveys in the villages.

CHALLENGES IN DATA COLLECTION

A longitudinal village study spanning over a decade poses several methodological challenges. One pertains to attrition of households as well as inclusion of new households that were originally not surveyed. Another pertains to the more granular elements of data about different themes relevant to our research. While some problems are intractable, many are manageable, and an account of both offers insights into the perils of administering village studies over an extended period. In what follows, we briefly present the methodological challenges in both these categories and how we learned to address them in due course of time.

Beyond challenges that are academic in nature, operational issues are an integral part of administering surveys, most of which are unanticipated. A major challenge in the surveys was recruiting the respondents for the survey and sustaining their benevolence, attention, and focus during the surveys in which respondent fatigue is common to set in. In particular, even within a survey round, the surveyors revisited a few households for correcting or checking some of the data points. Such frequent visits over these years were not always enthusiastically received by the respondents in all villages even with the provision of in-kind gifts for respondents as a token of appreciation for their time and patience, and the study taught us as much about human resource management as development economics. Challenges in data collection were not peculiar to our study as similar issues have been reported in other longitudinal studies.[30]

MEASUREMENT ISSUES

(i) Household type

The first challenge that impedes data collection in studies such as ours is the definition of categories of households—farm and non-farm or cultivator or non-cultivator. There are various definitions of farm, farmer, and farm households that are used by different surveys. A definition of farm households based on land-ownership alone, as discussed earlier, risks excluding landless tenants dependent on farming by way of tenancy arrangements. The 'absentee' landowners might also be included as farmers in this definition. Defining a farmer or farm household based on minimum farm income or share of total household income might be limited as the type of household will vary based on the inter-annual income variations. As an extreme example, a household only dependent on farming incurring a loss will not be classified as a farm household based on this definition. Such exclusion is tricky when we would want to analyse the risk and vulnerability of farm households in the region where losses in agriculture and allied activities are recurrent. It may be recalled that we defined a farm household based on land ownership and participation in cultivation. We defined the cultivator (farmer household) based on the household in which the head of the household owned and operated some land during the last 365 days preceding the date of our survey as a primary occupation. A limitation of this definition is that it does not account for the extent to which the labour employed in cultivation was supplied by household members as in a peasant family farm and by hired workers; a distinction that is crucial for a class-based understanding of agrarian relations. Since 2019, we began surveying non-cultivator households in which members were primarily dependent on agricultural and non-agricultural wage labour but despite not owning land undertook agricultural labour activities.

Problems similar to defining a cultivator household surfaced while defining non-cultivator households. The dilemma was regarding whether the definition should be based on primary occupation only or include secondary occupation, that is, principal or subsidiary activity status, or share of agricultural labour income in total household income. As discussed, we adapted a simpler definition of non-cultivator households. Non-cultivator households are those households in the village that did not operate owned land and did not have any member of the household primarily involved in cultivation over the past 365 days. The category comprises a broad range of occupations as primary occupational activity including agricultural labour and non-farm labour, as coded in our survey questionnaire.

(ii) Income

It is well known that there are several issues with measuring income in rural settings.[31] We measured household income based on the aggregation of labour incomes of all working individuals and income from all plots cultivated by household members. Household income was thus calculated as the sum of income from farm and non-farm activities, accounting for the earnings of all the members of the household. The former comprises net earnings (net of costs for purchased inputs) from a household's own cultivation, animal husbandry, farm enterprise, and wage earnings from farm employment as hired labour (that is, off-farm labour). The latter includes income from non-farm wage employment such as casual non-farm labour, salaried work in non-farm activity, earnings from one's own non-farm business or own-account work in the non-farm sector. In the absence of reliable records of agricultural incomes, which are exempt from tax in India, reported incomes require considerable validation.

There are issues of recall on certain types of occupations which the individuals in the household were involved in during a short period of time in the year. The definitions of farm business income are complicated, and it is important to be aware of various challenges in its estimation. Farm business income statistics have had a long history in the Indian context and a rich source of data and concepts exists.[32] In one of the farm income studies in India conducted post-independence in a village called Dodda Ganni in Tripura, Jambunathan quips, 'When a farmer is asked about the amount spent per acre on certain inputs, he will vaguely give a figure which he ought to spend rather than the actual amount spent.'[33] Arriving at estimates of remittances is of particular concern in the absence of information on household members who have migrated seasonally or permanently. There are also instances of family members residing in a village or town not far away but providing financial assistance to those staying behind in the village. Equally difficult is gleaning information about incomes from child labour and older adults in the household who may or may not be recipients of pensions. Although such concerns usually plague cross-sectional surveys, longitudinal studies with active data quality controls and back checks ensure completeness and validation of responses. The challenges to understanding the cost of cultivation of a crop are still quite high—aspects that we will describe in this chapter. We will also relate to how these challenges meant a pen and paper personal interview (PAPI) mode of data collection was more convenient for our survey. The issues involved in various modes of data collection will also be discussed in detail later.

(iii) Cost estimates, frequent activities, imputed values

In the early stages of our surveys, we were influenced by categories of cost of cultivation followed by the National Sample Survey Office (NSSO) and Commission for Agricultural Costs and Prices (CACP). To compute the incomes of farmers, of which cultivation costs are a substantial component, there are challenges in costs reported by farmers pertaining to different agricultural operations. Most often, farmers face difficulty with such questions. Subsequent visits and interactions informed us about the following reasons.

First, farmers rarely keep an account of the actual expenses, least by crop. If someone spent around 5,000 rupees (around 700 US dollars) for irrigating a plot of cotton and pigeon-pea in the kharif season, it is difficult to recall the amount spent on irrigation, particularly by crop, when an investigator knocks at their door six months later. Therefore, what farmers report as costs are approximations to the best of their ability to recall and understanding of what constitutes aggregation of costs. It takes considerable validation by investigators who are aware of the underlying prices and rules of thumbs or heuristics about quantities. Wherever corrections are necessary, they are made. Although such validation introduces delays in project timelines, they considerably improve the quality of survey data.

Second, there is the difficulty of aggregating costs in the case of activities undertaken multiple times. Activities such as irrigation and weeding are usually undertaken multiple times in a cropping season. Farmers incur myriad costs including wages for labour, rental payments for equipment as well as interest payments for capital expenses associated with the activity. As a result, it becomes difficult for them to separate the cost incurred on labour and any equipment taken on rent. To circumvent this problem, multiple visits during the cropping season and the wisdom of the resident investigators turned out to be handy.

Third, wherever one's own labour or equipment and non-purchased materials were utilized, it was challenging for the farmers to report the costs involved. In such cases, appropriate imputations were done by using prevailing market prices. However, as is common in agricultural research, valuing by-products often pose challenges in arriving at a price for the imputation. For instance, farmyard manure or fodder often has prices that differ by season and availability within a season. Using an average price of farmyard manure for imputing the cost of farmyard manure from one's own cattle used in farming is a point in case.[34]

(iv) Consumption

Getting consumption expenditure is a challenging task given the issues involved with recall and sensitivity of certain items in a given context. Enumerating the consumption expenditure for various items in a household survey is a time-consuming task. In particular, it is difficult if we have other modules related to agricultural incomes and costs that have been collected in the survey already. We have enumerated consumption expenditure in five of the eight surveys we conducted as it is an important measure to understand the vulnerability of the households. There were various aspects related to consumption that had to be rechecked particularly in the last round of the survey. This round collected data for consumption when lockdown restrictions for COVID-19 were implemented. This meant that there were aspects related to consumption that might have seen some drastic changes given a pandemic. So, any aberration had to be vetted out if it was due to these abnormal circumstances or changes in behaviour of the households. There was also an added issue related to significant changes in expenditure on some fundamental goods which made validation of the consumption data a big challenge. When we found people were spending more on eating out during lockdown, we first had to validate it before we could even think of an explanation for such behaviour. The other consumption item that was always challenging to validate was that of consumption of intoxicating substances including *paan*, tobacco, and alcohol. The challenge was multiplied by the fact that Wardha district was a 'dry' district where consumption of alcohol was legally prohibited. But people did consume alcohol by purchasing it or consuming it in nearby districts. We still believe that not all the members provided the correct consumption expenditure related to alcohol.

(v) Assets and liabilities

Collecting data on the value of assets owned by the households was not straightforward. There are difficulties involved in figuring out the value of assets such as gold and jewellery where not only there are issues of under-reporting but also lack of information about quality. An associated problem pertains to the reported value being purchase value or the present value of the asset. There is very little agreement on which of the value is to be used, but in general we believed it is important to use a consistent measure across all assets. We confined data on assets to the following: farm equipment, movable assets, and unmovable assets including land. Information on land transactions over the past five–ten years was also collected. There were also issues related to the collection of information related to financial liabilities particularly when there were multiple loans. Not all farmers were able to recollect the credit outstanding with the input dealer while purchasing different inputs. These difficulties notwithstanding, the presence of resident investigators and multiple visits to households created an environment of trust that lends credibility to the respondents' self-reported figures about assets and liabilities.

NON-SAMPLING ERRORS

There were several other issues that were not specific to the modules in the survey instrument. Respondent fatigue while responding to long questionnaires is usually a concern in cross-sectional studies. However, in longitudinal studies, the possibility of multiple visits often allows investigators to partially fill survey forms and complete them during revisits. This also aids in data completion and validation on a regular basis.

One is often asked by the respondents as to what is the purpose of the data or what would be the benefit accruing to them for the time that they spend responding to our questions. There were always questions on what was the policy or scheme that we would bring with this information. All our surveys benefited from the presence of resident investigators who eventually got the training to lead teams of field investigators ranging from a size of three–five. Some resident investigators who started working with us in their early twenties and continue to do so, not only learned significantly from experienced investigators but also continue to train the younger generation. There was considerable peer learning not only about administering surveys but also agronomic practices (Image 3.2). The survey team also had their own share of fatigue and there was attrition on that front too. The long term involvement also taught us that dynamics among the field team members also change, and that between them and the supervisor. The seasonal nature of surveys also meant that the salaries of surveyors were also seasonal. Despite this, many surveyors have stayed with us during the whole survey period.

LOGISTICAL CHALLENGES

It will be illustrative to demonstrate how we adapted our survey or made use of technology to address the issues. Although surveys administered by computer-assisted personal interviews (CAPI) is a common practice in recent rural surveys, we relied on the old-fashioned PAPI method of surveys for longitudinal study. Our experience in administering the surveys suggests that the latter offers several advantages.

One of the most important advantages of the traditional method is the quality of remarks and notes that is relatively limited in the digitized version. Apart from the 'endowment effect' that storage of physical records of data over a decade induced in us, it introduces considerable flexibility in note-taking and the quality of remarks for investigators. In all our surveys,

Image 3.2 A resident investigator demonstrating concoction for ecological approach to pest management based on the concept of non-pesticidal management (NPM) to another resident investigator and farmers at Dorli village, Wardha, circa 2009

Source: Sarthak Gaurav.

investigators had less anxiety about implementing the surveys given their comfort with pen and paper. Respondents also inform us about their comfort with pen and paper instead of digital devices. In addition, digital devices have been observed to attract unwarranted attention among neighbours and acquaintances, thereby raising the risk of social desirability bias.

In the context of open-ended questions, investigators find it comfortable to leave detailed remarks beyond designated spaces for note-taking—at margins or blank spaces behind questionnaire blocks. This practice has time and again been integral to our validation process. Often it helped us validate the data and rectify any discrepancies in reporting or recall by respondents, which are corrected based on the richness of the qualitative remarks.

The PAPI survey also facilitates iterations as minor changes to forms are introduced every season. Our experience with CAPI however suggests that minor modifications as the ones we introduce iteratively are less flexible and there is no risk of survey failure to glitches if any. However, a flipside of the PAPI surveys, several times a year, for several years is that it may land one in considerable administrative trouble and to the chagrin of accountants as they try to make sense of bills for reimbursement that say 5,000 pages for photocopying. However, we hope for the future waves of our study, we gain access to affordable technology that provides us with the flexibility discussed earlier.

SAMPLE DESCRIPTION

DEMOGRAPHY

Table 3.2 presents the characteristics of the respondents surveyed in the first year of the three rounds of survey conducted in 2009, 2015, and 2019. In the final survey round starting from 2019, we surveyed non-cultivators too to analyse their labour supply, risks faced, and vulnerability of these households. Here, we present the characteristics of cultivators and non-cultivators separately for the last round of survey.

A typical household head in the study villages is a middle-aged male. In the 2009 and 2015 round, only 5 per cent of the households were female-headed households. However, in 2019 there was greater representation of female household heads in our sample: about one-eighth of both the cultivator and non-cultivator households were female-headed households. The share of male-headed households among the cultivator households is comparable to other studies pertaining to the region.[35] We also find that the household heads of non-cultivator households are younger than those of cultivator households. This is likely because non-cultivator households in the split into nuclear families considerably earlier than cultivator households owing to the absence of landholding. On the contrary, it is common for land-owning cultivators, who are senior citizens, to continue as head of the household even if there are two middle-aged married sons staying in the same household. It is only after the death of the male household head that the land is split among the sons or daughters irrespective of whether it was a joint or nuclear family.

Although daughters have legal rights over their ancestral property as per a ruling of the Supreme Court of India in 2005, daughters usually do not claim their share in their father's land following his demise.[36] Nevertheless, we have encountered incidents of the son-in-law vehemently demanding his

Table 3.2 Summary of sample households

	Round 1 (2009)	Round 2 (2015)	Round 3 (2019)	
			Cultivators	Non-cultivators
Age of the household head (years)	47.9	51.1	53.7	46.3
Male headed households (%)	94.2	94.6	88.3	87.5
Family size (Number)	4.3	4.3	3.3	3.5
Education of household head (%)				
Illiterate	14.2	13.2	20.3	19.6
Primary (1–5)	16.7#	3.0	3.1	5.4
Upper Primary (6–7)	10.8	16.9	15.3	13.0
Secondary (8–10)	31.7	25.9	22.7	33.2
Intermediate (11–12)	23.3	13.2	13.5	6.5
Diploma/Certificate	0.8	0.7	0.0	0.5
Graduation and above	2.5	3.7	0.6	0.0
Others (literate but not primary schooling)		23.3	24.5	21.7
Social groups (%)				
SC	28.3	15.2	11.7	8.2
ST	4.2	14.7	11.7	30.4
OBC	37.5	51.0	53.4	26.6
SBC	24.2	13.1	19.0	28.3
NT	5.0	5.4	4.3	6.0
Others	0.8	0.5	0.0	0.5
Land owned (acres)	6.7	5.1	4.7	0.0
Land inequality (Gini coefficient)	0.31	0.33	0.30	
Number of households	120	571	163	184

Source: Authors' calculation based on survey data.

Note: The table presents data pertaining to the first years of the three survey rounds.

This includes those who are literate without primary schooling only for this round of the survey. 'Age and Land owned' are averages. 'Social groups' are percentages in the sample. SC refers to scheduled caste, ST to scheduled tribe, OBCs to other backward classes, and NT to nomadic tribe. Gini coefficient is calculated on the basis of land owned by the households in a survey round to suggest the inequality in land distribution.

wife's share in her father's land resulting in family feuds. In case the family has only one daughter, her marital status notwithstanding, she becomes the natural heir to her father's property. It is also common to have *ghar jawai*s or sons-in-law co-residing with the in-laws even when the father-in-law is alive. This practice also serves the function of the son-in-law helping the father-in-law in agricultural activities, and there is no stigma associated with this practice.

The educational attainment of household heads also differed across the three rounds of surveys. In the first round of surveys, more household heads had completed 'intermediate' (eleven–twelve years of formal education) than the other two rounds of surveys. In the survey conducted in 2019, household heads in cultivator households were more educated in comparison with non-cultivator households. Few household heads had diplomas or certifications in industrial training. This is in consonance with the low prevalence of technical skills training among the middle-aged population in general.[37] However, the educational attainment as well as skills training among youngsters in these households has improved over time. There has also been an impressive improvement in the educational attainment of women in the study village following concerted efforts of the state.

In 2009, the Sarva Shiksha Abhiyaan or the Right of Children to Free and Compulsory Education Act or Right to Education Act was enacted by the Parliament of India to ensure the provision of free and compulsory education for children between the ages of six–eighteen years in the country. There has also been a proliferation of private English medium schools in the vicinity of each of the study villages. Interestingly, Wardha became an important centre for educational reforms since the Wardha Scheme of 1937 that became the first comprehensive national education policy as it gave the calling for free and compulsory education for seven years in their mother tongue, and that education should be anchored to manual and productive work. This glorious facet of Wardha and the region's history notwithstanding, we have come across serious gaps in learning outcomes, and employment opportunities for females have not improved considerably. Despite campaigns like 'Beti Bachao Beti Padhao', which are steps in the right direction, drop-out of girl children seem to be increasing at the all-India level.[38] Maharashtra has also been a laggard state in this scheme with actual utilization of funds less than 50 per cent of the allocated funds during the period from 2015–2016 to 2019–2020.[39]

In the study villages though, we have evidence of increasing participation of the women in economic activities, mostly in agricultural wage work and self-employment. In Yavatmal, we came across an *anganwadi* worker (*sevika*) who resided there for nearly four decades. Despite being a widow at an early age, she made sure her children got educated. Her son did a BSc in Agriculture and her daughter did a BA; another daughter did an MA (BEd). There are also stories of improved attitudes towards women's agency. In a Wardha village, we came across a divorced young lady. She had completed her polytechnic degree staying with her parents. She had recently started tutoring school students in her village and the nearby villages of which her educated parents were very encouraging and supportive. Participation in microfinance-related activities and livelihoods programmes such as participation in self-help groups (SHGs) is also commonplace for women in most of the study villages. Since 2006, there has also been greater participation of women in casual wage employment under the Mahatma Gandhi National Rural Employment Guarantee Scheme (MGNREGS)—the largest public works programme in the world. However, in the study villages, there was considerable variation in participation of women in MGNREGS projects that were few and far between. In fact, in 2009 MGNREGS employment was unheard of in several villages as projects had not been initiated as per the operational guidelines of the scheme. As recent as 2015, the number of workdays provided per household was around 45 days in Wardha—a poor performing district in the scheme despite the 100 days guaranteed under the act. Though Yavatmal provided greater employment under the scheme compared to Wardha, the average remained below two months. In 2020, MGNREGS provided wages to around 0.4 million workers across nearly 19,000 projects in Vidarbha during the COVID-19 pandemic of 2020.[40] The Government of Maharashtra resolved to provide employment to the rural population for 365 days a year. Wages were increased to 238 rupees (3.3 US dollars) per day from 206 rupees (2.9 US dollars), and the wages were transferred to the worker's bank account directly.

As the rural public health system underwent a significant transformation over the past several decades, women in households in our sample also work as village-level functionaries such as community health workers—accredited social health activists (ASHAs) and *anganwadi* workers under the Integrated Child Development Scheme (ICDS). In order to improve nutrition among children in the school-going age, the Mid-day Meal Scheme (MDMS)—the school meal programme for students enrolled in primary and upper primary in several categories of schools including public education centres has been implemented for over three decades in the state. However, malnutrition is a major concern in the state.

In Yavatmal, with a particularly high tribal population, nearly half of the children under the age of five were stunted in 2015–2016. The prevalence of underweight children in three districts of Vidarbha including Yavatmal was also particularly high.[41] Several studies indicate that the gains in malnutrition reduction since 2000 seem to have been lost during the last decade despite high economic growth and increased public action to arrest malnutrition.[42] At the same time, the Millennium Development Goals (MDGs) conditions—incidence of communicable diseases, maternal mortality, neonatal mortality, and nutritional deprivation—have reduced.[43]

A key demographic change over the span of our studies is that the age at first marriage for women has increased in general. This is largely attributed to greater enrolment in educational institutions and opportunities for participation in economic activities. While at the national as well as the state level there has in fact been a worsening of the labour force participation rate (LFPR) of women in rural India, we find active employment in agriculture, particularly cotton sowing, weeding, and picking activities.[44] Participation of women in non-agricultural employment remains persistently low.

A recurrent theme that emerges from interaction with youth in the villages is that as agriculture is becoming less sought after, so are the men in search of a match in the marriage market. There is a growing trend in rural society that farmers are finding it increasingly difficult to find a suitable match as the girl's families would rather prefer a non-farm worker to a farmer. This has also increased the age at first marriage for the male cohorts in the villages as they often experience multiple rejections owing to their occupation. In one such instance, a farmer in our sample managed to find a suitable match only after he convinced the girl's family that he will undertake poultry business before the marriage—which he eventually undertook as a secondary occupation along with his cotton farming.

The social group composition has varied over time in the sample in our three survey rounds. Some of the changes following the 2009 round, in the 2015 and 2019 rounds, are likely due to the fact that we sampled households from the Yavatmal district in the second and third rounds of our surveys, and resampled households in Wardha as discussed earlier. We also dropped a few villages from Wardha that were surveyed in the 2009 round. The proportion of scheduled castes (SCs) in the dropped villages has also altered the overall social group composition of the Wardha villages in our samples since 2015. In general, Yavatmal has a higher proportion of scheduled tribes (STs) compared to Wardha. The proportion of STs in Yavatmal is about 20 per cent.

Across different survey rounds, among the cultivator households, other backward classes (OBCs) are the most preponderant followed by special backward classes (SBCs). Among non-cultivator households, Scheduled Tribes (STs) and SBCs comprise a larger proportion. Along with OBCs, SBCs comprise around half the sample of non-cultivators. While SBCs in Wardha villages are nearly twice of that in Yavatmal villages, OBCs in Yavatmal villages are nearly thrice of that in Wardha villages. The Wardha sample also has more nomadic tribe (NT) households. As discussed in Chapter 1, Gonds—who ruled over several parts of the present-day region including the Gond king being the founder of Nagpur—are preponderant among STs in the sample. Bhuis and Beldars are preponderant among NTs. SCs/Dalits includes castes such as the Chambhars and religious groups such as those who converted to Neo-Buddhism. SBC comprises communities such as Gowaris, which is the predominant community in the region. Earlier SBCs were part of STs (Gond-Gowari). Maratha-Kunbi and Malis belong to OBC.

The Marathas have been a dominant group that was formed from an eclectic group of castes, and were crucial actors in the military service since the sixteenth century as discussed in Chapter 1. They primarily comprise the 'forward castes' following the classification by two commissions in the 1990s: the Bapat Commission and the Saraf Commission. The traditional cultivator castes comprising 'Kunbis' and the amalgamation of Kunbis and Marathas, 'Maratha-Kunbis' constitute the major castes in the OBC category.[45] It should be noted that the distinction between the Marathas and Kunbis are subtle and the caste identities are intricately linked to their class on the basis of position in the agrarian society, particularly through their landholding status. Maratha dynasties such as Gaekwads and Scindias are believed to have Kunbi roots but unlike certain groups of Marathas who assert affiliation to Kshatriya caste in the Varna system, Kunbis are considered to have a lower position. Historically, the largest landholders in the village, who are locally called the Patils, claim the Maratha caste status despite being believed to have Kunbi roots. The consolidation of Kunbis and Marathas was precipitated due to social reforms and development processes during the Raj.[46] In 2021, the Supreme Court ruled against the reservation of Marathas in government jobs and public educational institutes following the state passing a law in 2018 that created a special category of socially and economically backward class (SEBC). In 2019, the Bombay High Court had approved the law but trimmed the quota.[47]

The SCs in the region comprise the 'Dalits' who are mostly *nav*-Boudhas or 'neo-Buddhists'—the largest sub-group in India's Buddhist population.[48] The region had seen a major political response to caste oppression by the Dalits beginning in the colonial era. Initially, a large number of the landless population converted to Christianity in the 1930s. In the period from 1891–1931, the census data indicates an eightfold increase in the Christian population in Yavatmal. There was also a significant following for Jyotiba Phule's Satyasodhak Movement in the region. These movements were also followed by B. R. Ambedkar and his championing of the Buddhist revival movement in the 1950s had a significant impact on the social composition of Vidarbha. In fact, Ambedkar's public conversion into Buddhism at Nagpur on 14 October 1956 saw the conversion of 0.6 million Dalits, mostly Mahars into Buddhism.[49] Some members of dominant castes see this conversion by the Dalits as a matter of ingratitude and betrayal to their patronage even today.[50] The proportion of SCs in the population of Wardha and Yavatmal following the conversion reduced to 2.4 per cent and 3.9 per cent in 1961 compared to 17.2 per cent and 13.9 per cent in 1951.[51] Initially, a person who converted to Buddhism was not considered an SC, but after 1990 the legislation recognizes persons converted to Buddhism as members of a Scheduled Caste. From 1960, the neo-Buddhists who are the predominant SC population in Maharashtra benefited from reservation in state government schemes but continued to be ineligible as a beneficiary for central government's reservation schemes. Interestingly, there has not only been an evolution in our understanding of social structure of the villages but also in the laws pertaining to caste affiliation such as the Maratha reservation issue discussed earlier as well as the eligibility of neo-Buddhists for government schemes. Since 2017, the Maharashtra government legalized the eligibility of neo-Buddhists for minority schemes in the state, of which they had been deprived from for decades.

ASSETS

Land is the most valuable physical asset of the cultivators. In the study villages, 40 *aar*s of land makes an acre. The average land owned has decreased from 6.7 acres to 5.1 acres from the first to the second round. The agricultural census of Maharashtra indicates that the size of an average landholding in 2011 was 5.7 acres. In the 2015–2016 agricultural census, the average size of a landholding was 5.2 acres in both Wardha and Yavatmal.[52] The average size of a landholding for the state of Maharashtra is about 3.4 acres, much smaller than the average in our study region.[53] The land sizes have reduced as an outcome of the subdivision of landholdings due to household splits and division of land among brothers following fathers' death or due to family feuds. There has also been a general decline in the arable lands in the region as rural construction and infrastructure projects have shrunk the land available for agriculture. For a perspective, the net sown area of Wardha district was around 0.4 million hectares in the 1960s, and it fell by more than 35,000 hectares over four decades. Also, the area under the current fallow, that is the cropped area kept fallow during the current year, as well as other fallow, that is land uncultivated for a period of one to five years, are on the rise.[54] Although the pattern of reducing land size over time is a nationwide phenomenon, there are localized variations in the driving forces. Landlessness, which has been an important push factor for high supply of agricultural labour in Vidarbha, continues to be an important force shaping the urbanization patterns as well as class structure in the region.

Over the three rounds of survey, the land inequality among cultivators has remained at around 30 per cent. The Gini coefficient is quite less compared to an average of 0.47 for Maharashtra calculated at the state level using data from the land census.[55] This has been a result of the robust implementation of land reforms in the region of Vidarbha in the 1970s and 1980s. From 1970–1971 to 1990–1991, the Gini coefficient of operational holdings in Wardha reduced from 0.45 to 0.39 while that in Yavatmal reduced from 0.41 to 0.37. During the same period, the Gini coefficient of land distribution in Maharashtra reduced from 0.53 to 0.46.[56] The Gini in our sample is still lower than the Gini based on land distribution from the census. This could be because of further improvement in land distribution over the last two decades or due to the under-representation of farmers with large landholdings in our survey. For instance, in our sample of farmers there are no farm households with landholdings above 10 hectares in any of the survey rounds.

When we began our studies in 2009, around 60 per cent of the farm households in our sample were completely rain fed, which is locally known as *koradwahu*. The irrigated land is called *olit*. It should be noted that even though the study region is rain fed, with no surface irrigation sources such as canals or tanks, those farmers who had the resources to invest in harnessing groundwater through dugwells and borewells could irrigate their agricultural plots. Access to irrigation sources on neighbouring plots also developed a rental market for irrigation. Despite access to irrigation for the *olit* lands, in drought years or periods when the water table is severely depleted, the 'moisture advantage' of *olit* farmers over the *koradwahu* farmers disappears indicating that the irrigated fields are also rain dependent.[57]

Table 3.3 presents reported farm and physical assets of the households by the starting year of the survey round. In the first round of surveys from 2009 to 2012, we only collected data on a few assets. In the later rounds, we collected data related to a larger number of assets. There is a clear trend of decline in tractor ownership among cultivator households. In 2009, tractor sales across Vidarbha increased as large land-owning farmers could secure tractor-financing schemes offered by public and private sector banks. Financial institutions were eager to extend such secured loans where the tractor was mortgaged, unlike riskier unsecured credit to the households. Fieldwork in 2010–2011 indicated growth of tractor sales in the Nagpur division as farmers benefitted from the availability of tractor financing options. Purchases peaked during the March–May period as farmers were less liquidity constrained with the cash from remunerative prices of cotton, and preparations for the oncoming kharif season commenced.[58]

Table 3.3 Farm and non-farm assets

			2019	
	2009	**2015**	**Cultivators**	**Non-Cultivators**
Farm Assets				
Tractor	6.7%	3.0%	2.9%	0.0%
Diesel pump	0.0%	4.2%	1.8%	0.0%
Tube well		39.0%	39.4%	0.0%
Spray pump		45.8%	63.5%	2.2%
Bullock cart	59.2%	32.1%	38.8%	0.0%
Trolley		3.8%	3.5%	0.0%
Plough		35.5%	28.2%	0.5%
Physical Assets				
Car	0.0%	1.7%	1.8%	0.0%
Two-wheeler	30.8%	34.1%	38.8%	22.5%
TV	64.2%	76.7%	82.9%	68.7%
Mobile phone	46.6%	95.5%	95.7%	80.2%
Number of households	120	574	170	182

Source: Authors' calculation based on survey data.

We have often heard farmers complaining about growing labour costs in tilling operations and difficulty in securing bullocks for operations as a motivation for purchasing tractors. However, rental incomes from tractor services in land preparation and inter-cultivation operations—*dawran*—is a good additional source of income for the household (Image 3.3). Tractors also became a popular mode of transportation of the produce to the nearby market yards apart from carrying causal labourers to nearby towns and transporting bricks from the ever-increasing number of brick kilns in the vicinity of the villages. Infrastructure projects such as highways and rural road works also demand tractors with trailers for the transportation of materials. Discussions with tractor dealers in the nearby towns suggest that the 'second wave' of the pandemic in 2021 impacted tractor sales much more than the 'first wave' in 2020. The uncertainty about demand for tractors was much higher at the time of writing. Sales typically go up during festive seasons such as Gudi Padwa in the month of April, but the prospects looked grim for 2021 production as kharif agricultural operations commenced.

In the first round of surveys, there were more bullock carts than tractors in the Wardha villages with around 60 per cent of the households owning one. Ownership of bullocks, which is an indispensable asset for the Vidarbha cultivator, registered a marginal decline in 2011 compared to the 2009, although on average there was a pair of bullocks per household. Bullocks

Image 3.3 A father and son operating a bullock pair in a Wardha village during *dawran*, circa 2009

Source: Sarthal Gaurav.

continue to be an important productive asset for the households as a large number of agricultural activities cannot be conducted without their help.[59] Nevertheless, there has been a decline in the ownership of bullocks as farm mechanization owing to the development of rental market for tractors.

Tractors are used for various operations and along with various other machines. In most of the study villages, there were about one–three households with tractors. The other households rented tractors for various operations involving land preparation (*nagaran* for deep and shallow ploughing along with cultivator, *wakhar phaas*, and *panji* tiller[60]), sowing (along with *pherni yantra*), and for removal of cotton plants after harvest (along with *ekka*). The rental rates of tractors depend on the type of operation that is performed and also varies across villages. As of 2019, the rents for using tractors along with *nagaran* and rotovator varied from 800 to 1,000 rupees per day while for other operations the rent varied from 400 to 600 rupees across different study villages.

Among other major farm equipment that was available with a quarter of the households in the sample of cultivator households in 2015 and 2019 was a plough. Ownership of other farm equipment was low. Among non-cultivators, few reported owning spray pumps. The non-cultivator households that own the spray pumps are the ones likely to be involved in the labour of applying pesticides. Panel (*b*) in Table 3.3 describes the physical assets belonging to the sample in the three first years of the study rounds. As of 2019, mobile phone ownership was nearly universal among both cultivator and non-cultivator households. From about less than two-thirds of the households owning mobile phones in 2009, it went up to almost 96 per cent in 2019. Since the launch of India's largest 4G network service provider, Jio in 2016, there has been a spurt in smartphones as households have unprecedented access to affordable 4G data services, and use of apps such as WhatsApp is widespread. Several households however continue to use feature phones. Ownership of white appliances and two-wheelers is also common. We also find that the non-cultivator households have lesser access to physical assets as compared to the cultivator households in 2019.

The change in nominal value of financial assets over a decade are presented for the starting years of the first and last survey rounds conducted: 2009 and 2019 (Table 3.4). Over the years, there has been a significant increase in bank savings. Cash at home has declined while the value of jewellery and other savings at home has gone up for the cultivators. The SHG savings have also gone up during this decade. Between the cultivators and non-cultivators in

Table 3.4 Financial assets

	2009	2019	
		Cultivators	Non-cultivators
Bank savings	1,537.2	11,666.3	3,904.4
SHG	233.4	815.3	614.5
Cash	5,123.3	1,639.8	1,052.5
Jewellery and other savings at home	2,644.2	13,157.1	8,634.6
N	120	170	182

Source: Authors' calculation based on survey data.

Note: SHG savings are calculated for a year based on monthly savings reported. All figures are as on date of the survey. N denotes the number of respondents who provided the details of their financial assets.

Table 3.5 Livestock ownership

Year		Milch Cattle	Bullocks	Goats	Poultry
2009	*Cutivators*	2.9 (66)	2.3 (85)	3.4 (27)	3.5 (33)
2019	*Cutivators*	2.5 (58)	2.0 (67)	3.2 (33)	2.6 (29)
	Non-cultivators	1.7 (27)	2.0 (1)	2.4 (45)	3.0 (25)

Source: Authors' calculation based on survey data.

Note: Figures indicate average livestock ownership. Figures in parenthesis represent the number of households owning livestock. Total number of households for each sub-group is as per Table 3.4.

the 2019 round of the survey, we find that the cultivators had substantially higher levels of financial assets compared to non-cultivators. Their bank savings and small savings through SHGs where women mostly participate are higher. Asset holding in the form of jewellery predominantly in the form of gold is also high for cultivator households. Although cash holdings differ by which month of the year one is surveyed given the seasonality of agricultural operations, multiple visits suggest that the average holdings at the time of survey during the kharif season are representative of these stocks.

Table 3.5 presents the change in livestock ownership over the study period. There was growth in ownership of milch cattle including cows and buffaloes, poultry, and goats over three years of our first round (2009–2011) while bullocks registered a decline during the same period. Nevertheless, the stark decline in sorghum acreage over the years has resulted in episodes of fodder shortage. In 2011, a *dhep*, a packet of fodder costed 14–16 rupees (5 cents) per 2 kilograms, which used to be home produced earlier. Assuming a pair of bullocks need a quarter of a quintal of fodder every month, the farm household had to spend around 250 rupees (3.5 US dollars). Moreover, farmers complained of non-availability of fodder and feed on most occasions. Whenever fodder and feed were available, there were concerns about their quality. These factors are likely to have contributed to the decline of livestock rearing in the villages in general. We did not collect data related to livestock ownership in the second round of surveys starting 2015.[61]

However, the 2019 survey revealed that there is a reduction in both the proportion of households owning milch cattle and the average milch cattle per household. For bullocks, too, both the proportion of households owning bullocks and the average number of bullocks owned per household has reduced from 2009 to 2019 among the cultivators. This is also true for poultry and goats.

Very few non-cultivator households owned bullocks as compared to cultivators because they have limited agricultural operations, mostly based on leased-in land given their lower asset base and almost no ownership of land in our sample. Even in the case of milch cattle, non-cultivator households have lower ownership relative to cultivator households. However, a higher proportion of non-cultivator households own milch cattle compared to bullocks. They also have more goat and poultry compared to milch cattle. This is due to their increasing dependence on small livestock-based income diversification—a pattern that is clearly a major change in the region over the past decade. The livestock ownership patterns are intricately linked to the cropping patterns that we will dwell on in Chapter 4.

Table 3.6 reports the livestock ownership by size-class of land ownership among cultivators in 2009 and 2019. The notable patterns are as follows. First, there has been a drastic change in the composition of marginal, small, and larger farmers in livestock ownership. In 2019, we even find that marginal cultivators are investing more in milch cattle and goats. As discussed earlier, this is a major source of income for the households. However, time spent by women in these activities, although substantial, is considered as non-market activity. Second, there is no difference among the size-classes in terms of poultry ownership. Third, in terms of size of the stock of poultry, however, the larger size-class has a higher head count of livestock. Fourth, small as well as larger size-class of cultivators have a

Table 3.6 Livestock ownership by size-class of land owned

	2009				2019			
Size-Class	**Milch Cattle**	**Bullocks**	**Goats**	**Poultry**	**Milch Cattle**	**Bullocks**	**Goats**	**Poultry**
Marginal								
Livestock owned	2.0	0.0	5.0	2.0	2.0	2.0	2	2.5
Percentage owning livestock (% of households)	33.3%	0%	66.7%	66.70%	29.0%	16.1%	22.6%	19.4%
N		3				31		
Small								
Livestock owned	2.8	2.4	2.4	3.4	2.3	2.0	2.6	2.2
Percentage owning livestock (% of households)	25.6%	43.6%	12.8%	17.9%	27.8%	27.8%	20.0%	17.8%
N		39				90		
Semi-Medium and Medium								
Livestock owned	2.9	2.2	3.4	3.7	3.04	2.0	5.5	3.4
Percentage owning livestock (% of households)	70.5%	87.2%	25.6%	30.8%	53.7%	80.5%	19.5%	17.1%
N		78				41		

Source: Authors' calculation based on survey data.

Note: Livestock owned is the average livestock ownership by category of livestock. N denotes the number of households in each size-class.

pair of bullocks. The reliance on bullock has been limited to *dawran*, or intercultivation in particular.

Over the years, there has been a concerted attempt by the state government to promote animal husbandry in Vidarbha. The private sector's presence is limited to supply of finance, fodder and feed, veterinary services, and extension. In Vidarbha, the development of end-to-end dairy value chain in distressed districts, promotion of scientific goat meat value chains, and development of sericulture clusters have been attempted in recent years.[62] Despite attempts to strengthen private sector investment in the distressed districts in the form of Convergence of Agriculture and Industry in Maharashtra (CAIM), not much progress has been made over the years in the study region. However, limited impact evaluation studies indicate positive effects on livelihoods.[63] State Agricultural Universities such as the Dr Punjabrao Deshmukh Krishi Vidyapeeth (PDKV) at Akola along with the district level farm science centres: Krishi Vigyan Kendras (KVKs) and societies of stakeholders under the Agricultural Technology Management Agency (ATMA) have played an important role in extension services for farmers but several aspects of the extension provision are wanting as we will discuss in Chapter 6. Several non-governmental organizations (NGOs) in Wardha and Yavatmal have also facilitated the setting up of livestock rearing, particularly goatery and poultry. While medium-sized farmers have largely been participating in these initiatives to diversify their crop incomes, participation by smallholders, particularly marginal farmers, is also on the rise. However, there are several gaps in the knowledge about animal husbandry among farmers, which has policy implications as discussed in Chapter 7.[64] The dairy sector in Vidarbha has not received the desired impetus over decades and this has resulted in low interest in cattle-related investment in the region.[65]

For a region whose bustling cattle markets and fairs had been affected by the colonial impetus on cash crop expansion based on ecological degradation as seen in Chapter 2, failure of the cattle economy to grow as evident from our observations over the years is disconcerting. These developments notwithstanding, one would still find cattle fairs, as shown in Image 3.4, a standard fixture in small towns across the district. These fairs are not only a marketplace for buying and selling cattle of various breeds but also an important connect between the region's present and the past. As avenues for socialization, bragging about quality of the bulls on display, and price discovery, such cattle fairs play an important role in Vidarbha society. These are important sources of income not only for petty retailers selling food and drinks for the swell of

Image 3.4 A cattle fair in Deoli, Wardha, circa 2020

Source: Sarthak Gaurav.

visitors but also those selling traditional accessories and trinkets for decorating the bulls. The cattle fairs also retain their importance for purchases before religious festivals such as Pola, which is celebrated with fanfare over five days in the month of August, and involves elaborate rituals to symbolise thanksgiving to bullock and farm labourers, as discussed in Chapter 6.[66]

LIABILITIES

Owing to the cotton economy forming the base of the economic activities in the villages, the credit institutions have evolved to cater to the high external input system of production. Although farmers are increasingly dependent on credit for their agricultural operations, there is widespread exclusion from institutional credit. A decade before the commencement of our surveys, there was considerable evidence of indebtedness being a triggering factor in farmers' suicides in the region.[67] The agricultural credit environment in the first decade of the twenty-first century is critical from two perspectives. First, the decade is at the centre of the debate on whether the agricultural credit revival in India began since 2000 following the reversal of the achievements made in the 1980s by serious neglect of agriculture in the 1990s following the economic reforms.[68] Scholarly research suggests that the observed increase in the flow of credit to agriculture in the 2000s was largely an outcome of the growing share of indirect finance; a category that had broadened in scope to subsume new types of farm lending. Despite the growth of direct lending to agriculture, a noticeable increase in the share of large-sized advances catering to agri-business enterprises rather than smallholders emerged as the trend.[69] Nevertheless, despite general improvements in access to formal credit and digital transformation in the banking sector over the past decade, several gaps in improving farmers' access to institutional credit remain unaddressed.[70]

As the spate of farmers' suicides continues to ravage Vidarbha and other distressed regions, the role of indebtedness among cash-crop-growing smallholders in particular has been extensively scrutinized.[71] The issue of farmers' indebtedness however has gained political attention since the first reports of farmers' suicides began thirty-five years ago from Wardha. Both the Government of India and the Government of Maharashtra have responded with large-scale debt waivers and debt-relief schemes over the years. During our study, 2008–2009 and 2017 saw massive debt waivers and debt-relief schemes implemented by the central and state governments, respectively.

Households were substantially indebted to both formal as well as informal institutions, although the quantum of the former was significantly larger (Table 3.8). Timely repayment of formal loans (institutional credit), which is the cheapest source of credit, is crucial for securing fresh loans in the subsequent crop season. It is also the cheapest source of credit due to subsidies on the interest rate. The loans become cheaper if repayments are done promptly within a specified period under the interest subvention scheme introduced since 2006–2007. Under this scheme, the annual interest rate for the loans was about 4 per cent for farmers repaying promptly. A failure to repay an outstanding loan, as observed to a considerable extent in 2010 after a drought year, is a common reason for farmers to be ineligible for a loan the following season, thereby increasing their dependence on informal sources of credit or costlier sources of formal credit. Under such limiting conditions, reliance on credit and savings for consumption smoothing has had an adverse impact on farm investment and productivity not just in the short term, but also in the long run.

While the reliance on formal credit was low, informal credit from kinship network, that is, friends and relatives was common. In 2009, around one-fourth of the sample had loans from friends and relatives, averaging at 9,000

Table 3.7 Loan outstanding: 2009, 2015, 2019

	2009	2015	2019	
			Cultivators	Non-cultivators
Mean	Rs 32,408.3	Rs 80,003.7	Rs 14,147.9	Rs 2,692.3
N	120	570	170	182

Source: Authors' calculation based on field surveys.

Note: Figures are self-reported values as on date of the survey. Rs denotes Indian Rupees. Exchange rate at the time of writing was 1 US dollar = Rs 72. N denotes the number of observations.

rupees for those who borrowed from these informal sources. As in the case of formal credit, there were instances of defaults in informal credit as well. Villagers have high awareness about the higher interest burden of informal loans, and the informal ties are a much-needed lifeline during financial hardship. Informal loans are usually *dedhi*, where the creditor is expected to repay the loan around harvest and pay 150 rupees for a 100-rupee loan. There also exist *sawai* loans in which the creditor has to pay 125 rupees for a loan of 100 rupees.[72] Other popular forms of loan carry an interest burden of 5 rupees or 10 rupees per month, and the interest is calculated following the return of the principal. There are variations in the interest payment by crops for which loan is sought as well as the reputation of the creditor. There are also provisions for flexibility in loan repayment and a fresh line of credit in the eventuality of non-wilful default due to natural factors.

During fieldwork in 2018, a farmer made an impressive comment about the power of information asymmetry between the lender and the creditor in the village economy that contrasts markedly with the state of the non-performing assets (NPA) in the formal banking sector during those days:

> Whatever be the form of credit, the informal lenders have lower NPA than the big banks lending out thousands of crores to scrupulous defaulters.[73]

It is well known that rural financial institutions in India have grappled with issues of overdues and NPAs for several decades.[74] Indeed, the information asymmetries are considerably lower in the rural informal credit arrangement but there are also occasional violations of the verbal contract. We have come across cases of scuffle between the lender and the creditor due to delays in repaying the dates following completion of the harvesting operations when the lender is aware that the farmer would soon have the necessary cash from selling the produce to clear the dues. However, it is a general practice to repay outstanding informal loans at the earliest as no one wants to upset their lender of last resort in times of need.

It is evident that very few households are indebted to moneylenders. Moneylending in the state has two forms—legal and illegal, the latter being a punishable offence. It is likely that there is gross under-reporting of moneylender loans given the implementation of the Maharashtra Money-Lending (Regulation) Act, 2014, which carries a penalty of 50,000 rupees and five-year imprisonment for illegal moneylending activities. The law also has a punitive provision of two years of imprisonment and 10,000 rupees of fines on a repeat offence. Moreover, the moneylending law caps the interest rates from legal (registered) moneylenders at 12 per cent and 15 per cent for secured and unsecured loans, respectively. Discussions with the villagers revealed that despite the law being in place, there were covert moneylending operations at interest rates on the principal being as high as 100–120 per cent per annum. However, there is reasonable reluctance among villagers to openly discuss the identity of the moneylender fearing repercussions.

Among other sources of credit, time and again, we have also observed the agricultural input dealer in the nearby town as well as the *arhatiya*—middleman or commission agent in the market yard—are also important sources of informal credit, albeit charging exorbitant interest rates. The interest rates for credit from these sources could vary from 36 per cent to 60 per cent per year.

Subsequent to the first round of survey, the average loan outstanding fell significantly from 80,000 rupees in 2015 to 14,148 rupees for cultivators in 2019. Over the past twelve years that have witnessed three major debt-waiver schemes including the Agricultural Debt Waiver and Debt Relief Scheme (ADWDRS) implemented by the United Progressive Alliance (UPA) government at the centre in 2008, we have been informed about the pros and cons of all these schemes. There is a general acknowledgement that such loan waivers offer a respite to farmers who were genuinely facing financial hardships and indebtedness due to non-wilful default, but it is unfair for the wilful defaulters to benefit. Several farmers in both Wardha and Yavatmal have also expressed their concern that such recurrent loan waivers, whilst necessary given the low and uncertain returns in agriculture, eventually affect repayment behaviour, usually mentioned as 'repayment culture'.

There has been a marked change in the participation of women in the SHG bank linkage programme. SHGs have been set up under the aegis of

UMED, the Maharashtra State Rural Livelihoods Mission (MSRLM).[75] Over the decade there has been a mushrooming of microfinance institutions, mostly the Andhra Pradesh based as well as those with national presence such as SKS Microfinance and BASIX. Local microfinance institutions (MFIs) such as D-Matrix Development Foundation have also contributed to livelihood generation among the underserved population in different parts of Wardha. Following the demonetization in 2016, repayment behaviour has been affected across the board for MFIs. There have also been tensions flared against MFIs with allegations of their charging exorbitant and hidden interest rates.

Farmer Producer Companies (FPCs) or Farmer Producer Organizations (FPOs) have also grown significantly over the past decade with the distressed regions of Vidarbha and Marathwada accounting for half of all the FPCs in the state.[76] With the promise of an end-to-end value chain, FPCs offer a promising institutional arrangement for aggregation of produce and value added services but there are several challenges that need to be addressed.[77] We discuss our observations in Chapter 7.

Farmers have access to subsidized short-term credit (loans up to 3,00,000 rupees for one year, with an effective interest rate of 4 per cent per annum [Graph 3.1] from commercial banks, cooperative banks, and

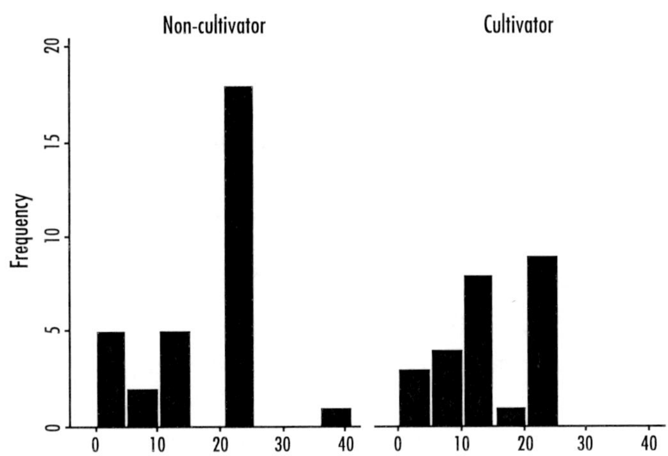

Graph 3.1 Interest rate (% per annum) on loans by household type: 2019

Source: Authors' calculation using survey data.

Note: Loans outstanding as on date of the survey. It includes both institutional and non-institutional credit.

Table 3.8 Source of credit

			2019		
Source	**2009** (N = 137)	**2015** (N = 438)	**Cultivator** (N = 82)	**Non-cultivator** (N = 45)	**All** (N = 127)
Government	-	2.5	2.4	0.0	1.6
Cooperative society	-	40.2	6.1	0.0	3.9
Commercial bank	78.1	31.3	59.8	0.0	38.6
RRB	-	13.7	0.0	4.4	1.6
Moneylender	0.7	0.2	3.7	0.0	2.4
Kinship network	19.7	0.7	1.2	4.4	2.4
SHGs	-	7.5	20.7	46.7	29.9
MFI	-	3.7	6.1	40.0	18.1
Others	1.5	0.2	0.0	4.4	1.6
Total	100.0	100.0	100.0	100.0	100.0

Source: Authors' calculation based on survey data.

Note: Figures are percentages. The percentages add up to 100 per cent.

regional rural banks [RRBs] [Table 3.8]). There has also been a proliferation of small banks and business correspondent (BC) models of financing in the region. Nearly everyone also has a Pradhan Mantri Jan-Dhan Yojana (PMJDY) account—a financial inclusion programme of the NDA central government launched in 2014. In terms of the purpose of the loan (Table 3.9), cultivators primarily borrow for capital expenditure on farm and farm business along with operational expenditure for farms—the subsidized credit discussed earlier. Non-cultivators on the other hand borrow mostly for the education of children and house construction at market interest rates. Non-cultivators also reported borrowing for farm business such as setting up poultry business and animal husbandry as discussed in the context of assets of the households and incomes in Chapters 3 and 4, respectively. This clearly indicates the importance of access to livelihood credit that helps diversify incomes beyond agricultural wage work for non-cultivator households.

From a risk management perspective, non-cultivators had significantly higher borrowing for health and education expenditure in 2019. In 2020, too, we observe a higher expenditure on health due to diagnostics and preventive medications given the pandemic. However, loans for

Table 3.9 Purpose of loan

Purpose	2015 (N = 438)	2019 Cultivator (N = 82)	2019 Non-cultivator (N = 45)
Capital expenditure for farm	2.1	44.6	15.9
Operational expenditure for farm	94.1	48.2	0.0
Non-farm business	0.2	1.2	0.0
Consumption expenditure	0.7	1.2	0.0
Social spending	0.2	0.0	9.1
Education	1.4	1.2	31.8
Health	0.0	0.0	6.8
House construction	0.2	3.6	29.5
Other purpose	1.4	0.0	6.8
Total	100.0	100.0	100.0

Source: Authors' calculation based on survey data.

Note: Figures are percentages. The percentages add up to 100 per cent.

large spending on in-patient treatment requiring hospitalization due to surgeries or chronic diseases is also a source of idiosyncratic risk among the households. In households with members having disabilities and chronic health issues, borrowing to meet expenses related to specialist consultation and diagnostics at secondary and tertiary hospitals in the city is common. Several among the non-cultivator households however benefited from the public health insurance programme for the poor, namely Rashtriya Swasthya Bima Yojana (RSBY). Although instances of high out-of-pocket expenditure related to complicated deliveries and caesarean section deliveries in private hospitals have been reported, conditional cash transfers such as Janani Suraksha Yojana (JSY) for institutional deliveries are believed to protect households from financial hardship due to underlying healh shocks. Whilst cultivators did not report having borrowed for social spending (for example, marriages, festivals, social functions), non-cultivators financed their social spending through loans. These patterns suggest that the lower asset base of non-cultivators makes them more vulnerable to reliance on high-cost non-institutional credit. This is also one of the reasons, as we will see in Chapter 6, for their reliance on credit for risk coping.

CONCLUSION

In this chapter, we described the research methodology and longitudinal study design in detail. We have described the timelines for the quantitative survey and fieldwork conducted in the Wardha and Yavatmal districts of Vidarbha that we have been conducting since 2009 over three survey rounds following exploratory fieldwork in the region in 2008. The inclusion of the Yavatmal district in the second round of survey brought with us some new challenges. Since most field investigators were from the Wardha district, we had to hire somebody who could manage the surveys across both districts. Also, there were issues related to conducting the surveys within a specified period of time for recall purposes. There were gaps in field surveys between the three rounds which made it difficult for us to get a balanced panel across all years. The financial resources available to us were also varying over the three rounds of survey; this also meant we could not have constant sample sizes over all these years. When we wanted to broaden the research questions, it needed a different kind of sample which restricted our scope to have a larger balanced sample.

The resident investigator allayed fears and suspicions that villagers had related to concerns about misuse of the data. Both the respondent and investigators have expressed their frustration with our asking the same questions repeatedly. Cooperation among hardworking enumerators resulted in quality data but conflicts also arose at times. The effort at cross-validation may enrich quality but an aspect of a longitudinal study is that there is an intimate understanding of people and how their lives change over time. We are fortunate to be a part of this story at a critical juncture of this transformation.

NOTES

1. See L. D. Satya, *Cotton and Famine in Berar 1850–1900* (New Delhi: Manohar, 1997), 261–271.
2. Ibid., 281–291.
3. M. Punch, 'Politics and Ethics in Qualitative Research', in *Handbook of Qualitative Research*, ed. N. K. Denzin and Y. S. Lincoln (Newbery Park, CA: Sage, 1994), 162.
4. Before fieldwork in Vidarbha, we had travelled across the country between 2007 and 2008 as part of our professional assignments at the Centre for

Insurance and Risk Management (CIRM) at the Institute for Financial Management and Research (IFMR), Chennai, related to developing microinsurance for the base of the pyramid markets.

5. Our sheer ignorance about qualitative research as graduate students in economics and development studies with a strong quantitative orientation is evident from the fact that the first time we heard of 'grounded theory', we imagined it to be something related to testing theories on the ground—the field. There were also occasions when we would hear economists at seminars claiming to have done grounded theory while what they actually did was far from generating theories grounded in systematic data collection and analysis. We are grateful to Srijit Mishra for encouraging us to conduct ethnography in Vidarbha instead of relying on sample-survey-based primary research alone. We nevertheless conducted several analyses using secondary data pertaining to agricultural households in the region.
6. Our introduction to this perspective on fieldwork was H. F. Wolcott, *The Art of Fieldwork*, 2nd ed. (Walnut Creek, CA: Altamira Press, 2005), 5.
7. C. Geertz, 'Thick Description: Toward an Interpretive Theory of Culture', in *The Interpretation of Cultures: Selected Essays* (New York: Basic Books, 1973), 3–30.
8. M. Shubik, 'Risk, Society, Politicians, Scientists, and People', in *Risk, Organization, and Society* (Dordrecht, Netherlands: Kluwer, 1991), 7–30, 12.
9. For a review of the literature on village studies, see R. Mukherjee, 'On "Village Studies" in India', *Indian Journal of Social Research* 29, no. 4 (1988): 281–294. Seminal social anthropological studies include M. N. Srinivas, ed., *India's Villages* (Bombay: Asia Publishing House, 1955); F. G. Bailey, *Caste and the Economic Frontie*r: *A Village in Highland Orissa* (Manchester: Manchester University Press, 1957); A. Béteille, *Studies in Agrarian Social Structure* (New Delhi: Oxford University Press, 1974); J. Harriss, *Capitalism and Peasant Farming: Agrarian Structure and Ideology in Northern Tamil Nadu* (New Delhi: Oxford University Press, 1982), among others.
10. An early influential study to argue so was M. N. Srinivas, 'The Social System of a Mysore Village', in *Village India: Studies in the Little Community*, ed. M. Marriott (Chicago: The University of Chicago Press, 1995), 1–35. Also see L. Dumont and D. F. Pocock, 'Village Studies', *Contributions to Indian Sociology* 1, no. 1 (1957): 23–41.
11. For a perspective on village studies in larger multi-sited ethnography, see E. Gallo, 'Village Ethnography and Kinship Studies: Perspectives from India and Beyond', *Critique of Anthropology* 35, no. 3 (2015): 248–262.

12. A. Shah and B. Harris-White, 'Resurrecting Scholarship on Agrarian Transformations', *Economic and Political Weekly* 46, no. 39 (2011): 13–18.
13. S. S. Jodhka, 'Nation and Village: Images of Rural India in Gandhi, Nehru and Ambedkar', *Economic and Political Weekly* 37, no. 32 (2002): 3343–3353.
14. Village studies are spread across the country and conducted by scholars from varied disciplines. For studies of village economy in north India, see Himanshu, P. Lanjouw, and N. Stern, *How Lives Change: Palanpur, India, and Development Economics* (Oxford: Oxford University Press, 2018); G. B. Rodgers, 'Nutritionally Based Wage Determination in the Low-Income Labour Market', *Oxford Economic Papers* 27, no. 1 (1975): 61–81; G. Rodgers and J. Rodgers, 'A Leap across Time: When Semi-feudalism Met the Market in Rural Purnia', *Economic and Political Weekly* 36, no. 22 (2001): 1976–1983; G. Rodgers and J. Rodgers, 'Inclusive Development? Migration, Governance and Social Change in Rural Bihar', *Economic and Political Weekly* 46, no. 23 (2011): 43-50. Village studies in south India focusing on agrarian change include T. S. Epstein, *Economic Development and Social Change in South India* (Manchester: Manchester University Press, 1962); T. S. Epstein, A. P. Suryanarayana, and T. Thimmegowda, *Village Voices: Forty Years of Rural Transformation in South India* (New Delhi: Sage Publications, 1998); V. K. Ramachandran, *Wage Labour and Unfreedom in Agriculture: An Indian Case Study* (Oxford: Clarendon Press, 1990). Sociological studies include A. R. Beals, 'Gopalpur: A South Indian Village', in *Case Studies in Cultural Anthropology*, ed. George and Louise Spindler (New York: Holt, Rinehard and Winston, 1962); R. Wade, *Village Republics: Economic Conditions for Collective Action in South India*, Cambridge South Asian Studies, series no. 4 (UK: Cambridge, 1988); S. S. Jodhka, 'From "Book View" to "Field View": Social Anthropological Constructions of the Indian Village', *Oxford Development Studies* 26, no. 3 (1998): 311–331; J. Breman, *The Poverty Regime in Village India: Half a Century of Work and Life at the Bottom of the Rural Economy in South Gujarat*, vol. 13 (New Delhi; Oxford: Oxford University Press, 2007), among others.
15. See J. Breman, P. Kloos, and A. Saith, *The Village in Asia Revisited* (Delhi; Oxford: Oxford University Press, 1997). For an excellent review of lessons from several village studies over time, see H. P. Jha and G. Rodgers, eds., *The Changing Village in India: Insights from Longitudinal Research* (Oxford: Oxford University Press, 2016). Despite not being village studies, Laxman D. Satya's studies on qualitative change under colonial rule in Berar, and works of scholars such as Crispin Bates and D. E. U. Baker offer rich

insights on Central Provinces in the late nineteenth and early twentieth centuries.

16. See C. J. Bliss and N. Stern, *Palanpur: The Economy of an Indian Village* (Oxford: Oxford University Press, 1983); P. Lanjouw and N. Stern, eds., *Economic Development in Palanpur over Five Decades* (Oxford: Oxford University Press, 1998).
17. Two villages of Vidarbha are included in socio-economic surveys of the Project on Agrarian Relations in India (PARI) conducted by the Foundation for Agrarian Studies (FAS). For a study based on Warwat Khanderao in Buldhana in Amravati division, see M. Swaminathan and V. Rawal, 'Is India Really a Country of Low-Income Inequality? Observations from Eight Villages', *Review of Agrarian Studies* 1, no. 1 (2011b): 1–22; and M. Swaminathan and V. Rawal, 'Are There Benefits from the Cultivation of Bt Cotton? A Comment Based on Data from a Vidarbha Village', *Review of Agrarian Studies* 1, no. 1 (2011a): 101–124. For a study based on a resurvey of Dongargaon in Akola district in the Amravati division, see R. Ramakumar and K. Raut, 'Agricultural Employment in a Vidarbha Village: Results from a Resurvey', *Review of Agrarian Studies* 1, no. 1 (2011). The two villages in ICRISAT-VDS, namely Kanzara and Kinkhed, are also in Akola districts.
18. For a study on the relationship between techno-material transformation in cotton and debt in Wardha based on two years of fieldwork, see A. Sethi, 'The Life of Debt in Rural India' (unpublished PhD thesis, UC Berkeley, 2017).
19. See J. Hardikar, *Ramrao: The Story of India's Farm Crisis* (Noida: HarperCollins, 2021).
20. See, for example, Meeta and Rajivlochan, *Farmers Suicide: Facts and Possible Policy Interventions* (Pune: Yashada Publications, 2006); and M. Rajivilochan, 'Farmers Suicide—Facts and Possible Policy Interventions' (Pune: YASHADA, Government of Maharashtra, Yashwantrao Chavan Academy Development Administration), http://www.yashada.org/organisation/FarmersSuicideExcerpts.pdf (accessed on 8 June 2020).
21. For details of the study of village economies in ICRISAT studies, see Thomas S. Walker and James G. Ryan, *Village and Household Economics in India's Semi-arid Tropics* (Baltimore, MD: Johns Hopkins University Press, 1990). For details of the Townsend-Thai Project, see R. M. Townsend, S. Sakunthasathien, and R. Jordan, *Chronicles from the Field: The Townsend Thai Project* (Cambridge, MA: MIT Press, 2013).
22. T. G. Kessinger, *Annals of Rural Punjab – Vilyatpur 1848–1968: Social and Economic Change in a North Indian Village* (Berkeley; Los Angeles;

London: University of California Press, 1974). Among the first village-level studies to be conducted in India was that of Pimple Saudagar near Poona (Pune) in Maharashtra, by Harold H. Mann in 1917. Mann's work included H. H. Mann, *Land and Labour in a Deccan Village*, University of Bombay Economic Series, no. 1 (London: H. Milford, Oxford University Press, 1917), https://dspace.gipe.ac.in/xmlui/bitstream/handle/10973/19804/GIPE-000458.pdf?sequence=3 (accessed on 24 April 2022). Mann also followed it up with a study of another village in Deccan as he felt the first village was not representative of a typical village in the region. See Harold H. Mann and N. V. Kanitkar, *Land and Labour in a Deccan Village, Study No. 2*, University of Bombay Economic Series, no. 3 (London: H. Milford, Oxford University Press, 1921). For significance of Mann's work in agricultural economics, refer to F. C. Bawden, 'Dr Mann's Contribution to Science and Agriculture (reprinted)', *Economic and Political Weekly* 2, no. 13 (1967): 639–641. Also see D. Thorner, 'Social and Economic Studies of Dr Mann', *Economic and Political Weekly* 2, no. 13 (1967): 642–645; and E. J. Russell, 'Dr H. H. Mann', *Nature* 193, no. 4813 (1962): 321–322. Slater was the first economics professor at the University of Madras (present-day Chennai) whose work was G. Slater, *Economic Studies (Volume 1): Some South Indian Villages* (Madras: Oxford University Press, 1918). Unlike Mann, who surveyed all the households in the study village, Slater selected sample households in larger numbers of villages. Since the 1930s, several revisits of the villages, renowned as 'Slater villages' have been conducted. Between the two approaches laid down by these two pioneers, we chose the household sample survey at different points of time against a village census.

23. Over the thirteen years of our study, we had institutional funding and research grants for half of the period. For the remaining half, we managed to fund the study by bootstrapping.
24. Since we plan to continue our investigations of risk and vulnerability in the region on a larger scale and incorporate alternative research strategies, we do not rule out the possibility of a village census nor the use of mixed methods in future studies. The trajectory that our research takes would largely depend on prospects of research funding as well as enthusiastic students and researchers willing to collaborate.
25. Kalyan K. Sanyal, 'Review of Production Conditions in Indian Agriculture by Krishna Bharadwaj', *Economic and Political Weekly* 11, no. 30 (1976): 1113.
26. R. Sanjek, *Ethnography in Today's World: Color Full before Color Blind* (Philadelphia: University of Philadelphia Press, 2014), 66.

27. R. Rukmani and M. Manjula, *Designing Rural Technology Delivery Systems for Mitigating Agricultural Distress: A Study of Wardha District* (MS Swaminathan Research Foundation, Chennai, and Office of the Principal Scientific Adviser to the Government of India, New Delhi, 2009).
28. Seven refers to Form VII containing several ownership details and 12 refers to Form XII in the extract containing details of crops and area under the crops among other details. A related document is 'aath-a' or 8A extract that records the ownership history. In Maharashtra, these records are digitized.
29. Given the impossibility of conducting fieldwork and data collection due to the pandemic, we are grateful to the MOE and ICSSR for extension of the deadline for submission. However, the author also contracted COVID-19 and had to be hospitalized, undergoing recovery at the time this report was submitted.
30. Refer to Townsend, Sakunthasathien, and Jordan, *Chronicles from the Field*; and Walker and Ryan, *Village and Household Economics*.
31. For more details on the difficulties in measuring incomes in rural settings, refer to Himanshu and S. Gaurav, 'Changing Activities, Changing Markets: Agriculture', in *How Lives Change*, ed. Himanshu, Lanjouw, and Stern, 161–195; and A. Saith and A. Tankha, 'Economic Decision-Making of the Poor Peasant Household', *Economic and Political Weekly* 1, no. 1 (1972): 351–360.
32. See V. Surjit, 'The Evolution of Farm Income Statistics in India: A Review', *Review of Agrarian Studies* 7, no. 2 (2008): 1–23, http://www.ras.org.in/the_evolution_of_farm_income_statistics_in_india (accessed on 16 September 2021), for a detailed review of farm income, various concepts involved, and emergence of various surveys in the Indian context.
33. M. V. Jambunathan, *An Economic Survey of Dodda Ganni Village* (Mysore: Seshadri Press, 1950), cited in V. Surjit, 'The Evolution of Farm Income Statistics in India: A Review', *Review of Agrarian Studies* 7, no. 2 (2017).
34. For details of various challenges involved in estimating farm incomes, refer to Saith and Tankha, 'Economic Decision-Making'; and M. Swaminathan, 'In Focus: Crop Incomes in India', *Review of Agrarian Studies* 7, no. 2 (2017).
35. See Ramakumar and Raut, 'Agricultural Employment in a Vidarbha Village'.
36. As per the Hindu Succession (Amendment Act), 2005, daughters in a joint Hindu family, governed by the Mitakshara law, were granted statutory right in the 'coparcenary property' that is father's property, not partitioned or alienated. Furthermore, originally it was applicable if the father died after 2005, but in a 2020 ruling the Supreme Court held that daughters have a

birth right to inherit joint Hindu family property like their brothers. 'Right by Birth: On Daughters and Hindu Succession Act', *The Hindu*, 14 August 2020, https://www.thehindu.com/opinion/editorial/right-by-birth-the-hindu-editorial-on-daughters-and-hindu-succession-act/article32347299.ece (accessed on 3 April 2021).

37. For gaps in skilling in Wardha and Yavatmal across the several skill sectors, see National Skill Development Corporation (NSDC), Government of India, *District-wise Skill Gap Study for the State of Maharashtra (2012–2017, 2017–2022)* (2013), 50, https://skillsip.nsdcindia.org/sites/default/files/kps-document/maha-sg-reports.pdf (accessed on 18 January 2021).
38. The issues related to the scheme and the changes since implementation in school enrolment is mentioned in Sneha Alexander and Surbhi Bhatia, 'Has Beti Bachao Beti Padhao Reduced Gender Imbalance?', *Mint*, 6 February 2020, https://www.livemint.com/news/india/has-beti-bachao-beti-padhao-worked-11580901150760.html (accessed on 26 April 2022).
39. The abysmal utilization of funds by different states is described in detail in Radheshyam Jadhav, 'Beti Bachao, Beti Padhao: 55% of the Funds Remain Unutilised', *Hindu Business Line*, 12 January 2021, https://www.thehindubusinessline.com/data-stories/data-focus/beti-bachao-beti-padhao-55-of-the-funds-remain-unutilised/article33561058.ece (accessed on 26 April 2022).
40. See 'MGNREGS Provides Work to 4.10 Lakh Workers in Vid', *Hitavada*, 22 May 2020, https://www.thehitavada.com/Encyc/2020/5/22/MGNREGS-provides-work-to-4-10-lakh-workers-in-Vid.html (accessed on 26 April 2022).
41. Based on the National Family Health Survey (NFHS) 5.
42. For evidence on the relationship between economic growth and malnutrition in India, see A. Malavika Subramanyam, Ichiro Kawachi, Lisa F. Berkman, and S. V. Subramanian, 'Is Economic Growth Associated with Reduction in Child Undernutrition in India?', *PLOS MEDICINE* 8, no. 3 (2011), https://doi.org/10.1371/journal.pmed.1000424.
43. O. C. Kurian and S. Suri, 'Weighed Down by the Gains: India's Twin Double Burdens of Malnutrition and Disease' (ORF Occasional Paper no. 193, Observer Research Foundation, May 2019). Also see Endang Achadi et al., *Global Nutrition Report: From Promise to Impact: Ending Malnutrition by 2030* (International Food Policy Research Institute, 2016).
44. For studies on declining female LFPR in India, see Vinoj Abraham, 'Employment Growth in Rural India: Distress-Driven?', *Economic and*

Political Weekly 44, no. 16 (2009): 97–104; Farzana Afridi, Taryn Dinkelman, and Kanika Mahajan, 'Why Are Fewer Married Women Joining the Work Force in Rural India? A Decomposition Analysis Over Two Decades', *Journal of Population Economics* 31, no. 3 (2018): 783–818; Sonalde Desai and Omkar Joshi, 'The Paradox of Declining Female Work Participation in an Era of Economic Growth', *Indian Journal of Labour Economics* 62, no. 1 (2019): 55–71; Rahul Lahoti and Hema Swaminathan, 'Economic Development and Women's Labor Force Participation in India', *Feminist Economics* 22, no. 2 (2016): 168–195.

45. For the complex socio-political aspects of Kunbis, Marathas and the related 'Maratha Kunbi' caste categories in Maharashtra, see R. Deshpande, 'Kunbi Maratha as OBC: Backward Journey of a Caste', *Economic and Political Weekly* 39, nos. 14/15 (2004): 1448–1449.
46. For a rich description of characteristics of the caste and sub-castes in the region and their relationship with agriculture, from a colonial perspective, see Robert Vane Russell and Rai Bahadur Hiralal, *Tribes and Castes of the Central Provinces of India*, vol. 4 (London: Macmillan & Co., 1916).
47. See Kiran Tare, 'Maharashtra: Despite SC Ruling That Maratha Reservation Is Unconstitutional, the Demand Again Gathers Momentum', *India Today*, 14 May 2021, https://www.indiatoday.in/magazine/up-front/story/20210524-maharashtra-despite-sc-ruling-that-maratha-reservation-is-unconstitutional-the-demand-again-gathers-momentum-1802533-2021-05-14 (accessed on 24 May 2021).
48. See Government of India, 'C-1 Population by religion community – 2011', The Registrar General & Census Commissioner, India, for religion-wise distribution in Maharashtra and India. Available at https://censusindia.gov.in/2011census/C-01.html (accessed on 18 June 2021).
49. Maren Bellwinkel-Schempp, 'Roots of Ambedkar Buddhism in Kanpur', in *Reconstructing the World: B. R. Ambedkar and Buddhism in India*, ed. Surendra Jondhale and Johannes Beltz (New Delhi: Oxford University Press, 2004), 221–244.
50. B. B. Mohanty, '"We Are Like the Living Dead": Farmer Suicides in Maharashtra, Western India', *Journal of Peasant Studies* 32, no. 2 (2005): 243–276.
51. See *Maharashtra Gazetteers: Yavatmal* and *Maharashtra Gazetteers: Wardha*.
52. The district-wise land-size data for the state of Maharashtra in the Agricultural Census of 2010–2011 is provided in http://krishi.maharashtra.

gov.in/Site/Upload/Pdf/Publications/Argi.pdf (accessed on 26 April 2022); and the details of the 2015–2016 Agricultural census for the state of Maharashtra is provided in http://krishi.maharashtra.gov.in/Site/Upload/Pdf/Agriculture%20Census%202015-2016%20Final%20for%20website_part3_pages36-60.pdf (accessed on 26 April 2022).

53. Information based on the agricultural census 2015–2016 for India is available at https://agcensus.nic.in/document/agcen1516/T1_ac_2015_16.pdf (accessed on 26 April 2022).
54. Rukmani and Manjula, 'Designing Rural Technology Delivery Systems'.
55. For estimates of the Gini coefficient of land ownership at the district level in India, refer to Y. Li, 'Land Inequality and the Provision of Public Works: Evidence from National Rural Employment Guarantee Scheme in India' (2019), available at SSRN 3347482.
56. For a detailed analysis of regional land distribution in Maharashtra, see N. Rajasekaran, 'Land Reforms in Maharashtra: A Regional Analysis', *Review of Development and Change* 3, no. 2 (1998): 238–263.
57. By 'moisture advantage' we refer to the ability of the *olit* farmers to provide their seeds and plants with greater moisture in comparison to the *koradwahu* farmers.
58. Mahindra and Mahindra (M&M) is the most popular tractor brand in the villages whereas other brands including TAFE (Eicher and Massey Fergusson), Sonalika, Escort, Swaraj, and John Deere also have their presence. Thirty to forty-seven HP tractors are mostly available in the market. There is also an active used-tractor market in both the study districts.
59. Historically, bullocks have played an important role in the life of the cultivators in Wardha (see Russell and Hiralal, *Tribes and Castes of the Central Provinces of India*) and continue to do so even today.
60. Few farmers also use rotavators along with tractors for ploughing.
61. This was owing to the thematic focus of the survey round being on understanding of agricultural inputs, particularly insecticides, weedicides, and tonics.
62. NABARD, 'Doubling Farmers' Income: Issues and Strategies for Maharashtra State', National Bank for Agriculture and Rural Development and Yes Bank (2019), 103–110, https://www.nabard.org/auth/writereaddata/tender/2406190028Doubling%20Farmers%202019%20Income%20-%20Issues%20and%20Strategies%20for%20Maharashtra.pdf (accessed on 23 June 2020).

63. The consortium for CAIM consists of the Government of Maharashtra, the International Fund for Agricultural Development (IFAD), and the Sir Ratan Tata Trust (SRTT). The programme was implemented between 2012 and 2018. Gaurav had the opportunity of attending the all-stakeholder meeting to discuss the possibilities of CAIM at Amravati district. For evidence from impact evaluations, see S. Bandyopadhyay, L. Joshi, P. K. Chaudhuri, T. Buragohain, and A. Sharma, *Impact Evaluation of the Maharashtra CAIM Programme* (National Council of Applied Economic Research [NCAER], New Delhi, 2019); and A. G. Angaitkar, 'Impact of Convergence of Agricultural Interventions in Maharashtra (CAIM) Programme on Beneficiaries of Distress-Prone District in Vidarbha' (PhD thesis, PDKV, Akola, 2018), https://krishikosh.egranth.ac.in/handle/1/5810117621 (accessed on 21 May 2021).
64. A. C. Lohakare, B. P. Kamdi, M. K. Nakadei, V. K. Basunathae, and V. Banthiya, 'Extent of Knowledge of Improved Animal Husbandry Practices and Socio-economical, Psychological Characteristics of Dairy Farmers of Yavatmal District of Vidarbha (Maharashtra)', *Veterinary Science Research Journal* 6, no. 1 (2015): 23–31.
65. For details related to the issues related to the dairy sector development in Vidarbha, see T. Shah, Y. Mehta, V. Kher, and A. Palrecha, 'Generating Agrarian Dynamism: Saurashtra's Lessons for Vidarbha', *Economic and Political Weekly* 49, nos. 26/27 (2015): 86–94.
66. For a detailed description of the rituals involved in the Pola festival, and how it symbolises bullocks as important members of the agricultural community in Vidarbha, see A. Sethi, 'Mahadev's Gift: Men, Bullocks and the Community of Cultivation in Central India', *Journal of South Asian Studies* 42, no. 6 (2019): 1173–1191.
67. For studies on farmers' suicides in Vidarbha and Maharashtra that identify the issue of indebtedness, see S. Mishra, 'Farmers' Suicides in Maharashtra', *Economic and Political Weekly* 41, no. 16 (2006): 1538–1545; S. Mishra, 'Risks, Farmers' Suicides and Agrarian Crisis in India: Is There a Way Out?', *Indian Journal of Agricultural Economics* 63, no. 1 (2008): 38–54; Mohanty, '"We Are Like the Living Dead"'; R. M. Mohan Rao, *Suicides among Farmers: A Study of Cotton Growers* (New Delhi: Concept Publishing Company, 2004), among several others. For studies on indebtedness and farmers' suicides in other regions and states, see R. S. Deshpande, 'Suicide by Farmers in Karnataka: Agrarian Distress and Possible Alleviatory Steps', *Economic and Political Weekly* 37, no. 25 (2002): 2601–2610; K. G. Iyer and M. S. Manick,

Impoverishment and Suicides in Rural Punjab (New Delhi: Indian Publishers Distributors, 2000).

68. For an authoritative account of the distributional issues in institutional credit delivery in India, see S. L. Shetty, 'Distributional Issues in Bank Credit: Multi-Pronged Strategy for Correcting Past Neglect', *Economic and Political Weekly* 39, no. 29 (2004): 3265–3269.
69. For an excellent analysis of the trends in agricultural credit during the period and a contextualization of the debate, see P. Chavan and R. Ramakumar, 'Revival of Agricultural Credit in the 2000s: An Explanation', *Economic and Political Weekly* 42, no. 52 (2007): 57–63. Also see A. Gulati and S. Bathla, 'Institutional Credit to Indian Agriculture: Defaults and Policy Options' (Occasional Paper no. 23, NABARD, Mumbai, 2002); and K. G. Kshirsagar and D. Shah, *Flow of Credit to Small and Marginal Farmers in Maharashtra* (AERC Study Report, Gokhale Institute of Politics and Economics, Pune, 2002). For a perspective on issues in priority sector lending and challenges faced by the public sector banks in the 1990s, see N. A. Mujumdar, 'Financial Sector Reforms: An Exercise in Introspection', *Economic and Political Weekly* 31, no. 12 (1996): 727–730; and N. A. Mujumdar, 'Credit Support to Priority Sectors: A Macro Perspective', *Economic and Political Weekly* 33, no. 4 (1998): 147–150.
70. Renita D'Souza, 'Improving Access to Agricultural Credit: New Perspectives' (ORF Occasional Paper no. 230, Observer Research Foundation, January 2020).
71. J. Kennedy and L. King, 'The Political Economy of Farmers' Suicides in India: Indebted Cash-Crop Farmers with Marginal Landholdings Explain State-Level Variation in Suicide Rates', *Globalization and Health* 10, no. 16 (2014), https://doi.org/10.1186/1744-8603-10-16. Also see Government of India, *Report of Fact-Finding Team on Vidarbha: Regional Disparities and Rural Distress in Maharashtra with Particular Reference to Vidarbha* (New Delhi: Planning Commission, Government of India, 2006); and N. Deshmukh, 'Cotton Growers: Experience from Vidarbha', in *Agrarian Crisis and Farmer Suicides*, ed. R. S. Deshpande and S. Arora (New Delhi: Sage, 2010), 175–191.
72. *Dedhi* refers to the literal meaning of 1.5 times, and *sawai* has reference to its literal meaning of 1.25 times.
73. Any quotation not accompanied by a formal citation is taken from interviews conducted by the author.

74. See M. V. Gadgil, 'Formal Agricultural Credit System in India: Shape of Things to Come', *Indian Journal of Agricultural Economics* 49, no. 3 (1994): 476–490; V. Puhazhendhi and B. Jayaraman, 'Rural Credit Delivery: Performance and Challenges Before Banks', *Economic and Political Weekly* 34, nos. 3/4 (1999): 175–182.
75. In 2013, the Government of India launched the National Rural Livelihood Mission (NRLM) by restructuring the Swarnjayanti Gram Swarojgar Yojana (SGSY). It was renamed DAY-NRLM (Deendayal Antyodaya Yojana – National Rural Livelihoods Mission) since 2016. The objective of this flagship programme is poverty reduction strong institution building. Women are active stakeholders in these institutions that have improved access to several financial services and livelihood generation initiatives. For details of the financing mechanisms and norms of good SHGs, see 'Circulars', NABARD, https://www.nabard.org/CircularPage.aspx?cid=504&id=5237 (accessed on 26 April 2022).
76. Radheshyam Jadhav, 'Why FPCs Are a Ray of Hope for Distressed Farmers in Maharashtra', *Hindu Business Line*, https://www.thehindubusinessline.com/news/why-fpcs-are-a-ray-of-hope-for-distressed-farmers-in-maharashtra/article34139545.ece (accessed on 30 January 2021).
77. R. Govil, A. Neti, and M. R. Rao, *Farmer Producer Companies: Past, Present and Future* (Bangalore: Azim Premji University, 2020), https://archive.azimpremjiuniversity.edu.in/SitePages/pdf/Farmer_Producer_Companies_Past_Present_and_Future.pdf (accessed on 17 July 2021).

4

GAMBLES OF FARMERS

On a mid-May afternoon in 2018, as the usual scorching heat greeted us during our visit to a village in Wardha district, we witnessed a disturbing event. A tractor was dragging a dead bullock along the stretch of an all-weather road bisecting farmlands en route to the village. As we wondered how the tragic visuals symbolized the essence of agrarian change and continuity—tractors replacing bullocks and human labour increasingly giving way to machines—we spotted a group of villagers consoling the visibly distressed farmer who had just lost an important asset and an animal he had shared a bond with. After all, bullocks and oxen have been valuable assets for Vidarbha cultivators, and are an integral part of their cultural identity, as discussed in Chapters 2 and 5.

What struck us at this instance, however, was that each farmer had a theory about the cause of the young bullock's sudden demise. The competing theories of the bullock's death notwithstanding, the farmer's misfortune was aggravated by the fact that he had lost one of his pair of bullocks right before the commencement of land preparation for the major agricultural season (kharif). Before tragedy struck, we were told he had hoped of repaying his debts, and marrying off his daughter with the income that he would earn from cultivating cotton on his two acres of land. To make matters worse, vagaries of monsoon, risk of pest infestation, and uncertainties of the market loomed large on the horizon. We could not help but wonder if, at the end of the cotton-picking season, he would manage to get the money he had hoped for. During a follow-up visit that year, we found out that though he could recover from the loss at the start of the agricultural season by managing agricultural operations with a rented pair of bullocks, he ran out of luck months later when a drought-like situation prevailed. His cotton yields were low, and it was only with the financial support of his kith and kin that he could wade through the year. Without recourse to any earning from rabi cultivation due to poor retained moisture on his plot, he waited for the next season hoping it would bring better outcomes and help him finance his daughter's wedding. He was unable to repay the loans he had borrowed. Of course, he was not alone as there were several others in the village who were affected by some misfortune or the other apart from the losses due to deficit rainfall that season, and carried on with their tryst with precarity. Unfortunately, they continue to do so in the absence of effective risk mitigation and sustainable solutions for protecting farmers from the brunt of frequent financial risks that render farm incomes unstable and aggravate their precarity.

Examination of historical cropping patterns (Chapter 2) as well as our observations over the years demonstrate that agricultural households including cultivator and non-cultivator households routinely diversify their sources of income. Even though cotton cultivation is the predominant agricultural activity, households also derive incomes from other crops grown on their own farm or leased-in land, working on the farms of others, and engaging in several non-farm activities in their village as well as outside. Although non-farm diversification patterns in the villages are embedded in the trajectory of India's structural transformation, it is hard to generalize the occupational profiles as well as distribution by farm size or caste. Understanding these livelihood strategies of agricultural households necessitates understanding why and how they diversify their livelihoods among farm and non-farm opportunities. There is no doubt that the yield of the crops primarily depends on the quantity and quality of inputs applied, biotic and abiotic stresses, as well as agronomic practices followed. However, uncertainty about yield becomes a source of anxiety for farmers (unless otherwise stated, we use cultivator and farmer interchangeably), season after season irrespective of whether they consider themselves as 'good' or 'progressive' relative to others of their ilk in the village.

Following the input intensive production systems that have become the norm since the Green Revolution, farmers have embraced a high external input system of production. In primarily the irrigated tracts, the emphasis on hybrid seeds since the 1970s, intensification of irrigation, and widespread farm mechanization set in motion a pattern of increasing commercialization of agricultural inputs that deepened the farmers' dependence on the market for agricultural inputs and, consequently, on credit. However, with predominantly rain-fed agriculture, Vidarbha farmers gamble by betting their hard-earned savings and borrowed capital despite high risk of indebtedness to increase their incomes from cultivation.

The past two decades witnessed the proliferation of genetically modified cotton seeds—Bt cotton, whose legitimacy leveraged on heightened levels of yield anxiety as we elaborate in Chapter 5. Further, failures of agricultural extension systems to address the informational needs of farmers as well frailty of their traditional knowledge in a fast-changing agricultural input landscape has eroded farmers' confidence in crop and input choices. The current environment is one where the cotton farmer struggles to eke out a livelihood from typically low and uncertain income from agriculture. Undoubtedly, the same fate has afflicted growers of other crops across the country as much of our own research and that of contemporary scholars suggests. However, the distress centred on cotton in Vidarbha in particular becomes the fulcrum for our discussion.

To make matters worse, the average landholdings are now too small for the farmer to either benefit from size economies or use the small parcels of land as collateral for substantial long-term credit for capital investment in farm improvement. Given the production technology, attaining economies of scale wherein all inputs are changed in the same proportion for more than proportionate increase in crop output is also challenging for the smallholders. At the same time, the structural transformation and educational development has not offered enough remunerative opportunities for non-farm diversification, a theme that runs uniformly throughout our discussion in Chapters 6 and 7.

Given the centrality of crops in determining incomes of farmer households and the potentially catastrophic consequences of lower-than-expected yields and crop failures, we ask the following questions in this chapter: How do farmers decide which crops to grow? What has been the experience of farmers with the yield and prices of these crops over the years? What have been the changes in agricultural input usage over time? What are the sources of income other than cultivation? These are some of the key questions central to characterizing the gambles that farmers routinely face.

In order to frame these gambles meaningfully, it is necessary to understand what is at stake or what the farmers stand to lose or gain from their decisions; what are the odds of fortuitous and ruinous events; what are the informational structures under which farmers strategize; and most importantly, what is the nature of 'choice' in these gambles. In this chapter, we begin by detailing the circumstances of the households with regard to their agricultural operations and examine cropping patterns and crop incomes related to it. We dwell on the phenomenon of increasing intensity of purchased agricultural inputs, and how their use has changed over the duration of our study. We especially discuss how, over the years, different agricultural inputs have assumed varied significance in the farmers' decision matrix.

Every season new seeds and chemical inputs are introduced; each promising higher returns or 'bang for the buck'. Thousands of seed brands, pesticides, chemical growth-promoters, and novel farm equipment such as battery-operated spray pumps are among several products that are sold through smart marketing tactics and advisory of the agricultural inputs retail outlets called the *krishi vikas kendra* or *krishi kendra* (agriculture development centres) in the nearby towns. At the start of every season, farmers become part of a bustling bazaar (market) of agricultural inputs where the agrochemicals and farm equipment companies vie for a greater share in the growing market for agricultural inputs. For a perspective, the value of Indian agrochemicals market in 2021 was estimated to be about 7.2 billion US dollars with the farmers using about 62,000 metric tonnes of pesticides.[1]

It is not that farmers simply resign to their fate in the changing climate and market, rather they actively undertake ex ante risk management that allows risk hedging such as crop diversification apart from ex post risk management including labour market adjustments, borrowing, and asset sales, among others. Whenever there is a squeeze, which is quite frequent, farmers tide over by their reliance on multiple coping strategies as elaborated in Chapter 6. As a stylized fact of cotton growing in Vidarbha, there are several mechanisms through which the fluctuations in income occur. Even in years when revenue might have been less variable, input price or quality changes alone can determine whether the farmer incurred profits or losses.

In this chapter, we also explore variations in crop economics across farmer households and land-size classes. This analysis is critical given the heterogeneity in capacity to deal with income shocks. Over the years, we also find that farmers' willingness to adopt new technologies has generally increased. It is not simply the aspiration for higher household income but also stabilization of incomes that often motivates farmers' cropping patterns and livelihood diversification strategies. This behaviour has been evident ever since historic times as we saw in Chapters 1 and 2.

CROPPING PATTERNS

The most striking features of the changes in cropping pattern over our study period are nested in the context of a significant decline in the size of land cultivated in the pooled sample. Between 2009 and 2020, there was a stark decline in average cultivated land (Graph 4.1) in our pooled sample respondents. The average size of cultivated land (also operational land) since 2011 in fact implies that the average farmer in the sample can be classified as smallholder based on land cultivated.

Data from eight out of the twelve years over which the study was conducted reflect the trend of declining landholdings across the sample. Three primary reasons are plausible. First, owing to partitioning of households or subdivision of lands which is a stylized fact in rural India, size of landholdings is expected to be lower over generations. Second, changes in land-use patterns over short periods of time like shifting land for brick kilns and new houses may also result in a reduction in total area under the plough

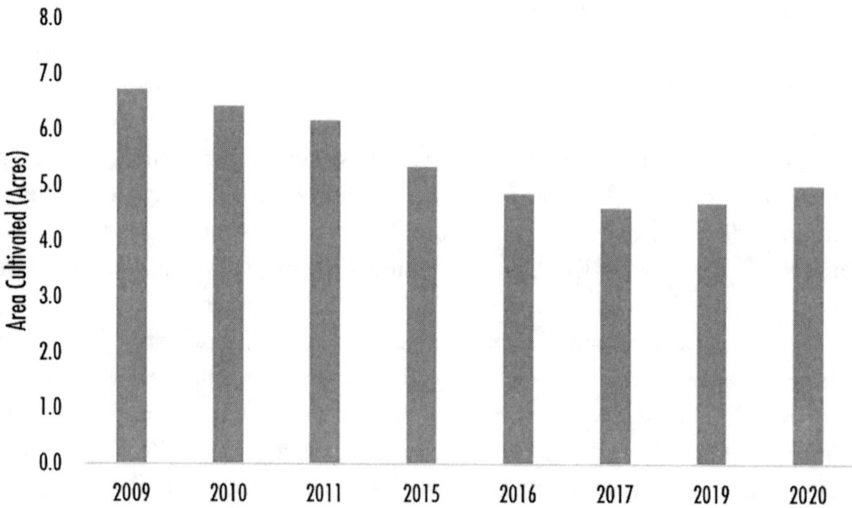

Graph 4.1 Cultivated area: 2009–2020

Source: Survey data.

Note: Average cultivated area of cotton, *tur*, and soybean only. These are not panel households , but the pooled sample. Nevertheless, the patterns are qualitatively similar for the panel households over a smaller period. Across all our analysis, we have indicated the data of survey years, which involves gaps, in a contiguous manner for representative convenience.

if the available culturable land shrinks, ceteris paribus. Third, the former two reasons notwithstanding, exposure to systematic shocks such as drought or other natural disasters may also constrain households in expanding the area cultivated. Engagements with farmers suggest that the steady decline in land in the villages is largely a consequence of household subdivision of land typically following the death of the household head or feuds among brothers even when the parents are alive. Such changes are commensurate with the trend of reduction in household land ownership over time as discussed in Chapter 3.

In 2019 and 2020, there was a slight increase in average cultivated area. Part of the reason might be due to the pandemic in 2020 during which there was an out of the ordinary increase in area sown across the whole country.[2] This has been caused largely due to the reverse migration of family members all over the country—a phenomenon labelled as movement from factories to farms.[3] Over the years, farmers have also leased in land for cultivation. In the study villages, the typical leasing in contract is in the form of a fixed rent. Very little sharecropping is found in these villages. It is typically observed that farmers owning a large area of land (greater than 10 acres) and with tractors and sufficient family labour are the ones who lease in land. The leasing out is usually done by the absentee landlords with salaried jobs and urban residence. Given the difficulties involved in monitoring, the lease contract is typically in the form of a *makta* contract (fixed rent lease). The rent is paid at the beginning of the traditional new year on the day of Gudi Padva (around March or April) for a year. As of 2021–2022, the lease for an acre of irrigated land was 7,000 rupees while that for rain-fed land was 4,000–5,000 rupees. The rent for the irrigated land increased by about 40 per cent over the last five years. In very few instances where we observed sharecropping, the cost of inputs and outputs were shared by the landowner and the lessee in a ratio of 50:50. These contracts were usually prevalent in the rabi season where the households cultivated wheat for their own consumption. It was also not uncommon for outsiders to lease-in land on *makta*.

On the issue of land use patterns resulting in decline in area available for cultivation, several major developments associated with urbanization and infrastructural development have taken place in the study villages and their vicinity. There has been a proliferation of brick kilns over the years. With the road from Wardha to the village cluster, there are scores of brick kilns, usually owned by residents of Wardha (Image 4.1). While most brick kilns

Image 4.1 Brick kiln along the road to Wardha villages, circa 2018
Source: Sarthak Gaurav.

are owned by non-residents on land bought or leased in from villagers, even study village residents own a few brick kilns. The labour in these brick kilns is mostly migrant worker families from the eastern Vidarbha districts of Bhandara, Chandrapur, and Gadchiroli.

Luck also appears in a peculiar form of loss of land due to infrastructural development that has been a jackpot for a few. In 2019, under the Maharashtra Samruddhi Mahamarg—the Mumbai–Nagpur super-expressway—*koradwahu* (rain-fed) lands were acquired for 12 lakh rupees an acre whereas *olit* (irrigated) land were obtained at a rate of 18 lakh rupees an acre.[4] If there was a well on the land but it was dry, the value was 16 lakh rupees per acre. The payments were done through direct bank transfer, obviating the concerns about bribery and commissions that land deals in cash are commonly associated with. There are stories of arbitrage opportunities and allegations of 'insider' information about potential route plans that strongly influenced land deals prior to land acquisition under eminent domain given the high stakes involved. In the study villages in Wardha, four–five households are reported to have benefitted from around 35 acres of land acquired for infrastructure projects.

Jealousy and regret about land deals are often rife. In 2010–2011, similar land deals for the Lanco thermal power plant saw agricultural land being sold for 3–30 lakh rupees per acre in the villages of Mandwa and Pulahi near Lonsavli and Shekapur that resulted in overnight fortune reversals. However, these fortune reversals were often not permanent as some are known to have gambled away their fortune and splurged on houses and SUVs. Alcoholism also became an issue for a few. A farmer in the vicinity got 60 lakh rupees by selling his land, which he is believed to have blown away. Some villagers quip that the biggest impact for him was that 'he switched to foreign liquor from desi *daaru*'. The individual who had a windfall from the land acquisition, unfortunately, committed suicide a few years later.

CROP DIVERSITY

Farmers in the study villages mainly grow three crops under predominantly rain-fed conditions in the main agricultural season, that is the kharif season: cotton, soybean (also soyabean), and *tur* (pigeon pea or red gram). Cotton and soybean are the major cash crops whilst *tur* is primarily used for household consumption while the marketable surplus is sold. Farmers having access to irrigation or those without access to irrigation but retained moisture from the monsoon rains grow two major crops in the rabi season: wheat and *chana* (chickpea or Bengal gram).[5] Among other grams, black gram (*udid*) and green gram (*mung*) are also grown sparsely. A small fraction of the irrigated farmers grows horticultural crops such as orange (mandarin), sweet lime, lemon, pomegranate, banana, papaya, custard apple, guava, mango, watermelon, and musk melon among others. Sugarcane is also grown by a few. Fewer still grow vegetables such as brinjal, tomato, ladies finger, onion, cabbage, cauliflower and seasonal green leafy vegetables as their main crop. Indeed, there are village-wide variations in the horticultural crops and vegetable growing patterns, and there are instances of outliers within a village as well.

Whilst we have spent considerable time explaining the history of cotton in the region in Chapter 2, the emergence of soybean as a major cash crop in the region is no less fascinating. Initially introduced as a rich source of protein, defeating the raison d'etre of its introduction, it quickly became a cash crop catering to the protein requirement of cattle—as processed into cattle feed. In the Malwa region of Madhya Pradesh, it was introduced in the early 1970s around the time when the *mandi* system was established.[6] Since the late 1980s, with developments in soybean-processing infrastructure that resulted in traders (commission agents) contracted by the companies procuring at the *mandi* through auctions, soybean emerged as a popular cash crop. In the mid-1990s, changing trade policy relating to the import of edible oils resulted in high prices of soybean oil in domestic markets. Furthermore, the opening of soybean futures trading since 1999 through the SBOT exchange of Soybean Processors Association of India (SOPA) and National Commodity & Derivatives Exchange Limited (NCDEX) in the mid-2000s influenced spot market prices significantly.[7]

In Vidarbha, soybean began competing with cotton in acreage. It has replaced *jawari* (sorghum) that was cultivated in large area until the 1980s. In fact, in Chapter 2, we also described how in different districts of the Central Provinces, *jawari* was a crop of significance not only from a food security perspective but also for fodder for livestock. Without doubt, the widespread replacement of *jawari* by cotton was a defining feature of the late nineteenth- and early twentieth-century Vidarbha.[8] Graphs 4.2 and 4.3 show the dynamics of the acreage of cotton, soybean, *tur*, and sorghum—the four major crops over the past five decades in Wardha and Yavatmal districts, respectively.

Cotton has significantly higher acreage than soybean in both districts, with Yavatmal being the larger cotton district among the two. However, in Wardha, soybean acreage had been higher than cotton for several years in the past two decades. With increasing acreage of soybean, which competed with the dominant cotton crop, it substituted the acreage of major food and fodder crop sorghum in kharif.[9] It is surprising that despite producing soybean for the industry that processes it to prepare deoiled cakes (DOC) which are a major export to meet the growing demands of livestock industry in the United States, most farmers in Vidarbha are oblivious of the trade and its destination. Such lack of awareness notwithstanding, several factors have contributed to the emergence of soybean as a major crop, more so in Wardha than in Yavatmal.

First, soybean cultivation is less costly than cotton cultivation. In our surveys, we find that the per acre cost of cultivation for cotton has ranged from 1.4 times to 2.4 times that of soybean. This implies farmers could cultivate soybean with lesser input costs, and probably lesser credit. Second, soybean has a higher seeding rate (more seeds per acre of produce) compared to the competing crops. Third, soybean being a short maturity crop (around 90 days) is less exposed to the vagaries of monsoon in comparison to cotton,

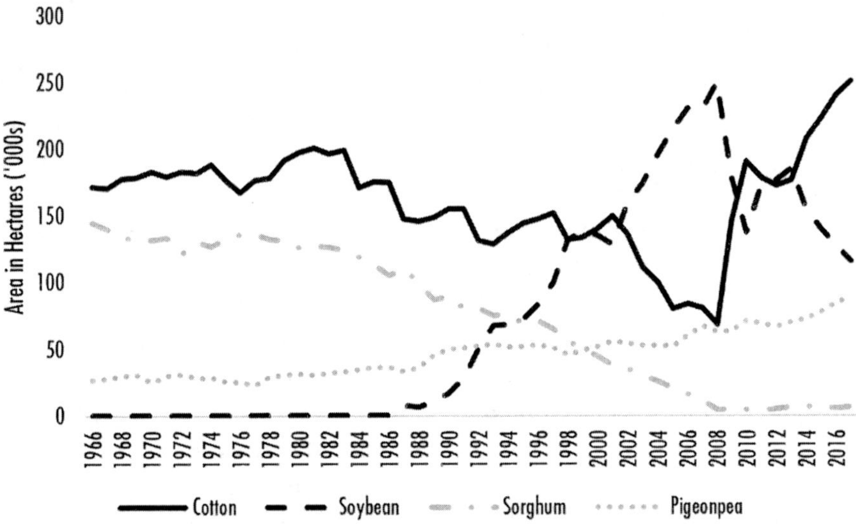

Graph 4.2 Area under major crops in Wardha: 1966–2017

Source: District Level data (DLD) collected by ICRISAT-TCI, http://data.icrisat.org/dld/src/about-dld.html (accessed on 28 May 2021).

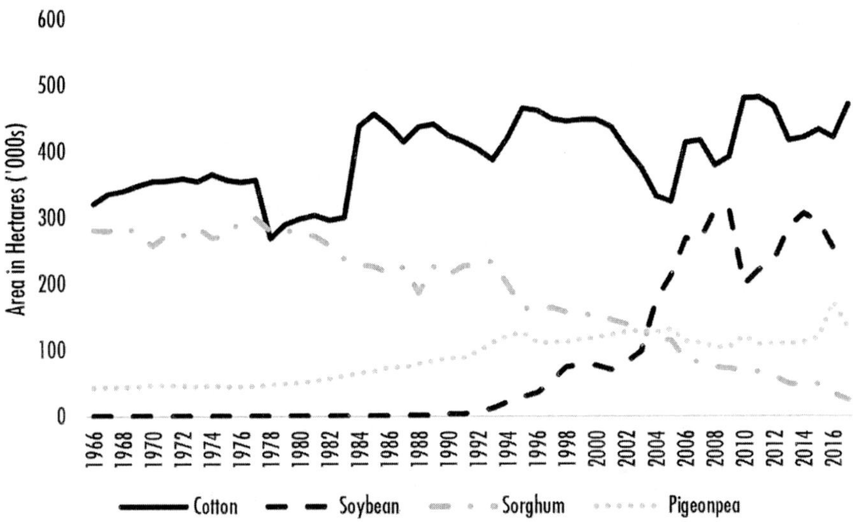

Graph 4.3 Area under major crops in Yavatmal: 1966–2017

Source: District Level Data (DLD) collected by ICRISAT-TCI, http://data.icrisat.org/dld/src/about-dld.html (accessed on 30 May 2021).

which varies from maturity periods in the range of 140 to 180 days. Fourth, as discussed earlier, farmers in low-lying areas frequently experience waterlogging during excess rainfall periods. However, soybean has been observed to be more resilient to the problem of waterlogging, unlike cotton. Farmers growing soybean manage to salvage some value in the eventuality of waterlogging while cultivating cotton in such instances results in substantial losses. Fifth, growing food crops like wheat and gram which were grown as dry rabi crops became less lucrative on account of more tedious and costly land preparation operations. Soybean substituted the acreage of those plots which would have been left fallow in the kharif season. Sixth, consequent to soybean production being preferred to sorghum production over the last three decades, even the few who continued to grow sorghum faced the risk of frequent damages by *dukar* (wild boars) and *rohi* (wild deer) venturing into the field from the bordering forest areas.[10] In recent years, there have been increasing reports of such animal–human conflict that has resulted in many choosing to adopt electrical fencing to protect their crops from damage inflicted by the foraging animals, which are however protected under wildlife protection laws of the land.

Until the late 1980s, sorghum along with cotton accounted for two-thirds of the gross cropped area. Soybean started replacing sorghum since the 1980s and the share of sorghum in the gross cropped area (GCA) reduced from about one-third to 6 per cent in a span of two decades.[11] In relation to the decline of the *jawari* acreage, the following issues are notable. First, the reduction in acreage and availability of an important food crop like sorghum carries substantial 'nutritional security risk' for households reliant on predominantly cash crops for their livelihood. It has been found that the six districts of the severely distressed western Vidarbha region experienced substantial undernutrition and households acknowledge the role of growing food crops in promoting higher nutritional security.[12] Since sorghum produced was mostly consumed by the household, its absence from the diet could have had some ramifications on households' nutritional safety as dietary diversity reduced significantly. However, with the disappearance of sorghum, households in the region substituted it with the softer alternatively namely *gahu chapatti* (wheat breads). Interestingly, such concerns of nutritional security of the Vidarbha farm households have been raised earlier in the historical context of substantial switching of acreage from food crops, particularly pulses, to cash crops such as cotton.[13] Second, with the dramatic decline in sorghum acreage, there has been a fodder as well as feed crisis. Moreover, farmers complained of the non-availability of fodder and feed on most occasions or availability of poor-quality fodder and feed: factors which have invariably contributed to the decline of livestock rearing in the villages in general. Third, sorghum being a rain-fed crop, its water (moisture) requirements are low. Being substituted by high water requiring crops like soybean, there emerges a problem of 'inefficient water utilization' in a rain-fed region, and aggravation of water stress in agriculture.

As in other regions, the cultivable land is typically divided into plots, and there is diversification both at the plot level as well as across plots. Every crop season, farmers adjust their area allocated to these crops. In the initial study years, few households in our sample were cultivating *jawari*. However, over a decade, it nearly vanished in the study villages. As we will see in our examination of household consumption data in Chapter 6, *jawari* consumption whilst reduced significantly has not vanished as it purchased by several households for the preparation of a traditional bread—*bhakri*.[14]

How do farmers allocate land among the aforementioned crops every season? Over the years, farmers have patiently explained to us how the area share of crops are determined largely by subsistence requirements of the family and their experiences in the previous years: yield, prices, duration of the crop growth, access to irrigation, and timely availability of credit and agricultural inputs. One of the biggest stories of change in the agricultural development of Vidarbha over the past two decades has been the diffusion of Bt cotton. Graphs 4.2 and 4.3 show that since 2008, the acreage of cotton grew markedly due to the diffusion of Bt cotton. However, a period of five years—2010–2014—saw a stagnation of cotton acreage. Both 2014 and 2015 were poor rainfall years, and cotton yields had been poor. Pink bollworm (PBW) infestation and the issue of secondary pests continue to be a serious concern for farmers.[15] The initial response to this emergence was excessive spraying of pesticides. Since this did not provide much damage control, some farmers have resigned to the ineffectiveness of pesticides, and have refrained from pesticide spraying in some years. The complexities involved in adoption of damage control practices is highlighted in Chapter 5.

Variations in soil type also influence the crop choice across the districts. There is considerable variation within a district as well. Three-fourths of the cultivable area in Wardha is endowed with medium-deep black and coarse shallow soil of nearly similar extent, while deep black soils constitute the remaining quarter of the area. Yavatmal, on the other hand, has nearly three-fourths of its cultivable area as coarse shallow soil; nearly a quarter as deep black soil, and a minuscule fraction of the land is medium-deep black soil.[16] Farmers in both the districts with whom we have interacted believe that soil in Yavatmal is heavier and hence better quality compared to that in Wardha.

Variations in experience with specific seeds, crops, and attributes of soil aside, agronomic practices also vary. It is evident that farmers have been practising intercropping for centuries (see Chapter 2). In the early rounds, we documented elaborate intercropping systems for cotton and soybean production, predominantly with *tur* as an intercrop. The intercropping patterns are a classic example of ex ante risk management through spatial diversification at the plot level, comprising precise spatial arrangements of the plants on a plot and are discussed at length in a subsequent chapter when we discuss agronomic practices—*paddhat*. While, cotton–*tur* and soybean–*tur* intercropping systems were the predominant cropping systems in the villages, sole cropping or monocropping of cotton, soybean, and *tur* was also prevalent. Soybean is typically cultivated in a plot other than the one in which cotton is cultivated.[17] Contrary to cotton and soybean, whatever little sorghum was grown, it was not intercropped. Instead, farmers practised mixed farming of sorghum with green gram. This practice does not consider specific spatial arrangements as in the case of intercropping. It was observed that some farmers add a few lines of pigeon pea to their sorghum farms as well to have a more diversified cropping system.

At this juncture, it would be informative to understand how cropping patterns in the study villages compare with that of the two districts. From the shares of area cultivated in our study sample, it is evident that cotton is the mainstay of the village economy, with about half to two-thirds of kharif area under cotton over the study years (Graph 4.4)—similar to the patterns observed at the district level. As in the case at the district level (Graphs 4.2 and 4.3), the share of area under cotton cultivation has largely been increasing while that of soybean has been declining. The share of soybean has also been on the decline in the more recent years. The decline in area under soybean has been prominent over the past six–seven years despite the rise in soybean prices. It is notable that the share of *tur* area is more than that of soybean since 2017. The declining yields of soybean and cotton and higher prices are a few reasons for farmers diversifying more into *tur*. There has also been a slight increase in *tur* monocropping in the study sample since 2017.

In 2020, the pandemic year, the share of cotton in area cultivated declined slightly and there was a moderate increase in share of soybean area cultivated. This change was observed to be on account of PBW infestation in

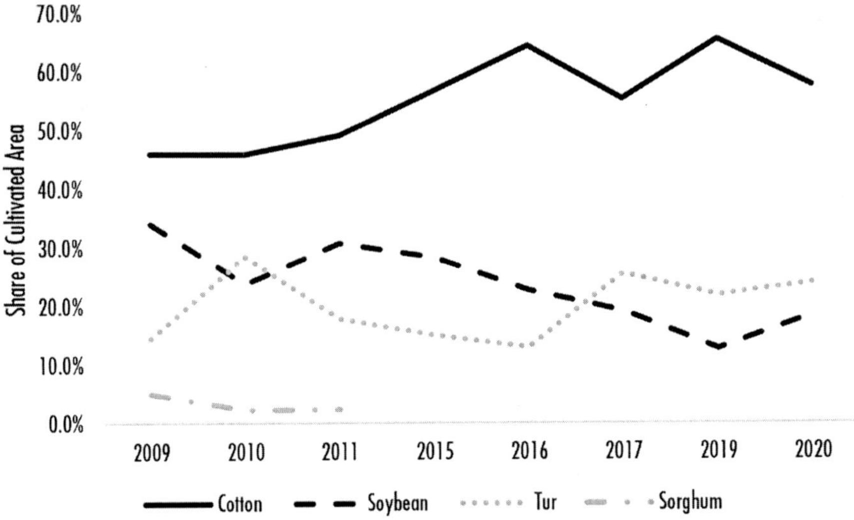

Graph 4.4 Area share of crops in cultivated area: 2009–2020

Source: Survey data.

Note: Cultivated area pertains to kharif season only.

the previous year—a serious concern for yield risk among farmers. Similar to district level trends, sorghum's share in area decreased from about 5 per cent in 2009 to about 2 per cent in 2011 and it became very negligent in the other years—corroborating our qualitative insights based on interactions with farmers over the decade.

Over the study years, there has been a significant decrease in share of soybean—which was once grown in more area than cotton in Wardha (see Graph 4.2), and whose acreage had increased steadily all through the decade of the 2000s in Yavatmal (see Graph 4.3). Since 2013, area under soybean has been on the decline in both the districts due to poor yield.[18] Reasons behind the poor yield range from high germination failure on account of poor seed quality to *khod keeda* (stem borer) infestation in 2020. As the yield anxiety with soybean increased due to these reasons in the recent past, more farmers resorted to chemical seed treatment. Weather shocks have also played a role in the reduced yields of soybean as unseasonal rains have also wreaked havoc in recent years.

The *tur* intercrop decision has the following logic that sheds light on the importance of local ecological knowledge. Since *tur* harvest starts around December and January, those who have access to irrigation do not sow *tur*

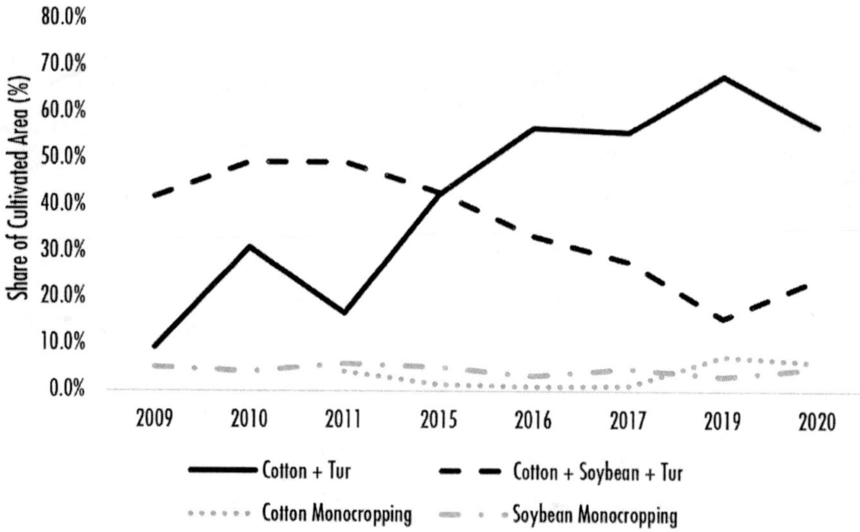

Graph 4.5 Major intercropping patterns: 2009–2020

Source: Survey data.

Note: Cultivated area pertains to kharif season only.

because they find it reasonable to take up rabi cultivation on those plots. Farmers typically cultivate soybean as a monocrop in plots which allows them to cultivate wheat and *chana* in rabi following the harvest of soybean. From a risk perspective, sole cropping being more risky than diversified cropping, these farmers explain having additional income from rabi cultivation as a 'risk cover' or 'buffer' that does not deter them from practising sole cropping. Although some are adopting short-duration cotton (short-maturity cotton) the duration is not short enough to allow for rabi cultivation. The short-duration varieties (Bt and straight varieties) seem to mature after a duration of 140–160 days. Even though this is lower than the typical variety, which stands for more than 170 days, the emphasis by scientists at the Central Institute for Cotton Research (CICR) is to reduce this further as it has a great potential to reduce the risk of PBWs.[19]

It is well understood over generations of the growing the crop that use of *tur* or pigeon pea as an intercrop offers several advantages. First, from their experience, farmers argue that the use of pigeon pea as an intercrop increases the yield of not only the main crop in comparison to monocropped crop but also offers yield advantages to pigeon pea production. A possible channel through which pigeon pea could be enhancing the yield of the main crop in the intercropping systems is that there is a symbiotic relationship between the main crop and the intercrop whereby there are nutritional complementarities from the planting of pigeon pea, which is leguminous and thus helps in nitrogen fixation. Second, the 'leaf fall' from the pigeon pea plants not only contributes to soil fertility in the current growing season but the stalks and residues also act as organic manure for the next season. Third, pigeon pea also acts as a 'trap crop' for some of the pests of the main crop, particularly the *Helicoverpa armigera* or cotton bollworms. These pests are common to both cotton and pigeon pea and damage both the crops; but with the presence of pigeon pea, the probability and severity of pest attack on the major cash crop of the farmers, cotton, comes down substantially. Fourth, some knowledgeable farmers explain that pigeon pea acts as a windbreaker for the cotton crop. Last but not least, pigeon pea serves a practical purpose. Dividing a plot into clear-cut lines, given the spatial arrangement of the intercropping system, helps the farmers have a rough estimate of their yield and labour productivity: both own and hired labour. However, it should be borne in mind that the relationship between the main crop and intercrop could differ by endogenous factors like spatial arrangement of the two crops, plant density, cultivars (varieties) and farm management practices.

CULTIVATION INCOME

Decisions around crop choice; the area to be allotted for each crop; and the type of inter-cropping to be adopted are some of the routine decision problems farmers face every crop season. The past two decades have seen sweeping changes in Vidarbha agriculture: diffusion of Bt cotton and more intensive use of chemical fertilizers and pesticides. This period has also been concomitant with several experiments with non-chemical agronomic practices as well as organic farming. The changing cropping patterns also reflect the food security considerations of the farm household. With the entitlement of subsidized food grains under the Public Distribution System (PDS), growing wheat in rabi is no more a concern for the household food security considerations of small and marginal cultivator households. All these determine the fortunes of the farmers dynamically as they not only form the basis of the asset accumulation over their life cycle but also the nature and extent of liabilities for the households. They are also crucial in determining vulnerability which is the central theme of Chapter 6. Every season, it is the income accruing from agricultural and non-agricultural activities that is at risk, and of particular concern is the most important source of income for cultivator households, namely net incomes from kharif cultivation.

KHARIF INCOME

The net incomes of the cultivator households are an outcome of area, yield, price, and input costs incurred by the households.[20] Inter-temporal changes in the crop economics indicates that the costs of cultivation increased at a higher rate than the revenue over these years (Table 4.1). For instance, the revenue from kharif cultivation increased 1.8 times while the costs increased by 3.5 times from 2009 to 2020. The first year of the COVID-19 pandemic, that is, 2020 was a bad year with low net returns from farming. But, even if we consider 2019; a relatively better year, revenues went up by 2.3 times while the costs went up by 3.4 times from 2009. This implies the real incomes of the farmers was stagnant during this whole period of study.[21] The period also saw a higher increase of net income per acre among small and marginal farmers in comparison with other subgroups of land-size class based on ownership (Table 4A.1). However, in good years in terms of general levels of yield, the semi-medium and medium farmers had higher profitability than the small and marginal farmers. These variations notwithstanding, across all land-size classes, we observed a slow rise in net incomes, largely due to rapidly rising costs.

Along with a general trend of slow rise in net incomes from kharif cultivation, we also observe significant variability in these incomes. The variability of net incomes from crop cultivation has generally been high over the study years (coefficient of variation [CV] > 100 per cent). In only two of the eight years under consideration, CV has been lower than 100 per cent (Table 4.1). Over the years, net income from crop cultivation was highest in 2017 and also with very low variability. The year 2020 was especially unpropitious with crop failure in cotton and soybean. Over the years, on average about one in ten households earned a revenue less than the costs, that is, incurred losses. In 2015 and 2020, almost one in five households bore losses in cultivation. As one would anticipate, the medium farmers were less likely to incur losses (Table 4A.1). It is also evident that variability does not necessarily imply more households experiencing losses. For instance, while the variability across cultivation incomes is similar in 2009 and 2020, only 6 per cent of households

Table 4.1 Economics of kharif cultivation: 2009–2020

Year	2009	2010	2011	2015	2016	2017	2019	2020
Area cultivated (acres)	6.4	6.4	6.1	5.3	4.9	4.6	4.7	5.0
Revenue (Rs)	56,240.9	74,830.7	79,714.9	113,341.1	125,517.1	122,032.5	131,542.0	102,017.0
Cost of cultivation (Rs)	17,210.9	39,642.7	38,307.8	60,661.1	60,629.7	54,237.3	58,855.8	60,484.1
Net income from cultivation in kharif (Rs)	39,030.1	35,188.1	41,407.1	52,680.0	64,887.4	67,795.2	72,686.2	41,687.8
CV of income (%)	138.9	140.0	112.4	162.5	122.1	82.2	99.0	135.8
Loss making households (%)	5.9	16.0	2.5	19.6	12.7	1.0	5.6	17.3
N	119	119	119	567	518	396	161	162

Source: Authors' calculations based on survey data.

Note: All costs are purchased inputs.

incurred losses in 2009 compared to 17 per cent in 2020. In the scheme of things in the villages, it is clear that those with higher capital in the form of more land are less likely to incur losses. As a case in point, in both 2009 and 2020, which were generally bad years, none of the medium farmers incurred losses (Table 4A.1).

Compared to the cost concepts of the Commission for Agricultural Costs and Prices (CACP), our use of purchased inputs (see Chapter 3 for details) alone as the relevant cost of cultivation makes it closer to the A1 cost which includes the value of the following inputs: hired human labour, hired bullock labour, owned bullock labour, owned machinery labour, hired machinery charges, seed (both farm-produced and purchased), insecticides and pesticides, manure (owned and purchased), fertilizers, depreciation on implements and farm buildings, irrigation charges, land revenue, cesses and other taxes, interest on working capital, and miscellaneous expenses. Related cost concepts including A2 cost comprises A1 cost and rent paid for leased-in land; B1 cost comprises A1 cost and interest on value of owned fixed capital assets (excluding land); B2 cost is the sum of B1 cost and rental value of owned land (net of land revenue) and rent paid for leased-in land; and C1 cost is the sum of B1 cost and imputed value of family labour. Viewed from this perspective, our costs are underestimates and imputations for family labour would result in an even lower level of net returns.

Although our data and information about depreciation rates and interest charges would have allowed calculation of the different cost concepts, two considerations drove our choice of using a subset of A1 cost.

First, the core components of A1 were readily available across the survey rounds, allowing comparison over time. Second, tenancy markets in the study villages are thin, and the rental value of owned land and rent paid for leased-in land did not emerge as major concerns in our discussions with farmers. It is however not unusual for land to be leased on *makta* or *theka* (fixed-rent tenancy) or *batai* (share-cropping) even in the rabi season. The rents differ by irrigation status of the plots. In share-cropping, the most common sharing rule is 50:50 for input costs as well as produce. Informal labour contracts such as that of the *saaldar* and of late, *mahine* contract wherein farm labourers are paid 8,000–9,000 rupees per month for exclusive work on the plots of the farmer, are also prevalent. Considering our estimates of cost of cultivation as lower bounds relative to the alternative measures in fact strengthens our arguments about the sustainability of agricultural incomes of the households.

A comparison of cultivation incomes from situation assessment surveys (SAS) conducted by the National Sample Survey Office (NSSO) in 2012–2013 and 2018–2019 is useful.[22] In 2012–2013, agricultural households in India, on an average, earned 36,972 rupees from cultivation which went up to 45,576 rupees in 2018–2019.[23] By comparison, cultivator households in our study, undertaking mostly rain-fed cultivation, earned 41,407 rupees from cultivation in 2011–2012 while they earned 72,686 rupees in 2019–2020. Meanwhile, the NSSO data indicates that the non-farm incomes from labour and enterprise increased from 3,142 rupees per month in 2012–2013 to 6,420 rupees per month in 2018–2019. Our estimates indicate that non-farm income reduced from 1,541 rupees per month in 2011–2012 to 1,078 rupees per month in 2019–2020 in our study sample. This is a vindication of relatively poor development of income-generating opportunities in our region with regard to livestock and other non-farm opportunities. The lack of non-farm opportunities seems to particularly stem from challenges with regard to low productivity and value chain development in the region. While there have been efforts to enhance supply chain for dairy products in the region, there have also been issues related to development of reliable marketing facilities for goat and poultry sales in the region. Few households in our study villages though have begun growing goats and poultry for sale in recent years. Issues related to lack of non-farm opportunities and their implications are discussed in Chapters 6 and 7.

Analysing the economics of the three major crops, an interesting trend emerges (Graphs 4.6–4.8). The cost of cultivation had a higher growth rate than the revenue per acre for all the crops. The rise in revenue per acre of cotton during this period was 2.5 times whilst the cost per acre quadrupled. In 2015 and 2020 net income per acre was negative for soybean, and 2016 yields were also low, but 2020 was a particularly poor year for soybean because of unseasonal rains. In that year, despite rising prices, the revenue per acre for the crop was almost half of that in 2009—a drought year—while the costs incurred were 2.8 times that of 2009. We found several instances of farmers not harvesting the crop in 2015 and 2020 as they reasoned that the value they could salvage from the produce would be much lower than the cost of labour employed in harvesting. In the case of *tur*, the revenue per acre went up by just over two times while the cost per acre rose by 8.4 times. These trends

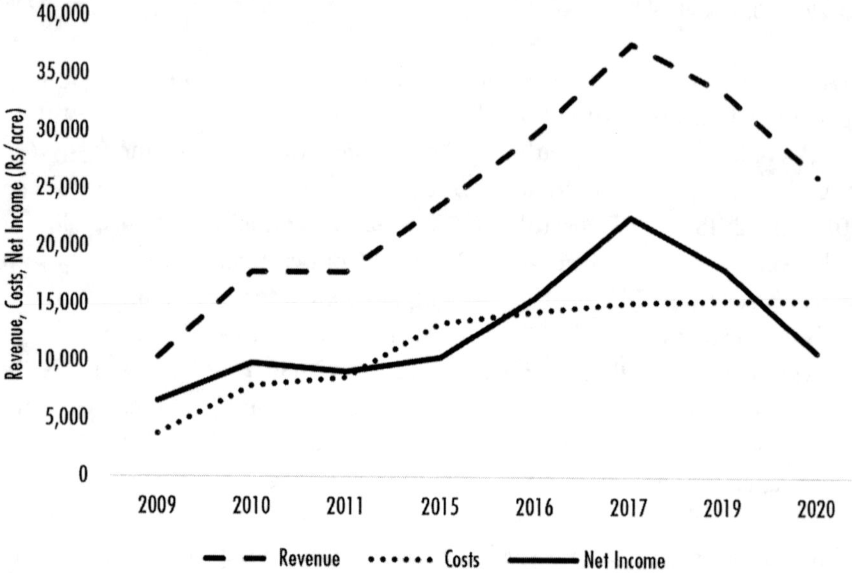

Graph 4.6 Economics of cotton cultivation: 2009–2020

Source: Authors' calculations based on survey data.

Note: Revenue, costs, and net income are calculated as average values across those who cultivated cotton in these years. Cultivated area is used in the denominator to arrive at corresponding per acre values. These are not panel households.

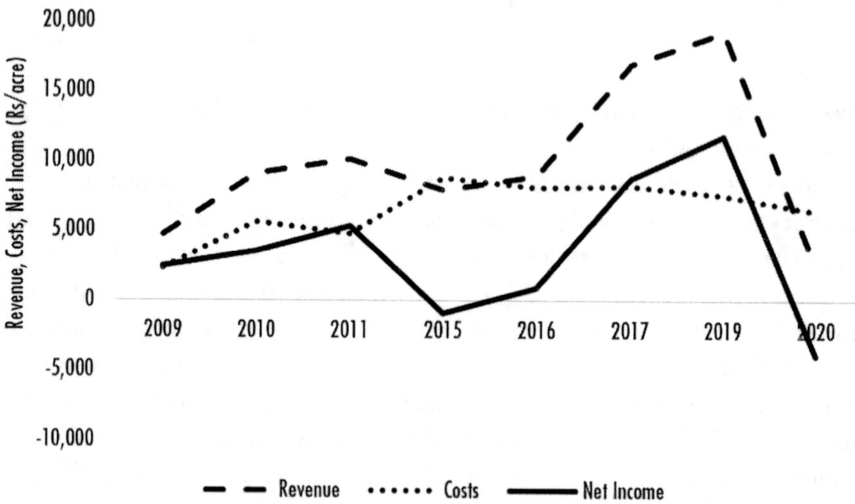

Graph 4.7 Economics of soybean cultivation: 2009–2020

Source: Authors' calculations based on survey data

Note: Revenue, costs, and net income are calculated as average values across those who cultivated soybean in these years. Cultivated area is used in the denominator to arrive at corresponding per acre values. These are not panel households.

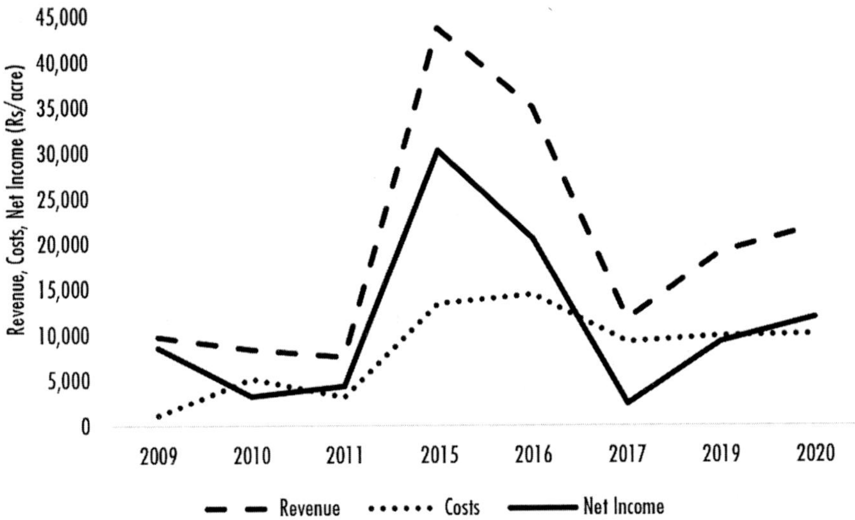

Graph 4.8 Economics of *tur* cultivation: 2009–2020

Source: Authors' calculations based on survey data

Note: Revenue, costs, and net income are calculated as average values across those who cultivated *tur* in these years. Cultivated area is used in the denominator to arrive at corresponding per acre values. These are not panel households.

indicate a rising input intensification in farming in the region which is not necessarily compensated by a proportional increase in revenues.

During our research, we often wondered why cotton is so alluring for the farmers despite the growing cost of cultivation. The answer emerged from the profitability dynamics of the crop. The net returns from cotton grew steadily until 2017, matching the narrative from the field about higher yields associated with Bt cotton (Graph 4.5). Since 2018, however, returns from cotton cultivation reduced largely owing to the emergence of the PBW. The vagaries of nature dealt a deadly blow to the cultivators in 2020. Still, cotton returned the highest income compared to all crops—for all the years. Moreover, prospects of higher prices and windfall keep the farmers invested in the crop even if there are streaks of losses.

In Chapter 2 we saw how windfalls from cotton because of historical accidents resulted in their hysterical expansion in the region. Over 160 years later, the ability of cotton to generate windfalls continues. High returns, even for one or two years, in a decade seems strong enough an incentive for farmers to bet on cotton in their portfolio of crops. Insights from fieldwork as well as survey data suggest that the attractiveness of cotton is further strengthened by the instability in returns from the competing cash crop—soybean. Net returns from soybean fell drastically more than once over the decade. In particularly bad agricultural seasons, net returns were sub-zero or almost zero in 2015, 2016, and 2020 (Graph 4.6). By contrast, the sturdiness of *tur*—another relic of the centuries-old cropping patterns in the region—is also evident from the survey and secondary data. Substantial *tur* incomes indicate the importance of crop diversification as a risk management strategy discussed at length in Chapter 6. Moreover, part of the *tur* produce is also consumed by the households and it comprises an important source of protein. Further, it has also insulated the households from food inflation caused due to high pulse prices in recent times.

There are significant interannual variations in the average yield and prices (Graphs 4.9 and 4.10). In terms of yield realizations over the period, cotton yield more than doubled from 3.4 quintals per acre to 7.5 quintals per acre from 2010 to 2017. The yields have gone downhill since then, reducing to 4.8 quintals per acre in 2020. The growing menace of PBWs severely impacted cotton yields since 2017. We learnt of the infestation of PBWs in 2015. Since then it has been clear that its resistance to Bt cotton is one of the reasons why farmers have begun looking for alternatives to Bt cotton. Consequently, illegal herbicide tolerant Bt cotton (HTBt) seeds were planted by many. We will discuss more on illegal and spurious seed usage in Chapter 5. Soybean yields remained erratic varying from 4.6 quintals per acre in 2011 to 0.7 quintals per acre in 2020, and were a major source of disappointment to farmers in some of the bad years as previously discussed. Persistent problems such as seed germination failures and stem-borer pest attacks took a severe toll on the farmer's expectations.

The typical response to such yield declines has been an adjustment in area allocated to different crops. Following the poor yields in 2020 that resulted in several farmers realizing losses in soybean and cotton, methods to treat the seeds before sowing became popular. Some farmers have been found to treat the seeds with fungicides and insecticides (involving the Thiamethoxam chemicals) before sowing. Anecdotal evidence suggests that the incidence of *khod keeda* pests were lower among those who practised these seed treatments.

Unlike yields, prices of all three crops have shown a steady increase over these years (Graph 4.10). In fact, the retail prices of *tur* went up substantially in 2015. It is speculated that the rise in prices in that year was due to

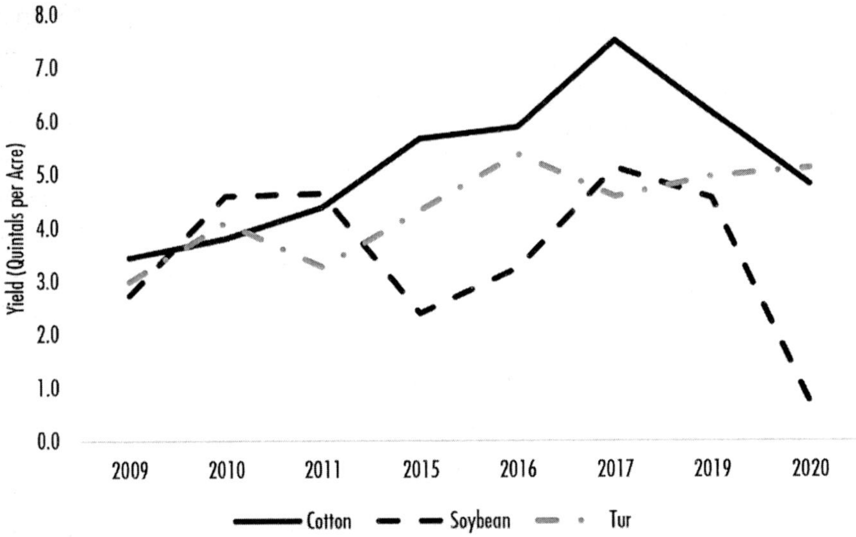

Graph 4.9 Yield of major kharif crops

Source: Survey data.

Note: The figures are averages. These are not panel households.

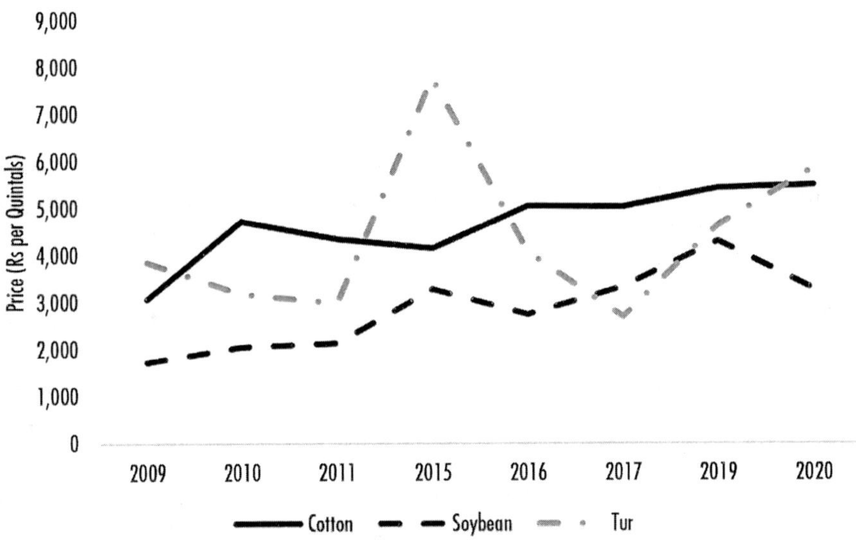

Graph 4.10 Price of major kharif crops

Source: Survey data.

Note: The figures are averages. These are not panel households.

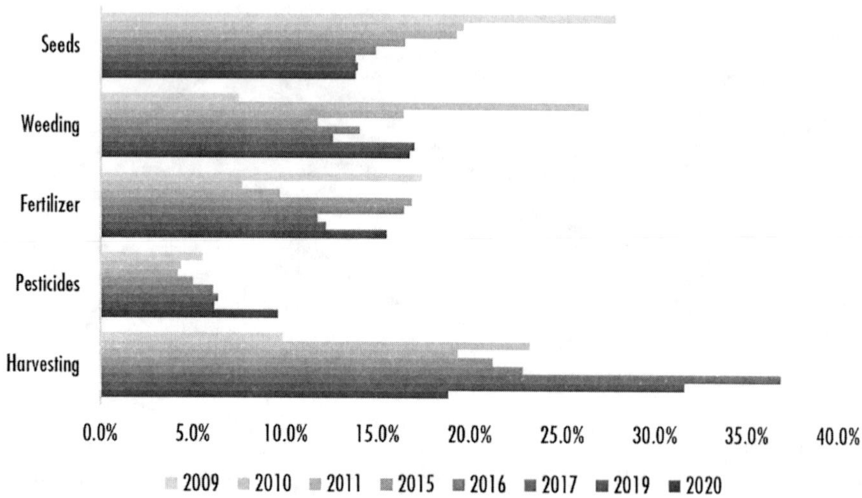

Graph 4.11 Share of major cost components: Cotton

Source: Survey data.

cartelization by major procurers of the commodity.[24] Following the spike in *tur* price, farmers' supply response behaviour has resulted in an increased area under *tur* cultivation ever since.

In terms of profitability, the most important story in this period is the rising input costs associated with greater intensification of purchased inputs in agriculture. Various components of the cost of cultivation have seen a marked change; including Bt cotton seeds and the illegally distributed HTBt cotton seeds. Rising costs of pesticides, an increase in the use of weedicides and plant growth promoters are some of the major changes in terms of input use. With higher wages contributing to higher labour costs, agricultural operations involving human labour experienced cost escalation. Indeed, government regulations also played a role in the changing agricultural input scenario. For instance, the regulations by the central and state governments have reduced the share of seed costs in total expenditure over time. Even though the adoption of Bt cotton was anticipated to reduce the pesticide expenditure, the promise was not realized in the region. The poor response of yield to fertilizers has also increased the share of fertilizer costs across all crops in this period. Here, we explore the dynamics of cost components as a share in total cost of cultivation for all the kharif crops over the study period (Graphs 4.11–4.13).

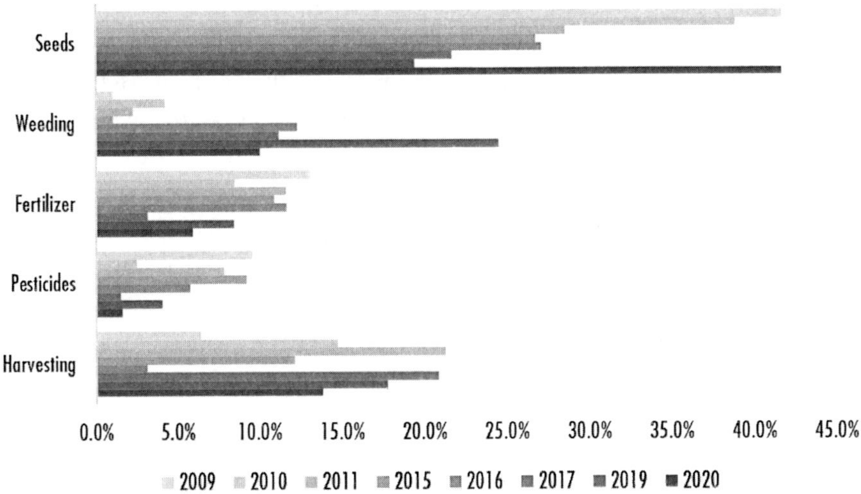

Graph 4.12 Share of major cost components: Soybean

Source: Survey data.

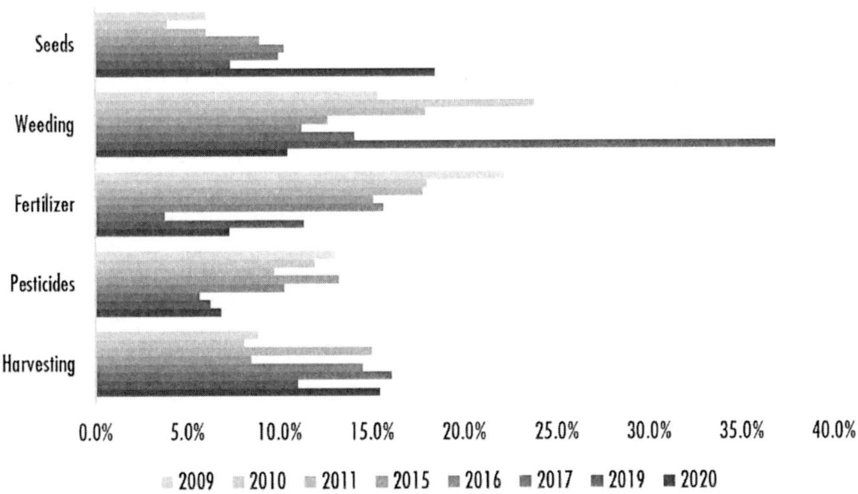

Graph 4.13 Share of major cost components: *Tur*

Source: Survey data.

The share of pesticides in costs has increased in cotton cultivation during this period due to the incidence of secondary pests and the emergence of pink bollworm resistance. Farmers also spend significantly more on weedicides and plant growth promoters. The labour costs form a significant component in harvesting and weeding and we observe their shares in total cost of cultivation going up in these years. With regard to soybean cultivation, seed costs comprise a major share of the total cost of cultivation. A high share in bad years indicates that it may be due to germination failures which might make the farmers resow and increase the seed costs. In the case of *tur*, the share of seed costs in total cost of cultivation has reduced reasonably over the years while the cost share of all the other components (fertilizer, pesticides, and weeding) has significantly increased over time. The underlying dynamics of the major inputs in cotton cultivation is a topic explored in detail in Chapter 5.

RABI INCOME

Over the years, there has been a slight increase in area cultivated during rabi season. This has happened with the impetus provided by public schemes that have attempted to improve irrigation in the region as well as greater private investment in accessing groundwater for protective irrigation. Secondary data over the past three decades indicate that the area under cultivation of typical rabi crops (wheat and gram) has been increasing since 2004. This increase is more pronounced in Yavatmal than in Wardha (Graphs 4.14–4.15). However, area under cultivation for these crops has experienced significant variability over the years. This is largely due to the lack of assured irrigation. Farmers typically purchase inputs for rabi crops with earnings from kharif. Hence, it was evident from our fieldwork that misfortune in the kharif affects the ability of farmer households to invest in rabi production. This also increases the dependency on good kharif incomes in determining the extent of rabi cultivation. Those farmers who are incapable of undertaking rabi cultivation and rely on only kharif incomes for sustaining their livelihoods typically have lower capital base and could be considered to be relatively more vulnerable within the village economy.

There have been various efforts by the government and non-government sectors to improve the irrigation infrastructure in the region. Among the various recent government schemes targeted at improved irrigation, the Vidarbha Intensive Irrigation Development Programme (VIIDP) and the Pradhan Mantri Krishi Sinchayee Yojana have large capital outlays. Schemes for water conservation such as the Jalyukt Shivar Abhiyan (JSA) have promised improvements in groundwater levels. The project was

Graph 4.14 Area under major rabi crops in Wardha: 1990–2017

Source: District Level Data (DLD) collected by ICRISAT-TCI, http://data.icrisat.org/dld/src/about-dld.html (accessed on 8 July 2021).

Graph 4.15 Area under major rabi crops in Yavatmal: 1990–2017

Source: District Level Data (DLD) collected by ICRISAT-TCI, http://data.icrisat.org/dld/src/about-dld.html (accessed on 7 May 2021).

launched in 2015 across Maharashtra and aimed to make 5,000 villages in the state free of water scarcity. It focused on a multitude of aspects improving water retention involving the construction of water-harvesting structures like check dams and small ponds, and removing silts from ponds and canals.[25]

Realizing the improved rabi cultivation in recent years, we collected information on rabi cultivation in 2020. In the ten study villages surveyed, about 42 per cent of the households cultivated in the 2020 rabi season. Typically, the farm households cultivated wheat and *chana* in about 2 acres of land. The per acre costs for cultivating wheat and *chana* were 5,000 and 7,000 rupees respectively. The yield for wheat was roughly 12 quintals per acre and that of *chana* was 6 quintals per acre. The price of wheat was in the range of 1,400 to 1,500 rupees per quintal and that of *chana* was 4,000 to 6,000 rupees per quintal. All in all, this meant that a farm household that cultivated wheat and *chana* as rabi crops could be earning 35,000 rupees as additional income in the rabi season. The average rabi income for all households was about 14,000 rupees in 2020. This is a substantially important source of income for the households. However, the importance of the produce goes beyond the earnings from marketable surplus as both the rabi crops are consumed as food for the households, while those unable to produce the same depend on markets for purchase or PDS for wheat.

LIVELIHOOD DIVERSIFICATION

The livelihood of farm households in the villages is nested in the pathways of the region's development. An important reason for rural distress in the region is the slow development of non-farm opportunities. The amount of labour and time that the cultivator households spend on their own cultivation is high given that the land sizes in their region are relatively larger compared to irrigated tracts of the country, and the labour demand in cotton cultivation has not only been high but also increasing. As we will see in Chapter 5, which delves into agricultural inputs, human labour continues to be an integral input in cotton cultivation despite general patterns of farm mechanisation across the region. The number of labour days generated in cotton cultivation is quite high and in general livelihood diversification during the kharif season is limited compared to other regions of the state.

LIVESTOCK AND NON-FARM ENTERPRISES

In Chapter 3, we sketched the changes in the livestock sector of the village economy since our surveys began. In 2009 we did not see much development in the livestock sector in the region. There were several accounts of fodder crisis with declining sorghum cultivation and growing acreage of Bt cotton. There were concerns about droughts affecting the cattle economy; however, the conditions were not as severe as the neighbouring Marathwada region where large-scale cattle shelters are arranged by the government to provide fodder and water for the survival of cattle during seasons of scarcity. In the later rounds, few households reported income from livestock and other non-farm enterprises.

Livestock-based livelihoods mostly comprise poultry, dairy, and rearing small ruminants such as goats and sheep, as discussed in Chapter 3. Though many households rear backyard poultry (mostly hens) meant for home consumption of eggs and occasionally chicken, goats are usually sold for meat. There is no large scale dairy unit in the village, but a few hatcheries and commercially viable poultry units are gradually being set up. A challenge with calculating earnings from livestock enterprises was that there was considerable household consumption, which could not be imputed due to delays in cross-verification due to the pandemic. The details of the income from these sources are provided below. A little over three-fourths of the cultivator households owned livestock, some of whom rely on it as an income-generating activity while others retain them for agricultural operations. Few respondents also reported having livestock for religious reasons. Considerable heterogeneities exist in the generally low incomes from livestock across social groups and size-class of landholding (Tables 4.2 and 4.3). Negative values for livestock is common because there are several instances of households incurring operational expenses exceeding value of the produce, even if imputed.

Although there has been an increase in non-farm activities, the level of non-farm diversification in the villages is limited. Year after year we increasingly hear arguments from the youth in the villages that they prefer non-farm work over toiling in the farms that have become increasingly fragmented on the one hand and the drudgery remains with limited farm mechanization, particularly for cotton. Their parents concur. However, limited industrial and service sector jobs mean that many still depend on agriculture. The skills training infrastructure in the villages is also lacking

Table 4.2 Household income from livestock and non-farm enterprises

District		Nominal (Rs) 2019	2020
Wardha	Livestock	426.1	858.8
	N	53	37
	Business	18,966.7	4,211.2
	N	3	6
Yavatmal	Livestock	–179.8	804.7
	N	56	61
	Business	11,000	8,780
	N	2	5
All	Livestock	114.8	825.2
	N	109	98
	Business	15,780	6,287.9
	N	5	11

Source: Authors' calculation using survey data.

Note: Income from livestock includes imputed values of the produce. Negative values are possible as we have reported net incomes, deducting costs from revenues. Business refers to non-farm enterprises, registered or otherwise. N denotes the sample size used in the calculation of mean incomes.

despite several initiatives by the government, civil society, and the private sector. Many young men from the villages find work as a 'JCB driver', a catch-all phrase to indicate that someone is the operator of heavy earth moving machinery that got this name from the ubiquity of the ones manufactured by the JCB company.

Few also worked as *hamal*, or porter, in market yards such as the APMC yard at Wardha and Yavatmal where wages are set by market yard officials, and several regulatory provisions for employment conditions are instituted (Image 4.2). The role of social networks in finding jobs in infrastructure and projects near and far is often acknowledged. It is not surprising to find many youngsters having left the village en masse for such opportunities. The pay is relatively handsome compared to the uncertain prospects and drudgery in cultivation. Another often-cited reason is the changing norms of the marriage market, namely that there is a reluctance to have a son-in-law who is a farmer. Since outside agriculture, employment opportunities

Table 4.3 Earnings from livestock and non-farm enterprises by social group: 2019 and 2020

	2019					2020				
	NT	OBC	SBC	SC	ST	NT	OBC	SBC	SC	ST
Livestock	−429.2	−88.5	529.6	−115.0	468.0	−178.0	455.9	438.0	1813.8	2392.5
Non-farm enterprises	3918	354	370	-	667	-	551	183	450	651
N	7	76	28	8	18	8	69	43	20	22

Source: Authors' calculation using survey data.

Note: Income from livestock include imputed values of the produce. The figures indicate the average income from livestock and non-farm enterprises among households which were engaged in atleast one of these activities. N denotes the sample size. Negative values are possible as we have reported net incomes, deducting costs from revenue.

Table 4.4 Earnings from livestock and non-farm enterprises by size-class of land owned: 2019 and 2020

		2019				2020			
District		Marginal	Small	Semi-Medium	Medium	Marginal	Small	Medium	Semi-Medium
All	Livestock	−0.7	212.1	−569.5	−251.3	216.8	378.8	573.7	81.8
	Non-farm enterprises	1676.3	91.2	-	-	579	197.2	-	263.2
	N	28	79	5	33	27	88	8	39

Source: Authors' calculation using survey data.

Note: Income from livestock include imputed values of the produce. The figures indicate the average income from livestock and non-farm enterprises among households which were engaged in atleast one of these activities. N denotes the sample size. Negative values are possible as we have reported net incomes, deducting costs from revenues.

Image 4.2 *Hamal* labour wage rates in Yavatmal APMC yard in 2020

Source: Sarthak Gaurav.

have been growing and there is greater ability of households to protect their incomes from the vagaries of nature and markets, such changing norms are not surprising.

With the economic transformation of Vidarbha, the social fabric of the villages is transforming in a manner that is not atypical of other villages in the region. Many have migrated to nearby towns and cities in search of better employment opportunities. It is also not uncommon to find brothers residing in villages and towns in the same district. In such situations, usually the brother residing in the urban area contributes financially to the other brother's agricultural operations and gets a share in the produce. This arrangement resembles the tenancy arrangement of *batai* (sharecropping) albeit within the family.

Only sixteen cultivators in our study sample in the last round of survey owned and managed a business enterprise: including farm and non-farm business. The range of the non-farm business was limited to the rural economy such as salon, *kirana* store (mom-and-pop grocery store), tailoring shop, flour mill, and self-employment as autorickshaw drivers. Apart from income from livestock and non-farm businesses, Pradhan Mantri Kisan Samman Nidhi (Prime Minister's Farmer's Tribute Fund) or PM-KISAN scheme announced in 2019 provides a direct benefit transfer (DBT) of 6,000 rupees per annum (around 80 US dollars) to farmers (excluding tenants) in three equal installments.

LABOUR INCOME

Despite an overarching dependence on cultivation income that involces a household's own labour as well as labour hired for different activities, cultivator households—particularly small and marginal land owners—also supply labour to other farms, that is, they engage in off-farm work. Owing to the seasonality of agricultural operations, farm employment opportunities are rife during the peak season, coinciding with the months between June and September (JJAS). As discussed in Chapter 3, we estimated the labour supply of cultivator and non-cultivator households during the JJAS months in the last round of surveys only as we began collecting data on labour supplied for households since 2019 as explained in Chapter 3. In the sample comprising cultivator and non-cultivator households, there was a marked increase in total labour supply between 2019 and 2020, a finding that was corroborated by insights from ethnography. Total labour supplied in the monsoon period increased by over a week in Wardha while it increased by over three weeks in Yavatmal. Juxtaposing the labour supplied by cultivator and non-cultivator households in both the years (Table 4.5), few heterogeneous patterns emerge.[26]

Table 4.5 Labour supply (days in JJAS) by non-cultivator and cultivator households: 2019 and 2020

	Non-cultivator Households (N = 159)		Cultivator Households (N = 132)	
	2019	**2020**	**2019**	**2020**
Total labour days (Men)	93.4	104.1	92.1	107.9
Total labour days (Women)	64.7	69.3	48.1	59.9
Total labour days (Household)	158.1	173.3	140.2	167.8

Source: Authors' calculation based on survey data.

While the former supply considerably more labour compared to the latter as expected, gendered division of labour between the two is evident. For the non-cultivator households who were landless and for whom labour incomes are the most important source of income, female labour supply for paid work was around 40 per cent of the total household labour supply in both years. Any paid agricultural labour work by cultivator households comprises off-farm in the sense that it is 'off own farm'. In other words, off-farm work for cultivator households includes work on farms of others as well as non-farm employment. By contrast, the share of labour supplied by women in the cultivator households is lower than that among the non-cultivator households, which is in accordance with the patriarchal norms determining women's labour force participation: women from larger farm households or higher castes such as Deshmukhs or Patils are relatively less likely to participate in the local labour market compared to those from small and marginal farm households or caste categories such as SC, OBC, ST, and NT.

In 2020, which was a pandemic year, we came across several cases of non-farm workers even among cultivator households experiencing difficulty in finding work due to prolonged lockdowns in the lean season. Therefore, the substantial increase in labour supplied by cultivator households by around four additional weeks is indicative of labour market adjustments due to the pandemic as well as the high labour demand in agriculture at the start of the season. However, among the cultivator households, there was a slight decline in the share of labour supplied by women relative to men even though the total labour supply increased for both men and women over the year. Furthermore, examining the allocation of labour days to own-farm and off-farm work for cultivator households and that to off-farm (agricultural wage work on plots of others) for non-cultivator households (Table 4.6) reveals the following.

Although we gathered insights about labour market participation from the households over telephonic surveys and intermittent visits to the villages between the two waves of the pandemic (2020–2021), which were validated by resident investigators, it was evident that agricultural operations were not severely affected due to exemptions as per the Essential Commodities Act (ECA). However, there were several localized variations. The incidence of COVID-19 infections in the villages was also negligible. However, Yavatmal villages experienced the return of significantly larger number of migrant workers from urban areas unlike in the Wardha villages. Those returning

Table 4.6 Labour supply by non-cultivator and cultivator households in own farm and off-farm: 2019 and 2020

	Non-cultivator Households (N = 159)		Cultivator Households (N = 132)	
	2019	2020	2019	2020
Off-farm (Men)	65.9	71.5	30.9	13.0
Off-farm (Women)	62.2	68.2	32.9	32.0
Off-farm (Household)	128.1	139.7	63.7	45.0
Own farm (Men)	-	-	51.3	64.2
Own farm (Women)	-	-	12.7	22.0
Own farm (Household)	-	-	64.0	86.2

Source: Authors' calculation using survey data.

Note: Own-farm labour is only applicable for cultivator households. Non-cultivator households in the study sample were landless.

from work in Nagpur and other cities had to undergo institutional quarantine in the outskirts of the village. This was organized by the Gram Panchayat and village accredited social health activists (ASHAs).

In the kharif season months of JJAS, demand for manual labour in agriculture is generally high as workers find gainful employment opportunities in ongoing agricultural operations. While drought or drought-like conditions depress demand for agricultural work, early stage heavy rains may increase demand for weeding, which is exclusively done by women from and around the village. For non-cultivator households, nearly all wage employment of women was found in agriculture. However, for men belonging to non-cultivator households, agriculture employs them for nearly 70 per cent of their wage employment days. Put together, in 2020, agriculture provided 80 per cent of the employment of non-cultivator households, the remaining one-fifth of their wage labour days being supplied to non-farm activities.

By contrast, for women in cultivator households, own-farm work comprises one-third of the labour days supplied and around half of the work is supplied to agricultural work on farms of others.[27] These activities mostly comprise sowing, weeding, and picking. This implies that around a quarter of the total labour days of women from cultivator households is supplied to non-farm activities. For men from cultivator households, of all labour supplied, work done on own-farm is significantly higher—60 per cent of total labour days. For men, work done on the farms of others is 12 per cent of their total labour days. This suggests there is considerable non-farm diversification among cultivator households—a valuable risk-hedging alternative for farm-based livelihoods.

The wages as in most parts of the state and the country are differentiated by gender (Table 4.7). Even in the study villages, there is considerable gender-based division of labour in the agricultural operations that reflects in the wage rates. We have already described how the micro-processes in agriculture, particularly cotton cultivation involve specialization of labour by gender. The changes in wage structure over time however warrant attention. In the first round of our study (2009–2012), the average agricultural wage rate for women was nearly half of the average of men. Wage rates for activities such as weeding which is exclusively undertaken by women were around 80 rupees

Table 4.7 Average wage rates (rupees/day) of agricultural labour by gender: 2020

Month	Men	Women
June	240.3	152.6
July	242.6	155.3
August	241.6	152.6
September	238.4	148.4
October	244.0	148.7
November	245.1	155.5
December	244.0	143.2
January	244.0	143.2
February	200.0	130.0
March	200.0	130.0
April	200.0	130.0
May	200.0	130.0

Source: Authors' calculation using survey data.

Note: Reported figures are averages of all agricultural operations reported by households in the survey in 2020–2021. June to December pertains to 2020 calendar year. January refers to the 2021 calendar year and the last month for wages available based on our survey as the field surveys ended in February 2021, given concerns about the COVID-19 pandemic. Therefore, wage rates reported for February–May 2021 are based on prevailing wage rates for representative agricultural operations as informed by resident investigators, and not on survey data.

(around 1 US dollar) per day. By contrast, in 2019 the per day wage rate for weeding was around 150 rupees. These wage trends suggest that it has taken women a decade to obtain a wage of what the men used to get back then. Over this period, per day wage rates of men in agriculture have gone up from 150 to around 250 rupees on an average, indicating a narrowing of the wage gap, the absolute of which is nevertheless substantial. In 2020, we also found some men engaged in weeding, receiving a 30-rupee premium over that of women for a day's work. Upon enquiring why they would take up such work which is conventionally done by women, the men cite 'we get easy earning from this work' as the most common response. However, cotton picking continues to be done by women, and despite it being illegal, employment of child labour in cotton picking has been occasionally reported.

An interesting change over the decade is the changing attitude of farmers towards agricultural labourers. During fieldwork related to recent rounds, we often heard farmers complain that agricultural labourers were deliberately putting in less time per day for the same tasks. However, minutely observing the operations over seasons, we found that it is indeed so. For instance, in Wardha villages weeding commences at eight in the morning and ends by an hour past noon unlike earlier when it started by seven and ended by an hour past noon. Those who work in the second shift—two hours in the afternoon—demand an extra 90-rupee wage which many farmers are reluctant to pay. Nominal wages have increased over time as expected but we did not have reason to believe that for weeding an acre of land, agricultural labourers demonstrate slack or take longer than what they would have ended up doing a decade ago. The practice of the farmer supervising the weeding operations on her or his land has not changed either. What then explains these changes in the attitudes of farmers towards labourers? Two reasons are apparent. First, farmers argue that since agricultural labourers started receiving subsidized food grains (wheat and rice) under the PDS as per the National Food Security Act (NFSA), agricultural labour households 'do not need to put in effort and have higher bargaining power'. While agricultural labourers do not contest this, they do not accept the farmers' view either. With real incomes growing for labour households due to subsidized food, income effect in labour–leisure trade off is likely to have changed preferences of manual farm labour that involves considerable drudgery. Second, greater entitlements through right to work under the Mahatma Gandhi National Rural Employment Guarantee Scheme (MGNREGS) have increasingly allowed additional labour incomes to eligible households, and the minimum wage set in MGNREGS anchors wage expectations in the farm labour where demand for agricultural labour has increased (for example, in cotton).

Second, these attitudinal changes are not surprising as farmers are anchored to lumpy wage bills which is the biggest component of the cost of cultivation, and most paid before the cash from the harvest is realised. As they experience the nominal wages going up, without a proportionate increase in their incomes as shown earlier, they have a sense of being unfortunate compared to agricultural labourers who do not face the kind of livelihood uncertainty like the farmers. Many times we have come across a response from Hindi-speaking farmers in Wardha along the following lines: 'Labour ko paisa mil jaata hai lekin kisan ko milega ki nahin koi guarantee nahin,' which translates to: 'The labourers get their money but the farmer does not have a guarantee on whether there will be any income.' Regarding the first logic, it is surprising to know the argument being made by farmers as even farmers are included as beneficiaries in the PDS scheme. In relation to the second logic, such has been the nature of earnings of the two occupations for long, and there has not been any structural change in the sequence of income accruing for the two groups. Investigating the wage setting process in rural labour markets, we infer that the four-hour day instead of six-hour day has largely been the outcome of bargaining process in which the growing demand for labour on cotton farms along with avenues for non-farm employment resulted in the labour suppliers to have the upper hand. To sum up, while the interaction between farmers and agricultural labourers is an

Table 4.8 Labour income (rupees) (JJAS months)

	Non-cultivators (N = 159)		**Cultivators (N = 132)**	
	2019	**2020**	**2019**	**2020**
Men labour income (Rs)	21,866.5	26,005.5	9,333.9	7,051.1
Women labour income (Rs)	7,655.1	10,575.0	3,970.3	3,827.4
Household labour income (Rs)	29,521.6	36,580.5	13,304.2	14,732.3

Source: Authors' calculation using survey data.

Note: Figures are in rupees.

essential element of the gamble with cotton, it has undergone considerable changes in the relationship has occured with growing farm mechanization and cropping pattern changes on the one hand, and rising opportunity cost for farm labourers as non-farm employment increases.

Comparing labour income of the households, key insights emerge from labour incomes of the cultivator and non-cultivator households (Table 4.8). First, the wage earnings of non-cultivator households were over three times that of cultivator households. Although farmers and family members belonging to the marginal and small size-class of land ownership actively supply labour in agricultural operations on farms of others, larger farmer households and family members seldom do so. Non-cultivator households, primarily those dependent on agricultural labour as their principal activity status as well as the source of income, find considerable employment in the cotton farms in their own and neighbouring villages. Although there has been an increase in non-farm employment for family members of both cultivator and non-cultivator households, very few households have instances of higher education resulting in upward economic mobility over the past twelve years.

Second, gender gradient in earnings is evident. The differences are particularly stark in agricultural wage work where there is a clear division of tasks by gender. While women mostly work in sowing, weeding, and cotton picking, men find employment in land preparation, fertilizer application, spraying of pesticides, and operating bullocks and tractors. In post-harvest operations, women find employment in threshing of *tur* and wheat as well as cleaning up fields after harvesting. They also find work in assistance with transport of produce to carts and trailers on tractors. Over the centuries, surprisingly, there has been no change in the gendered division of labour in agricultural operations, and the wage differential continues to be substantial.

Third, nominal wage earnings of non-cultivator households grew over 12 per cent over the period whilst the earnings of cultivator households rose by a smaller margin. Indeed, the absolute levels of wage earnings of cultivator households remain low in greater extent of participation in non-farm activities. Much of the non-farm work is in the informal sector and involves low-skill jobs. A pattern that emerges from our analysis of individual-level employment among cultivator households suggests that it is typical for parents, who are currently household heads, to be involved in farm-based livelihoods whilst children engage in non-farm activities or actively seek work outside the farm sector. Nevertheless, children, particularly females assist families with own-farm activities substantially. Their counterparts in non-cultivator households however have greater workforce participation given their relatively lower asset base.

CONCLUSION

In this chapter, we described the stylized facts pertaining to incomes of cultivator households based on surveys in Wardha and Yavatmal districts of Vidarbha between 2009 and 2020. The set of findings attest to the variations in cropping patterns, crop yields, cost of cultivation, and cultivation income over time. In doing so, we shed light on the gambles that farmers in the region routinely partake in. Given the slow pace of improvement in irrigation infrastructure and low industrial growth in the region, the predominant gamble by farmers is on the cultivation of external input intensive crops. The changes in cropping pattern are of overriding importance.

Changes in cropping patterns including the rise and fall of soybean cultivation; near disappearance of *jawari* (sorghum); and the fall and rise of cotton cultivation suggest two critical dimensions of the ongoing agrarian transformation. First, farmers enthusiastically adopted Bt cotton, but over the past decade yield stagnation has arrested its area expansion whilst the promise of soybean has been thwarted by recurring poor yields. Second, the stark reduction in area under millets such as *jawari* has adversely affected the cattle economy. These changes have a direct economic effect on the local labour market owing to reduced demand for farm labour as well undesirable social consequences that remain to be examined.[28] In terms of the structural transformation that the villages are an integral part of, it is evident that there has been an increase in diversification of income sources over the years. We investigated these changes and focused on income and income diversification by size-class and social group.

Surveys spanning over a decade allow us to observe and comment on major developments in agricultural input and output markets that had overarching influence on the cotton economy. The most remarkable development over the period was the proliferation of Bt cotton cultivation, covered in great detail in Chapter 5. Although thousands of brands of Bt hybrids for two commercialized traits—BGI and BGII—diffused rapidly, there was a clear decline in yields during this period following a decade of rise in yields. The apparent rise in average yields concomitant with reduction in losses in yield from the protection provided against lepidopteran bollworm infestation had clearly waned by 2021. This has happened due to various reasons such as PBW resistance, secondary pest outbreaks, and likely reduction in the yield-response of fertilizers. There has been a tendency of input intensification, fertilizer application per acre of land is on the rise; more so among the marginal and smallholders. There has also been growth in expenditure on chemical pesticides—weedicides, herbicides, fungicides, and even what the farmers call 'tonic' which are basically plant growth promoters.

Over the past decade, public investment in management of natural water resources has improved the extent of protective irrigation for hitherto rain-fed cotton. Programmes such as the Vidarbha Intensive Irrigation Development Programme (VIIDP) have restored, renovated, and augmented rainwater conservation and harvesting structures that have allowed intensive irrigation. Irrigation has also intensified for those with access to dug wells or borewells. All these factors have, however, been accompanied by increasing labour costs which has pushed the weeding and harvesting (picking) costs up, contributing to a steep rise in the cost of cultivation.

To make matters worse, the real prices of cotton did not go up much in this period whereas the real cost of cultivation increased sharply. Herein lies the dilemma of the farmers in their gamble with cotton.

On the one hand, declining yield, increasing costs, and unremunerative prices have meant that the real income from the cultivation of cotton has not grown, and even fallen for many farmers. On the other hand, as the economy grows and the village society witnesses structural changes in economic mobility and living arrangements, borrowing, dissaving, and asset sales become a reasonable option to make ends meet or enable household consumption patterns to 'keep up with the Joneses'. No doubt, recourse to these strategies dent the productive capacity of the farm or weaken the ability of households to cope with shocks in the absence of safeguards against them. It is not that farmers have not experimented with improved varieties or genetically modified seeds or intensified their input use hoping to get higher yields; however it is recurrent losses and unstable incomes that worsen their precarity. As a case in point, three decades ago farmers in the region adopted soybean with the hope of a steady stream of revenue and owing to the short duration of the crop (90 days) many with access to irrigation could undertake a second crop in the winter—rabi season. However, over the past decade, the return to soybean has been declining. Extremely poor yields and zero or negative net returns are not uncommon in the villages. In particular, the small and marginal farmers have been hit badly. The good old *tur* (pigeon pea) continues to be an effective hedge and source of nutrition for households; however its prices have also been notably volatile in the period of our primary research. These developments have unequivocally added to the woes of farmers as they search for remunerative livelihood alternatives to replace or supplement their low and uncertain incomes from cultivation.

Amidst concerns about the viability of cotton cultivation, there is some optimism in the development of irrigation infrastructure and improved crop management for greater water use efficiency, which has helped a section of the farmers to earn incomes in rabi cultivation. However, there is not much optimism for those farmers with no irrigation—the Koradwahu farmers. The quality of irrigation and availability of water from the irrigation sources is not something that the farmers could rely heavily on. There is more investment needed in irrigation in the region along with overcoming backlogs in irrigation projects—a theme that we will elaborate on in subsequent chapters. Since 2019, information on non-cultivator households offers novel quantitative insights on the village labour markets.

Labour income variations for cultivators and non-cultivators reveals cotton absorbing considerable months of labour for agricultural labour households who are either residents of the same village or from nearby villages. There is also a gender-based segregation of critical tasks in cotton's growing and picking operations. Wage variations between men and women in agricultural activities in the study villages continue to be high. If farmers are concerned about growing labour costs on account of weeding and picking, there is a possibility of technological solutions attempting to do away with these activities. Reports of employment of child labour in cotton weeding and picking are disconcerting; a practice not unheard of either in the villages. As cultivator households diversify into non-farm economic activities, there is a gradual decoupling of incomes from agricultural risks. Markets play a critical role in price uncertainty and instability of household incomes, which is the topic of discussion in Chapters 5 and 6.

To a certain extent, the crisis in agriculture is linked to the crisis in yield, and, it is in this context that techno-managerial solutions with a narrow focus on crop productivity and income growth that have gained policy attention (for example, 'doubling farmers' income') become problematic due to a disproportionate emphasis on increasing crop yields without due attention to the increase in cost of agricultural inputs.[29] Often the gambles by farmers are in response to the incentives that are an outcome of these policies. At the same time, structural issues such as the deficiencies of agricultural insurance including multi-peril crop insurance scheme and weather insurance provide neither timely nor adequate compensation in the eventuality of losses that are covered. Several structural and institutional factors confounding farmers' behaviour and characteristics of markets may also be hard or impossible to observe. With this caveat in place, in the next chapter we examine major agricultural inputs to understand farmers' input choices and their implications on risk and vulnerability of households.[30] We will also return to the issue of agricultural insurance that has taken the form of a 'wicked problem'.

APPENDIX

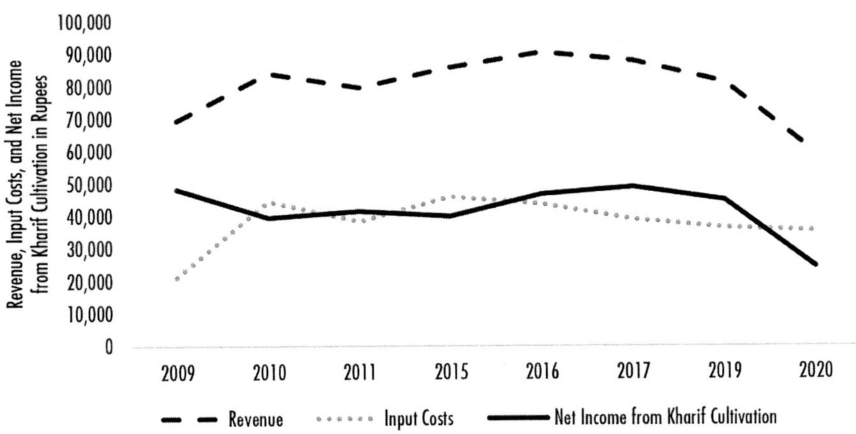

Graph 4A.1 Economics of kharif cultivation (constant prices, 2011 prices): 2009–2020

Source: Survey data.

Table 4A.1 Kharif cultivation economics across land-size classes: 2009–2020

	2009	2010	2011	2015	2016	2017	2019	2020
Revenue per Acre (Rs)								
Marginal (< 2.5 acres)	9,610.0	11,769.4	10,268.9	23,339.9	27,860.5	25,428.5	26,241.5	21,737.1
Small (2.5–5 acres)	7,046.4	11,339.9	13,056.5	20,243.4	24,526.2	26,353.6	28,446.5	21,280.0
Semi-medium (5–10 acre)	8,055.1	12,140.8	12,608.9	20,026.0	24,398.6	27,184.8	27,847.3	19,979.5
Medium (> 10 acre)	10,296.1	11,750.7	13,613.6	23,286.8	30,504.7	25,538.7	28,068.0	18,846.2
Cost of Cultivation per Acre (Rs)								
Marginal (< 2.5 acres)	5,033.8	5,923.2	5,184.4	13,862.2	14,133.5	12,234.8	15,241.5	13,390.7
Small (2.5–5 acres)	2,700.2	6,330.5	6,248.6	11,672.2	12,727.2	12,178.9	13,102.9	12,303.2
Semi-medium (5–10 acre)	2,661.1	6,514.9	5,527.8	10,956.8	12,157.8	11,499.3	12,273.6	11,596.4
Medium (> 10 acre)	2,538.9	5,971.0	7,411.1	11,301.1	12,325.1	10,720.9	9,874.2	11,837.4
Net Income per Acre (Rs)								
Marginal (< 2.5 acres)	4,576.2	5,846.3	5,084.4	9,477.7	13,727.1	13,193.8	10,999.9	8,718.1
Small (2.5–5 acres)	4,346.2	5,009.4	6,807.9	8,571.1	11,799.0	14,174.8	15,343.7	8,976.8
Semi-medium (5–10 acre)	5,394.0	5,625.8	7,081.1	9,069.1	12,240.8	15,685.5	15,573.6	8,383.1
Medium (> 10 acre)	7,757.2	5,779.7	6,202.5	11,985.7	18,179.6	14,817.8	18,193.8	7,008.8

CV of Income								
Marginal (< 2.5 acres)	20.0%	22.2%	0.0%	24.4%	11.4%	1.6%	9.7%	11.1%
Small (2.5–5 acres)	76.8%	95.0%	68.7%	126.1%	95.4%	50.6%	77.3%	96.0%
Semi-medium (5–10 acre)	77.3%	106.8%	63.6%	114.2%	81.9%	41.4%	51.7%	129.3%
Medium (> 10 acre)	100.6%	112.4%	92.6%	90.6%	85.9%	81.8%	66.9%	134.6%
Loss-Making Households								
Marginal (< 2.5 acres)	20.0%	22.2%	0.0%	24.4%	11.4%	1.6%	9.7%	11.1%
Small (2.5–5 acres)	6.9%	16.7%	3.7%	21.4%	16.0%	1.2%	5.6%	19.3%
Semi-medium (5–10 acre)	5.0%	15.8%	0.0%	20.3%	11.0%	0.0%	3.0%	20.5%
Medium (> 10 acre)	0.0%	11.1%	6.7%	1.8%	2.3%	0.0%	0.0%	0.0%

Source: Authors' calculation based on primary survey.

Note: Loss-making households are those with negative net returns from cultivation in a particular year.

Table 4A.2 Individual level employment among household members

	Household Head (N = 162)		Spouse of Household Head (N = 124)		Third Member of Household (N = 76)		Fourth Member of Household (N = 36)		Fifth Member of Household (N = 12)	
JC (Job Code)	**Job Description**	**%**	**JC**	**%**	**JC**	**%**	**JC**	**%**	**JC**	**%**
1	Cultivation	85.19	1	37.1	1	31.58	1	33.33	1	33.33
2	Agricultural labour	3.09	2	54.84	2	47.37	2	50	2	58.33
3	Farm enterprises	2.47	3	3.23	3	6.58	5	5.56	3	8.33
4	Government jobs	0.62	5	2.42	5	5.26	7	5.56		
5	Casual non-farm job		6	1.61	6	3.95	8	2.78		
6	Private job (monthly salary)	1.23	999	0.81	7	2.63	999	2.78		
7	Professional	1.85			8	1.32				
8	Own non-farm enterprises	1.23			11	1.32				
11	Cowherd/shepherd	3.7								
999	*Saaldar* (annual farm labour)	0.62								
Total	162	100	Total	100	Total	100	Total	100	Total	100

Source: Authors' calculations based on primary survey.

NOTES

1. Vikash Agarwal, 'India Can Be a Star in Agrochem Market If the Government Encourages Collaboration', *Economic Times*, 4 July 2022, https://economictimes.indiatimes.com/small-biz/trade/exports/insights/india-can-be-a-star-in-agrochem-market-if-the-government-encourages-collaboration/articleshow/92646676.cms (accessed on 3 August 2022).
2. See H. Sharma, 'Area under Kharif Crop Rises to Record 1,082 Lakh Ha', *Indian Express*, 29 August 2020, https://indianexpress.com/article/india/area-under-kharif-crop-rises-to-record-1082-lakh-ha-6574408/#:~:text=Agriculture%20Minister%20Narendra%20Singh%20Tomar,under%20Kharif%20crops%20during%202019 (accessed on 30 April 2021).
3. See M. Vyas, 'An Increasingly Agrarian Society', Centre for Monitoring Indian Economy, https://www.cmie.com/kommon/bin/sr.php?kall=warticle&dt=20210809122441&msec=850 (accessed on 30 April 2021).
4. This was scheme of compensation provided for the 8,311 hectares of land procured for the development of a 701-kilometre-long expressway between Nagpur and Mumbai called the Samruddhi Mahamarg. For further details, refer to Shruti Ganapatye, 'Samruddhi Expressway Land Acquisition Complete', *Mumbai Mirror*, 11 June 2019, https://mumbaimirror.indiatimes.com/mumbai/crime/samruddhi-expressway-land-acquisition-complete/articleshow/69732322.cms (accessed on 14 May 2022).
5. Some farmers grow rabi crops in waterlogged plots, locally known as *pan basan*. These plots are left fallow in the kharif season and the rabi cultivation is carried out on the retained moisture, mostly from the waterlogging. Such crops are also known as 'dry rabi' crops.
6. R. Kumar, *Rethinking Revolutions: Soyabean, Choupals and the Changing Countryside in Central India* (Delhi: Oxford University Press, 2016a), 232.
7. Ibid., 233. SBOT, or SOPA Board of Traders, which later became NBOT, or National Board of Traders.
8. P. Harnetty, 'Crop Trends in the Central Provinces of India, 1861–1921', *Modern Asian Studies* 11, no. 2 (1977): 341–377.
9. R. Rukmani and M. Manjula, *Designing Rural Technology Delivery Systems for Mitigating Agricultural Distress: A Study of Wardha District* (report by MS Swaminathan Research Foundation, Chennai, and Office of the Principal Scientific Adviser to the Government of India, New Delhi, 2009), http://59.160.153.188/library/sites/default/files/Study-of-Wardha-RR10-25.pdfA (accessed on 30 October 2019).

10. For a similar dilemma related to sowing date of sorghum in the Palanpur village in Uttar Pradesh, India, refer to S. Bowles, *Microeconomics: Behavior, Institutions, and Evolution* (Princeton: Russell Sage Foundation, 2003), 23–24.
11. See S. Gaurav, 'Risk and Vulnerability of Agricultural Households in India' (unpublished PhD thesis, IGIDR, Mumbai, 2014).
12. For description of severe under-nutrition in the region among people across all land classes, see S. Parasuraman and T. Rajaretnam, 'Agriculture, Food Security and Nutrition in Vidarbha: A Household Level Analysis', *Economic and Political Weekly* 46, no. 19 (2011): 42–50.
13. See M. Davis, *Late Victorian Holocausts: El Niño Famines and the Making of the Third World* (London; New York: Verso Books, 2001).
14. Also known as *jawarichi bhakri* that translates into *bhakri* made of *jawari.*
15. In previous research, we have analysed both these aspects. The use of pesticides by cotton farmers across the country using a nationally representative data is presented in T. Ranganathan, S. Gaurav, and I. I. Halder, 'Pesticide Usage by Cotton Farmers in India: Changes Over a Decade', *Economic and Political Weekly* 53, no. 19 (2018). For an analysis focusing on the emergence of secondary pests and increased expenditure on pesticides in the study villages based on our survey data, refer to T. Ranganathan and S. Gaurav, 'Pest Management Practices of Cotton Farmers in Vidarbha: The Curious Case of Cocktails, Weedicides, and Tonics', *Economic and Political Weekly* 54, no. 44 (2019).
16. A. S. Tingre, A. S. Ingole, P. D. Thakare, and P. V. Shingrup, 'Cropping Pattern Changes and Crop Diversification in Akola District of Vidarbha', *Journal of Soils and Crops* 18, no. 1 (2008): 240–244.
17. This practice is irrespective of the intercrops grown with cotton or soybean.
18. Data regarding total cultivated area in kharif area for Wardha are official statistics available at https://www.zpwardha.in/departments_agriculture.php (accessed on 30 April 2022). Data for total kharif area cultivated for Yavatmal as official statistics available at http://kvkyavatmal.pdkv.ac.in/?page_id=309 (accessed on 30 April 2022).
19. Personal communication with Gaurav in 2020.
20. For the input costs, we include the costs incurred for land preparation, seeds, sowing, irrigation, weeding, cost of fertilizers, pesticides, and harvesting costs. We estimate costs for these heads across costs incurred for labour (human and animal, family and hired), materials, machinery obtained at the plot level. The detailed methodology followed in estimating the cost of inputs and limitations have been discussed in Chapter 3.

21. The changes in incomes of the farmers over the study period at constant 2011–2012 prices are provided in Graph 4A.1. We use the Consumer Price Index-Agricultural Labourers (CPI-AL) index for the state of Maharashtra to calculate the revenue, costs, and net income in real terms.
22. There are issues related to comparability of farm incomes across the two rounds of the surveys as the costs collected in the 2012–2013 was just the 'paid-out' costs, similar to the costs we have collected; while in 2019–2020, the costs included imputed costs of farm labour, land, and assets. However, the 2019–2020 report provides the economics of cultivation in which they estimate the net income that is comparable based on 'paid-out' costs too. We refer to these in our analysis. For details, see MoSPI, *Situation Assessment of Agricultural Households and Land and Livestock Holdings of Households in Rural India, 2019* (NSS 77th Round, Report no. 587, 2021), http://mospi.nic.in/sites/default/files/publication_reports/Report_587m.pdf (accessed on 12 May 2021). For details related to cultivation incomes in 2012–2013, refer to MoSPI, *Income, Expenditure, Productive Assets and Indebtedness of Agricultural Households in India, 2013* (NSS 70th Round, Report no. 576, 2015), http://mospi.nic.in/sites/default/files/publication_reports/nss_rep_576.pdf (accessed on 12 May 2021).
23. It is important to note that these are incomes in the NSS are from cultivation in both the kharif and rabi season, whereas the incomes from our study pertain only to kharif season in a predominantly rain-fed region. Also, in 2018–2019, the NSS uses imputed costs related to saved inputs and unpaid family labour for estimating the net income, hence the net incomes estimated are much lower.
24. S. Ghosh, 'Surge in 2015 Pulse Prices Was a Result of Cartelisation', *The Wire*, 6 July 2017, https://thewire.in/economy/surge-in-2015-pulse-prices-was-a-result-of-cartellisation (accessed on 25 June 2021).
25. The Jalyukt Shivar Abhiyaan (JSA) project faced issues related to various discrepancies in its works and was scrapped in 2020. Refer to Anjali Marar, 'Explained: Why a Mission to Make Maharashtra Villages Drought-Free Has Been Shelved', *Indian Express*, 23 February 2020, https://indianexpress.com/article/explained/explained-jalyukta-shivar-maharashtra-villages-drought-free-scrapped-6282236/ (accessed on 30 April 2022).
26. Although we collected labour data for three months in 2019, we are able to estimate labour supplied in other months based on labour data available from June to January 2020.

27. Details of individual-level employment across members of the households for the year 2020 is provided in Table 4A.2.
28. While studies on the agrarian transformation of Vidarbha are conspicuously absent, for a discussion on the social costs of the agrarian transformation and ambiguity about economic gains in the context of western Maharashtra, see B. B. Mohanty, *Agrarian Transformation in Western India: Economic Gains and Social Costs* (New York: Routledge, 2019).
29. R. Kumar, 'The Perils of Productivity: Making "Good Farmers" in Malwa, India', *Journal of Agrarian Change* 16, no. 1 (2016): 104.
30. Wicked problems are complex social and planning problems that are difficult to solve, and may not have a solution. See H. W. Rittel and M. M. Webber, 'Dilemmas in a General Theory of Planning', *Policy Science*s 4, no. 2 (1973): 55–169.

5

INPUTS IN THE COTTON GAMBLE

Are the dice loaded against the Vidarbha farmer in the gambles with cotton? Does the agrarian crisis stem from the nature of cotton cultivation? Taken together, the insights from the preceding chapter brought to the fore the limited livelihood diversification options for households and the overarching dependence on cotton cultivation. Even the outcomes of landless non-cultivator households hinge on the fate of cotton every season, given its importance in absorbing agricultural labour from the villages and their vicinity.

In this chapter, we discuss the changes related to agricultural inputs and agronomic practices of cotton cultivation. These changes have elements of accidentality as well as gambling akin to developments that have transpired in the history of the region's cotton economy. While doing so, we connect the findings to technological changes, policy environment, and behavioural motivations of farmers in their input choices. In particular, we address the following questions: How do farmers choose their inputs in cotton cultivation? What have been the changes in the input use patterns over the last decade? What has been the implications of these changes on farmer incomes?

Having examined several experiments with cotton seeds during the colonial period in Chapter 2, we begin by focusing on the input that has amassed the most attention in recent times—seeds. Over the past two decades, the seed market for cotton has undergone tremendous changes that have generated intense debates. At the centre of the debates has been the issue of proliferation of Bt cotton. The debates have revolved around issues of yield effects, monocultures, monopoly of multinational and agribiotech firms such as Monsanto, regulation, health hazards, and seed sovereignty, among others. In this backdrop, as if history has repeated itself, there has been an emergence of 'loose', 'stealth', and 'illegal' cotton seeds in the form of herbicide tolerant (HT) Bt seeds (HTBt henceforth).[1]

These debates notwithstanding, what was the experience of Vidarbha's cotton farmers with growing Bt cotton? Following our discussion of seeds, we move on to an equally critical input in cotton cultivation—pesticides. In particular, we explore the patterns of Bt cotton and pesticide usage in cotton cultivation. We comment on the rationale of decision-making by farmers in relation to pesticides by examining their use over a two-year period. Another principal component of cost of cultivation is related to the management of weeds, and in that regard, we discuss how weedicide use and labour have gained prominence in our study period. In fact, we trace the reasons behind the proliferation of illegal HTBt seeds. We also observe changes in cultivation practices that have accompanied the management of weeds—a growing concern in the region's cotton story. Finally, we explore the issue of labour use in cotton. For centuries, labour has been a critical input in the cultivation of cotton, particularly for weeding and cotton picking.[2] In this context, we also examine how the technological change in cotton cultivation has impacted the gendered division of labour.[3] Much of the drudgery-inducing and backbreaking work is performed by women involved in sowing, weeding, and picking whilst tasks undertaken by men that are drudgery-inducing have been increasingly mechanized.

AGRICULTURAL INPUTS

Expenditure on seeds accounts for a significant share of total spending on agricultural inputs. Two decades since the Genetic Engineering Appraisal Committee's (GEAC's) approval of commercial use of Bt cotton in India, nearly all the cotton cultivation involves Bt hybrid seeds. Cotton farmers began using Bt seeds sold 'illegally' in 2001 against a backdrop of serious bollworm infestation.[4] Referring to the incident, Sharad Joshi, a prominent farmer union leader and founder of the farmers' organization, Shetkari Sanghatana described the company as the 'Robinhood' who smuggled the gene when the farmers were reeling under severe pest attack.[5]

In 2002, three transgenic cotton hybrids were introduced under the brand name Bollgard (MECH-12, MECH-162, and MECH-184) by

Mahyco–Monsanto Biotech Ltd (MMBL)—a joint venture between the Indian seed company Maharashtra Hybrid Seeds Company Ltd (Mahyco) and Monsanto. Mahyco—a seed company headquartered in Jalna district of Marathwada region of Maharashtra—was primarily a vegetable seed company that pioneered hybrid maize and *jawari* seeds with technical cooperation from the Rockefeller Foundation and the Government of India during the Green Revolution. Monsanto, which was then the leading global supplier of herbicides and seeds, was acquired by Bayer in 2019.[6]

Over time, newer technology within Bt was introduced in the Indian seed market. The first generation Bt construct—Bollgard I (BGI) that belonged to Monsanto—with the single gene event MON531 featured the gene *cry1Ac*. This was followed by the two-gene event (second generation) MON15985, commonly known as Bollgard II (BGII), which featured the two genes *cry1Ac* and *cry2Ab2*, was approved for sale for the first time in 2006. BGII was promoted as a response to the pink bollworm (PBW) developing resistance to BGI. By this time, three prominent competitors to Mahyco's monopoly in Bt cotton had emerged, namely Rasi Seeds in Tamil Nadu, Nuziveedu in Andhra Pradesh, and Ankur in Maharashtra. Around the time our exploratory fieldwork began in 2008, non-Bt hybrid seeds and varieties were increasingly vanishing from the market.

By our second round of survey in 2015 and 2016, certain farm practices catalysed the development of PBW pressure. As noted in a recent study in 2018:

> Since three to four years, some farmers had left the cotton crops standing in the field till March for more pickings instead of pulling them out in December which is the usual practice. This allows the pink bollworm, which makes an appearance in winter, to stay on in the soil since its cycle is not disrupted, allowing it to return early at the time of sowing. The problem is exacerbated in irrigated areas.[7]

Though the problem originated in irrigated cotton, rain-fed cotton too has started bearing the brunt of the insect pest.

Much has been debated about the effects of Bt hybrids on yield and farmers' incomes. Two narratives have dominated much of the debates: 'triumph' and 'failure' narrative. The 'triumph' camp showed considerable reduction in bollworm infestation due to the use of Bt seeds, arguing that this reduction in losses raised cotton productivity (yield per acre), resulting in substantial savings in chemical pest control and higher net returns. Lower pest management effort and reduction in incidence of pesticide poisoning among farmers were highlighted as the marvel of the Bt seed technology. Even at the village level, it was posited to have resulted in favourable distributional outcomes with improvements in female wage earnings and incomes of vulnerable households.

Meanwhile, the 'failure' camp has raised concerns about increased seed costs, incidence of insecticide resistance and secondary pests, distortion of pest ecology, loss of varietal diversity, loss of seed sovereignty, genetic contamination, and human and livestock health hazards due to increased exposure to plant toxicity. Risk and uncertainties associated with the new technology have also been highlighted. The plausible link between the growing use of Bt cotton and farmers' suicides has also been mooted. There have also been questions raised on the evidence-making related to improved incomes due to Bt seeds alone as farmers could have increased their use of other inputs such as fertilizers along with adoption of Bt cotton. In this ongoing debate, a critical point is to note that the Bt traits are available exclusively in hybrids in India. Within a decade of adoption of Bt, area under hybrid cotton increased from 40 per cent to 90 per cent. Hence, the improved yields could not be attributed exclusively to the Bt trait unless appropriate causal inferences are drawn by having non-Bt hybrids as counterfactuals instead of non-Bt varieties.[8]

As of today, emergence of PBW's resistance to BGII technology has triggered the illegal cultivation of HT cotton, which might seem like a déjà vu of events that unfolded two decades ago with the introduction of BGI technology in India. Back then, a steady increase in Bt cotton adoption happened over a few years across the country including Vidarbha. By the time our first round of survey began in 2009, over three-fourths of cultivators had adopted Bt cotton (Graph 5.1).

The cost of Bt seeds was initially high. The companies charging between 1,600 and 1,850 per 450 grams (1 pound) packet at a time when non-Bt hybrids were priced at around a quarter to a fifth of the Bt hybrid seed prices and varieties were much cheaper.[9] Consequently, in 2009, farmers spent nearly 30 per cent of the total cost of cultivation on seeds. In 2010 and 2011, the seed costs constituted about one-fifth of the total costs (Graph 4.11). Around the time we began the second round of survey, Bt cotton seed prices were regulated by the central government. Following the issue of the Cotton

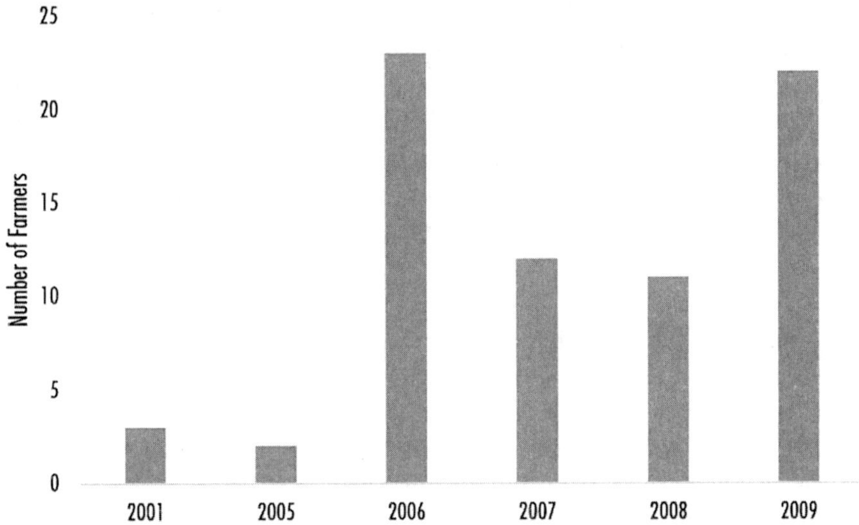

Graph 5.1 Year of Bt cotton adoption in Wardha sample: 2009

Source: Authors' calculation using survey data.

Note: Number of farmers refers to the farmers who cultivated cotton in kharif 2009 and reported their year of adoption of Bt-hybrids.

Seed Price (Control) Order, 2015, under the Essential Commodities Act, 1955, the Government of India notified the Bt cotton prices before the end of every financial year. This substantially reduced the seed costs in cotton cultivation.

In 2016 the central government again imposed a cap on prices of Bt cotton that varied across the country. The maximum retail price of the 450-gram packet of BGI seeds was set at 635 rupees and zero trait fees, and that of BGII seeds at 800 rupees. To the chagrin of Monsanto, which holds the intellectual property of the seed technology, the 'trait fee' was cut to 49 rupees from around 184 rupees per packet while farmers paid 830 rupees until this regulation was notified.[10] Since 2016, consecutive years of price cuts (barring 2017) were imposed by the central government to such an extent that, in 2019, the price of a 450-gram packet of BGII seed fell to 730 rupees. The royalty to Monsanto, which by then had been acquired by the agrochemical behemoth Bayer, was cut to 20 rupees per packet. By contrast, the price of BGI seeds was capped at 635 rupees per packet without any fee. By the end of the first quarter of 2020, the trait value for BGII was slashed to zero.

State intervention in the pricing of Bt cotton was not new. In fact, political economy factors were crucial in the subsequent dilution of Monsanto's market power in the Indian cotton seed industry. The price of Bt cotton seeds had been fixed since 2006 by Andhra Pradesh, Maharashtra, and Gujarat—three major cotton-growing states—following the Monopolies and Restrictive Trade Practices (MRTP) Commission . These states ordered Bt seed prices to be lowered, in response to a case against exorbitant prices filed by the Andhra Pradesh government. Until 2004, Mahyco had a monopoly over Bt seed production but since then several Indian seed companies incorporated MMBL's traits in the Bt seeds they produced and sold as sub-licensees.[11] Monsanto did appeal to the Supreme Court regarding the MRTP Commission's order but the latter refused to intervene, as a result of which MMBL had to bear a huge reduction in trait fee per packet.[12]

In 2010 the price of BGI was capped at 650 rupees and that of BGII at 750 rupees. Almost a decade later, the price of the genetically modified (GM) seed decreased, as discussed earlier. Upon careful examination of the evolution of market for Bt seeds, it is evident that the inability of the public sector to develop viable hybrids placed MMBL in a powerful position in the first decade of the twenty-first century to influence the profitability of its rival companies through sub-licencing the Bt construct. In the saga of Monsanto's dominance in Bt seed industry in the country, it is incredible that even though MMBL did not have a patent on Bollgard in India, it managed to extract high trait fees in its licencing arrangements with other seed companies, thereby revealing serious regulatory loopholes.[13] While the Bt seed market structure was being fundamentally altered, there was a minor rise in cotton prices from 2009 (Graph 4.10). However, the yield increases that were observed since the introduction of Bt cotton had started fizzling out by then.

The state intervention in seed prices expectedly resulted in a flurry of litigation in the three states. Conflict between the central and state governments was also evident during this tumultuous period as far as the transgenic seed industry was concerned. In 2011 the Gujarat High Court struck down the Gujarat Cotton Seed Act, which controlled the cotton seed prices including transgenic seeds on the grounds that it conflicted with the central government's legislation of Bt cotton seed prices.[14] The aforementioned regulatory developments generated an environment of uncertainty about the timely availability of seeds for farmers.[15] As the state control over transgenic seed pricing continued, in 2016 Monsanto threatened to exit the Indian market in response to the price capping by the central government, but it also got involved in a protracted legal battle with its Indian licensee—Nuzhiveedu Seeds Ltd (NSL)—over the latter's default on the payment of licensee fees for BGII in the light of the regulatory changes. In 2018 a ruling by the high court of Delhi regarding a 2017 appeal by Monsanto against NSL prohibited Monsanto from claiming patents for its GM seeds in India, which prompted it to appeal to the Supreme Court of India. The Supreme Court, in its 2019 verdict, overturned the verdict of the Delhi High Court that Monsanto's patent was invalid in India.[16]

While Bt seed price reductions hailed by farmers, price interventions in the transgenic seeds have time and again raised concerns about incentives for innovation in the agribiotech industry and prospects of attracting investments. Industry seed associations have also raised alarms about the viability of the industry citing growing labour costs in seed production.[17] However, the government's larger stance has been that the exorbitant seed prices have benefitted the industry at the cost of the farmers.

No doubt, the lack of parity in transgenic seed prices across the states as well as growing concerns about the link between Bt cotton and farmers' suicides have been contentious issues that motivated the government's intervention. However, despite the deficiencies of the public sector seed breeding initiatives that have not enabled the release of viable Bt hybrids and varieties, it need not be forgotten that the private sector seed industry developed with government support. Therefore, demands for non-intervention of the state as well as repeated threats to withdraw from the market by multinationals like Monsanto need to be interpreted in the light of the characteristics of the seed industry and role of the state therein. As of March 2022, the Government of India increased the maximum sale price of BGII seeds to 810 rupees. Such interventions have nonetheless been strongly opposed by farmer organisations such as Shetkari Sanghatana.

Reflecting on the cap on the Bt cotton prices, the amount spent on seeds per acre was more or less constant during the second and third rounds of our surveys as there were no serious variations in the quantity of seed used per acre of land. Indeed, whenever farmers resorted to resowing due to germination failure in years of delayed onset of monsoon or prolonged dry spells, the total seed costs incurred by farmers increased. The low variation in seed costs per acre over the period notwithstanding, the decision-making process behind the choice of seeds is far from being a simple process. Throughout our study period, Bt cotton hybrids available in the market exploded. Between 2009 and 2011, various seeds with gene construct MON

15985, which expresses 'Cry' proteins licenced by Monsanto as Bollgard II, were approved by the GEAC.[18] Of the 899 gene constructs approved between 2002 and 2011, 677 were approved between 2009 and 2011.[19] As of today, more than 3,000 cotton hybrids are available in the market. The rapid increase in seeds and widespread use of Bt hybrids might indicate that farmers have unquestioningly embraced the Bt technology and that there is a high latent demand for Bt hybrids. However, this could not be further from the truth. The trend of the growing supply of Bt hybrids masks several issues. First, the inability of farmers to sufficiently experiment with the seed varieties is a serious concern. Over the study period, farmers have demonstrated not only their frequent adoption and disadoption of seed brands but also their inability to know whether any yield improvement arose because of the seed or conducive natural factors and prudent farm management. This has hampered social learning as well as self-learning—aspects that are critical in the practice of agriculture. Furthermore, there has been a process of 'deskilling' as farmers' traditional knowledge going for a spin in the face of the emergent issues with new varieties and seasonal variations is common.

Second, in the absence or shortage of effective non-Bt hybrids and *desi* varieties, farmers also procure seeds from the black market. 'Loose' or 'illegal' seeds are typically sold directly by the agent, often in ingenious ways. They are sometimes referred to as 'Bt III seeds' or HT seeds promising to reduce the weeds and hence lead to large saving on weeding expenses. There are reports that 15 per cent of the area cultivated by cotton in the states of Maharashtra, Telangana, Andhra Pradesh, and Gujarat are found with illegal HT cotton in 2017. These varieties have not yet been approved legally in India and the issue of some of the seeds being spurious is also a concern among policymakers.[20] The extent of spurious seeds is not limited to HT cotton alone.

There are various spurious and counterfeit Bt cotton seeds sold across India and some of them do not have the Bt gene. There is no knowledge of the extent and spread of these 'stealth' seeds.[21] In a test of Bt seeds using kits in 2006, the Central Institute for Cotton Research (CICR henceforth) at Nagpur found that 28 per cent of the sampled illegal seed brands were actually non-Bt hybrids.[22] In addition to illegal and spurious seeds, seasonal changes in seed varieties and the attributes of the marketing seeds often confuse farmers about the yield potential and suitability of specific varieties on their plots. The recent passing of the Seed Bill, 2019, has provision for more stringent regulation of the seed markets. Despite this, the bill has generated debates on seed sovereignty.[23]

Third, the technological uncertainty related to effectiveness is manifested in the development of resistance of pests to Bt cotton. For dealing with this, it is often suggested that one-fifth of the area around Bt cotton is sown with refuge non-Bt hybrids which are kept protected against pest infestation or one-twentieth of the area is sown with refuge non-Bt hybrids which are left unsprayed. In our study region starting from 2017, the Bt cotton seeds were sold along with refuge seeds to farmers. Along with a packet containing 450 grams of Bt seeds, farmers were provided with a 120-gram pack of non-Bt seeds. Though farmers purchased these seeds, they rarely complied with cultivating the refuge cotton plants in their farms. To avert this problem, the Government of India advocated implementation of 'refuge-in-bag' (RIB) for Bt cotton where 5–10% of non-Bt seeds are mixed in a 475-gram Bt seed bag.[24] These developments have however not significantly prevented the development of pink bollworm resistance across the country.[25]

CHOICE OF SEED

In 2016 and 2017 we examined plot-level use of cotton seed brands used by farmers.[26] Farmers typically adopted multiple seed brands.[27] Across different *taluka*s, farmers used up to five seed brands in a season (Graphs 5.2 and 5.3). Rather than multiple trials of a single seed brand as was the practice when they had limited options, farmers used multiple seed brands as a 'rule of thumb' in the absence of knowledge on what works and what does not in a fast-changing and uncertain production environment. Discussing with neighbours and those in their social network, we figured out that this heuristic becomes a shortcut to know which combinations work and which do not as new brands emerge every season. Farmers are well aware that the germination rates of new varieties are not guaranteed. Moreover, farmers hope if one did not provide protection against the pests, the other might. This trial-and-error approach to seed choice has dimensions of deskilling that we will discuss later.

Our findings conform to the evidence from other cotton tracts of the country.[28] Apart from farmers' experiences and motivations of risk diversification, the brands adopted are also heavily dependent on the marketing and sales push made by the companies. The number of sales

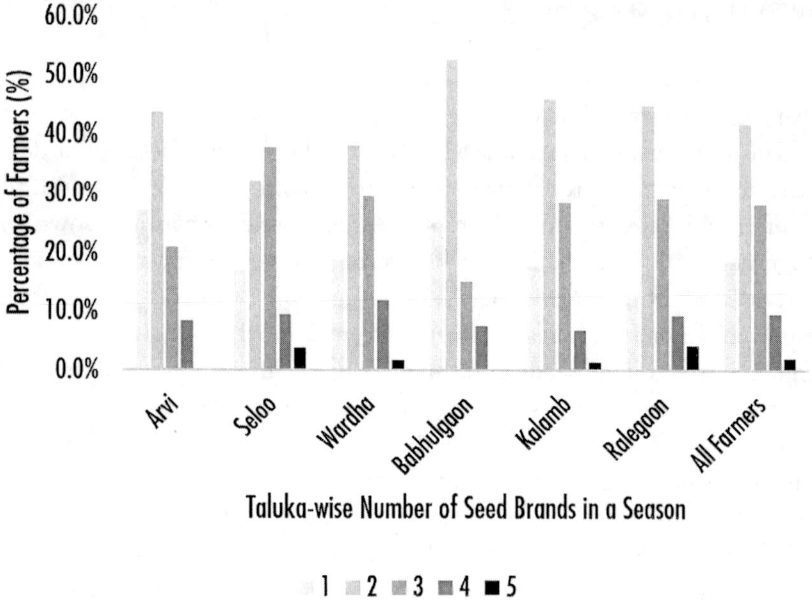

Graph 5.2 Plot-level number of cotton seed brands: 2016

Source: Authors' calculations based on survey data.

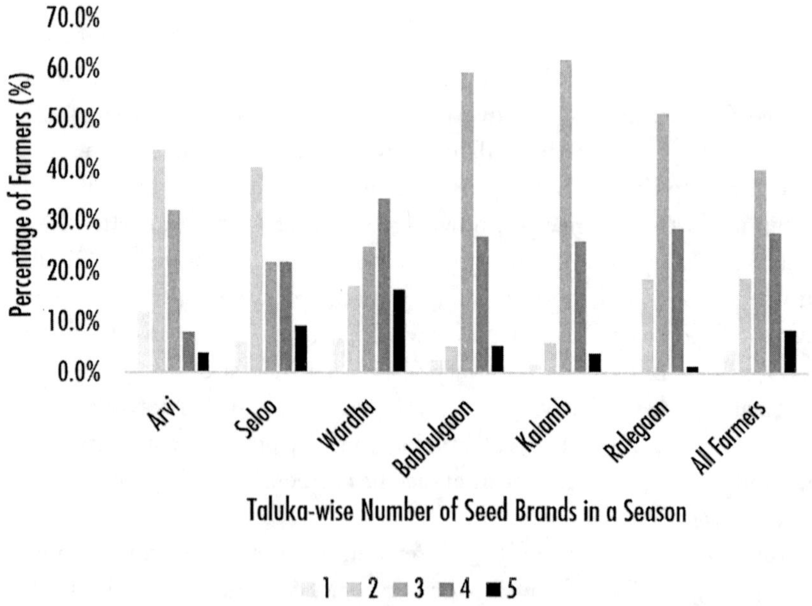

Graph 5.3 Plot-level number of cotton seed brands: 2017

Source: Authors' calculations based on survey data.

demonstrations conducted by the seed companies particularly have an influence on large farmers or 'progressive' farmers who in turn facilitate the diffusion of the brand in their village and their social network. However, there is considerable evidence of supplier-induced demand on account of higher margins that certain seed brands provide to the input dealers. The seed companies also exploit the seed diversification strategy of farmers to create various brand names for seeds with the same hybrid code.[29] The choice of seeds and seed brands involves various forms of legitimization.[30] The choices of farmers belonging to marginalized groups are based on the choices made by larger, wealthy, and so-called 'progressive' farmers in the village. Given the heterogeneous strategies of risk management across farmers belonging to various land size classes, choices made by the larger farmers or the progressive farmers need not be optimal for others. This could have dire consequences, particularly in bad years.

Awareness about variants of Bt cotton was low. Farmers were largely ignorant of the difference between the BGI and BGII varieties. In the first round of survey, we came across farmers who believed that since the relatively new BGII seeds were expensive, they were likely to double the yield. However, when problems of pest resistance and secondary pests arose with the BGII seeds, farmers hoped for 'Bt-3' which would solve most of the emerging problems. In fact, the illegal HT seeds and other spurious seeds in the region were sold to the farmers as 'Bt-3 seeds', sometimes as 'BG4 seeds' and 'Bt-5 seeds' in loose packets, starting from about 2017.

The popularity of specific seed brands too kept varying over time, indicating the prevalence of 'seed fad'. It was not uncommon for a particular brand to be popular in a year but later get replaced by another brand in the subsequent year. This was happening in a scenario where there are significant ambiguities in learning from the environment, with very low knowledge of different types of seeds. Consequently, seed choices were largely driven by social emulation. For instance, the dominant seed brand belonging to the Nagpur-based seed company Ankur in 2016 was adopted by a much lesser number of farmers in 2017. While almost 40 per cent of the farmers used Ankur in 2016 (Graph 5.4), only 12 per cent cultivated Ankur in 2017.[31] Rashi was the most popular brand in 2020. During the first round of our surveys from 2009 to 2011, Bunny, Sunny, Ankur, and Super Mallika were popular seed brands in the five Wardha villages. As of 2021, they had ceased to be popular, and a few other brands emerged as popular: Solar 96, Waghoba, and Rasi 608. Rasi 608 in particular was supposed to yield cotton with big bolls

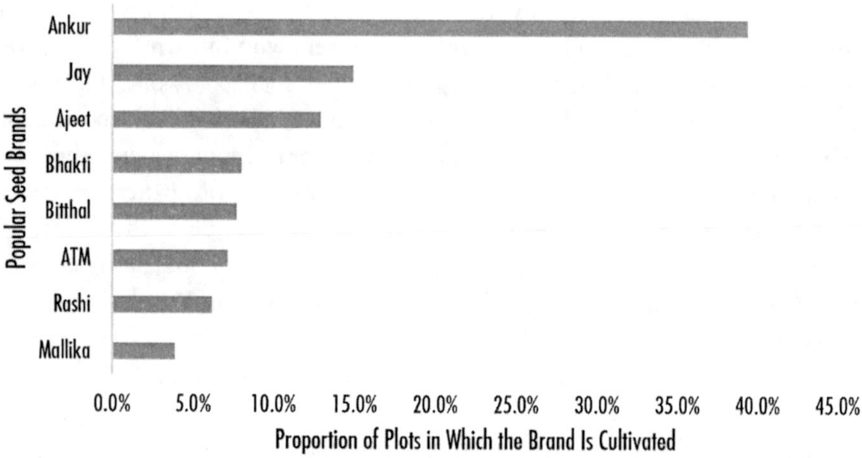

Graph 5.4 Seed brands used by cultivators: 2016

Source: Authors' calculations based on survey data.

Note: Total adds up to 100 per cent.

and many farmers had cultivated it with the hope of this new seed brand providing higher yield because of it.

An important feature of cotton seed marketing is ingenious seed brand names that rely on metaphors that farmers relate to or are rather lured by. For instance, names that symbolize power, prosperity, abundance, and masculinity among others include Balwan, Kabaddi, Panga, Lottery, Money Maker. Another popular brand name—Mallika by NSL—has feminine connotations, literally. It even puts a smile on the face of mostly the male farmers when they talk about its pros and cons. Another marketing strategy is illustrating extraordinarily large cotton bolls to appeal to the subconscious of the farmers while they visit the *krishi kendra* or the input dealer to purchase seeds and other agricultural inputs.

During fieldwork, we have come across several posters brandishing the apparently supreme gimmicky attributes of the seeds. We distinctly reminisce about such a poster of a seed brand. There was a larger-than-life poster of a farmer wearing a spick suit sitting on large bolls of cotton and displaying loads of cash in his hand, tacitly implying that those who miss out on this seed brand might as well miss out on the opportunity to earn big. During our second round of survey, we found an advertising pamphlet which had a cotton boll and a Sumo wrestler on two arms of a weighing machine with the boll pulling down the wrestler. Such imageries and the associating marketing strategies are often successful in persuading the farmers and subtly influence seed choices.

As mentioned before, there has been a rise in the cultivation of illegal HTBt seeds in the region. With the increasing use of herbicides, demand for herbicide-resistant seeds has gained momentum in various parts of the country. It is anticipated that this technology will reduce labour requirements for weeding, but this technology has not yet been approved by the GEAC. The legal status notwithstanding, farmers all over the country are using these seeds. In Vidarbha too there has been an inflow of HT cotton seeds. Even though Monsanto has withdrawn its application for GEAC clearance of HTBt seeds (Roundup Ready Flex), a lot of seeds are available as HTBt seeds in the region and are sold at a price of 1,200 rupees per 450-gram pack. The state action against its sale has also been sporadic.[32] The total estimated value of seeds seized in the state of Maharashtra up to 9 June 2021 was close to 20 million rupees. Some scrupulous input dealers also sold non-cotton seeds as HTBt seeds. About 6,200 quintals of soybean, *chana*, and *tur* were sold as cotton seeds in the Yavatmal district.[33] Owing to concerns about potential legal implications, there was very little self-reporting of the use of HT seeds and hence we could not collect the data in our primary survey. We did however amass anecdotal evidence on the proliferation of HT seeds.[34]

In January 2021 a farmer in a Wardha village who grows cotton and *tur* on his rain-fed plot (*koradwahu*) of land narrated to us the evolution of HTBt seeds that had already been grown by farmers. He described animatedly how some adventurous youngsters from a neighbouring village went on a motorcycle trip to Telangana to procure around 30 kilograms of such seeds.[35] A barrage of questions later, he informed us that no one really knows who manufactured those seeds, whether they were legal, and where they were grown. While we have come across innumerable descriptions about Bt cotton and how it influenced the region and the farmers' ecological validation, two instances stand out. First, a septuagenarian farmer in a Yavatmal village who had witnessed the marked changes in the agrarian systems in the village over decades gave a satirical response to our question about where he foresaw the future of Bt cotton for Vidarbha farmers. He said:

> I could see Bt-3, and hope that I live long enough to see Bt-9.

The naiveté of the farmer is not surprising as many believe that BGIII hybrids exist. This also reveals low awareness about cotton seeds. Second, a young farmer in a Wardha village drew comparison between pedigree and indigenous dog breeds to explain how a farmer risks the lure of Bt cotton and the subsequent expenses and losses. According to him, the comparison between Bt hybrids and the indigenous varieties resembled that of the experience of adopting a pedigree—*pardeshi jaaticha kutra* and a *desi kutra*—the Indian pariah dog. In the farmer's words, while the

> *pardeshi jaaticha kutra* is high maintenance and requires frequent spending on food, vet, and grooming, *the desi kutra* is sturdy and survives on much less attention and care. The loyalty of the two however unchanged, the expenses on the former is considerably higher. However, why someone without the means may even borrow to own the former rather than adopt the freely available breed is because of it as a status symbol.

PESTICIDES

Another critical input related to cotton cultivation that has had significant influence on economy, ecology, and health is pesticides—a catch-all phrase including insecticides of several groups including pyrethroids, organophosphates, and cyclodiens, weedicides, fungicides, and herbicides. The emergence of Bt cotton occurred in the context of widespread American bollworm (*Helicoverpa armigera*) infestation and high resistance to pyrethroids in cotton cultivation. Relentless spraying of synthetic pesticides was ineffective for managing this large-scale infestation, and Bt cotton emerged as a promising alternative. The promise of Bt cotton was to reduce bollworm infestations, consequently reducing pesticide use by farmers. It is often argued that the seed companies had initially thought of charging a higher price which would account for a share of farmers' savings on pesticides that would accrue to the farmer. The new technology of damage control was expected to improve yields and profitability in cotton cultivation.

Two types of insect pests—bollworms (*bond ali*) that feed on the cotton and sap-sucking pests that suck the sap from the leaves—infest a cotton plant during different growth phases. The problem of bollworm in cotton cultivation has existed for more than a century and have been handled in various ingenious ways in history. As far as back in 1915 the exotic cotton varieties were found to be more susceptible to bollworms than the *desi* varieties. In experimental plots, cultivating *bhindi* (ladies' fingers) on the plot in a proportion of 1:100 was found helpful in managing pest attacks with *bhindi* acting as the trap crop.[36] At that time, it was also noted that immediately after the worms appeared on *bhindi* plant, the vegetable had to be destroyed. Else, it could become a breeding ground for more bollworms. Proper management of pests, over the years, has evolved in a complex manner where newer solutions at times give rise to newer problems. While Bt cotton was anticipated to provide protection against bollworms, the *hiristum* hybrids that were introduced with the Bt gene are known to be more vulnerable to sap-sucking pests, unlike the public-sector-produced *desi* varieties.[37]

During the early days of fieldwork in 2008, farmers in Wardha expressed concerns about *pithya* (mealy bug) which was known to have caused severe damages in Punjab cotton by then. Over the years, issues of insecticide pests such as *lashkari* (military bug) and sucking pests such as *jassid*s and *aphid*s emerged. Given we found an almost universal adoption of Bt cotton in the study region, we examined the pest incidence and pesticide use in the second round of surveys, that is 2015 and 2016. We found that 80 per cent and 95 per cent of cotton growers in 2015 and 2016, respectively, faced one or more insect pest incidence.[38] The dominant pest infestation in both years was by sap-sucking pests. In these two years, there was very limited incidence of bollworm infestation. In fact, in the eight years from 2010 to 2017, *mawa, jassid*s and *aphid*s were the major pests in half of these years, and *pandhri mashi* (whiteflies) was the major pest in 2012. The pink bollworm, developing resistance to BGII, has emerged as the major pest mostly since 2018.

A crucial aspect of insect pest management by farmers is the identification of pests and pest incidence. Most farmers identified pest incidence by symptoms that appear at different stages of the plant's growth. Farmers also evaluated the effectiveness of pesticides based on how these symptoms had subsided. With *mawa/churda* (*jassids/aphids*) and *thurthude* (leafhopper/thrips), farmers observed the curling of leaves. Whiteflies were more clearly visible on the plants given its distinct colour. Bollworm attacks were more distinct than these two pests. Interestingly, in the social context of agrarian realities, a signal of 'performance' of pest management related to sap-sucking pests was the 'green'-ness of the cotton plants.

Discussions with farmers as well as entomologists suggest that the *krishi kendra* or input dealers have successfully manipulated farmer perceptions to sell fertilizers like potash to be added along with pesticides. Application of potash made leaves appear greener and farmers perceived it to be a signal for higher effectiveness of pesticides. What the indiscriminate application of pesticides has also affected is the indigenous agriculture knowledge about ecological farming practices. For instance, most farmers could not identify benevolent insects since broad-spectrum chemical pesticides killed non-harmful and non-target insects too. Typically, these insects developed resistance slower than bollworms, and sucking pests such as plant-eating (phytophagous) pests develop resistance earlier than the insect-eating (entomophagous) natural enemy population. This led to excessive pest pressure and consequently a pesticide treadmill which made the development of pest resistance easier.[39] The approved package of practices suggested by the Directorate of Cotton Development warns against excessive use of certain pesticides which could lead to resurgence of specific pests, but farmers do not seem to pay much heed to these guidelines.[40]

From discussions with input dealers in 2016 at Wardha, we draw the following insights. Apart from pesticides, farmers had been applying weedicides for the last three years not only for cotton but also soybean and *tur*. Some farmers applied weedicides while sowing even before the weeds occured. This was plausibly one of the reasons for a drop in soybean yield. Tonics were regularly applied in October and November. A farmer in a study village applied three different tonics in 2015, hoping to have 'greener' leaves that are a sign of good yield. Although some of the input dealers mentioned that the pesticide monocrotophos (locally known as 'Mono') was banned, the use of the same was rampant. Ironically, Mono happens to be the most commonly consumed pesticide in farmers' suicides in Vidarbha.

Despite availability of biological and physical alternatives to control insect pests, only a few farmers in the study villages adopted them. Some used 'yellow sticky pads' for managing whitefly incidence. The attractiveness of this measure is that insects could not develop resistance against this, but the effectiveness is dependent on various climatic factors and the type of glue used in the sticky pads.[41] Apart from this, very few farmers were aware of 'pheromone traps' for pest management. Few used organic pastes such as *nimbu arka* made with chilli, lemon, and other ingredients for insect pest management. It is generally believed that these pastes are effective if they remain stuck to the leaves for twenty-four hours. If it rains in the intermittent period, these pastes have to be applied again making it a cumbersome method to manage pests.

The use of alternative damage control methods such as non-pesticidal management (NPM) was restricted not just due to uncertainty in their effectiveness but also by limited availability of ingredients to prepare the alternatives. These practices require preparation of concoctions based on locally sourced materials that were made available when the non-governmental organizations (NGOs) and local agricultural universities trained farmers about insecticide resistance management (IRM) strategies, though farmers showed little interest after the intervention pilots were over. All the non-chemical applications could be prepared at home, but they required a substantial amount of time, labour, and materials that made them unpopular. According to farmers and extension workers, these requirements for the NPM spraying is one of the biggest bottlenecks to their diffusion. In earlier studies we found attempts by interventions such as integrated pest management (IPM) programmes in certain pockets of the study region. Despite attempts to disseminate information about scouting the field and deciding to spray the recommended dosage of pesticides based on economic threshold limit (ETL), awareness about these practices remained low.[42] In fact, Subash Palekar, one of the pioneers of the zero budget natural farming (ZBNF) method of farming without chemicals, hails from Amravati. While farmers were aware of the methods for rejuvenating soil health through applications prepared from natural and locally found ingredients such as *jeevamrut*, adoption of ZBNF, renamed to Subhash Palekar Natural Farming (SPNF), was abysmal. There were also recommendations to use sucking pest resistant hybrid seeds for cultivation by CICR, but we did not come across mention of the same either from the input dealers or farmers in our study region, and effective insecticide resistance management remained a complicated problem.[43]

In this background, almost all farmers used chemical pesticides to manage the incidence of pests. Farmers usually used broad-spectrum pesticides which were sprayed for all types of pests. Typically, pesticides were approved by the Central Insecticides Board and Registration Committee (CIBRC) in India.[44] The committee registers and approves pesticides for particular crop and pest combinations or for a particular pest. But the use of these pesticides manifested in the field differently. Most pesticides were used for pest management across various pests and crops despite the specific approved use.[45] There are large number of pesticides registered and approved by CIBRC every year. As of 31 December 2014, about 256 pesticides were registered for use in India. This number went up to 299 as of 1 July 2021.[46] These pesticides are also provided with different brand names by companies producing them. The result of such a speedy increase in number of pesticides and brands is that the farmer is faced with a choice overload when deciding on the appropriate pesticide. Farmers in our study mentioned that they kept changing pesticides frequently. In our survey in 2015, 95 per cent of the farmers indicated that they kept changing pesticides. The choice of pesticide is typically mediated by inputs from the input dealer. As for the input dealers who sold pesticides to the farmers, holding a large inventory of new varieties of seeds and pesticides was perceived as a good quality.

Farmers typically used three chemical pesticides—monocrotophos (an organophosphate), acephate, and imidacloprid—to manage the pests. Monocrotophos is a toxic pesticide that is banned for use for vegetables and food crops in India.[47] The pesticides were available in various brands and importantly, different brands were sold at different prices. Farmers preferred using specific brands even though the chemical composition was generally the same. Monocrotophos was available as Monostar, Monocil, and Monorin.

The use of 'cocktails' of pesticides that is mixing pesticides before application is widely prevalent. For instance, farmers mix water-soluble fertilizers such as 19.19.19 (mono ammonium phosphate, or MAP) with pesticides. They also mix plant growth enhancers, popularly known as 'tonic' along with the cocktail of pesticides. Though farmers frequently prepare these cocktails, they do not have knowledge of what is mixed nor the rationale behind the ingredients. An input dealer in Yavatmal said:

> When a farmer demands humic (a plant growth enhancer) and I offered him 96 per cent humic at a price 1400 rupees per litre, some of them declined the purchase of the same. They contest that the price is only 300 rupees per litre. I explain that this has 96 per cent humic while the one which costs 300 rupees per litre has only 6 per cent humic. But they do not get it. Eventually they purchase the 6 per cent humic at 300 rupees per litre.

As 'cocktails' of pesticides, farmers typically used monocrotophos or a combination of monocrotophos and acephate to deal with pest infestation. Few farmers used pesticides containing diafenthiuron and flonicamid to manage whiteflies. However, there was a large discrepancy in how farmers referred to pesticides. They mostly knew the brand names albeit with colloquial variations. Only a few farmers used imidacloprid, which is relatively safer and more effective.[48] Imidacloprid, though, is costlier than monocrotophos and acephate. It is likely that farmers mix other pesticides to reduce their expenditure, but it poses the same problem of knowledge of effectiveness of ingredients as in the case of mixing of Bt hybrid seeds brands.[49] These routine practices raise questions about how farmers in the region learn from others in the social network or through their own experiments. This is also an indictment of the public agricultural extension system; a theme that we will return to later.

Farmers spend a substantial amount per acre on an array of pesticides: insecticides, weedicides, herbicides, and plant growth promoters. In our sample, more farmers had their crops infested by pests in 2016 but also that they spent less on insecticides. The usage of weedicides and tonics increased in 2016 as compared to 2015. It could be the case that when expenditure on insecticides was lower, they spend more on plant growth promoters (Table 5.1).

We also explored the differences in pesticide expenditure per acre across various parameters (Table 5.2). Perceptions towards pesticides seem to play a key role in spending on pesticides. In addition, farmers who reported changing pesticides frequently spent more on pesticides in both years. Farmers who believed that pesticide application increased the yield also spent more per acre. Farmers who perceived pesticides as a damage control input tended to use lesser pesticides than those who perceived it as a yield-enhancing input. This logic cuts through to the perceptions about Bt cotton's role in yield enhancement as well.

Farmers who bought pesticides on credit invariably spent more on pesticides. In a survey of input dealers at *krishi vikas kendra*s, as the stores are locally called, we found that the shops sold more than half of their pesticide based on credit.[50] For some of the input dealers, as much as 80 per cent of their pesticides were sold on credit. From the farmers, we also observed that the prices of pesticides were different when bought

Table 5.1 Expenditure on pesticides (rupees per acre): 2015 and 2016

	2015	2016
Insecticide expenditure	535	406
Weedicide expenditure	50	182
Tonic (plant growth promoters)	71	249
All items	657	837
N (cotton growers)	440	460

Source: Authors' calculations based on survey data.

Note: Sample includes villages in both Wardha and Yavatmal.

Table 5.2 Variations in pesticide expenditure per acre

	2015				2016			
	Yes	No	Difference	t-Statistic for Difference in Means	Yes	No	Difference	t-Statistic for Difference of Means
Small and marginal farmer	588.3 (358)	501.4 (158)	–86.9	–1.36	766.8 (358)	768.8 (157)	1.9	0.03
Irrigated	597.9 (277)	519.7 (239)	–78.3	–1.33	867.5 (276)	651.8 (239)	–215.6	–3.64***
Farmer keeps changing the pesticides frequently	571.7 (476)	433.3 (26)	–138.4	1.02	777.9 (475)	545.2 (26)	–232.8	–1.73*
Farmer believes pesticide application increases the yield	580.5 (472)	300.9 (29)	–279.6	–2.18**	784.2 (471)	495.4 (29)	–288.8	–2.27**
Farmer bought pesticides on credit	630.6 (232)	508.3 (274)	–122.2	2.05**	808.3 (232)	722.2 (273)	–86.1	1.45

Source: T. Ranganathan and S. Gaurav, 'The Curious Case of Cocktails, Weedicides, and Tonics Pest Management Practices of Cotton Farmers in Vidarbha', *Economic and Political Weekly* 54, no. 44 (2019).

Note: Figures in parentheses indicate the number of farmers in the particular category. *, **, and *** indicate statistical significance at 1 per cent, 5 per cent, and 10 per cent, respectively.

on credit and when bought on cash. Demonstrating an age-old strategy of moneylenders, for those who bought pesticides on credit, the input dealers did not charge any interest until the time of harvest. Beyond that, they charge about 2–3 per cent per month as interest. Typically, the differential price acted as an interest for the period up to harvest. Also, most farmers repaid credit only after harvest.

The *krishi vikas kendra*s also kept accounts of individuals who locked in the farmer with the specific input dealer. Among several acts of performance associated with cotton cultivation, farmers perceive the purchase of pesticides by cash as a sign of their progress or status. One of the farmers we have been interacting with regularly during fieldwork proudly asserted that his family could purchase pesticides with cash in recent years and it was for him a sign of their upward economic mobility. The notions of cash and pride interactions aside, the role of credit in purchase of agricultural inputs cannot be undermined. Credit was very much intertwined with purchase of inputs, in particular pesticides by farmers. When farmers purchased on credit, the input dealers could also push high-priced or high-margin pesticides. Farmers buying input on credit have also experienced 'push sales' of products that they initially did not have any intention to buy. This is closely related to the input dealer increasingly becoming the most important source of agricultural extension in the region as elaborated later.

Pesticide spraying carries the hazard of affecting the health of the cultivator or the labourer who sprays the pesticides.[51] In 2015, almost two-fifths of farmers in our study sample felt that spraying pesticides caused health issues. Interestingly, in contrast, the input dealers did not worry about toxicity of pesticides while selling them. Even though the input dealers indicated imidacloprid and acephate as the more efficient pesticides, they held a larger stock of the more hazardous monocrotophos.[52] Discussions with older adults, typically in their seventies, revealed that a few decades ago there had been widespread use of now-banned toxic chemicals—endosulfan and endrin.[53] They considered these highly toxic chemicals 'very effective against pests'. These assertions were affirmed in focus group discussion (FGDs).

The widespread use of hazardous pesticides has severe short-term and long-term health effects.[54] Pesticides are used by farmers to commit suicides and banning hazardous pesticides like endosulfans have resulted in reduced suicides across India.[55] Apart from this, farmers are routinely exposed to pesticide poisoning while spraying it on the fields. Many experience symptoms of headache, nausea, and skin problems. In some years, these cases become severe and some of the farmers or farm workers lose their lives due to poisoning caused during pesticide spraying.

Yavatmal experienced a tragic loss of human lives in 2017 due to toxic pesticide spraying. During 2017–2018, there were 886 hospitalizations due to pesticide spraying in the district. It is to be noted that the numbers are not much less in other years. Even in the year prior to this, the number of hospitalizations for pesticide poisoning due to spraying was 433. In 2017–2018 though, at least 14 farmers and 7 farm labourers lost their lives and the hospitalizations and deaths became a larger political issue in the state. The Maharashtra state government then constituted a seven-member special investigation team (SIT) for determining the cause of the poisoning and provided recommendations for the improvement of the situation in the region.[56]

The committee came up with the following findings related to the cause of high levels of pesticide poisoning in the region that year.[57] First, the temperature and humidity were relatively higher that year which could have caused more perspiration resulting in larger absorption of pesticides in the body while spraying. Second, cotton plants in the district grew over 6 feet, 1–1.5 feet taller than usual, which meant spraying had to be done at the mouth or face level of those spraying pesticides which could have resulted in poisoning. Interestingly, high usage of plant growth promoters could have had a role in this growth. Third, too much spraying, often in doses much above the recommendations is common, and farmers or farm workers were seen to be spraying pesticides until 8:00 p.m.; well beyond the usual time for spraying in some places. Fourth, there was a serious lapse in health and safety measures as sprayers only tied napkins to their mouths and hardly wore any protective clothes while preparing and spraying the hazardous chemicals. Image 5.1 shows a labourer spraying pesticides on *tur* in a cotton–*tur* intercrop in a Yavatmal village in 2020. The lack of appropriate protective gear is common. Farmers and farm workers complain of inconvenience in wearing protective wear, particularly in hot and humid conditions during the season. Fifth, the mixing of pesticides and plant growth promoters could have resulted in the possible formation of a new compound that was more poisonous than the individual chemicals. Raids by authorities also revealed the sale of unauthorized tonics that were peddled to unsuspecting farmers through input dealers in the region. Sixth, there was a shift towards using ultra-low volume spray pumps instead of high-volume spraying pumps. The use of these pumps creates a dense mist from the droplets out of them, increasing the risk of poisoning.

Image 5.1 A labourer spraying insecticides on *tur* in a cotton–*tur* intercropping in a Yavatmal village, circa 2020

Source: Sarthak Gaurav.

Note: Since crops are intercropped, the precision application of pesticides on specific crops is common. However, safety and health considerations are often ignored while spraying toxic chemicals. The practice of wearing protective gear is ignored although those involved in spraying often refer to the heuristics of 'reading the wind direction' while spraying to have kept them safe.

The SIT also made note of lack of state capability to monitor quality in the region. There were unapproved tonics sold by the input dealers in the region. The quality control inspector is supposed to monitor the use of only approved pesticides in the region. There was only one full-time quality control inspector for the sixteen *taluka*s of Yavatmal and that post was lying vacant for over two years. This is a cause of concern across the country. As of 2019, only 10,496 pesticide inspectors were notified, and this would mean a severe under-capacity to deal with more than 2,00,000 input dealers across the country.[58] The recently approved Pesticide Management Bill, 2020, aims to bring in new rules and regulations in registering and monitoring pesticides. But constraints of state capacity offer formidable implementation challenges.[59] Among other issues related to the government, government hospitals in the district did not have antidotes for poisoning caused due to all the pesticides used in the region. It also lacked adequate facilities for cholinesterase tests which would allow for diagnosing chemical poisoning.

Nonetheless, the SIT did enact a few things. Licences of a few pesticide producers and input dealers were revoked. However, the report does not mention the reasons for specifically revoking the licence of those producers and input dealers. The lack of transparency only indicates that the government wanted to signal its intent but was not much concerned about addressing the structural issues. The SIT also suggested the banning of monocrotophos immediately. At the time of writing, this had not materialized.[60] The team also allocated funds for the distribution of protective kits in the villages. We have not observed any noticeable increase in the uptake of protective equipment by the sprayers in the region. The committee also made some recommendations related to the regulation of pesticide registration and licencing in the region. But there has been not much change in the way pesticide spraying has been happening in the region. Occasional reports of toxic reactions, mostly dermatological problems and acute headaches, are mentioned but reluctance to wear protective gear while spraying still remains widespread. The farmers and the farm workers are continuing to gamble on their incomes and health every year in pretty much the same way as before.

WEEDING

There is an important difference in the use of synthetic pesticides in India as compared to many other countries. While herbicides form a major part of pesticide use in other countries, insecticides are the most widely used pesticides in India. As of 2015, Indian farmers spent 2.5 billion US dollars on insecticides while spending only 350 million US dollars on herbicides.[61] Another related market is that of HT seeds, as discussed earlier. Typically, glyphosate is the weedicide of choice for farmers across the world. Use of these weedicides might affect the yield of cotton crops as the weeds grow alongside the cotton crops and it is difficult to spray the weedicides only on the weeds. The typical HT seeds are resistant to glyphosate and 86 per cent of the world's GM acres is resistant to these weedicides.[62]

An important reason for lower use of weedicides in India is that most of the weeding is carried out by human labour. Manual weeding (*nindan*) is an important activity in cotton cultivation and has been so for centuries. Agronomic practices and ongoing wages influence farmers' expenditure on manual weeding; there are often trade-offs between bullock-based hoeing for weeding or inter cultivation (*dawran*), and weedicides. This has important consequences on yield and incomes. *Dawran* is undertaken by men whilst *nindan* is done by women. However, the agronomic practices have evolved to accommodate these critical time-bound operations or micro-processes in interconnected and complex agricultural processes.

Typically, cotton is planted in lines such that there is a gap between the plants on both sides. Seeds are sown at a distance (typically through square grids of 3 feet by 3 feet) so that the plants could be seen as growing on the edges of a square. Such a practice is called *fulli paddath*. Such spacing allows for manual weeding as there is enough space for the labourer to move and remove weeds. Also, it allows *dawran*—oxen-based inter cultivation—across the rows and columns which is done before manual weeding. In recent years, a new form of lining, a single-lining technique, is gaining prominence. In this lining called *patta paddath*, the plants are spaced at gaps of 5 feet or 7 feet in rows and only 1-foot distance in the column (Image 5.2). This means there is a gap only across one direction and not much space for the oxen pair to

Image 5.2 *Yeli*, a lining tool used in *patta paddath*

Source: Sarthak Gaurav.

move across the column for *dawran*. In such cases, the spacing is supposed to provide a higher density planting. However, this *paddath* does not allow for completing weeding operations by human labour or bullock labour. In such instances, use of weedicides is the more convenient way to control weeds.

Given the high labour costs, there is a clear shift towards weedicides. Over the years, the proportion of farmers using *patta paddath* has been on the rise. This shift is important for the proliferation of herbicide or weedicide markets and also paves the way for HT-trait cotton seeds. Though there was no consensus among farmers about the impact of the type of line-spacing (*paddath*) on yield, there was a growing sense that *patta paddath* could also have a positive impact on yield of the cotton crop.

The proportion of farmers adopting *patta paddath* increased from about two-thirds to four-fifths over a year (Table 5.3). However, there was no significant difference in area under cotton cultivation among both groups of farmers. Also, the adoption of *patta paddath* did not decrease the expenditure on manual weeding but spent more on weedicides. There are variations in costs and income from cotton cultivation across the common sample of farmers adopting *patta paddath* and *fulli paddath* (Table 5.3). Farmers adopting *patta paddath* spacing spent more, had higher yields, and received higher net incomes from cotton cultivation in 2017, which was the best cropping year among our study years since 2009 (Table 5.3).

LABOUR

Labour formed a significant input in cotton cultivation in the study years. In many of our field visits, we kept repeatedly hearing about issues related to labour availability and wage increases. To understand labour input both from the cultivator's point of view and that of the non-cultivator households which supplied labour, we conducted a survey of cultivator and non-cultivator households in Wardha and Yavatmal for the years 2019 and 2020. This gave us valuable insights related to both the cultivator and non-cultivator households. The findings related to labour supply and labour incomes are presented in this section.

The cotton economy offers considerable wage employment to labour-supplying households. Despite changes in the nature and extent of labour absorption in Vidarbha agriculture, several characteristics of the agricultural labour in the region deserve attention.[63] As mentioned earlier, historically, the proportion of agricultural labourers and cultivators in Vidarbha villages

Table 5.3 Economics of cotton cultivation by *paddath*: 2016–2017

	2016			2017		
	Fulli Paddath	***Patta Paddath***	**Difference**	***Fulli Paddath***	***Patta Paddath***	**Difference**
Number of farmers	96	185		55	226	
Area cultivated (acres)	3.4	3.6	−0.2	3.1	3.1	0.0
Costs per acre (rupees)						
Seeds	1,966.9	2,120.1	–153.3**	2,069.6	2,098.4	–28.8
Fertilizer	2,142.9	2,480.6	–337.7***	1,456.8	1,854.4	–397.6***
Inter-culture	1,164.4	1,076.7	87.7	591.8	632.9	–41.0
Manual weeding	1,864.3	2,079.1	–214.7*	1,723.6	1,960.6	–237.1**
Weedicides	102.9	270.1	–167.1***	161.3	120.4	40.9
Harvesting (picking)	2,927.2	3,436.8	–509.6**	5,072.8	5,696.9	–624.1**
All inputs	13,379.4	15,007.0	–1627.6***	13,849.1	15,303.1	–1,454.0***
Yield (quintals per acre)	5.4	6.1	–0.7**	6.7	7.6	–0.9**
Net income per acre (rupees)	14,130.3	15,766.6	–16,36.3	20,194.4	22,991.4	–2,797.0*

Source: Authors' calculations based on survey data: 2016–2017.

Note: Figures are averages at the household level. Costs and net income are nominal values. All inputs reported are purchased inputs. *, **, and *** indicate the statistical significant of the t-statistics at 10 per cent, 5 per cent, and 1 per cent confidence levels.

have been more or less similar. This results in rare occasions of labour shortage for agricultural operations. On the other hand, the high demand for employment in the cotton economy has also attracted migrant farm workers from neighbouring regions. Over the past decades, there has been an increase in not only the number of agricultural workers but also their proportion in the population. Consequently, an individual worker does not experience an increase in number of days of labour supplied to agriculture despite growing labour demand at the macro level.

A decade and a half ago, a primary agricultural worker in a Vidarbha village would find less than 120 days of gainful employment in agriculture. However, with changes in cropping patterns fostered by the intensification of irrigation and new crop technologies such as Bt cotton that require greater weeding and higher rounds of pickings than traditional non-Bt varieties, agricultural employment in Vidarbha has far from stagnated. In fact, it has absorbed more labour over time.

The most striking characteristic of the farm labour in the villages is gender-based differentiation in agricultural operations. This differentiation has a considerable bearing on the wage rates. Table 5.4 illustrates the gender-based division of agricultural operations as well as differences in wages for men and women for the most common cropping pattern: cotton and *tur* intercropping in the kharif season. Depending on the cropping pattern, several weeks of employment is available for a worker from an agricultural household to supply labour in the agricultural activities. As has been the history of cotton cultivation, it deepens the gendered difference in agricultural tasks (see Chapter 2) and differentials in wages of men and women.

Women exclusively supply labour for *kadhi kachra* (cleaning of fields as part of land preparation), sowing, weeding (*nindan*), and picking of cotton—over three–four rounds of picking in the case of the near universally adopted Bt cotton. The other operations are dominated by men. Another feature of agricultural labour supply is that there is not only a gender-based allocation of agricultural activities but also seasonality which is central to the cash flows for the agricultural labour households.

Higher employment generation due to Bt cotton relative to non-Bt cotton, and greater on-farm wage employment for female labourers relative to male agricultural labourers is also evident in the literature.[64] During the phase when Bt cotton reduced crop losses due to pest damages, there were labour-saving effects of Bt cotton for own-farm labour due to reduced pesticide

Table 5.4 Cost per acre for the most common cropping pattern: Cotton and *tur* intercropping (2020 wage rates/costs)

Month	Activity	Sub-activity	Cost per acre (rupees) 2020	Assumptions
April	Land preparation	*Nagran* (deep ploughing)	900	
		Wakhran (V pass/ cultivator)	600	*Nagran* is done in three–four years depending on the hardness of the soil. Cultivator cost is 450 rupees per acre's work. *Wakhran* is done every year except for the years when *nagran* is done.
May	Land preparation	Cleaning (*kadhi kachra*)	600	Four women labour at 150 rupees wage rate
June	Land preparation	Cultivator	500	The cultivator is used for normal ploughs with shallow depth. The cost of hiring a cultivator is 500 rupees for an acre's work
	Sowing	Ox plough	250	Ox plough and one operator charges 1,000 rupees for one day and completes ploughing of 4 acres in a day
		Sowing	300	Two women labour at 150 rupees per day. Cotton and *tur* sowing are done by female labour. Ox plough for lines where seeds will be applied. Soybean sowing is done by tractors using seed drills but not with cotton.
July	*Dawran*	*Dawran*	500	Operator of ox plough is paid the amount and he covers more than 1 acre in a day
		Weeding	1,200	Eight women at 150 rupees wage rate
	Fertilizer application	Mixing urea and NPK fertilizers	300	Three men at 100 rupees per person, in 3–4 hours
August	Pesticide spraying	Weedicide spray one time	300	Three–four hours for 1 acre by a male

(*continued*)

Table 5.4 Cost per acre for the most common cropping pattern: Cotton and *tur* intercropping (2020 wage rates/costs) (*continued*)

Month	Activity	Sub-activity	Cost per acre (rupees) 2020	Assumptions
		Pesticide spray one time	300	Three–four hours for 1 acre by a male
	Fertilizer application	Mixing fertilisers + potash	300	Three men at 100 rupees per person complete the task in 3–4 hours
September	Weeding	Weeding	1,500	Ten women at 150 rupees wage rate
		Dawran	500	Operator of ox plough is paid the amount and he usually completes more than 1 acre in a day
	Pesticide spraying	Pesticide spray one time	300	One male labour takes two days to spray 1 acre of land. In 2020, the wage was 300 rupees per six hours (ten times emptying the 20-litre spray pump: the mix of which is pesticide and water).
November	Cotton picking	Wechne/Picking (all rounds)	400	Picking begins in November. For all three or four pickings. Picking labour cost is production dependent. Around 800 rupees per quintal output. On an average, 40 kilograms–0.5 quintal of *kapas* per day is picked by a female labourer.
December	*Tur* harvesting	Harvesting	600	*Hunda padhat* (piece-rate) as in the case of soybean and wheat.
December –January	Threshing	*Tur* threshing	250	One male labour with a thresher called Hadimba. Two hundred rupees per quintal for Hadimba's rent. Earlier method was done by female labour called *thokun*. Cost was based on 60 rupees per *peti* (20 kilograms). It was discontinued about seven–eight years ago due to delays in processing.
December–January	Transportation	Cotton transport	250	One male labour for loading output in tractor trolley. Additional cost includes 500–1,000 rupees per trolley and additional charges in the market yard.

Source: Author's calculation based on insights from fieldwork.

spraying. However, with an increase in pesticide spraying on account of growing pink bollworm infestation and secondary pests, such indirect effects of Bt cotton on labour-saving of males have weakened now.[65]

Even in the month of September, labour is required for spraying of pesticides (second or third spray). A labourer usually takes two days to spray 1 acre of land. In 2020, at the peak of the COVID-19 pandemic, the wage rate was 300 rupees for six hours of work comprising emptying the 20-litre spray pump ten times. Soybean harvest typically begins in mid-September and gets over by the first week of November. This provides around three weeks of agricultural work for the labour.

In the month of October, around one-fifth of farmers begin rabi operations involving land preparation such as *wakhran*, *dawran*, and *kadhi kachra* (cleaning). Labour is also demanded for soybean harvesting, threshing, transport to house. Three labourers finish the work on an acre of land in two days. Rabi sowing that commences in October goes on until the end of the month and early November (Image 5.3).

Image 5.3 Land preparation before rabi sowing in a Wardha village, circa October 2019

Source: Sarthak Gaurav.

Note: Tractors have increasingly replaced bullocks for land preparations. With an increase in tractor ownership, often financed by a new scheme of the government or many of the several auto-finance schemes offered in the region, the rental market for tractors has developed rapidly.

Around the end of October, irrigation of standing cotton plants requires labour. Two days for irrigation of an acre of cotton is not uncommon. In November, rabi work includes irrigation, spraying, and *dawran*. Usually, the second picking and cotton irrigation also demands labour. In this month, around seventeen–eighteen days of wage work is possible for a labourer. In the month of December, there is *tur* harvest, threshing, and transporting to home for storage. Cotton only has picking activity in December. Around eighteen days of labour is demanded by the cultivator household in this month.

In the month of January, harvest of *chana* begins. Cotton's last picking goes on, and wheat receives a round of irrigation. Around fifteen days of farm employment is available for a worker. In February, labour is mostly employed in the harvesting and threshing of wheat. About ten days of labour can be supplied by a member of the household in these operations. In the month of March, demand for labour in agriculture wanes considerably. There is demand for around five days of labour in the harvest of wheat and land

Image 5.4 Women agricultural workers engaged in cotton-picking activity at a field in a Wardha village, circa December 2020

Source: Sarthak Gaurav.

Note: It is common for female cotton-pickers to carry handmade bags to collect the bolls during picking. These bags carry up to half a quintal of cotton, and there are several variations that one may come across. It is also common for women to receive cuts on their fingers and palms from the bracteoles and branches during the picking activity.

preparation (ploughing using *nagaran/tirhi/panji* tiller). Unlike other parts of India, rotavator is not commonly used in these districts. The land is left fallow for two months—April and May—before the kharif sowing begins in June. This is also the lean period for agricultural labour households who find employment in the Mahatma Gandhi National Rural Employment Guarantee Scheme (MGNREGS) or non-farm work in the vicinity. After pre-monsoon showers, farmers start land preparation in the month of April/May by conducting operations such as *nagaran* (deep ploughing) or *wakharan* (shallow ploughing using a *wakhar* or a cultivator). Such land preparation requires around fifteen labour days. A new season of agriculture more or less offers the same prospects of agricultural work conditional on how the weather plays out over the next few months.

CONCLUSION

In this chapter, we have analysed patterns of input usage in cotton cultivation. We have also analysed various issues involved in seeds, pesticides, weedicides, and labour use in cotton cultivation. The key debates and concerns over the last decade or two have been about the extensive use of Bt cotton and chemical pesticides. There have been various efforts to portray the Bt cotton seeds as the 'suicide seeds' or the seeds that have brought in a yield 'revolution' in Indian cotton.[66] In this context, an exploration of how farmers engage with decision-making in the seeds is critical to understanding the ground realities. Moreover, we have investigated some of the changes in cultivation practices that have accompanied the input use changes related to weeding to explain the interdependence of seed technology and agronomic practices. In addition, we have examined the use of labour for cotton in the region during the last two years of our study.

Our findings suggest that farmers indeed consider damage control by use of Bt cotton as effective and associate it with higher yields. Farmers routinely navigate the agricultural input choice space with several new seeds and pesticides that are introduced every year and such a choice overload does not seem to be making decision-making easier for the farmer. While reliance on experimenting with combination of seeds is common, development of resistance and emergence of secondary pests in the study period has meant that cotton farmers are constantly on the search newer varieties of seeds and pesticides every year. Pink bollworm continues to bother farmers for many years. The HT cotton seeds that have proliferated despite their illegality owing to rising labour costs for weeding give a sense of déjà vu about 'stealth seeds' that invaded Indian cotton fields two decades ago before the legal commercialization of Bt cotton. However, despite widespread diffusion of Bt cotton, consumption of pesticides continues unabated, more so with the emergence of secondary pests and of late, the pink bollworm menace. The benefits could not be sustained over the decade. Across the two inputs, it is evident that farmers have been continuously experimenting with seeds and pesticides.

We argue that the urge to try out newer seeds by farmers is neither new nor unique to cotton or Vidarbha. This phenomenon has been documented for several crops and regions including soybean in the state of Madhya Pradesh.[67] Economic considerations aside, new and improved varieties of seeds are also seen as a necessary condition for becoming a 'good farmer'. Usually a progressive farmer is considered a good farmer but the expertise and specializations may influence social perceptions about who a 'good farmer' is.[68] Even when organic crop cultivation is pursued, the urge remains again to be a 'good farmer' for the organizations promoting that kind of cultivation.[69] In essence, the seed and agricultural input choices seem to stem from the idea of agriculture as performance to become 'good' farmers achieving 'good' yields.[70] In the study villages, farmers typically knew which farmer in their village had the best yield and which farmer had the worst yield in a year. It was also imperative that the farmers having bad yields in the year change certain practices in the next year to avoid being seen as a 'bad' farmer. This is the context in which experimentation by farmers takes place in the villages. An enormous role is also played by the marketing agents and input dealers who are many a time part of the farming ecosystem in the study region.[71] The experimentation is also recently accelerated as there is the widespread tapering of yield gains from Bt cotton.[72] In itself, trying out or experimenting is not necessarily a bad thing, but a large amount of 'experimentation' happened with an aim for measuring up to the choices made by others and that is a serious concern with these choices.

Despite the late adoption of Bt cotton in Vidarbha compared to Gujarat, by the time our survey commenced in 2021 there was near universal adoption of Bt cotton. The transgenic seeds initially resulted in lower usage of chemical pesticides but since 2011, there have been growing reports of insecticide resistance. Secondary pests and of late pink bollworm (PBW) infestation have forced farmers to spray high doses of pesticides again. Often the experimentation with pesticides takes the form of 'cocktails' based on the advice of agricultural input dealers.[73] The pesticide treadmill is continuing with farmers not just using different pesticides, but also mixing multiple pesticides as cocktails. Perceptions related to the functioning of pesticides and institutional aspects like purchasing on credit seems to influence the choice of pesticides significantly. There are significant health costs involved in the use of pesticides which does not receive significant attention from the stakeholders. Even a significant loss of human lives has not led to much progress in this regard. The state has failed to address the systemic issues in this regard and has approached this with a mindset of relief and recommendation provision.

To what extent these experiments are a consequence of regulatory and institutional changes coupled with the need for the farmer to be 'performing' good agriculture remains an open question.[74] Indeed, the expenditure on seeds stabilized due to state regulation in the form of price ceilings for Bt hybrids. However, spending on seeds goes up whenever the vagaries of weather result in lower seed germination rates and farmers resorting to resowing. Farmers diversify across seed varieties and brands. In recent rounds of our surveys, we have found that given the low efficacy of Bt seeds in the face of insecticide resistance and secondary pests and increasing labour costs for weeding, farmers have also begun experimenting with HTBt seeds that are illegal. Such developments are telltale signs of the industrial seed treadmill that cotton farmers have not been able to jump off from.

The prevalence of 'cocktails' and tonics in pesticide application practices resembles that of mixing Bt seed types. Prevalence of such practices is catalysed by the rapidly changing market for seeds and agricultural inputs and an absence of the ability to have extended trials with specific varieties or pesticides. Again, economic and non-economic logics interact to result in such behaviour. Taken together, these practices raise serious concerns about how farmers learn from experiments of the self and that of others, and the ability of extant extension systems to address these challenges. As farmers experiment with agricultural inputs, they are also adapting their *paddhat* (agronomic practice). There is a move towards a different lining method for planting in the hope to increase yields and provide better weed management. Preliminary analysis indicates that these changes have resulted in positive effects on yield; however, effects of such changes are better studied over the long run. The experience of Bt hybrids over the decade should inform us better to be cautious while analysing impacts of any such changes in the short term. In the absence of assured protection from weather-related shocks because of failures in the crop insurance market, farmers demonstrate risk-reduction practices as well as hedging in their cropping practices. CICR at Nagpur—the leading cotton research institute in the country—has been at the forefront of innovations in seed technology and agronomic practices. CICR has also been actively demonstrating high density planting system (HDPS) for cotton cultivation. Based on our interactions with scientists at the institute, canopy management as well as reliance on early maturity varieties are critical agronomic practices from which the Vidarbha farmers are likely to benefit.[75] CICR has also introduced new straight cultivars of Bt cotton and continues its effort at improving agricultural extension in the region.

Despite the gamut of technologies adopted by farmers and various experimentation done by them, cotton cultivation is highly labour intensive. The amount of human labour that goes into the various operations of cotton cultivation is enormous. From activities of land preparation to cleaning of the land after harvest, cotton cultivation involves labour for over eight months of the year. Although several processes such as land preparation have witnessed growing farm mechanization, the progress has been slow in terms of mechanization of cotton picking. The Indian Council of Agricultural Research's (ICAR's) Central Institute for Research on Cotton Technology (CIRCOT) at Mumbai has been experimenting with mechanized cotton harvesters and spreading awareness among farmers about this farm equipment.

We find several issues with agricultural extension, particularly public sector extension. In the absence of timely and localized advisory from the public agencies including the Krishi Vigyan Kendra (KVK), farmers have heavily relied on the *krishi vikas kendra* (agricultural input dealer store). Over time, farmers have also made changes to certain agronomic practices like inter-cultivation patterns which lock them into use of weedicides. While there are few credible private extension services offering limited advisory, many farmers have been duped by unscrupulous extension service providers as well. On the one hand, the problem of effective and affordable is exacerbated by the broad array of locally relevant extension services that farmers demand. On the other hand, the process of deskilling in a rapidly changing agricultural input market scenario has aggravated the agricultural extension challenges. Such dynamics once again indicates that farmers in the study region are frequently adapting and experimenting with new practices and techniques which could improve their cultivation incomes. However, in a situation where there are multiple causes that could impact the crop yield, farmers are experimenting with very limited expert advisory. The absence of a proper extension, lax regulation, and attendant uncertainties involved has meant that most of the gambles by farmers are largely a shot in the dark. In this context, the words of wisdom of an experienced cotton grower who was working with an NGO promoting NPM in 2009 frequently appears in our conversations with farmers: 'Pehle kheti hoti thi, abhi karna padta hai' (Earlier farming used to happen, now one needs to farm). How the changing agriculture and the institutions relevant for cotton cultivation bear on the risks and vulnerability of cotton farmers is the essence of our discussion in Chapter 6.

NOTES

1. The first generation Bt seeds were adopted after seeds with Bt trait were released illegally in Gujarat. It is remarkable to note that even with the HTBt seeds, adoption is happening before legal approval.
2. Recent literature on the new history of capitalism places huge importance of relative costs of production for cotton under slavery in the United States and 'free' labour in other countries. The estimates of labour costs of cotton cultivation in the nineteenth century is available in K. Rönnbäck and D. Theodoridis, 'Cotton Cultivation under Colonial Rule in India in the Nineteenth Century from a Comparative Perspective', *Economic History Review* 75, no. 2 (2021).
3. For a recent work on the gendered nature of mechanization on employment in the Indian context, refer to F. Afridi, M. Bishnu, and K. Mahajan, 'Gender and Mechanization: Evidence from Indian Agriculture', *American Journal of Agricultural Economics* 105, no. 1 (January 2023).
4. K. S. Jayaraman, 'Illegal Bt Cotton in India Haunts Regulators', *Nature Biotechnology* 19, no. 12 (2001): 1090–1091.
5. R. J. Herring, 'Stealth Seeds: Bioproperty, Biosafety, Biopolitics', *Journal of Development Studies* 43, no. 1 (2007): 130–157.
6. For an excellent overview of evolution of Mahyco and the phenomenal rise of its founder, Badrinarayan Barwale, as well as proliferation of seed companies within the Marwari community that Barwale belonged to, see A. Aga, *Genetically Modified Democracy: Transgenic Crops in Contemporary India* (New Haven, CT: Yale University Press, 2021), 186–188. For an overview of the development of the MECH varieties, see P. Ramasundaram and S. Vennila, 'A Decade of Bt Cotton Experience in India: Pointers for Transgenics in Pipeline', *Current Science* 104, no. 6 (2013): 697–698.

7. M. Menon, 'Over the Years, Bt Cotton Has Exacerbated Vidarbha's Existing Vulnerabilities', *Economic and Political Weekly* 53, no. 21 (2018).
8. P. Priyanka, 'A Perfect Storm in the Cotton Field', *The Hindu*, 4 December 2021, https://www.thehindu.com/opinion/op-ed/a-perfect-storm-in-the-cotton-field/article62111808.ece (accessed on 3 May 2022).
9. For a concise discussion on the contestations around licencing fee or trait fee of Bt hybrids in India, see Aga, *Genetically Modified Democracy*, 192–195.
10. Trait value is the technology fee or royalty that Monsanto charged for seed technology transfer to other Bt cotton producers, who in turn included it in their maximum retail price (MRP) that farmers paid. This value is inclusive of taxes.
11. It is in this context that the licencing fee charged by Monsanto gained prominence.
12. Aga, *Genetically Modified Democracy*, 195–196.
13. K. Peschard and S. Randeria, 'Taking Monsanto to Court: Legal Activism around Intellectual Property in Brazil and India', *Journal of Peasant Studies* 47, no. 4 (2020): 792–819.
14. The Gujarat Cotton Seeds (Regulation of Supply, Distribution, Sale and Fixation of Sale Price) Act, 2008, aimed to regulate the supply, distribution, sale, and fixation of the sale price of cotton seeds in the state.
15. See ET Bureau, 'Maharashtra Says No to Cotton Seed Price Hike', *Economic Times*, 11 May 2011, https://economictimes.indiatimes.com/markets/commodities/maharashtra-say-no-to-bt-cotton-seed-price-hike/articleshow/8236063.cms (accessed on 18 January 2021).
16. For an excellent discussion on the legal aspects of the patent violation issue and broader implications on the livelihoods of Indian farmers, see K. Kurungati, 'Was There a Victory for Monsanto in India's Supreme Court on a Patent Matter?', *Down to Earth*, 13 January 2019, https://www.downtoearth.org.in/blog/agriculture/was-there-a-victory-for-monsanto-in-india-s-supreme-court-on-a-patent-matter--62800 (accessed on 20 January 2021). For legal aspects of the case, refer to Peschard and Randeria, 'Taking Monsanto to Court', 792–819; L. Van Dycke and G. Van Overwalle, 'Genetically Modified Crops and Intellectual Property Law: Interpreting Indian Patents on Bt Cotton in View of the Socio-Political Background', *JIPITEC* 8 (2017): 151.
17. See M. Sally, 'Government to Review Cotton Seed Price', *Economic Times*, 2020, https://economictimes.indiatimes.com/news/economy/agriculture/

government-to-review-cotton-seed-price/articleshow/74240990.cms?from =mdr (accessed on 3 March 2020).

18. For the list of seeds that were approved between 2002 and 2011 by the GEAC, India, see 'Yearwise List of Commercially Released Varieties of Bt Cotton Hybrids by GEAC', GEAC, https://geacindia.gov.in/resource-documents/approved-products/Final_commercially_approved.pdf (accessed on 1 May 2022).
19. For details of various gene constructs approved by the GEAC during the decade, refer to A. Flachs, *Cultivating Knowledge: Biotechnology, Sustainability, and the Human Cost of Cotton Capitalism in India* (Tucson: University of Arizona Press, 2019a).
20. For a detailed overview of planting of illegal seeds in the recent years, refer to M. Meena, 'Planting of Illegal Crops', *Economic and Political Weekly* 54, no. 42 (2019a): 16–19.
21. On the spread of stealth seeds with regard to Bt Cotton in India refer to Herring, 'Stealth Seeds'; and R. J. Herring and Milind Kandlikar, 'Illicit Seeds: Intellectual Property and the Underground Proliferation of Agricultural Biotechnologies', in *Politics of Intellectual Property*, ed. Sebastian Haunss and Kenneth C. Shadlen (Cheltenham, UK; Northampton, USA: Edward Elgar Publishing, 2009).
22. T. V. Padma, 'GM in India: The Battle over Bt Cotton', 2006, https://www.scidev.net/global/features/gm-in-india-the-battle-over-bt-cotton/ (accessed on 27 April 2022).
23. The draft of the seed bill, 2019, is available at https://prsindia.org/billtrack/draft-seeds-bill-2019 (accessed on 29 April 2022). The bill has generated intense debates, particularly with regard to the definition of a farmer and seed sovereignty. For various critiques of the seed bill, refer to M. Mandal, 'The Problem with the Draft Seed Bill, 2019, for Indian Farmers', *The Wire*, 14 October 2020, https://science.thewire.in/economy/agriculture/draft-seed-bill-2019-indian-farmers/ (accessed on 27 April 2022).
24. The government move is described in detail in S. Mohan Komarlingam, ' Refuge-in-Bag for Bt Cotton', *Current Science* 114, no. 4 (2018): 726.
25. The return of pink bollworms in various parts of India is described in K. Najork, S. Gadela, P. Nadiminti, S. Gosikonda, R. Reddy, E. Haribabu, and M. Keck, 'The Return of Pink Bollworm in India's Bt Cotton Fields: Livelihood Vulnerabilities of Farming Households in Karimnagar District', *Progress in Development Studies* 21, no. 1 (2021): 68–85.

26. On various aspects related to seed selection by farmers, refer to S. Gaurav, 'Risk and Vulnerability of Agricultural Households in India' (unpublished PhD thesis, Indira Gandhi Institute of Development Research (IGIDR), Mumbai, 2014). The specific theme on Bt seed selection is elaborated further in S. Mishra and S. Gaurav, 'To Bt or Not to Bt? Risk and Uncertainty Considerations in Technology Assessment', in *India's Tryst with Bt Cotton: Learning from the First Decade*, ed. N. Lalitha and P. K. Viswanathan (New Delhi: Concept Publishing Company Pvt. Ltd, 2015).
27. By brand, we refer to types of both Bt cotton hybrids and non-Bt straight varieties.
28. For an extensive description of fad nature and intensive herding behaviour of seeds in the Warangal district of Andhra Pradesh over more than a decade, see G. D. Stone, A. Flachs, and C. Diepenbrock, 'Rhythms of the Herd: Long Term Dynamics in Seed Choice by Indian Farmers', *Technology in Society* 36 (2014): 26–38; and Flachs, *Cultivating Knowledge.*
29. A. Flachs, 'Planting and Performing: Anxiety, Aspiration, and "Scripts" in Telangana Cotton Farming', *American Anthropologist* 121, no. 1 (2019): 48–61.
30. For an understanding of various legitimizations in the context of adoption of Bt cotton seeds in Warangal, Andhra Pradesh, refer to E. Desmond, 'The Legitimation of Risk and Democracy: A Case Study of Bt Cotton in Andhra Pradesh, India' (PhD Thesis, University College Cork, 2013).
31. There were more than ten brands used by farmers in 2017 including Ankur, Ajeet, Vithal, Rashi, Bhakti, Jay, Balban, Bindhas, Ashtha, and Yuva.
32. S. Arya, 'HT Cotton Seeds Available in Almost All Rural Areas', *Times of India*, 9 June 2020, https://timesofindia.indiatimes.com/city/nagpur/ht-cotton-seeds-available-in-almost-all-rural-areas/articleshow/76271733.cms (accessed on 4 May 2022).
33. *The Hitavada*, 'Agriculture Department Cracks Down on Unapproved HTBt Cotton Seeds', 14 June 2021, https://www.thehitavada.com/Encyc/2021/6/14/Agriculture-Department-cracks-down-on-unapproved-HTBt-cotton-seeds.html (accessed on 30 April 2022).
34. In Gujarat, farmers had reported a willingness to pay 1,123 rupees per packet of HT seeds, which was closer to the price at which the illegal HT seeds were purchased. It did seem to provide certain savings in labour time and costs to the farmers including a 17 per cent reduction in labour time (including family, casual, and permanent labour) and 35 per cent reduction in hired labour cost. For details of the study in Gujarat, refer to N. Mehta,

Dynamics of Labour Use and Role of Genetically Modified Crops in Cotton Cultivation (New Delhi: Academic Foundation, 2019).

35. Interestingly, in the neighbouring state of Andhra Pradesh, the use of herbicides was banned to curb illegal HT cotton seeds in 2018. See S. Arya, 'To Curb Illegal HT Cotton, Andhra Bans Herbicide', *Times of India*, 14 February 2018, https://timesofindia.indiatimes.com/city/nagpur/to-curb-illegal-ht-cotton-andhra-bans-herbicide/articleshow/62906991.cms (accessed on 3 May 2022).
36. See A. S. Pearse, *Report on Indian Cotton Prepared for the International Federation of Master Cotton Spinners and Manufacturers Associations* (University of Toronto, 1914), 133, https://archive.org/details/indiancotton00inte/page/110/mode/2up (accessed on 4 May 2022).
37. For a critical analysis of Bt cotton's impact on various pests and cotton yield, refer to K. R. Kranthi and G. D. Stone, 'Long-Term Impacts of Bt Cotton in India', *Nature Plants* 6, no. 3 (2020): 188–196. They claim that the cost of insecticide per hectare in 2013 was on par with pre-Bt levels of 2001. This was due to increased spray of insecticides for sucking pests beginning in 2007. The major sucking pests that thrive on cotton are *aphid*s/*jassid*s (*mava*), *thrips* (*thurthude*), and *whiteflies* (*pandhi masjhi*).
38. We present the findings from the survey over a common pool of 516 farmers in the survey over the first two years of the survey round. In the first year, we surveyed 574 farmers while only 516 responded in the second year. We collected data related to pest incidence among the farmers growing cotton. We collected information of up to three pest attacks on their cotton plant in both the years. Very few farmers had incidence of three pest attacks, hence we summarise information related to two pest attacks in the study households.
39. K. R. Kranthi and D. A. Russell, 'Changing Trends in Cotton Pest Management', in *Integrated Pest Management: Innovation-Development Process* (Dordrecht: Springer, 2009), 499–541.
40. Directorate of Cotton Development, *Status Paper of Indian Cotton* (Maharashtra: Ministry of Agriculture & Farmers Welfare, 2017), https://www.nfsm.gov.in/StatusPaper/Cotton2016.pdf (accessed on 4 May 2022).
41. These pads attract insects as yellow colour typically attracts most of the insects. The glue in the sticky pads traps the insects. The effectiveness of these pads in controlling whiteflies in field conditions have not been great in the trapping trials in other countries. But recent trials in India indicate that the rectangular yellow sticky pads to be effective for management of *aphid*s and whiteflies. The Indian trails investigating the effects of shapes and

colours of sticky pads is presented in I. J. Nair, S. Sharma, and P. S. Shera, 'Impact of Sticky Traps of Different Colours and Shapes against Sucking Pests of Tomato under Protected Conditions: A Randomized Controlled Trial', *International Journal of Tropical Insect Science* 41, no. 4 (2021): 2739–2746. For details of a trapping trial in the greenhouse and the field, refer to Y. Lu, Y. Bei, and J. Zhang, 'Are Yellow Sticky Traps an Effective Method for Control of Sweet Potato Whitefly, Bemisia tabaci, in the Greenhouse or Field?', *Journal of Insect Science* 12, no. 1 (2012): 113.

42. According to ETL, economic threshold is reached when the value of the damaged crops exceeds the cost of pest control.
43. Approved package of practices for cultivating cotton in the state of Maharashtra is available at 'Approved Package of Practices for Cotton: Maharashtra State', https://www.cicr.org.in/pop/mh.pdf (accessed on 21 November 2020).
44. For critical issues related to pesticide registration and modifications made in the recent Pesticide Management Bill, 2020, see A. D. Kumar and D. N. Reddy, 'The Pesticide Management Bill 2020', *Current Science* 121, no. 3 (2021): 348.
45. For a specific case of misuse of paraquat, see Dileep Kumar, *Conditions of Paraquat Use in India, IUF, Berne Declaration, PAN AP and PAN India* (Kerala: PAN India, 2015), https://pan-india.org/wp-content/uploads/2017/03/PAN-India_paraquat_4-15_def-WEB.pdf (accessed on 1 May 2022).
46. The list of registered pesticides is available at http://ppqs.gov.in/sites/default/files/insecticides_registered_under_section_-_93_as_on_01.07.2021.pdf (accessed on 3 September 2020).
47. WHO has recommended classification of pesticides based on the toxicity of their formulations: Class Ia (Extremely Hazardous), Class Ib (Highly Hazardous), Class II (Moderately Hazardous), Class III (Slightly Hazardous), and Class U (Unlikely to present acute hazard). Monocrotophos falls under Class Ib which implies it is a highly hazardous pesticide. For the complete WHO list of recommended classification of pesticides as of 2019, refer to https://www.who.int/publications/i/item/9789240005662 (accessed on 5 May 2022).
48. Refer to J. A. Gervais, B. Luukinen, K. Buhl, and D. Stone, 'Imidacloprid Technical Fact Sheet' (National Pesticide Information Centre, Oregon State University Extension Services, 2010), http://npic.orst.edu/fact sheet/imidacloprid.pdf (accessed on 21 September 2022). WHO recommends Imidacloprid as a Class II (moderately hazardous) pesticide. Refer to

https://www.who.int/publications/i/item/9789240005662 (accessed on 21 September 2022).

49. In a study among farmers in Gujarat, it was found that the use of a combination of pesticides might be ineffective. For the detailed description of the study and its findings, see Hee Kwon Seo, 'Can Behavioral Biases Explain Demand for a Harmful Pesticide? Evidence from India' (discussion paper, Harvard Environmental Economics Program, Cambridge, Massachusetts, USA, 2013).
50. We surveyed seventy-eight input dealers selling pesticides to farmers in Wardha district in the 2016–2017 season to understand aspects related to the selling of pesticides and weedicides. The *kendra*s are usually run by individuals with capital and belonging to farming castes. Forty-three of the seventy-seven shops were owned by individuals belonging to backward castes (BCs), twenty-two belonged to other castes, and three belonged to the Jains. Such an evolution petty retail created by agrarian surplus is observed in other places too. For an account of the evolution of petty retailers in western Maharashtra, refer to A. Aga, 'Merchants of Knowledge: Petty Retail and Differentiation without Consolidation among Farmers in Maharashtra, India', *Journal of Agrarian Change* 18, no. 3 (2018): 658–676.
51. An important study in the context of risk perceptions and health hazards of pesticides for agricultural labourers in this context is P. I. Devi, 'Health Risk Perceptions, Awareness and Handling Behaviour of Pesticides by Farm Workers', *Agricultural Economics Research Review* 22, no. 2 (2009): 263–268.
52. About 48 per cent (1,962 litres out of 4,096 litres) of all the pesticide stock were organophosphates (monocrotophos, monocil, and monostar) indicating probably a high usage of these pesticides in the region.
53. Endosulfan is currently banned in India following a protracted legal tussle involving farmers in Kerala, Centre for Science and Environment (CSE), and the pesticide company. The chronology of events over a decade that led to the ban of endosulfan is provided in 'Endosulfan Industry's Dirty War: A Chronology of Events', Centre for Science and Environment, https://www.cseindia.org/endosulfan-industrys-dirty-war-a-chronology-of-events--1927 (accessed on 14 July 2021). Endrin was banned or highly prohibited as a pesticide across the world. The WHO recommends it under O class—obsolete as pesticide, not classified.
54. For an analysis of health effects of spraying toxic pesticides, refer to P. L. Pingali and P. A. Roger, eds., *Impact of Pesticides on Farmer*

Health and the Rice Environment, vol. 7 (New York: Springer Science & Business Media, 2012); P. L. Pingali, C. B. Marquez, and F. G. Palis, 'Pesticides and Philippine Rice Farmer Health: A Medical and Economic Analysis', *American Journal of Agricultural Economics* 76, no. 3 (1994): 587–592. For a recent detailed study of the effects of pesticides on health in the Chinese context, see R. Hu, X. Huang, J. Huang, Y. Li, C. Zhang, Y. Yin, Z. Chen, Y. Jin, J. Cai, and F. Cui, 'Long- and Short-Term Health Effects of Pesticide Exposure: A Cohort Study from China', *PloS One* 10, no. 6 (2015): e0128766, https://doi.org/10.1371/journal.pone.0128766. The effects of pesticides on the health of farm workers in Thailand is analysed using mixed methods in C. A. Forté, J. Colacino, K. Polemi, A. Guytingco, N. J. Peraino, S. Jindaphong, T. Kaviya, J. Westrick, R. Neitzel, and K. Nambunmee, 'Pesticide Exposure and Adverse Health Effects Associated with Farm Work in Northern Thailand', *Journal of Occupational Health* 63, no. 1 (2021): 1–13.

55. For a study that analyses the impact of pesticide bans on suicide reduction across India and Kerala, refer to T. Bonvoisin, L. Utyasheva, D. Knipe, D. Gunnell, and M. Eddleston, 'Suicide by Pesticide Poisoning in India: A Review of Pesticide Regulations and Their Impact on Suicide Trends', *BMC Public Health* 20, no. 1 (2020): 1–16. For a study that incorporates substitution effects of methods to commit suicide, refer to V. Arya, A. Page, D. Gunnell, and G. Armstrong, 'Changes in Method Specific Suicide Following a National Pesticide Ban in India (2011–2014)', *Journal of Affective Disorders* 1 (January 2021): 592–600.
56. The report of the special investigation team (SIT) is available at https://www.publiceye.ch/fileadmin/doc/Pestizide/20180412_Report_Special-Investigation-Team-Yavatmal-Poisoning.pdf (accessed on 14 July 2021).
57. The pesticide action network also has a report on the same incident. The report pretty much mentions the same reasons as the SIT except it also puts the blame on specific pesticides used in that year. The complete report by the network is D. N. R. Reddy and A. D. Dileep Kumar, *Pesticide Poisonings in Yavatmal District in Maharashtra: Untold Realities*, PAN Network, 2017, https://www.pan-india.org/wp-content/uploads/2017/10/Yavatmal-Report_PAN-India_Oct-2017_web.pdf (accessed on 5 July 2021).
58. The number of insecticide inspectors is available at http://ppqs.gov.in/sites/default/files/number_of_insecticide_inspectors_of_central_state_govt.pdf (accessed on 23 June 2022).

59. For a summary and critical analysis of the Pesticide Management Bill, 2020, refer to https://prsindia.org/billtrack/the-pesticide-management-bill-2020 (accessed on 15 November 2021).
60. Eighteen other pesticides were banned though, few immediately and few from 2020. See Sonam Taneja, 'India Bans 18 Pesticides, Has Many More to Go', *Down to Earth*, 16 August 2018, https://www.downtoearth.org.in/news/agriculture/india-bans-18-pesticides-has-many-more-to-go-61405 (accessed on 15 November 2021).
61. S. Sapale and N. Malani, *Ushering in the 2nd Green Revolution: Role of Crop Protection Chemicals* (New Delhi: Federation of Indian Chambers of Commerce & Industry and TATA Strategic Management Group, 2015).
62. C. James, '20th Anniversary (1996 to 2015) of the Global Commercialization of Biotech Crops and Biotech Crop Highlights in 2015' (International Service for the Acquisition of Agri-Biotech Applications). For details related to the herbicide market and herbicide tolerant (HT) seed market across the world, see G. D. Stone and A. Flachs, 'The Ox Fall Down: Path-Breaking and Technology Treadmills in Indian Cotton Agriculture', *Journal of Peasant Studies* 45, no. 7 (2018): 1272–1296.
63. For a resurvey of a village in the Vidarbha region and analysis of labour supply in the village, refer to R. Ramakumar and K. Raut, 'Agricultural Employment in a Vidarbha Village: Results from a Resurvey', *Review of Agrarian Studies* 1, no. 1 (2011).
64. For a study of 341 farmers across four states in India, refer to M. Qaim, A. Subramanian, G. Naik, and D. Zilberman, 'Adoption of Bt Cotton and Impact Variability: Insights from India', *Applied Economic Perspectives and Policy* 28, no. 1 (2006): 48–58.
65. For a study of pesticide use changes over a decade, see T. Ranganathan, S. Gaurav, and I. I. Halder, 'Pesticide Usage by Cotton Farmers in India: Changes Over a Decade', *Economic and Political Weekly* 53, no. 19 (2018).
66. Bt cotton has been portrayed as seeds of suicide in Vandana Shiva, 'Seeds of Suicide and Slavery versus Seeds of Life and Freedom', *AlJazeera*, 30 March 2013, https://www.aljazeera.com/opinions/2013/3/30/seeds-of-suicide-and-slavery-versus-seeds-of-life-and-freedom (accessed on 23 June 2022); and Vandana Shiva, 'Seed Monopolies, GMOs and Farmers Suicides in India', *Counter Currents*, 10 January 2014, https://www.countercurrents.org/shiva100114.htm (accessed on 23 June 2022), while yield increases and positive distributional impacts have been documented in J. Kathage and M. Qaim, 'Economic Impacts and Impact Dynamics of Bt (Bacillus

thuringiensis) Cotton in India', *Proceedings of the National Academy of Sciences* 109, no. 29 (2012): 11652–11656; A. Subramanian and M. Qaim, 'The Impact of Bt Cotton on Poor Households in Rural India', *Journal of Development Studies* 46, no. 2 (2010): 295–311.

67. For studies on experimentation in soybean in the Malwa region of Madhya Pradesh, refer to R. Kumar, 'The Perils of Productivity: Making "Good Farmers" in Malwa, India', *Journal of Agrarian Change* 16, no. 1 (2016b): 70–93.
68. The idea of a good farmer however dates back to the colonial period and the Green Revolution era. For insights about 'good farmer' in other parts of India, see Kumar, 'The Perils of Productivity', 109–110.
69. For an idea of 'performance' in the context of organic farming, refer to Flachs, *Cultivating Knowledge.*
70. This idea of agriculture as performance is developed in various literatures starting with P. Richards, 'Agriculture as a Performance', in *Farmer First: Farmer Innovation and Agricultural Research*, ed. R. Chambers and L. A. Thrupp (London: Intermediate Technology Publications, 1994), 39–43. Recent literature in the Indian context include Kumar, 'The Perils of Productivity', 70–93; Flachs, 'Planting and Performing'; and A. Flachs, '"Show Farmers": Transformation and Performance in Telangana, India', *Culture, Agriculture, Food and Environment* 39, no. 1 (2017), 25–34.
71. For a contextualization of graded informality where the proliferation of agrochemicals cannot be necessarily seen as tension between global capital and petty production, refer to A. Aga, 'The Marketing of Corporate Agrichemicals in Western India: Theorizing Graded Informality', *Journal of Peasant Studies* 46, no. 7 (2019): 1458–1476.
72. For a discussion on tapering of yields from Bt cotton since 2012, see A. Sethi, 'The Life of Debt in Rural India' (Unpublished thesis, Columbia University, 2018). For a more critical evaluation of Bt cotton on agronomic practices, yield and capital-intensiveness of production, refer to Kranthi and Stone, 'Long-Term Impacts'.
73. T. Ranganathan and S. Gaurav, 'Pest Management Practices of Cotton Farmers in Vidarbha: The Curious Case of Cocktails, Weedicides, and Tonics', *Economic and Political Weekly* 54, no. 44 (2019).
74. Flachs, 'Planting and Performing'.
75. See *Crop Production Agronomy, Physiology and Biochemistry* (annual report, ICAR-All India Coordinated Research Project on Cotton, 2018–2019), http://aiccip.cicr.org.in/CD_18_19/5-Crop-Production.pdf (accessed on 6 May 2022).

6

RISK AND VULNERABILITY

We have come a long way in our understanding of the changing circumstances of cotton growing in Vidarbha, and livelihood of agricultural households comprising cultivator and non-cultivator households. An inquiry into the historical roots of the region's cotton economy from a *longue durée* perspective revealed how constant alteration of the region's boundaries owing to political instability and sustained conflict in the precolonial era and subsequent colonial takeover in the second half of the nineteenth century transformed the region and its economy (Chapters 1 and 2).

We examined how the region witnessed an agrarian transformation that encompassed dismantling of feudal institutions such as *balutedari*, granting of property rights to cultivators under *ryotwari* in Berar, and rising demands of land revenue under the *khatedari* system that compelled cultivators to be dependent on usurious credit and commercialized agriculture.

We also saw how the colonial economic interests and American Civil War; historical events and processes that we characterise as accidents from the farmers' perspective catalysed the integration of Vidarbha into the 'Empire of Cotton'.[1] We illustrated how the colonial efforts to convert the Bombay Presidency, Berar, and central India as an important source of raw cotton for Britain's industrial demand through crop improvement initiatives as well as investment in roads and railways that had begun before the American Civil War gathered momentum in the post-bellum period. The devastating effects of the famines in the late nineteenth century and epidemics exacted a severe toll on the region's demography along with the ecological impacts of the cotton expansion. Although the region went through phases of trade integration, the late nineteenth-century and early twentieth-century global integration established it as a vibrant cotton economy. Credit markets as well as cotton towns flourished. The region however was bereft of irrigation works unlike in other regions during the late nineteenth and early twentieth centuries.

In Chapter 3 we described our fieldwork and data collection in the villages of Vidarbha over the period 2009–2021. Having described the nature of our surveys and characteristics of the sampled households in detail, we examined the changes in cropping patterns, input use, and household incomes of cotton farmers (Chapters 4 and 5). An extensive scholarly debate on the question of Bt cotton notwithstanding, there was a proliferation of Bt cotton for a decade since its commercialization in the early 2000s, followed by an ongoing phase of yield stagnation and decline due to growing resistance of pink bollworm (PBW) and secondary pest pressure.

In terms of the rural labour market transformation, changing structure of agriculture has influenced growth of non-farm activity in the villages and vice-versa. Arguably, based on the discussion so far, it can be inferred that cotton farming has remained precarious even after 160 years since the outbreak of the American Civil War—that momentous event in world history which transformed the region's relationship with cotton cultivation and cotton trade. The rise and fall of the cotton economy in the following decades that saw the reconfiguration of the cotton manufacturing and trade as well as the developments since India's independence suggested that the gamble continued as farmers experimented with new cash crops such as hybrid cotton and soybean and gradually abandoned traditional crops like *jawari*.

For nearly 30,000 farmers of the Vidarbha and Marathwada regions who ended their lives between 2001 and 2018 primarily due to the general state of despair and distress in the hinterland, the path of agricultural development has been dystopian.[2] It is as if there is a perennial element of risk and vulnerability for farmers in the region that successive states and market-based reforms, particularly since the broad-based neoliberal reforms of 1990s. Following India's joining of the World Trade Organization (WTO) in 1995, there has been a gradual withdrawal of the state from agricultural investment on the one hand and opening up the farm sector to global competition on the other hand. At the same time, there has been a clear capitalistic development trajectory associated with changes in the traditional agrarian structures. To what extent have these factors exacerbated the vulnerability of agricultural households? How have they impacted the resilience of these households?

Irrespective of the institutions in place and the governments in power, Vidarbha farmers have undertaken agriculture against odds that are by any stretch of imagination perilous. Year after year, for more than one and a half centuries, farmers in the region have been growing water-intensive crops such as cotton under predominantly rain-fed conditions on increasingly smaller parcels of land that make them susceptible to chronic indebtedness. To make matters worse, the soil health has grievously deteriorated following centuries of continual farming and disregard for soil conservation. Moreover, the external input intensive system of production that has been systematically encouraged since the Green Revolution has aggravated their vulnerability to ecological duress. Although the post-independence era has so far witnessed decades of targeted policies and reforms measures, agrarian distress still persists. Policy response to the agrarian distress has however attempted to fix symptoms rather than the underlying structural issues. Therefore, it is not surprising that even when farmers continue to adjust to changing circumstances, their vulnerability has not diminished. The gamble with cotton continues to be a gamble with the rains and gamble with the markets. Those who have been unable to cope with the distress and its attendant worries have unfortunately become mere figures in Vidarbha's farmers' suicides statistics. For hundreds of thousands of others who are dealing with the distress, the hope of high stable returns from cash crops such as cotton and soybean continues.

Against this backdrop of a crisis-prone agricultural environment, we attempt to answer the following questions in this chapter. What are the risks in cultivating cotton in Vidarbha? What are the welfare consequences of these risks? Who is particularly more vulnerable in Vidarbha agriculture if the sector itself is in a state of distress? What institutional and non-institutional risk management structures are in place? What is the effectiveness of these formal and informal insurance mechanisms?

We first explore a crucial source of agricultural production risk (yield risk) and income risk, namely weather variability. Then we explore the consequences of yield risks by examining panel data of households over a five-year period, which allows us to control for unobserved heterogeneities associated with time invariant household factors. We demonstrate what happens to households that face adverse yield shocks in the study years relative to those who were fortunate not to have experienced any shock over this period.[3] Since the downside price risk for the marketed produce is another source of income risk, we study the variability in prices over time. In doing so, we locate the price movements in the context of the general decline in cotton prices over the past quarter century as well as trade policies of leading export destinations and domestic trade policy that have historically been crucial. We also discuss farmers' perceptions of risk and the risk management strategies that households rely on. Through insights from fieldwork and survey data, we present the limitations of informal risk sharing and risk coping strategies along with market failures in formal risk management instruments as households prepare for anticipated losses and cope with unanticipated losses in the absence of effective insurance against losses. Of particular concern is the limitations of market-based insurance such as multi-peril crop insurance and parametric weather insurance interpreted through the experiences of farmers. Ultimately, having delved into questions of risk and its management, we comment on the vulnerability of households to risk through analysis of consumption patterns of cultivator and non-cultivator households that not only establishes the importance of characterizing agricultural households as consumption units but also raises questions on intersectionality of vulnerability along the lines of gender, caste, and class.

RISK

An obvious issue in characterizing risk is the problem one runs into while defining the phenomenon. We empathize with the following comment by Joseph Stiglitz:

> Risk is like love; we have a good idea of what it is, but we can't define it precisely.[4]

For the sake of our discussion, we consider risk as adverse outcomes whose probability of occurence is known in contrast to uncertainty where the potential outcomes are unknown. Therefore, risks imply the chance that actual outcomes differ from expected outcomes. Considered thus, risk has a connotation of being associated with loss and damages. However, wherever we refer to an alternative definition of risk, we will specify the notion of risk if it is not self-explanatory.

WEATHER RISKS

Based on our discussion of changes in cropping patterns during the colonial period (Chapter 2) and incidence of catastrophic droughts and climate variability in the past (Chapter 1), it is evident that the expansion of cotton cultivation in Vidarbha has been accompanied by weather risks of various kinds. In Chapter 2 we demonstrated the climate variability in the region using long rainfall series and discussed recent evidence on susceptibility of the region to adverse impacts of climate change. In Chapter 4 we saw that even in a normal monsoon year, extreme weather events can wreak havoc on household incomes. In years of rainfall deficit, the riskiness of undertaking cotton production considerably amplifies unless prices rise substantially to compensate for the yield loss. In this sense, the decision to grow cotton in a high-risk environment is a gamble on not just a single risky outcome but multiple outcomes related to vagaries of the weather and market. This raises questions as to how farmers perceive risks and whether they are able to ascertain the root causes of losses attributed to the underlying risks. As we will elaborate later, it is important to see risks as stretching beyond financial losses as something embedded in the local ecological knowledge.

It is a traditional practice in the region to start kharif sowing around the seventh of June every season. This usually coincides with the onset of the southwest monsoon. The decisions relating to sowing are based on the traditional knowledge passed over generations. The timing of sowing is usually predetermined by consulting astrological almanacs. In particular, *mrigashira nakshatra*, typically a window of two weeks starting on 8 June,[5] is considered the best time for sowing in the region.[6] Another recommendation of the traditional knowledge system about sowing is that it should be sown on or around full moon days and the orientation of the rows should be in the north–south direction. The conventional wisdom behind the north–south orientation is that it provides better sunlight penetration for the plant and reduces the risk of crop disease.[7] As discussed in Chapters 4 and 6, farmers also convey their thanks to bullocks or oxen during the festival of Pola on a specific new moon day (*pithori amavasya*) of the last day of Shravan month (typically August). At the beginning of the Shravan month, Vidarbha farmers also celebrate Naga Panchami, symbolic of the ecological importance of snakes in the farm ecosystem. Another ritual that is of extreme symbolic relevance for cotton farmers of the region is that of

'Sitadevi' before the commencement of cotton picking; it exemplifies farmers' belief in supernatural powers in blessing them with abundant cotton every season.[8] For much of the year, festivals and traditional cultural practices are widely celebrated in Vidarbha. On 14 January every year, Makar Sankranti celebrations see women offering gifts on trays (*vaans*) including sundry items such as a comb, bowl, tea strainer, and soap stand to other women. Sesame candies (*tilguls*) made with jaggery are also made at home and exchanged with others. In February, Shri Gajanan Maharaj Manifest Day and Chhatrapati Shivaji Maharaj's birth anniversary are widely celebrated. March is marked by Mahashivratri and Holi celebrations, whereas in April the traditional lunar new year celebration Gudi Padwa symbolizes the rabi harvest season. On this day, the year of the annual farm worker, *saaldar* begins. There are several rituals involved that symbolize the symbiotic relationship between a cultivator and farm labourer. Traditional sweets such as *puran poli* (sweet flatbread) and *dalpaan* (pulse-based sweet dish) made of flour, jaggery, chickpea, and *ghee* (clarified butter) are prepared at home. Ram Navami is also a popular Hindu festival in late March and early April. In the month of May, Eid and Buddh Purnima is celebrated with great vigour by Muslims and Buddhists, respectively. Among other major festivities, Shri Krishna Jayanti, Raksha Bandhan; Ganesh Chaturthi in September; and Dussehra, Diwali, and Laxmi Puja in October are associated with significant spending on food and non-food items by households. There are not only community-specific festivals but also the rituals differs for events such as birth, marriage, and funerals.

However, the belief of farmers in astrology notwithstanding, there are frequent deviations in monsoon onset dates. For instance, when we began fieldwork in 2009, which was a drought year, the onset of monsoon was substantially delayed. Most farmers began sowing towards the end of June. Often, some farmers go ahead with early sowing with the occurrence of pre-monsoon showers in the first week of June. However, they have also been found to go for a second sowing if prolonged dry spells followed. Those having recourse to protective irrigation escape this ordeal unless the rainfall deficit is particularly high in the season. We have also observed intermittent rains after three weeks of dry spell immediately followed by another week of dry spell. In such circumstances, the risk of germination failure heightens significantly, heightening the likelihood of a crop failure. By contrast, the arrival of monsoon around 7 June in 2010 was normal and the overall distribution of the rainfall was conducive to crop production.

Table 6.1 reports the distribution of southwest monsoon rainfall in Wardha *taluka* of Wardha district in the first round of our study.[9] The year 2009 was a drought year, and the deviation from the long-range normal rainfall in the region was more than 50 per cent for the southwest monsoon season as per data from the India Meteorological Department (IMD) in 2011. Analysing the daily rainfall data for the *taluka*, in June 2009 the cumulative monthly precipitation was 80 millimetres while in July it was 256 millimetres in comparison to the higher June and July values in 2010 and 2011. Furthermore, precipitation in August 2009 was less than one-third of 2010 and 2011, while the September 2009 precipitation was less than half of that in the following two years. The variability in June and August rainfall was also high as evident from the respective coefficient variation (CV).

Table 6.2 shows the proportion of 'dry days', that is, days with no rainfall for the months of the southwest monsoon (JJAS as in Chapter 2) during the study period. The probability of a dry day in June and July (in 2009) was 73 per cent and 32 per cent, respectively. This was clearly higher than the probability of having a dry day in those months of 2010 as well as 2011. Also, the probability of a dry day in any of the months of the southwest monsoon period was higher in 2009 (68 per cent) in comparison with the following two years. The risk of slow-onset disasters such as drought was considerable.[10] In subsequent years of our study, the inexactness of monsoon onset on 7 June was the exception rather than the rule. Apart from the onset of monsoon, the level and intensity of dry spells also have a bearing on crop yield. In the first round of our survey, we observed wide variation in probability of dry

Table 6.1 Distribution of monsoon rainfall (in millimetre) in Wardha: 2009–2011

	2009			2010			2011		
Month	**Total**	**Mean**	**CV**	**Total**	**Mean**	**CV**	**Total**	**Mean**	**CV**
June	81	11	1.2	143	13	0.9	107	12	0.8
July	256	13	0.8	533	23	1.1	190	9	1.0
August	103	8	1.6	375	17	1.1	354	16	1.1
September	108	27	0.7	219	17	0.8	299	23	1.1
All	119	13	1.0	263.13	17	1.1	191	14.25	1.2

Source: Sarthak Gaurav, 'Risk and Vulnerability of Agricultural Households in India' (unpublished PhD thesis, Indira Gandhi Institute of Development Research (IGIDR), Mumbai); calculations are based on daily rainfall data from the Office of the District Collector, Wardha.

Note: Total is the total rainfall in the month. Mean is the average daily rainfall. CV is the coefficient of variation measured as the ratio of standard deviation and mean of daily rainfall.

Table 6.2 Probability of a dry day in Wardha: 2009–2011

Month	2009	2010	2011
June	0.73	0.63	0.70
July	0.32	0.26	0.29
August	0.58	0.29	0.29
September	0.87	0.57	0.57
All	0.68	0.51	0.56

Source: Sarthak Gaurav, 'Risk and Vulnerability of Agricultural Households in India' (unpublished PhD thesis, Indira Gandhi Institute of Development Research (IGIDR), Mumbai); calculations are based on daily rainfall data from the Office of the District Collector, Wardha.

Note: Probabilities are calculated on the basis of daily rainfall data as in Table 6.1.

Table 6.3 Average rainfall and dry days in automated weather station (AWS) villages: 2017 and 2018

	Mean Daily Rainfall (mm)		Dry Days		Consecutive Dry Days	
Village	**2017**	**2018**	**2017**	**2018**	**2017**	**2018**
Yavatmal villages						
Inzapur	4	7	57	57	31	38
Sankarpur	5	7	54	54	32	33
Ichora	5	8	52	51	38	32
Wardha villages						
Wathoda	5	5	55	53	38	35
Shekapur	6	6	51	54	31	35
Sawad	3	4	46	52	26	37

Source: Data are from S. Gaurav and V. Chaudhary, 'Do Farmers Care about Basis Risk? Evidence from a Field Experiment in India', *Climate Risk Management* 27 (2020): table 4, DOI: 100201.

Note: Mean Daily Rainfall is the average rainfall over all the days of the 4 months from June to September.

days across all the months (Table 6.3). Typical of the nature of agro-climatic phenomena, there is considerable spatial variation even within a district.

As discussed in Chapter 3, to analyse the weather variability across the villages in our sample, we installed automated weather stations (AWSs) in six study villages across Wardha and Yavatmal in the third round of the surveys. There is considerable variability in both the amount of rainfall and dry spells across the villages as well as over the two years: 2017 and 2018 (Table 6.3). The riskiness of the southwest monsoon season is evident from the substantially high number of dry days within a short period of time. This bodes well with our earlier findings on the declining trend in rainfall over a long timescale as seen in Chapter 2. Spatial variability in precipitation as well as probability of dry days and consecutive dry days contributes to 'basis risk' in weather insurance that arises whenever there is poor correlation between the weather event experienced at the weather station used for determining the insurance payouts and that experienced at the farms.

Weather risks that households in the villages are exposed to is representative of those at the regional scale. The region is susceptible to frequent droughts with studies predicting a moderate drought every five years.[11] Moreover, beyond weather, climatic risks aggravate the vulnerability of agrarian communities. With predictions of Vidarbha's districts becoming climate hotspots, the risk of droughts as well as extreme weather events is likely to worsen the riskiness of agricultural production.

Having said this, farmers were more worried about immediate concerns over much shorter time horizons namely rainfall at different stages of crop growth. This is indeed a reflection of the fact that moisture requirements vary across different phases of crop growth and the 'effective moisture' determines the relationship between weather and crop yield.[12] For example, let us take the case of the hybrid cotton grown in the villages, which are usually 160-to-210-day crops. During the first seven weeks of the plant growth—from germination to the vegetative stage (July to early August)—the fields receive around three-fourths of the monsoon showers when the moisture requirement is not that high. On the other hand, while the remaining phases such as the reproductive and flowering phases (early August to early September) have higher moisture requirements, about one-fourth of the seasonal rains fall during this period. Cotton varieties follow a different growth cycle, and although the critical relationship between a crop's moisture requirement and growth phase of hardy varieties was well known, the proliferation of Bt hybrids rendered that knowledge futile. In this context, how households manage weather risk is crucial because weather reinforces other production and post-harvest risks often through distortions in the timeliness of farm operations and associated micro processes.

Unseasonal and excess rains result in damages to standing crops which is a sight becoming far too common in recent times. Prolonged waterlogging in low-lying plots result in yield losses. In recent times, unseasonal rains in

November of 2017 and excess rains in September of 2020 and 2021 severely affected crop yields as the standing crops were affected. It is not only that the heavy showers result in bolls dropping off before they are ready to be picked but the moisture content of the surviving bolls also goes up if the showers happen closer to or during the picking season. Fieldwork at the start of the cotton marketing season in October 2021 suggests that damages in cotton in the 2021–2022 season are apprehended by farmers to the extent of 50 per cent as compared to 20 per cent in 2020. Losses in soybean cultivation in 2020 due to the unseasonal rains were extremely high, which depressed the household incomes. In the light of successive bad years, it is beyond anyone's guess what fate awaits the farmers at the end of the next marketing season in terms of their prospects of indebtedness. The only saving grace for farmers in the face of such losses was that the lower supply resulted in higher cotton prices—around 10,000 rupees per quintal in January 2022. Interestingly, such patterns of excess and unseasonal rains have been observed over more than a century ago as is evident from colonial administrative records (Chapter 2) as well as the *Gazetteer of the Central Provinces and Berar*.[13]

That even a normal rainfall year could be associated with significant losses due to unseasonal rains at a critical stage of the crop's growth is a recurrent finding. However, these shocks add to the farmers' worries as they have consequences on the ability of farmers to repay debts. One such terrible prospect was evident in 2010. Farmers who had defaulted on their crop-loan payments after the drought of 2009 lost their ability to repay even in a good year on account of such idiosyncratic losses. Furthermore, an economic implication of such a complex relationship between the intra-seasonal distribution of rainfall and riskiness of crop production is that farmers, who hope to have good rainfall in the second phase of the crop's growth, invest in fertilizers and pesticides, and a mismatch between their hopes and reality results in substantial monetary losses. From a household finance perspective, on the one hand, consecutive years of default on crop loans could spell disaster as they lose their ability to get 'fresh' short term credit from banks—the cheapest source of credit. On the other hand, such shocks also result in a reduced asset position if households sell off assets for making ends meet or repaying costlier outstanding debt. Such scenarios deplete the farmers' ability to invest on farm or other productive purposes. When the levels of debt are high or there are big-ticket farm investments or social functions such as marriages, the propensity of farmers to engage in asset depletion or mortgage them for high-cost borrowing is not uncommon, as we will see later in the context of risk coping strategies of sampled households. The welfare consequences of unmitigated weather risks are aggravated by the fact that the productive capacity of the farm households has knock-on effects on their future income streams.

There are also potential pest-weather interactions that induce yield uncertainty and render the relationship between weather and crop yields non-linear and complex.[14] For instance, during the prolonged dry spell of 2009 mentioned earlier, incidents of reddening of leaves (*lalya*) and attacks by the insect pest—mealybug (*pithya*)—were reported in different plots in the study villages as well as neighbouring villages. Early maturing varieties of cotton are known to have lower chances of suffering from late-stage pest attacks which could be triggered by weather. Poring over our field notes that are replete with several such cases of inter-related shock, it is apparent that the dynamic interactions of the weather cycle, the crop cycle, and the insect pest life cycle introduce substantial ambiguity in the conventional notion of yield risk.

Another important source of yield risk that is mediated through weather risk is fall in groundwater level. There is considerable variation in the depth of water levels of the wells across villages and over seasons and years.[15] Although few farmers have invested significantly in sinking wells or rejuvenating existing wells, mostly through financial support under new schemes, cases of wells drying up or well failures are common. Yavatmal villages in general face the issue of groundwater depletion compared to Wardha villages as there has been an increase in groundwater extraction for irrigation as shown in preceding chapters. Given greater reliance on groundwater rather than surface irrigation, an increase in tube wells or borewells has posed a serious concern regarding the sustainability of aquifers. Size-class-wise distinctions exist in access to groundwater-based irrigation, but marginal and smallholders have increased access to groundwater irrigation even if they typically operate on *koradwahu* (rain-fed) plots of land. However, the risk of dug wells running dry and borewell failures is ever-present. During a visit to farms, it is common to come across a large number of wells that are temporarily as well as permanently unused. Farmers as well as groundwater experts we have interacted with suggest that inadequate discharge of wells continues to be a major constraint for wells that are temporarily unused. Farmers attribute such well failures to bad luck and internalise their loss of capital and future crop yield potential. More importantly, the risk of crop yield losses remains unmitigated without timely and protective irrigation. The inability of several small and marginal farmers to pump the water for irrigation using electric pumps due to credit constraints has also been observed.

In the absence of access to canal irrigation, those who could afford it, rely on groundwater for their irrigation purposes. However, it has resulted in a situation akin to 'tragedy of commons' with rampant groundwater exploration taking place at a rate greater than the replenishment rate. In this context, it is not surprising to hear borewells are being dug deeper to reach the aquifers. From the power utilization perspective, the pumping wattages also go up over time, increasing the cost of irrigation. This issue has created ample opportunities for making political statements by way of waiving off electricity bills. Since the period of our study had seen growing acreage of Bt hybrids, high water requirements of Bt cotton on the one hand and differential energy efficiency of the farmers on the other are also likely to be factors that compound the riskiness of the overarching reliance on groundwater for irrigation. As discussed in Chapter 3, very few households have diesel pumps for irrigation, and dependence on electricity for pumping water to the fields is high. In this context, the following peculiar challenges emerge.

First, despite a general improvement in intensity of irrigation, reliability of power for irrigation troubles farmers, who have to schedule their farm activities to suit the often-odd hours for power supplied to farms. Second, the political economy of irrigation development that is nested in the region's developmental backlogs and lack of political assertiveness that we elaborate in Chapter 7, has limited farmers' crop options as well as yield potential. The growth of cotton under low but assured rainfall conditions has historically been an argument against development of irrigation infrastructure in Vidarbha, thereby skewing the irrigation infrastructure towards western Maharashtra to support water-guzzling crops such as sugarcane. With elite capture of the cooperatives that have deep political connections, it is not surprising that western Maharashtra ended up having a lion's share in the irrigation projects of the state while regions such as Vidarbha and Marathwada continue to suffer. That the politically connected sugarcane cooperatives of western Maharashtra do not have a comparable cohort in cotton tracts of Vidarbha is a crucial factor that we will return to.

Another dimension of riskiness of the production is linked to the growing fertilizer use over time (Table 6.4). The manner in which weather risks interact with fertilizer applications is varied. In a season with prolonged dry spells or when farmers apprehend a drought or drought-like situation, they

Table 6.4 Fertilizer use among farmers of different land-size classes

	2019				2020			
	N (kg/acre)	P (kg/acre)	K (kg/acre)	Fertilizer (kg/acre)	N (kg/acre)	P (kg/acre)	K (kg/acre)	Fertilizer (kg/acre)
Marginal	41.2	20.8	11.3	151.1	37.7	24.4	8.8	143.2
Small	32.2	16.3	8.0	126.6	35.4	19.1	12.7	136.2
Semi-medium	20.1	13.4	6.2	80.7	30.9	18.6	11.3	120.3
Medium	8.4	4.6	0.0	26.5	20.9	11.8	4.5	78.9
All	29.7	15.9	7.8	115.3	33.8	19.6	11.2	130.2

Source: Authors' calculations based on survey data.

Note: Marginal, small, semi-medium, and medium size-classes corresponding to land ownership of less than 2.5 acres, 2.5–5 acres, 5–10 acres, and 10–25 acres, respectively.

reduce application of fertilizers to minimize potential losses. We have already seen the considerably high share of fertilizers in total cost of cultivation in Chapter 4. Timing of fertilizer applications as well as different ways in which fertilizers are applied including mixing with pesticides as seen in Chapter 5 are also influenced by weather risk.

Compared to the generally low application of chemical fertilizers in Wardha villages during our first round, villages in Wardha and Yavatmal reported significant increases in fertilizer application during subsequent survey rounds. Marginal farmers use substantially high quantities of subsidized fertilizers in their gambles to get high yields from the cash crops. Since fertilizers are risk-increasing inputs, this propensity of marginal farmers could manifest in greater inequality in yields and agricultural incomes. In terms of composition of the fertilizers used, high use of nitrogen seems to emanate from low prices of subsidized urea compared to other fertilizers (Table 6.5).[16] Apart from the price factor, an estimate of fertilizer response based on our data in the last round of survey indicates that cotton yield increased with the amount of fertilizer applied by farmers (Table 6.7, column 1). Particularly, a kilogram of nitrogen applied per acre increased the yield by 0.05 quintals (Table 6.7, column 2).

One may wonder why marginal farmers are so intensively applying chemical fertilizers in their cotton cultivation. It is evident from pooled regression estimates from the panel data in 2019 and 2020 that fertilizer response as well as nitrogenous response to yield is statistically significant (Table 6.6). Differences by size-class of owned land are also significant. Marginal farmers apply more fertilisers as well as more N and P per acre

Table 6.5 Content of N, P, and K in fertilizers

Fertilizer	Nitrogen (N)	Phosphorus (P)	Potassium (K)
Urea	0.46	0.00	0.00
DAP	0.18	0.46	0.00
SSP	0.00	0.15	0.00
Potash	0.00	0.00	0.60

Source: Authors' calculation based on survey data.

Note: If a farmer uses 10:26:26 NPK fertilizer complex, then it contains 10 per cent N (nitrogen), 26 per cent P (phosphorus), and 26 per cent K (potassium). Say a farmer uses 100 kilograms of urea and 100 kilograms of DAP (Di-ammonium Phosphate), then N content used by the farmer is 64 kilograms (46 kilograms from Urea + 18 kilograms from DAP), P content is 46 kilograms (46 kilograms from DAP), and K content is 0 kilograms as neither contains potassium.

compared to medium and semi-medium farmers (Table 6.7). Labour cost involved in fertilizer and pesticide application however is negatively associated with cotton yield, suggesting the inherent riskiness of more intensive fertilizer applications (Table 6.6).[17] There are other concerns as well. Fieldwork brings out several stories of degradation of soil health and fatigue having set in for plots of several farmers. Although soil health cards (SHCs)

Table 6.6 Cotton yield response to fertilizer (pooled OLS): 2019–2020

Dependent Variable: Yield of Cotton (kg/acre)	**Fertilizer Model**	**N Content Model**	**P Content Model**	**K Content Model**
Fertiliser Qty (kg/acre)	0.014*			
	(–0.01)			
Nitrogen Qty (kg/acre)		0.050**		
		(–0.02)		
Phosphorous Qty (kg/acre)			0.017	
			(–0.03)	
Potassium Qty (kg/acre)				0.007
				(–0.03)
Land class (Base class - Marginal)				
Medium	–6.440*	–5.949*	–7.003*	–7.032*
	(–2.91)	(–2.88)	(–3.09)	(–3.11)
Semi-medium	–2.087	–1.769	–2.605	–2.656
	(–2.00)	(–1.97)	(–2.11)	(–2.11)
Small	–1.382	–0.791	–1.394	–1.365
	(–2.19)	(–2.16)	(–2.33)	(–2.34)
Irrigation cost (Rs/acre)	0.003	0.004	0.003	0.003
	(0.00)	(0.00)	(0.00)	(0.00)
Pesticide/weedicide (Rs/acre)	0.000	0.000	0.000	0.000
	(0.00)	(0.00)	(0.00)	(0.00)
Fertilization and spraying (Rs/acre)	–0.002**	–0.002**	–0.001*	–0.001*
	(0.00)	(0.00)	(0.00)	(0.00)
Constant	5.902**	5.576**	7.471***	7.645***
	(–1.91)	(–1.90)	(–1.93)	(–1.92)
N	211	211	211	211
R-squared (Adjusted)	0.37	0.39	0.29	0.29
P-value	0.00	0.00	0.02	0.03

Source: Author's calculation using survey data.

Note: N denotes number of observations in the pooled sample. * p<0.05, ** p<0.01, *** p<0.001. P-value refers to P-value of F-test of overall significance.

Table 6.7 Fertilizer use among farmers by land-size classes

Dependent Variable: Fertilizer Intensity (kg/acre)	Fertilizer Model	N Content Model	P Content Model	K Content Model
Land class (Base class - Marginal)				
Medium	–80.5*** (–3.72)	–21.2** (–3.27)	–13.5** (–3.01)	–6.4 (–1.58)
Semi-medium	–37.7** (–2.96)	–11.3** (–2.95)	–6.3* (–2.39)	0.20 (0.08)
Small	–11.7 (–1.02)	–4.3 (–1.24)	–5.0* (–2.11)	1.7 (0.78)
Year 2020 (Base year: 2019)	16.3 (1.86)	4.50 (1.71)	3.70* (2.05)	3.60* (2.24)
Constant	134.10*** (11.50)	35.60*** (10.21)	20.80*** (8.57)	7.00** (3.22)
N	173	173	173	173
R-squared	0.12	0.10	0.08	0.05
P-value	0.000	0.001	0.005	0.056

Source: Author's calculation using survey data.

Note: * $p<0.05$, ** $p<0.01$, *** $p<0.001$. Figures in parenthesis indicate t-statistics. Fertilizer Model has total fertilizer used (kg/acre) as dependent variable. N Content Model, P Content Model, and K Content Model have the respective N, P, and K used (kg/acre) as per composition of fertilizers as shown in Table 6.5 as dependent variable. P-value refers to P-value of F-test of overall significance.

have been provided for most farmers in the since 2015 the consensus is that there is a lack of dynamic and affordable testing facilities in the vicinity which renders the SHC exercise pointless.

PRICE RISKS

Farmers who have to negotiate a multitude of production risks continue to face myriad of post-harvest risks as well. Lack of storage infrastructure often makes households vulnerable to losses and renders them incapable to sell their produce at remunerative prices. At the marketing yards, perceptions of the quality of the produce also determine the prices that farmers receive after months of hard work and uncertainty. Our historical analysis demonstrated that the ups and downs in cotton prices became a stylized fact of cotton cultivation with growing market integration and exposure to conditions of the trade in raw cotton. Unlike the late nineteenth century or early twentieth century where a large proportion of cotton was destined for international markets (Chapter 2), a substantial share of cotton produced meets domestic consumption demand.

The fluctuations in demand and supply of cotton in domestic and international markets do give rise to price volatility which have to be managed by the farmers. Vidarbha cotton farmers have been affected by the high level of subsidies by the United States to its cotton growers since the mid-1990s that have depressed world cotton prices. Since the 2015 Farm Act, the United States has initiated several support measures for its cotton growers that have been fiercely debated in the WTO whose rules have been biased and asymmetric against the cotton growers of the developing world. The plight of the group of cotton growing African countries (C-4) comprising Burkina Faso, Benin, Chad, and Mali is a case in point.[18]

Prevailing trade policies, domestic cotton output and industry demand, global import demand, and carry-forward stocks frequently influence market prices of cotton as they have been for centuries. For instance, in 2008 high cotton prices were affecting the spinning mills and textile sectors reeling under higher cost of raw cotton. To lower prices, India abolished the 10 per cent customs duty on raw cotton imports along with the 4 per cent special additional duty to boost domestic supply. World cotton consumption picked up after the 2008 financial crisis. However, in 2009, the domestic cotton industry faced an artificial crisis as local textile mills were unable to procure at market prices. The rising prices were an outcome of the 40 per cent hike in the minimum support price (MSP). Prices were 1,000–2,000 rupees per candy higher than international prices.[19] In 2010–2011, due to a combination of high oil and polyester prices and increased Chinese demand for cotton, international cotton prices more than doubled.[20] The MSP for cotton was hiked in the following three years. There was also a delay in receiving export subsidies, and the subsidy from the Technology Upgradation Fund Scheme, thus hindering cotton mills from procuring more cotton. Fieldwork suggested that mills also began to reduce inventory levels from three–six months to one–two months because of the price volatility. The high carry-forward stock in 2015–2016 caused a crash in world cotton prices to 2009 levels. The domestic prices fell below international prices due to rising exports and concerns about the Chinese supply of cotton reserves. Domestic cotton prices rose 2021–2022, despite pressure from China's direct subsidy policies and low domestic demand. China releasing its stocks remained a concern. Cotton prices also rose thanks to lower domestic supplies.

Farmers in the study villages sell their produce at the market yards or *mandis* in nearby towns, which we introduced in Chapter 4. Some traders also visit the villages and procure the goods from the farmers' doorstep, by offering prices higher than the government's MSP. For example, at a time in the 2009 marketing season, when the government was offering 2,400 rupees per quintal of cotton, the traders who had tie-ups with the ginning mills offered 2,700 rupees per quintal of cotton to farmers. However, during the period of the study, we observed high variability in the activity of the public procurement system.

The Cotton Corporation of India (CCI) intervenes in the cotton output markets by procuring *kapas* (seed cotton) through competitive auctions conducted by the Agricultural Produce Market Committees (APMCs) in notified market yards across the country. Since 1963, notified agricultural commodities began being marketed through regulated markets in Maharashtra. By the time CCI was setup by the Government of India in 1970, agriculture in Maharashtra was already on a path of modernization under the chief ministership of Vasantrao Phulsing Naik from the Indian National Congress party. It is ironic that the state government appointed task force to address issues of agrarian crisis in Vidarbha and Marathwada districts, namely the Vasantrao Naik Sheti Swavlamban Mission (VNSSM) is named after a champion of the Green Revolution from Vidarbha, and someone who held three consecutive terms as chief minister.[21] CCI undertakes MSP operations on an event prices of fair average quality (FAQ) grade falling below the MSP.[22] Between the period 2014–2015 to 2020–2021, when cotton prices were generally low, CCI played an important role in procurement. This was in contrast to the general dissatisfaction among farmers in the first round (2009–2011) of our survey in the Wardha villages. More importantly, during the first wave of the COVID-19 pandemic, CCI played an important role in procuring nearly one-third of the annual produce of 36 million bales cultivated in 13.5 million hectares in 2020–2021.[23] A visit to a private ginning unit in Wardha which was also a satellite processing centre in the 2020–2021 marketing season helped us understand the role of CCI officials supervising the grading, weighing, and procurement from local farmers (Images 6.1 and 6.2). Typically, the cotton ginning and pressing units are owned by those from the Marwari Bania community who have strong networks with other ginners in the region. This allows them to have some degree of collusive power in pricing the cotton which is graded, ginned, and packed at their units, which are also referred to as 'ginning and pressing factories' in Gazetteers of the districts. It is useful to remember that in the early twentieth century these ginning and pressing factories in districts such as Wardha were dominated by the Marwari Banias with a few owned by Maratha Brahmins and Kunbis.

In contemporary settings, three interesting aspects of these units are worth mentioning. First, the local cotton supply chain has sound knowledge of the villages from where they get cotton of high ginning outturn ratio, that is the ratio of lint–seed cotton as it has implications on their profit margins. Second, the units have automated systems that separate the seed, lint, kernel, and hull, thereby making them an important source of cotton seeds for the cotton oil industry. Third, these units are an important source of livelihood for mostly casual workers who clean up conveyor belts; assist in semi-automated processes; operate machines; provide labour for unloading of raw cotton and loading of pressed cotton bales, and other processes in the units. The manager and supervisors are usually from nearby towns and villages whereas casual workers are predominantly migrant labourers. The importance of CCI officials' presence from the first day of arrivals to the last day in a marketing season is often acknowledged by farmers. Unlike cotton, for pulses and oilseeds, the National Agricultural Cooperative Marketing Federation of India Ltd (NAFED) procures through its marketing federation in the state by way of MSP operations to stabilize prices and avoid distress sales among farmers.

In stark contrast to the general satisfaction with CCI's operations during the pandemic, there was gross disappointment with NAFED. In May 2020, several farmers from Wardha reported delays in receiving payment for the *tur* they had sold to NAFED despite higher prices of 5,800 rupees per quintal as MSP. During subsequent field visits after the lockdown was lifted, farmers confirmed that the pending bills were paid off despite worrisome delays. Another behemoth of the public procurement system, the Food Corporation of India (FCI) procures pulses as well as food grains through its procurement centres on which *tur* and wheat-growers for the rabi season rely. These contemporary developments, however, mask decades of dirigisme in agricultural markets that protected cotton growers in the region from price fluctuations and competition. The Raw Cotton (Procurement, Processing, and Marketing) Act, 1971, was promulgated with the objective of ensuring fair and remunerative prices to cotton farmers. This became the basis for implementation of the Monopoly Cotton Procurement Scheme (MCPS) through the Maharashtra State Cooperative Cotton Growers Marketing Federation (MSCCGMF) in 1972. Farmers received guarantee price for specified varieties of cotton but neither were they allowed to sell their cotton to anyone but the government nor was *kapas* allowed to be transported outside the state. Setting up cotton business or ginning and pressing unit was also prohibited. MCPS and its subsequent dismantling several decades later impacted Vidarbha's cotton economy and lives of nearly 200,000 cotton farmers drastically, and aggravated the agrarian crisis. We will discuss this in the context of political economy of Vidarbha cotton in Chapter 7.[24]

Over the decade, there has been limited improvement in the public and private storage infrastructure. Those without access to a godown in the village or nearby towns store the produce in their houses. These stocks run the risk of fire, high moisture, rodents, and theft, and there is no insurance available for the stocks. Depending on the price expectations in the nearest local markets, farmers bring their product to the market yard and bear the transportation cost. As expected, the holding capacity of the produce is higher for wealthier households, and they are more capable of holding on to their stocks until they believe the prices are remunerative. However, the less wealthy households who cannot hold on to their produce for long tend to sell it earlier, often missing out on any opportunity for windfalls. These households are more prone to distress sale of their produce. In the absence of proper storage facilities in the villages, the farmers are eager to sell their produce at the earliest and the APMC auctioning floor in the nearest town becomes an important arena where post-harvest risks play out. At the APMC yard in Wardha and Yavatmal, the processes such as assaying and weighing are standardized and farmers seem to have a preference for such transparent practices. Private cotton gins, that have increased remarkably over the past decade, also procure raw cotton and many have CCI agents procuring at the same site. Our visit to one such gin during the COVID-19 pandemic helped understand how the cotton marketing operations were affected by the pandemic (Images 6.1 and 6.2).

From our visits to a few market yards at different points of time, it is evident that the moment the farmers enter the marketing yard, they lose their bargaining power in a manner that exemplifies the helplessness of a farmer for whom the price expectation influenced crop and acreage choices that season. The traders (buyers) usually have better price information (of spot, forward and futures market price trends) than the farmers. Once the lots of the produce brought by the farmers are lined up on the auction floor at some

Image 6.1 Cotton bales getting ready to be transported from a ginning and pressing unit in Wardha, circa 2020

Source: Sarthak Gaurav.

indeterminate time of the day, a group of traders walk down the floor with the auctioneer, momentarily stopping by each of the lots (heaps). At each lot, in a chaotic ambience lasts over a few seconds where scores of traders assess the quality of the stock and the auctioneer makes the bidding calls amidst the din and roar of the yard, until the produce is auctioned off. In this context, it should be noted that failure to sell off the produce in a single day also carries the risk of lower prices the next day apart from additional costs for overnight storage and lodging for the farmer or her/his attendants. So, the farmers who are not content with the going rates do not appear to have the incentive to try their luck another day.

Close examination of the functioning of the regulated markets sheds lights on several manifestations of price risk. There are a few observations made during visits to the market yards in Vidarbha that are worth noting. First, the perception of the bidders (traders) about the quality of the produce plays an important role in determining the price of the output. For instance,

Image 6.2 Ranganathan at a cotton gin in Wardha district, circa December 2020

Source: Sarthak Gaurav.

Note: There has been an increase in the number of ginning and spinning units in the region as the government has provided subsidized credit to promote such units as MSME (micro, small, and medium enterprises).

during one of our visits to the APMC marketing yard in Wardha in 2010 with the farmers of the study villages, a farmer who expected his quintal of soybean to go for 2,200 rupees per quintal ended up getting 1,750 rupees per quintal at 2009 prices. This was because of the perceived low quality of his produce on account of visible residues which he had not bothered to separate. Second, anecdotal evidence suggests that smaller lots with visibly less leftover stalks, stones, or residuals fetch a better price as they signal better quality. However, variations as high as 500–2,000 rupees per quintal on the same auction floor in a given day are not uncommon. Furthermore, as in the case of yield or production risks, such price risks can be considered to be idiosyncratic in nature as they affect the individuals and the misfortunes of the farmers are not correlated. Third, the role of the middleman, or *arhatiya*, also deserves a mention. At the APMC yard, every farmer is associated with an APMC-certified agent—*arhatiya*—who charges a commission of 1.5 per cent on the receipts and links the traders to the farmers.[25] Usually the *arhatiya* pays the farmers in cash on the same day, but at times there are delays up to a month. While the farmer believes that the *arhatiya* plays the role of connecting the traders to them given their connections with them, the *arhatiya* believes that he plays a facilitating role and makes life easy for the farmer in receiving his revenues without much hassle. Farmers' dependence on the *arhatiya* and apparent exploitation by the same became the basis for one of the three controversial farm laws that were recently repealed. However, fieldwork in 2009 as well as 2019 in the *mandi* confirmed that in the absence of well-functioning credit markets, the *arhatiya* continues to be an important source of instant credit for the farmers in times of their need. Further, indicative of interlocked markets, many *arhatiya*s also assume the role of experts and push the sales of costly chemical inputs to the farmer.

That the *arhatiya* is an influential actor in agricultural markets to the extent that it is believed that they played a significant role in orchestrating the protests against the controversial farm laws in India that were repealed recently. Of the three farm laws—the Farmers' Produce Trade and Commerce (Promotion and Facilitation) Act, the Essential Commodities (Amendment) Act, and the Farmers (Empowerment and Protection) Agreement on Price Assurance and Farm Services Act—the first law became the main reason for discontent among agitating farmers. The main argument forwarded by several groups was that it threatened to dismantle the intermediation by *arhatiya*s in states such as Punjab and Haryana where government procurement of wheat, paddy, and mustard had largely depended on them. Since these middlemen play an important role in the procurement and payment of prices across the network of *mandi*s, the prospects of farmers' selling anywhere outside the *mandi* to anyone became untenable to the *arhatiya*s who are mostly politically connected. With the three farm laws repealed, as per new mechanisms instituted by the central government, farmers continue to get payment for the procured amount as direct bank transfer to their account whilst the *arhatiya*s get paid separately for their commission fee, cost of labour and sacks. This move also brings incomes of *arhatiya*s from these commission under the tax net unlike earlier when they declared their sales income as agricultural income, which is untaxed in India. In stark contrast to the protests on the outskirts of New Delhi, the protests in Vidarbha were lukewarm, despite the prolonged agrarian crisis that has marred the region. Although there were few instances of mass agitation by different groups, *mandi*s more or less continued to function uninterrupted, and support for call for *bandh*s and *chakka* *jams*—common forms of strikes—did not have much impact. Nor was there any notable protest beyond a month or two. However, in January 2021, a group of around sixty women from a *taluka* in Yavatmal travelled to Delhi to join the larger group of protesters. In February that year around 15,000 farmers from different parts of the state gathered at Mumbai's Azad Maidan to extend solidarity with protesters in bordering areas of New Delhi. Why were there no large-scale protests against the contentious farm laws in Vidarbha?

Traveling across the region just before the lockdown and travel restrictions in the first wave of the pandemic were in place, and once during the second wave when there was frequent changes in travel restrictions, we inferred the following reasons might explain the timid response by farmers in the region. First, there was no restriction on farmers to sell their produce outside the *mandi*s that anyway have been functioning fairly well without serious concerns about expropriation by the *arhatiya*s. Second, unlike in Punjab, Haryana, or western Uttar Pradesh, there was a clear lack of political interest in protesting against the farm laws. Several fringe groups mobilized farmers and activists for the cause, but the protests failed to attain scale without convergence among larger political parties and farmer unions. Third, individuals or groups in favour of the new farm laws primarily because of their unflinching support for the Bharatiya Janata Party (BJP) or Prime Minister Narendra Modi instead of the government's logic behind the enactment of the laws failed to protest despite insecurity around risk of MSP being irrelevant or concerns of collusion between large private buyers. Many such individuals that we could interact with during our visits immediately after the lockdown and travel restrictions were lifted in 2020 and 2021, blamed the pandemic for their inability to coordinate a mass agitation instead.

In terms of policy uncertainties, tepid response to the controversial farm laws notwithstanding, farmers in the region have to deal with price uncertainty on account of policy changes pertaining to commodity markets and trade. To add to the farmers' uncertainties, an unexpected 'policy shock' in the form of an export ban on cotton was imposed by the central government on 5 March 2011.[26] Although the ban was temporary and lifted on account of political pressures, many farmers lost substantially as prices plummeted to levels below 4,500 rupees over a period of two weeks of imposition of the export restriction. This piece of finding shows that farmers in Vidarbha not only have to grapple with yield risk and uncertainty due to the weather but also face substantial price risk and uncertainty due to market and policy shocks. This seems like déjà vu, as we have already seen in Chapter 2 how yield and price uncertainty characterized cotton cultivation in the region in the nineteenth and twentieth centuries. In what follows, we present further insights from quantitative evidence on losses, risk coping, and vulnerability to risk.

WHEN GAMBLES GO WRONG

Farming, like gambling, can go wrong given uncertainties associated with the income-generating process. Undoubtedly, farmers cultivating under risky conditions are aware of the stakes involved. In particular, cotton yield which is subject to the vagaries of weather and the price that a farmer realizes can fall from what a farmer anticipates owing to idiosyncratic and systemic factors. To begin with, the rain-fed nature of cultivation makes households particularly prone to frequent losses. A typical farmer household goes through a cycle of gains and losses characterizing the income fluctuations in high-risk farming. The lack of non-farm opportunities leaves farmers with little option to stabilize their incomes or even compensate for losses incurred in farming, instead only to gamble on cotton. A panel data of cultivator households that were sampled in our surveys over the course of five years allows us to explore these trajectories in detail.

The dominant source of financial loss for the farmers has been poor yields for cotton. Things have gone wrong quite frequently due to weather vagaries, particularly unseasonal rains and insect pest attacks. Most years in the last decade can be considered as subjectively 'bad' from the farmers' perspective, and pest incidence remained considerably high. Of the five years under consideration for our panel data (2015, 2016, 2017, 2019, and 2020), three were higher than normal rainfall years—2017, 2019, and 2020. However, a good monsoon season did not guarantee high crop yields as farmers experienced considerable losses due to unseasonal excess rains starting from September. The years 2015 and 2016 were deficit rainfall years for the region when yield losses were high. Yield losses in two years were manifested due to infestation by *jassids* and *aphids*, while 2019 and 2020 saw the re-emergence of pink bollworm (PBW), as discussed in Chapter 5, resulting in significant yield losses. While such composite weather and pest-related risks have become common, the resemblance to similar circumstances in the Central Provinces in the late nineteenth century is uncanny:

> From 1894 the cultivation and export of linseed begin to decline. In that year excessive rains and hot, damp weather during the sowing

> season provided conditions for the appearance and spread of fungoid diseases and for the propagation of insect pests such as caterpillars. As a result, the linseed crop of 1894–95 was absolutely ruined in the northern districts and there was a drastic fall in exports. This led to a sharp contraction of the area under linseed in 1895, aided by poor rains that year.[27]

As weather risks remained unmitigated, some households were better equipped to face specific risks. Households with land in low-lying areas suffered more from excess rains. The exposure to risk also varies dependent on the array of decisions made by the farmers including crop diversification, the seed choice, levels of fertilizers, a mix of pesticides, and timely weeding. In view of multiple sources of risk in cotton cultivation, no year is likely to be a good or bad year for all farmers who put in hard work and year-round supervision in tending their fields. Apart from the covariate risks which will build the anxiety of everyone in the village, the idiosyncratic exposure to risks and differential adaptive capabilities brings in varied anxieties at the level of individual farmers.

With this background, we analyse the losses incurred by the ninety-five farmers who we surveyed in all the five years of the second and third rounds of the survey. We define cotton yield loss as a function of expectations of yield based on the village yield and the variation around the same.[28] The yield loss to the household is estimated using the following formula:

$$\textit{Yield loss in a particular year} = 1 \ \textit{if} \left(\frac{X_{ivt} - \bar{X}_{v}}{X_{vt}^{SD}} \right) < -0.5$$

Where X_{ivt} is the yield of i household in v village in the year, $\bar{X}_{v}$ is the expected yield of v village level yield over the five years leaving out the household,[29] and X_{vt}^{SD} is the standard deviation of crop yield of v village in the year t. Based on this definition, we find widespread experience of losses by households each year. Even in a relatively good year in 2017, 15 per cent of the cotton cultivators experienced yield losses while 2020 was a really bad year with almost two-thirds of the farmers experiencing yield losses in that year (Table 6.2). A substantial number of households in our sample incurred losses for more than one year (Graph 6.1). There have also been a few unfortunate households that have experienced sequential yield loss as in the case of three households with no cotton yield in both 2015 and 2016. The reason for the same was destruction of crops by wild animals such as *rohi* (Nilgai, a species

Table 6.8 Yield losses

Year	Households Facing Yield Losses
2015	45% (80)
2016	44.2% (86)
2017	15.2% (79)
2019	35.6% (90)
2020	64.0% (86)

Source: Authors' calculations based on survey data.

Note: This is the data on losses among those who cultivated cotton. The numbers in parenthesis indicate the number of farmers out of 95 who cultivated cotton in that year.

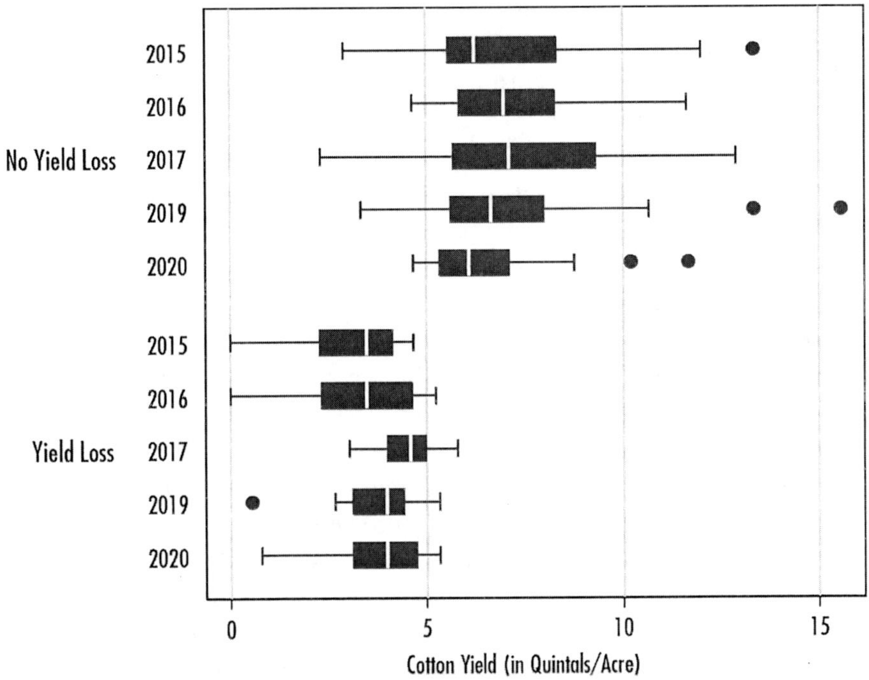

Graph 6.1 Yield variation: 2015–2020

Source: Primary survey.

of antelope) and *dukkar* (wild boar) that are a major source of crop losses in villages in the region but against which farmers are helpless to protect their crops given the wildlife protection laws of the land that prohibits killing of these animals. They incurred a loss of 20,000 rupees from cotton cultivation and a loss of 22,000 rupees from agriculture. It is crucial to note that among the households that did not incur losses, the yields went up to as high as 16 quintals per acre for a few farmers. Such an array of outcomes clearly indicates that cotton farming in rain-fed conditions is very much akin to a game of snakes and ladders where a potential for making a great fortune exists along with a serious possibility of ruin.

How have the farmers adapted to these risks? The households that incur losses cope with them in that year and adapt their cultivation practices in the next years. Those who averted losses plan for another season, with renewed optimism. As mentioned before, households can vary their cropping patterns in response to losses. Changes in agronomic practices have also evolved in response to losses. Farmers sometimes use a different plot in the land for cotton cultivation following a bad year as a response to losses. Since they do not generally keep the land fallow completely for a year, the land in which soybean was cultivated typically remains fallow for a longer time. Cultivating cotton and *tur* in those plots sometimes helps in revival of the yield. In response to specific problems like waterlogging, farmers change some of the farm practices. As waterlogging has become more frequent, farmers practise sloped line spacing (*varham paddath*),[30] which reduces the yield losses in case of excessive rains. That the farmers adapt routinely and the roll of the dice varies every year means some of the households recover after losses in a year. It also means some of the households that do reasonably well in one year might face deterioration of incomes in future. The trajectory of the household and cotton cultivation incomes indicates that most households incurring losses in 2015 but not in 2016 and 2017, recovered over time to earn a relatively higher income from cotton cultivation (Graph 6.2) and agriculture in the subsequent years (Graph 6.3). The households that did not encounter a loss in 2015 earned much lesser than other categories of households defined on the basis of loss experience in both cotton cultivation and agriculture in 2019 and 2020. It is noteworthy that households that experienced two and three consecutive kharif losses could also recover over the next two rounds, and did not necessarily get trapped in losses.

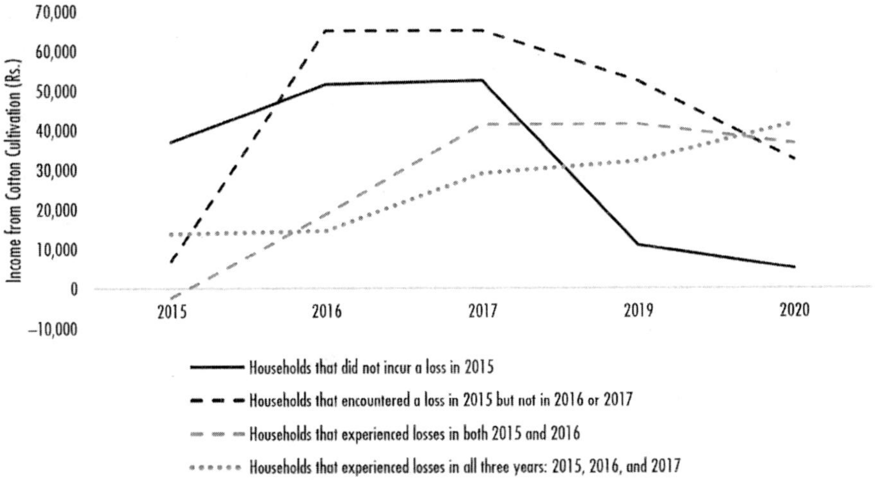

Graph 6.2 Trajectories of income from cotton cultivation: 2015–2020

Source: Authors' calculations based on survey data.

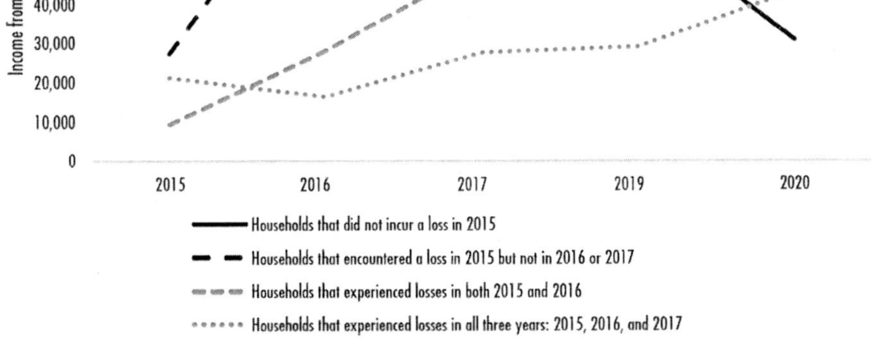

Graph 6.3 Trajectories of income from cultivation: 2015–2020

Source: Authors' calculations based on survey data.

LOSS DISTRIBUTION

It is evident from the foregoing discussion that some of the households experience losses in more than one year. Despite the adaptation and possible reversal of fortune in the future, such multiple losses could have severe welfare consequences. These effects could be related to the stress and anxiety of recurrent losses which becomes even more magnified by the need to 'perform' agriculture to the household, farmers in the village, input dealers, and anybody else who visit them. But it could also have material consequences related to consumption in future.

In the second round of our survey conducted between 2015 and 2017, about twenty-one of the ninety-five cultivator households faced losses in two or more years. These households are likely to be more vulnerable and a further loss in 2019 would push their consumption severely down. As anticipated, experiencing a yield loss in 2019 pulled their consumption drastically down.[31] Among the households who did not encounter multiple shocks in 2015–2017, there was no big difference in monthly per capita expenditure. However, among the vulnerable households, a yield loss in 2019 meant their monthly per capita expenditure on food was 17 per cent lesser than those who did not face a loss that year; the same on non-food was 30 per cent lesser (Graphs 6.4 and 6.5). These households also had a much higher dependence on the public distribution system (PDS) in that year (Graph 6.6). Indeed, there is seasonality in consumption in the villages as festivals and social events are interspersed across the calendar year as discussed in Chapter 3.

The households that coped with multiple yield losses from 2015 to 2017 continued growing cotton in 2019 and 2020. They allocated on average three-fourths of their cultivated land to cotton in 2019 and over two-thirds of the cultivated land to cotton in 2020. In fact, these households had a higher share of cultivated area devoted to cotton in both years than the households that did not face multiple losses over the same period. This finding underlines the lure of cotton among farmers in the region. Given the various options that were detailed in Chapter 5, a farmer having poor yield in cotton goes back to trying out either a new seed brand of cotton (host of Bt seed brands for most and, more recently, the illegally approved HTBt cotton seeds for some); newer cultivation practice related to cotton (organic cultivation, *fulli* or *patta* or *varham paddath*); plot diversification; and trying out newer 'cocktails' of pesticides. However, it is not necessary that the farmers abandon or cultivate less cotton even after incurring losses. Even when some commentators pointed

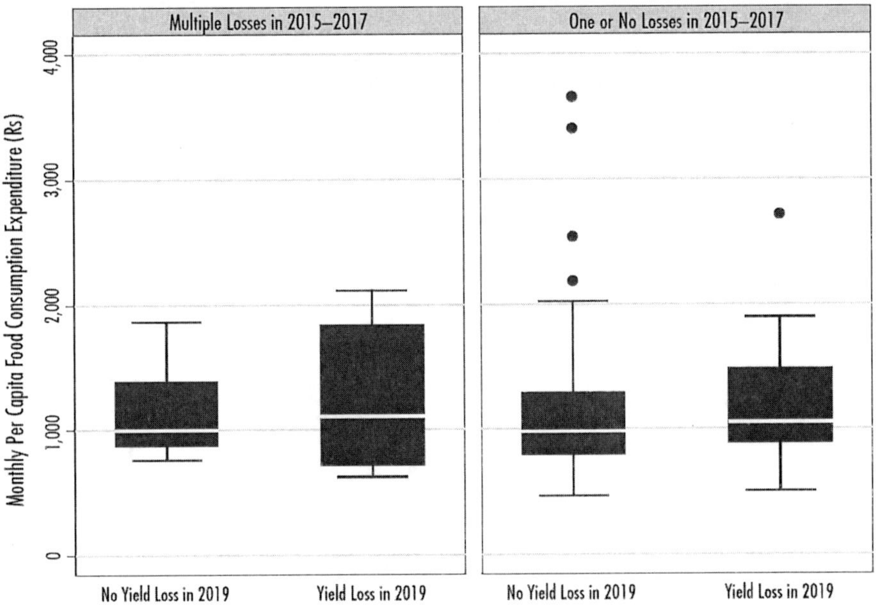

Graph 6.4 Monthly per capita food consumption expenditure and losses: 2019

Source: Authors' calculations based on primary survey.

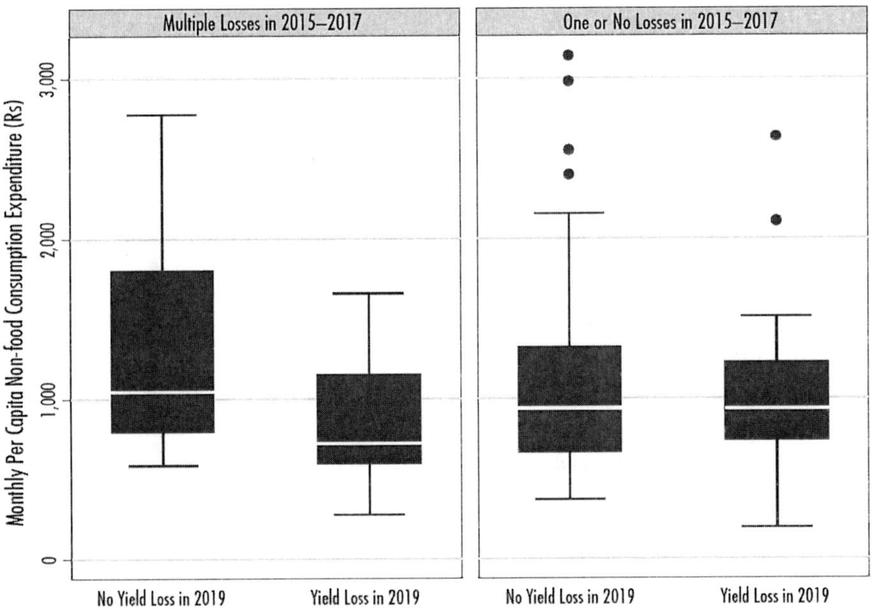

Graph 6.5 Monthly per capita non-food consumption expenditure and losses: 2019

Source: Authors' calculations based on primary survey.

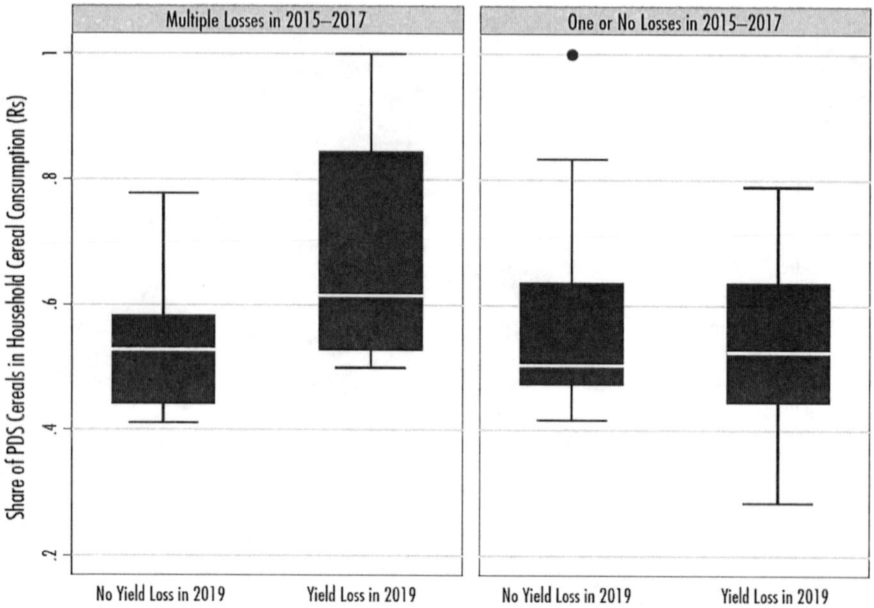

Graph 6.6 Share of PDS cereals in household cereal consumption: 2019

Source: Authors' calculations based on primary survey.

to large scale shift away from cotton to soybean in the region based on what they observed in 2017, such a shift did not persist as seen in Chapter 4. Farmers seemed to have moved back to cotton over the last couple of years in the absence of viable alternatives.[32] Farmers clearly internalized the fact that everyone cannot win this game every time and prospects of loss loom large every year. Therefore, despite losses and sometimes multiple losses, farmers go back to gambling with cotton in the hope of a good yield. This propensity to take multiple gambles with possibility of loss could possibly be explained by 'choice bracketing'. Though people might be averse to taking a single gamble with a possibility of a loss, they might be more prone to taking multiple gambles of same chance. This could happen as they bracket their outcomes over multiple risky events. With the farmers in the study region, though they might be wary of a loss in a single year, they might keep taking gambles over many years as the possibility of sustained losses over many years is less.[33]

We see stories of recovery and stories of vulnerability get played out again and again in our study region and across various farmers. Although we have presented findings at an aggregate level, there are differences by gender and class in particular that warrant attention. Many of the adaptation practices discussed earlier may not be feasible for households who do not have the relevant able-bodied farm workers to undertake the farm practices. We have found women-headed households, particularly those where household heads are widows, elderly, and where children (married or otherwise) are employed in non-farm activities, to be prone to risks on the one hand and facing difficulties in coping with any shock on the other hand. Similarly, near landless and marginal cultivator households have limited financial strength to cope with idiosyncratic and covariate shocks compared to those with the means to cope with the same. In terms of vulnerability of landless households are concerned, it is primarily linked to yield shocks in agriculture given their earnings from farm labour is substantial. We will discuss the same in the context of risk coping by non-cultivator households later.

RISK PERCEPTIONS AND RISK MANAGEMENT

RISK PERCEPTIONS

It is to be noted that households face risks both in and outside the domain of agriculture. In the context of risks faced by agricultural households, a distinction is typically made between *covariate* (aggregate, common or correlated) and *idiosyncratic* (independent or uncorrelated) risks.[34] Such a distinction is critical because depending on whether the risk is idiosyncratic or covariate, the ex ante or the ex post response to the risk is determined. Moreover, the multiple waves of the COVID-19 pandemic also became a rare phenomenon in which agricultural risks intersected with that of a pandemic, thereby demonstrating wide variation in shocks experienced by households and their ability to prevent and cope with these shocks.

While idiosyncratic risks such as illness (health shock) for a particular household can be managed through informal risk sharing or risk pooling arrangements, on the contrary, covariate risks such as drought or downside price risk due to macro-level variations cannot be effectively hedged by informal risk pooling arrangements as everyone is exposed to the risk. Given the likelihood of informal risk management mechanisms breaking down given the severity of certain covariate shocks, the justification for formal risk management mechanisms such as market-based insurance arises. However, as we will demonstrate later, access to formal insurance mechanisms does not guarantee indemnification or payoffs even if farmers experienced losses associated with the insured events. It should be borne in mind that agricultural production and price risks can vary between covariate and idiosyncratic shocks depending on the degree of correlation between the risks in a village or community. This would allow for the simultaneous existence of both idiosyncratic and covariate yield and price risks.[35]

This brings us to the topic of risk management by agricultural households, which is central to households' lives and livelihoods under risk and uncertainty. Over time, there were variations in the risk exposure the cultivator households. While in 2009, 81 per cent of the households were affected by drought, this proportion was 21 per cent in 2019 (Table 6.8). The more prominent risk in 2019 was that of a fall in output price. Instead, the risks related to health shocks increased due to the pandemic, and there was wide variation whether these health shocks had a transitory or permanent effect on household incomes. Excess rainfall risks as perceived by farmers have also gone up over this decade.

In 2020, during the pandemic that prevented us from frequently visiting the villages, resident investigators conducted FGDs, on the basis of which we were able to identify whether rainfall and pest pressure were high or low over the study years. There is a clear match between farmers' perceptions

Table 6.9 Risk perceptions: 2009 and 2019

Risks Faced	2009 %	2019 %
Fall in output price	13.0	45.0
Drought	81.0	21.0
Health shocks	2.0	13.0
Excess rainfall	3.0	12.0
Rise in input costs	13.0	8.0
Deficit rainfall	10.0	6.5
Unseasonal rainfall	14.0	2.8
Others	2.0	1.8
N	120	110

Source: Authors' calculation based on survey data.

Note: Multiple options were allowed.

and the actual state of rainfall and pest infestation in those years. This is not surprising as the fluctuations in rainfall and pest pressure would have affected the farmers considerably. Recall of exceptionally good or bad years is also a frequent topic of conversation during field visits.

RISK COPING MECHANISMS

Farm households in Vidarbha aim to reduce or insulate consumption variability from the vagaries of incomes. This is the central purpose of various informal strategies that have evolved over generations and the more recent formal market-based or public insurance programmes. As they do so, these households aim to smooth their incomes through strategizing their livelihood options or smooth their consumption post the realization of low incomes.[36]

Income smoothing involves ex ante strategies to mitigate adverse income shocks and is often achieved by diversification of income sources and conservative production and occupation choices. Consumption smoothing refers to the ex post risk coping mechanisms by way of borrowing, dissaving, asset depletion and accumulation of non-financial assets, labour supply adjustments, and reliance on formal and informal insurance arrangements. There is an inherent difficulty in determining whether income smoothing or consumption smoothing contributed to the smoothness of the consumption and the two types can act as substitutes for each other.

Income smoothing strategies include spatial (plot-level) and cultivar (variety-level) diversification, diversification of income sources; tenancy contracts such as sharecropping; weather insurance; and precautionary savings.[37] However, it has been argued that such strategies are costly in terms of high-income opportunities foregone by 'risk averse' households who tend to make 'conservative' production choices and prefer safer activities (portfolios) in their endeavour to minimize their exposure to risk and uncertainty.[38] Moreover, if we have reasons to believe that wealthier households have better risk bearing capabilities, there could be distributional consequences of income shocks apart from their effective productivity.[39]

On the other hand, consumption smoothing strategies such as cutting down on household consumption, dissaving, asset depletion, credit transactions, and labour supply adjustments have also been observed among rural households.[40] Reliance on asset accumulation and decumulation, and use of assets as 'buffer stocks' as inter-temporal 'consumption smoothing' strategies have been identified.[41] Credit transactions, both formal and informal, have also been identified as consumption smoothing options for rural households.[42] However, households could be credit constrained or credit markets would be imperfect, limiting the consumption smoothing abilities of some households. Furthermore, for inter-temporal as well as cross-sectional risk-sharing, informal arrangements such as dependence on kinship groups or solidarity networks,[43] which are based on principles of 'generalised reciprocity',[44] are also relevant. Alternative cross-sectional risk pooling mechanisms in the community have also been observed.[45] In an event of an aggregate and extreme weather shocks such as droughts, which affect a large number of households in the village, the traditional adjustment strategies based on kinship and solidarity might not be as effective as in case of idiosyncratic and low-magnitude losses. It is these aspects of risk management that emanate in the vulnerability of households.[46]

Farm households in the region have changed the strategy of consumption smoothing over the last decade. Our study over more than decade throws a light into these transitions (Table 6.10). While formal credit was the predominant risk coping mechanism in 2009—a drought year, dissaving was the most common risk coping mechanism in 2019—a normal rainfall year. Consumption cuts as well as unilateral transfers within the kinship network (friends and relatives) were prevalent and relied upon much more compared to reliance on formal credit or asset depletion. Reliance on informal credit is the least common. This points to the growth in the number of self-help groups

Table 6.10 Risk coping mechanisms: 2009 and 2019

	2009	2019	
	Cultivator	**Cultivator**	**Non-cultivator**
Dissaving	66.0%	71.0%	82.0%
Increasing labour supply	24.0%	69.0%	73.0%
Consumption cuts	34.0%	36.0%	43.0%
Unilateral transfers	31.0%	35.0%	30.0%
Formal credit	71.0%	22.0%	9.0%
Asset depletion	47.0%	20.0%	9.0%
Borrowing from kinship	30.0%	18.0%	8.0%
Informal credit	18.0%	9.0%	6.0%
N	120	170	174

Source: Authors' calculation based on survey data.

Note: Multiple options allowed; totals may exceed 100 per cent.

(SHGs), particularly women SHGs that have mobilized household savings, offered livelihood finance by linkages with public schemes, and inculcated credit discipline among members. In the time of adverse shocks, there is greater dependence on loans from SHGs at lower cost as women SHGs are eligible for credit up to 3 lakh rupees at 7 per cent per annum under certain government programmes. In a survey during the COVID-19 pandemic year of 2020–2021, we found that drawn on household savings was the most common risk coping strategy. This raises serious concerns about the ability of households to weather extreme shocks in the absence of well-functioning insurance markets.

A striking feature of our discussions with farmers over the years is that they do not acknowledge crop insurance or weather insurance as a risk coping mechanism. Perhaps the biggest barrier to adoption of market-based agricultural insurance lies in the inability of the insurance industry to alleviate the trust issues based on poor past experience with insurance payouts. Much of this lack of acknowledgement of formal insurance is attributed to poor experience with crop insurance over the years. Despite several modifications to the agricultural insurance schemes and experimentation with weather insurance, farmers continue to have low awareness and a general sense of being 'short changed' by the insurance company.[47] In 2010, discussion with multiple farmers suggested that those farmers who had availed formal loans, and hence had mandatory premium enrolment in crop insurance, failed to develop a sense of demand for insurance. Even though there are provisions for voluntary adoption, we rarely encountered a farmer who had voluntarily purchased weather insurance. A decade later, a similar situation prevails. In studies, such adverse emotions towards insurance not only in this region but also in other cotton-growing regions such as Gujarat have been well documented.[48]

The 2019–2020 round of survey indicated important differences between risk management strategies of cultivator and non-cultivator households. Unlike cultivator households, non-cultivator households do not have many ex ante risk management strategies. Risk coping becomes critical to these households. Consumption cuts are more common among non-cultivator households.

There was a considerable increase in reliance on consumption cuts by non-cultivator households in 2020. This is likely to be the effect of the pandemic as it may have increased precautionary saving in the households who witnessed uncertainty in non-farm labour incomes as well as business operations, if any.

Labour supply adjustments in the form of increasing labour supply (both within and outside the village) continue to be a major coping mechanism for the non-cultivator households. Unilateral transfers—a strategy that takes myriad forms in both kind as well as cash—also continue to be relied upon in a sense that borrowing from kinship and social networks as well as costlier borrowing from formal and informal sources is less prevalent. In assessing the effectiveness of risk management strategies pertaining to labour market adjustments, it is essential to take note of intersectionalities associated with gender, age, and caste due to the insights about heterogeneities along these dimensions.

VULNERABILITY TO RISK

How do we conceptualize vulnerability? Vulnerability of households has been conceived as 'uninsured exposure to risk' (VER) in some of the studies. Unlike alternative vulnerability measures that are ex ante and forward looking, VER is ex post-oriented and hence backward looking.[49] A clarification is needed here on the disciplinary variation in conceptualizing vulnerability. The climate change literature approaches vulnerability as both socio-economic and a bio-physical phenomenon.[50] In the 'risk-assessment' or 'hazard' literature, vulnerability is implicit in exposure to any hazard and sensitivity of the exposed units, and vulnerability indicators specific to a particular hazard are widely developed.[51] Within Sen's 'capability approach' framework, an argument could be made that it is not the failure of production, rather the failure of entitlements or endowments which renders an individual or household vulnerable.[52] Furthermore, vulnerability could be contextualized at inter- and intra-household levels. The multi-faceted approaches to vulnerability across disciplines provide a broad framework for measuring vulnerability of households. It also means that any quantitative metric is unlikely to capture the essence of vulnerability and we are cognizant of such a limitation of our analysis.

Evidence on vulnerability of households to uninsured exposure to risk emerged from analysis of panel data of 120 households in the five Wardha villages over the consecutive kharif seasons of 2009 to 2011.[53] This analysis indicated substantial variability of household incomes on the one hand and limited off-farm income opportunities on the other. Analysis of correlations among different sources of income revealed that the existing off-farm livelihood alternatives did not suffice as effective ex ante income risk management strategies for the Wardha households. Public works programmes such as MGNREGS were yet to become popular in the study villages a decade ago and the limited livelihood base governed the ability of non-farm incomes to stabilize household incomes. In such a context, our quantitative tests of 'full insurance' hypothesis—which posits risk management strategies in the villages ensure perfect sharing of idiosyncratic shocks as a result of which consumption of all the households moves similarly over time—was summarily rejected. As we estimated various metrics (food consumption, non-food consumption, and total consumption) of the household as a function of village consumption, it was evident that these measures had a distinct idiosyncratic component. This implies that the vagaries of household consumption that emanated from risks faced by them were not smoothed enough by the various risk management strategies adopted by the households.

Taken together, these empirical results implied that upon controlling village-level shocks, households were significantly vulnerable to idiosyncratic shocks. Furthermore, there was significant wealth differentiated sensitivity of consumption growth. Farmers belonging to higher land quartiles were associated with significantly lower growth of per capita real consumption. Households with access to off-farm income and greater access to credit were more likely to experience higher consumption growth.

Tests of the full-insurance model by alternative specifications that controlled for covariate income shocks and idiosyncratic health shocks showed that households were significantly susceptible to covariate shocks while there seemed to be limited informal insurance against idiosyncratic health. A decade later when average land sizes have fallen and Bt cotton yields have declined, the vulnerability of households to covariate shocks is likely to have worsened over the past decade. Moreover, non-farm employment has grown much lesser than what one would have anticipated, constraining the ability of non-farm incomes to hedge farm risks. The welfare implications of these findings are immense as failures in insulating household incomes from covariate shocks such as crop failures due to droughts or widespread pest attacks as well as catastrophic health shocks at the household level are likely to reduce household food consumption growth. Therefore, in the absence of well-functioning formal insurance markets, the role of PDS in safeguarding the food security of households is commendable.

Studying the relationship between consumption and income of both cultivator and non-cultivator households in the third round of our study

(2019–2021), share of PDS food grains (wheat and rice) in food grain consumption of households had a significant negative association with both non-food and food consumption. This suggests that relatively less well-off households (who have a greater dependence on PDS cereals rather than market-purchased ones) are vulnerable in terms of their consumption being lower but the access to PDS entitlements at subsidized rates has safeguarded such households' food grain consumption needs.[54] Even for non-cultivator households, the relationship between consumption and income was found to be positive and significant. However, own income for food consumption of cultivator households was not statistically significant, suggesting that food security concerns were greater for non-cultivator households. In fact, none of the households in the surveys during the pandemic year reported food insecurity. There were however a few cases of households skipping a meal or two due to acute liquidity constraints on account of income shocks; however, there was no such incidence of transforming into chronic food insecurity. That food consumption did not significantly influence household income however does not rule out the risk of food inflation—particularly for the cash crop growing households who have significant dependence on the market for purchase of food grains such as rice and wheat. Moreover, even though dependence on PDS is high, those concerned about poor quality of the food grains provided under the scheme end up buying at market rates.[55]

However, there are several observations about the farmer household as a consumption unit rather than a production unit alone that warrants attention. As discussed earlier, the region has experienced devastating droughts, natural calamities, and epidemics over the long historical period covered in Chapters 1 and 2. However, the post-independence era has also witnessed slow-onset disasters like droughts that aggravate crop failures. Although the immediate concerns of scarcity and food shortages accompanying earlier droughts and disasters have been ameliorated to a large extent, the resultant damages and losses gnaw off large parts of household savings and asset base.[56]

Coping strategies such as asset sales and dissaving also affect the household's ability to invest in improving farm productivity. If households experience asset depletion to pay off debts, their ability to raise capital from formal institutions is severely constrained. Landlessness has often been an outcome of cyclical drought, and in the absence of remunerative alternatives individuals from these households usually migrate for informal employment in urban areas. However, in cotton economies that provide considerable employment over an extended period, the tendency to migrate due to landlessness in the villages has been low compared to other regions such as Marathwada. Droughts nevertheless dent the demand for agricultural labour on the farms. Though horticultural crops are not grown widely in the study villages, few who have grown horticultural crops in the past report excess heat as a risk factor.

Over the decade, we have witnessed the seasonal variations in households' fortunes through income fluctuations. These fluctuations are in fact nested in cyclical fluctuations including drought cycles and business cycles. To understand the long-term welfare consequences of these risks, it is important to learn from the severity of these shocks on the economic mobility of households. Often these shocks are reinforced by institutional changes that accentuate entitlement failures as discussed earlier. There have been few attempts at documenting downward mobility due to a series of farm losses in drought-prone areas of Maharashtra. Moreover, it is not well understood how institutional change and weather shocks affect farmers' welfare over a prolonged period.

A recent account from the neighbouring Marathwada demonstrates how institutional factors such as land ceiling laws enacted in the mid-1970s interacted with social norms and sequence of farm losses in the downward mobility of a Patil household belonging to the Maratha community. The household that had farmland ownership of 400 acres in the 1970s experienced its ownership fall to less than 10 acres in 2020 due to the land reforms as well as recurrent farm losses. Social norms four decades ago also discouraged upper caste women who also happened to be from a higher class from taking up agricultural work following widowhood. Such tendencies motivated asset sales including land.[57] Losses from attempts at entrepreneurship of farmers are also often not chronicled. Although a few cultivator households and fewer non-cultivator villages in the Wardha and Yavatmal villages have cattle, many do not consider cattle as an asset in a farm enterprise. Localized dairy activities have gained attention but the milk cooperatives in the region have not developed to the extent one notices in Gujarat or even in western Maharashtra. Sourcing quality cattle feed, veterinary expenses, and logistical considerations often deter households from undertaking dairy activities. Aggregation mechanisms to develop the poultry business in the region as part of the state's plans of 'yellow revolution' also hold immense potential, particularly for women SHGs. The neighbouring state of Telangana undoubtedly offers stiff competition but assured markets and capital support are vital for encouraging rural entrepreneurs.

While crop insurance payouts have been meagre or absent, the state nonetheless has continued the provision of financial assistance to distressed farmers in the aftermath of large-scale losses in the administrative divisions. Vidarbha has received ex gratia assistance from the state government for crop damages in the recent past. Since the damage assessment is based on average damages per acre basis, and there is an upper limit of around 2 hectares per farmer, compensations usually fall short of the actual damages considerably. Continual demands for damage compensation following a round of financial assistance is also not uncommon. Further, loss of productive capacity goes beyond damages incurred in a growing season, and such compensations that are received after a lag, often fail to safeguard farmers from borrowing at higher interest rates. The role of the state in aiding farmers in times of financial hardship however cannot be ignored. From 2016, the Vasantrao Naik Sheti Swavlamban Mission (VNSSM) set up by the Government of Maharashtra's (GoM's) attempts to ameliorate farmers' suicides by provision of new crop loans of 0.4 trillion rupees to all farmers with the financial support of the National Bank for Agriculture and Development (NABARD) and the state government. It also attempts to restructure institutional credit. There has been a thrust on the completion of pending irrigation (borewell) works in farmlands and food and health security schemes. In addition, as mentioned in Chapter 3, debt waivers and debt relief schemes were implemented in 1990 and 2008 by the central government, and in 2017 by the state government. Despite these 'packages' being politically motivated, they serve as a lifeline to the beneficiaries. However, access to formal credit remains a challenge for smallholders and concerns about these waivers affecting credit discipline are also often heard of.

Farmers have been provided with frequent assistance due to crop damages. While 2008 and 2009 were drought years triggering financial assistance from the state, 2011 also resulted in widespread crop damages due to prolonged dry spells. In 2013, Vidarbha received 6.42 billion rupees for damages in the 2011–2012 agricultural season. In 2014, drought assistance was much higher, and 2015 and 2018 also witnessed adverse crop outcomes that brought in assistance.[58] Over and above the challenges faced due to the pandemic, 2020 and 2021 have also not been favourable for agriculture in the *taluka*s owing to unseasonal and excess rains affecting cotton and soybean. State support also takes the form of waivers of electricity bills for agricultural purposes and waiver of educational fees in public schools and colleges.

CONCLUSION

Having arrived at the conclusion that crises have been a perennial feature of Vidarbha's agriculture for several reasons as described in the preceding chapters, in this chapter we analysed the risks by focusing on insights from our longitudinal study of households in the villages of Wardha and Yavatmal. We also explored how variability around mean and 'adverse shocks' in the form of deviation of yield from a specified level of village mean yield affects cultivator households' welfare over time.

We find that as in the centuries before (Chapters 1 and 2) there are significant production risks involved in cultivation that are particularly related to weather variability. Deficit rains as well as excess and untimely rains result in considerable losses quite frequently. Over the period of our analysis based on survey data, that is 2009–2020, there is significant variability in yield of various crops. In particular, soybean cultivation has become particularly unpredictable in terms of yields obtained by the farmer. A major source of poor yields in soybean in the past decade is the poor quality of seeds. Cotton yields seem more stable but have started to decline since the emergence of high PBW pressure in the region. This is striking given the near universal adoption of Bt cotton in the study villages for nearly two decades as discussed in Chapter 5.

Apart from the yield risk, prices too vary due to extant market risks and policy changes related to MSP and public procurement. In the context of price risks for Vidarbha's cotton farmers, an element of continuity with its colonial past is the constant presence of downward risk in cotton prices due to deeper trade inter-linkages. In the post-colonial period, India's compliance with WTO rules has indisputably exposed farmers to greater uncertainty in cotton prices within a trend of declining global prices in the past three decades in particular. Since the WTO policies regarding price support for farmers is inherently skewed against developing country agriculture in comparison to developed countries such as the United States, farmers' gamble with cotton is anchored in their hopes of getting a windfall in an average lower price and average loss in cultivation as the baseline. In essence, what matters to the farmer is the variability in incomes. With more liberalization of procurement, the 'natural' hedge that was existent between the prices and yields have reduced.[59] This means that there are farmers who could face both low yield shocks and price shocks in a year. We find that the income variability is increasing among the small and marginal farmers, which is a cause of concern. In Chapter 4, we have already seen that small and marginal farmers experience higher income variability compared to large farmers. Since the dismantling of the MCPS, farmers continue to express their vulnerability to downside price risk. In fact, our findings suggest that downside price risk is perceived as the most critical risk factor rather than yield variability or other risk factors. That such unmitigated risks exist unaddressed in the twenty-first century raises several questions.

There has been a failure of insurance markets over the period of analysis. Be it the innovative Weather-Based Crop Insurance Scheme (WBCIS) or the Modified National Agricultural Insurance Scheme (MNAIS) or its latest version, the Pradhan Mantri Fasal Bima Yojana (PMFBY), fundamental issues in design and implementation of weather and agricultural insurance remain unaddressed. During a field visit to Yavatmal in 2018 we were informed about the case of how some insurance company personnel was beaten up by farmers and a first information report (FIR) was filed against the private insurer for failing to pay claims despite significant losses experienced by the farmer. The inability of market-based insurance to protect farm incomes in the region warrants attention. In a randomized controlled trial (RCT) study in villages where we installed automated AWS, farmers are sensitive to flaws in the weather insurance contract design. Households routinely adapt to weather and income variability and follow various risk management strategies to cope with shocks whenever they arise. Both systematic and idiosyncratic shocks continually affect household welfare in the absence of well-functioning insurance markets.

The set of findings in this chapter suggests that despite several adaptation strategies, households continue to be exposed to unmitigated risks. Using panel data on households, we demonstrated that on an average households experiencing yield shocks in 2015 were able to recover and even surpass the incomes of those who did not experience these shocks over a short span of five years. Few households also faced multiple years of shocks, often sequentially, and these multi-year shocks have substantial consequences on the future well-being of the household related to consumption and labour supply. Most importantly, vulnerability to such shocks is asymmetrically borne by the small and marginal farmers, and women in the household compared to other sub-groups of the village population. Women-headed households and households belonging to marginalized communities are also at particular risk to yield shocks. So far as representation of SCs and STs is higher among the landless households relative to other caste groups in the villages, their vulnerability and risk coping strategies are of immense significance. Indeed, there was improvement in land holding position of SCs and STs in Maharashtra until the neoliberal reforms of 1990–1991 due to decades of land reforms measures and strong movements against upper caste landed interests that enabled land redistribution to the lower caste and tribes. However, since the 1990s, tribal movements around protection of land rights have weakened whilst Dalit movements have deviated from land redistribution issues to greater representation in educational institutions and formal employment.[60] The external input intensive system of cultivation not only aggravates the financial risk inherent in agricultural production or post-harvest losses, but also generates ecological risks that are present when agricultural systems are taken into consideration.

No doubt the long history of cotton in Vidarbha has been interspersed with years of remunerative prices and yield improvements owing to technological progress, conducive weather, institutional support, and market forces. However, these seasons of positive outcomes have largely been exceptions rather than the norm. Over a decade of primary research in the region has irrefutably established that households frequently rely on a host of informal risk management strategies that may offer some protection in the eventuality of idiosyncratic shocks. However, these strategies do not adequately insure households in the face of systemic or covariate shocks.

From the perspective of vulnerability of households to unanticipated shocks, risk coping strategies such as sale of productive assets and consumption smoothing through dissaving is likely to have depleted the ability of households to deal with future shocks. Therefore, it is not surprising that recurrent crop failures and limited non-farm employment opportunities trap vulnerable households in a vicious circle of indebtedness and many find it difficult to escape the despair. It is not that cotton farmers or agricultural households of Vidarbha do not aspire for higher standards of living plan for their future and that of their children as do millions of farmers in other regions of the country and the world. Rather, lack of accumulated savings to absorb the shocks given unmitigated risks in agriculture and other spheres of life thwart their plans looked at from a life-cycle perspective. The growing cost of cultivation and non-increasing real income as discussed in Chapters 4 and 5 render the gambles of the cotton farmers unsustainable.

In terms of VER, studies in the first round for Wardha villages rejected the full-insurance hypothesis or the full risk sharing model, providing evidence on the vulnerability of households to covariate shocks. Access to PDS food grains at subsidized rates offers commendable protection against food insecurity in the villages. However, catastrophic health shocks, particularly of the kind that have been associated with COVID-19 hospitalization and death of kith and kin of households in the sample, there are serious concerns among uninsured households to safeguard their incomes. By drawing attention to our findings on risk and vulnerability, we argue that farmers' choice of crops as well as agricultural inputs have responded to the changing social structures as well as improved access to formal sources of credit in general. Any analysis of risk and vulnerability of farmers in the region would therefore be incomplete without acknowledging the wide-ranging changes in the village society as well as role of non-farm incomes in mediating the risk management strategies of households. Also, we emphasize two understudied aspects of risk and vulnerability.

First, questions of class-based differences are of considerable importance given the risk management strategies of non-cultivator households, particularly landless agricultural labour households. Second, gendered response to risk as well as vulnerability in Vidarbha cotton justifies the need for appropriate social protection measures. From an institutional perspective, the COVID-19 pandemic demonstrated the ability of the agricultural sector to withstand catastrophic shocks if there is strong state support and the institutions are robust enough to cope with such eventualities. However, it has regressed the growth trajectory of several households facing health shocks and the death of earning members. In the absence of indemnification from insurance or adequate state support, it is not difficult to imagine the hardships that would have befallen the households.

From a political economy perspective, the risks and vulnerability of the farmers in Vidarbha is embedded in its socio-political realities. At one end, the Marathas, Kunbis, Rajputs, Marwaris, and Deshmukhs have failed to form politically relevant alliances, despite decades of agrarian crisis, in a manner that the interests of the agrarian communities of the region are protected. At another end, unlike in western Maharashtra, the elites of Vidarbha have not forged alliances that can demand a larger share of resources for the region that continues to be backward and suffer from development lags that we elaborated on in the Introduction, and to which we will return in Chapter 7. As households recover from individual tales of tragedy and loss as the country bounces back to a business-as-usual scenario following multiple waves of the pandemic, the course of action for the cotton farmers of Vidarbha hinges precariously on the pathways of economic development and stemming the market failures in formal risk management. They await another season of their gamble with nature, markets, and the state.

APPENDIX

Table 6A.1 Monthly household expenditure on food items and non-durables (rupees): 2019 and 2020

	Non-Cultivator Households				Cultivator Households			
Item	**2019**	**N**	**2020**	**N**	**2019**	**N**	**2020**	**N**
Food								
Wheat (PDS)	42.8	140	28.7	128	41.0	146	31.9	154
Wheat (Market)	383.2	133	457.2	150	366.4	140	418.1	146
Rice (PDS)	28.6	119	30.2	129	24.2	137	33.1	154
Rice (Market)	171.1	53	163.0	39	182.3	29	159.7	35
Jowar	102.4	20	118.5	50	154.2	28	84.2	67
Bajra			95.0	2			37.5	2
Maize			40.0	1				
Tur	232.8	182	217.7	165	289.1	46	374.1	27
Urad	92.5	12	161.3	8	112.8	9	110.5	19
Mung	98.9	68	87.1	89	129.0	62	119.2	93
Chickpea	96.2	140	98.6	157	113.5	149	112.3	148
Milk	124.0	86	159.7	92	130.6	98	280.2	120
Butter	269.1	11	216.0	44	270.0	27	253.8	91
Other milk products	235.5	20	251.2	34	261.2	33	164.6	87
Edible oil	515.9	176	543.0	164	557.8	163	664.9	162
Eggs	117.8	135	100.0	129	120.9	124	97.7	121
Fish	231.2	74	239.2	51	245.5	56	234.3	40
Meats	360.7	130	402.4	110	399.4	120	382.1	123
Vegetables	348.7	170	332.5	163	379.4	162	448.0	159
Fruits	133.6	45	94.5	66	119.3	56	116.5	114
Dry Fruits	500.0	1	135.0	8	140.0	1	140.0	16
Sugar	238.1	179	232.2	165	263.6	164	254.5	162
Garlic	125.5	162	116.6	164	119.9	152	234.9	162

(*continued*)

Table 6A.1 *(continued)*

Item	Non-Cultivator Households				Cultivator Households			
	2019	N	2020	N	2019	N	2020	N
Spices	155.0	182	164.3	166	174.0	170	244.3	162
Tea	106.9	170	79.3	160	114.4	154	102.7	161
Other groceries	334.5	182	498.6	165	396.3	166	565.7	162
Supari/Tobacco	77.4	70	308.4	95	83.9	71	265.4	110
Cigarette/*Bidi*	262.5	2	775.0	3	400.0	2	256.7	3
Alcohol	272.0	42	268.9	36	289.4	32	485.4	41
Outside food	250.6	32	236.8	19	242.5	16	236.9	96
Non-food: Non-durable								
Home power bill	451.9	156	362.9	166	500.7	162	521.5	158
Cable TV	127.5	4	241.7	6	203.3	6	262.5	4
Mobile phone bill	139.9	146	159.9	166	165.1	150	239.0	151
Fuel (Transportation)	751.5	137	534.8	166	783.0	149	495.3	155

Source: Authors' estimates based on data from primary survey.

Note: Missing values have not been replaced as zero. This gives an idea of the exact number of cases used in finding an average of each item of consumption.

Table 6A.2 Annual household expenditure on durables (rupees)

Item	Non-Cultivator Households				Cultivator Households			
	2019	N	2020	N	2019	N	2020	N
Non-food: Durables								
Education	5,917.0	100	4,075.8	164	8,222.5	71	10,805.3	57
Clothes and footwear	4,733.7	181	4,631.9	166	5,920.7	164	3,965.8	161
Medicines	4,574.0	179	4,650.6	166	4,743.0	165	6,519.1	161
Health	1,596.4	179	1,018.3	166	1,886.7	165	1,338.9	160
Social events	5,480.3	178	4,318.7	161	7,435.8	165	4,034.0	162

Source: Authors' estimates based on data from primary survey.

Note: Medicines includes outpatient and doctor consultation fees. Health comprises inpatient or hospitalization related expenses.

NOTES

1. S. Beckert, *Empire of Cotton: A Global History* (New York: Vintage; Penguin, 2014).
2. Ibid.
3. Unless otherwise stated, shocks refer to adverse shocks or those have negative connotations.
4. Cited in J. A. Roumasset, J. M. Boussard, and I. Singh, *Risk, Uncertainty, and Agricultural Development* (Southeast Asian Regional Centre for Graduate Study and Research in Agriculture [SEARCA] and Agricultural Development Council [ADC], Laguna, Philippines, 1979), 4.
5. This practice of depending on *nakshatra*s, or lunar mansions, in Hindu astrology is not unique to Vidarbha. Farmers in different regions have different heuristics based on almanacs and environmental conditions surrounding them, and it is well established by scientists that the coefficient of variation is usually low in the specific period. See U. S. De, U. R. Joshi, and G. S. P. Rao, 'Nakshatra Based Rainfall Climatology', *Mausam* 55, no. 2 (2004): 305–312.
6. A year is divided into 27 *nakshatra*s, a period of 13–14 days. The *nakshatra*s are used by farmers as a reference for understanding rainfall variability across the country. For an analysis of rainfall variability across the *nakshatra*s in a district in Andhra Pradesh, refer to K. Narahari Rao, Sulochana Gadgil, P. R. Seshagiri Rao, and K. Savithiri, 'Tailoring Strategies to Rainfall Variability: The Choice of the Sowing Window', *Current Science* 78, no. 10 (2000): 1216–1230. On how farmers in Madhya Pradesh refer to rainfall across the *nakshatra*s, refer to V. Yogasri Poorna, 'For Monsoon, Farmers Hopes Still Met by Age-Old Wisdom', *Economic Times*, 29 June 2010, https://economictimes.indiatimes.com/news/economy/agriculture/for-monsoon-farmers-hopes-still-met-by-age-old-wisdom/articleshow/6103672.cms?from=mdr (accessed on 7 May 2022).
7. These insights based on fieldwork from 2009 to 2011 are discussed at length in S. Gaurav, 'Risk and Vulnerability of Agricultural Households in India' (Unpublished PhD Thesis, Indira Gandhi Institute of Development Research [IGIDR], Mumbai, 2014).
8. The *Wardha Gazetteer* notes on the age-old practice thus: 'The first picking is called Sitadevi because when the cultivator goes to the field, he makes a small mound of earth, places a little cotton on its top and offers curds and milk to the goddess.' See Government of Mahashtra, 'Fibres', *Central*

Provinces and Berar District Gazetteers: Wardha District, https://cultural.maharashtra.gov.in/english/gazetteer/WARDHA/agri_fibres.html (accessed on 7 May 2020).

9. Yavatmal was included in the second round onwards.
10. The distinction between meteorological, hydrological, and agricultural drought often emerged from our interactions with IMD officials as well as farmers during the first round of our study. See P. G. Gore, T. Prasad, and H. R. Hatwar, *Mapping of Drought Areas over India* (NCC Research Report no.12, National Climate Centre, India Meteorology Department, Pune, 2010).
11. Defining three categories of a 'slow onset disaster' such as drought, namely, severe drought (over 75 per cent deviation from normal rainfall); moderate drought (between 50 and 75 per cent deviation from normal rainfall); and minor drought (between 25 and 50 per cent deviation from normal rainfall), studies indicate that the probability of a 'moderate drought' in the district is 20 per cent, that is, one in five years; the rainfall deficit in the area is more than 25 per cent but less than 50 per cent of the climatological or long-range normal. See Gore, Prasad, and Hatwar, *Mapping of Drought Areas over India*. Another predicts the probability of having any kind of drought in the region to be around one in every three years. The probability of severe drought is less than 5 per cent, that of moderate drought is around 12 per cent, and minor or low drought is around 15 per cent in a given year. For details, see S. Gaurav, 'Assessing Risk and Vulnerability of Farm Households in Vidarbha Region of India' (Unpublished YSSP Report, International Institute for Applied Systems Analysis [IIASA], Laxenburg, Austria, 2010).
12. Effective moisture refers to the moisture availability to the crops in terms of rainfall, less the effective evapotranspiration (ET), and surface run-off.
13. For example, the *Gazetteer of Central Provinces and Berar* notes:

    > On the other hand it is said that a heavy rainfall would injure or even ruin cultivation in some parts of the District, and that some villages in Pusad taluk formerly went out of cultivation from this cause.

    See Government of Maharashtra, 'Rainfall', *Central Provinces and Berar District Gazetteers: Yavatmal District*, 2006, https://cultural.maharashtra.gov.in/english/gazetteer/YAVATMAL/agri_rainfall.html (accessed on 7 May 2022).
14. Temperature, rainfall, and humidity interactions influence pest pressure.

15. Government of India, *Groundwater Year Book of Maharashtra and Union Territory of Dadra and Nagar Haveli* (Draft Report/GWM/2016 Ministry of Water Resources, River Development and Ganga Rejuvenation, Central Ground Water Board, 2016), 12–22, http://cgwb.gov.in/Regions/GW-year-Books/GWYB-2015-16/GWYB%20CR%202015-16.pdf (accessed on 7 May 2022).
16. For an overview of fertilizer subsidy and its implication on imbalanced use of nitrogen, see Ashok Gulati and Pritha Banerjee, 'Rationalising Fertiliser Subsidy in India: Key Issues and Policy Options' (ICRIER Working Paper Number 307, 2015), https://www.think-asia.org/bitstream/handle/11540/11017/Working_Paper_307.pdf?sequence=1 (accessed on 7 May 2022).
17. However, analysis using the fixed effects model of a balanced panel data for 130 households, which has not been presented for brevity, results in lack of significance of fertilizers in influencing cotton yield, indicating that unobserved heterogeneity plays a crucial role in the empirical relationship between fertilizer application and cotton yields in the study villages.
18. The value of cotton subsidy as a ratio of the total monetary value of cotton produced prevailing in 1986–1988 being the basis for flexibility in support to farmers for a country skews the policy in favour of the United States, which inflated its base subsidy to 85 per cent of total value of cotton produced by using only the 1986 value instead of average value for the period 1986–1988. By contrast, in India the ratio of cotton subsidy to value of cotton produced was negligible or negative back in 1986–1987, giving it little space to introduce trade distorting subsidies to its cotton farmers without violating WTO rules unlike the United States. See S. K. Sharma, A. Sawant, and T. Lahiri, 'Unfair Fields: Asymmetric WTO Rules Let US Inflate Cotton Subsidies Must Be Reformed', *Down to Earth*, 22 February 2021, https://www.downtoearth.org.in/blog/agriculture/unfair-fields-asymmetric-wto-rules-let-us-inflate-cotton-subsidies-must-be-reformed-75622 (accessed on 18 September 2021).
19. S. G. Mehta, 'Govt under Pressure to Lower Cotton Prices', *Economic Times*, 6 January 2009, https://economictimes.indiatimes.com/markets/commodities/govt-under-pressure-to-lower-cotton-prices/articleshow/3939990.cms?from=mdr (accessed on 4 September 2021).
20. Polyester has been price-competitive with cotton since the early 1970s.
21. Vasantrao Naik belonged to the Banjara community from Yavatmal district in Vidarbha. He championed agricultural and industrial modernization in

the state and is considered the father of Green Revolution in Maharashtra. He was instrumental in promoting hybrid cotton production as well as expansion of credit for cotton growers.

22. Before the start of the marketing season, MSP of different varieties of *kapas* are fixed for FAQ grade *kapas* that specifies minimum parameters on staple length and mic value as indicators of quality.
23. In November 2021 the Cabinet Committee for Economic Affairs (CCEA) took the decision to reimburse CCI's losses to the tune of 174 billion rupees for the MSP operations it undertook during the cotton season (October–September) from 2014–2015 to 2020–2021. See Press Trust of India, 'CCI to Get Rs. 17,049 Crores for Cotton Procurement in 7 Seasons to 2020–21', *Business Standard*, 10 November 2021, https://www.business-standard.com/article/economy-policy/cci-to-get-rs-17-409-cr-for-cotton-procurement-in-7-seasons-to-2020-21-121111000907_1.html (accessed on 12 November 2021).
24. For a succinct summary of the policy priorities regarding agriculture over the first four decades of India's Five-Year Plans, and the evolution of agricultural and rural development under different chief ministers of Maharashtra, see B. B. Mohanty, *Agrarian Transformation in Western India: Economic Gains and Social Costs* (New York: Routledge, 2019), 37–46.
25. There is no commission on cotton sales, but vegetables carry higher commission rates. Some *mandi*s or market yards do not have these middlemen but have issues with transparent weighing and timely payment of the due receipts.
26. The ban was lifted on 9 March 2011. On 9 April 2010 the government had imposed export duties of 2,500 rupees per tonne on raw cotton, following it up with an export ban on 19 April 2010. The export ban in 2010 was lifted on 1 October 2010.
27. P. Harnetty, 'Crop Trends in the Central Provinces of India, 1861–1921', *Modern Asian Studies* 11, no. 3 (1977): 355.
28. The definition of loss we develop is closer to that defined in M. Amare, N. D. Jensen, B. Shiferaw, and J. D. Cissé, 'Rainfall Shocks and Agricultural Productivity: Implication for Rural Household Consumption', *Agricultural Systems* 166 (October 2018): 79–89. They define the event as a shock as rainfall shock is completely unanticipated by the household whereas in our context the yield losses may be due to a combination of anticipated and unanticipated shocks and after consequent adaptation made by the household. In our case, we first estimate expected cotton yield as the average

yield at the village level over the five study years. This is calculated based on yield and price of all the households surveyed in these years. This gives a better estimate of the expected cotton yield of the household.

29. Note that in order to avoid the issue of potential endogeneity on account of using a household's cotton yield in calculation of the aggregate or village yield, we drop the household specific observations while calculating the village mean. This is what 'leave out' means as it excludes the specific households in calculating the average. See B. J. Mace, 'Full Insurance in the Presence of Aggregate Uncertainty', *Journal of Political Economy* 99, no. 5 (1991): 928–956; R. Townsend, 'Risk and Insurance in Village India', *Econometrica* 62, no. 3 (1994): 539–591; and A. Deaton, 'On Risk, Insurance, and Intra-village Consumption Smoothing' (research program in Development Studies, Preliminary Draft, Princeton University, 1990), http://www.princeton.edu/~deaton/downloads/On%20risk_insurance_and_intravillage_consumption_smoothing.pdf (accessed on 8 June 2021).
30. This *paddath* is similar to a ridge and furrow system of planting referred to in A. L. Basediya, S. Mishra, P. Gupta, and S. S. Basediya, 'Performance of Ridge and Furrow System on the Growth and Yield Attribution of Soybean in Barwani District of M. P. India', *International Journal of Current Microbiology and Applied Sciences* 7, no. 8 (2018): 499–505.
31. The details of food consumption of the cultivator households in 2019 and 2020 are presented in Table 6A.1 and Table 6A.2.
32. For the predictions of movement out of cotton and into soybean in Vidarbha, see R. Ramakumar, K. Raut, and T. Kamble, 'Moving Out of Cotton: Notes from a Longitudinal Survey in Two Vidarbha Villages', *Review of Agrarian Studies* 7, no. 1 (2017); and M. Menon and Uzramma, *A Frayed History: The Journey of Cotton in India* (New Delhi: Oxford University Press, 2017).
33. Choice bracketing is a behavioural aspect popularized by the Nobel prize winning behavioural economist Richard Thaler. For a reference to the concept and in particular an explanation of how bracketing of gambles influences the attractiveness of bets, refer to Richard Thaler, 'Mental Accounting Matters', *Journal of Behavioral Decision Making* 12, no. 3 (1999): 183–206.
34. Refer to World Bank, *Managing Agricultural Production Risk: Innovations in Developing Countries* (ESW report by the Agricultural and Rural Development Department, The World Bank, Washington, DC, 2005), https://openknowledge.worldbank.org/bitstream/handle/10986/8797/3

27270Managing1Ag1Risk01PUBLIC1.pdf?sequence=1&isAllowed=y (accessed on 8 May 2020).

35. See S. Gaurav, 'Are Rainfed Agricultural Households Insured? Evidence from Five Villages in Vidarbha, India', *World Development* 66 (February 2015): 719–736.
36. For a discussion on income smoothing and consumption smoothing, see J. Morduch, 'Income Smoothing and Consumption Smoothing', *Journal of Economic Perspectives* 9, no. 3 (1995): 103–114.
37. There is an extant literature on income smoothing by rural households. Some of the studies that could be referred are S. Cole, X. Gine, J. Tobacman, P. Topalova, R. Townsend, and J. Vickery, 'Barriers to Household Risk Management: Evidence from India', *American Economic Journal: Applied Economics* 5, no. 1 (2013): 104–135; M. Ghatak and P. Pandey, 'Contract Choice in Agriculture with Joint Moral Hazard in Effort and Risk', *Journal of Development Economics* 63, no. 2 (2000): 303–326; ICRISAT, *Socioeconomic Constraints to Development of Semi-arid Tropical Agriculture* (Hyderabad: ICRISAT, 1979); and D. Newbery and J. Stiglitz, *The Theory of Commodity Price Stabilisation: A Study in the Economics of Risk* (Oxford: Clarendon Press, 1981).
38. For inefficiencies involved in income smoothing, refer to S. Dercon, ed., *Insurance against Poverty* (Oxford: Oxford University Press, 2005); S. Dercon, 'Risk, Crop Choice, and Savings: Evidence from Tanzania', *Economic Development and Cultural Change* 44, no. 3 (1996): 485–513.
39. The distributional consequences are explored in J. Jalan and M. Ravallion, 'Are the Poor Less Well Insured? Evidence on Vulnerability to Income Risk in Rural China' (Policy Research Working Paper no. 1863, Development Research Group, The World Bank, Washington, DC, 1997); and M. R. Rosenzweig and H. Binswanger, 'Wealth, Weather Risk and the Composition and Profitability of Agricultural Investments', *Economic Journal* 103, no. 416 (1993): 56–78.
40. Consumption smoothing is explored in A. Deaton, 'Saving and Liquidity Constraints', *Econometrica* 59, no. 5 (1991): 1221–1248; M. R. Rosenzweig and K. Wolpin, 'Credit Market Constraints, Consumption Smoothing, and the Accumulation of Durable Production Assets in Low Income Countries: Investments in Bullocks in India', *Journal of Political Economy* 101, no. 2 (1993): 223–244; R. Townsend, 'Consumption Insurance: An Evaluation of Risk-Bearing Systems in Low-Income Countries', *Journal of Economic Perspectives* 9, no. 3 (1995): 83–102.

41. For adjustment in the form of asset depletion in the Indian context, see asset depletion and other risk management strategies explored in detail in N. Jodha, 'Effectiveness of Farmers' Adjustment to Risk', *Economic and Political Weekly* 13, no. 25 (1978): A38–A48. This theme is further developed in Deaton, 'Saving and Liquidity Constraints'; M. Fafchamps, C. Udry, and K. Czukas, 'Drought and Saving in West Africa: Are Livestock a Buffer Stock?', *Journal of Development Economics* 55, no. 2 (1998): 273–305; T. Kurosaki, *Risk and Household Behavior in Pakistan's Agriculture* (Tokyo: Institute of Development Economics, 1998); T. Kurosaki, 'Consumption Smoothing and the Structure of Risk and Time Preferences: Theory and Evidence from Village India', *Hitotsubashi Journal of Economics* 42, no. 2 (2001): 103–117; T. Kurosaki, 'Consumption Vulnerability to Risk in Rural Pakistan', *Journal of Development Studies* 42, no. 1 (2006): 70–89.
42. See N. S. Jodha, 'Role of Credit in Farmers' Adjustment against Risk in Arid and Semi-arid Tropical Areas of India', *Economic and Political Weekly* 16, nos. 42/43 (1981): 1696–1709; C. Udry, 'Risk and Insurance in a Rural Credit Market: An Empirical Investigation in Northern Nigeria', *Review of Economic Studies* 61, no. 3 (1994): 495–526.
43. For studies on kinship-based networks, refer to B. Agarwal, 'Social Security and the Family in Rural India: Coping with Seasonality and Calamity', *Journal of Peasant Studies* 17, no. 3 (1990): 341–412; P. Dubois, B. Jullien, and T. Magnac, 'Formal and Informal Risk Sharing in LDCs: Theory and Empirical Evidence', *Econometrica* 76, no. 4 (2008): 679–725; M. Fafchamps, 'Cash Crop Production, Food Price Volatility, and Rural Market Integration in the Third World', *American Journal of Agricultural Economics* 74, no. 1 (1992): 90–99; F. Grimard, 'Household Consumption Smoothing through Ethnic Ties: Evidence from Cote d'Ivoire', *Journal of Development Economics* 53, no. 2 (1997): 391–422.
44. See M. Sahlins, *Stone-Age Economics* (Chicago: Aldine-Atheton, 1972).
45. Refer to E. Cashdan, ed., *Risk and Uncertainty in Tribal and Peasant Economies* (Boulder: Westview Press, 1990); M. R. Rosenzweig and O. Stark, 'Consumption Smoothing, Migration, and Marriage: Evidence from Rural India', *Journal of Political Economy* 97, no. 4 (1989): 905–926.
46. On limitations of informal risk management strategies for agricultural risk management, see A. Alderman and C. Paxson, 'Do the Poor Insure? A Synthesis of Literature on Risk and Consumption in Developing Countries' (Policy Research Working Paper no. 1008, The World Bank, Washington, DC, 1992); T. S. Walker and J. G. Ryan, *Village and Household Economies*

in India's Semi-Arid Tropics (Baltimore: Johns Hopkins University Press, 1990).

47. See S. Gaurav and V. Chaudhary, 'Do Farmers Care about Basis Risk? Evidence from a Field Experiment in India', *Climate Risk Management* 27 (2020).
48. See S. Gaurav, S. Cole, and J. Tobacman, 'Marketing Complex Financial Products in Emerging Markets: Evidence from Rainfall Insurance in India', special issue, *Journal of Marketing Research* 48 (2011): 150–162; Gaurav, 'Risk and Vulnerability among Agricultural Households in India'.
49. There are three important perspectives of vulnerability that have shaped empirical work in the economics literature, namely, vulnerability as expected poverty (VEP); vulnerability as low expected-utility (VEU); and, vulnerability as uninsured exposure to risks (VER) (Hoddinott and Quisumbing 2003a; Hoogeveen et al. 2004). According to the VEP theory, vulnerability of a household can be measured in two ways. First, vulnerability can be measured as the probability of the household's consumption level falling below a poverty line at a future point of time (Shubham Chaudhuri, Jyotsna Jalan, and Asep Suryahadi, 'Assessing Household Vulnerability to Poverty from Cross-Sectional Data: A Methodology and Estimates from Indonesia' [Department of Economics Discussion Paper Number 0102-52, Columbia University, 2002], https://academiccommons.columbia.edu/doi/10.7916/D85149GF [accessed on 8 May 2022]; L. Christiansen, V. Hoffmann, and A. Sarris, 'Gauging the Welfare Effects of Shocks in Rural Tanzania' [Policy Research Working Paper 4406, The World Bank, Washington, DC, 2007]; L. S. Chiwula, R. Witt, and H. Waibel, 'An Asset-Based Approach to Vulnerability: The Case of Small-Scale Fishing Areas in Cameroon and Nigeria', *Journal of Development Studies* 47, no. 2 [2011]: 338–353). Second, vulnerability of a household could be specified as a risk in the sense of the probability of observing at least one spell of poverty (Lant Pritchett, Asep Suryahadi, and Sudarno Sumarto, 'Quantifying Vulnerability to Poverty: A Proposed Measure, Applied to Indonesia' [Policy Research Working Paper No. 2437, The World Bank, 2000], https://documents1.worldbank.org/curated/en/131651468751147913/pdf/multi-page.pdf [accessed on 8 May 2022]; Cesar Calvo and Stefan Dercon, 'Measuring Individual Vulnerability' [Department of Economics Discussion Paper Number 229, University of Oxford, 2005], https://www.rrojasdatabank.info/calvo.pdf [accessed on 8 May 2022]; L. J. Christiaensen and K. Subbarao, 'Toward an Understanding of Household

Vulnerability in Rural Kenya', *Journal of African Economies* 14, no. 4 [2005]: 520–558; Isabel Günther and Kenneth Harttgen, 'Estimating Households Vulnerability to Idiosyncratic and Covariate Shocks: A Novel Method Applied in Madagascar', *World Development* 37, no. 7 [2009]: 1222–1234). This approach is forward looking in the sense that it estimates the future vulnerability of individuals or households and measures their susceptibility to future poverty. According to the VEU theory, vulnerability is defined with reference to the utility derived from some level of certainty-equivalent consumption; at and above which the household would not be considered vulnerable (Ethan Ligon and Laura Schechter, 'Measuring Vulnerability: The Director's Cut' [Discussion Paper No. 2002/86, UNU/WIDER, 2002], https://www.wider.unu.edu/sites/default/files/dp2002-86.pdf [accessed on 8 May 2022]; Ethan Ligon and Laura Schechter, 'Measuring Vulnerability', *Economic Journal* 113 [March 2003]: C95–C102).

50. See N. Brooks, 'Vulnerability, Risk and Adaptation: A Conceptual Framework' (working paper no. 38, Tyndall Centre for Climate Change Research, University of East Anglia, Norwich, 2003); K. L. O'Brien, R. Leichenko, U. Kelkar, H. Venema, G. Aandahl, H. Tompkins, A. Javed, S. Bhadwal, S. Barg, L. Nygaard, and J. West, 'Mapping Vulnerability to Multiple Stressors: Climate Change and Globalisation in India', *Global Environmental Change* 14, no. 4 (2007): 303–313.
51. See B. L. Turner et al., 'A Framework for Vulnerability Analysis in Sustainability Science', *Proceedings of the National Academy of Sciences of the United States of America* 100, no. 4 (2003): 8074–8079.
52. See A. K. Sen, *Poverty and Famines: An Essay on Entitlements and Deprivation* (Oxford: Clarendon Press, 1982); A. K. Sen, *Commodities and Capabilities* (Amsterdam: North Holland, 1985); A. K. Sen, 'Food Economics and Entitlements' (WIDER Working Paper no. 1, World Institute for Development Economics Research, Helsinki, 1986).
53. Based on the findings of Gaurav, 'Risk and Vulnerability of Agricultural Households in India'; and S. Gaurav, 'Are Rainfed Agricultural Households Insured? Evidence from Five Villages in Vidarbha, India', *World Development* 66 (February 2015): 719–736.
54. Since implementation of the NFSA (National Food Security Act) in 2016, rules of the public distribution system (PDS) have changed. In contrast with multiple ration card categories of different colours as well as different entitlements for each type, the new system of PDS simplified the distribution rules. The entitlement of the priority households is 35

kilograms of cereals per month for a household at the subsidized price of 3 rupees for rice and 2 rupees for wheat. Non-priority households are entitled to 15 kilograms of the cereals per month at the same subsidized price. There are nevertheless variations in the quality of cereals across regions.

55. S. Gaurav, *IMPRESS Project P2276: Risk and Vulnerability of Agricultural Households in Vidarbha, Maharashtra: A Longitudinal Study* (Indian Council of Social Science Research [ICSSR], New Delhi, 2021).
56. For policy response to droughts in the early 1970s, see S. E. Sukthankar, *Report of the Fact-Finding Committee for Survey of Scarcity Areas, Maharashtra State, 1973*, vol. 1 (Government Central Press, Bombay, 1973), 8. The report documents several famines in the nineteenth century. However, the severity of the famines increased drastically between 1860 and 1908 during which the likelihood of famine was nearly 50 per cent. This was also a period of rapid expansion of cotton in Berar and the Central Provinces and some of the worst famines of the postbellum period as discussed in Chapter 2.
57. K. Iyer, *Landscapes of Loss: The Story of an Indian Drought* (New Delhi: Harper Collins, 2020), 28–29.
58. Ibid., 32.
59. For a discussion on the changes in price-yield correlations and its impact on farm revenue risk, refer to T. Ranganathan and S. Gaurav, 'An Inquiry into the Composition of Farm Revenue Risk: The Case of Six Vidarbha Districts', *Economic and Political Weekly* 48, nos. 26/27 (2013): 125–128.
60. For a discussion on the evolution of land reforms and representation of SCs and STs in operated land as well as average area of land operated for Maharashtra, see Mohanty, *Agrarian Transformation in Western Maharashtra*, 127–134.

7

CONCLUSION

Over the past two and a half decades, literature pertaining to Vidarbha region in central India largely focused on the story of agrarian distress manifested in the form of farmers' suicides, as elaborated in the foregoing chapters. In this context, the predominantly rain-fed cotton tracts of Vidarbha appeared on the map of agrarian crisis primarily because of a spate of farmers' suicides. Scholarly discourse and popular writing on the crisis in Indian agriculture has found neoliberal policies since the economic reforms of the early 1990s and the state's withdrawal from agriculture as a corollary of neoliberalism that centred on removing obstacles to free market capitalism, as the prime suspects for the grim situation.[1] Rising cost of cultivation, falling profitability, growing indebtedness, susceptibility to market and natural forces, and general developmental backlogs are recurrent themes in analyses of economic distress of farmers. While this narrative describes the plight of farmers by emphasizing agrarian distress and farmers' suicides, a mere focus on the grim realities of agrarian life, though necessary, misses out on three critical dimensions of life and livelihood of agricultural households central to the cotton economy.

First, in a production system that has been historically exposed to considerable risks owing to it being nested in interconnected systems of global demand and supply, contemporary discourse has focused on a time horizon that is confined to neoliberal policies and the post-colonial Indian state. Therefore, ascribing culpability to the state and broader economic paradigms although ideologically expedient owing to the proximity to what has transpired in recent times, lacks critical awareness of inveterate historical forces that have shaped institutions and political antecedents of the cotton economy of the region. True, there are several accounts of social distress attributed to neoliberal reforms in the Global South, namely in Asia, Africa, and Latin America. However, the evolution of institutions, state actions, and capitalist development are intertwined in a complex manner that makes it naïve to simply infer that neoliberalism is the root cause of agrarian distress. Moreover, contrarian views on the opportunities created by neoliberalism also abound, a cross-examination of which is crucial for scholarly progress.[2] Second, among the tales of tragedy unfolding in the region in the form of the agrarian crisis and farmers' suicides, there are stories of upward mobility and optimism. Understanding the routine adjustments that farm households undergo to cope with changing environment, policies, and market speaks to the resilience of the Vidarbha cotton farmer. Third, while economic distress is undeniably a significant component of agrarian crisis, most analyses tend to ignore the socio-political context in which the risks and vulnerabilities are embedded. Additionally, treating farmers as a homogenous group fails to account for wide variation in vulnerability and risk management. Often, farmers' vulnerability as well as response to negative shocks has intersectionality with gender, caste, and class that warrants attention.

This book is an attempt to examine the historical 'accidents' that shaped the gambles by generations of farmers in the region getting lured by cotton—'white gold'—despite its dystopian connotations. The central thesis of the book is that the history of the development of cotton economy has a deeper connection with state and capitalism that a few decades of a timescale are unable to accomplish in their explanatory ability. Despite a vast literature on farmers' suicides and agrarian distress, it is difficult to obtain an overall picture of the agrarian landscape of Vidarbha in the past. Particularly troubling is the lack of characterization of agrarian crises in the past, and why suicides became prominent as a form of farmers' response to the contemporary crisis rather than other forms including protests and rebellion as discussed in Chapter 6. Hence, an intimate understanding of the regional history—particularly its colonial past and more recently the post-colonial developments—helps unpack underlying causes of the present duress in a nuanced manner. Furthermore, the book argues that there is a need to shift the narrative in the agrarian crisis discourse from that of a crestfallen farmer to that of a farmer routinely adapting and learning in the face of uncertainties. Indeed, valuable scholarly as well as journalistic contributions have frequently noted the manifestation of an underlying crisis in the form of farmers' suicides that cannot be ignored. However, despite the focus on the grim realities of trajectory of Vidarbha's agrarian transformation, several serious questions that extant investigations have fallen short of answering are: What are the historical roots of the crisis? Have there been persistent agrarian crises in the past? Does crisis preclude possibility of recovery and prosperity? What are the gambles in cotton production in a risky environment? How do farmers adapt and learn in an ever-changing production and market environment?

In this book, we address these questions by weaving together two interrelated approaches. First, we delve into the history of the region and the development of its cotton economy. We present a long historical account of erstwhile Berar and Central Provinces from which present-day Vidarbha is carved out. Over a period of interest spanning pre-colonial, colonial, and post-colonial phases of economic development and agrarian transformation, we examine the role of historical accidents in shaping the cotton economy of the region. Although we acknowledge the importance of specific events such as the American Civil War and the expansion of railways as turning points in Vidarbha's economic history, our approach resembles the *longue durée* perspective of historical writing in terms of its emphasis on long duration that allows an examination of long-term historical structures.[3] Second, we explain the changes that have taken place over the past twelve years of our primary research in the villages of Vidarbha. The historical engagement is motivated by the need to intimately engage with economic history of a region that qualifies to be a 'commodity frontier' to the extent that cotton capitalism and state policies have profoundly restructured its countryside and ecology.[4] Yet at the same time, it also allows an examination of the evolution of agrarian crisis in the region from a political ecology perspective. The longitudinal study allows a micro understanding of the changes over a crucial period in the history of cotton as well as that of India in which the post-colonial crisis has been squarely attributed to globalization, global rules of trade, and withdrawal of the state under the influence of neoliberalism. The rich insights from both these approaches can be briefly recapitulated as follows.

KEY FINDINGS

We present our arguments in two parts. In Part I of the book, we found that the region's agrarian conditions and manifestation of agrarian crisis are outcomes of the complex interplay of historical accidents and gambles that farmers participated in by way of reliance on cotton as a cash crop since the middle of the eighteenth century, which became increasingly commercialized since the late nineteenth century. Chapter 1 dealt with how present-day Vidarbha was carved out of two administrative building blocks namely Berar and the Central Provinces, each with its rich cultural heritage and political history. We also delved into the agro-climatic conditions and peculiarities of the soils of the region. The long historical perspective demonstrated that the region has witnessed continuous territorial reconfiguration over the centuries, often brokered by 'outsider influences'.

Berar and the parts that later became the Central Provinces have had a distinct cultural, social, and political heritage that present inherent contradictions usually ignored in imagining the region as a homogenous administrative or electoral entity. While demands for separate statehood for Vidarbha have erupted intermittently for over a century, an analysis of risk and vulnerability in cotton cultivation in the region is incomplete without a deeper engagement with the region's history.

Since the thirteenth century, the region's distinct sociocultural, political, and institutional antecedents shaped the agrarian economy irretrievably. Following the downfall of the Yadava dynasty, the erstwhile Berar and Central Provinces came under the rule of Muslim sultanates, Mughals, Marathas, the Nizam of Hyderabad, the Company, and the British Crown before India gained independence. We dwelled on the key developments at different phases of the region's history and changes in the political alliances that prevented the formation of stable polities for centuries. While there were intermittent attempts at reforming agrarian institutions and occasional remissions from revenue demands, the pre-capitalist and feudal agrarian institutions had a significant bearing on the nature of institutions and social structures that evolved in the region.

An understanding of the inveterate distinction between Berar and the Central Provinces also took us to courtroom intrigues and political factions involving Gond kings, Marathas, Mughals, and the Nizam of Hyderabad. The long historical account, which by no means is comprehensive, nevertheless clarified several aspects of the Vidarbha economy and state until its colonial takeover.

Our investigation of how Vidarbha became a 'cotton frontier' since the middle of the nineteenth century began with a deeper examination of the geopolitical developments in the region since the thirteenth century. Contrary to contemporary descriptions of the region's struggling cotton economy, the historical account showed how it was a vibrant centre of raw cotton cultivation and trade owing to its integration into raw cotton trade with China since the late eighteenth century. The region was part of a bustling network of markets central to the cotton trade such as Mirzapur and Calcutta. It also witnessed the expansion of domestic capitalism that saw the growth of Indian mercantile and trading centres such as Calcutta and Bombay. Different communities such as Marwari Banias and Komtis emerged as important actors in the trade, commerce, and credit system that evolved in response to the growth of demand for cash crops such as raw cotton. In Chapter 2 we delved into historical accidents that stood out since the colonial takeover of Berar and the Central Provinces, and how it transformed the cotton economy. The interests of the mercantile class from Manchester in unsheathing raw cotton from the region to feed the mills in the county of Lancashire following the Industrial Revolution in the late eighteenth century played an important role in the region's transformation.

Following the colonial takeover, significant institutional changes were introduced by the British Raj that recasted traditional modes of production and transformed the social organization of labour in the hinterland. Granting property rights to the cultivators along with access to credit resulted in expansion of area under cash crops. Although there was unprecedented increase in revenue for the state from commercialization of agriculture—farmers became susceptible to vagaries of the market. In general, the dynamics of modernized agriculture created winners, particularly among the large class comprising caste groups such as Marathas, Kunbis, and Deshmukhs. These classes could access capital at relatively lower cost to expand area and invest in purchased inputs.

In contrast, peasants belonging to historically backward communities such as SCs and STs with small parcels of land and the landless were often pushed to the edge given their inability to cope with crop failures and price risks. These unfortunate sub-groups in Vidarbha's population were the losers in the agrarian transformation. As indebtedness to rapacious moneylenders became widespread, *sahukar* communities such as Marwaris thrived in the absence of formal sources of credit. Indeed, the colonial state intervened with laws and courts to curb usurious moneylending in rural areas. However, growing dependence on purchased inputs and unmitigated risks in cash crop cultivation meant that there was no respite from the risk of indebtedness, and the attendant worry of losing mortgaged land.

In terms of the macroeconomy of cotton, episodes of panics and mania frequently recurred in the globalized cotton economy. It is in this context that there was a momentous accident in the 'empire of cotton' namely the outbreak of the American Civil War in 1861. With the abrupt stoppage of raw cotton exports from the American South to Lancashire, India became the main supplier of raw cotton to Britain until the civil war lasted. During this short period, there was an unprecedented rise in demand for raw cotton from India, and subsequently the rising cotton prices and changed institutional structures in Berar and Central Provinces created unforeseen prosperity among a few cotton farmers. The boom in cotton was catalysed by the colonial investment in railways, roads, and telegraph that not only connected the hinterland to the ports but also improved price discovery of commodities including cotton. The cotton boom created fortunes and contributed significantly to the growth of Bombay. The subsequent crash in cotton prices, although brief, caused a financial crisis and ruined the fortunes of many well-known merchants and capitalists in the city. In Vidarbha, the growth of railway infrastructure and cotton marts fostered remarkable emergence of cotton towns such as Khamgaon (depicted in our book cover), Malkapur, Amravati, Akola, and Nagpur, among others.

Accounts of prosperity ushered in by the American Civil War notwithstanding, cotton farmers became increasingly susceptible to price shocks and financial losses. Moreover, the cotton expansion that was brought about by rampant deforestation and monoculture had lasting impacts in terms of soil degradation and ecological damage, which was terribly felt during the famines of the late nineteenth century. In the early twentieth century, the cotton economy withstood turbulence of the two World Wars and the Great Depression as well as the fervour of nationalism and freedom struggle. Despite the rise and fall of textile mills in Nagpur and Bombay as well as changing contours of the rural and urban labour markets due to epidemics and migration, Vidarbha's cotton farmers did not abandon cotton.

The post-colonial phase of agricultural development was associated with decades of planned development, agrarian transformation marked by changing degrees of state intervention. Green Revolution, public investment in irrigation, dirigisme in rural credit markets became prominent features of the rural economy for three decades since 1960s. Since 1991, neoliberal economic policies became concomitant with dismantling of state support systems such as MCPS, rationalization of farm subsidies, and removing barriers to international trade. Vidarbha's cotton growers undoubtedly faced gargantuan difficulties in adjusting to the sweeping agrarian transformation, whose different facets are covered in detail in Chapters 4, 5, and 6.

Our account of transformation of the region's cotton economy highlights the following significant developments that warrant attention. First, far from being a static agrarian system, the cotton economy has been considerably dynamic. Cotton farmers switched crops as well as seed types for over a century. For instance, linseed, despite the remarkable growth in cotton acreage following the American Civil War, had a higher area share than cotton in the late nineteenth century. Within two decades there was a major shift, with cotton having a much higher share. Also, it would be incorrect to presume that it has been only a few decades that farmers have adopted new seed varieties. Long before the diffusion of hybrids following the Green Revolution and the near universal diffusion of Bt cotton two decades ago, farmers of the region experimented with several cotton varieties that the Company and British Raj actively promoted. For instance, the short staple cotton variety (*bani*) gradually ousted the long staple variety (*jari*) in Nagpur and Wardha villages and Berari *jari* in Berar villages by the late nineteenth century. The colonial agenda of fostering cotton expansion that we discussed in detail is also proof of the important role of state policy in cotton expansion.

Second, over the centuries, farmers have responded to rising cotton prices by increasing the area under cotton cultivation. Whenever cotton production was more profitable, farmers demonstrated enthusiasm to increase area under cotton. In this story, the colonial state facilitated the expansion of cotton by investment in research and development, sprucing up physical infrastructure, especially railways, and institutional reforms to enable market development. For instance, following the colonial takeover of Berar, property rights were assigned to farmers through the *khatedari* system and significant credit market regulation was introduced. These changes were aimed at creating incentives for individual farmers to grow cotton in an unencumbered manner unlike under former institutional arrangements such as *balutedari*, which was the caste-based system of organizing agrarian production.

Third, while farmers adapted to fluctuations in weather and price, their vulnerability to fluctuations in global demand and supply continued to be a defining feature of the cotton economy. The booms and bust in cotton were associated with speculation for centuries, and there were no markets to mitigate the risks of farmers. Derivatives markets in cotton and speculation in cotton trading however were rife. The prospects of windfall and fortuitous gains were mostly harnessed by merchant classes in entrepôt such as Bombay.

Although events such as the Cotton Panic and Cotton Famine affected the industry since the early nineteenth century, the prospects of abnormally high earnings that accrued due to the American Civil War in 1861 transformed the region's cotton economy in an unprecedented manner. The Cotton Mania and the subsequent busting of the speculative boom made and marred fortunes in western India as well as Berar. The conduciveness of rich black cotton soil and climatic conditions of the region aided the cotton boom to such an extent that Berar, or Varhad as the region was known in the vernacular, had a popular saying: 'Varhad, sonyachi kurhad' (Berar is a golden axe).[5] Although there are colonial accounts of prosperity in the cotton tracts of the Central Provinces and Berar, it is evident that despite few years of high returns from cotton cultivation, the transformation of the economy rendered rural households more vulnerable to economic fluctuations and environmental degradation.[6] The environmental crisis accentuated in the post-colonial period with rapid diffusion of Green Revolution technologies. The price fluctuations and the consequent vulnerabilities also worsened in the post-WTO period in the twentieth century. These aspects form the background to our findings from the field in the Part II of the book.

In Part II, we presented findings from our analysis of longitudinal data collected over the past twelve years in villages of two districts of Vidarbha—Wardha and Yavatmal. In Chapter 3, we described the longitudinal study which was motivated by our interest in understanding and bringing to light farmers' risk and vulnerability. We laid bare our motivations for the long-term research undertaking in Vidarbha, particularly our affinity to village level study. We also discussed key epistemological foundations, and our methods of data collection in the villages of Wardha and Yavatmal. We presented the sampling strategy of our primary research, summarized the characteristics of the sample over multiple rounds. We elaborated on demography, educational attainment, land ownership, caste structure, farm and non-farm assets, and liabilities that varied across villages in the two districts. We also commented on development programmes and non-governmental initiatives observed during the period of study that also included two waves of the COVID-19 pandemic.

We introduced several rounds of our surveys along with a description of thematic focus in specific years. To recap, we also discussed the challenges in fieldwork and administering long-term studies in village settings. In doing so, we highlighted the importance of the resident investigator and cooperation among enumerators in sustaining data quality. That said, we also noted that since longitudinal studies offer an intimate understanding of changes taking place in the lives of participating individuals belonging to the households, they should not be merely considered as data points in the scheme of the research. Instead, they should be looked upon as valuable partners in the research journey who trusted us in opening up about their plights, predicaments, hopes, and aspirations.

Findings presented in Chapter 4 that elaborated the gambles with cotton cultivation based on our field surveys and ethnography suggest that farmers follow elaborate inter-cropping patterns that not only respond to changes in past yield and price realizations but also act as a hedge against income variability. Cotton, soybean, and *tur* (red gram/pigeon pea) dominated the cropping pattern in the study villages. Every season, most farmers begin agricultural operations that are associated with elaborate time-bound operations or microprocesses with considerable debt and the hope of higher returns. However, cultivation incomes grew sluggishly over the last decade whilst cost of cultivation increased disproportionately, putting downward pressure on cultivation incomes.

The rising cost of cultivation contributed to farmers incurring large financial losses in cultivation while non-farm incomes have not grown enough over the years to compensate for the farm losses. Size-class based variations in cropping patterns as well as intensity of input usage also indicate that smallholders do not have significant productivity advantages relative to larger size-classes of land owned in the study villages. The cattle economy that was once bustling in the region has experienced a marked decline over the decades. Furthermore, the growth of non-farm sources of income is representative of the structural transformation in the economy.

Interestingly, demand for agricultural labour remains high because of high demand for weeding and cotton picking—activities that have a clear gendered division of labour. As labour-saving technologies continue to be increasingly adopted, women are confined to the drudgery of agricultural operations. This is unequivocally an underexamined aspect in our story of gamble with cotton.

That there are considerable failures in the market for inputs and the cost of cultivation as elaborated in Chapter 5 underlines the gambles that are a central focus of the book. Although Bt cotton expansion was rampant over the years, unavailability of non-Bt hybrids and varieties continues to reflect failures of the seed policy aligned with neoliberalism, since 2017 there has been a secular decline in yield due to growing pink bollworm (PBW) pressures and insecticide resistance. The ecological imbalances brought about by destruction of beneficial insects and emergence of secondary pests has also raised its ugly head in the fields of Vidarbha that farmers have become increasingly concerned about. Organic and non-chemical methods to pest management have not emerged as credible alternatives and important constraints related to drudgery and availability of these inputs have persisted for too long. Furthermore, as in the case of illegal seeds before the commercialization of Bt cotton in Gujarat two decades ago, the widespread illegal HTBt cotton seeds has gained prominence. There has been a crackdown on the practice as expected, but loose seeds continue to be sown discreetly. Nonetheless, the set of findings about changes in the seed options and choices by farmers remind us about the narratives of 'deskilling' and 'performance' as emerging from anthropological inquiries into India's cotton economy.

Chapter 6 described the risk and vulnerability of agricultural households in the study villages by focusing on variability as well as negative shocks to crop yield as well as household income. In sum, due to predominantly rain-fed nature of agriculture in the region, there is considerable variability in weather that results in recurrent yield shocks, and hence income shocks recurrently. In this scenario, small and marginal farmers have intensively applied large amounts of fertilizers than the larger farmers, which has paved the way for increasing vulnerabilities in absence of robust fertiliser response. The provision of soil health cards (SHCs), which were supposed to rationalise the use of chemical fertilizers, have not been taken up adequately and have failed to make any noticeable impact in the region.

Apart from unmitigated production risks, uninsured downside risks in the price of outputs also emerge as a source of concern for our quantitative surveys as well as ethnography. Crop losses inflicted by wild animals is also a growing concern for farmers in both Wardha and Yavatmal, albeit some villages are more vulnerable to the same compared to others. The chapter also presented the changing patterns of risk-management and risk-coping strategies of households. In doing so, it raised serious doubts on the functioning of formal risk-management alternatives such as crop insurance and weather insurance in Vidarbha. Furthermore, using panel data of households for a subset of the study years it demonstrated the vulnerability of households to multi-year shocks and identified heterogeneity in exposure to the farmer's vulnerability by size-class of landholding. Additionally, comparison of consumption patterns of cultivator and non-cultivator households shed light on the importance of PDS and rising non-farm incomes in protecting households against agricultural risks. The findings from the surveys and fieldwork offered incisive insights into vulnerability along the lines of gender, caste, and class.

LESSONS FROM ACCIDENTS AND GAMBLES

It may be tempting to ask the following questions at this juncture: So what is the way of out of the agrarian crisis which is the biggest adversity facing Vidarbha cotton farmers? What have we learned from the historical exploration of the cotton economy? First, we demonstrate how even before the outbreak of the American Civil War in 1861 Berar's (present-day Amravati division) integration with global raw cotton trade began in the country trade with China in the middle of the eighteenth century. It had important trade links with Calcutta through the Mirzapur route. Britain's search for alternative sources of raw cotton for the growing demand in the Lancashire mills resulted in several experimentations with seed varieties that mostly failed. However, introduction of the railways and telegraph deepened the colonial access to Indian cotton following colonial takeover in the 1850s. The American Civil War catalysed institutional reforms such as land administration and infrastructure investment in the region that was systematically transformed into an export-oriented region. These developments were driven by the objective of expanding cotton cultivation to meet the interests of cotton manufacturers in Lancashire. Investment in railways especially fostered rapid area expansion of cotton in the hinterland. Experimentation with new cultivars and traits in the cotton tracts was institutionalized by a concerted cotton improvement programme that included the formation of agricultural universities and crop research stations. The production surge resulted in the recasting of capital and labour relations in the countryside along with the rise of domestic capitalism in the urban areas—in centres such as Bombay and Nagpur. While there was sluggishness in agricultural growth between 1860 and 1947, cotton offered prospects of profit owing to growing world and domestic demand. Growth in cotton production was associated with unprecedented developments, which Tomlinson aptly notes as

> capital accumulation by peasants, landlords, merchants, bankers and industrialists, and some investment in productivity—and profit enhancing production processes.[7]

Whilst there are parallels with the developments in the American South—area expansion, episodes of windfall, price volatility, lobbying by cotton interests, railways, and state support—there are obvious dissimilarities such as the absence of slavery and the 'mining' of land to utter exhaustion of productive capacity. We describe how the American Civil War stimulated cotton growing and exports in the region but argue that its integration with the global cotton supply chains predates the American Civil War by over a century. It is surprising that in the story of Vidarbha's agricultural development, an account of the eighteenth-century expansion of raw cotton exports to China is conspicuous by its absence in the discourse. In sum, the cotton economy of the nineteenth century was a culmination of past developments, as succinctly noted by a colonial commentator, Baden-Powell:

> Muhammadan rule and Maratha conquest, the institutions of ancient Gondwana and those of Northern as well as Orissa Rajputs, have all contributed something to the production of the present condition of things.[8]

In the nineteenth century, Berar began its tryst with the cotton trade. Initially, it was part of the cotton trade of Mirzapur and Calcutta as part of the bustling raw cotton trade with China. In the domestic trade, raw threads locally spun rather than raw cotton was in fact an important commodity from the region. What transpired later in Vidarbha had its origins in the way cotton was cultivated in the southern states in the nineteenth century United States. Among several factors that we identify, a key factor that differentiated the Southern slaveholders from cotton planters in other parts of the world was that the planter aristocracy had considerable influence on the state. This enabled them to lobby with the state for expansion of slavery in the new territories where cotton growth took place. It also positioned them strategically to bargain with the state for improved infrastructure such as roads and railroads.[9] The American Civil War of 1861–1865 'saw the planter aristocracy crushed by the industrial giant of the North'.[10] The decline in cotton trade from America and need for cotton accelerated the spread of cotton in Vidarbha.

The proliferation of cotton cultivation and trade exposed farmers and other actors in the global supply chain to cycles of boom and bust. It also deeply entrenched the dependence on credit for growing this cash crop, which in turn aggravated vulnerability to shocks. The expansion of area under cotton came at the cost of environmental and ecological degradation. The unprecedented expansion was attained by widespread deforestation and bringing wastelands under the plough—a land use transformation that had adverse environmental and ecological costs. The consequences of the environmental degradation were borne by generations of cotton farmers—aggravating the riskiness of cotton production.

The story of development and change in the twentieth and twenty-first centuries strengthens our central thesis. Even following the crash of cotton prices in 1865, farmers continued to gamble in the form of export-oriented cotton cultivation in a rain-fed region. The Raj catalysed the market integration by dismantling traditional institutions and promoting infrastructure development in the form of railway expansion and telegraph, among others. The institutional reforms took the form of changes in revenue administration and private property rights in land, that transformed agrarian relations in the region in an unprecedented manner. Accompanying this transformation was the marketization of agricultural inputs—which was a harbinger of the external input intensive system of production. The introduction of courts and regulation of the moneylender also meant a formalization of land grab by licenced moneylenders and banks in the eventuality of defaults. This worsened the problem of indebtedness for the peasantry. The rapid expansion of area under cotton was attained at the cost of large-scale deforestation and degradation of natural endowments such as pastures and manure—which eventually became part of the market as well.[11] The late nineteenth-century 'Victorian Holocausts' in the form of recurrent famines became a cost that the rural households of the region had to heavily pay.[12] Owing to the export orientation, cash crop production replaced food grain production to a large extent which not only affected dietary diversity but also the fodder crisis decimated Berar's cattle economy.

Since 1947 Indian agriculture has undergone major transformations. Prospective development planning resulted in planned allocations to agriculture and industry. In the pre-reforms period, welfare capitalism and the thrust on poverty alleviation programmes gained momentum. The regional imbalances in development however were an outcome of the national and state level political contestations. The Indian National Congress (INC) was in power in the centre until its defeat by the Janata coalition in 1977 following the Emergency that lasted twenty-one months since 25 June 1975. At the state level, this period was of great instability as a series of chief ministers failed to complete their full term of five years. That such instability followed the long stint of V. P. Naik as discussed in Chapter 6, is not surprising as there was rampant rent seeking among politicians primarily from western Maharashtra who vied for power with mercurial alliances to get a largesse from economic growth of the country's richest state. Political patronage and its consequences on regional inequality was evident in the political clout of sugarcane cooperatives in western Maharashtra unlike Vidarbha or Marathwada. The latter regions withered in terms of development indicators as they failed to secure a significant share in resource allocation. In the context of agricultural development, most importantly, there was an absence of political alliances or pressure groups that could bargain adequate irrigation development, as we elaborate later. The growth of non-farm economy also lagged in comparison with western Maharashtra.[13]

While the green revolution of the 1960s and 1970s set the path for sufficiency in food grains, it also normalized input intensive cultivation. Owing to its massive developmental backlogs attributed primarily to political negligence, the agricultural development of Vidarbha faltered. In this book, our endeavour has been to situate the agricultural development of Vidarbha in the context of these development backlogs. In doing so we demonstrate that the political economy of the region's development resulted in decades of underinvestment in the farm and non-farm sectors. Irrigation projects in fact suffered the most in terms of backlogs that aggravated the agrarian stagnation of the region.[14]

In 1972, as discussed in Chapter 6, the Monopoly Cotton Procurement Scheme (MCPS) was implemented, giving considerable price support to farmers. Since the late 1980s soybean emerged as an important cash crop that substituted for acreage of sorghum (*jawari*). Despite cotton being primarily grown under rain-fed conditions, there was a trend of increasing exploitation of groundwater owing to intensive irrigation of cotton. Following the Green Revolution of the 1960s, this process of groundwater exploitation intensified. History is witness to the policy emphasis on an input intensive system of farming that has normalized intensive use of chemical fertilizers and pesticides in a water-stressed landscape.

The economic reforms of the 1990s did not generate non-farm employment to the extent a planner would have desired. In the post–World Trade Organization (WTO) era, the issue of farmers' suicides gained prominence in the discourse, which unsurprisingly drew considerable political attention. Large-scale debt waiver and debt relief schemes, watershed programmes, and considerable civil society involvement to alleviate agrarian distress commenced given the spate of farmers' suicides. The dismantling of the MCPS in the early 2000s and the increasing cost of cultivation exposed farmers to significant price and income shocks. Since 1970s, cotton lint imports had been canalized through CCI but in 1994, with the economy opening up and compliance with WTO, it meant that cotton lint exports came under an Open General Licence (OGL), allowing free import. Since 2001, raw cotton exports were also put under OGL, making Indian cotton farmers prone to global price shocks.

In profitability squeeze due to growing cost of cultivation, cost of production (rupees per quintal) is often lower than the MSP, and even if produce were procured at MSP rates during times of price crash, farmers would not necessarily recover their cost of cultivation. Due to unmitigated price risk, risk of indebtedness lurches in the corner every season. It is at this juncture that there was a spate of farmers suicides for which the region has gained notoriety. True, economic distress contributed to the suicides but, as several scholars have stressed before us, social phenomena including the Durkheimian concepts of anomie and alienation cannot be ignored. Moreover, innumerable insights from fieldwork also suggest that suicides are a complex phenomenon involving several predisposing and proximate causes.[15]

Developments over the past three decades are of considerable importance in linking the agricultural development of Vidarbha with sweeping changes in the country and the rest of the world. In the early twenty-first century genetically modified cotton—Bt cotton—was approved for commercialization in India, which we consider yet another accident in the region's agrarian history. There have also been several institutional changes over this period that have shaped the circumstances of cash crop cultivation. Prominent among them is the implementation of the WTO guidelines in international trade, dismantling of the MCPS, emergence of cheaper substitutes of cotton such as synthetic fibres, and state intervention in mitigating agrarian crisis in the form of debt waiver and debt relief schemes in the context of the transformation of the cotton economy of Vidarbha in recent times.

Whilst increasing productivity for certain periods such as in the first decade of the twenty-first century that was associated with the introduction of genetically modified cotton, namely Bt cotton, there have been undeniable adverse impacts on soil health and insect ecology; outcomes that have jeopardized the sustainability of cotton production. Although improved seed varieties and cotton hybrids saw widespread diffusion by the 1970s, since the first decade of the 2000s Bt hybrids have proliferated. Apart from the impact on the ecology, the changes also altered traditional knowledge systems. This phase of Vidarbha's agricultural development saw the legitimization of treadmills and fads in agricultural inputs such as seeds and pesticides. In such a scenario, access to PDS, despite its limitations, have played an important role in ensuring food security that could otherwise have been catastrophic in the prolonged gamble with cotton.[16]

POLICY IMPLICATIONS

In the light of the set of findings from the analysis and our observations, we ask the following questions that are fundamental to the characterization of cotton farmers in Vidarbha as 'accidental gamblers'. What are the institutional forces that influence the payoffs from gambles with cotton? What factors render the farmers vulnerable on behalf of their participation in this gamble? To answer these questions, we break up the complex problem of cotton growing and marketing in an environment of risk as well as a structural transformation on the economy along the following dimensions.

SEED SOVEREIGNTY

Historical insights in Part I suggest that centuries of experimentation with cotton seeds predate the introduction of Bt cotton in 2002. While in the distant past the colonial administration of the nineteenth and early twentieth centuries was in charge of experimentation and diffusion of cotton seeds, post-independence efforts on experimentation were led by State Agricultural Universities (SAUs) such as Dr Panjabrao Deshmukh Krishi Vidyapeeth (PDKV) in Akola and Nagpur, and central institutes such as the Central Institute for Cotton Research (CICR), Nagpur. By the time our fieldwork began in 2009, Monsanto had released BGII hybrids. Over the period of our study, BGI hybrids—what farmers were introduced to as Bt cotton—was phased out.

Farmers were made to believe that as in the case of upgrades of smartphones, newer versions are better in the sense that they are more potent in providing crop protection against bollworms. Few farmers were aware of the legal battle that Monsanto was fighting with Nuzhiveedu seeds; however, we rarely came across discussions about the inability of Monsanto to claim royalty fees over BGI given that its patent rights had expired. There was confusion about Mahyco-Monsanto Biotech Ltd (MMBL) having patent rights over BGI, but it is hard to understand how Monsanto could charge royalty fees from its joint venture in India, and ultimately from the Indian farmer, if indeed it did not have the royalty over BGI to begin with. We were often informed about regulatory loopholes including the approval procedures; however, the developments in the Bt cotton story suggest that farmers are not only oblivious to the regulatory realities but also have to bear unnecessary costs for the same. However, the price ceiling on Bt cotton since 2008 implemented by various state and central governments have offered respite to farmers from overpaying for the seeds.

While in the first round (2009–2010 to 2011–2012) yield increases associated with Bt cotton could be observed, in the following rounds of surveys high losses due to pest infestation despite using Bt cotton was commonplace. Anecdotal accounts and scientific studies indicate that the response to fertilizers has dwindled over time across the country, and Vidarbha is no exception to this. Also, a sense of optimism among farmers that prevailed a decade ago had given way to pessimism. As a case in point, a farmer from a village in Yavatmal who claimed that Bt cotton would sustain a yield around 12–14 quintals an acre was distraught when over the past two years his yields dropped to around 4–5 quintals an acre. There was an acknowledgement that perhaps the quality of Bt seeds have worsened over time or that the soil fertility has taken a hit. While our empirical findings (Chapters 5 and 6) demonstrate considerable yield risks including PBW infestation, anecdotal evidence offers much deeper insights into what could have possibly gone wrong with the promise of Bt cotton. Recent research vindicates the emerging voices from the field.[17]

An interesting observation regarding the evidence for and against Bt cotton is that in the last several years the debate on Bt cotton has subsided. In the early years since the introduction of Bt cotton, there were heated debates between the 'pro-Bt' and 'anti-Bt' camps[18] with even evidence from Vidarbha.[19] However, somehow since the narratives of problems with Bt hybrids emerged over the past decade, the academic and scholarly interest in the issues seems to have considerably waned. There seems to be an asymmetry in the context of agricultural technologies such as Bt cotton that we consider as 'knowledge asymmetry'. This means that the top-down research taking place in the scientific labs of research institutes and farmers' learning about the seeds is not synchronized. This warrants attention in the context of evidence of deskilling in Bt cotton seeds.[20]

As issues with Bt cotton emerge and there is growth of illegal HTBt seeds as 'loose seeds' in an ironical recreation of the process that Bt cotton went through, it should be borne in mind that experimentation with cotton varieties that was also evident in the colonial period is a significant element of the story of its evolution. In recent times, while India imports over 5 lakh bales of extra-long staple (ELS) cotton for the production of high-quality yarn, the government has prioritized the revival of 'Suvin'—a hybrid of the Sea Island variety from the Caribbean Islands and the indigenous Sujatha variety.[21] However, conversations with scientists at the CICR suggests that there are considerable challenges in the production of seeds at the scale required for desired expansion of area under Suvin.

DROUGHT MITIGATION AND GOVERNANCE

Famines have ceased to be a concern for Vidarbha, but recurrent droughts continue to affect the farmers in the state.[22] Given the susceptibility of the districts of the region to climate change, particularly in the light of the fact that most Vidarbha districts are 'hot spots', there is an immediate need for policy attention on not only drought-proofing agriculture but also mitigation measures for climate-smart agriculture such as the Project on Climate Resilient Agriculture (POCRA) in Maharashtra. Beneficiary farmers who received financial and technical assistance as part of projects under POCRA expressed a general level of satisfaction with the initiatives in their village. Farmers have also been trained about sustainable water conservation practices.

Lack of irrigation was a major problem in the region and the study villages were no exception. Analysis of the political economy of irrigation even during the colonial period suggests that public investment in irrigation in the past has lacked intent. For a perspective, the Berar Commission as well as Irrigation Commission argued against need for irrigation.[23] In the post-colonial period, although Vidarbha was the first region outside the Green Revolution belt where watershed development emerged in India, the water stress levels continue to be a concern for farmers in several drought-prone areas. Since the Holistic Watershed Development Programme was launched by the National Bank for Agriculture and Rural Development (NABARD) in 2006, several initiatives for soil and water conservation have been implemented in the region. We have not specifically evaluated the impact of the watershed development programmes that some study villages are a part of. However, farmers report that NABARD's Holistic

Watershed Development Programme for watershed management (*paanlot*) has impacted water availability through improvements in existing structures as well as installation of new farm ponds. An innovation of the project is that livelihood support in the form of activities of *wadi* (horticulture) and livestock development have also been integrated. Beneficiaries in the villages have received support for farm mechanization, irrigation, and sericulture, among other purposes.

A thematic survey on women entrepreneurship conducted in 2010 indicates that few women in our study sample have benefitted from welfare and livelihood support programmes for the landless as envisaged by the programme. Conforming to insights from the qualitative study, evidence from studies in distressed districts of Vidarbha suggest that the extent of community participation in the watershed programme is moderate during the planning and implementation phase but high during the maintenance phase.[24]

Another project for drought mitigation—Jalyukt Shivar Abhiyaan (JSA)—was launched by the state government in 2014, a terrible year for villages across due to acute water scarcity. The objective of the scheme was to drought-proof villages by reducing runoffs, increasing the groundwater table, creating decentralized water storage, and fostering irrigation and efficient water use. The scheme was operationalized through integration and convergence of other schemes implemented by various line departments for creation and renovation of old water conservation structures. Structures such as *mati nala bandh* (earthen stop dams or *nullah*), cement *naala bandh* (CNB), farm ponds, and loose boulder structure (LBS) have been built across the thousands of villages with the objective of improving the water table by reducing runoff and drought proofing the villages by 2019.

The scheme also mobilized community participation in water budgeting and awareness campaigns for soil and water conservation. In some study villages, farm ponds and deepening or widening of existing streams took place as per work allotted under the scheme. Focus group discussions (FGDs) suggest several instances of improvement in water availability in villages to the extent that rabi cultivation could be taken up or water crisis for cattle was alleviated. However, despite the good intent of the scheme and success stories, it has been mired in controversy due to allegations of corruption.

Key informant interviews suggest that despite the provision to have a variety of structures, flouting the technical recommendations, costlier structures took precedence due to rampant rent-seeking.[25] Another likely consequence of the rent-seeking, as reported by the informants, is that instead of appropriate structures being built on plain and hilly areas as per technical recommendations, LBS mostly came up, thereby violating the geological and watershed considerations. Several procedural lapses in the selection of contractors who were often politically connected have also been reported. These anecdotes confirm several concerns raised by the report of the comptroller and auditor general of India (CAG) on the planning and outcomes of the scheme.[26] JSA was envisaged to implement the Maharashtra Groundwater (Development and Management) Act, 2009. However, due to lack of regulatory guidelines, Gram Sabhas do not consult the Agriculture Department because of which area under cash crops has in fact increased in response to rise in exploitation of groundwater—in deviance with the law. Nevertheless, as the state got relief from the first wave of the COVID-19 pandemic, a special investigation team (SIT) was approved by the incumbent government to probe into the alleged irregularities in JSA. In the context of corruption mired institutions such as the Vidarbha Irrigation Development Corporation (VIDC) as part of the alleged irrigation scam since 2012, these developments may well be another case in point in the narrative of 'everyone loves a good drought'.[27]

During fieldwork in Wardha and Yavatmal, we also travelled to other districts of Vidarbha that suggested wide variations in approaches to water conservation in the villages. One such insight came from the early benefits from the Jal Gram scheme under the Jal Kranti Abhiyan programme that was initiated in 2015. Attempts to rejuvenate water bodies and community management are important interventions in water-scarce villages that need scientific impact evaluation. In the light of the evidence on water stress in the district, the nexus between cropping patterns and water stress on the one hand and the role of community management of natural resources on the other hand deserves attention.

Focus on cropping pattern changes is crucial but as discussed earlier, the cotton, soybean, *tur*-based cropping systems persist. The high water intensity of cotton continues to be an ecological concern, but without an increase in area under soybean or other competing crops, the onslaught of cotton on the region's groundwater resources persists. With increasing prices of soybean, it is difficult to anticipate farmers to switch to alternative crops despite falling soybean yields. Several villages have some area under vegetables and horticultural crops but there is a need for improvement in supply chain and crop insurance coverage which was minuscule. There is some encouragement from the state and NGOs asking farmers to diversify their cropping to turmeric and drumstick trees. In terms of intensification of irrigation, although several large-scale irrigation projects and micro-irrigation projects have been implemented and projected to grow in number, it is critical to revive traditional community-based water management systems.[28]

Revival of community-based irrigation systems such as *phad* (Chapter 2) systems is critical as local impacts are evident. Non-profit organizations such as Dilasa have been working on reviving *phad* irrigation, particularly in Yavatmal. *Phad* irrigation offers protective irrigation during dry spells. In several areas, it has enabled farmers to grow rabi crops and take up a third crop in the summer. Based on our interactions with the late founder of Dilasa Madhukar Jhas during fieldwork in 2009–2010, *phad* irrigation has also curtailed seasonal migration among the Dhangar nomadic tribes residing in Dhangwardi.[29] In eastern Vidarbha, renovation of the *malguzari* tanks (Chapter 2) can also offer protective irrigation to the paddy growers. Following the Madhya Pradesh Abolition of Proprietary Rights (Estates, Mahals, Alienated Lands) Act, 1950, or Abolition of *Malguzari* Act by Madhya Pradesh, rights over the tanks were transferred from the *malguzar*s and village committees to the government, which took on the task of modernization of the tanks. Despite efforts to renovate the tanks, there were several issues with maintenance of traditional water structures.[30] The verdict of the Bombay High Court in the litigation involving the descendants of *malguzar*s of Navegaon Bandh (Bhandara District) and the state of Maharashtra in 1978 gave free rights to the *malguzar*s but thwarted the modernization of over 1,000 *malguzari* tanks in the area.[31] By the end of the twentieth century, there were over 43,000 such tanks but they have been on the decline given the surge in borewells and dug-wells.[32]

CREDIT MARKET

Over the long timescale, it is evident that credit market imperfections have persisted. During the colonial period there were several institutional changes in credit markets. Credit market regulations, decrees, and laws became increasingly important in rural Vidarbha (Chapter 2). These changes resulted in a tendency of loss of land—the most valuable asset that the borrowers could mortgage for their loan. In the post-independence period, there have been several developments in ensuring financial inclusion and access to timely and adequate crop loans (Chapter 4). The growth of microfinance and non-banking financial companies (NBFCs) in Vidarbha over the past two decades is a major development in the banking and credit market that warrants attention.

Three pertinent observations emerge in this regard. First, the purpose of loans from the formal and informal sectors differ considerably. Reliance on formal loans meant for agriculture and livelihood-generating activities are often utilized for social expenses or contingencies, leaving the farmers susceptible to high-cost sources of borrowing such as moneylenders. Second, the cost of debt servicing varies considerably, and farmers are constantly worried about the possibility of falling into a debt trap if yields or prices do not play out favourably. Indeed, there have been massive debt waiver and debt relief schemes promulgated by the central and state governments; however, the question of sustainable agricultural credit in a high-risk environment continues to be unanswered. Third, while short-term agriculture credit availability and increase in *kisan* credit cards (KCC) may be a welcome move from a supply-side perspective, the ability to avail long-term credit for investment on farm and livelihood activities has consequences on asset accumulation of growth of a household's financial position.

There is an inherent welfare consequence of utilizing credit for consumption smoothing.[33] We believe that there is potential for bundling credit and insurance; however, this is not possible without fixing the market failures in both these markets. Moreover, as we elaborate in the dimension of political economy, both credit and insurance markets are susceptible to elite capture and rent-seeking activities that the state as well as the region have not been able to eliminate yet.

INSURING RISKS

Households have significant exposure to systemic and idiosyncratic production shocks. With less than 5 per cent of the area under cotton being irrigated, the need for insuring crop incomes is particularly high.

Despite decades of experimentation with which design of agricultural insurance, several bottlenecks to voluntary adoption of insurance persist. Though the subsidized index-based weather insurance scheme—Weather-Based Crop Insurance Scheme (WBCIS)—was introduced in the district in the kharif 2015 season, low awareness and concerns with due dates for payment of premium (even for voluntary participants) was reported.[34] The area-yield multi-peril crop insurance scheme—the Pradhan Mantri Fasal

Bima Yojana (PMFBY)—was implemented in both Wardha and Yavatmal in 2016 but it was mandatory for farmers having institutional credit only.

During fieldwork in the rabi season of 2021, reports of dissatisfaction with crop insurance were ubiquitous. Not only less than half of the cultivable area in Vidarbha is insured but also there has been a large dip in this figure in the 2021 season to around one-fifth which was likely due to the deadline for deduction of premium on bank accounts coinciding with lockdown during the second wave of the COVID-19 pandemic.[35] Even prior to this, there had been considerable issues with the implementation of the flagship crop insurance programme PMFBY.[36] The WBCIS, which was considered promising at the time of its implementation in the country over a decade ago, has also not performed and resulted in large-scale discontinuations and dissatisfaction.

Beyond agricultural income shocks, even personal shocks such as health shocks continue to be a major source of financial hardship and indebtedness. The COVID-19 pandemic has exposed the fragility of health systems and livelihood support mechanisms. However, local governance and institutions have nonetheless been resilient and learnt from the tragedy. Considering the variations in risk management strategies as well as risk coping strategies of smallholders and larger farm households, it is important to bear in mind the disparities that uninsured shocks are likely to result in. In the eventuality of unanticipated shocks, there is the possibility of divergent welfare implications of these shocks. In this context, it is necessary to assess the adaptation strategies as well as risk coping strategies of households with different levels of asset base. Although informal risk management strategies are weakening, how formal insurance interacts with informal strategies for smallholders needs careful assessment.[37] In this context, the role of farmer producer organizations (FPOs) and cooperatives become critical in insuring farm incomes. With growing public investment in irrigation projects under the aegis of VIDC, possibility of leveraging on community management institutions such as Water User Associations (WUA) as commodity aggregators can also be explored. However, learning from the history of institutional failures in the region, good governance and accountability become ever so critical for the sustainability of such initiatives.

An important observation that may have implications on community-based risk management initiatives as well as natural resource management efforts is that there is a general acknowledgment of environmental degradation and limits to growth of yield of crops that was not so in the surveys a decade ago. Surprisingly, during the first two rounds surveys when Bt cotton yields were generally high and the issue of PBW infestation was not as pronounced, farmers were visibly confident that Bt cotton would continue to give sustained yields and there are no ecological issues from the practices followed in cotton cultivation. However, with the decline in the Bt's potency, such change in attitudes towards environmental and ecological effects is interesting.

LIVELIHOOD AND SKILLING

The growth of non-farm incomes and non-farm occupational diversification in Vidarbha is intricately linked to the trajectory of India's structural transformation. Although we provide evidence on the growing importance of earnings from small-scale livestock enterprises and dairy initiatives of agricultural households, there is a need for concerted effort to train and fund rural initiatives in dairy and livestock. Sericulture has been experimented with by several households in the study villages, and subsidies are available for the promotion of sericulture. Lack of inputs (mulberry leaves) and readily available markets is a concern that needs to be addressed.

During our last visit to the field before lockdown in the second wave of the pandemic in 2021, we also became aware of several villagers having received substantial sums of support from the state government for sericulture activities. A few have also reverted to traditional crops after burning their fingers in the sericulture business. Discussions with key informants in the villages as well as insights from our data suggest that there is not only a general lack of demand but also poor awareness about the gamut of activities undertaken under the JSA. However, the state government's focus shifted to the JSA for drought-proofing instead of the Mahatma Gandhi National Rural Employment Guarantee Scheme (MGNREGS). Vidarbha did not perform well under the erstwhile Employment Guarantee Scheme (EGS) in the state. In fact, between 1977 and 1997, none of the eleven districts of Vidarbha featured in the top ten districts in terms of their EGS performance. However, there have been improvements in the MGNREGS implementation over the last decade. In 2013–2014, Amravati district received the excellence award for a district from the Ministry of Rural Development. With the National Democratic Alliance (NDA) coalition coming to power at the centre in 2014, there was a cut in resource allocation to MGNREGS as well.

There is gradual increase in employment of the youth in the 'gig economy'. This necessitates examination of the landscape of skilling as soft skills, interpersonal skills, and offers considerable advantages in the service sector job market. Although youngsters have been finding short-term contractual jobs in the growing infrastructural projects including highways and expressways—often as JCB operators or as construction labourers depending on their household financial conditions and aversion to drudgery—there is a need for mainstreaming the Indian government's vision articulated in the National Education Policy (NEP), 2020.[38]

EXTENSION

Digital transformation in the form of access to affordable and high-speed internet connectivity on mobile devices and smartphones was the single most significant technological development following the widespread adoption of Bt cotton. Free message service apps such as WhatsApp have become ubiquitous. Not only do farmers frequently share information about prices or availability of inputs during the season but they also actively participate in several group chats. While a decade ago we observed the *chaupal*s (village centre points which are popular spaces to socialize) were deserted as the cable television access was near universal, cable TVs have now been disrupted by smartphones and the services on offer. Still several households in our survey do not have smartphones and continue to use their feature phones (see Chapter 3). While this offers immense opportunities for price information and marketplace platforms for farmers, inequalities in the form of digital divides, data privacy, and data protection remain unabated.

An important area where digital transformation has the promise to be transformative for cotton farmers and other agricultural households in Vidarbha is its instrumentality in agricultural extension. While ICT-based innovations have been experimented with for decades and the evidence has not been encouraging in terms of scalability of these innovations,[39] there is ample scope for local entrepreneurs to employ the digital medium in meeting agricultural extension demands for the farmer.

MORAL ECONOMY VERSUS POLITICAL ECONOMY

The state has been a constant presence in the agriculture in the region. The pre-colonial and colonial states had extractive revenue systems, but the latter invested in infrastructure for market development albeit to its own advantage. The post-independence state has shaped agricultural development through a plethora of policies, programmes, and schemes.

The subsidy approach to agricultural development and political economy considerations assume significance in the context of withdrawal of the state from agriculture. Indeed, the state has intervened in the dimensions, however there is a need for a reimagination of the role of the state in agricultural development and structural transformation pathways. The long historical account of changing regime, political turmoil, unscrupulous moneylending, and agrarian transition suggests that generations of peasants in Vidarbha withstood centuries of exploitative revenue extraction, impoverishment, famines, and agrarian transition marred with crises, but the region was never an epicentre of farmers' suicides unlike in the past three and half decades.[40] In fact, as colonial agriculture became increasingly market oriented, distress resulting from rapacious moneylenders and unremitting revenue demand of the state lead to farmers' response to crises in the form of revolts and uprisings in the late nineteenth century such as the Deccan Riots of 1875.[41] The nationalism of the first half of twentieth century also saw mass peasant support to the INC in the freedom movement. Organized farmer movements in the 1970s in response to the droughts and impoverishment as well as in 1980s in response to growing commercialization of agriculture following the Green Revolution and challenge to urban–industrial elites demanding remunerative prices meant farmers could form effective alliances and bargain with the state for their interests, obtaining several concessions from the government.[42] The recent protests against the now repealed farm laws also did not garner much support from Vidarbha farmers as discussed in Chapter 6. Thus, a question that begs an answer is what has changed since the mid-1990s that farmers' response to crises took the form of suicides rather than protests?

From a theoretical perspective, two competing models have gained prominence to explain the collective action of the peasants namely Scott's 'moral economy' and Popkin's 'political economy', which led to the Scott–Popkin debate.[43] According to the moral economy perspective, peasants as risk averse and follow 'safety-first' and disaster avoidance. The 'safety-first' principle posits that peasants do not rebel until and unless their 'ethics of subsistence' and 'ethics of reciprocity' are violated by transformations on account of capitalism and the modern state.[44]

Given their proximity to the subsistence margin, in pre-capitalist peasant society settings motivation for revolts by peasants was often to compel the elites to meet their moral obligation rather than to destroy the elites.[45] The latter, however, argues that 'peasants are often willing to gamble on innovations when their position is secure against the loss and when a success could measurably improve their position'.[46] This is in stark contrast to the moral economy argument in that peasants seek something better through cost-benefit calculations on their inputs, in their bid for upward mobility. In this framework, short-term declines or drops in welfare are neither necessary nor sufficient for protest. Rather than restoring traditional systems, peasant struggles aim to tame markets and bureaucracies.[47] Viewing thus, according to political economy theory, peasants are rational utility maximizers, conniving and competitive individuals who act within several constraints including pre-capitalist as well as those societies deeply integrated into the global economy.[48] However, in the context of Maharashtra in general, and Vidarbha in particular, we believe that the assumptions of the two models are inappropriate, if not irrelevant. Indeed, at different stages of the region's agricultural development, some of the attributes of both the theories would be applicable. In this regard, we concur with the conclusion of Mohanty.[49]

The peasants' behaviour goes beyond the Scott–Popkin debate which is based on economics' narrow and self-imposed rejection of alternatives and its incapacity to see more than a single dimension of most phenomenon. The stereotypical binary between profit and subsistence, rational and moral, risk and safety, and individual and collective welfare overlooks many discursive social dimensions of peasants' response to agrarian change. It is true that peasants by and large follow safety first principle, and they go by subsistence ethics and moral values. On the contrary, they also make risky investments and do not necessarily resist change. In the colonial period they went for commercial crops, particularly during the American Civil War; during the post-colonial period they adopted new technology; and during the post-reform period they changed their agricultural practices in response to market conditions. When they experienced the adverse effects of these changes, they responded differently considering the existing socio-political conditions and their immediate enemies.

Peasants made cost-benefit calculations but not in pure economic sense, as argued by Popkin. They were motivated to earn profit to secure subsistence, to maximise subsistence or to make profit to meet the rising aspirations in the changing socio-economic context.[50]

While for two decades since the Green Revolution, several farmer protests and agitations were organized by farmer groups such as Shetkari Sanghatana in 1980s in response to the agrarian dynamism, in the post-reforms era—the one which overlaps with the onset of farmers' suicides in Vidarbha—agrarian distress was not associated with organized protests even by the left parties (CPI and CPI-M) who mobilized peasants during the droughts crisis of 1970s. The inability of farmers to mobilize themselves along caste, class, kinship, and regional lines can be attributed to the contradictions and polarization emerging in the countryside with neoliberal transformation.

The class of rich farmers emerging in in the 1970s and 1980s appropriated benefits of the Green Revolution and developmentalism associated with Panchayati Raj Institutions and cooperatives as in western Maharashtra. Furthermore, rising assertiveness of members of the lower castes in view of their wider mobilization and organization resulted in hostility with the upper castes. Regional disparities intersected with caste and kinship networks hindered development of state-wide solidarity among farmers.[51]

The disconnect among the farming communities was bolstered by the process of mass consumerism that distorted collective identity of the village, and individualism and competitiveness became the norm.[52]

By the end of the 1990s, when high input intensive system of agriculture and shift to high value cash crops had become widespread, differences within factions of farmer groups such as Shetkari Sanghatana, particularly around flippant political alliances despite initial resolve to remain apolitical, and endorsement of neoliberalism and open support of peasant displacing policies such as formation of SEZs, led to the decline. Several sources of discontent among the farmers have emerged from the laments of erstwhile active members of the organization whom we have had deep conversations with. Broadly put, the discontent revolves around loss of direction and shift in focus of the farmer organizations from issues that were central to the agrarian distress to those that catered to political ambitions of the leaders.

On countless occasions over the decade, we have been intimated about the sense of disillusionment in Vidarbha villages with the political alliances being forged among large farmers, corporate interests, and trading communities with utter disregard for smallholder and vulnerable among the farming community. Even national farmers' organizations such as the Bharatiya Kisan Union (BKU) lack a connect with Vidarbha farmers who are apprehensive of its pro-rich farmer bias. By the time our study began, withdrawal of the state from agriculture was imminent and the process of consumerism and commercialized agriculture had become the norm. The pressures to enhance social prestige and safeguard self-esteem in a structurally transformed social context that was increasingly individualized and competitive meant that those in distress were desperate to reach out for help. However, in the absence of collective effort to protest unmitigated risk and vulnerability, suicides became a form of farmers' response to crisis.[53]

HOW ARE HOUSEHOLDS FROM THE FIRST ROUND DOING?

Although most of the original households (2009–2012) were not sampled in the second and third rounds of our study, we kept in touch with the household heads and family members. Also, a casual encounter during fieldwork in nearby villages or the same village would often result in extended conversations about what has transpired in their lives and that of their other family since 2012. Catching up on developments in agriculture and issues of politics were common topics of these conversations. Local political developments often lightened up the conversations. Based on our follow-up survey among these households in 2020, several insights emerge on how life has turned out for their households, among which three major insights stand out.

First, the children of those in households surveyed in the first wave have generally moved away from agriculture. Although most farmers repeatedly express a conscious decision to not have their children involved in agriculture as their primary vocation, it is not uncommon for educated children to lend a hand or two in agricultural activities every now and then. In fact, examining the labour supplied to own farm agriculture as well as agricultural wage labour work, educated children also feature in the list. Engineering education institutes or industrial training institutes (ITI) for several engineering and non-engineering trade training after completion of matriculation have emerged as a popular way of moving out of agriculture or as several villagers put it, 'escaping agriculture'. The importance of education is evident from the high expense on education as well as the mushrooming of private educational institutes as evident from the patterns of consumption expenditure (Chapter 6).

It has been heartening to know that several family members of the original households who were children (five years or below) and pre-adolescents during the first round of the study have benefitted from these training programmes or have entered the formal education system. We wager that education will continue to be the most important avenue to meet the aspirations of households and provide opportunities for non-farm work. However, high expenses on education as well as the practice of borrowing to finance children's education are aspects of risk that warrant policy attention.

Second, farmers in the study villages have increasingly invested in a girl child's education. Attitudes towards the girl child have also improved over the last twelve years. It was not surprising for a few to indicate their unwillingness to continue the education of their girl child; however, such responses have conspicuously fallen over time. There are several cases of daughters becoming engineers and findings jobs in the private sector. Although the average age of marriage in the villages has increased and there is a general sense of acceptability of mobility of unmarried daughters to work, as in the case of the country and the state at large, marriage continues to be the primary reason for migration among women of the village.

Third, prima facie there may not appear bustling non-farm employment in the study villages but investment and more importantly experimentation with non-farm employment have risen gradually. For example, many household heads from the original sample have successfully or unsuccessfully set up *kirana* stores, poultry units, brick kilns, bike repair shops, or retail outlets in nearby towns. Some have dabbled with allied activities such as sericulture and retailing vermicompost or organic manure. There are even cases of some progressive farmers finding employment with non-governmental organizations (NGOs). The diversity of the non-farm jobs in the next generation is considerably higher.

A small farmer purchased 4 acres of land using savings from daily wage earnings. He also benefitted from the windfall in the Mahamarg Samruddhi scheme in lieu of 10 acres of land, which enabled him to purchase 16 acres of land. Another farmer purchased 4 acres of land using daily wage earnings. There have also been stories of failure. For instance, a farmer set up a *kirana* store by investing 10,000 rupees from savings accumulated from farm profits in 2015, but it failed. Another household sold off their 2.5 acres of land after the sub-division of their paternal land of 5 acres. This has brought the household despair and the farmer's children remain unemployed.

We often wondered if agriculture in the region had been under such duress, how did the households manage to invest in non-farm avenues or how did they finance their children's education or enterprises and the likes. The exploration over time and enquiries in villages of Vidarbha bring us to the conclusion that the answer lies in the accumulated profits and the financial savings that the households managed despite the frequent shocks to income. Ironically, the role of the state in providing safety nets despite the state's withdrawal from agriculture because of the adoption of neoliberal policies has been a critical factor in protecting the farmers from 'drowning' in the sense like the one described by R. H. Tawney and which James Scott reproduced in *The Moral Economy of the Peasant: Rebellion and Subsistence in Southeast Asia*: '... that of a man standing permanently up to the neck in water, so that even a ripple is sufficient to drown him.'

UNFINISHED AGENDA

Following the restrictions on mobility and lockdowns in place due to the COVID-19 pandemic, we were unable resume our fieldwork in kharif season, 2021. As we were finalizing the draft of the manuscript, we received a call from our resident investigator from Wardha. He informed us of the heavy losses in cotton because of unseasonal rains in September 2021 that damaged crops all over. Although he and others in his village who had availed crop insurance had not received any indemnification for the losses, they were hopeful that prices will shoot to 10,000 rupees per quintal around January 2022 and that such high prices may help them overcome imminent financial hardships and they will continue to adjust the cropping patterns along with non-farm income opportunities. This and several other conversations with farmers over the years have convinced us that enterprising cotton farmers of Vidarbha, while not much of a rural bourgeoisie or cotton baron, continue their search for high as well as stable incomes through the cotton route which had its fastest predictive validation. There are three strands of studies that we have planned in the post-pandemic period with an objective of extending the research presented in the book. First, we intend to delve into details of tenancy arrangements and social networks to examine their relationship with risk and vulnerability. Second, we believe geospatial analysis of health and nutrition indicators, of women and children in particular, will offer new insights into sub-regional vulnerabilities that could be linked to our broader conclusions presented here. Last but not least, we hope that we will be able to deeply engage with questions of caste, class, politics, and agrarian change to an extent that these aspects are not evident in our work.[54]

While farmers' dependence on cotton despite the attendant worries and risks involved may seem like an elusive quest for prosperity and a longshot at realizing aspirations, it is an important chapter in the history of the region's farmers as accidental gamblers. We believe that several such chapters will unfold in the times ahead as the agrarian transition of the region is far from over. The history of cotton in the region and its integration with the global markets suggest that the lure of cotton is likely to persist despite the booms and bust that 'King Cotton' will put its retainers through.

As cotton outlives generations of farmers, regimes, institutions, and crises, the uncertainties linked with climate change and climate extremes will hold the key to its sustainability in the rain-fed regions such as Vidarbha. It can be conjectured that as Vidarbha's development backlogs are overcome, the trajectory of technology change and quality of institutions will significantly determine the winners and losers in the gambles with cotton. Having been fortunate to have started our longitudinal study at a relatively young age, assuming we survive long enough, we will be fortunate to witness and chronicle the economic development and social transformation of Vidarbha. We end the book with the hope that a new cohort of academics, practitioners, policymakers, and whoever is interested in understanding how a long historical account can be blended with longitudinal studies for a deeper understanding of the causes, consequences, and mechanisms of agricultural development will be motivated to engage with the fascinating story of 'Accidental Gamblers'.

NOTES

1. For a critical review of neoliberalism, see D. Harvey, *A Brief History of Neoliberalism* (New York: Oxford University Press, 2007); and U. Patnaik, 'Neoliberalism and Rural Poverty in India', *Economic and Political Weekly* 42, no. 3 (2007): 3132–3150; and U. Patnaik and S. Moyo, *The Agrarian Question in the Neoliberal Era: Primitive Accumulation and the Peasantry* (Oxford: Pambazuka Press, 2011).
2. See, for example, D. F. Bryceson, 'Sub-Saharan Africa's Vanishing Peasantries and the Spectre of a Global Food Crisis', *Monthly Review* 61, no. 3 (2009): 48–62; C. Oya, 'Agro-Pessimism, Capitalism and Agrarian Change: Trajectories and Contradictions in Sub-Saharan Africa', in *Political Economy of Africa*, ed. V. Padayachee (London: Routledge, 2010), 85–109; T. M. Li, *Land's End: Capitalist Relations on an Indigenous Frontier* (London: Duke University Press, 2014).
3. For a review of the *longue durée*, see F. Braudel and I. Wallerstein, 'History and the Social Sciences: The Longue Durée', *Review (Fernard Baudel Centre)* 32, no. 2 (2009): 171–203.

4. S. Beckert, U. Bosma, M. Schneider, and E. Vanhaute, 'Commodity Frontiers and the Transformation of the Global Countryside: A Research Agenda', *Journal of Global History* 16, no. 3 (2021): 435–450.
5. J. Hardikar, *Ramrao: The Story of India's Farm Crisis* (India: HarperCollins, 2021), 33.
6. On how the commercialization ushered in by the colonial state did not improve the conditions of the peasantry, see T. Roy, 'Unyielding Land', in *How British Rule Changed India's Economy*, Palgrave Studies in Economic History (Cham: Palgrave Pivot, 2019), 81–98.
7. B. R. Tomlinson, *The Economy of Modern India, 1860–1970* (Cambridge, UK: Cambridge University Press, 2008 [1993]), 9.
8. B. H. Baden-Powell, *The Land-Systems of British India: Being A Manual of the Land-Tenures and the Systems of Land-Revenue Administration Prevalent in the Several Provinces*, vol. 2, book 3, *The System of Village or Mahal Settlements* (Oxford: Clarendon Press, 1892), 369.
9. For a historical account of how expansion of railroads in even remote regions of the American South expanded slavery-based cotton cultivation, see Kenneth Noe, *Southwest Virginia's Railroad: Modernization and the Sectional Crisis* (Champaign, IL: University of Illinois Press, 1994); and Mark Wetherington, *Plain Folk's Fight: The Civil War and Reconstruction in Piney Woods Georgia* (Chapel Hill, NC: University of North Carolina Press, 2005). There is evidence of considerable presence of slave labour in the railroad expansion of the South in the mid-nineteenth century. For example, see Theodore Kornweibel Jr., *Railroads in the African American Experience: A Photographic Journey* (Baltimore, MD: Johns Hopkins University Press, 2010).
10. R. W. Griffin, 'Problems of the Southern Cotton Planters After the Civil War', *Georgia Historical Review* 39, no. 2 (1995): 103–117, 117.
11. L. D. Satya, *Cotton and Famine in Berar 1850–1900* (New Delhi: Manohar, 1997).
12. M. Davis, *Late Victorian Holocausts: El Niño Famines and the Making of the Third World* (London: Verso, 2001).
13. In fact, over the past fifty years, it has occurred only once that a chief minister could complete a full term. Devendra Fadnavis of the BJP, representing Nagpur South West constituency, was chief minister for two terms; his second term lasting only three days. The incumbent coalition Maha Vikas Aghadi (MVA) government headed by Chief Minister Uddhav Thackeray does not favour a separate Vidarbha statehood unlike their long-

term political ally BJP, with whom they severed ties in 2019, a few months before the COVID-19 pandemic struck.

14. T. Shah, Y. Mehta, V. Kher, and A. Palrecha, 'Generating Agrarian Dynamism: Saurashtra's Lessons for Vidarbha', *Economic and Political Weekly* 49, nos. 26/27 (2014): 86–94.
15. See D. N. Reddy and S. Mishra, *Agrarian Crisis in India* (Nagpur: Oxford University Press, 2010), and the references therein.
16. For a critique on the food insecurity concerns of export-oriented agriculture, see U. Patnaik, 'Export-Oriented Agriculture and Food Security in Developing Countries and India', *Economic and Political Weekly* 31, nos. 35/37 (1996): 2429–2449.
17. K. R. Kranthi and G. D. Stone, 'Long-Term Impacts of Bt Cotton in India', *Nature Plants* 6, no. 3 (2020): 188–196.
18. G. D. Stone, 'Both Sides Now: Fallacies in the Genetic Modification Wars, Implications for Developing Countries, and Anthropological Perspectives', *Current Anthropology* 43, no. 4 (2002a): 611–630; G. D. Stone, 'Field versus Farm in Warangal: Bt Cotton, Higher Yields, and Larger Questions', *World Development* 39, no. 3 (2011): 387–398; G. D. Stone, 'Constructing Facts: Bt Cotton Narratives in India', *Economic and Political Weekly* 47, no. 38 (2002b): 62–70.
19. M. Swaminathan and V. Rawal, 'Are There Benefits from the Cultivation of Bt cotton? A Comment Based on Data from a Vidarbha Village', *Review of Agrarian Studies* 1, no. 1 (2011a): 101–124.
20. G. D. Stone, 'Agricultural Deskilling and the Spread of Genetically Modified Cotton in Warangal', *Current Anthropology* 48, no. 1 (2007): 67–103.
21. M. Menon, 'The Long and the Short of Quality Cotton', *Hindu Business Line*, 17 May 2019, https://www.thehindubusinessline.com/specials/india-interior/the-long-and-the-short-of-quality-cotton/article27164693.ece (accessed on 17 February 2020).
22. For example, see P. Udmale, Y. Ichikawa, S. Manandhar, H. Ishidaira, and A. S. Kiem, 'Farmers' Perception of Drought Impacts, Local Adaptation and Administrative Mitigation Measures in Maharashtra State, India', *International Journal of Disaster Risk Reduction* 10, no. A (2014): 250–269.
23. Secretary of Public Works Department, 'Irrigation as a Protection against Famine', Indian Famine Commission (1880), 52.
24. For evidence from a recent study, see G. L. Bagdi and R. S. Kurothe, 'People's Participation in Watershed Management Programmes: Evaluation

Study of Vidarbha Region of Maharashtra in India', *International Soil and Water Conservation Research* 2, no. 3 (2014): 57–66. For political ecology perspectives on the JSA, see S. H. Shah and L. M. Harris, 'Beyond Local Case Studies in Political Ecology: Spatializing Agricultural Water Infrastructure in Maharashtra Using a Critical, Multimethods, and Multiscalar Approach', *Annals of the American Association of Geographers* 112, no. 4 (2021): 988–1007.

25. One LBS costs around 1.2 million rupees (around 16,000 US dollars). Contractors are believed to give a 0.5 per cent 'cut' or share of the payment they receive for completion of the structure. Despite audit mechanisms, allegations of corruption are evident.
26. The CAG report however does not refer to irregularity or corruption in the implementation. See Government of Maharashtra, *Report of the Comptroller and Auditor General of India on General and Social Sector and Public Sector Undertakings for the year ended 31 March 2019*, report no. 3 of the year 2020 (2019), 9–18. For a scholarly review of the literature on corruption and development, see P. Bardhan, 'Corruption and Development: A Review of Issues', *Journal of Economic Literature* 35, no. 3 (1997): 1320–1346.
27. P. Sainath, *Everyone Loves a Good Drought* (New Delhi: Penguin India, 1996). In 2012, a Vidarbha-based NGO, Jan Manch, spearheaded the petition against the Government of Maharashtra, which became the genesis of the so-called Maharashtra Irrigation Scam. VIDC was alleged to have escalated costs of scores of irrigation projects in Vidarbha by four times within a short span in 2009. These allegations resulted in resignation of NCP leader Ajit Pawar who was the irrigation minister of Maharashtra in 2009. In November 2019, Ajit Pawar became the deputy chief minister following the MVA government releasing a white paper exculpating him from the corruption charges.
28. For details of traditional water management systems in eastern Vidarbha, see M. Rajankar, 'Traditional Water Management Systems of Eastern Vidarbha: Community Conservation–1', *South Asia Network on Dams, Rivers and People* 9 (November 2011a): 5–8; and M. Rajankar, 'Traditional Water Systems of Eastern Vidarbha–II: Current Status', *South Asia Network on Dams, Rivers and People* 9 (November–December 2011b): 14–17.
29. A. Pallavi, 'A Maharashtra Village Revives Itself by Reviving a Tank', *Down To Earth*, 30 June 2008.
30. A. Kumar, 'Ramtek's Water Woes', *Economic and Political Weekly* 38, no. 3 (2003): 186–187, 187.

31. *Madhavrao Sitaram Kohali and Ors. vs The State of Maharashtra*, on 21 February 1978, https://indiankanoon.org/doc/758777/ (accessed on 23 April 2021).
32. M. Rajankar and Y. Dolke, 'Decline of a Grand Tradition', in *Making Water Everybody's Business: Practice and Policy of Water Harvesting*, ed. A. Agarwal, S. Narain, and I. Khurana (New Delhi: Centre for Science and Environment, 2001), 30–32.
33. C. Udry, 'Risk and Insurance in a Rural Credit Market: An Empirical Investigation in Northern Nigeria', *Review of Economic Studies* 61, no. 3 (1994): 495–526.
34. The Restructured Weather-Based Crop Insurance Scheme (RWBCIS) was implemented in both districts in kharif 2018.
35. S. Arya, 'Area under Crop Insurance Further Down in Vidarbha', *Times of India*, 29 July 2021, http://timesofindia.indiatimes.com/articleshow/84841183.cms?utm_source=contentofinterest&utm_medium=text&utm_campaign=cppst (accessed on 19 August 2021).
36. Jitendra, 'Punctured Cover: India's Crop Insurance Scheme Loses Sheen', *Down to Earth*, 6 January 2020, https://www.downtoearth.org.in/news/agriculture/punctured-cover-india-s-crop-insurance-scheme-loses-sheen-68379 (accessed on 18 August 2021).
37. T. S. Walker and N. S. Jodha, 'How Small Farm Households Adapt to Risk', in *Crop Insurance for Agricultural Development*, ed. P. Hazel, C. Pomareda, and A. Valdes (Baltimore: Johns Hopkins University Press, 1986), 17–34.
38. N. Sengupta, S. Gaurav, and J. Evans, 'The Skills Space in Informal Work: Insights from Bangalore Slums', *Journal of Development Studies* 57, no. 10 (2021): 1662–1689.
39. R. Kumar, 'Elusive Empowerment: Information Provision and Disintermediation in Soyabean Markets in Malwa, India', *Development and Change* 45, no. 6 (2014): 1332–1360.
40. For details of suicides in the region due to the distress in agrarian sector, refer to S. Shroff and S. Mitra, 'Farmers' Suicides in Maharashtra', *Economic and Political Weekly* 42, no. 49 (2007): 73–77; P. Sainath, 'In 16 Years, Farm Suicides Cross a Quarter Million', *The Hindu*, 29 October 2011, https://www.thehindu.com/opinion/columns/sainath//article60641412.ece (accessed on 23 May 2021); K. Nagaraj, P. Sainath, R. Rukmani, and R. Gopinath, 'Farmers' Suicides in India: Magnitudes, Trends, and Spatial Patterns, 1997–2012', *Review of Agrarian Studies* 4, no. 2 (2014): 53–83.

41. For details of the Deccan Riots of 1875, refer to D. N. Dhanagre, *Peasant Movements in India, 1920–1950* (New Delhi: Oxford University Press, 1983); David Hardiman, *Peasant Resistance in India, 1858–1914* (New Delhi: Oxford University Press, 1992).
42. See G. Omvedt, '"We Want the Return for Our Sweat": The New Peasant Movement in India and the Formation of a National Agricultural Policy', *Journal of Peasant Studies* 21, nos. 3/4 (1994): 126–164; and D. N. Dhanagare, *Populism and Power: Farmers' Movement in Western India, 1980–2014* (London; New York: Routledge, 2015).
43. For intricacies of the debate, refer to Jonathan Lieberson, 'Peasant Values and Rural Development: An Unresolved Controversy' (Working Papers, no. 73, Centre for Policy Studies, Population Council, New York, 1981a); C. F. Keyes, 'Peasant Strategies in Asian Societies: Moral and Rational Economic Approaches; A Symposium', *Journal of Asian Studies (pre-1986)* 42, no. 4 (1983): 753–786; also refer to J. C. Scott, *The Moral Economy of the Peasant: Rebellion and Subsistence in Southeast Asia*, vol. 315 (New Haven: Yale University Press, 1977); Samuel Popkin, *The Rational Peasant: The Political Economy of Rural Society in Vietnam* (Berkeley: University of California Press, 1979).
44. For elaboration of the safety-first principle, refer to J. A. Roumasset, *Rice and Risk: Decision Making among Low-Income Farmers* (Amsterdam: North Holland Publications, 1976).
45. Scott, *The Moral Economy of the Peasant*, 192.
46. Popkin, *The Rational Peasant*, 21.
47. Ibid., 35.
48. Keyes, 'Peasant Strategies in Asian Societies', 756.
49. B. B. Mohanty, *Agrarian Transformation in Western India: Economic Gains and Social Costs* (New York: Routledge, 2019), 262.
50. See Mohanty, *Agrarian Transformation in Western India*.
51. For peculiarities of classes and social groups in the region, refer to B. B. Mohanty, 'Land Distribution among Scheduled Castes and Tribes', *Economic and Political Weekly* 36, no. 40 (2001): 3857–3868; B. B. Mohanty, 'Regional Disparity in Agricultural Development of Maharashtra', *Economic and Political Weekly* 44, no. 6 (2009): 63–69.
52. See K. Johnson, 'Globalisation at the Crossroads of Tradition and Modernity in Rural India', *Sociological Bulletin* 54, no. 1 (2005): 40–58.
53. For an engaging articulation of the changing response to agrarian crisis in Maharashtra, see B. B. Mohanty, *Agrarian Transformation in Western India:*

Economic Gains and Social Costs (New Delhi: Routledge, 2021). For those who did not contemplate committing suicide or continued with optimism about a future in farming, the struggle is far from over in light of market and policy uncertainties as well as climate change.

54. For a recent scholarly contribution on the issue of caste, class, and agrarian policies in three states of India namely Gujarat, Karnataka, and Chhattisgarh, see S. Das Gupta, *Class, Politics, and Agrarian Policies in Post-liberalisation India* (Cambridge, UK: Cambridge University Press, 2019).

GLOSSARY

aantarpeeka	intercropping
aar	local unit of land measurement; an acre comprises 40 *aars*
aath-A	8A document in land records
arhatiya/adhatiya	middleman in the market yard
bajra	pearl millet
balutedari	caste-based master–servant system covering twelve trades in villages of Maharashtra that was dismantled in the colonial era
bani/ghat kapas	*Gossypium indicum* cotton variety
barad	shallow soils that are black, brown, and reddish in colour
bazar bhav	market price
beej	seed
batai/bhagbati/bhagidari	sharecropping
bharkali	deep black soil with good moisture retention property
bhoodan	land gift
bima	insurance
bond	cotton boll
bond ali	bollworm (cotton bollworm)
buri	*Gossypium hirsutum* cotton variety

byaj dar	interest rate
chana/harbara	chickpea/Bengal gram
charkha/churka	traditional Indian spinning wheel
chaupal	village centre points which are popular spaces to socialize
chauth	annual tax or tribute levied by the Marathas, at a quarter of the produce or revenue from lands that were nominally under Mughal rule
chirda	flat rice
chunna/wechne	picking (handpicking of cotton)
Dalit/Harijan	historically disadvantaged/backward castes
dalpaan	pulse-based sweet dish
dawran	bullock-based hoeing for weeding/inter cultivation
desi	indigenous
dhep	cattle feed, typically in 2-kilogram packets
Diwali	Hindu festival of lights
dukkar	wild pig/boar
ekka	cotton silk remover
faujdar	a military officer with functions including land revenue collection and maintenance of law and order during the Mughal rule although pre-Mughal references ascribe a *faujdar* to a military officer in charge of an army
fawwarni	pesticide spraying
firman	royal decree
khod keeda	stem borer
gahu/gehu	wheat
ghari	crop produce stored for home consumption
ghee	clarified butter
ghogli	*Gossypium hirsutum* cotton variety
Gudi Padwa	lunar new year
gutkha	tobacco
hamal	porter in market yard

hawaamaan yantra	weather station
iqta	a form of revenue farming started by the Khaljis of the Delhi sultanate in which the holder of the right, *iqtedar/muqti* had temporary revenue rights over a unit of land
jagir	area assigned to Mughal nobles as payment for maintenance of law and order under the *jagirdari* system which was part of the non-hereditary m*ansabdari* system that underwent several changes during Mughal era
jama/jamabandi	rent roll/rent roll directory
jowar/jawari/juari	sorghum; in Hindi sorghum is *jowar* and colonial administrators of the region referred to it as *juari*
kadhi kachra	cleaning of fields as part of land preparation
kapas/parathi	seed cotton
kharaj	land tax that was originally paid only by non-Muslims during the Delhi sultanate but subsumed other forms of taxes paid to the Muslim rulers
kharif	summer sowing season coinciding with the southwest monsoon
khatedar	registered tenant in a village
khod keeda	stem borer
koradwahu	rain-fed plot of land
kkrishi mitra	farmer friends to assist in credit access and debt management
krishi vikash kendra	agricultural input dealer store
Kunbi/Kunbi-Maratha	a predominantly OBC group adept at cultivation
laga	cess
lalya	reddening of leaves
lashkari	military bug
mahine	monthly labour contract for few months
makta	fixed rent lease
mandi	market yard

mansabdar	ranked official in charge of a *mansab* under the *mansabdari* system since Akbar's reign and predominantly assigned to Kolis in Maratha administration and followed in the Bahamani sultanate and Nizam Shahi sultanate; the *mansabdar* maintained soldiers out of his salary from the *jagirdari* and maintained stipulated quota of horses, elephants, camels, mules, and carts; salary was determined by rank of a *mansabdar*
Maratha	a predominantly forward caste sub-group belonging to OBC
maund	20 kilograms
mawa/churda jassids/aphids	sucking pests
mitra kida	friendly insect
moghda	blade harrow (heavy)
muccadum	carting agent and ware-houseman in cotton trade; not to be confused with *muqaddam* that refers to the administrative post of village headman during the Sultanate and Mughal period
mung	bean
murmad	medium black soil containing lime
nagar	plough
nagaran/tirhi/panji	deep-ploughing operations using specific equipment
nav-Boudha	neo-Buddhist
*navaratna*s	nine gems
nindan	manual weeding
nisarg	nature
olit	irrigated plot of land
paanlot	watershed management
paddath	agronomic technique
pan	betel (leaf)
pan basan	water-logged plots of land

pargana/parganah	an administrative unit in the subcontinent, introduced by Delhi sultanate and followed during Mughal and colonial period
patil	large landowner in village/colonial village revenue officer
paus	rainfall
peeka	crop
peekanchi pher palat	crop rotation
phandi	farm equipment tied to the back of a bullock or tractor
pherni yantra	seed-sowing machine
pithya	mealybug
Pola	thanksgiving festival for bullocks/oxen
pucca	solid and permanent housing structure
puja	ritual/festival
puran poli	sweet flatbread
rabi	winter sowing season
regur	black cotton soil
rohi	wild deer
roti	bread
saaldar	annual farm worker
sanad	agreement between government and the owner of property such as land
sardeshmukhi	a cess of one-tenth levied over and above the *chauth*, levied by the Marathas
sarkar	administration and revenue division
sarta	seed dibbler
saatbaara	7/12 land deed in revenue records
shetkari/kastakar	farmer
subah	province in Mughal Empire, governed by the *subahdar*
supari	areca nut

shatru keeda	harmful insect pest
Sitadevi	ritual before cotton-picking
taluka	administrative unit below the district
tilgul	sesame candy
tudtuda	leaf hopper
tur/arhar	pigeon pea/red gram
udid	black gram
vaan	gift tray offered during Makar Sankranti
wadi	horticulture
wakhar	blade harrow (light)
wakharan	harrowing
zila	district

BIBLIOGRAPHY

Abraham, V. 2009. 'Employment Growth in Rural India: Distress-Driven?' *Economic and Political Weekly* 44 (16): 97–104.

Acemoglu, D., and J. Robinson. 2012. *Why Nations Fail: The Origins of Power, Prosperity and Poverty*. New York: Crown.

Acemoglu, D., P. Aghion, L. Bursztyn, and D. Hemous. 2012. 'The Environment and Directed Technical Change'. *American Economic Review* 102 (1): 131–166.

Achadi, E., A. Ahuja, M. A. Bendech, Z. A. Bhutta, L. M. De-Regil, J. Fanzo, et al. 2016. *Global Nutrition Report: From Promise to Impact; Ending Malnutrition by 2030*. Washington, DC: International Food Policy Research Institute.

Afridi, F., M. Bishnu, and K. Mahajan. 2023. 'Gender and Mechanization: Evidence from Indian Agriculture'. *American Journal of Agricultural Economics* 105, no. 1 (January). https://onlinelibrary.wiley.com/doi/10.1111/ajae.12315.

Afridi, F., T. Dinkelman, and K. Mahajan. 2018. 'Why Are Fewer Married Women Joining the Work Force in Rural India? A Decomposition Analysis over Two Decades'. *Journal of Population Economics* 31 (3): 783–818.

Aga, A. 2018. 'Merchants of Knowledge: Petty Retail and Differentiation without Consolidation among Farmers in Maharashtra, India'. *Journal of Agrarian Change* 18 (3): 658–676.

———. 2019. 'The Marketing of Corporate Agrichemicals in Western India: Theorizing Graded Informality'. *Journal of Peasant Studies* 46 (7): 1458–1476.

———. 2021. *Genetically Modified Democracy: Transgenic Crops in Contemporary India*. New Haven, CT: Yale University Press.

Agarwal, B. 1990. 'Social Security and the Family in Rural India: Coping with Seasonality and Calamity'. *Journal of Peasant Studies* 17 (3): 341–412.

Ahir, H. G. 2008. The Commission for the Formation of the State of Vidarbha Bill. http://164.100.47.4/billstexts/lsbilltexts/asintroduced/153ls-8.pdf. Accessed on 6 January 2021.

Aiyar, V. N. 1914. *A Historical Sketch of the Central Provinces and Berar from the Earliest Times*. Allahabad: Pioneer Press.

Aldcroft, H. D., and H. W. Richardson. 1968. *The British Economy 1870–1939*. London: Macmillan.

Alden, E., and C. Swann. 'US Proposes to Abolish Cotton Subsidy Scheme'. *Financial Times*, 6 July 2005. https://www.ft.com/content/41c01c66-ed8a-11d9-9ff5-00000e2511c8. Accessed on 17 May 2021.

Alderman, A., and C. Paxson. 1992. 'Do the Poor Insure? A Synthesis of Literature on Risk and Consumption in Developing Countries'. Policy Research Working Paper no. 1008, The World Bank, Washington, DC.

Aldrich, M. 1973. 'Flexible Exchange Rates, Northern Expansion, and the Market for Southern Cotton: 1866–1879'. *Journal of Economic History* 33 (June): 399–416.

Alexander, S., and S. Bhatia. 2020. 'Has Beti Bachao Beti Padhao Reduced Gender Imbalance?' *Mint*, 6 February 2020. https://www.livemint.com/news/india/has-beti-bachao-beti-padhao-worked-11580901150760.html. Accessed on 27 November 2021.

Ali, M. A. 1966. *The Mughal Nobility under Aurangzeb*. Bombay: Oxford University Press.

Ali, S. S. 1996. *The African Dispersal in the Deccan: From Medieval to Modern Times*. New Delhi: Orient Blackswan.

Alkire, S., P. Conceição, C. Calderón, J. Dirksen, M. Evans, R. Gonzales, et al. n.d. *Global Multidimensional Poverty Index 2020: Charting Pathways Out of Multidimensional Poverty: Achieving the SDGs*. Oxford Poverty & Human Development Initiative (OPHI), Oxford, UK. https://ophi.org.uk/wp-content/uploads/G-MPI_Report_2020_Charting_Pathways.pdf. Accessed on 7 May 2022.

Allami, A. F. 1949. *The Ain-i-Akbari*. Translated from the original Persian by H. S. Jarrett, annotated by Rev. J. N. Sarkar. Vol. 2. Calcutta: The Asiatic Society.

Allirajan, M. 2016. 'Cotton Prices Will Stay under Pressure in 2016–17: India Ratings'. *Times of India*, 9 February 2016. https://timesofindia.indiatimes.com/business/india-business/cotton-prices-will-stay-under-pressure-in-2016-17-india-ratings/articleshow/50919528.cms. Accessed on 24 May 2021.

Altekar, A. S. 1960. *The Early History of the Deccan. VIII: Yādavas of Seuṇadeśa*, edited by Ghulam Yazdani. London: Oxford University Press, 516–551.

Alvi, R. A. 1975. 'Mughal Geographical Accounts of Khandesh'. *Medieval India: A Miscellany* 3: 127–151.

Amare, M., N. D. Jensen, B. Shiferaw, and J. D. Cissé. 2018. 'Rainfall Shocks and Agricultural Productivity: Implication for Rural Household Consumption'. *Agricultural Systems* 166 (August): 79–89.

Amrutkar, P. 2009. 'The Backwardness and Demand for a Statehood of Vidarbha'. *Indian Journal of Political Science* 70 (2): 521–528.

Anderson, G. M., and R. D. Tollison. 1985. 'Ideology, Interest Groups, and the Repeal of the Corn Laws'. *Zeitschrift für die gesamte Staatswissenschaft/ Journal of Institutional and Theoretical Economics* 141 (2): 197–212.

Andrabi, T., and M. Kuehlwein. 2010. 'Railways and Price Convergence in British India'. *Journal of Economic History* 70 (2): 351–377.

Aney, S. 2021. *Vidarbhanama: Early Period to British Rule*. Nagpur: Vidarbha Mirror Prakashan.

Angaitkar, A. G. 2018. 'Impact of Convergence of Agricultural Interventions in Maharashtra (Caim) Programme on Beneficiaries of Distress Prone District in Vidarbha'. PhD thesis, Akola, 2018. https://krishikosh.egranth.ac.in/handle/1/581011762. Accessed on 21 May 2021.

Appleyard, D. J. 2006. 'The Terms of Trade between the United Kingdom and British India, 1858–1947'. *Economic Development and Cultural Change* 54 (3): 635–654.

Arnold, Sir Arthur. 1864. *The History of the Cotton Famine, from the Fall of Sumter to the Passing of the Public Works Act (1864)*. London: Saunders, Otley, and Co.

Arya, S. 2018. 'To Curb Illegal HT Cotton, Andhra Bans Herbicide'. *Times of India*, 14 February 2018. https://timesofindia.indiatimes.com/city/nagpur/to-curb-illegal-ht-cotton-andhra-bans-herbicide/articleshow/62906991.cms. Accessed on 27 August 2021.

———. 2020. 'HT Cotton Seeds Available in Almost All Rural Areas'. *Times of India*, 2020. https://timesofindia.indiatimes.com/city/nagpur/ht-cotton-seeds-available-in-almost-all-rural-areas/articleshow/76271733.cms. Accessed on 15 September 2021.

———. 2021a. 'Area under Crop Insurance Further Down in Vidarbha'. *Times of India*, 29 July 2021. http://timesofindia.indiatimes.com/articleshow/84841183.cms?utm_source=contentofinterest&utm_medium=text&utm_campaign=cppst. Accessed on 19 August 2021.

———. 2021b. 'Cotton Rates at an All-Time High but No Bonus for Vid's Farmers'. *Times of India*, 3 November 2021. https://timesofindia.indiatimes.com/city/nagpur/cotton-rates-at-an-all-time-high-but-no-bonus-for-vids-farmers/articleshow/87495612.cms. Accessed on 20 November 2021.

Arya, V., A. Page, D. Gunnell, and G. Armstrong. 2021. 'Changes in Method-Specific Suicide Following a National Pesticide Ban in India (2011–2014)'. *Journal of Affective Disorders* 278 (September): 592–600.

Asher, C. B., and C. Talbot. 2006. *India before Europe*. New York: Cambridge University Press.

Astarabadi, M. Q. H. S. (Firishtah). 1981. *History of the Rise of the Mahomedan Power in India*. Translated by John Briggs. Vol. 2. New Delhi: Oriental Books.

Atkinson, F. J. 1909. 'Rupee Prices in India, 1870 to 1908; With an Examination of the Causes Leading to the Present High Level of Prices'. *Journal of the Royal Statistical Society* 72 (3): 496–573.

Attwood, D. W. 2005. 'Big Is Ugly? How Large-Scale Institutions Prevent Famines in Western India'. *World Development* 33 (12): 2067–2083.

Baden-Powell, B. H. 1892. *The Land-Systems of British India: Being a Manual of the Land-Tenures and the Systems of Land-Revenue Administration Prevalent in the Several Provinces*. Vol. 2, book 3, *The System of Village or Mahal Settlements*. Oxford: Clarendon Press.

Bagchi, A. K. 1976. 'De-industrialization in India in the Nineteenth Century: Some Theoretical Implications'. *Journal of Development Studies* 12 (2): 135–164.

Bagdi, G. L., and R. S. Kurothe. 2014. 'People's Participation in Watershed Management Programmes: Evaluation Study of Vidarbha Region of Maharashtra in India'. *International Soil and Water Conservation Research* 2 (3): 57–66.

Bailey, F. G. 1957. *Caste and the Economic Frontier: A Village in Highland Orissa*. Manchester: Manchester University Press.

Baker, D. E., and D. E. U. Baker. 1979. *Changing Political Leadership in an Indian Province: The Central Provinces and Berar, 1919–1939*. Delhi: Oxford University Press.

Bandyopadhyay, S., L. Joshi, P. K. Chaudhuri, T. Buragohain, and A. Sharma. 2019. *Impact Evaluation of the Maharashtra CAIM Programme*. New Delhi: National Council of Applied Economic Research.

Banerjee, T. 1972. 'The Marathas and the Pindaris: A Study in Their Relationship'. *Quarterly Review of Historical Studies* 11 (2): 71–82.

Bardhan, P. 1997. 'Corruption and Development: A Review of Issues'. *Journal of Economic Literature* 35 (3): 1320–1346.

Basediya, A. L., S. Mishra, P. Gupta, and S. S. Basediya. 2018. 'Performance of Ridge and Furrow System on the Growth and Yield Attribution of Soybean in Barwani District of M. P. India'. *International Journal of Current Microbiology and Applied Sciences* 7 (8): 499–505.

Bates, C. N. 1985. 'Regional Dependence and Rural Development in Central India: The Pivotal Role of Migrant Labour'. *Modern Asian Studies* 19 (3): 573–592.

———. 1988. 'Class and Economic Change in Central India: The Narmada Valley, 1820–1930'. In *Arrested Development in India: The Historical Perspective*, edited by C. J. Dewey, 241–282. New Delhi: Manohar.

Battutah, I., and T. Mackintosh-Smith. 2002. *The Travels of Ibn Battutah*. London: Picador.

Bawden, F. C. 1967. 'Dr Mann's Contribution to Science and Agriculture'. *Economic and Political Weekly* 2 (13): 639–641.

Bayly, C. A. 1983. *Rulers, Townsmen and Bazaars: North Indian Society in the Age of British Expansion: 1770–1870*. Cambridge, UK: Cambridge University Press.

———. 1985. 'State and Economy in India over Seven Hundred Years'. *Economic History Review* 38 (4): 583–596.

Beals, A. R. 1962. 'Gopalpur: A South Indian Village'. In *Case Studies in Cultural Anthropology*, edited by George Spindler and Louise Spindler, 47–49. New York: Holt, Rinehard and Winston.

Beckert, S. 2001. *The Monied Metropolis: New York City and the Consolidation of the American Bourgeoisie, 1850–1896*. Cambridge, UK: Cambridge University Press.

———. 2004. 'Emancipation and Empire: Reconstructing the Worldwide Web of Cotton Production in the Age of the American Civil War'. *American Historical Review* 109 (5): 1405–1438.

———. 2014. *Empire of Cotton: A Global History*. New York: Penguin.

Beckert, S., U. Bosma, M. Schneider, and E. Vanhaute. 2021. 'Commodity Frontiers and the Transformation of the Global Countryside: A Research Agenda'. *Journal of Global History* 16 (3): 435–450.

Beggs-Humphreys, M., H. Gregor, and D. Humphreys. 2005. 'The Revolution in Spinning and Weaving'. In *The Industrial Revolution*, 126–155. Economic History. Oxfordshire: Taylor and Francis.

Bellwinkel-Schempp, M. 2004. 'Roots of Ambedkar Buddhism in Kanpur'. In *Reconstructing the World: Dr Ambedkar and Buddhism in India*, edited by S. Jondhale and J. Beltz, 221–244. New Delhi: Oxford University Press.

Bernier, F. 1891. *Travels in the Mogul Empire AD 1656–1668*. Translated by Archibald Constable. Westminister: Archibald Constable & Co.

Berteselen, K. J. 1984. 'Indian Slavery in Colonial Virginia and South Carolina'. Masters' thesis, College of William & Mary-Arts & Sciences, Williamsburg, Virginia.

Béteille, A. 1974. *Studies in Agrarian Social Structure*. New Delhi: Oxford University Press.

Bhagat, A. 2022. 'Stephen Hislop: Discovering the Wonders of Central India'. *Live History India*, 19 May 2022. https://www.livehistoryindia.com/story/people/stephen-hislop. Accessed on 25 October 2022.

Bhambi, R. P. 2016. *The Great Indian Peninsula Railway: A Journey through Time (1853–1871)*. New Delhi: Bharti Publications.

Binswanger-Mkhize, H. P. 2013. 'The Stunted Structural Transformation of the Indian Economy: Agriculture, Manufacturing and the Rural Non-Farm Sector'. *Economic and Political Weekly* 48 (26/27): 5–13.

Black, J. 2006. *A Military History of Britain: From 1775 to the Present*. Westport, Connecticut: Greenwood Publishing Group.

Bliss, C. J., and N. H. Stern. 1982. *Palanpur: The Economy of an Indian Village*. Oxford: Oxford University Press.

Blunt, J. T. 1803. 'Narrative of a Route from Chunarghur to Yertnagoodum, in the Ellore Circar'. *Asiatic Researches; or, Transactions of the Society Instituted in Bengal for Inquiring into The History and Antiquities, The Arts, Sciences, and Literature of Asia* 7: 57–169. https://fabiomesquita.files.wordpress.com/2017/01/asiatic-researches-volume-7-1803.pdf. Accessed on 7 May 2022.

Blyn, G. 1966. *Agricultural Statistics of British India, 1891–1947*. Philadelphia: University of Pennsylvania.

Board of Governors of the Federal Reserve System (US), 1935–, and Federal Reserve Board, 1914–1935. 1923. 'American Cotton Production, Exports and Percentages of Cotton Exported'. *Federal Reserve Bulletin: 'May 1923'*, 566–567.

Bogart, D., and L. Chaudhary. 2015. 'Railways in Colonial India: An Economic Achievement?' In *A New Economic History of India*, edited by Latika Chaudhary, Bishnupriya Gupta, Tirthankar Roy, and Anand V. Swamy, 140–160. New York: Routledge.

Bonvoisin, T., L. Utyasheva, D. Knipe, D. Gunnell, and M. Eddleston. 2020. 'Suicide by Pesticide Poisoning in India: A Review of Pesticide Regulations and Their Impact on Suicide Trends'. *BMC Public Health* 20 (1): 1–16.

Boot, H. M. 1995. 'How Skilled Were Lancashire Cotton Factory Workers in 1833'. *Economic History Review* 48 (2): 283–303.

Bose, S., U. Ghosh, H. K. Chauhan, N. C. Narayanan, and D. Parthasarathy. 2018. 'Uncertainties and Vulnerabilities among the Koli Fishers in Mumbai: A Photo Voice Study'. *Indian Anthropologist* 48 (2): 65–80.

Bowen, H. V. 2009. 'British Exports of Raw Cotton from India to China during the Late Eighteenth and Early Nineteenth Century'. In *How India Clothed the World*, edited by Giorgio Riello and Tirthankar Roy, 115–137. Leiden; Boston: Brill.

Braudel, F., and I. Wallerstein. 2009. 'History and the Social Sciences: The Longue Durée'. *Review (Fernand Braudel Center)* 32 (2): 171–203.

Breman, J. 2007. *The Poverty Regime in Village India: Half a Century of Work and Life at the Bottom of the Rural Economy in South Gujarat*. Vol. 13. New Delhi; Oxford: Oxford University Press.

Breman, J., P. Kloos, and A. Saith. 1997. *The Village in Asia Revisited*. Delhi; Oxford: Oxford University Press.

Brien, J. 2013. 'The Role of Causation in History'. *History in the Making* 2 (1): 72–81.

Broadberry, S., and B. Gupta. 2006. 'The Early Modern Great Divergence: Wages, Prices and Economic Development in Europe and Asia, 1500–1800, 1'. *Economic History Review* 59 (1): 2–31.

———. 2009. 'Lancashire, India, and Shifting Competitive Advantage in Cotton Textiles, 1700–1850: The Neglected Role of Factor Prices, 1'. *Economic History Review* 62 (2): 279–305.

Brooks, N. 2003. 'Vulnerability, Risk and Adaptation: A Conceptual Framework'. Working Paper no. 38, Tyndall Centre for Climate Change Research, University of East Anglia, Norwich.

Brown, C., and A. E. Nelson. 1910. *Central Provinces and Berar District Gazetteers: Akola District*. Calcutta: Baptist Mission Press. https://indianculture.gov.in/gazettes/central-provinces-and-berar-district-gazetteers-akola-district-vol-descriptive. Accessed on 16 April 2021.

Brown, C., and R. V. Russell, eds. 1979. *Central Provinces District Gazetteers (Facsimile Reproduction): Yeotmal District*. Vol. A. Government Photozinco Press: Pune. https://indianculture.gov.in/gazettes/central-provinces-district-gazetteers-facsimile-reproduction-yeotmal-district-1908-vol. Accessed on 24 May 2022.

Bruchey, S., ed. 1967. *Cotton and the Growth of the American Economy, 1790–1860*. New York: Harcourt, Brace & World.

Bryceson, D. F. 2009. 'Sub-Saharan Africa's Vanishing Peasantries and the Spectre of a Global Food Crisis'. *Monthly Review* 61 (3): 48–62.

Buchanan, D. H. 1934. *The Development of Capitalistic Enterprise in India*. New York: The Macmillan Company, 196.

Bulley, A. 2013 *The Bombay Country Ships 1790–1833*. Richmond, VA: Curzon.

Bush, J. A. 2002. 'The British Constitution and the Creation of American Slavery'. In *Slavery and the Law*, edited by Paul Finkelman, 379–418. Lanham, MD: Rowman & Littlefield.

Business Standard. 2021. 'Press Trust of India (2021) CCI to Get Rs. 17,049 Crores for Cotton Procurement in 7 Seasons to 2020–21'. 10 November 2021. https://www.business-standard.com/article/economy-policy/cci-to-get-rs-17-409-cr-for-cotton-procurement-in-7-seasons-to-2020-21-121111000907_1.html. Accessed on 12 April 2022.

Calvo, C., and S. Dercon. 2005. 'Measuring Individual Vulnerability'. Department of Economics Discussion Paper Number 229, University of Oxford. https://www.rrojasdatabank.info/calvo.pdf. Accessed on 8 May 2022.

Campbell, G. 2013. 'Deriving the Railway Mania'. *Financial History Review* 20 (1): 1–27.

Campbell, J. M., I. C. S. 1883. *Gazetteer of the Bombay Presidency: Nasik*. Bombay: Government Central Press.

Carr, E. H. 1961. *What Is History?* London: Penguin.

Carrano, M. T., J. A. Wilson, and P. M. Barrett. 2010. 'The History of Dinosaur Collecting in Central India, 1828–1947'. *Geological Society, London, Special Publications* 343 (1): 161–173.

Carroll, J. M. 2010. 'The Canton System: Conflict and Accommodation in the Contact Zone'. *Journal of the Royal Asiatic Society Hong Kong Branch* 50, fiftieth anniversary issue: 51–66.

Cashdan, E., ed. 1990. *Risk and Uncertainty in Tribal and Peasant Economies*. Boulder: Westview Press.

Cassell, W. R. 1862. *Cotton: An Account of Its Culture in the Bombay Presidency, Prepared from Government Records and Other Authentic Sources, in Accordance with a Resolution of the Government of India*. Vol. 103. Bombay: Bombay Education Society's Press.

Central Provinces and Berar (India). 1922. *The Central Provinces and Berar: A Review of the Administration of the Province*. Nagpur: Govt Printing. https://www.jstor.org/stable/saoa.crl.25235956#metadata_info_tab_contents. Accessed on 2 June 2022.

———. 1869. *Report on the Cotton Department for the Year 1868–69*. Bombay: Education Society's Press.

Central Provinces District Gazetteers: Buldana Gazetteer. 1910. Calcutta: Baptist Mission Press.

Chakrabarti, P. 2019. 'Gondwana and the Politics of Deep Past'. *Past and Present* 242 (1): 119–153.

Chakrabarti, P. N. 1979. 'Myth of the Date of Establishment of the First English Factory (1613) and Its Baneful Effect on Mughal Economy'. *Proceedings of the Indian History Congress* 40 (1979): 487–490.

Chambers, R., and L. A. Thrupp. 1994. *Farmer First: Farmer Innovation and Agricultural Research*. London: Intermediate Technology Publications.

Chandavarkar, R. 2002. *The Origins of Industrial Capitalism in India: Business Strategies and the Working Classes in Bombay, 1900–1940*. Vol. 51. Cambridge, UK: Cambridge University Press.

———. 2008. 'The Decline and Fall of the Jobber System in the Bombay Cotton Textile Industry, 1870–1955'. *Modern Asian Studies* 42 (1): 117–210.

Chandra, S. 2004. *Medieval India: From Sultanat to the Mughals-Delhi Sultanat (1206–1526)*. Part 1. New Delhi: Har-Anand Publications.

———. 2007. *History of Medieval India:(800–1700)*. New Delhi: Orient Blackswan.

Chaplin, J. E. 1991. 'Creating a Cotton South in Georgia and South Carolina, 1760–1815'. *Journal of Southern History* 57 (2): 171–200.

Chaudhuri, K. N. 1978. *The Trading World of Asia and the English East India Company: 1660–1760*. Cambridge, UK: Cambridge University Press.

Chaudhuri, S., J. Jalan, and A. Suryahadi. 2002. 'Assessing Household Vulnerability to Poverty from Cross-Sectional Data: A Methodology and Estimates from Indonesia'. Department of Economics Discussion Paper Number 0102-52, Columbia University. https://academiccommons.columbia.edu/doi/10.7916/D85149GF. Accessed on 8 May 2022.

Chaurasia, R. S. 2004. *History of the Marathas*. New Delhi: Atlantic Publishers & Dist.

Chavan, P., and R. Ramakumar. 2002. 'Micro-Credit and Rural Poverty: An Analysis of Empirical Evidence'. *Economic and Political Weekly* 37 (10): 955–965.

———. 2007. 'Revival of Agricultural Credit in the 2000s: An Explanation'. *Economic and Political Weekly* 42 (52): 57–63.

Chew, M. R. 1884. *History of the Kingdom of Cotton and Cotton Statistics of the World*. New Orleans: W. B. Stansbury & Co.

Chiwula, L. S., R. Witt, and H. Waibel. 2011. 'An Asset-Based Approach to Vulnerability: The Case of Small-Scale Fishing Areas in Cameroon and Nigeria'. *Journal of Development Studies* 47 (2): 338–353.

Choi, N. 2012. 'Ahmedabad Textile Laborers Win Strike for Economic Justice, 1918'. Online case study published by Global Nonviolent Action Database. https://nvdatabase.swarthmore.edu/content/ahmedabad-textile-laborers-win-strike-economic-justice-1918#case-study-detail. Accessed on 8 May 2022.

Choksey, R. D. 1968. *Economic Life in the Bombay Gujarat, 1800–1939*. Bombay: Asia Publishing House.

Choudhary, B., and K. Gaur. 2010. *Bt Cotton in India: A Country Profile*. New Delhi: The International Service for the Acquisition of Agri-biotech Applications (ISAAA). http://www.isaaa.org/resources/publications/biotech_crop_profiles/bt_cotton_in_india-a_country_profile/download/Bt_Cotton_in_India-A_Country_Profile.pdf. Accessed on 22 March 2011.

Christiansen, L, V. Hoffmann, and A. Sarris. 2007. 'Gauging the Welfare Effects of Shocks in Rural Tanzania'. Policy Research Working Paper 4406, The World Bank, Washington, DC.

Christiaensen, L. J., and K. Subbarao. 2005. 'Toward an Understanding of Household Vulnerability in Rural Kenya'. *Journal of African Economies* 14 (4): 520–558.

Cole, S., X. Giné, J. Tobacman, P. Topalova, R. Townsend, and J. Vickery. 2013. 'Barriers to Household Risk Management: Evidence from India'. *American Economic Journal: Applied Economics* 5 (1): 104–135.

Colebrooke, H. T. 1884. *Remarks on the Husbandry and Internal Commerce of Bengal*. Chowringhee, Calcutta: Statesman Steam Printing Works; reprint.

Commission, S. R. 1955. *Report of the States Reorganisation Commission*. New Delhi: Government of India Press.

Committee, B. A.-P. 1931. *Berar's Position in Indian Federation: A Case*. Prepared by the Berar All-Parties' Committee for consideration by the members of the Round Table Conference. Bombay: Vaibhav Press.

Committee, G. E. A. 2011. 'Seed Approval List'. https://geacindia.gov.in/resource-documents/approved-products/Final_commercially_approved.pdf. Accessed on 17 May 2021.

Conway, V. M. 1039. 'The Panic of 1837'. Master's thesis, Loyola University, Chicago.

Cooper, W. J. 2012. *We Have the War upon Us: The Onset of the Civil War, November 1860 – April 1861*. New York City, NY: Vintage.

D'Monte, D. 2006. *Mills for Sale: The Way Ahead*. Mumbai: Marg Publications.

D'Souza, R. 2020. 'Improving Access to Agricultural Credit: New Perspectives'. Occasional Paper 230, Observer Research Foundation, January 2020.

Dalrymple, W. 2019. *The Anarchy: The East India Company, Corporate Violence, and the Pillage of an Empire*. New York: Bloomsbury Publishing.

Dantwala, M. L. 1947. *A Hundred Years of Indian Raw Cotton*. Bombay: Orient Longman for the East India Cotton Association.

Das Gupta, S. 2019. *Class, Politics, and Agrarian Policies in Post-liberalisation India*. Cambridge, UK: Cambridge University Press.

Davis, L. E., and H. L. Stetller III. 1966. 'The New England Textile Industry, 1825–60: Trends and Fluctuations'. In *Output, Employment, and Productivity in the United States after 1800*, edited by Dorothy S. Brady, 213–242. Studies in Income and Wealth Series. Cambridge, MA: NBER.

Davis, M. 2001. *Late Victorian Holocausts: El Niño Famines and the Making of the Third World*. London; New York: Verso Books.

Day, W. M. 1949. 'Relative Permanence of Former Boundaries in India'. *Scottish Geographical Magazine* 65 (3): 113–122.

De, U. S., U. R. Joshi, and G. S. P. Rao. 2004. 'Nakshatra Based Rainfall Climatology'. *Mausam* 55 (2): 305–312.

Deaton, A. 1990. 'On Risk, Insurance, and Intra-Village Consumption Smoothing'. Research Program in Development Studies, Preliminary draft, Princeton University. http://www.princeton.edu/~deaton/downloads/On%20risk_insurance_and_intravillage_consumption_smoothing.pdf. Accessed on 15 October 2021.

———. 1991. 'Saving and Liquidity Constraints'. *Econometrica* 59 (5): 1221–1248.

Deo, S. B. 1973. 'New Evidence of Hinayana Buddhism in Vidarbha'. *Puratattva* 1972–1973 (6): 84–86.

Deotare, B. C. 2006. 'Late Holocene Climatic Change: Archaeological Evidence from Purna Basin, Maharashtra'. *Man and Environment* 35 (1): 87–102.

Deotare, B. C., P. S. Joshi, and C. N. Parchure. 2013. *Glimpses of Ancient Maharashtra through Archaeological Excavations*. Pune: Bharatiya Itihas Sankalan Samitee and Deccan College Post-Graduate and Research Institute.

Deotare, B., G. Shete, R. Sawant, V. Kathale, and S. Naik. 2007. 'Discovery of Structural Stupa at Bhon, District Buldana, Maharashtra'. *Puratattva* 2006–2007 (37): 176–185.

Department of Agriculture. 2014. *Agricultural Census 2010–11 (Phase-I)*. http://krishi.maharashtra.gov.in/Site/Upload/Pdf/Publications/Argi.pdf. Accessed on 14 November 2021.

———. 2019. *Agricultural Census (2015–16)*. http://krishi.maharashtra.gov.in/Site/Upload/Pdf/Agriculture%20Census%202015-2016%20Final%20for%20website_part3_pages36-60.pdf. Accessed on 14 November 2021.

Dercon, S. 1996. 'Risk, Crop Choice, and Savings: Evidence from Tanzania'. *Economic Development and Cultural Change* 44 (3): 485–513.

———, ed. 2005. *Insurance against Poverty*. Oxford: Oxford University Press.

Dercon, S., and P. Krishnan. 2000. 'Vulnerability, Seasonality and Poverty in Ethiopia'. *Journal of Development Studies* 36 (6): 25–53.

Desai, A. V. 1972. 'Population and Standards of Living in Akbar's Time'. *Indian Economic and Social History Review* 9 (1): 43–62.

———. 1978. 'Population and Standards of Living in Akbar's Time: A Second Look'. *Indian Economic and Social History Review* 15 (1): 53–79.

Desai, S., and O. Joshi. 2019. 'The Paradox of Declining Female Work Participation in An Era of Economic Growth'. *Indian Journal of Labour Economics* 62 (1): 55–71.

Deshmukh, C. 1976. 'Bombay Cottons On (A Case Study of the Economic Revolution in Bombay with Special Reference to Cotton and the Textile Industry, 1850–1914)'. *Proceedings of the Indian History Congress* 37: 321–326.

Deshpande, R. 2004. 'Kunbi Maratha as OBC: Backward Journey of a Caste'. *Economic and Political Weekly* 39 (14/15): 1448–1449.

Deshpande, R. S. 2002. 'Suicide by Farmers in Karnataka: Agrarian Distress and Possible Alleviatory Steps'. *Economic and Political Weekly* 31 (25): 2601–2610.

Deshpande, R. S., and S. Arora, eds. 2010. *Agrarian Crisis and Farmer Suicides*. New Delhi: Sage Publications.

Deshpande-Mukherjee, A., P. K. Thomas, and R. K. Mohanty. 2010. 'Faunal Remains from the Iron Age and Early Historical Settlement at Mahurjhari, District Nagpur, Maharashtra'. *Man and Environment* 35 (1): 87–102.

Desmond, E. 2013. 'The Legitimation of Risk and Democracy: A Case Study of Bt cotton in Andhra Pradesh, India'. PhD Thesis, University College Cork.

———. 2018. 'Legitimation in a World at Risk: The Case of Genetically Modified Crops in India'. Singapore: Springer.

Devi, P. I. 2009. 'Health Risk Perceptions, Awareness and Handling Behaviour of Pesticides by Farm Workers'. *Agricultural Economics Research Review* 22 (2): 263–268.

Dhanagre, D. N. 1983. *Peasant Movements in India, 1920–1950.* New Delhi: Oxford University Press.

———. 2015. *Populism and Power: Farmers' Movement in Western India, 1980–2014.* London; New York: Routledge.

Diamond, J. 1997. *Guns, Germs, and Steel: The Fates of Human Societies.* New York: W. W. Norton & Company.

Directorate of Cotton Development. 2017. *Status Paper of Indian Cotton.* Maharashtra: Ministry of Agriculture & Farmers Welfare. https://www.nfsm.gov.in/StatusPaper/Cotton2016.pdf. Accessed on 4 May 2022.

Dierksheide, C. 2008. 'The Great Improvement and Civilization of That Race: Jefferson and the "Amelioration" of Slavery, ca. 1770–1826'. *Early American Studies* 6 (1): 165–197.

Donaldson, D. 2018. 'Railroads and the Raj: Estimating the Economic Impact of Transportation Infrastructure'. *American Economic Review* 108 (4/5): 899–934.

Dubois, P., B. Jullien, and T. Magnac. 2008. 'Formal and Informal Risk Sharing in LDCs: Theory and Empirical Evidence'. *Econometrica* 76 (4): 679–725.

Duff, J. G. 1878. *A History of the Mahrattas.* 2 vols. New Delhi: Times of India Office.

Dumbel, S. 1927. 'The Origin of Cotton Futures'. *Economic Journal* 37 (suppl. 1): 259–267.

Dumont, L., and D. F. Pocock. 1957. 'Village Studies'. *Contributions to Indian Sociology* 1 (1): 23–41.

Dutt, R. C. 1969. *The Economic History of India.* Vol. 2. New York: Augustus M. Kelley.

Dyson, T., ed. 1989. *Studies in Famine, Disease and Society.* 1st ed. London: Routledge.

Earle, E. M. 1926. Egyptian Cotton and the American Civil War'. *Political Science Quarterly* 41 (4): 520–545.

Eaton, R. M. 2005. *A Social History of the Deccan, 1300–1761: Eight Indian Lives.* Part 1, vol. 8. New York: Cambridge University Press.

Economic Times. 2011. 'Maharashtra Says No to Bt Cotton Seed Price Hike'. 11 May 2011. https://economictimes.indiatimes.com/markets/commodities/maharashtra-say-no-to-bt-cotton-seed-price-hike/articleshow/8236063.cms. Accessed on 18 January 2021.

Edmondson, L. 1976. 'Trans-Atlantic Slavery and the Internationalization of Race'. *Caribbean Quarterly* 22 (2/3), 'Essays on Slavery': 5–25.

Edwards, M. M. 1967. *The Growth of the British Cotton Trade, 1789–1815.* Manchester: Manchester University Press.

Eichengreen, B. 1995. 'Financing Infrastructure in Developing Countries: Lessons from the Railway Age'. *World Bank Research Observer* 10 (1): 75–91.

Ellis, F. W. 2005. 'In What Way, and to What Degree Did the Mughal State Inhibit Smithian Growth in India in the Seventeenth Century?' Working Papers of the Global Economic History Network (GEHN) (14/05), Department of Economic History, London School of Economics and Political Science, London, UK.

Ellison, T. 1968. *The Cotton Trade of Great Britain*. New York: Augustus M. Kelley.

Epstein, T. S. 1962. *Economic Development and Social Change in South India*. Manchester: Manchester University Press.

Epstein, T. S., A. P. Suryanarayana, T. Thimmegowda. 1998. *Village Voices: Forty Years of Rural Transformation in South India*. New Delhi: Sage Publications India Pvt. Ltd.

Eraly, A. 2015. *The Age of Wrath: A History of the Delhi Sultanate*. New Delhi: Penguin.

Ernst, C. W. 1992. *Eternal Garden: Mysticism, History, and Politics at a South Asian Sufi Center*. Albany, New York: SUNY Press.

Ericson, D. F. 2000. *The Debate over Slavery: Antislavery and Proslavery Liberalism in Antebellum America*. New York: NYU Press.

ET Bureau. 2011. 'Maharashtra Says No to Cotton Seed Price Hike'. *Economic Times*, 11 May 2011. https://economictimes.indiatimes.com/markets/commodities/maharashtra-say-no-to-bt-cotton-seed-price-hike/articleshow/8236063.cms. Accessed on 18 January 2021.

Fafchamps, M. 1992. 'Cash Crop Production, Food Price Volatility, and Rural Market Integration in the Third World'. *American Journal of Agricultural Economics* 74 (1): 90–99.

Fafchamps, M., C. Udry, and K. Czukas. 1998. 'Drought and Saving in West Africa: Are Livestock a Buffer Stock?' *Journal of Development Economics* 55 (2): 273–305.

Farnie, D. A. 1979. *The English Cotton Industry and the World Market, 1815–1896*. Oxford: Clarendon Press.

———. 2004. 'The Role of Cotton Textiles in the Economic Development of India, 1600–1990'. In *The Fibre That Changed the World: The Cotton Industry in International Perspective, 1600–1990s*, edited by D. A. Farnie and D. J. Jeremy, 395–430. Oxford: Oxford University Press.

Faruqui, M. D. 2009. 'At Empire's End: The Nizam, Hyderabad and Eighteenth-Century India'. *Modern Asian Studies* 43 (1): 5–43, 17.

———. 2012. *The Princes of the Mughal Empire, 1504–1719*. New York: Cambridge University Press.

Fay, P. W. 2000. *The Opium War, 1840–1842: Barbarians in the Celestial Empire in the Early Part of the Nineteenth Century and the Way by Which They Forced the Gates Ajar*. Vol. 1. Chapel Hill, North Carolina: University of North Carolina Press.

Ferling, J. E. 2002. *Setting the World Ablaze: Washington, Adams, Jefferson, and the American Revolution*. Oxford: Oxford University Press.

Fields, B. J. 1985. 'The Advent of Capitalist Agriculture: The New South in a Bourgeois World'. In *Essays on the Postbellum Southern Economy*, edited by Thavolia Glymph and John J. Kushma, 73–94. Tex.: College Station.

Fitzgerald, S. V., and A. E. Nelson. 1983 (1911). *Central Provinces District Gazetteers: Amraoti District*. Vol. 1. Pune: The Government Photozinco Press. https://indianculture.gov.in/gazettes/central-provinces-district-gazetteers-facsimile-reproduction-amraoti-district-volume-0. Accessed on 16 April 2022.

Flachs, A. 2017. '"Show Farmers": Transformation and Performance in Telangana, India'. *Culture, Agriculture, Food and Environment* 39 (1): 25–34.

———. 2019a. *Cultivating Knowledge: Biotechnology, Sustainability, and the Human Cost of Cotton Capitalism in India*. Tucson: University of Arizona Press.

———. 2019b. 'Planting and Performing: Anxiety, Aspiration, and "Scripts" in Telangana Cotton Farming'. *American Anthropologist* 121 (1): 48–61.

Foley, N. 1997. *The White Scourge: Mexicans, Blacks, and Poor Whites in the Cotton Culture of Central Texas*. Oakland, CA: University of California Press.

Foner, E. 1988. *Reconstruction: America's Unfinished Revolution, 1863–1877*. New York: Harper Collins.

Forbes, R. J. 1850. *On the Culture and Commerce of Cotton in India*. London: Smith, Elder, & Co.

Forté, C. A., J. Colacino, K. Polemi, A. Guytingco, N. J. Peraino, S. Jindaphong, T. Kaviya, J. Westrick, R. Neitzel, and K. Nambunmee. 2021. 'Pesticide Exposure and Adverse Health Effects Associated with Farmwork in Northern Thailand'. *Journal of Occupational Health* 63 (1): 1–13. https://www.jstage.jst.go.jp/article/joh/63/1/63_e12222/_pdf. Accessed on 7 May 2022.

Foster, W. 1927. *Early Travels in India, 1583–1619*. London: Oxford University Press.

Fukazawa, H. 1972. 'Rural Servants in the 18th Century Maharashtrian Village—Demiurgic or Jajmani System?' *Hitotsubashi Journal of Economics* 12 (2): 14–40.

———. 1982. 'Standard of Living 2: Maharashtra and the Deccan'. In *The Cambridge Economic History of India: Volume 1, c.1200–c.1750*, edited by T. Raychaudhuri and I. Habib, 471–477. Cambridge, UK: Cambridge University Press.

Fuller, J. B. 1922. *Introduction to the Land Revenue and Settlement Systems of the Central Provinces*. Nagpur: Government Press.

Gadgil, M. V. 1994. 'Formal Agricultural Credit System in India: Shape of Things to Come'. *Indian Journal of Agricultural Economics* 49 (3): 476–490.

Gazetteer of Akola. https://cultural.maharashtra.gov.in/english/gazetteer/AKOLA/his_mediaeval%20period.html. Accessed on 20 April 2021.

Gazetteer of Bhandara. https://cultural.maharashtra.gov.in/english/gazetteer/BHANDARA/his_mediaeval%20period.html. Accessed on 8 May 2021.

Gazetteer of Buldhana. https://cultural.maharashtra.gov.in/english/gazetteer/BULDHANA/his_mediaeval%20period.html. Accessed on 10 April 2021.

Gazetteer of Poona. https://cultural.maharashtra.gov.in/english/gazetteer/Poona/PART%20II/Chap%20(2)/Muslim%20Period.htm. Accessed on 23 March 2021.

Gallo, E. 2015. 'Village Ethnography and Kinship Studies: Perspectives from India and Beyond'. *Critique of Anthropology* 35 (3): 248–262.

Gaurav, S. 2010. 'Assessing Risk and Vulnerability of Farm Households in Vidarbha Region of India'. Unpublished YSSP Report, International Institute for Applied Systems Analysis (IIASA), Laxenburg, Austria.

———. 2014. 'Risk and Vulnerability of Agricultural Households in India'. Unpublished PhD Thesis, Indira Gandhi Institute of Development Research (IGIDR), Mumbai.

———. 2015. 'Are Rainfed Agricultural Households Insured? Evidence from Five Villages in Vidarbha, India'. *World Development* 66 (C): 719–736.

———. 2021. *IMPRESS Project P2276: Risk and Vulnerability of Agricultural Households in Vidarbha, Maharashtra: A Longitudinal Study*. New Delhi: Indian Council of Social Science Research (ICSSR).

Gaurav, S., and V. Chaudhary. 2020. 'Do Farmers Care About Basis Risk? Evidence from a Field Experiment in India'. *Climate Risk Management* 27.

Gaurav, S., S. Cole, and J. Tobacman. 2011. 'Marketing Complex Financial Products in Emerging Markets: Evidence from Rainfall Insurance in India'. Special issue, *Journal of Marketing Research* 48: 150–162.

Geertz, C. 1973. 'Thick Description: Toward an Interpretive Theory of Culture'. In *The Interpretation of Cultures: Selected Essays*, edited by Clifford Geertz, 3–30. New York: Basic Books.

Gentry, J. F. 1970. 'A Confederate Success in Europe: The Erlanger Loan'. *Journal of Southern History* 36 (2): 157–188.

Gervais, J. A., B. Luukinen, K. Buhl, and D. Stone. 2010. 'Imidacloprid Technical Fact Sheet'. National Pesticide Information Center, Oregon State University Extension Services, no. 5, 1–7.

Ghatak, M., and P. Pandey. 2000. 'Contract Choice in Agriculture with Joint Moral Hazard in Effort and Risk'. *Journal of Development Economics* 63 (2): 303–326.

Ghose, B. 1960. 'The Colonial Beginnings of Calcutta Urbanisation without Industrialisation'. *Economic and Political Weekly* 12 (33): 1255–1260.

Gladwell, M. 2000. *Tipping Point: How Little Things Can Make a Big Difference.* New York: Little Brown.

Glasner, D. 1997. *Business Cycles and Depressions: An Encyclopedia.* New York: Taylor & Francis.

Glover, D. 2010a. 'Exploring the Resilience of Bt Cotton's "Pro-poor Success Story"'. *Development and Change* 41 (6): 955–981.

———. 2010b. 'Is Bt Cotton a Pro-poor Technology? A Review and Critique of the Empirical Record'. *Journal of Agrarian Change* 10 (4): 482–509.

———. 2010c. 'The Corporate Shaping of GM Crops as a Technology for the Poor'. *Journal of Peasant Studies* 37 (1): 67–90.

Gordon, S. 1994. *Marathas, Marauders, and State Formation in Eighteenth-Century India.* Delhi: Oxford University Press.

———. 2007. *The Marathas 1600–1818.* Cambridge, UK: Cambridge University Press.

Gordon, S., and G. Johnson. 1993. *The New Cambridge History of India.* Cambridge, UK: Cambridge University Press.

Gore, P. G., T. Prasad, and H. R. Hatwar. 2010. *Mapping of Drought Areas over India.* NCC Research Report no. 12, National Climate Centre, India Meteorology Department, Pune.

Government of India. 1898. *Report of The Indian Famine Commission, 1898.* Simla: Government Central Printing Office.

———. 1911. *Census of India 1911.* New Delhi: Office of the Registrar General and Census Commissioner.

———. 1955. *Report of the States Reorganisation Commission.* New Delhi.

———. 2006. *Report of Fact-Finding Team on Vidarbha: Regional Disparities and Rural Distress in Maharashtra with Particular Reference to Vidarbha*. New Delhi: Planning Commission, Government of India.

———. 2011. *Census of India 2011, Provisional Population Totals*. New Delhi: Office of the Registrar General and Census Commissioner.

———. 2016. *Groundwater Year Book of Maharashtra and Union Territory of Dadra and Nagar Haveli*. Draft Report/GWM/2016, Ministry of Water Resources, River Development and Ganga Rejuvenation, Central Ground Water Board.

Government of Maharashtra. 2006. 'Rainfall'. *Central Provinces and Berar District Gazetteers: Yavatmal District*. https://cultural.maharashtra.gov.in/english/gazetteer/YAVATMAL/agri_rainfall.html. Accessed on 7 May 2022.

———. 2013. *Report of the High Level Committee on Balanced Regional Development: Issues in Maharashtra*. https://dspace.gipe.ac.in/xmlui/bitstream/handle/10973/33424/KCR-English.pdf?sequence=1&isAllowed=y. Accessed on 31 May 2021.

———. 2015. *Rights of Women in Hindu Joint and Coparcenery Property after 2005 Amendment – Effects of Recent Judicial Pronouncements*. Maharashtra Judicial Academy and Indian Mediation Centre and Training Institute. http://mja.gov.in/Site/Upload/GR/Title%20NO.78(As%20Per%20Workshop%20List%20title%20no78%20pdf).pdf. Accessed on 31 May 2021.

———. 2019. *Report of the Comptroller and Auditor General of India on General and Social Sector and Public Sector Undertakings for the year ended 31 March 2019*. Report No. 3 of the year 2020, 9–18.

———. n.d. 'Fibres'. *Central Provinces and Berar District Gazetteers: Wardha District*. https://cultural.maharashtra.gov.in/english/gazetteer/WARDHA/agri_fibres.html. Accessed on 7 May 2020.

Govil, R., A. Neti, and M. R. Rao. 2020. *Farmer Producer Companies: Past, Present and Future*. Bangalore: Azim Premji University.

Gráda, C. Ó. 2007. 'Making Famine History'. *Journal of Economic Literature* 45 (1): 5–38.

Gray, J. 1858. *General Administration Report of Hyderabad Assigned Districts, 1856–57*. Calcutta: John Gray.

———. 1863. *General Administration Report of Hyderabad Assigned Districts, 1861–62*. Calcutta: John Gray.

Greenberg, M. 1969. *British Trade and the Opening of China 1800–1842*. New York: Cambridge University Press Archive.

Griffin, R. W. 1995. 'Problems of the Southern Cotton Planters After the Civil War'. *Georgia Historical Review* 39 (2): 103–117.

Grimard, F. 1997. 'Household Consumption Smoothing through Ethnic Ties: Evidence from Cote d'Ivoire'. *Journal of Development Economics* 53 (2): 391–422.

Guha, A. 1972. 'Raw Cotton of Western India: 1750–1850'. *Indian Economic and Social History Review* 9 (1): 1–41.

Guha, S. 1987a. 'Commodity and Credit in Upland Maharashtra, 1800–1950'. *Economic and Political Weekly* 22 (52): A126–A140.

———. 1987b. 'The Land Market in Upland Maharashtra c. 1820–1960-I'. *Indian Economic and Social History Review* 24 (2): 117–144.

Guhathakurta, P., and E. Saji. 2013. 'Detecting Changes in Rainfall Pattern and Seasonality Index Vis-à-Vis Increasing Water Scarcity in Maharashtra'. *Journal of Earth System Science* 122 (3): 639–649.

Gulati, A. 1987. 'Effective Incentives and Subsidies for Cotton Cultivators in India'. *Economic and Political Weekly* 22 (52): A177–A187.

Gulati, A., and P. Banerjee. 2015. 'Rationalising Fertiliser Subsidy in India: Key Issues and Policy Options'. ICRIER Working Paper no. 307. https://www.think-asia.org/bitstream/handle/11540/11017/Working_Paper_307.pdf?sequence=1. Accessed on 7 May 2022.

Gulati, A., and S. Bathla. 2002. 'Institutional Credit to Indian Agriculture: Defaults and Policy Options'. Occasional Papers no. 23, National Bank for Agriculture and Rural Development (NABARD), Mumbai.

Günther, I., and K. Harttgen. 2009. 'Estimating Households Vulnerability to Idiosyncratic and Covariate Shocks: A Novel Method Applied in Madagascar'. *World Development* 37 (7): 1222–1234.

Habib, I. 1963. *The Agrarian System of Mughal India 1556–1707*. 3rd ed. Oxford: Oxford University Press.

———. 1982. 'Northern India under the Sultanate: Agrarian Economy'. In *The Cambridge Economic History of India: Volume 1, c.1200–c.1750*, edited by T. Raychaudhuri and I. Habib, 48–76. Cambridge, UK: Cambridge University Press.

———. 1983. 'The Peasant in Indian History'. *Social Scientist* 11 (3): 21–64.

———. n.d. 'Usury in Medieval India'. *Comparative Studies in Society and History* 6 (4): 393–419.

Habib, M. 1963. *The Agrarian System of Mughal India (1556–1707)*. New Delhi: Oxford University Press.

Habib, M., and K. A. Nizami, eds. 1970. *A Comprehensive History of India: The Delhi Sultanat (AD 1206–1526).* Vol. 5. New Delhi: People's Publishing House.

Hahn, S. 1983. *The Roots of Southern Populism: Yeoman Farmers and the Transformation of the Georgia Upcountry, 1850–1890.* New York: Oxford University Press.

Haig, T. W. 1909. *Imperial Gazetteers of India: Berar.* Calcutta: Calcutta Superintendent of Govt Printing.

Hammond, J. L., and B. Hammond. 1919. *The Skilled Labourer 1760–1832.* London: Longmans, Green, and Co.

Hanlon, W. W. 2015. 'Necessity Is the Mother of Invention: Input Supplies and Directed Technical Change'. *Econometrica* 83 (1): 67–100.

Hardikar, J. 2021. *Ramrao: The Story of India's Farm Crisis.* Noida: HarperCollins.

Hardiman, D. 1992. *Peasant Resistance in India, 1858–1914.* New Delhi: Oxford University Press.

Harman, T. T., and W. Showell. 2004 (1885). 'Calico, Cotton, and Cloth'. In *Showell's Dictionary of Birmingham: A History and Guide Arranged Alphabetically.* Project Gutenberg, ebook.

Harnetty, P. 1971. 'Cotton Exports and Indian Agriculture, 1861–1870'. *Economic History Review* 24 (3): 414–429.

———. 1972. *Imperialism and Free Trade: Lancashire and India in the Mid-Nineteenth Century.* Manchester: Manchester University Press.

———. 1977. 'Crop Trends in the Central Provinces of India, 1861–1921'. *Modern Asian Studies* 11 (3): 341–377.

———. 2014. 'The Imperialism of Free Trade: Lancashire, India, and the Cotton Supply Question, 1861–1865'. *Journal of British Studies* 6 (1): 70–96.

Harriss, J. 1982. *Capitalism and Peasant Farming: Agrarian Structure and Ideology in Northern Tamil Nadu.* New Delhi: Oxford University Press.

Harvey, D. 2007. *A Brief History of Neoliberalism.* New York: Oxford University Press.

Hazareesingh, S. 2016. '"Your Foreign Plants Are Very Delicate": Peasant Crop Ecologies and the Subversion of Colonial Cotton Designs in Dharwar, Western India, 1830–1880'. In *Local Subversions of Colonial Cultures: Commodities and Anti-commodities in Global History*, edited by S. Hazareesingh and H. Maat, 97–124. Cambridge Imperial and Post-colonial Studies Series. London: Palgrave Macmillan.

Heckscher, E. F. 1994. *Mercantilism.* Vol. 1. London; New York: Routledge.

Herring, R. J. 2007. 'Stealth Seeds: Bioproperty, Biosafety, Biopolitics'. *Journal of Development Studies* 43 (1): 130–157. https://doi.org/10.1080/00220380601055601.

Herring, R. J. K., and M. Kandilkar. 2009. 'Illicit Seeds: Intellectual Property and the Underground Proliferation of Agricultural Biotechnologies'. In *Politics of Intellectual Property*, edited by S. S. C. Kenneth Haunss, 56–79. Cheltenham: Edward Elgar Publishing.

Heston, A. W. 1977. 'The Standard of Living in Akbar's Time: A Comment'. *Indian Economic and Social History Review* 14 (3): 391–396.

Hickey, D. R. 1981. 'American Trade Restrictions during the War of 1812'. *Journal of American History* 68 (3): 517–538.

Himanshu, and S. Gaurav. 2018. 'Changing Activities, Changing Markets: Agriculture'. In *How Lives Change? Palanpur, India, and Development Economics*, edited by Himanshu, P. Lanjouw, and N. Stern, 161–195. Oxford: Oxford University Press.

Himansu, P. Lanjouw, and N. Stern. 2018. *How Lives Change? Palanpur, India, and Development Economics*. Oxford: Oxford University Press.

Hindu Business Line. 2021. 'Why FPCs Are a Ray of Hope for Distressed Farmers in Maharashtra'. 23 March 2021. https://www.thehindubusinessline.com/news/why-fpcs-are-a-ray-of-hope-for-distressed-farmers-in-maharashtra/article34139545.ece. Accessed on 27 November 2021.

Hoddinott, J., and A. Quisumbing. 2003a. 'Methods for Microeconometric Risk and Vulnerability Assessments'. Social Protection Discussion Series Paper no. 0324, The World Bank, Washington, DC.

———. 2003b. 'Data Sources for Microeconometric Risk and Vulnerability Assessments'. Social Protection Discussion Series Paper no. 0323, The World Bank, Washington, DC.

Holt, P. M., A. K. S. Lambton, and B. Lewis. 1977. *The Cambridge History of Islam: Islamic Society and Civilization*. Vol. 2B, Vol. 2. Cambridge, UK: Cambridge University Press.

Hoogeveen, J., E. Tesliuc, R. Vakis, and S. Dercon. 2004. 'A Guide to the Analysis of Risk, Vulnerability and Vulnerable Groups'. Washington, DC: The World Bank.

Hoppit, J. 1987. *Risk and Failure in English Business, 1700–1800*. Cambridge: Cambridge University Press.

Hu, R., X. Huang, J. Huang, Y. Li, C. Zhang, Y. Yin, Z. Chen, Y. Jin, J. Cai, and F. Cui. 2015. 'Long- and Short-Term Health Effects of Pesticide Exposure: A Cohort Study from China'. *PloS One* 10 (6): 1–13. https://journals.plos.

org/plosone/article/file?id=10.1371/journal.pone.0128766&type=printable. Accessed on 7 May 2022.

Hugo, G., and B. Currey. 1984. *Famine as a Geographical Phenomenon*. Boston, MA: D. Reidel Publishing Company.

Hunter, S. W. W. 1839. *The Imperial Gazetteer of India*. Vol. 17, *Mahbubabad to Moradabad*. New ed. New Delhi: Clarendon Press.

———. 1886. *Imperial Gazetteer of India*. Vol. 10, *Multan to Palhalli*. London: Trubner & Co.

Hurd II, J. 1975. 'Railways and the Expansion of Markets in India, 1861–1921'. *Explorations in Economic History* 12 (3): 263–288.

Husain, Z. 1999. 'The "Zamindars" in the Deccan under Aurangzeb'. *Proceedings of the Indian History Congress* 60:315–331.

ICRISAT. 1979. *Socioeconomic Constraints to Development of Semi-arid Tropical Agriculture*. Hyderabad: ICRISAT.

Ingco, M. D., and J. D. Nash, eds. 2004. *Agriculture and the WTO: Creating a Trading System for Development*. New Delhi: World Bank/Atlantic.

Irwin, D. A., and M. G. Chepeliev. 2020. 'The Economic Consequences of Sir Robert Peel: A Quantitative Assessment of the Repeal of the Corn Laws'. NBER Working Paper, NBER, Cambridge, MA.

Ishwaran, K. 1966. *Tradition and Economy in Village India*. Vol. 74. New York, US: Routledge and Kegan Paul Ltd.

Iyer, K. 2020. *Landscapes of Loss: The Story of an Indian Drought*. New Delhi: Harper Collins.

Iyer, K. G., and M. S. Manick. 2000. *Indebtedness, Impoverishment and Suicides in Rural Punjab*. Delhi: Indian Publishers Distributors.

Jackson, P. 2003. *The Delhi Sultanate: A Political and Military History*. Cambridge: Cambridge University Press.

Jalan, J., and M. Ravallion. 1997. 'Are the Poor Less Well Insured? Evidence on Vulnerability to Income Risk in Rural China'. Policy Research Working Paper no. 1863, Development Research Group, The World Bank, Washington, DC.

Jambunathan, M. V. 1950. *An Economic Survey of Dodda Ganni Village*. Mysore: Seshadri Press.

James, C. 2015. *20th Anniversary (1996 to 2015) of the Global Commercialization of Biotech Crops and Biotech Crop Highlights in 2015*. Brief no. 51, International Service for the Acquisition of Agri-Biotech Applications. https://www.isaaa.org/resources/publications/briefs/51/. Accessed on 7 June 2021.

Jayaraman, K. S. 2001. 'Illegal Bt Cotton in India Haunts Regulators'. *Nature Biotechnology* 19 (12): 1090.

Jenkins, D. 2003. 'The Western Wool Textile Industry in the Nineteenth Century'. In *The Cambridge History of Western Textiles*, edited by David Jenkins, 2:761–789. Cambridge: Cambridge University Press.

Jervis, T. B. 1840. 'Report: Historical and Geographical Account of the Western Coast of India, Revenue and Land Tenure'. *Journal of Bombay Geographical Society, Calcutta, India*. Cited in G. T. Kulkarni, 'Land Revenue and Agricultural Policy of Shivaji: An Appraisal', *Bulletin of the Deccan College Post-Graduate and Research Institute* 31, nos. 3/4 (1976): 73–82.

Jha, H. P., and G. Rodgers, eds. 2016. *The Changing Village in India: Insights from Longitudinal Research*. Oxford: Oxford University Press.

Jitendra. 2020. 'Punctured Cover: India's Crop Insurance Scheme Loses Sheen'. *Down to Earth*, 6 January 2020. https://www.downtoearth.org.in/news/agriculture/punctured-cover-india-s-crop-insurance-scheme-loses-sheen-68379. Accessed on 18 August 2021.

Jodha, N. 1978. 'Effectiveness of Farmers' Adjustment to Risk'. *Economic and Political Weekly* 13 (25): A38–A48.

———. 1981. 'Role of Credit in Farmers' Adjustment against Risk in Arid and Semi-arid Tropical Areas of India'. *Economic and Political Weekly* 16 (42/43): 1696–1709.

Jodhka, S. S. 1998. 'From "Book View" to "Field View": Social Anthropological Constructions of the Indian Village'. *Oxford Development Studies* 26 (3): 311–331.

———. 2002. 'Nation and Village: Images of Rural India in Gandhi, Nehru and Ambedkar'. *Economic and Political Weekly* 37 (32): 3343–3353.

Johnson, K. 2005. 'Globalisation at the Crossroads of Tradition and Modernity in Rural India'. *Sociological Bulletin* 54 (1): 40–58.

Johnson, L. H. 1966. 'Northern Profit and Profiteers: The Cotton Rings of 1864–1865'. *Civil War History* 12, no. 2 (June): 101–115.

Johnson, W. 2013. *River of Dark Dreams: Slavery and Empire in the Cotton Kingdom*. Cambridge, MA: Harvard University Press.

Joshi, P. M. 1966. 'Ala-ud-Din Khalji's First Campaign against Devagiri'. In *Dr Ghulam Yazdani Commemoration Volume*, edited by H. K. Sherwani, 203–211. Hyderabad: Maulana Abul Kalam Azad Oriental Research Institute.

Karve, I. K. 1968. *Maharashtra, Land and its People*. Vol. 60. Maharashtra: Directorate of Government Printing, Stationery and Publications.

Kathage, J., and M. Qaim. 2012. 'Economic Impacts and Impact Dynamics of Bt (Bacillus thuringiensis) Cotton in India'. *Proceedings of the National Academy of Sciences* 109 (29): 11652–11656.

Kaur, D. 1990. 'Iqtadari System and the Growth of Towns in Medieval India'. *India Quarterly* 46 (2/3): 188–196.

Keay, J. 2001. *India: A History*. New York: Atlantic Monthly Press.

Kelly, J. 2018. *Marooned: Jamestown, Shipwreck, and a New History of America's Origin*. New York: Bloomsbury Publishing.

Kennedy, J., and L. King. 2014. 'The Political Economy of Farmers' Suicides in India: Indebted Cash-Crop Farmers with Marginal Landholdings Explain State-Level Variation in Suicide Rates'. *Globalization and Health* 10 (1): 1–9.

Kessinger, T. G. 1974. *Annals of Rural Punjab – Vilyatpur 1848–1968: Social and Economic Change in a North Indian Village*. Berkeley; Los Angeles; London: University of California Press.

Keyes, C. F. 1983. 'Peasant Strategies in Asian Societies: Moral and Rational Economic Approaches; A Symposium'. *Journal of Asian Studies (pre-1986)* 42 (4): 753–786.

Klein, I. 2008. 'British Reforms, Commercial Agriculture, and Agrarian Distress in India'. *The Historian* 70 (4): 732–752.

Komarlingam, M. S. 2018. 'Refuge-in-Bag for Bt Cotton'. *Current Science* 114 (4): 726–727.

Kornweibel Jr., T. 2010. *Railroads in the African American Experience: A Photographic Journey*. Baltimore, MD: Johns Hopkins University Press.

Kosambi, M. 2000. *Intersections: Socio-cultural Trends in Maharashtra*. New Delhi: Orient Blackswan.

Kranthi, K. R., and D. A. Russell. 2009. 'Changing Trends in Cotton Pest Management'. In *Integrated Pest Management: Innovation-Development Process*, edited by R. Peshin and A. K. Dhawan, 499–541. Dordrecht: Springer.

Kranthi, K. R., and G. D. Stone. 2020. 'Long-Term Impacts of Bt Cotton in India'. *Nature Plants* 6 (3): 188–196.

Krishna, V. V., and M. Qaim. 2007. 'Estimating the Adoption of Bt Eggplant in India: Who Benefits from Public–Private Partnership?' *Food Policy* 32 (5/6): 523–543.

———. 2008. 'Potential Impacts of Bt Eggplant on Economic Surplus and Farmers' Health in India'. *Agricultural Economics* 38 (2): 167–180.

Kruk, M. E., M. Myers, S. T. Varpilah, and B. T. Dahn. 2015. 'What Is a Resilient Health System? Lessons from Ebola'. *The Lancet* 385 (9980): 1910–1912.

Kshirsagar, K. G., and D. Shah. 2002. *Flow of Credit to Small and Marginal Farmers in Maharashtra*. AERC Study Report, Gokhale Institute of Politics and Economics, Pune.

Kulkarni, A. R. 1967. 'Village Life in the Deccan in the 17th Century'. *Indian Economic and Social History Review* 4 (1): 38–52.

———. 2000. 'The Mahar Watan: A Historical Perspective'. In *Intersections: Socio-Cultural Trends in Maharashtra*, edited by Meera Kosambi, 121–140. London: Sangam.

Kulkarni, G. T. 1991. 'Land Revenue Settlement under the Nizam Shahis (1489–1636) – With Special Reference to Malik Ambar: A Preliminary Study'. *Proceedings of the Indian History Congress* 52: 369–377.

Kulkarni, S. 1995. *The Satara Raj, 1818–1848: A Study in History, Administration, and Culture*. New Delhi: Mittal Publications.

Kumar, A. 2003. 'Ramtek's Water Woes'. *Economic and Political Weekly* 38 (3): 186–187.

Kumar, A. D. D., and D. N. Reddy. 2021. 'The Pesticide Management Bill 2020'. *Current Science* 121 (3): 348–349.

———. 1966. *India and the European Economic Community*. New Delhi: Asia Publishing House.

Kumar, D. 2015. *Conditions of Paraquat Use in India, IUF, Berne Declaration, PAN AP and PAN India*. Kerala: PAN India.

Kumar, N. 2011. 'Egoism, Anomie and Masculinity: Suicide in Rural South India (Andhra Pradesh)'. PhD thesis, London School of Economics and Political Science, London, UK.

Kumar, N. K. 1979. 'Hydraulic Agriculture in Peninsular India (c. 300 BC—1300 AD)'. *Proceedings of the Indian History Congress* 40: 211–214, 212.

Kumar, R. 2014. 'Elusive Empowerment: Information Provision and Disintermediation in Soyabean Markets in Malwa, India'. *Development and Change* 45 (6): 1332–1360.

———. 2016a. *Rethinking Revolutions: Soyabean, Choupals and the Changing Countryside in Central India*. Delhi: Oxford University Press.

———. 2016b. 'The Perils of Productivity: Making "Good Farmers" in Malwa, India'. *Journal of Agrarian Change* 16 (1): 70–93.

Kunte, B. G., ed. 1974. 'Maharashtra State Gazetteers: Wardha District, Rev. ed.' Government Central Press, Bombay. https://indianculture.gov.in/gazettes/maharashtra-state-gazetteers-wardha-district-rev-ed. Accessed on 24 May 2021.

Kurian, O. C., and S. Suri. 2019. 'Weighed Down by the Gains: India's Twin Double Burdens of Malnutrition and Disease'. ORF Occasional Paper no. 193, Observer Research Foundation, May 2019. https://www.orfonline.

org/wp-content/uploads/2019/05/ORF_OccasionalPaper_193_Double_Health_Burden.pdf. Accessed on 14 July 2021.

Kurosaki, T. 1998. *Risk and Household Behavior in Pakistan's Agriculture*. Tokyo: Institute of Development Economics.

———. 2001. 'Consumption Smoothing and the Structure of Risk and Time Preferences: Theory and Evidence from Village India'. *Hitotsubashi Journal of Economics* 42 (2): 103–117.

———. 2006. 'Consumption Vulnerability to Risk in Rural Pakistan'. *Journal of Development Studies* 42 (1): 70–89.

Kurungati, K. 2019. 'Was There a Victory for Monsanto in India's Supreme Court on a Patent Matter?' *Down To Earth*, 13 January 2019. https://www.downtoearth.org.in/blog/agriculture/was-there-a-victory-for-monsanto-in-india-s-supreme-court-on-a-patent-matter--62800. Accessed on 20 January 2021.

Lahoti, R., and H. Swaminathan. 2016. 'Economic Development and Women's Labor Force Participation in India'. *Feminist Economics* 22 (2): 168–195.

Lakwete, A. 2003. *Inventing the Cotton Gin: Machine and Myth in Antebellum America*. Baltimore: Johns Hopkins University.

Lal, K. S. 1950. *History of the Khaljis (1290–1320)*. Allahabad: The Indian Press.

Lal, N. 2015. 'Mirzapur: Did the Railways Change Its Commercial Narrative?' *Proceedings of the Indian History Congress* 76: 408–425.

Lalitha, N., and P. K. Viswanathan. 2015. *India's Tryst with Bt Cotton: Learning from the First Decade*. New Delhi: Concept Publishing Company Pvt. Ltd.

Lanjouw, P., and N. Stern. 1998. *Economic Development in Palanpur over Five Decades*. Oxford: Oxford University Press.

Leacock, S., and D. G. Mandelbaum. 1955. 'A Nineteenth Century Development Project in India: The Cotton Improvement Program'. *Economic Development and Cultural Change* 3 (4): 334–351.

Lebergott, S. 1981. 'Through the Blockade: The Profitability and Extent of Cotton Smuggling, 1861–1865'. *Journal of Economic History* 41 (4): 867–888.

Leonard, K. 2013. 'Palmer and Company: An Indian Banking Firm in Hyderabad State'. *Modern Asian Studies* 47 (4): 1157–1184.

Lester, R. 1974. 'An Aspect of Confederate Finance during the American Civil War: The Erlanger Loan and the Plan of 1864'. *Business History* 16 (2): 130–144.

Li, T. M. 2014. *Land's End: Capitalist Relations on an Indigenous Frontier.* London: Duke University Press.

Li, Y. 2019. 'Land Inequality and the Provision of Public Works: Evidence from National Rural Employment Guarantee Scheme in India'. https://

papers.ssrn.com/sol3/papers.cfm?abstract_id=3347482. Accessed on 25 May 2021.

Lieberson, J. 1981a. 'Peasant Values and Rural Development: An Unresolved Controversy'. Working Papers, no. 73, Centre for Policy Studies, Population Council, New York.

Lindbeck, J. 2018. 'Slavery's Holy Profits: Religion and Capitalism in the Antebellum Lower Mississippi Valley'. Electronic theses and dissertations, no. 1424, PhD dissertation, Department of History, University of Mississippi.

Ligon, E., and L. Schechter. 2002. 'Measuring Vulnerability: The Director's Cut'. Discussion Paper No. 2002/86, UNU/WIDER. https://www.wider.unu.edu/sites/default/files/dp2002-86.pdf. Accessed on 8 May 2022.

———. 2003. 'Measuring Vulnerability'. *Economic Journal* 113 (March): C95–C102.

———. 2004. 'Evaluating Different Approaches to Estimating Vulnerability'. Social Protection Discussion Paper Series no. 0410, The World Bank, Washington, DC.

Logan, F. A. 1956. 'The American Civil War: An Incentive to Western India's Experiments with Foreign Cotton Seeds?' *Agricultural History* 30 (1): 40–50.

———. 1958. 'India–Britain's Substitute for American Cotton, 1861–1865'. *Journal of Southern History* 24 (4): 472–480.

———. 1965. 'India's Loss of the British Cotton Market after 1865'. *Journal of Southern History* 31 (1): 40–50.

Lohakare, A. C., B. P. Kamdi, M. K. Nakade, V. K. Basunathe, B. Vaishali, et al. 2015. 'Extent of Knowledge of Improved Animal Husbandry Practices and Socio-economical, Psychological Characteristics of Dairy Farmers of Yavatmal District of Vidarbha (Maharashtra)'. *Veterinary Science Research Journal* 6 (1): 23–31.

Longmore, P. K. 1988. *The Invention of George Washington*. Berkeley, California: University of California Press.

Lu, Y., Y. Bei, and J. Zhang. 2012. 'Are Yellow Sticky Traps an Effective Method for Control of Sweet Potato Whitefly, Bemisia tabaci, in the Greenhouse or Field?' *Journal of Insect Science* 12 (1): 113.

Lyall, A. C. 1870. *Gazetteer of Haidarbad Assigned Districts, Commonly Called Berar, 1870*. New Delhi: Archaeological Survey of India, 136.

Lyons, J. S. 1979. 'The English Cotton Industry and the World Market, 1815–1896. By DA Farnie. Oxford: Clarendon Press, 1979. Pp. xiii, 399. $41.00'. *Journal of Economic History* 39 (4): 1033–1035.

Macartney, G. 1962. *An Embassy to China: Being the Journal Kept by Lord Macartney During His Embassy to the Emperor Ch'ien-lung, 1793–1794*. London: Longmans.

Mace, B. J. 1991. 'Full Insurance in the Presence of Aggregate Uncertainty'. *Journal of Political Economy* 99 (5): 928–956.

Mackenna, J., N. N. Wadia, F. Hodgkinson, G. S. Henderson, W. Roberts, H. F. Ashton, and F. Noyce. 1920. *Report of the Indian Cotton Committee, 1919*. Calcutta: Superintendent Government Printing.

Mahajan, V. D. 2007. *History of Medieval India, Part II*. New Delhi: S. Chand Publishing.

Maharashtra (India) Gazetteers Dept. 1977. *Maharashtra State Gazetteers*. Director of Govt Printing, Stationery and Publications, Maharashtra State, 951.

Mampatta, S. P., and R. Bhayani. 2015. 'How Abraham Lincoln Triggered India's First Stock Market Crash'. *Business Standard*, 22 July 2015. https://www.business-standard.com/article/beyond-business/150-years-later-115071001354_1.html. Accessed on 17 July 2021.

Mandal, M. 2020. 'The Problem with the Draft Seed Bill 2019, for Indian Farmers'. *The Wire*, 14 October 2020. https://science.thewire.in/economy/agriculture/draft-seed-bill-2019-indian-farmers/. Accessed on 13 December 2021.

Mani, M., S. Bandyopadhyay, S. Chonabayashi, A. Markandya, and T. Mosier. 2018. *South Asia's Hotspots: The Impact of Temperature and Precipitation Changes on Living Standards*. Washington, DC: World Bank Publications.

Mann, H. H. 1917. *Land and Labour in a Deccan Village*. University of Bombay Economic Series, no. 1. London: H. Milford, Oxford University Press.

Mann, H. H., and N. V. Kanitkar. 1921. *Land and Labour in a Deccan Village, Study No. 2*. University of Bombay Economic Series, no. 3. London: H. Milford, Oxford University Press.

Mann, J. de L., and Al. P. Wadsworth. 1931. *The First Cotton Spinning Factories: The Cotton Trade and Industrial Lancashire, 1600–1780*. Manchester: Manchester University Press.

Mantoux, P. 1963. *The Industrial Revolution in the Eighteenth Century: An Outline of the Beginnings of the Modern Factory System in England*. Oxfordshire: Routledge.

Marar, A. 'Explained: Why a Mission to Make Maharashtra Villages Drought-Free Has Been Shelved'. *Indian Express*, 23 February 2020. https://indianexpress.com/article/explained/explained-jalyukta-shivar-maharashtra-villages-drought-free-scrapped-6282236/. Accessed on 30 April 2022.

Marriott, M., and A. R. Beals. 1955. *Village India; Studies in the Little Community*. Chicago: The University of Chicago Press.

Marx, K. 1852. 'The Eighteenth Brumaire of Louis Bonaparte'. https://www.marxists.org/archive/marx/works/1852/18th-brumaire/ch01.htm. Accessed on 10 April 2021.

Maw, P., P. Solar, A. Kane, and J. S. Lyons. 2022. 'After the Great Inventions: Technological Change in UK Cotton Spinning, 1780–1835'. *Economic History Review* 75 (1): 22–55. https://doi.org/10.1111/ehr.13082.

McAlpin, M. B. 1974. 'Railroads, Prices, and Peasant Rationality: India 1860–1900'. *Journal of Economic History* 34 (3): 662–684.

McCloskey, D. N. 2010. *Bourgeois Dignity: Why Economics Can't Explain the Modern World*. Chicago: University of Chicago Press.

McEldowney, P. F. 1966. 'Pindari Society and the Establishment of British Paramountcy in India'. Master's thesis, Department of History, University of Wisconsin–Madison. https://asianstudies.github.io/area-studies/SouthAsia/Ideas/pindaris.html. Accessed on 14 March 2021.

———. 1980. 'Colonial Administration and Social Developments in Middle India, the Central Provinces, 1861–1921'. PhD thesis, Corcoran Department of History, University of Virginia.

Meeta and Rajivlochan. 2006. *Farmers Suicide: Facts and Possible Policy Interventions*. Pune: Yashada Publications.

Mehta, B. H. 1984. *Gonds of the Central Indian Highlands*. Vol. 1. New Delhi: Concept Publishing Company.

Mehta, J. L. 2005. *Advanced Study in the History of Modern India: Volume One: 1707–1813*. Noida, Uttar Pradesh: Sterling Publishers Pvt. Ltd.

Mehta, N. 2019. *Dynamics of Labour Use and Role of Genetically Modified Crops in Cotton Cultivation*. New Delhi: Academic Foundation.

Mehta, S. G. 2009. 'Govt under Pressure to Lower Cotton Prices'. *Economic Times*, 6 January 2009. https://economictimes.indiatimes.com/markets/commodities/govt-under-pressure-to-lower-cotton-prices/articleshow/3939990.cms?from=mdr. Accessed on 12 October 2021.

Menon, M. 2018. 'Over the Years, Bt Cotton Has Exacerbated Vidarbha's Existing Vulnerabilities'. *Economic and Political Weekly* 53 (21).

———. 2019a. 'Planting of Illegal Crops'. *Economic and Political Weekly* 54 (42): 16–19.

———. 2019b. 'The Long and the Short of Quality Cotton'. *Hindu Business Line*, 17 May 2019. https://www.thehindubusinessline.com/specials/india-interior/the-long-and-the-short-of-quality-cotton/article27164693.ece. Accessed on 17 February 2020.

Menon, M., and Uzramma. 2017. *A Frayed History: The Journey of Cotton in India*. New Delhi: Oxford University Press.

Miller, J. O. 1912. 'The Central Provinces'. *Journal of the Royal Society of Arts* 60 (3103): 611–630.

Mills, I. D. 1986. 'The 1918–1919 Influenza Pandemic: The Indian Experience'. *Indian Economic and Social History Review* 23 (1): 1–40.

Ministry of Statistics and Programme Implementation (MoSPI). 2015. *Income, Expenditure, Productive Assets and Indebtedness of Agricultural Households in India, 2013*. NSS 70th Round, Report no. 576. http://mospi.nic.in/sites/default/files/publication_reports/nss_rep_576.pdf. Accessed on 12 May 2021.

———. 2021. *Situation Assessment of Agricultural Households and Land and Livestock Holdings of Households in Rural India, 2019*. NSS 77th Round, Report no. 587. http://mospi.nic.in/sites/default/files/publication_reports/Report_587m.pdf. Accessed on 12 May 2021.

Mishra, A. K. 2015. 'Premchand Roychand: Mumbai's Original Share King'. *Mint*, 29 May 2015. https://www.livemint.com/Sundayapp/R5BUHntOmItyIJ2yE4G09M/Premchand-Roychand-Mumbais-original-share-king.html. Accessed on 10 October 2021.

Mishra, S. 2006. 'Farmers' Suicides in Maharashtra'. *Economic and Political Weekly* 41 (16): 1538–1545.

———. 2008. 'Risks, Farmers' Suicides and Agrarian Crisis in India: Is There a Way Out?' *Indian Journal of Agricultural Economics* 63 (1): 38–54.

Mishra, S., and S. Gaurav. 2015. 'To Bt or Not to Bt? Risk and Uncertainty Considerations in Technology Assessment'. In *India's Tryst with Bt Cotton: Learning from the First Decade*, ed. N. Lalitha and P. K. Viswanathan, 123–155. New Delhi: Concept Publishing Company Pvt. Ltd.

Mohanty, B. B. 2005. '"We Are Like the Living Dead": Farmer Suicides in Maharashtra, Western India'. *Journal of Peasant Studies* 32 (2): 243–276.

———. 2009. 'Regional Disparity in Agricultural Development of Maharashtra'. *Economic and Political Weekly* 44 (6): 63-69.

———. 2013. 'Farmer Suicides in India: Durkheim's Types'. *Economic and Political Weekly* 48 (21): 45–54.

———. 2019. *Agrarian Transformation in Western India: Economic Gains and Social Costs*. New York: Routledge.

———. 2021. *Agrarian Transformation in Western India: Economic Gains and Social Costs*. New Delhi: Routledge.

Mohanty, B. B., and S. Shroff. 2004. 'Farmers' Suicides in Maharashtra'. *Economic and Political Weekly* 41 (16): 5599–5606.

Mohanty, S. K., and A. Kastor. 2017. 'Out-of-Pocket Expenditure and Catastrophic Health Spending on Maternal Care in Public and Private Health Centres in India: A Comparative Study of Pre and Post National Health Mission Period'. *Health Economics Review* 7 (1): 31.

Mokyr, J. 1992. 'Technological Inertia in Economic History'. *Journal of Economic History* 52 (2).

———. 2016. *A Culture of Growth: The Origins of the Modern Economy*. Princeton, NJ: Princeton University Press.

Moosvi, S. 1987. *The Economy of the Mughal Empire, c. 1595*. Oxford: Oxford University Press.

———. 2011. 'The World of Labour in Mughal India (c. 1500–1750)'. *International Review of Social History* 56 (S19): 245–261.

Morduch, J. 1995. 'Income Smoothing and Consumption Smoothing'. *Journal of Economic Perspectives* 9 (3): 103–114.

Moreland, W. H. 1926. 'Sher Shah's Revenue System'. *Journal of the Royal Asiatic Society* 58 (3): 447–459.

———. 2011. *The Agrarian System of Moslem India*. Cambridge, UK: Cambridge University Press, reprint of 1929.

Morgan, E. S. 1975. *American Slavery, American Freedom: The Ordeal of Colonial Virginia*. New York: W. W. Norton and Company.

Morris, J. H. 1870. *Report on the Administration of the Central Provinces for the Year 1869–1870, Nagpur*. The Chief Commissioner's Office Press, Nagpur.

———. n.d. *Report on the Administration of the Central Provinces for the Year 1902–03*. The Chief Commissioner's Office Press, Nagpur.

———.n.d. *Report on the Administration of the Central Provinces for the Year 1903–04*. The Chief Commissioner's Office Press, Nagpur.

Morris, M. D. 1965. *The Emergence of an Industrial Labour Force in India: A Study of the Bombay Cotton Mills, 1854–1947*. Berkeley; Los Angeles: University of California Press.

Morse, H. B. 1926. *The Chronicles of the East India Company, Trading to China 1635–1834*. Cambridge, UK: Harvard University Press.

Mujumdar, N. A. 1996. 'Financial Sector Reforms: An Exercise in Introspection'. *Economic and Political Weekly* 31 (12): 727–730.

———. 1998. 'Credit Support to Priority Sectors: A Macro Perspective'. *Economic and Political Weekly* 33 (4): 147–150.

Mukherjee, D. 2020. *Bombay Hustle*. New York: Columbia University Press.

Mukherjee, R. 1988. 'On "Village Studies" in India'. *Indian Journal of Social Research* 29 (4): 281–294.

NABARD. 2019. *Doubling Farmers' Income: Issues and Strategies for Maharashtra State.* National Bank for Agriculture and Rural Development & Yes Bank. https://www.nabard.org/auth/writereaddata/tender/2406190028Doubling%20Farmers%202019%20Income%20-%20Issues%20and%20Strategies%20for%20Maharashtra.pdf. Accessed on 23 June 2020.

———. 2021. *Master Circular on Deendayal Antyodaya Yojana – National Rural Livelihoods Mission (DAY-NRLM) and Interest Subvention Scheme for Women SHGs under DAY-NRLM for the Year 2021–22.* https://www.nabard.org/CircularPage.aspx?cid=504&id=5237. Accessed on 12 February 2022.

Nagaraj, K., P. Sainath, R. Rukmani, and R. Gopinath. 2014. 'Farmers' Suicides in India: Magnitudes, Trends, and Spatial Patterns, 1997–2012'. *Review of Agrarian Studies* 4 (2): 53–83.

Nair, I. J., S. Sharma, and P. S. Shera. 2021. 'Impact of Sticky Traps of Different Colours and Shapes against Sucking Pests of Tomato under Protected Conditions: A Randomized Controlled Trial'. *International Journal of Tropical Insect Science* 41 (4): 2739–2746.

Najork, K., S. Gadela, P. Nadiminti, S. Gosikonda, R. Reddy, E. Haribabu, and M. Keck. 2021. 'The Return of Pink Bollworm in India's Bt Cotton Fields: Livelihood Vulnerabilities of Farming Households in Karimnagar District'. *Progress in Development Studies* 21 (1): 68–85.

Nanekar, K. R. 1968. *Land Reforms in Vidarbha: An Enquiry into the Implementation of Land Reforms in the Vidarbha Region.* Calcutta: Oxford; IBH Publishing Company.

Naoroji, D. 1901. *Poverty and Un-British Rule in India.* London: Swan Sonnenschein.

Naravane, M. S. 2006. *Battles of the Honourable East India Company: Making of the Raj.* New Delhi: APH Publishing.

Narang, T. 2013. 'Cotton Pricing Best Left to the Market'. *Hindu Business Line*, 26 March 2013. https://www.thehindubusinessline.com/opinion/cotton-pricing-best-left-to-the-market/article22995782.ece. Accessed on 17 April 2022.

National Archives of India. 1918a. 'Further Papers from the R and A Department Regarding the Appointment of a Committee in India to investigate the Possibility of Increasing the Production of Long Stapled Cotton in India'. Department of Commerce and Industries, PR_000004008643, file no. 25, 1–2.

———. 1918b. 'Papers Regarding the Import of Cotton into Japan from India'. PR_000004008644, file no. 7. Accessed through *Abhilekh Patal.*

National Skill Development Corporation. 2013. *District-wise Skill Gap Study for the State of Maharashtra (2012–17, 2017–22).* https://skillsip.nsdcindia.

org/sites/default/files/kps-document/maha-sg-reports.pdf. Accessed on 18 January 2021.

Narayanan, N. C. 2002. 'Technical Fixes and Social Relations: The Case of Group Farming in Kerala, India'. *Review of Development and Change* 7, no. 2 (July–December): 314–362.

Narayanan, N. C., and Jean-Philippe Venot. 2009. 'Drivers of Change in Fragile Environments: Challenges to Governance in Indian Wetlands'. Natural Resources Forum (A United Nations Journal for Sustainable Development), 33: 320–333.

Newbery, D., and J. Stiglitz. 1981. *The Theory of Commodity Price Stabilisation: A Study in the Economics of Risk*. Oxford: Clarendon Press.

Nightingale, P. 2008. *Trade and Empire in Western India*. Cambridge, UK: Cambridge University Press.

Noe, K. 1994. *Southwest Virginia's Railroad: Modernization and the Sectional Crisis*. Champaign, IL: University of Illinois Press.

O'Brien, K. L., R. Leichenko, U. Kelkar, H. Venema, G. Aandahl, H. Tompkins, et al. 2004. 'Mapping Vulnerability to Multiple Stressors: Climate Change and Globalisation in India'. *Global Environmental Change* 14 (4): 303–313.

O'Brien, P., T. Griffiths, and P. Hunt. 1991. 'Political Components of the Industrial Revolution: Parliament and the English Cotton Textile Industry, 1660–1774'. *Economic History Review New Series* 44 (3): 395–423.

OECD/FAO. 2020. *OECD-FAO Agricultural Outlook 2020–2029*. Paris/FAO; Rome: OECD Publishing. https://doi.org/10.1787/1112c23b-en.

OECD/ICRIER. 2018. *Agricultural Policies in India*. OECD Food and Agricultural Reviews, OECD Publishing, Paris. https://doi.org/10.1787/9789264302334-en.

Olmstead, A. L., and P. W. Rhode. 2018. 'Cotton, Slavery, and the New History of Capitalism'. *Explorations in Economic History* 67: 1–17.

Omvedt, G. 1994. '"We Want the Return for Our Sweat": The New Peasant Movement in India and the Formation of a National Agricultural Policy'. *Journal of Peasant Studies* 21 (3/4): 126–164.

Otto, J. S. 1989. *The Southern Frontiers, 1607–1860: The Agricultural Evolution of the Colonial and Antebellum South*. Westport, CT: Greenwood.

Oxford University Press. 1888. 'Statistics of Iron and Cotton 1830–1860'. *Quarterly Journal of Economics* 2 (3): 379–384.

Oya, C. 2010. 'Agro-Pessimism, Capitalism and Agrarian Change: Trajectories and Contradictions in Sub-Saharan Africa'. In *Political Economy of Africa*, edited by V. Padayachee, 85–109. London: Routledge.

Padma, T. V. 2006. 'GM in India: The Battle over Bt Cotton'. *Sci DevNet*, 20 December 2006. https://www.scidev.net/global/features/gm-in-india-the-battle-over-bt-cotton/. Accessed on 16 March 2021.

Pallavi, A. 2008. 'A Maharashtra Village Revives Itself by Reviving a Tank'. *Down To Earth*, 30 June 2008.

Parasuraman, S., and T. Rajaretnam. 2011. 'Agriculture, Food Security and Nutrition in Vidarbha: A Household Level Analysis'. *Economic and Political Weekly* 46 (19): 42–50.

Park, J.-S., and V. Shinde. 2013. 'Iron Technology of the Ancient Megalithic Communities in the Vidarbha Region of India'. *Journal of Archaeological Science* 40 (11): 3822–3833.

Parthasarathi, P. 2002. 'The Great Divergence'. *Past and Present* 176 (August): 275–293.

Parthasarathi, P., and I. Wendt. 2012. 'Decline in Three Keys: Indian Cotton Manufacturing from the Late Eighteenth Century'. In *The Spinning World: A Global History of Cotton Textiles, 1200-1850*, edited by G. Riello and P. Parthasarathi, 398–407. Delhi: Primus Books.

Patel, H., A. K. Pokharia, N. Nihildas, N. Rai, and R. P. Sinha. 2021. 'Rithi Ranjana: Reconstructing Crop Economy Based on Archaeobotanical Evidence and Radiocarbon Dates from an Early Iron Age Site in Semi-arid Vidarbha, Maharashtra, India'. *Current Science* 120 (11): 1728–1739.

Patnaik, U. 1996. 'Export-Oriented Agriculture and Food Security in Developing Countries and India'. *Economic and Political Weekly* 31 (35/37): 2429–2449.

———. 2007. 'Neoliberalism and Rural Poverty in India'. *Economic and Political Weekly* 42 (3).

Patnaik, U., and S. Moyo. 2011. *The Agrarian Question in the Neoliberal Era: Primitive Accumulation and the Peasantry*. Oxford: Pambazuka Press.

Pavaskar, M. 1985. *Saga of The Cotton Exchange*. Bombay: Popular Publications.

Pearse, A. S. 1915. *Report on Indian Cotton Prepared for the International Federation of Master Cotton Spinners' and Manufacturers' Associations*. Bombay: University of Toronto (Sponsor), 133.

Pearson, M. N. 1976. 'Shivaji and the Decline of the Mughal Empire'. *Journal of Asian Studies* 35 (2): 221–235.

Pearson, M. N., and Ashin Das Gupta, eds. 1987. *India and the Indian Ocean, 1500–1800*. Oxford: Oxford University Press.

Peschard, K., and S. Randeria. 2020. 'Taking Monsanto to Court: Legal Activism around Intellectual Property in Brazil and India'. *Journal of Peasant Studies* 47 (4): 792–819.

Phadke, M. 2017. 'I Am for a Separate Vidarbha State: Maharashtra CM Fadnavis'. *The Print*, 16 November 2017. https://theprint.in/theprint-otc/separate-vidarbha-maharashtra-fadnavis/16582/. Accessed on 16 July 2021.

Piele, J. B. 1880. 'Note on the Economic Condition of the Agricultural Population of India'. Indian Famine Commission.

Pingali, P. L. 2012. 'Green Revolution: Impacts, Limits, and the Path Ahead'. *Proceedings of the National Academy of Sciences* 109 (31): 12302–12308.

Pingali, P. L., C. B. Marquez, and F. G. Palis. 1994. 'Pesticides and Philippine Rice Farmer Health: A Medical and Economic Analysis'. *American Journal of Agricultural Economics* 76 (3): 587–592.

Pingali, P. L., and P. A. Roger, eds. 2012. *Impact of Pesticides on Farmer Health and the Rice Environment*. Vol. 7. New York: Springer Science & Business Media.

Pomeranz, K. 2000. *The Great Divergence: China, Europe, and the Making of the Modern World Economy*. Princeton: Princeton University Press.

Popkin, S. 1979. *The Rational Peasant: The Political Economy of Rural Society in Vietnam*. Berkeley: University of California Press.

Powell, L. N. 1980. *New Masters: Northern Planters during the Civil War and Reconstruction*. New Haven: Yale University Press.

Prakash, O. 1998. *European Commercial Enterprise in Pre-colonial India*. Vol. 5. New Delhi: Cambridge University Press.

Prasad, Akash. K. 2015. 'Gondwana Movement in Post-colonial India: Exploring Paradigms of Assertion, Self-determination and Statehood'. *Journal of Tribal Intellectual Collective India* 3 (1): 37–61.

Prasad, C. S. 1999. 'Suicide Deaths and Quality of Indian Cotton Perspectives from History of Technology and Khadi Movement'. *Economic and Political Weekly* 34 (5): PE12–PE21.

Prasad, G. V. R., and A. Sahni. 1988. 'First Cretaceous Mammal from India'. *Nature* 332 (6165): 638–640.

Pritchett, L., A. Suryahadi, and S. Sumarto. 2000. 'Quantifying Vulnerability to Poverty: A Proposed Measure, Applied to Indonesia'. Policy Research Working Paper No. 2437, The World Bank. https://documents1.worldbank.org/curated/en/131651468751147913/pdf/multi-page.pdf. Accessed on 8 May 2022.

Priyanka, P. 2021. 'A Perfect Storm in the Cotton Field'. *The Hindu*, 4 December 2021. https://www.thehindu.com/opinion/op-ed/a-perfect-storm-in-the-cotton-field/article62111808.ece. Accessed on 3 May 2022.

Puhazhendhi, V., and B. Jayaraman. 1999. 'Rural Credit Delivery: Performance and Challenges before Banks'. *Economic and Political Weekly* 34 (3/4): 175–182.

Punch, M. 1994. 'Politics and Ethics in Qualitative Research'. In *Handbook of Qualitative Research*, edited by N. K. Denzin and Y. S. Lincoln, 83–95. Newbery Park, CA: Sage.

Purohit, M. 2016. 'Rejuvenating Traditional Water System in Maharashtra'. *Down to Earth*, 2 August 2016. https://www.indiawaterportal.org/articles/rejuvenating-traditional-water-system-maharashtra. Accessed on 17 March 2020.

Qaim, M., A. Subramanian, G. Naik, and D. Zilberman. 2006. 'Adoption of Bt Cotton and Impact Variability: Insights from India'. *Applied Economic Perspectives and Policy* 28 (1): 48–58.

Quddusi, M. Y. 2007. *Berar under the Mughals*. Nagpur: Vishwabharti.

Rajankar, M. 2011a. 'Traditional Water Management Systems of Eastern Vidarbha: Community Conservation–1'. *South Asia Network on Dams, Rivers and People* 9 (November): 5–8. https://sandrp.files.wordpress.com/2018/03/traditional_water_management_systems_of-e_vidarbha_community_conservation.pdf. Accessed on 19 March 2021.

———. 2011b. 'Traditional Water Systems of Eastern Vidarbha–II: Current Status'. *South Asia Network on Dams, Rivers, and People* 9 (November–December): 14–17.

Rajankar, M., and Y. Dolke. 2001. 'Decline of a Grand Tradition'. In *Making Water Everybody's Business: Practice and Policy of Water Harvesting*, edited by A. Agarwal, S. Narain, and I. Khurana, 30–32. New Delhi: Centre for Science and Environment.

Rajasekaran, N. 1998. 'Land Reforms in Maharashtra: A Regional Analysis'. *Review of Development and Change* 3 (2): 238–263.

Rajivilochan, M. 2006. *Farmers Suicide—Facts and Possible Policy Interventions*. Pune: YASHADA, Government of Maharashtra, Yashwantrao Chavan Academy Development Administration. http://www.yashada.org/organisation/FarmersSuicideExcerpts.pdf. Accessed on 8 June 2020.

Ramachandran, V. K. 1990. *Wage Labour and Unfreedom in Agriculture: An Indian Case Study*. Oxford: Clarendon Press.

Ramakumar, R., and P. Chavan. 2014. 'Bank Credit to Agriculture in India in the 2000s: Dissecting the Revival'. *Review of Agrarian Studies* 4 (1).

Ramakumar, R., and K. Raut. 2011. 'Agricultural Employment in a Vidarbha Village: Results from a Resurvey'. *Review of Agrarian Studies* 1 (1).

Ramakumar, R., K. Raut, and T. Kamble. 2017. 'Moving Out of Cotton: Notes from a Longitudinal Survey in Two Vidarbha Villages'. *Review of Agrarian Studies* 7 (1).

Ramasundaram, P., and S. Vennila. 2013. 'A Decade of Bt Cotton Experience in India: Pointers for Transgenics in Pipeline'. *Current Science* 104 (6): 697–698.

Ranganathan, T., and S. Gaurav. 2013. 'An Inquiry into the Composition of Farm Revenue Risk: The Case of Six Vidarbha Districts'. *Economic and Political Weekly* 48 (26/27): 125–128.

———. 2019. 'Pest Management Practices of Cotton Farmers in Vidarbha: The Curious Case of Cocktails, Weedicides, and Tonics'. *Economic and Political Weekly* 54 (44).

Ranganathan, T., S. Gaurav, and I. I. Halder. 2018. 'Pesticide Usage by Cotton Farmers in India–Changes Over a Decade'. *Economic and Political Weekly* 53 (19): 43–51.

Rao, K. Narahari, Sulochana Gadgil, P. R. Seshagiri Rao, and K. Savithiri. 2000. 'Tailoring Strategies to Rainfall Variability: The Choice of the Sowing Window'. *Current Science* 78 (10): 1216–1230.

Rao, R. M. M. 2004. *Suicides Among Farmers: A Study of Cotton Growers*. New Delhi: Concept Publishing Company.

Rao, V. M. 1972. 'Land Transfers in Rural Communities: Some Findings in a Ryotwari Region'. *Economic and Political Weekly* 7 (40): A133–A144.

Rashid, A. 1964. 'Famine in the Turco-Afghan Period'. *Proceedings of the Indian History Congress* 26 (2): 84–89, 86.

Ray, I. 2009. 'Identifying the Woes of the Cotton Textile Industry in Bengal: Tales of the Nineteenth Century'. *Economic History Review* 62 (4): 857–892.

Raychaudhuri, T. 1982. 'State and the Economy: The Mughal Empire'. In *Cambridge Economic History of India* edited by T. Raychaudhuri and I. Habib, 1:172-193. Cambridge, UK: Cambridge University Press.

Raychaudhuri, T, and I. Habib, eds. 1982. *The Cambridge Economic History of India: Volume 1, c.1200–c.1750*. Cambridge, UK: Cambridge University Press.

Raza, S. J. 2008. 'Tughlaq Administration in the Light of Epigraphic Evidence'. *Proceedings of the Indian History Congress* 69: 230–239.

Reddy, C. R. 1990. 'The Incidence of Agricultural Labourers in India: Variations over Time and Space (with a Study of Varhad in Maharashtra)'. Doctoral dissertation, Jawaharlal Nehru University, New Delhi.

Reddy, D. N., and D. Kumar. 2017. *Pesticide Poisonings in Yavatmal District in Maharashtra: Untold Realities*. Thrissur: PAN India Report.

Reddy, D. N., and S. Mishra, eds. 2010. *Agrarian Crisis in India*. Nagpur: Oxford University Press.

Reid, A. 2013. 'Southeast Asian Consumption of Indian and British Cotton Cloth, 1600–1850'. In *How India Clothed the World: The World of South Asian*

Textile, 1500–1850, edited by Giorgio Riello and Tirthankar Roy, 31–51. Leiden and Boston: Brill.

Report on the Administration of the Central Provinces for the Year 1902–1903. 1903. Nagpur: Government Central Press.

Report on the Administration of the Central Provinces for the Year 1903–1904. 1904. Nagpur: Government Central Press.

Report of the Fact-Finding Committee for Survey of Scarcity Areas, Maharashtra State, 1973. Vol. 1. Bombay: Government Central Press

Richards, J. F. 1993. *The Mughal Empire*. Vol. 5. Cambridge, UK: Cambridge University Press.

———. 1995. *The Mughal Empire: New Cambridge Economic History of India*. Vol. 1.5. Cambridge: Cambridge University Press.

Riello, G., and T. Roy. 2009. *How India Clothed the World: the World of South Asian Textiles, 1500–1850*. Lieden, Netherlands: Brill.

Rittel, H. W., and M. M. Webber. 1973. 'Dilemmas in a General Theory of Planning'. *Policy Sciences* 4 (2): 55–169.

Rivett-Carnac, J. H. 1910. *Many Memories of Life in India at Home and Abroad*. Scarborough; London: Blackwood and Sons.

Robins, N. 2012. *The Corporation That Changed the World: How the East India Company Shaped the Modern Multinational*. London: Pluto Press.

Rodgers, G. B. 1975. 'Nutritionally Based Wage Determination in the Low-Income Labour Market'. *Oxford Economic Papers* 27 (1): 61–81.

Rodgers, G., and J. Rodgers. 2001. 'A Leap across Time: When Semi-feudalism Met the Market in Rural Purnia'. *Economic and Political Weekly* 36 (22): 1976–1983.

Rodgers, G., and J. Rodgers. 2011. 'Inclusive Development? Migration, Governance and Social Change in Rural Bihar'. *Economic and Political Weekly* 46 (23): 43–50.

Rodrik, D., A. Subramanian, and F. Trebi. 2004. 'Institutions Rule: The Primacy of Institutions Over Geography and Integration in Economic Development'. *Journal of Economic Growth* 9 (2): 131–165.

Rönnbäck, K., and D. Theodoridis. 2021. 'Cotton Cultivation under Colonial Rule in India in the Nineteenth Century from a Comparative Perspective'. *Economic History Review* 75 (2): 374–395. DOI: https://doi.org/10.1111/ehr.13094.

Rose, W. L. N. 1999. *A Documentary History of Slavery in North America*. Athens, Georgia: University of Georgia Press.

Rosenzweig, M. R., and H. Binswanger. 1993. 'Wealth, Weather Risk and the Composition and Profitability of Agricultural Investments'. *Economic Journal* 103 (416): 56–78.

Rosenzweig, M. R., and O. Stark. 1989. 'Consumption Smoothing, Migration, and Marriage: Evidence from Rural India'. *Journal of Political Economy* 97 (4): 905–926.

Rosenzweig, M. R., and K. Wolpin. 1993. 'Credit Market Constraints, Consumption Smoothing, and the Accumulation of Durable Production Assets in Low Income Countries: Investments in Bullocks in India'. *Journal of Political Economy* 101 (2): 223–244.

Ross, J. 1900. *The Marquis of Hastings, K. G. and the Final Overthrow of the Maratha Power.* Oxford: Clarendon Press.

Rothman, J. D. 2012. *Flush Times and Fever Dreams: A Story of Capitalism and Slavery in the Age of Jackson.* Athens: University of Georgia Press.

Roumasset, J. A., J. M. Boussard, and I. Singh. 1979. *Risk, Uncertainty, and Agricultural Development.* Southeast Asian Regional Centre for Graduate Study and Research in Agriculture (SEARCA) and Agricultural Development Council (ADC), Laguna, Philippines.

Roy, T. 2019. 'Unyielding Land'. In *How British Rule Changed India's Economy*, edited by Tirthankar Roy, 81–98. Palgrave Studies in Economic History. Cham: Palgrave Pivot.

Royle, J. F. 1851. *On the Culture and Commerce of Cotton in India and Elsewhere: With an Account of the Experiments Made by the Hon. East India Company Up To the Present Time.* London: Smith, Elder, & Co.

Rukmani, R., and M. Manjula. 2009. *Designing Rural Technology Delivery Systems for Mitigating Agricultural Distress: A Study of Wardha District.* MS Swaminathan Research Foundation, Chennai, and Office of the Principal Scientific Adviser to the Government of India, New Delhi. http://59.160.153.188/library/sites/default/files/Study-of-Wardha-RR10-25.pdf. Accessed on 30 October 2019.

Rungta, S. 1985. 'Bowreah Cotton and Fort Gloster Jute Mills, 1872–1900'. *Indian Economic and Social History Review* 22 (2): 109–137.

Russell, E. J. 1962. 'Dr H. H. Mann'. *Nature* 193 (4813): 321–322.

Russell, R. V., and R. B. Hiralal. 1916. *Tribes and Castes of the Central Provinces of India.* Vol. 4. London: Macmillan & Co.

Sahlins, M. 1972. *Stone-Age Economics.* Chicago: Aldine-Atheton.

Sainath, P. 1996. *Everyone Loves a Good Drought.* New Delhi: Penguin India.

———. 2011. 'In 16 Years, Farm Suicides Cross a Quarter Million'. *The Hindu*, 29 October 2011. https://www.thehindu.com/opinion/columns/sainath//article60641412.ece. Accessed on 23 May 2021.

Saith, A., and A. Tankha. 1972. 'Economic Decision-Making of the Poor Peasant Household'. *Economic and Political Weekly* 1 (1): 351–360.

Saksena, B. P. 1992 (1970). 'The Khaljis: Alauddin Khalji'. In *A Comprehensive History of India: The Delhi Sultanat (AD 1206–1526)*, edited by Mohammad Habib and Khaliq Ahmad Nizami, 5:326–425. 2nd ed. New Delhi: The Indian History Congress/People's Publishing House.

Sally, M. 2020. 'Cotton Seeds Price: Government to Review Cotton Seed Price'. *Economic Times Bureau*, 21 February 2020. https://economictimes.indiatimes.com/news/economy/agriculture/government-to-review-cotton-seed-price/articleshow/74240990.cms?from=mdr. Accessed on 17 March 2021.

Sanjek, R. 2014. *Ethnography in Today's World: Color Full before Color Blind.* Philadelphia: University of Philadelphia Press.

Santhanam, V., and V. Sundaram. 1997. 'Agri-history of Cotton in India: An Overview'. *Asian Agri-History* 1 (4): 235–251.

Sanyal, Kalyan K. 1976. 'Review of Production Conditions in Indian Agriculture by Krishna Bharadwaj'. *Economic and Political Weekly* 11 (30): 1112–1114.

Sapale, S., and N. Malani. 2015. *Ushering in the 2nd Green Revolution: Role of Crop Protection Chemicals.* New Delhi: Federation of Indian Chambers of Commerce & Industry, and TATA Strategic Management Group.

Sardesai, G. S. 1948. *New History of the Marathas: The Expansion of the Maratha Power, 1707–1772.* Vol. 2. Bombay: Phoenix Publications.

Sarkar, J. 1906. 'Aurangzeb's Farman to Rasikdas'. *Journal of the Asiatic Society of Bengal.* 1st ed. https://famineanddearth.exeter.ac.uk/displayhtml.html?id=fp_00386_fa_rasikdasfarmanjasb. Accessed on 21 June 2021.

———. 1924. *History of Aurangzib: Based on Original Sources.* Vol. 5. Calcutta: M. C. Sarkar & Sons.

———. 1960. *Military History of India.* Calcutta: M. C. Sarkar and Sons.

Saswadkar, P. L. 1967. 'The Dawn of Modernization in the Maratha State on the Eve of its Extinction, 1790–1840'. *Proceedings of the Indian History Congress* 29 (2): 127–131.

Satya, L. D. 1997. *Cotton and Famine in Berar 1850–1900.* New Delhi: Manohar.

———. 1998. 'Colonial Encroachment and Popular Resistance: Land Survey and Settlement Operations in Berar (Central India), 1861–1877'. *Agricultural History* 72 (1): 55–76.

Sawant, R. 2010. 'Review of Archaeological Investigations in the Protohistoric and Historical Archaeology of Vidarbha'. *Man and Environment* 35 (2): 45–65.

———. 2011. 'Buddhism in a Regional Perspective: A Glance at Early Historic Vidarbha'. In *Monasteries Shrines and Society: Buddhist and Brahmanical Institutions in India in their Socio-Economic Context*, edited by Birendra Nath Prasad, 84–115. New Delhi: Manak.

Schlingloff, D. 1974. 'Cotton-Manufacture in Ancient India'. *Journal of the Economic and Social History of the Orient/Journal de l'histoire Economique et Sociale de l'Orient* 17 (1): 81–90.

Schonhardt-Bailey, C. 1991. 'Lessons in Lobbying for Free Trade in 19th-Century Britain: To Concentrate or Not'. *American Political Science Review* 85 (1): 37–58.

———. 2006. *From the Corn Laws to Free Trade: Interests, Ideas, and Institutions in Historical Perspective*. Cambridge, MA: MIT Press.

Schottenhammer, A. 2007. *The East Asian Maritime World, 1400–1800: Its Fabrics of Power and Dynamics of Exchanges*. Vol. 4. Wiesbaden, Germany: Otto Harrassowitz.

Scott, J. C. 1977. *The Moral Economy of the Peasant: Rebellion and Subsistence in Southeast Asia*. Vol. 315. New Haven: Yale University Press.

Secretary of Public Works Department. 1880. 'Irrigation as a Protection against Famine'. Indian Famine Commission.

Sen, A. K. 1982. *Poverty and Famines: An Essay on Entitlements and Deprivation*. Oxford: Clarendon Press.

———. 1985. *Commodities and Capabilities*. Amsterdam: North Holland.

———. 1986. 'Food Economics and Entitlements'. WIDER Working Paper no. 1, World Institute for Development Economics Research, Helsinki.

Sen, S. 2013. *Textbook of Medieval Indian History*. New Delhi: Primus Books.

Sengupta, N., S. Gaurav, and J. Evans. 2021. 'The Skills Space in Informal Work: Insights from Bangalore Slums'. *Journal of Development Studies* 57 (10): 1662–1689.

Seo, H. K. 2013. 'Can Behavioral Biases Explain Demand for a Harmful Pesticide? Evidence from India'. Discussion paper, Harvard Environmental Economics Program, Cambridge, MA, May 2013. https://citeseerx.ist.psu.edu/viewdoc/download?doi=10.1.1.638.1566&rep=rep1&type=pdf. Accessed on 27 March 2021.

Sethi, A. 2018. 'The Life of Debt in Rural India'. Unpublished PhD thesis, UC Berkeley.

———. 2019. 'Mahadev's Gift: Men, Bullocks and the Community of Cultivation in Central India, South Asia'. *Journal of South Asian Studies* 42 (6): 1173–1191.

Sexton, J. 2005. *Debtor Diplomacy: Finance and American Foreign Relations in the Civil War.* Oxford: Oxford University Press.

Shah, A., and B. Harriss-White. 2011. 'Resurrecting Scholarship on Agrarian Transformations'. *Economic and Political Weekly* 46 (39): 13–18.

Shah, S. H., and L. M. Harris. 2021. 'Beyond Local Case Studies in Political Ecology: Spatializing Agricultural Water Infrastructure in Maharashtra Using a Critical, Multimethods, and Multiscalar Approach'. *Annals of the American Association of Geographers* 112 (4): 988–1007.

Shah, T., Y. Mehta, V. Kher, and A. Palrecha. 2014. 'Generating Agrarian Dynamism: Saurashtra's Lessons for Vidarbha'. *Economic and Political Weekly* 49 (26/27): 86–94.

Sharma, R. S. 1987. *Urban Decay in India, Circa 300–1200.* New Delhi: Munshiram Manoharlal Publishers Pvt. Ltd.

Sharma, S. K., A. Sawant, and T. Lahiri. 2021. 'Unfair Fields: Asymmetric WTO Rules Let US Inflate Cotton Subsidies Must Be Reformed'. *Down to Earth*, 22 February 2021. https://www.downtoearth.org.in/blog/agriculture/unfair-fields-asymmetric-wto-rules-let-us-inflate-cotton-subsidies-must-be-reformed-75622. Accessed on 18 September 2021.

Sharma, S. R. 1951. *The Making of Modern India: From AD 1526 to Present Day.* New Delhi: Orient Longman.

Shashtri, P. 2015. 'American War Set Gujarat Cotton Afire 150 Years Ago'. *Times of India*, 23 June 2015. https://timesofindia.indiatimes.com/city/ahmedabad/american-war-set-gujarat-cotton-afire-150-years-ago/articleshow/47790075.cms. Accessed on 12 July 2021.

Shefveland, K. M. 2014. 'The Many Faces of Native Bonded Labor in Colonial Virginia'. *Native South* 7: 68–91.

Shetty, S. L. 2004. 'Distributional Issues in Bank Credit: Multi-Pronged Strategy for Correcting Past Neglect'. *Economic and Political Weekly* 39 (29): 3265–3269.

Shiva, V. 2013. 'Seeds of Suicide and Slavery Versus Seeds of Life and Freedom'. *Al Jazeera*, 30 March 2013. https://www.aljazeera.com/opinions/2013/3/30/seeds-of-suicide-and-slavery-versus-seeds-of-life-and-freedom. Accessed on 24 February 2022.

Shiva, V. 2014. 'Seed Monopolies, GMOs and Farmer Suicides in India'. *Counter Currents*, 10 January 2014. https://www.countercurrents.org/shiva100114.htm. Accessed on 24 February 2022.

Shroff, S., and S. Mitra. 2007. 'Farmers' Suicides in Maharashtra'. *Economic and Political Weekly* 42 (49): 73–77.

Shubik, M. 1991. 'Risk, Society, Politicians, Scientists, and People'. In *Risk, Organizations, and Society*, edited by M. Shubik, 7–29. Calcutta: Springer-Verlag.

Siddiqi, N. A. 1960. 'The Dastur-ul-Amal-i-Baikas: An Administrative Manual of Muhammad Shah's Reign'. *Proceedings of the Indian History Congress* 23: 243–247.

Silver, A. W. 1966. *Manchester Men and Indian Cotton, 1847–1872*. Manchester: Manchester University Press.

Singh, P., and M. S. Kairon. n.d. 'Cotton Varieties and Hybrids'. CICR Technical Bulletin no. 13, Central Institute for Cotton Research (CICR), Nagpur. https://www.cicr.org.in/pdf/cotton_varieties_hybrids.pdf. Accessed on 24 November 2020.

Sinha, K. N. 1966. British Relations with the Nagpur Court (1799–1806). *Proceedings of the Indian History Congress* 28: 346–353.

Slater, G. 1918. *Some South Indian Villages*. Vol. 1 of *Economic Studies*. Madras: Oxford University Press.

Smith, C. T., and P. A. Van Dyke. 2004. 'Muslims in the Pearl River Delta, 1700 to 1930'. *Review of Culture* 3 (10): 6–15.

Smith, J. D. 2003. 'The Enduring Myth of "Forty Acres and a Mule"'. *Chronicle of Higher Education* 49 (24). https://www.chronicle.com/article/the-enduring-myth-of-forty-acres-and-a-mule/. Accessed on 27 February 2021.

Somers, R. 1871. *The Southern States since the War, 1870–1*. London; New York: Macmillan & Co.

Sparks, W. H. 1870. *Memories of Fifty Years*. Philadelphia: Claxton, Remsen and Haffelfinger.

Spate, O. H. K., and A. T. A. Learmonth. 1954. *India and Pakistan: A General and Regional Geography*. London: Methuen.

Spodek, H. 1965. 'The Manchesterisation of Ahmedabad'. *Economic Weekly* 17 (13): 483–490.

———. 2011. *Ahmedabad: Shock City of Twentieth-Century India*. Bloomington: Indiana University Press.

Srinivas, M. N. 1955. 'The Social System of a Mysore Village'. In *Village India: Studies in the Little Community*, edited by McKim Marriott, 1–35. Chicago: University of Chicago Press.

———, ed. 1955. *India's Villages*. Bombay: Asia Publishing House.

Stephen, S. G. 1976. 'The Origins of Sea Island Cotton'. *Agricultural History* 50 (2): 391–399.

Stewart, G. 1993. 'The Marathas 1600–1818'. In *The New Cambridge History of India*, edited by Gordan Stewart, 2:73–74. Cambridge, UK: Cambridge University Press.

Stone, G. D. 2002a. 'Both Sides Now: Fallacies in the Genetic Modification Wars, Implications for Developing Countries, and Anthropological Perspectives'. *Current Anthropology* 43 (4): 611–630.

———. 2002b. 'Constructing Facts: Bt Cotton Narratives in India'. *Economic and Political Weekly* 47 (38): 62–70.

———. 2007. 'Agricultural Deskilling and the Spread of Genetically Modified Cotton in Warangal'. *Current Anthropology* 48 (1): 67–103.

———. 2011. 'Field versus Farm in Warangal: Bt Cotton, Higher Yields, and Larger Questions'. *World Development* 39 (3): 387–398.

Stone, G. D., and A. Flachs. 2018. 'The Ox Fall Down: Path-Breaking and Technology Treadmills in Indian Cotton Agriculture'. *Journal of Peasant Studies* 45 (7): 1272–1296.

Stone, G. D., A. Flachs, and C. Diepenbrock. 2014. 'Rhythms of the Herd: Long-Term Dynamics in Seed Choice by Indian Farmers'. *Technology in Society* 36 (November): 26–38.

Stowe, H. B. 1852. *Uncle Tom's Cabin; or, Life Among the Lowly*. Vol. 1. Boston: John P. Jewitt.

Subramanian, A., and M. Qaim. 2010. 'The Impact of Bt Cotton on Poor Households in Rural India'. *Journal of Development Studies* 46 (2): 295–311.

Subramanyam, M. A., I. Kawachi, Lisa F. Berkman, and S. V. Subramanian. 2011. 'Is Economic Growth Associated with Reduction in Child Undernutrition in India?' *PLoS Medicine* 8 (3): e1000424.

Sugihara, K. 2013. 'The Resurgence of Intra-Asian Trade, 1800–1850'. In *How India Clothed the World: The World of South Asian Textiles, 1500–1850*, edited by Giorgio Riello and Tirthankar Roy, 139–169. Leiden; Boston: Brill.

Sukhtankar, S. 2012. 'Sweetening the Deal? Political Connections and Sugar Mills in India'. *American Economic Journal: Applied Economics* 4 (3): 43–63.

Sukhtankar, S. E. 1973. *Report of the Fact-Finding Committee for Survey of Scarcity Areas: Maharashtra State*. https://dspace.gipe.ac.in/xmlui/handle/10973/52242. Accessed on 26 April 2022.

Sundaram, V. 1974. *Fifty Years of Research [at the] Cotton Technological Research Laboratory, Bombay, 1924–1974*. New Delhi: Indian Council of Agricultural Research.

Surdam, D. G. 1998. 'King Cotton: Monarch or Pretender? The State of the Market for Raw Cotton on the Eve of the American Civil War'. *Economic History Review* 51 (1): 113–132.

Surjit, V. 2017. 'The Evolution of Farm Income Statistics in India: A Review'. *Review of Agrarian Studies* 7 (2).

Swami, D., P. Dave, and D. Parthasarathy. 2021. 'Analysis of Temperature Variability and Extremes with Respect to Crop Threshold Temperature for Maharashtra, India'. *Theoretical and Applied Climatology* 144 (3/4): 861–872.

Swami, D., and D. Parthasarathy. 2021. 'Dynamics of Exposure, Sensitivity, Adaptive Capacity and Agricultural Vulnerability at District Scale for Maharashtra, India, 2021'. *Ecological Indicators* 121 (107206): 1–17. DOI: 10.1016/j.ecolind.2020.107206.

Swaminathan, M. 2017. 'In Focus: Crop Incomes in India'. *Review of Agrarian Studies* 7 (2).

Swaminathan, M., and V. Rawal. 2011a. 'Are There Benefits from the Cultivation of Bt Cotton? A Comment Based on Data from a Vidarbha Village'. *Review of Agrarian Studies* 1 (1).

———. 2011b. 'Is India Really a Country of Low-Income Inequality? Observations from Eight Villages?' *Review of Agrarian Studies* 1 (1).

Swierenga, R. P. 1968. *Pioneers and Profits: Land Speculation on the Iowa Frontier.* Ames: Iowa State University Press.

Talule, D. 2020. 'Farmer Suicides in Maharashtra, 2001–2018'. *Economic and Political Weekly* 55 (25): 116–125.

Taneja, S. 2019. 'India Bans 18 Pesticides, Has Many More to Go'. *Down to Earth*, 16 August 2018. https://www.downtoearth.org.in/news/agriculture/india-bans-18-pesticides-has-many-more-to-go-61405. Accessed on 21 May 2022.

Taylor, M. 1863. 'Sketch of the Topography of East and West Berar, in Reference to the Production of Cotton'. *Journal of the Royal Asiatic Society of Great Britain and Ireland* 20: 1–21.

Temple, R. 1882. *Men and Events of My Time in India*. London: J. Murray.

Thaler, R. 1999. 'Mental Accounting Matters'. *Journal of Behavioral Decision Making* 12 (3): 183–206.

Thankappan, N. P. 1990. 'The Growth and Development of Old Calcutta'. In *The Living City, 2 Vols*, edited by S. Chaudhuri, 10–23. New Delhi: Oxford University Press

The Hindu. 2020. 'Right by Birth: The Hindu Editorial on Daughters and Hindu Succession Act'. 14 August 2020. https://www.thehindu.com/opinion/

editorial/right-by-birth-the-hindu-editorial-on-daughters-and-hindu-succession-act/article32347299.ece. Accessed on 27 November 2021.

The Hitavada. 2020. 'MGNREGS Provides Work to 4.10 Lakh Workers in Vid'. 22 May 2020. https://www.thehitavada.com/Encyc/2020/5/22/MGNREGS-provides-work-to-4-10-lakh-workers-in-Vid.html. Accessed on 27 November 2021.

———. 2021. 'Agriculture Department Cracks Down on Unapproved HTBt Cotton Seeds'. 14 June 2021. https://www.thehitavada.com/Encyc/2021/6/14/Agriculture-Department-cracks-down-on-unapproved-HTBt-cotton-seeds.html. Accessed on 21 May 2022.

Thorner, D. 1951. 'Capital Movement and Transportation: Great Britain and the Development of India's Railways'. *Journal of Economic History* 11 (4): 389–402.

———. 1955. 'The Pattern of Railway Development in India'. *Journal of Asian Studies* 14 (2): 201–216.

———. 1967. 'Social and Economic Studies of Dr Mann'. *Economic and Political Weekly* 2 (13): 642–645.

Thornton, E. 1854. *Gazetteer of the Territories under the Government of the East India Company, and of the Native State on the Continent of India*. Vol. 1. London: William H. Allen & Co.

Timberlake, R. H. 1997. 'Panic of 1837'. In *Business Cycles and Depressions: An Encyclopedia*, edited by David Glasner and Thomas F. Cooley, 514–516. New York: Garland Publishing.

Tingre, A. S, A. S. Ingole, P. D. Thakare, and P. V. Shingrup. 2008. 'Cropping Pattern Changes and Crop Diversification in Akola District of Vidarbha'. *Journal of Soils and Crops* 18 (1): 240–244.

Tomlinson, B. R. 2008 (1993). *The Economy of Modern India, 1860–1970*. Cambridge, UK: Cambridge University Press.

Townsend, R. 1994. 'Risk and Insurance in Village India'. *Econometrica* 62 (3): 539–591

———. 1995. 'Consumption Insurance: An Evaluation of Risk-Bearing Systems in Low-Income Countries'. *Journal of Economic Perspectives* 9 (3): 83–102.

Townsend, R. M., S. Sakunthasathien, and R. Jordan. 2013. *Chronicles from the Field: The Townsend Thai Project*. Cambridge, MA: MIT Press.

Tripathi, D. 1980. 'A Shot from Afar: India and the Failure of Confederate Diplomacy'. *Indian Journal of American Studies* 10 (2): 74–89.

———. 2004. *The Oxford History of Indian Business*. New Delhi: Oxford University Press.

Turnbull, N. 1917. 'The Beginning of Cotton Cultivation in Georgia'. *Georgia Quarterly History* 2 (1): 39–45.

Turner, B. L., R. E. Kasperson, A. P. Matson, J. McCarthy, R. W. Corell, L. Christensen, et al. 2003. 'A Framework for Vulnerability Analysis in Sustainability Science'. *Proceedings of National Academy of Sciences of the United States of America* 100 (4): 8074–8079.

Twomey, M. J. 1983. 'Employment in Nineteenth Century Indian Textiles'. *Explorations in Economic History* 20 (1): 37–57.

Udmale, P., Y. Ichikawa, S. Manandhar, H. Ishidaira, and A. S. Kiem. 2014. 'Farmers' Perception of Drought Impacts, Local Adaptation and Administrative Mitigation Measures in Maharashtra State, India'. *International Journal of Disaster Risk Reduction* 10 (A): 250–269.

Udry, C. 1994. 'Risk and Insurance in a Rural Credit Market: An Empirical Investigation in Northern Nigeria'. *Review of Economic Studies* 61 (3): 495–526.

Upadhyay, S. B. 1989. 'Communalism and Working Class: Riot of 1893 in Bombay City'. *Economic and Political Weekly* 24 (30): PE69–PE75.

———. 1990. 'Cotton Mill Workers in Bombay, 1875 to 1918: Conditions of Work and Life'. *Economic and Political Weekly* 25 (30), 87–99.

UP Front News. 'Maharashtra: Despite SC Ruling that Maratha Reservation is Unconstitutional, the Demand Again Gathers Momentum'. 24 May 2021. https://www.indiatoday.in/magazine/up-front/story/20210524-maharashtra-despite-sc-ruling-that-maratha-reservation-is-unconstitutional-the-demand-again-gathers-momentum-1802533-2021-05-14. Accessed on 27 November 2021.

Vajpeyi, R. 1989. 'Areas of Set-Back and Tension in Agrarian Relations in Vidarbha in the Fifth Century: A Causality Analysis'. *Proceedings of the Indian History Congress* 50: 96–104.

Van Dycke, L., and G. Van Overwalle. 2017. 'Genetically Modified Crops and Intellectual Property Law: Interpreting Indian Patents on Bt Cotton in View of the Socio-Political Background'. *JIPITEC* 8: 151–165.

Voelcker, J. A. 1893. *Report on the Improvement of Indian Agriculture*. London: Eyre and Spottiswoode.

Wacha, D. E. 1910. *A Financial Chapter in the History of Bombay City*. Bombay: Commercial Press.

———. 1918. 'Indian Cotton and the Cotton-mill Industry'. *Journal of the Royal Society of Arts* 66 (3426): 544–564.

Wade, R. 1988. *Village Republics: Economic Conditions for Collective Action in South, India*. Cambridge South Asian Studies, series no. 4. Cambridge, UK: Cambridge University Press.

Wadsworth, A. P., and J. de L. Mann. 1931. *The Cotton Trade and Industrial Lancashire, 1600–1780*. Manchester: Manchester University Press.

Walker, T. S., and N. S. Jodha. 1986. 'How Small Farm Households Adapt to Risk'. In *Crop Insurance for Agricultural Development*, edited by P. Hazel, C. Pomareda, and A. Valdes, 17–34. Baltimore: Johns Hopkins University Press.

Walker, T. S., and J. G. Ryan. 1990. *Village and Household Economics in India's Semi-arid Tropics*. Baltimore, MD: Johns Hopkins University Press.

Ward-Perkins, C. 'The Commercial Crisis of 1847'. *Oxford Economy Papers* 2 (1): 75–94.

Ware, C. 1931. *The Early New England Cotton Manufacture*. Boston: Houghton Mifflin Company.

Washbrook, D. A. 1988. 'Progress and Problems: South Asian Economic and Social history c. 1720–1860'. *Modern Asian Studies* 22 (1): 57–96.

Waters, D. 2010. 'The Fiftieth Anniversary of the "Journal" of the Royal Asiatic Society Hong Kong Branch, 1961–2010'. *Journal of the Royal Asiatic Society Hong Kong Branch* 50: 21–49.

Watson, F. 1879. *Report on Cotton Gins and on the Cleaning and Quality of Indian Cotton*. London: William H. Allen & Co..

Watson, J. F. 1858. 'On the Growth of Cotton in India, Its Present State and Future Prospects, with Special Reference to Supplies to Britain'. *Journal of the Society of Arts, London* 7 (2): 293.

———. 1859. 'On the Growth of Cotton in India, its Present State and Future Prospects, with Special Reference to Supplies to Britain'. *Journal of the Society of Arts, London* 7 (331): 277–293.

Watt, G. 1966 (1908). *The Commercial Products of India*. London: J. Murray, 276.

Wetherington, M. 2005. *Plain Folk's Fight: The Civil War and Reconstruction in Piney Woods Georgia*. Chapel Hill, NC: University of North Carolina Press.

Whale, P. B. 1944. 'A Retrospective View of the Bank Charter Act of 1844'. *Economica New Series* 11 (43): 109–111.

WHO. 2020. *The WHO Recommended Classification of Pesticides by Hazard and Guidelines to Classification 2019*. Geneva, Switzerland: World Health Organization.

Wink, A. 1997. *Al-Hind, Volume 2: Slave Kings and the Islamic Conquest, 11th–13th Centuries*. Leiden, Netherlands: E. J. Brill.

Wittfogel, K. A. 1957. *Oriental Despotism: A Comparative Study of Total Power.* London: Oxford University Press.

Wolcott, H. F. 2005. *The Art of Fieldwork.* 2nd ed. Walnut Creek, CA: Altamira Press.

Woodman, H. D. 1966. 'The Decline of Cotton Factorage after the Civil War'. *American Historical Review* 71 (4): 1219–1236.

———. 1968. *King Cotton and His Retainers: Financing and Marketing the Cotton Crop of the South, 1800–1925.* Lexington: University Press of Kentucky.

Woodward, G. S. 1976. *Pocahontas.* Oklahoma: University of Oklahoma Press.

World Bank. 2005. *Managing Agricultural Production Risk: Innovations in Developing Countries.* ESW Report by the Agricultural and Rural Development Department, The World Bank, Washington, DC. http://siteresources.worldbank.org/INTARD/Resources/Managing_Ag_Risk_FINAL.pdf. Accessed on 22 July 2021.

Wright, G. 1974. 'Cotton Competition and the Post-bellum Recovery of the American South'. *Journal of Economic History* 34 (3): 610–635.

———. 1978. *The Political Economy of the Cotton South: Households, Markets and Wealth in the Nineteenth Century.* New York: Norton.

Yadav, S. 2018. *Precarious Labour and Informal Economy: Work, Anarchy, and Society in an Indian Village.* New York: Springer.

Yazdani, G. 1961. *The Early History of the Deccan.* Vol. 1. Published for the Government of Andhra Pradesh by Oxford University Press, London.

INDEX

aar, 190
Abdali, Ahmad Shah, 25
abiotic stress, 219
accident/historical accidents, 3–4, 6, 8, 32, 61, 123, 239, 375–377
accredited social health activists (ASHAs), 157, 187, 253
acephate, 286, 289
Achalpur (Elichpur), 22
Adil Shah, Adil Shahi sultanate, 24, 49n71
administrative records, 7, 93–94, 324
adoption, 41, 152n224, 156n270, 166, 175, 229, 242, 272–273, 276, 283, 285, 294, 302, 305n1, 308n30, 313n64, 351, 357, 394, 397, 402–403
Africa, 114, 374, 404n2
agrarian crisis, 2–3, 6–10, 15–16, 64, 118, 120, 125, 127, 156–157n273, 168, 171, 215n67, 216n71, 269, 332, 334, 337, 360, 373–375, 383, 387, 406n15, 409n53
agrarian distress, 2, 4, 10, 13–14, 19–20, 63, 118, 149n184, 215n67, 317, 373–374, 399–400
agrarian history, 123, 187
agrarian transformation, 7, 19, 163, 208n12, 258, 268n28, 315, 366n24, 372n60, 375, 377
agrarian transition, 3, 398, 403–404
agreement on agriculture, 118
Agricultural Debt Waiver and Debt Relief Scheme (ADWDRS), 202
agricultural development, 5, 7–8, 14–15, 19, 31, 36, 41–42, 127, 148n166, 164, 215n63, 229, 316, 363n4, 378, 384, 386–387, 397–399, 404, 408n37, 409n51
agricultural extension
  krishi kendra/krishi vikash kendra, 221, 280, 283
  Krishi Vigyan Kendra (KVK), 198, 304
  private extension, 304
agricultural labourers, 38, 94, 97, 104, 149n179, 149n185, 161–162, 255–257, 267n21, 294–296, 311n51
Agricultural Loans Act, 1891, 107
Agricultural Produce Market Committees (APMCs), 332
Agricultural Technology Management Agency (ATMA), 198

agriculture
acreage, 86, 226–228
agronomic practices, 5, 90, 112, 182, 219, 230, 233, 269, 292–293, 301, 303–304
commercialization, 7, 9, 34, 61, 119, 124, 316
credit, 5, 119–120, 124, 199, 216n69
cropping pattern, 5, 8, 70, 73, 90
income, 2, 5, 220, 236–237
inputs, 270–277
insurance, 261, 318
irrigated, 319
irrigation, 96, 128, 314
loss, 31, 115
markets, 34
net returns, 296–298
own production, 115
rain-fed, 39
technology, 71
agrochemicals, 221, 273, 314n71
agroclimatic zone, 172–173
Ahmad Shah, Sultan, 23
Ahmedabad, 61, 108–109, 111, 126, 145n132, 152n222, 153n235, 154n237
Ahmedabad Mill Owners Association, 109, 111
Ahmednagar, Ahmednagar sultanate, 23
ainkali, 33–34
Ajantha range, 73
Akbar, 23–24, 33, 40, 49n73, 56n143, 59n177, 414
Alabama, 66, 134n36, 137–138n70
Ala-ud-din Husain Bahamani Gangu (Hasan Shah and Bahaman Shah), 22
Ala-ud-din Khalji (Khilji), 21, 31, 47n48, 47n52
alcohol, 94–95, 181, 225, 362
Alexandria Mill, 109
Ali Mardan Khan, 25
All India Congress Committee, 18
alluvial plains, 73
Amaravati Gazetteer (Amraoti Gazetteer), 46n41, 49n69, 100, 146n148, 149n187
Ambar, Malik, 23, 34–35, 41, 56n145
Ambedkar, B. R., 46n34, 190, 208n13, 213n49
American Civil War, 3, 7, 60–62, 64, 68, 70–71, 81, 83, 88, 103–104, 108, 112, 123–126, 127n2, 128n5, 136n61, 137n64, 138n71
American South, 38, 60, 62–68, 71–72, 78, 83–85, 95, 112, 123, 128n7, 137n69
amils, 32, 34–35
amirs, 22, 23
Amoy, 76
Amravati, 13, 15–17, 20, 22, 24, 80, 82–84, 99, 171
Amravati division, 13, 16, 99, 120, 209n17, 383
ancient history, 19
anganwadi worker (*sevika*), 187
Anglo-Maratha Wars, First, Second, Third, Fourth, 51n95
anicuts, 39
animal husbandry, 178, 198, 204, 215n64
animal–human conflict, 228
animals, 43n10, 178, 198, 204, 215n64
Ankur seeds, 271, 279, 308n31
Annales/Annales school, 14–15
antebellum period, 70, 81, 135n52
antecedents, 5, 14, 41–42, 61–62, 123, 373–374
anti-usury regulation, 158
aqueducts, 36
archaeological evidence, 43n12, 72–73

arhatiya, 202, 336–338
Arkansas, 66
Arkwright's water frames, 131n21
asami, 38, 39
ashram, 49n72, 145n129, 153n236, 162
assets, 1, 6, 165–166, 181, 190–199, 201, 204–205, 218, 221, 233–234, 236, 257–259, 267n22
astrology, 320, 363n5
Atlantic slave trade, 66
attrition, 176–177, 182
auctions, 226, 332, 334–336
Aurangzeb, 24–25, 29, 34–37, 40, 49n76, 49n79, 50n86, 53n112, 56n143
automated weather station (AWS), 175–176, 322, 358
aykari, 38, 58n171

back checks, 179
Backbay Reclamation, 85
backyard poultry, 247
Bahamani sultanate, 3, 21–23, 32, 41, 48n65
Bahamas, 65–66
Bajaj, Bachhraj, 109–110, 152n227
Bajaj, Jamnalal, 109–110, 145n129, 152n227
Baji Rao I, 25, 28, 30
Baji Rao II, 28
bajra, 73, 361
Baker, D. E. U., 45n26, 208n15
Bakht Buland Shah, 25, 27, 35–36, 50n86, 57n152
Balapur, 24
Balasore, 28
bales, 62, 69, 87, 113, 136n56, 332–333, 335, 390
baluta/*balutedar*/*balutedari* system, 38, 58n171
Bania, 106, 108–109, 126, 151n210, 157n283, 332–333, 377
bank
  banking correspondent, 204
  cooperative banks, 203–204
  regional rural bank (RRB), 203–204
  small finance bank, 204
bankruptcy, 125
Bapat Commission, 189
Barabhai, 26, 51n91
basis risk, 166, 322–323, 370n47
batai, 34, 236, 250
Bates, Crispin, 208n15
battles
  Battle of Koregaon and Khadki, 28
  Battle of Mahidpur, 28
  Battle of Palkhed, 30
  Battle of Plassey, 26, 76, 142n108
  Battle of Shakar Kheda, 30
  Battle of Sitabuldi, 28
  Third Battle of Panipat, 25–27
Bayer, 271, 273
bazaars, 161, 221
Beckert, Sven, 127n2, 128n7, 133n31, 134n40, 144n116, 150n204, 155n258, 363n1, 405n4
beegha (*bigha*), 96
behavioral motivations, 269
  Bengal Subah, 25
Bentinck, William, 96
Berar
  annexation, 23, 82, 94, 126
  Berar Commission, 94, 390
  Berar Protector of Debtors Act, 107
  Berar Subah, 25, 54n131
  Berar Wastelands Act, 1865, 95
  Central Provinces and Berar, 7, 17, 45n26, 50n82, 55n140, 57n153, 91, 93, 95–96, 105, 107, 109, 111, 114–116, 118–119, 147n156, 148n169
  Hyderabad Assigned Districts (HAD), 30, 147n159, 148n172

north Berar, 23
south Berar, 23, 28
Berar Protector of Debtors Act, 107
Berar Province, 13, 15–16, 117
Berar Waste Land Rules, 1865, 97–98
Betul, 22
bhagindar, 96–97, 148n171
Bhandara, 15, 36, 44n18
Bhangi, 97
Bharatiya Janata Party (BJP), 17, 338
Bharatiya Kisan Union (BKU), 400
Bhat, Balaji Vishwanath, 25
Bhat, Madhavrao I, 26, 51n91
Bhat, Narayanrao, 26
Bhat, Raghunathrao (Raghoba), 26
bhindi, 282–283
bhoja, 105, 151n206
Bhonsale, Mudhoji, 27
Bhonsale, Raghoji II, 27
Bhonsale, Shahaji, 24
Bidar, 24, 48n61, 49n67, 52n106
bigha, 33, 56n144, 96, 148n168
Bihar, 34, 94, 147n164
Bijapur, 23–24, 49n67
bills of lading, 70
biotic stress, 219
black gram, 73, 225
Bliss, C., 209n16
Bloch, Marc, 43
blockade runners, 69
Blyn, G., 89
Bollgard, 270–271, 274
Bollgard I (BGI), 271
Bollgard II (BGII), 271, 276
Bollywood, 125
Bombay Chamber of Commerce and Industry, 80
Bombay Deccan, 100, 148n165, 151n211
Bombay High Court, 19, 189, 393
Bombay Money-Lenders Act, 107
Bombay Presidency, 29, 55n142, 77, 80, 85, 90, 112–113, 126, 128n4, 154n239
Bombay Province, 21, 85–87
Bombay Stock Exchange (BSE), 85, 145n134, 152n223
Bombay Tenancy and Agricultural Lands Act, 1948, 118
Bombay Weaving and Spinning Company, 108
boom, 4, 62–64, 66–67, 78, 80–81, 86, 104–106, 108–110, 113–115, 125–126, 129n12, 162, 378–380, 384, 404
borrowing, 204–205, 221, 259, 324–325, 349–350, 352, 356, 394, 401
Bourbon, 77
Bowreah Mills, 108
Braudel, Fernand, 43n8, 404n3
Brazil, 70, 93, 138n78, 306n13
bribery, 224
brick-kilns, 193, 222–224, 402
Britain, 61–63, 65, 67–68, 71, 78, 80, 83–84, 100–101
British Crown, 20, 102, 376
British East India Company, 20
British Raj, 107, 115, 127, 377, 379
British Resident, 27, 30, 52n102, 85
British textile industry, 81
British trade policy, 60
Broach (Bharuch), 26
brokers, 85, 376
BSE, 85, 145n134, 152n223
Bt cotton seeds, 6, 9, 119, 152n221, 220, 240, 242, 273–274, 276, 277, 301
Bt III seeds, 276
Bt-3 seeds, 279
bubonic plague, 111
Buddh Purnima, 320
Buddhism, 14, 42n6, 46n34, 189–190, 213n49

buffaloes, 195
Buldhana, 15, 17, 48n65, 82–83, 99, 144n117, 155n250, 209n17
bullock carts, 192–193
bullocks, 103, 105, 161, 192, 193–199, 197, 214n59
bumper crops, 69
Bundelkhand, 78
Bunny, 279
Burhan Shah, 27
Burial Act of 1666, 130n14
business enterprise, 250
bust, 4, 62–64, 82, 110, 113, 125, 198, 221, 377, 379–381, 384
Byramji (Behramji) Hormusji Cama, 88

Calcutta, 44n15, 48n62, 50n82, 51n87, 52n97, 54n119, 76, 78, 80–82, 103, 108, 114, 123, 142n101, 142n106, 144n115, 149n178, 156n267, 377, 383–384
calico
  Calico Act, 1721, 65, 130n16
  calicoes, 65, 114, 130n16
  calico printing industry, 65
canals, 36–37, 55n141, 191, 246, 326, 387
candy (*khandi*), 154n247
Canton/Canton system, 76–78, 80, 94, 141n95
cantonments, 94
capability approach, 352
capital expenditure, 204–205
capitalist development, 61, 81, 108, 110, 316, 374
capitalists, 61, 65, 71, 81, 105–106, 108–110, 112, 116, 125–126, 137n64, 150n194, 316, 374, 376, 378, 398–399, 404n2
caravans, 114
carding, 82
cargo, 77, 103
Carnatic, 29, 30
Carr, E. H., 124, 157n278
cart, 63, 80–81, 104, 145n135, 161, 192–193, 257
cart carriers, 33
cart roads, 80–81
case studies, 167, 208n14, 406–407n24
cash crop, 200, 216n71, 354
casino, 60, 139n81
caste
  Banjara, 161, 365n21
  Beldar, 189
  Bhuis, 189
  Brahmin, 22, 46n38
  Dalit, 190, 359
  Gond-Gowari, 189
  Gowari, 189
  Kunbi, 97, 151n210, 162, 189
  lower caste and upper caste, 38, 97, 359, 400
  Mahar, 97, 148n173
  Maratha-Kunbis, 189
  Marathas, 3, 20, 24–28, 30, 35–36, 40–41, 51n90, 51n95, 53n107, 189, 213n45, 360, 376–377
  NT, 185, 189, 249
  OBC, 185, 189, 213n45, 249, 252
  Rajput, 23–24, 51n94
  SBC, 185, 189, 249
  SC, 118, 174, 185, 190, 249
  ST, 118, 174, 185, 249
caste and class, 318, 374, 383, 410n54
cattle
  cattle-breeding, 115
  cattle dung, 97
  cattle economy, 98, 125, 161, 198, 247, 258, 381, 385
  cattle fairs, 198–199
  cattle population, 117
census of 1881, 98

Central Insecticides Board and Registration Committee (CIBRC), 285
Central Institute for Cotton Research (CICR), 128n3, 232, 276, 285, 303–304, 388, 390
Central Institute for Research on Cotton Technology (CIRCOT), 304
Central Provinces/Central Provinces and Berar, 7, 17, 45n26, 55n140, 91, 93, 95–96, 105, 107
cess, 30, 85, 101, 145n136
*chakka jam*s, 337–338
Chalukyas, 20
Chambhars, 189
chana, 225, 232, 246, 281, 300
Chand Bibi, Sultana, 23
Chand Sultan, 27
Chanda, 24–25, 27
Chandrapur, 15–16, 24, 44n18, 73, 76, 224
Chandu Lal, Raja, 100, 149n188
charai, 31
*chari*s, 36
charitable activities, 93–94
charkha (*churka*), 82, 112, 145n129
Charter Act of 1813, 78
*chaudhuri*s, 32, 37
*chaupal*s, 397
chauth, 30, 36, 41
check dams, 36, 246
chemical growth-promoters, 221
chemical inputs, 221, 337
Chhindwara, 25, 116
Chhotalal, Ranchhodlal, 108
chief commissioner, 17, 45n25, 85
child labour, 109, 179, 255, 260
China, 1, 61–62, 66–67, 76–82, 103, 123, 126, 140n91, 141n93, 141n97, 142n101, 143n111
China trade, 80–81, 123
Chinchpokli, 109
chintzes, 65, 114
choice bracketing, 346, 367n33
choice overload, 285–286, 301
cholinesterase test, 292
churda, 283
churka, 82–83
civil society, 4, 173, 247–248, 386–387
class, 36, 38, 41, 96–97, 99, 117, 178
cleaning, 78, 82, 88, 112, 257, 296, 297
climate/climate change, 76, 319, 352, 371n50, 390, 404, 409–410n53
coefficient of variation (CV), 73–74, 234, 321, 363n5
Colebrooke, H. T., 27–28, 144n115
collateral, 30, 106, 220
collective failure, 162
colonial era, 3, 13–14, 16, 61, 63–64, 124, 190
colonial history, 14, 30
colonies, 45–46n33, 67, 82, 100–101, 132n23, 132n26, 133n33, 133n34
commerce, 61, 65, 80–82, 95, 115, 138n72, 142n107, 153n233, 313n61, 337, 377
commercialization, 7, 9, 34, 61, 119, 123–124, 219, 302, 313n62, 316, 377, 382, 387, 398, 405n6
commission agents, 133n31, 202, 226
Commission for Agricultural Costs and Prices (CACP), 179, 236
commodity, 3, 8, 60, 119, 136n60, 151n208, 226, 241–242, 338, 368n37, 375, 384, 395, 405n4
common pea, 73
communicable diseases, 188
communication
  internet, 10n1, 397
  Jio, 194
  mobile phone, 192, 194, 362

smart phone, 10n1, 194, 388, 397
telegraph, 69, 71, 104, 110, 125, 378, 383, 385
telephone, 71
communist, 112
Commutation Act of 1784, 77, 141n97
compensation, 261, 265n4, 356
competitiveness, 119, 131n20, 400
complex systems, 10, 61
compound, 99, 105, 290, 326
comptroller and auditor general of India (CAG), 392, 407n26
computed assisted personal interviews (CAPI), 182–184
confederate states, 69
Consolidation of Landholdings, 133n31
consumption expenditure, 166, 180–181, 345, 401
consumption smoothing, 200, 349–350, 359, 367n29, 368n36, 394
Convergence of Agriculture and Industry in Maharashtra (CAIM), 198
cooperative credit, 107
corn, 68, 70
Corn Laws, 130n14
Coromandel Coast, 35, 114
corruption, 69, 391–392, 407n26
cost of cultivation, 9, 117, 165, 179, 226, 234–239, 242–244, 256, 258–259, 262, 272, 328, 359, 373, 381, 387
cotton
acreage, 85–87, 89–90, 100, 116, 136n56, 173, 195–196, 226, 228–229, 231, 247, 326, 334, 379, 386
adulteration, 61, 112
agronomy, 314n75
Cotton Commissioner, 91, 95–96, 105, 114–115, 151n209
cultivation cost, 387
Dharwad cotton, 90
diffusion, 229, 233, 279, 285
experimental farms, 112
export, 123
ginning and pressing, varieties, 109–110
Gossypium arboreum, 62, 72, 128n3
Gossypium barbadense, 67, 128n3
Gossypium herbaceum, 62, 128n3
Gossypium indicum, 113
Gossypium neglectum, 113
hybrids, 3, 272, 316
input intensive, 3
marketing, 5, 35
pesticides, 233
pests, 285–286
post-harvest, 257, 323, 330, 334, 359
price ceiling, 303, 389
rain-fed, 33, 39, 55n141, 56n144, 82, 90, 119, 171, 173, 219–220, 223–225, 229
royalty, 388–389
trader, 2, 811
trait, 272–273
transgenic, Bt, BGI, BGII, GEAC, 270, 276, 281
'Sea Island' cotton, 65–66
staple length, 366n22
warehouse, 145n135
cotton belt, 70, 74–75, 137n63, 137n70
cotton capitalism, 71, 81, 132–133n30, 307n19, 375
cotton commissioner of the Central Provinces and Berar, 91, 95–96, 105
cotton compressors, 70–71
Cotton Corporation of India (CCI), 332–334, 366n23, 387
cotton development programme, 81
Cotton Frauds Act, 88
cotton hybrids
BGI and BGII, 258, 279
Bt cotton, 6, 9, 119
Bt hybrid, 270–273

cultivar, 233, 304
transgenic, 9, 270
See also cotton
cotton towns, 144n117, 161, 316, 378
cotton varieties
bani (*bhunee/ghat kapas/Hinganghat*), 113, 154n247, 155n250
buri (*G. hirsutum*), 113
cotton improvement programme, 62, 383
Cotton Supply Association, 81, 125n145
desi, 62, 225, 276, 282–283
ghogli (*G. hirsutum*), 113
jari (*jhuree/Kati Vilayati*), 113, 154n247
organic, 345–346
Council Bills, 110–111
counterfeit, 276
country trade, 76–77, 383
courts, 19, 26, 30, 52n100, 81, 108, 124, 161, 184, 189, 211n36, 274–275, 306n13
covariate shocks, 32, 173, 347–348, 353, 359–360, 370–371n49
COVID-19, 1, 9, 166, 175–176, 181, 187, 211n29, 234, 252, 254, 299, 332, 334, 347, 351, 360, 380, 392, 395, 403, 405–406n13
cows, 195
credit risk, 91
creditors, 70, 201
crop advisory, 304
crop diversification, 221, 240, 266n16, 340
crop failure, 220, 234, 320, 353–354, 359, 377
crop loan, 324, 356, 393–394
crop rotation, 32
crop yields, 2, 75–76, 165, 258, 261, 304, 321–325, 339–340, 382
cropping patterns, 5, 8, 70, 73, 90, 104, 125, 140n85, 165, 196, 219, 221–233, 240, 257–258, 266n16, 296–298, 316, 319, 342, 378, 381, 392, 403
cross-sectional survey, 164, 169, 179
cry1Ac, 271
cry2Ab2, 271
cultivars, 233, 304, 349, 383
cultivated land, 61, 177, 191, 222, 344
cultivation income, 233–246, 251, 258, 267n22, 304, 342, 381
culturable land, 97, 222–223
cultural groups, 15
current fallow/fallow/other fallow, 32, 36, 191, 228, 265n5, 301, 342
customs duty, 331
Cuttack, 27–28

dahshala system, 33, 55n136
dairy sector, 198, 215n65
dakhin. *See* Deccan
Dalhousie, Lord, 53n109, 101
Dalit Panther Movement, 190
dam (currency), 36
dam (irrigation), 36
Dastur-ul-Amals, 34
data collection, 163, 165, 168–171, 176–184, 207n5, 211n29, 316, 380
data quality, 169, 179, 206, 380–381
Daulatabad, 21–22, 46n46, 48n61
Davar, Cowaszee Nanabhoy, 108
Davis, Jefferson, 136n54
dawran, 193, 197–198, 292–294, 297–300
dearness allowance, 111
debt bondage, 99
debt relief, 120, 200, 202, 356, 386–387, 394
debt traps, 130, 394
debt waiver, 4, 120, 200, 202, 356, 386–387, 394

debt/indebtedness, 2, 37, 67, 91, 97, 99–100, 105–108, 119–120, 199–200, 202, 215n67, 219–220, 267n22, 317, 324, 359, 373, 377, 385, 387, 395
Deccan
  Deccan Agricultural Relief Act, 100
  Deccan famine (*see* famines)
  Deccan Riots, 398, 409n41
  Deccan traps, 73
  rulers, 7, 14, 21–23, 25, 27–31, 35, 41, 51n89, 53n109
decision-making, 164, 168, 170, 211n31, 270, 275, 301
dedhi, 201, 216n72
deductive paradigms, 164
Deep South, 66, 134n36
deforestation, 125, 378, 385
degradation, 92, 98, 137–138n70, 198, 329–330, 378, 380, 384–385, 395
deindustrialization, 110, 142–143n108
Delhi sultanate, 3, 21–22, 40, 46–47n46, 47n47, 47n48, 55n133
demilitarization, 97
democracy, 305n6, 306n9, 308n30
demography, 165, 184–190, 315, 380
demonetization, 174, 206
demonstration, 115, 278–279
Deogarh (Devagad), 25, 27, 35–36
deoiled cakes (DOC), 226
Department of Revenue and Agriculture, 115
depreciation, 236
depression, 110, 112, 142n108, 143n109, 144n120, 378
derivative, 68, 171, 226, 379
deshmukh, 32–33, 54n131, 95–96
deshpandias, 95–96
deskilling, 276–277, 304, 382, 389, 406n20
Deva Raya I, 23
Devagiri, 20–21, 46–47n46, 47n48
developmental backlogs, 13, 19, 326, 373, 386
Dhamangaon, 173
Dharwad, 90
Dharwar region, 112–113
dhimmi, 31
dialects, 58n171, 165
dice, 269, 342
diesel pumps, 192, 326
dietary diversity, 228, 385
diffusion, 9, 229, 233, 278–279, 285, 302, 379–380, 387–388
Dilasa, 393
Diler Khan, 24
dimmat, 38–39
dinosaurs, 15, 43n13
direct benefit transfer (DBT), 251
Directorate of Cotton Development, 284, 309n40
disaster avoidance, 398
disease, 93, 113, 149n181, 154n239, 162, 188, 205, 212n43, 319, 339–340
dispossession, 100
dissaving, 259, 349–351, 354, 359
Diwali, 320
D-Matrix Development Foundation, 203
do amli, 36
doctoral research, 162, 164, 170
doctrine of lapse
  dokras, 104
dollar, 1, 10n1, 70, 180, 187, 196, 201, 221, 251, 254–255, 292, 407n25
domestic factors, 61
dominant castes, 190
Dorli, 171, 173–174, 183
doubling farmers' income, 5, 214n62, 260–261
Dowlat Rao Scindia (Daulatrao Shinde), 28
downside risk, 106, 382

downward mobility, 355
Dr Panjabrao Deshmukh Krishi Vidyapeeth (PDKV), 140n85, 198, 215n63, 388
drought year, 173, 191–192, 200, 237, 320, 320, 350, 356
drought-proof, 390, 391, 396
droughts, 34, 98, 148n165, 173, 191–192, 200, 219, 223, 237, 247, 253, 267n25, 319–321, 323–327, 347–348, 350, 353–356, 364n10, 364n11, 372n56, 390–393, 396, 398–400, 406n22
drudgery, 2, 247–248, 255, 270, 381–382, 397
drumstick trees, 392–393
dry days, 321–323
dry spells, 275, 320–323, 325–327, 356, 393
dukkar, 342
Durgadevi Famine, 34, 55n142
Durrani Empire, 25
Dussehra, 320
Dutch VOC (Vereenigde Oostindische Compagnie), 35
duty-free trading rights, 35
Dyson, Tim, 99, 149n181

East India Company (EIC), 20, 43n14, 51n95, 57n148, 57n150, 140n91, 141n93, 142n107, 143n110
ecology/ecological degradation, 98, 198, 384–385
economic growth, 42n7, 188, 212n42, 212–213n44, 386
economic reforms, 199–200, 373, 386
economic threshold limit (ETL), 285, 310n42
economist, 145n129, 167–168, 207n5, 367n33
education, 18, 185–189, 204–205, 220, 257, 356, 359, 362, 380, 401–402
Eid, 320
electrical fencing, 228
Eli Whitney's gin, 65
emancipation, 70, 127n2, 135n51, 150n204
Embargo Act, 67
eminent domain, 224
Empire of Cotton, 128n7, 134n38, 144n116, 155n258, 315, 363n1, 378
employment, 2, 18, 68, 72, 103, 109–110, 135n50, 138n75, 166, 178, 186–188, 209n17, 211n35, 214n55, 248–253, 255–257, 260, 264, 268n27, 294, 296, 300–301, 305n3, 313n63, 353–355, 359, 386, 396
Empress Mill, 109, 152n224
endowment effect, 182
endrin, 289, 311n53
English piece goods, 104
entitlement failures, 91, 125–126, 355
entrepôts, 71–72, 101, 103, 126
entrepreneurs, 5, 108–109, 355–356, 391, 397
enumerators, 206, 380–381
environmental degradation, 82, 98, 380, 385, 395
epidemics, 119, 153n235, 315, 354, 378
episodic events, 15
epistemology, 166–167, 380
Erlanger bonds, 69, 136n61
Essential Commodities Act (ECA), 252, 273
ethnography, 8–9, 164–165, 207n5, 207n11, 251, 381–382
euphoria, 62
Europe, 1, 55n134, 59n175, 61–62, 65, 67–69, 113, 123, 131n21, 136n60
ex ante risk management, 221, 230, 351
ex post risk management, 221
experimentation, 62, 125, 302–304, 314n67, 351, 383, 388, 390, 394, 402

exploratory fieldwork, 162, 173, 206, 271
export/export subsidies, 61–62, 64, 67–68, 77, 79–81, 101, 103, 109–110, 112–115, 118, 126, 132n26, 154n247, 226, 318, 331, 338–340, 366n26, 383, 385, 406n16
expressway. *See* Samruddhi Mahamarg
extension, 98, 100–102, 104, 115, 198, 211n29, 220, 285, 287, 289, 303–305, 310n48, 397
extra-long staple cotton, 128n3, 390

factor/factorage, 70, 138n71
factorage systems, 70
factories, 81, 83, 108–109, 117, 129n13, 131n21, 223, 333
Factories Act, 117
Fafchamps, Marcel, 369n41, 369n43
failure narrative, 269
fair average quality (FAQ), 332, 366n22
fairs, 60, 94–95, 161, 198–199, 202, 332–333, 338
famines
  Cotton Famine, 64, 71–72, 81, 85, 138n76, 380
  Deccan famine, 23, 34, 55n142
  Durgadevi famine, 34, 55n142
  famine relief policy, 31
  Indian Famine Commission, 90, 146n151, 147n156, 406n23
  state response to famine, 31
farm business income, 179
farm laws, 1–2, 337–338, 398
farm mechanization, 246
Farm Services Act, 337
farman (*firman*), 35, 37, 57n160
Farmer Producer Companies (FPCs), 203, 217n77
Farmer Producer Organizations (FPOs), 5, 203, 395
farmer resistance, 243
farmers
  crop diversity, 225–233
  cropping patterns, 222–225
Farmers (Empowerment and Protection) Agreement on Price Assurance, 337
Farmers' Produce Trade and Commerce (Promotion and Facilitation) Act, 337
farmers' suicides, 2, 8, 10, 13–14, 16, 119, 127, 156–157n273, 161–162, 171, 199–200, 215n67
farmyard manure, 180
Farrukhsiyar, 29, 35
Fathullah Imad-ul-Mulk, 23
faujdar, 24, 29, 32–33
Febvre, Lucien, 43
female-headed households, 184
Fenwick, R. H., 81
fertility, 33, 97, 137n70, 233, 389
fertilizer response, 328
fertilizers, 298, 328–329, 365n16, 382
feudal land grants, 31
Fibres and Silk Branch, 115
field immersion, 168
fieldwork, 6, 161–217, 239–240, 244, 255, 271, 280, 283, 289, 298, 316, 318, 320, 324, 329, 331, 337, 363n7
financial crisis, 125, 164, 331, 378
financial panic, 68
financiers, 108–109
firewood, 97
Firuz (Firoz) Shah Bahamani, 22–23, 31–32, 36
five-year settlement, 95
flour mill, 250–251
fluctuations, 2, 34, 75–76, 88, 91, 105, 116, 126, 135n50, 221, 331, 333, 339, 349, 355, 379–380
focus group discussions (FGDs), 164, 289, 391

fodder/fodder crisis, 36, 90, 98, 180, 195–196, 198, 226, 228–229, 247, 385
Food Corporation of India (FCI), 333
food crop production, 32
food rationing, 31
food shortage, 77, 91, 147n155, 354
forest, 13–16, 20, 125, 228, 378, 385
'forty acres and a mule', 70, 137n67
forward castes, 189
fragmentation of holdings, 97
free market capitalism, 373
freedman families, 70
freight, 71, 103, 132n30, 141–142n100
frontier
  commodity frontier, 375, 405n4
  cotton frontier, 376
full insurance hypothesis, 353, 359–360
Fuller, J. B., 17, 147–148n164
fulli paddath, 293–295
furnishing merchant, 70
fustians, 65, 130n16
futures contracts, 85
futures market, 334
futures trading, 69, 226

Gadchiroli, 15–16, 44n18, 73, 76, 224
Gaekwads, 189
gahu chapatti, 228
gamble (also gambler, gamblers, gambling), 3–8, 39, 60–158, 162, 169, 218–314, 316–317, 319, 328, 339–344, 346, 357, 359, 374–376, 381, 383–388, 398–399, 403–404
Gandhi, Mahatma, 82, 109–112, 145n129, 152–153n227, 162, 187, 208n13, 255–256, 301, 308n26, 321–322, 363n7, 396
Ganesh Chaturthi, 320
Gavligad (Gawlighur), 23, 48n65
Geertz, Clifford, 207n7,
gene constructs, 275–276, 307n19
genetic contamination, 272
Genetic Engineering Appraisal Committee (GEAC), 270, 275–276, 281, 307n18
genetically modified cotton seeds, 220
geographic luck, 14, 42n7
Georgia, 65–66, 113, 132n23, 134n36, 137n63
germination failure, 231, 240, 244, 275, 320
ghalla-bakshi, 34
ghari (*ghurry*), 31, 38–39
ghas dana, 36
Ghazi Malik (Ghiyas-ud-Din Tughluq), 22
Gini coefficient, 185, 191, 214n55
ginned cotton/lint cotton, 82, 127n1, 155n249, 387
ginning, 66, 77, 109–110, 113, 332–336
ginning outturn, lint–seed ratio, 113, 333
Girni Kamgar Union (GKU), 112, 154n241
global capitalism, 63, 71
global financial crisis, 164
global integration, 64, 88
Global South, 374
global supply chain, 64, 66, 70, 76, 123, 125, 133n31, 384
glut, 71, 72, 136n56
goat, 195–198, 237, 247
Golconda, 30, 49n67, 53n112
gold bullion reserves, 67–68
Gondi (language), 15
Gondia, 15–16, 44n18, 73, 76, 120–122
Gonds, 14, 15, 22, 24, 25, 27, 36, 40, 44n16, 48n65, 50n85, 189, 376
Gondwana, 15, 44n15, 44n16, 45n25, 384
Gondwanaland, 15
goods and services tax (GST), 174

governance, 208n14, 390–393, 395
Government of Maharashtra, 187, 200, 209n20, 215n63, 356, 364n13, 407n26
government regulations, 242
grains, 33–34, 38, 55n141, 58n171, 67–68, 77, 86–87, 90–92, 103, 107, 117, 125, 161, 233, 255, 333, 354, 360, 385–386
gram, 73, 217n75, 225, 228, 230, 244, 253, 273, 277, 281, 381, 392
Gram Panchayat, 253
grass, 73, 90–91, 97
grazing land, 31
Great Bombay Textile Strike, 154n241
Great Depression, 110
Great Divergence, 41, 59n175, 141n93
Great Indian Peninsular Railway (GIPR), 102–104
Greater Bombay, 26
Greaves Cotton, 109
green gram, 73, 225, 230
Green Revolution, 3, 118, 127, 156n266, 219, 271, 313n61, 314n68, 317, 332, 365–366n21, 378–380, 386, 390, 398–400
gross cropped area (GCA), 98, 228
gross domestic product (GDP), 41
gross state domestic product, 13
groundwater, 9, 191, 244, 325–326, 365n15, 386, 391–392
Guangzhou, 76
Gudi Padwa, 193, 320
Guha, Amlendu, 79, 140n87, 144n115, 144n118, 144n119, 154n242
Guha, S., 151n211
Gujarat, 18–19, 21, 35, 40, 45n33, 76–77, 85, 87, 100, 106, 109, 114, 140n92, 141n94, 145n132
Gulbarga, 22, 48n61
Gwalior, 28
Habib, Irfan, 32, 37–38, 54n122, 54n130, 57n162, 140n83
hamal, 248, 250
Harapaladeva, 21
Harnetty, Peter, 86–87, 114, 128n6, 128n7, 138n78, 150n202, 155n253, 265n8, 366n27
harvest, 34–35, 57n161, 58n168, 67–68, 126–127, 137–138n70, 194, 201, 231–232, 237, 243–244, 246, 256–257, 259, 266n20, 289, 295, 298, 299–301, 304, 320, 323, 330, 334, 359
Haryana, 127, 337–338
Hastings, Governor-General Warren, 26
hazard, 269–270, 272, 289–290, 310n47, 310n48, 311n51, 352, 368n37
health, 9, 47n51, 166, 187, 204–205, 212n41, 253, 269–270, 272, 282, 285, 289–292, 303, 311n51, 311–312n54, 317, 329–330, 347–348, 353, 356, 360, 362, 382, 387, 395, 403
health card, 329–330, 382
health hazards, 272, 311n51
hectares, 119, 191, 265n4, 309n37, 332, 356
Helicoverpa armigera, 233, 282
herbicide tolerant Bt cotton, 240
herbicides, 259, 271, 281–282, 287, 292, 309n35
high density planting system (HDPS), 304
highway, 193, 397
Hinganghat, 113
hired workers, 178
historian, 32, 37, 41, 52n106, 53n115, 57n160, 67, 124, 129n12, 138n75, 143n114, 167
historiography, 6
Holi, 320

Holkar, Malharrao, III, 28
Holocene, 15, 43n12, 73
hons, 24
hoondakur/*hoondakuri*, 100
horticultural crops, 39, 225, 355, 392
hospital, 205, 211n29, 290–292, 360, 362
hours, 255–256, 284, 297–299, 326
household expenditure, 165
household income, 5, 177–178, 221, 246, 248, 260, 316, 319, 324, 348, 352–354, 382
HTBt, 240, 242, 270, 281, 303, 305n1, 308n33, 344–345, 382, 390
human capital, 105, 150n205
humic acid, 286
Hyderabad, 17–18, 21, 27, 29–30, 40, 46–47n46, 52n102, 53n111, 81, 85, 93, 100, 147n159, 148n172, 149n188, 151n208, 151n209, 368n37
hypothesis-testing, 164

Ibn Battuta, 31, 48n59
idiosyncratic risks, 9, 204–205, 347
Imad Shahi dynasty, 23
Imad Shahi rule, 49n68
imidacloprid, 286, 289, 310n48
imperialism, 3–4, 123
import tariffs, 65
imputation, 180, 236
inam/*inamdar*/*inamdari* system, 95, 148n173
income
  income diversification, 196, 258
  income generation, 237, 247, 339
  income risk, 317–318, 353, 368n39
  income shocks, 5, 9, 162, 221, 349, 353–354, 382, 387, 395
  income smoothing, 349, 368n36, 368n38
  measurement, 33–35, 97, 177–181
India
  central India, 2, 13, 22, 30, 39, 43n13, 44n16, 45n31, 50n82, 64, 109, 147n161, 157n277, 215n66, 315, 373
  south-central India, 30
  western India, 55–56n142, 58n166, 76–79, 85, 88, 101, 126, 128n5, 142n105, 144n115, 154n242, 366n24
India Meteorological Department (IMD), 74–75, 321, 364n10
Indian Cotton Committee (ICC), 114, 155n254
Indian Cotton Report, 113, 155n248
Indian Council of Agricultural Research (ICAR), 139n82, 304, 314n75
Indian National Congress (INC), 45n33, 332, 385, 398
Indian textile industry, 142–143n108
indigenous, 3, 62, 77–78, 80–81, 110, 113, 125–126, 144n117, 282, 284, 390
indigenous capitalism, 110
indigenous traders, 80
indigo, 94, 132n23
indirect agricultural credit, 119
industrial revolution, 42, 65, 123, 130n14, 130n19, 131n21, 134n37, 377
industrial training, 186
industrial training institutes (ITIs), 401
industrialists, 65, 383
inequality, 66, 185, 191, 209n17, 214n55, 328, 386
infestation, 9, 90, 218, 229–231, 240, 258–259, 270–272, 277, 282–283, 286, 299, 302, 339, 349, 389, 395–396
inflation, 1, 86–87, 94, 111, 129n8, 162, 240, 354
influenza, 99, 111, 154n239
informal risk sharing, 318, 347, 350, 369n43

information/information asymmetry, 53n107, 69, 71, 110, 115, 133n31, 165, 175, 179, 181–182, 201, 214n53, 220, 224, 236, 246, 260, 285, 309n38, 334, 358, 397
innovation, 1, 32, 64–65, 67, 70–71, 131n21, 134n40, 152n224, 275, 304, 391, 397–399
input dealer, 181, 202, 279–281, 283–287, 289–292, 302–304, 311n50, 344
insect-eating (entomophagous) pests, 284
insecticide resistance, 272, 285, 302–303, 381–382
insecticide resistance management (IRM), 285
institutional reforms, 4, 105, 125, 379, 383, 385
insurance
  crop insurance, 261, 303–304, 318, 351, 356, 358, 382, 392, 394–395, 403, 408n34
  microinsurance, 162, 206–207n4
  Modified National Agricultural Insurance Scheme (MNAIS), 358
  multi-peril crop insurance, 318, 394–395
  weather insurance, 166, 175, 261, 318, 323, 349, 351, 358, 382, 394
  Weather-Based Crop Insurance Scheme (WBCIS), 358, 394, 395, 408n34
Integrated Child Development Scheme (ICDS), 187
integrated pest management (IPM), 285, 309n39
intercropping, 90, 230, 232–233, 291, 296–298, 381
inter-cultivation operations, 193
interlocked markets, 337
International Crop Research Institute for the Semi-Arid Tropics (ICRISAT), 163, 168–169, 209n17, 209n21, 227, 245, 368n37
intertemporal dynamics, 169
investment, 36, 82, 104, 108, 110, 112, 115, 118, 125, 150n205, 152n221, 162, 198, 200, 220, 244, 259–260, 275, 315–316, 324, 368n40, 378–379, 383, 386, 390, 394–395, 399, 402
iqta/iqtadari system, 31–32, 54n126
iqtedar/muqti, 31
Ireland, 67–68, 154–155n247
irrigation, 36–39, 118–119
Irrigation Commission, 390
Ishvakus, 36
izara/izaradari, 98

jagir/jagirdar/jagirdari system, 24, 33, 50n83, 55n134
Jahangir, 23–24, 35
Jains, 126, 311n50
Jajmani, 58n172
Jalyukt Shivar Abhiyaan (JSA), 244, 267n25, 391–392, 396, 406–407n24
jama (colonial/Mughal), 33, 95
jamabandi, 95
Jejeebhoy, Rustomjee Jamsetjee, 88, 103, 146n146
Japan
  Indo-Japanese trade relations, 110
  Japan Cotton Trading Company, 111
  Toyo Menka Kaisha, 116
jawari/jowar, 73, 87, 90–93, 125, 226, 228–229, 258, 266n14, 271, 316, 361, 386
JCB, 248, 397
jeevamrut, 285
Jefferson, Thomas, 66–67
jewellery, 181, 194–195
jins-i-aalaa, 32

jins-i-kaamil, 32
jizya, 31
jobber, 108, 152n220
jobs, 189, 223, 247–248, 257, 264, 396–397, 402
Jubbulpore (Jabalpur), 103–104

kadhi kachra, 296–299
Kafur, Malik, 21, 47n49, 47n51
Kakatiyas, 21–22
Kalachuris, 20
kalaspati, 33–34
kankut, 34
kapas, 3, 113, 118, 127n1, 298, 332, 334, 366n22
Karnataka, 21–22, 45–46n33, 58n171, 215n67, 410n54
karpashi, 72
Khamgaon, 80, 82–83, 104–105, 144n117, 161, 378
Khan, Mir Qamaruddin Ali (Asaf Jah I, Chin Qilich Kamaruddin Khan, and Nizam-ul-Mulk), 29
Khan, Ulugh, 22
Khandesh, 24, 49n75
kharaj tax, 31
kharif income, 234–244
khatedar/khatedari, 95–99, 105, 124, 148n171, 161–162, 315, 379
Khedala (Kherla), 22
khel, 38–39
khod kheeda, 231, 240
Khurram, Prince. *See* Shah Jahan
King Cotton, 60, 64–71, 85, 126, 134n40, 136n54, 138n77, 404
Kingdom of Mysore, 26, 40, 52n101
kirana store, 250–251, 402
Koh-i-Noor diamond, 21, 52n96
Kolhapur, 30
Komtis, 377
Konkan, 110
koradwahu, 191–192, 214n57, 224, 260, 281, 325
Korku, 43n14
Krishna–Godavari basin, 23

labour
  agricultural labour, 5, 38, 94, 97, 100, 104, 149n179, 161–162, 178, 191, 252, 254–257, 260, 264, 269, 294–296, 301, 311n51, 355, 360, 381
  drudgery, 255, 270, 381–382
  farm labour, 120, 175, 178–179, 199, 236, 253, 255–258, 264, 267n22, 290, 296–297, 320, 347, 352
  gendered division, 9, 252, 257, 270, 381
  labour market, 38, 208n14, 221, 252, 256, 258, 260, 316, 352, 378
  specialization, 254
  wage, 252
labour force participation rate (LFPR), 188, 212–213n44
laga, 85
laissez-faire, 95
Lancashire/Lancashire mills, 3, 59n175, 60, 64–66, 68, 71–72, 77, 80–82, 84, 86, 90, 110, 112–114, 123–124, 128n6, 130n17, 131n20, 138n75, 142–143n108, 377–378, 383
Lanco, 225
land ceilings, 118, 355
land Gini, 185
Land Improvement Act, 1871, 107
land mortgages, 100, 377
land reforms, 23, 34, 41, 105, 118, 156n268, 191, 214n56, 355, 359, 372n60
land revenue system, 7, 31–38, 56n145, 61, 94–96, 98–100, 104–106, 124, 148n166, 236, 315
land size classes, 221, 234, 279, 327, 330

land surveys, 32, 41, 95
landholding, size class, 98–99, 190–191, 247, 382
landholdings, 98–99, 118, 184, 189–191, 216n71, 220, 222, 247, 382
landless, 110, 173–174, 177, 190–191, 252–253, 269, 347, 354–355, 358–360, 377, 391
landless household, 347, 358–359
landlords, 29, 95–96, 106, 147n164, 223, 383
language, 17, 45n33
large farmer, 196, 257, 278–279, 358, 382, 400
lashkari, 283
lawani, 106–107
Laxmi Puja, 320
leafhopper, 283
lease, 17, 98, 173, 196, 219, 223–224, 236, 275
legitimacy, 220
legume, 32, 73
leisure, 171, 255
liabilities, 165–166, 181–182, 199–205, 233, 380
life-cycle, 359
Lincoln, Abraham, 68, 146n147
linseed, 117, 339–340, 379
literary references to Vidarbha
  Mahabharata, 15, 45
  mythology, 15
  Puranas, 15
  Ramayana, 15
  Rig Veda, 15, 72
  Rukmini, 211n27, 214n54, 265n9
Liverpool, 78–79, 84, 106
livestock/livestock research, 115, 166, 195–198, 226, 229, 237, 247–252, 272, 369n41, 391, 396
Loan Limitation Act, 100
loan waiver, 174, 202
loans, 37, 41, 69, 94, 100, 105–108, 116, 119, 136n61, 174, 181, 192, 200–205, 219, 324, 351, 356, 393–394
lobbying, 130n14, 384
local institutions, 3, 16, 19–20, 30, 40, 61, 124
lockdowns, 1, 175, 181, 252, 333, 338, 395–396, 403
locust, 90
logistics, 161
London Stock Exchange, 67
long staple cotton, 153n233
long timescale, 323, 393
longitudinal study, 8, 163–170, 175–176, 182, 206, 357, 375, 380, 404
longue durée, 14–15, 43n8, 375, 404n3
loss distribution, 165, 344–347
lottery, 6, 139n81, 280
Louisiana, 66, 134n36
luck, 14, 42n7, 50n86, 218–219, 224, 325, 335
Lyall, A. C., 149n186, 150n204

macroeconomy, 378
Madhya Pradesh, 17–18, 21–22, 25, 44n22, 45n31, 225–226, 302, 314n67, 363n6, 393
Magan Sangrahalaya, 145n129
*mahajan*s, 37
Mahalwari system, 96
Maharashtra Groundwater (Development and Management) Act, 392
Maharashtra Hybrid Seeds Company Ltd (Mahyco), 270–271
Maharashtra Money-Lending (Regulation) Act, 2014, 202
Maharashtra Samruddhi Mahamarg, 224
Maharashtra State Rural Livelihoods Mission (MSRLM), 202–203

Mahashivratri, 320
Mahatma Gandhi National Rural Employment Guarantee Scheme (MGNREGS), 187, 212n40, 255–256, 301, 353, 396
Mahmud Gawan (Gavan), 23, 32
Mahur, 23, 48n65
Mahyco-Monsanto Biotech Ltd (MMBL), 270–271, 274, 388–389
Majlis-i-Aaali, 22, 48n65
Makar Sankranti, 320
makta, 223, 236
Malabar Coast of India, 23
Malacca Straits, 114
malguzari, 16, 36, 95–96, 157n277, 393
Malguzari Act, 393
malguzari tank, 57n157, 95, 393
*malguzar*s, 36–37
Malis, 189
Malkapur, 103–104, 378
Mallika, 279–280
malnutrition, 187–188, 212n42
managing agency, 109
Manchester, 81–82, 95, 112, 130n17, 131n21, 132n24, 145n125, 147n162, 207n9, 208n14, 377
Manchester Act, 65
Manchester Chamber of Commerce, 81–82, 95
Manchester Cotton Company, 132n24
*mandi*s, 332, 337–338, 366n25
mansabdar (*mansabdari*), 24, 33
manufactured cotton looms, 77, 116
manufacturing, 10n2, 13, 41, 64–65, 67–68, 71, 80–81, 108–110, 112, 114, 116, 126, 139n82, 153–154n236, 157n275, 316
manure, 97, 180, 233, 236, 385, 402
Manusmriti, 72
Maratha Confederacy, 26–27, 30, 40
Maratha Resurrection, 26
Marathi, 18, 21, 45–46n33, 46n36, 58n168, 110, 165
Marathwada, 127, 156n273, 203, 247, 271, 316, 326, 332, 355, 386
marginal farmer, 198, 216n69, 234, 260, 288, 325–326, 328, 357–358, 382
margins, 9, 34, 110, 183, 193, 196–198, 216n69, 233–234, 251–252, 257, 259–260, 279, 289, 325–326, 328–330, 333, 347
market failures, 5, 318, 360–361, 394
Marwari (Marwadi), 106, 109, 126, 151n210, 158, 305n6, 332–333, 360, 377
maternal mortality, 188
Marx, Karl, 124, 157n276
Mauryan dynasty, 19
mawa, 283
mealybug, 325
measurement/measurement issues, 177–181
mechanization, 110, 137–138n70, 194, 219, 247, 256–257, 304, 305n3, 391
medieval history, 19
medium farmer, 198, 234, 236, 328–329
medium staple cotton, 77
Melghat, 73
members of parliament (MPs), 19
members of the Legislative Assembly (MLAs), 19
mercantile capital, 66–67
merchants, 34, 65, 68, 70–72, 76–78, 80, 85–86, 88, 100–101, 103–106, 114–116, 126, 140–141n92, 142n106
Messrs Vikaji and Pestanji, 80
method, 90, 114, 163–164, 168–171, 182, 210n24, 240, 284–285, 303, 309–310n41, 312n55, 370–371n49, 380, 382, 406–407n24
methodology, 8–9, 164–171, 176–177, 206, 266n20, 370n49

microclimates, 173
microfinance, 156n271, 187–188, 203, 393–394
microfinance institution (MFI), 203–204
micro-irrigation projects, 393
Mid-day Meal Scheme (MDMS), 187
Middle East, 114
milch cattle, 195–197
military bug, 283
mill workers, 72, 108, 110, 152n218, 187
millennium development goals (MDGs), 188
millets, 73, 258
mills, 3, 60–61, 68, 70–71, 73, 77, 82, 90, 104, 108–117, 124–126, 131n21
mineral deposits, 13, 16
minimum support price (MSP), 2, 331
minority schemes, 190
Mirzapur, 78, 80–81, 103, 142n107, 143n114
Mississippi, 66–69, 132–133n30, 134n36
mixed farming, 230
mixed methods, 170, 210n24
mobility, 39, 150–151n205, 161, 257, 259, 288, 355, 374
Mohammed Bin Tughluq, 22, 48n59
MON15985, 271
MON531, 271
moneylender/Moneylender Act, 107
monocil, 286, 311n52
monocrop, 90, 232
monocrotophos, 284, 286, 289, 292, 310n47, 311n52
monoculture, 270–271, 378
monopoly, 78, 119, 135n46, 143n111, 269–271, 274, 333–334, 386
Monopoly Cotton Procurement Scheme (MCPS), 119, 333–334, 386
Monsanto, 269–271, 273–276, 281, 306n16
monsoon, 2, 4, 34, 73–75, 116–117, 153n235, 171–173, 218, 225–227, 251, 275
monthly per capita expenditure, 344
moral economy, 397–401, 403
Morduch, J., 368n36
Morocco round, 118
Morris, D. M., 152n219
mortality, 92–94, 154n239, 162, 188
motivation, 51n95, 163, 193, 269, 277, 380, 398
Mouzawur, Muqqadam, 95
mrigashira nakshatra, 319
muccadums, 85
Mughals, 3, 20, 23–25, 28, 30, 35, 37, 40–41, 47n47, 51n94
multinational firms, 269–270
Mumbai, 13, 153n230
Munro, Thomas, 96, 147n164
muqqadams, 32, 95
Murtizapur, 161
Muslim sultanates, 20–23, 39–40, 376
muslin, 114, 130n16
Maha Vikas Aghadi (MVA), 17, 405n13
Mysore, 21, 26–28, 40, 52n101, 207n10, 211n33

Naga Panchami, 319
nagaran, 194, 300–301
Nagpur division. *See* Vidarbha
Nagpur Pact, 18
nahars, 36
naib, 21
Naik, Vasantrao Phulsing, 332, 356, 365n21, 385–386
Nana Phadnavis, 26
naqdi, 33
Narasingdeva, 22
Narmada, 20, 27–28, 44n22, 157n277
Narsinghpur, 29, 80–81
nasaq, 35

National Agricultural Cooperative Marketing Federation of India Ltd (NAFED), 333
National Bank for Agriculture and Rural Development (NABARD), 214n62, 216n69, 217n75, 356, 390–391
National Council of Applied Economic Research (NCAER), 163, 215n63
National Democratic Alliance (NDA), 204, 396
National Education Policy (NEP), 2020, 186, 397
National Food Security Act (NFSA), 255, 371n54
National Sample Survey Office (NSSO), 179, 237
nationalistic movement, 111–112
Native Americans, 66
natural disasters, 223
naval blockade, 69
nav-Boudhas, 189
Nawab of Bengal, 26
Naxalite-Maoist, 13–14, 16
neo-Buddhists, 189, 190
neoclassical framework, 170
neoliberal policies, 373, 402–403
neonatal mortality, 188
Neoproterozoic Era, 15
net sown area, 171, 191
New England, 68, 135n50
new history of capitalism (NHC), 67, 134n41, 305n2
New Orleans cotton, 113
New World, 66–67, 128n3
Newcomen steam engine, 131n21
Nimar, 116
nimbu arka, 284
nimi sawai, 106–107
nindan, 292–293, 296
nitrogen, 73, 233, 328–329, 365n16
Nizam of Hyderabad, 17, 27, 29–30, 40, 53n111, 376
Nizam Shahi, 23–24, 32, 35, 49n71, 56n145
nominal wages, 91, 255–257
non-banking financial companies (NBFCs), 393–394
non-cultivator household, 166, 174–175, 178, 184, 189, 194, 196, 205, 219, 251–253, 257–258, 260, 269, 294, 315, 318, 347, 351, 354, 360–362, 382–383
non-farm diversification, 220, 247, 254
non-farm income, 237, 353, 360, 381–383, 396, 403
non-farm opportunities, 219, 237, 246, 339
non-pesticidal management (NPM), 183, 284–285, 305
North America, 61–62, 65–67, 70, 133n33
nutrition security risk, 228
nutritional deprivation, 188
Nuziveedu, 271

odds, 5, 139n81, 220–221, 317, 326
off-farm work, 251–252
oil extraction, 70
oilseeds, 104, 333
olit, 191–192, 214n57, 224
Open General Licence (OGL), 387
operational expenditure, 204–205
operational land, 222
opium. *See* opium wars
opium wars, 80, 143n111
oranges, 19, 225
organic farming, 233, 314n69
organic matter, 73
organophosphates, 282, 286, 311n52
oriental despotism, 39
Orissa (Odisha), 17

other backward classes (OBCs), 185, 189, 213n45, 249, 252
Ottoman Empire, 114
Oudh (Awadh), 27–28
outturn ratio, 333
ownership, 32, 70, 101, 150n193, 173–174, 177–178, 192–197, 211n28, 214n55, 223, 234, 257, 299, 327, 355, 380
oxen, 90, 218, 293–294, 319

paan, 181
paanlot, 390–391
pack bullocks, 103, 161
package, 120, 284, 310n43, 356
packet, 6, 196, 272–274, 277, 279, 308n34
packing, 78, 88, 141n100
paddhat, 230, 303
paddy, 16, 73–74, 116, 127, 157n277, 337, 393
paddy belt, 74–75
paddy-growing regions, 16
Palanpur, 168, 208n14, 209n16, 266n10
Palekar, Subhash. *See* Subhash Palekar Natural Farming
Pallavas, 36
Palmer & Co., 100, 149n188
Palmer, William, 100
panchayat, 39, 155n249
Panchayati Raj, 400
pandemic, 1, 9, 93, 99, 111, 125–126, 166, 173, 175–176, 181, 187, 193, 204, 211n29, 223, 230, 234, 247, 252, 254, 299, 332–334, 338, 347–349, 351–352, 354, 356, 360–361, 380, 392, 395–396, 403, 405–406n13
panel data, 8, 169–170, 317, 328, 339, 352, 358, 365n17, 382
parganas, 24, 32, 50n83
Parsi, 80, 85, 103, 108–109, 126, 146n146
pass system, 161
pastures, 98, 125
patil, 54n131, 95, 98
patta paddath, 293–295
patterns, 5, 8, 16, 70, 73–74, 81, 86, 90, 104, 125, 137–138n70, 165, 174, 191, 196, 205, 219, 221–225, 230, 232–233, 240, 246, 251, 257–259, 269–270, 296–299, 301, 304, 316, 318–319, 324, 342, 378, 381
patwaris, 32, 54n132, 95
Paunar, 49n72
Peacock Throne, 21, 52n96
pearl millet, 73
peasant rebellion, 402–403, 409n43
pen and paper personal interview (PAPI), 179, 182–184
pence, 68, 79–80
Penganga, 73
pension, 26, 179
periphery, 67, 134n40
Permanent Settlement Act of 1793, 147n164
peshkash, 34
peshwa, 25–30, 50n83, 51n89, 51n91, 52n101
pests
  American bollworm, 282
  aphids, 283, 309n41, 339
  bond ali (*see* pink bollworm)
  jassids, 283, 309n37, 339
  Lalya, Churda, Mawa, Thurthude, 283, 325
  pandhri mashi (*see* whitefly)
  pink bollworm (PBW), 9, 229, 243, 271, 277, 283, 299, 301–302, 307n25, 316, 339, 381–382
  thrips, 283, 309n37
pest ecology, 272
pest infestation, 90, 218, 277, 283, 286, 349, 389
pest resistance, 279, 284

Pesticide Management Bill, 2020, 291, 310n44, 313n59
pesticide spraying, 229, 289–290, 292, 297–299
pesticide treadmill, 284, 303
pesticide use, 166, 282–283, 286, 289, 291–292, 312n57, 313n65
pesticides
cocktails, 266n15, 286–287, 302–303, 314n73, 346
endosulfan, 292
endrin, 289, 311n53
fungicides, 240, 259, 282
glyphosate, 292
herbicides, 259, 271, 281–282, 287, 292, 309n35
insecticides, 214n61, 236, 240, 282, 285, 287, 291–292, 309n37, 310n46
tonics, 214n61, 266n15, 284, 287–288, 290–291, 303, 314n73
weedicides, 214n61, 242–243, 259, 266n15, 270, 282, 284, 287–288, 292–295, 301, 304, 311n50, 314n73
phad, 36, 393
Phadnavis, Nana, 26
phone/smart phone/mobile phone, 10n1, 192, 194, 362, 388, 397
phosphate, 73, 286, 328
phosphorous, 329
Phule, Jyotiba, 190
picking, 188, 218, 253, 255, 257, 259–260, 270, 271, 295–296, 298, 300, 304, 319–320, 324, 363n8, 381
piece goods, 80, 104, 129n8, 142–143n110
Piedmont, 66
pigeon pea, 73, 180, 225, 230, 232–233, 260, 381
pilot studies, 164
Pindari. *See* Pindari Wars
piracy, 88
pisciculture, 37
pithya, 283, 325
plague bonus, 111, 153n235
plant growth promoters, 242–243, 259, 287, 290
plant toxicity, 272
plant-eating (phytophagous) pests, 284
planters, 65–68, 70, 95, 133n31, 136n54, 384, 405n10
plateau, 73
plot diversification, 345–346
plough/ploughing, 29, 35, 67, 90, 155n249, 192, 194, 214n60, 222–223, 297–298, 300–301, 385
Pola, 199, 215n66, 319, 400
policy response, 317, 372n56
policymakers, 2, 6, 276, 404
political ecology, 41, 375, 406–407n24
political economy, 5, 9, 130n14, 137n65, 162, 216n71, 274, 326, 334, 360, 367n29, 368n40, 386, 390, 394, 397–401
political upheavals, 31, 61, 71
politics
coalition
Maha Vikas Aghadi, 17, 405n13
NDA, 204, 396
UPA, 202
political parties
BJP, 17, 338, 405n13, 405–406n13
INC, 385, 398
Shiv Sena, 17
poll tax, 31, 94–95
Poona, 26, 28, 52n101, 54n127, 209–210n22
population, 3, 16, 21, 31, 41, 42n1, 59n177, 66, 82, 91, 93–94, 97–100, 105, 110, 117–118, 125–126, 148n171, 173–174, 186–190, 203, 213n48, 284, 296, 358, 377
population growth rate, 99
port, 62, 66, 76–77, 84, 101, 112

port cities, 66
porter, 248
Portuguese traders, 114
post-bellum/post-bellum period, 61, 63, 70–71, 81, 84, 128n7, 137n65, 315
post-colonial, 44n16, 118, 154n245, 357, 373–375, 378, 380, 390, 399
post-independence era, 3, 317, 354
potash, 73, 283–284, 298, 328
potassium, 328–329
poultry, 188, 195–199, 204, 237, 247, 355, 402
poultry business, 188, 204, 355
poverty/poverty alleviation/BPL, 91, 217n75, 370n49, 370–371n49, 385
power, 14, 20–24, 27–30, 33, 35–36, 38–41, 51n89, 53n108, 69, 82–83, 85, 96–97, 112, 201, 225, 255, 274, 280, 317, 319–320, 326, 332–334, 337, 362, 385–386, 396
Pradhan Mantri Fasal Bima Yojana (PMFBY), 358, 394–395
Pradhan Mantri Jan-Dhan Yojana (PMJDY), 204
Pradhan Mantri Kisan Samman Nidhi (PM-KISAN), 251
Pradhan Mantri Krishi Sinchayee Yojana, 244
precautionary savings, 349, 352
precipitation, 74–75, 321, 323
Premchand Roychand, 85, 146n138
pressure, 1, 28–29, 46n35, 68, 95, 98, 101, 106, 271, 284, 316, 331, 338, 349, 357, 364n14, 381–382, 386, 400
price ceiling, 303, 389
price discovery, 71, 198, 378
price risks, 9, 119, 317–318, 330–339, 347–348, 357–358, 377, 387
price volatility, 78, 331, 369n43, 384
principal/subsidiary activity status, 178
private enterprise, 101
private hospital, 205
private property in land, 97, 385
privatization, 97
processing, 78, 226, 298, 332–333
production risk, 5, 8, 317, 330, 336, 357, 382
production system, 4, 38, 71, 219, 373
profit maximization, 170
progressive, 219, 279, 302, 402
Project on Climate Resilient Agriculture (POCRA), 390
property rights, 7, 35, 61, 95, 97, 104–105, 124, 161, 315, 377, 379, 385
protective kits, 292
protective tariffs, 109
protests, 1–2, 337–338, 374, 398–401
proximate events, 162
public distribution system (PDS), 233, 246, 255–256, 344–346, 353–354, 360–361, 371n54, 383–384, 388
public health, 187, 205
public investment, 118, 259, 378, 390, 395
public relief, 72
public sector, 216n69, 274–275, 283, 304
public works, 95, 187, 214n55, 353, 406n23
public works programme, 187, 353
pump sprayer, 192, 194, 221, 290–292, 299
Punjab, 127, 169, 283, 337, 338
Purna, 43n12, 73
purposive sample, 175
pyrethroids, 282

Qing China, 76
qualitative research, 164–165, 170, 207n5
quality, 78, 87–88, 104, 111–114, 117, 169, 179–183, 196, 198, 206, 219, 221, 228–231, 260, 286, 291, 330, 332, 335–336, 354–355, 357, 366n22, 371–372n54, 379–381, 389–390, 404

quality control inspector, 291
quintal, 113, 196, 240, 246, 281, 295, 297, 300, 324, 328, 332–333, 336, 342, 387, 389, 403

rabi sowing, 116–117, 244–246, 299
rack-renting, 28, 96–97
Raghuji I, 27
Raghoba, 26
Rashtrakutas, 20
Rashtriya Swasthya Bima Yojana (RSBY), 205
Raigarh, 25
railways
  rail freight, 103
  railway mania, 67, 100, 135n45
  railway mileage, 103
  railway securities, 67
  railway station, 104
  railway towns, 104
  train, 18, 102, 164, 171, 182, 186, 247, 390, 396, 401
rainfall deficit, 219, 319–320, 339, 348, 364n11
rainfall distribution, 324
rainfall variation, 73
rain-fed agriculture, 39, 219–220
raiyat, 37
Raj Gonds, 50n85
Raj Gond kings, 24, 25, 27, 50n85
Raja Simhana III, 21
Rajput king, 24, 51n94
Raksha Bandhan, 320
Ralli Brothers, 104
Ram Navami, 320
Ramachandra, 21, 208n14
Ramadeva, 21, 47n48, 47n50
Ramtek/Ramtek Model of Irrigation, 37
randomized control trial (RCT), 165, 309–310n41, 358
raqba, 34
Rashi, 279, 308n31
Rashtrakutas, 20
Rasi Seeds, 271
ration card, 371n54
rational choice, 170
raw cotton. See *kapas*
Raw Cotton (Procurement, Processing, and Marketing) Act, 1971. *See* cotton marketing
Rawdon-Hastings, Governor-General Francis, 29
real estate boom, 86
real incomes, 234, 255, 259, 359
real wages, 41, 59n175, 59n177, 91–92
reflexivity, 170
refuge seeds, 277
refuge-in-bag (RIB), 277, 307n24
regulation, 124, 158, 242, 269–270, 273, 276–277, 291–292, 303–305, 379, 385, 393
regulatory oversight, 269
relative humidity, 175
relief works, 93–94
religion, 132–133n30, 213n48
religious festivals, 199
rent roll, 95
rents, 19, 33, 86, 95–96, 117, 147–148n164, 180, 194, 223, 236, 298–299, 385–386, 391–392, 394
repayment culture, 202
reproductive and child health (RCH) issues, 166
research design, 164, 167, 169–170
research methodology, 163, 206
reservation, 77, 189–190, 213n47
reservoirs, 36
resident investigators, 165, 169, 173, 180–183, 206, 252, 254, 349, 380–381, 403
resilience, 2, 4, 316, 374

resistance, 47n50, 112, 240, 243, 259, 271–272, 277, 279, 282–285, 301–303, 381–382
respondent fatigue, 169–170, 177, 182
restoration, 65
revenue
 revenue administration, 7, 22, 30–38, 56n143, 98, 104, 385
 revenue assessment, 33, 35, 56n144, 61, 95–96
 revenue farming. See *iqtadari*
reverse migration, 21–22, 223
revisits, 167, 177, 182, 209–210n22
Revolt of 1857/Sepoy Mutiny, 158
Riddel, 113
Right to Education Act, 186
risk
 covariate risks, 340, 347–348
 health risk, 311n51
 idiosyncratic risks, 9, 204–205, 347
 price risk, 9, 119, 317–318, 330–339, 347–348, 357–358, 377, 387
 risk and uncertainty, 164, 308n26, 338, 348–349
 risk attitudes, 165–166
 risk aversion, 397
 risk coping mechanisms 166, 349–352
 risk hedging, 221, 254
 risk management, 5, 168, 204, 221, 230, 240, 279, 317–318, 347–356, 358–361, 369n41, 374, 382, 395
 risk perceptions, 166, 311n51, 347–349
 weather risk, 76, 319–330, 340
 yield risk, 230–231, 317, 325, 338, 357, 389
river mouths, 66
Rivett-Carnac, John Henry, 91, 95–96, 105, 146n153, 148n165, 150n200, 151n207
Roe, Thomas, 35
rohi, 228, 342
roller-spinning, 131n21
rotavator, 214n60, 301
Roundup Ready Flex, 281
ryotwari, 16, 95–96, 147n164, 315

saaldar, 264, 320
saatbaara utara (*saatbaara*), 173
sacred thread, 72
safety-first principle, 398, 409n44
*sahukar*s, 96, 106
salon, 250
Salsette, 26
Sambalpur, 28
sample, 8, 163, 168–169, 173–176, 184–206, 207n5, 222, 229–230
sample size, 206, 248–249
sample survey, 168–169, 207n5, 209–210n22, 237
sampling frame, 173–175
Samruddhi Mahamarg, Mumbai–Nagpur Expressway, 224
Samyukta Maharashtra Movement, 18–19
sanad (deed), 95
Sanskrit, 20–21, 43n9, 72
sap-sucking pests, 382–383
Saraf (Shroff), 108–109
Saraf Commission, 189
*sarang*s, 36
sardeshmukhi, 30, 36, 41
Sarva Shiksha Abhiyaan, 186
Satavahana Empire, 19
Satpura/Satpura Range, 20, 48n65, 73
Satyasodhak Movement, 190
savings, 194–195, 200, 220, 259, 276, 282, 296–297, 299, 308n34, 324, 349–352, 354, 359, 368n38
sawai, 106–107, 201, 216n72
Madhavrao, Sawai, II, 26, 51n91
sawar, 33
Saugor and Narmada territories, 28

Sayyid brothers, 29, 53n113
SBOT exchange, 226
schemes, 4, 69, 72, 96, 119, 182, 186–187, 190, 192, 200, 202, 212n38, 214n55, 235–236, 244, 251, 255–256, 261, 265n4, 299, 301, 325, 331, 333–334, 351, 354, 356, 358, 381, 386–387, 391–392, 394, 396
School Meal Programme, 187
Scindias, 28, 189
Scott, J. C., 402–403, 409n43
seasonality, 120, 140n87, 169, 195, 251, 296, 344, 369n43
secondary pests, 9, 229, 243, 259, 266n15, 272, 279, 299, 301–303, 316, 382
secured loans, 108, 192, 202
seed
  Seed Bill, 2019, 276–277, 307n23
  seed companies, 271, 274, 278–279, 282, 305n6
  seed cotton, 6, 9, 65–66, 70, 111, 115, 118–119, 127n1, 128n5, 220, 242, 269, 270, 273–274, 276–278, 280–281, 294, 301, 306n14
  seed experiments, 112–115
  seed fad, 279
  seed gardens, 114
  seed sovereignty, 269–270, 272, 277, 307n23, 388–390
  seed varieties, 61, 114–115, 125, 276, 303, 379, 383, 387
  seeding rate, 226
self-help groups (SHG), 187, 194–195, 202–204, 217n75, 351, 355–356
self-learning, 276
semi-arid region, 73
semi-arid tropics, 163, 168, 209n21, 368n37, 369n42
semi-medium farmer, 328–329
semi-structured interviews, 164
senior citizens, 184
separation movement, 18
sericulture, 198, 391, 396, 402
service sector jobs, 247, 396–397
Seuna dynasty, 20–21
Shah Alam II, 25
Shah Jahan, 24, 34, 49n79
Shah, Mubarak, 21
Shah, Muhammad, 22, 29–30, 48n65, 56n143
Shah, Murtaza Nizam, I, 23
Shahu, 25
Share and Stock Brokers Association 'share mania', 85
sharecropping, 19, 137–138n70, 223, 236, 250, 349
Shegaon, 103
Sher Shah Suri, 34
Sherman, General W. T., 137n66
Shetkari Sanghatana, 270, 275, 399–400
shipping, 77
Shiv Sena, 17
Shivaji
  Shivaji Bhonsale I (Bhosle and Bhonsala), 24, 49n71
  Chhatrapati Shivaji, 50n82, 320 (*see also* Marathas)
shocks/income shocks, 5, 9, 162, 221, 349, 353–354, 382, 387, 395
short maturity crop, 226–227
short staple cotton, 379
short-duration varieties, 232
short-term credit, 203–204
Shravan, 319
Shri Krishna Jayanti, 320
Shunga dynasty, 19
Shylock, 105
Siddi, 23, 34
Siegfrieds, 116
silks, 65, 113, 115, 141n97, 143n110

silts, 246
Simhana, Raja, III, 21
Singapore, 80
Singh, Man, I, 23–24, 49n73
Siraj-ud-Daulah, 25–26
Sistani, Safdar Khan, 22
Sitadevi, 319–320, 363n8
size economies, 220
size-class, 196–198, 247, 249, 257–258, 325, 327–328, 381–382
skills training infrastructure, 247–248
SKS Microfinance, 203
slavery, 38, 66–68, 70, 133n33–34, 134n36, 134n41, 135n52, 305n2, 313n66, 384, 405n9
slump, 34, 67, 70–72, 78, 105
small farmer, 402
small ponds, 246
smallholders, 118, 198, 200, 220, 222, 259, 325, 356, 381, 395, 400
smoothing, 200, 349–350, 359, 367n29, 368n36–38, 369n43
snakes and ladders, 342
social
  social capital, 109
  social desirability bias, 183
  social learning, 276
  social organization, 58n171, 175, 377
  social security, 369n43
  social spending, 205
socially and economically backward class (SEBC), 189
soil fertility
  soil health, 9, 285, 317, 329, 382, 387
  soil health cards (SHCs), 329–330, 382
  soil moisture, 175
soil types
  alkaline soil, 73
  barad, 73
  bharkali, 73
  coarse shallow soils, 73, 229–230
  deep black soil, 33–34, 73, 229–230
  lime (*murmad*), 73, 225
miankalas, 33–34
  medium black soil, 73, 229–230
  regur, 73
  very shallow soil, 73
solidarity, 338, 350, 400
sorghum. See *jawari/jowar*
South Carolina, 65–66, 68–69, 132n23, 133n34, 134n36
Southeast Asia, 76, 114, 402–403, 409n43
southwest monsoon, 405n9
soybean
  DOC, 226
  soybean futures trading, 226
  soybean oil, 226
  Soybean Processors Association (SOPA), 226, 265n7
spatial diversification, 230
specialization, 5, 116, 135n50, 254, 302
speculation, 68, 71–72, 82, 85, 111, 117, 125, 132–133n30, 379
speculative bubbles, 61, 67, 126
spindles, 108–109
spinning
  charkha, 82, 112, 145n129
  spinning jenny, 131n21
  spinning mule, 131n21
spray pumps, 192, 194, 221, 290, 298–299
State Agricultural Universities (SAUs), 198, 388
state government, 18, 101, 173–174, 190, 198, 200, 242, 274, 290, 332, 356, 391, 394, 396
State Reorganization Committee (SRC), 18
statehood, 13, 17–19, 42n5, 44n19, 46n35, 376, 405n13

stealth seeds, 276, 301–302, 305n5, 307n21
steamboat transportation, 67
stem borer, 231, 240
Stern, Nicholas H., 208n14, 209n16, 211n31
storage infrastructure, 330, 334
straight varieties, 232, 308n27
structural transformation, 2, 219–220, 258, 381, 388, 396, 398
structured questionnaire, 164
study villages, 168, 173–177, 184, 186–187, 190, 194, 209–210n22, 223–225, 229–230, 236–237, 246, 260, 266n15, 284, 302, 322–323, 325, 332, 335–336, 353, 355, 357, 365n17, 381–382, 390–391, 396, 402
stunted, 2, 10n2, 188
subah, 24–25, 32, 40, 54n131
subahdar, 24, 32–33, 54n132
Subash Palekar Natural Farming (SPNF), 285
subdivision, 22, 32, 97, 191, 222–223, 402
sub-licencing, 274
subsidy, 118–119, 231, 365n16, 365n18, 398
subsistence, 32–33, 90, 229, 398–399, 402–403
sucking pests, 282–285, 309n37, 309–310n41
sugarcane, 32, 37, 56n144, 127, 225, 326, 386
suicide seeds, 301, 303n66
suicides, 2–3, 8, 10, 13–14, 16, 63, 119, 120, 127, 156n273, 157n274, 161–162, 171, 199–200, 215n67, 216n71, 225, 272, 275, 284, 289, 301, 312n55, 313n66, 317, 356, 373–375, 386–387, 398–401, 408n40, 409–410n53
Sujatha variety, 390
Super Mallika, 279
supplier-induced demand, 279
supplies of raw cotton, 129n8, 157–158
Surat, 23–24, 26, 35, 73, 76–77, 79, 112, 117, 140n92, 142n101, 157n283
Surat cotton (Surats), 76–77, 79, 112
survey rounds, 166, 171–177, 184–185, 188–189, 191–192, 194, 206, 214n61, 236, 309n38, 328, 395–396
sustainability, 236–237, 325, 387, 395, 404
sutta contract, 106
Suvin, 390
Swadeshi movement, 111–112, 153n236
systemic shocks, 359

taccavi, 37, 41, 107
tailoring shop, 250–251
taluka/*taluka*s, 94, 107, 155n249, 174, 277, 291, 356
*talukdar*s, 37
tank irrigation systems, 36–37
tankhwa, 33
tanks, 36–37, 57n157, 95, 151n215, 191
Tarabai, 25
*tarafdar*s, 22, 48n65
*taraf*s, 22, 48n61
tariff, 65, 109
Tata, Jamsetji Nusserwanji, 109
Tatas, 109
tax regimes, 41
taxation, 28, 35–36
tax-free cultivation, 32
Taylor, Meadows, 154–155n247
tea, 77, 94, 141n97, 320, 362
technical change, directed technical change, 139n79
technical skills training, 186
technological change, 270
technological dynamics, 269
technological innovations, 1, 64–65, 67

technology
Green Revolution, 118, 127
Intermediate Technology Upgradation Fund Scheme, 331
Industrial Revolution, 65, 123
technological change, 270
Telangana, 21, 24, 276, 281, 308n29, 314n70, 355–356
Telinkheri, 115
temperature, 76, 140n88, 175, 290, 364n14
Temple, Sir Richard, 85, 145n133
tenancy, 118, 137–138n70, 173–174, 177, 236, 250, 349, 403
Tennessee, 66
Texas, 66, 132n23, 176
textile industry, 68, 71, 81, 100, 104, 110, 119, 126–127, 129n12, 130n14, 131n21, 135n50, 142n103, 142–143n108, 144n121, 152n220
Textiles Committee of the Board of Trade, 111
Thackeray, Uddhav, 405n13
Thane, 102
theka contract, 236
thematic focus, 163, 214n61, 380
tiger, 28
tilling, 192
Tipu Sultan, 28, 52n101
tobacco, 66, 132n23, 132n26, 181, 362
tobacco boom, 66
Todar Mal, Raja, 33
Townsend, Robert, 367n29, 368n37
Townsend-Thai Project, 169, 209n21
tractor, 137–138n70, 192–194, 214n58, 218, 223, 257, 297–299, 392, 407n25
trade integration, 112, 315–316
trade liberalization, 118
traditional knowledge, 220, 276, 319, 387–388
tragedy of commons, 326
trait fees, 273–274, 306n9
transportation costs, 68, 79, 334
transactions, 85, 105, 168, 181, 349–350
trans-Atlantic cable, 71, 85
transgenic seeds, 9, 274–275, 302
transoceanic trade, 68
trap crop, 233, 283
treaties
Treaty of Deogaon, 28
Treaty of Purandhar (Purandar), 24, 50n83
Treaty of Surat, 26
Treaty of Surji-Anjangaon, 28
tribal population, 188
tribes, 16, 132n26, 185, 188–189, 213n46, 214n59, 359, 393, 409n51
triumph narrative, 269
Tufail Khan, 23, 49n69
Tughluq/Tughlak, 21
Tughluq, Muhammad bin, 22, 47n47, 48n59
tur, 73, 90, 222, 225–226, 230–232, 237, 239–244, 257, 260, 281, 284, 290–291, 296–297, 300, 333, 342
turmeric, 392–393

underweight, 188
uninsured exposure to risk, 352
union, 68, 112, 270
union blockade, 68
unit of analysis, 163, 167–169
United Progressive Alliance (UPA), 202
United Provinces, 110
United States, 60–63, 65–67, 69, 72, 81, 84, 115, 123, 128n7, 129n8, 132n26, 135n50
unmitigated risks, 400–401
unseasonal rains, 231, 237, 323–324, 339, 348, 403
unsecured loans, 108, 202
upland cotton, 66–67, 128n3

upward mobility, 374, 399
Uruguay Round, 118
usury, 57n162, 161

Vakataka period, 19
validation, 165, 169, 171, 179–183, 206, 281, 403
Varhad, 15, 149n179, 380
varham paddath, 342, 345–346
variability, 9, 73–76, 119, 140n88, 175, 234–235, 244, 313n64, 317–319, 321–323, 332, 349, 352–353, 357–358, 363n6
varietal diversity, 272
Vasantrao Naik Sheti Swavlamban Mission (VNSSM), 332, 356
Vedic period, 19
Vidarbha
  agrarian condition, 5, 14, 30
  agrarian distress, 2
  agriculture, 2, 219–220, 233, 294, 317, 357
  Ajantha Range, 73
  alluvial plains, 73
  Amravati division, 16, 383
  Akola Pact, 18
  Bhandara, 36
  Buldhana, 15, 17
  Chandrapur, 24
  coal, 100
  developmental backlogs, 13, 19, 326, 373, 386
  dinosaurs, 15
  Eastern Vidarbha, 14, 16, 36, 73, 224
  farmers' suicides, 13–14
  forest, 125
  Gadchiroli, 16
  Gondia, 120
  irrigation, 36
  language, 17
  Maha Vidarbha, 18
  Melghat, 73
  minerals, 94
  Nag Vidarbha, 15, 44n19
  Nagpur division, 16
  Nagpur Pact, 18
  Naxalite-Maoist, 13–14
  rivers (*see* Wardha, Wardha river, Wainganga, Penganga, Purna)
  Satpura Range, 73
  society, 198
  soil (*see* soil types)
  State Reorganization Committee (SRC), 18
  statehood, 18, 405n13
  Samyukta Maharashtra Movement, 18–19
  Varhad, 380
  Vidarbha Intensive Irrigation Development Programme (VIIDP), 259
  Vidarbha Irrigation Development Corporation (VIDC), 392
  Wardha, 6, 8, 15–16, 19, 22, 49n72, 73, 76, 109–110, 114–116, 119, 145n129, 151n214, 162, 164–166, 171, 173–175, 181, 183, 186–191, 193, 198–200, 202–203, 206, 209n18, 212n37, 213n51, 214n59, 218, 223–227, 229–231, 244–245, 248, 251–253, 255–256, 258, 265n9, 266n18, 272–273, 279, 281–284, 287, 294, 299–300, 311n50, 321–322, 325
  Washim, 15
  western Vidarbha, 14, 16, 228
  Yavatmal, 8, 15, 17, 36, 44n17, 76, 119, 149n177, 164–166, 171–172, 174–175, 187–191, 198, 202, 206, 212n37, 215n64, 226–227, 229–231, 244–245, 248, 250–252, 258, 266n18, 281, 286, 290–291, 294,

312n57, 322, 325, 328, 334, 338, 355, 357–358, 364n9, 365n21
Vijayanagara Kingdom, 22–23, 49n69
village census, 168–169, 209–210n22
Village Dynamics Studies in South Asia (VDSA), 168–169
village economy, 9, 38, 40, 98, 167–168, 174–175, 201, 208n14, 230, 244, 247
village level studies (VLS), 163, 168, 209–210n22
village society
caste, 97
kinship, kinship network, 351
marriage, 402
social networks, 277
solidarity networks, 350
Vindhya, 20, 45n31
Voelcker Report, 115, 155n256
Volkart Brothers, 104, 116
vulnerability
climate change, 76, 352
measurement, 352, 371–372n49
VER, 352, 359–360, 370n49

wadi, 391
wage/wages, 32, 41, 59n175, 59n177, 85–86, 91–92, 94, 103, 111, 138n75, 139n81, 153n235, 178, 180, 186–187, 204, 208n14, 242, 248, 250, 252–253, 252–257, 272, 292, 294, 296–300, 381, 401–402
Waghoba, 279
Wainganga, 19, 35–37, 73
war capitalism, 67
wars
American Civil War (*see* American Civil War)
Deccan wars, 24
First Anglo-Maratha War, 26
Pindari Wars, 28–29
Second Anglo-Maratha War, 28
Third Anglo-Maratha War, 28–29
World War I and II, 108, 110–111, 153n235, 153–154n236
Waradatat, 22
Warangal, 21, 23, 47n49, 308n30, 406n20
Wardha Scheme, 186, 199
warships, 69
Washim, 15, 44n17, 99
Washington, George, 66, 133–134n35
watan, *watandar*, 38–39, 97, 148n173
water
logging, 228, 265n5, 323–324, 342
water management, 36, 57n157, 390–391, 393, 406n24, 407n28
water table, 191–192, 391
Water User Associations (WUA), 395
water utilization, 229
water-intensive crops, 317
Watershed, Watershed Development Programme (see *paanlot*)
wazir, 29, 32
wealth distribution, 66
weather shocks, 75, 231, 303–304, 350, 355
weather variability, 75, 317, 322, 357
weaving, 72, 78, 82–83, 108–109, 114, 131n21, 157n283, 375
weeding, 9, 107, 137–138n70, 180, 188, 243–244, 253–255, 257, 259–260, 266n20
weevil, 90, 137n70
welfare, 72, 76, 118, 120–121, 130n14, 309n40, 317, 325, 344, 346–347, 353, 355, 357–358, 370n49
welfare capitalism, 385
welfare schemes, 72
Wellesley, Governor-General Richard, 28–29
Wellesley, Sir Arthur, 28
Wellesley, Lord, 52n102

wells, 55n141, 325
WhatsApp, 194, 397
wheat, 34, 73, 86–87, 103, 117, 127, 157n277, 223, 225, 228, 232–233, 244, 246, 255, 257, 298, 300–301, 333, 337, 354, 361
wicked problem, 261, 268n30
wild animals, 342, 382
wildlife protection laws, 228, 342
wilt disease, 113
wind speed, 175
windbreaker, 233
windfall, 69, 72, 86, 126, 225, 239, 334, 357, 379–380, 384, 402
winter capital, 13, 19
women, 83, 91, 94, 110, 166, 186–188, 195–196, 202–203, 217n75, 252–257
wood shortage, 95
Wood, Sir Charles, 95
working capital, 236
working-class struggle, 111
world cotton trade, 60–61
world system, 42
World Trade Organization (WTO), 118, 316, 331, 357, 365n18, 380, 386–387
worsted cloth, 65
woven cloth, 65

Yadavas/Yadava dynasty, 20–21, 31, 376
yarn, 66–67, 71, 78, 83, 131n21, 142n106, 145n129, 390
yellow revolution, 355
yellow sticky pads, 284, 309n41
yield/yield risks, 230–231, 317, 325, 338, 357, 389

zabt/*zabti*, 34–35
zakat, 31
zamindar/*zamindari*, 34, 37, 55n134, 56n143, 96, 147n164
zat, 33
zero budget natural farming (ZBNF), 285
zirayati, 56, 144